HITLER'S
LEGIONS

ALSO BY Samuel W. Mitcham, Jr.

Triumphant Fox: Erwin Rommel and the Rise of the Afrika Korps
Rommel's Desert War: The Life and Death of the Afrika Korps
Rommel's Last Battle: The Desert Fox and the Normandy Campaign

HITLER'S LEGIONS

The German Army Order of Battle, World War II

Samuel W. Mitcham, Jr.

DORSET PRESS
New York

Copyright © 1985 by Samuel W. Mitcham, Jr.
Maps by the author
All rights reserved.

This edition published by Dorset Press,
a division of Marboro Books Corporation,
by arrangement with
Stein & Day/Publishers.
1987 Dorset Press

ISBN 0-88029-214-8
(formerly ISBN 0-8128-2992-1)

Printed in the United States of America
M 9 8 7 6 5 4 3 2 1

To
Robert R. Wyatt

ACKNOWLEDGMENTS

This book was the most difficult project I have ever undertaken. It took seven years to produce it, and, frankly, if I had known that when I started, I do not believe I would have done it. I have written several other books—primarily about Field Marshal Rommel, the "Desert Fox," and all those together did not require as much work as this single volume.

One problem was the German documents. Most of the time I was a graduate assistant, either at the Geoscience Department at Northeast Louisiana University or the Department of Geography at the University of Tennessee, so going to Germany to research was out of the question. (As some readers may not know, graduate assistants are typically paid about $300 per month: hardly enough to be able to commute to Germany.) I was able to acquire many valuable primary and secondary sources through interlibrary loan and the purchase of microfilm from the U.S. National Archives in Washington, D.C. I wish to thank the fine librarians at the United States Army's War College, Carlisle Barracks, Pennsylvania; at Sandel Library, Northeast Louisiana University; and the long-suffering staff of the Morehouse Parish Library, Bastrop, Louisiana, who had to put up with my insatiable demands. Jim Trimble of the United States National Archives was a tremendous help as well, and I wish to single him out for special praise and recognition. Any deficiencies the book might have are, of course, fully my own fault and responsibility.

I wish it had been possible to furnish a complete list of unit commanders for this book, with the exact dates of their tenure and a more complete biography of their careers, but it was not. There were 3,363 German generals in World War II, and researching all those personnel files would have taken years. For the listings of commanders I relied primarily on the excellent *Kriegstagebuch des Oberkommando der Wehrmacht* and the wartime files of the U.S. Military Intelligence Service, but even those were incomplete. The Intelligence Service, for example, discarded its records of dead German commanders from its rosters as the war progressed, and this figure amounted to 25 percent of the total by 1945. Erza Warner wrote two excellent books covering the lives of all Union and Confederate generals in the American Civil War. I hope someday someone does the same thing for the World War II commanders. There is a definite need for such a volume in the literature of World War II.

I wish to thank my editor, Benton Arnovitz, for all his excellent cooperation, advice, and assistance. A veteran officer and a reserve lieutenant colonel himself, he is unquestionably one of the best military editors in the United States today. I also want to thank Drs. John C. Lewis and Lorraine Heartfield for their support and help. Professor Charles S. Aiken—the most thorough researcher I have ever known—also deserves special acknowledgment and thanks, as does Dr. Ed Hammond, whose voluntary graduate student writing seminar I was "encouraged" to take has made all the difference in my career. I also wish to thank Drs. Sidney R. Jumper and John B. Rehder of the University of Tennessee for their kindness, encouragement, and help along the way.

I would be ungrateful indeed if I did not thank my parents, Mr. and Mrs. Wayne Mitcham, my brothers, Steve and Marq, and my very good friends Mr. and Mrs. Wayne D. Shows of Bastrop for everything they have done for me over the years.

Finally, I wish to thank the officers and men of the 269th Combat Aviation Battalion and the 528th Engineer Battalion (Combat) (Heavy) and especially those subordinate units that, in my younger days, I had the privilege of commanding.

Samuel W. Mitcham, Jr.

August 1984

CONTENTS

MAPS

PHOTOGRAPHS

Foot-sore infantry in the Polish campaign, 1939
A German medical unit in Poland, 1939
Adolf Hitler greets Wehrmacht troops, 1939
A German machine-gun team, 1939-40
Wehrmacht infantrymen under fire in France, 1940
Adolf Hitler with members of the 7th Air Division, Belgium, 1940
Signal troops on the Western Front, 1940
Colonel General von Reichenau and Lieutenant General Dietrich,
     Western Front, 1940
Tanks of Rommel's 7th Panzer Division, France, 1940
German horses being off-loaded, Norway, 1940
A heavy field piece on the African Front, 1941
A German half-track, the Balkans, 1941
A dispatch rider in the Balkan campaign, 1941
A tired, dirty private in the Balkans, 1941
A tank of the 1st SS Panzer Division, the Balkans, 1941
A formation of Afrika Korps panzer grenadiers, 1941
Erwin Rommel and General Ludwig Crüwell, 1942
A Russian highway, 1941
Divisional supply troops behind the Russian Front, 1941-42
German infantry on the Russian Front, 1942
A forward observer and his radio operator on the Russian Front, 1942
A German artillery piece on the Russian Front
Heavy artillery in action on the Russian Front
A convoy of the 100th Jäger Division pursuing the Soviets, 1942
A Soviet city after the Wehrmacht passed through
The huge fortress guns at Sevastopol

SS Lieutenant General Fegelein

Theodor Eicke, director of operations at Dachau as early as 1933

Lieutenant General Boldenstern being decorated with the Knight's Cross, 1942

The swastika goes up in Stalingrad, 1942

Major General Munoz Grandes being decorated with the Iron Cross

Ski troops in Russia, 1942 or 1943

A panzer unit during the Battle of Kursk, July 1943

Members of the 8th Panzer Regiment, 15th Panzer Division

A flame-thrower team on the Russian Front

A mortar crew on the Russian Front, 1943

An infantry fire team in Stalingrad, 1942

A German soldier examines the graves of compatriots

Field Marshal Rommel and Lieutenant General Hans Speidel, France, 1944

The spoils of battle, Western Front, 1944

Some of Rommel's infantrymen, Normandy, 1944

A German artilleryman, France, 1944

German gunners train their rocket launcher

Lieutenant General Karl Wilhelm von Schlieben, 1944

After the Battle of Argentan, 1944

Field Marshal Gerd von Rundstedt with U.S. Lieutenant General Alexander Patch, 1945

Taking boots from dead Americans during the Battle of the Bulge, 1944

Colonel General Alfred Jodl surrendering Germany to the Allies, 1945

HITLER'S LEGIONS

1

The German Division

The Divisional Staff. German divisions in World War II varied remark-ably in strength, composition, organization, transport, equipment and even in racial composition. The division staffs of most combat units, however, were very similar, and were divided into three operational group-ings: the Führungsabteilung, or tactical detachment; the Quartermeister, or supply group; and the Adjutantur, or personnel group.

The tactical group included the Chief of Operations (or Ia) and the Chief Intelligence Officer (Ic) and their respective staffs. The Ia served as chief of staff in divisional-sized units or lower, and the Ic was directly subordinate to him. Besides the intelligence officer, various other combat-oriented subordinates worked for the chief of operations, including the Ia for artillery, air liaison officers, and others. This tactical headquarters was also known as the division's Command Post (CP).

The supply headquarters, which was physically separated from the CP, was headed by the Ib (Chief Supply Officer, or Divisional Quartermaster). It included the IVa (Chief Administrative Officer), the IVb (Chief Medical Officer), the IVc (Chief Veterinary Officer) and the V (Motor Transport Officer). All of these officers were in charge of their own sections. Most of them were not General Staff officers; however, to hold an I-type position (i.e., Ia, Ib, or Ic), an officer had to be a member of the General Staff.

The third operational grouping was the personnel or Adjutantur group, which was headed by the IIa, the Chief Personnel Officer, or Adjutant. Subordinate to him were the IIb or Second Personnel Officer (Adjutant Two), the III (Chief Judge Advocate), the Chaplain (IVd) and various other sections necessary for the functioning of the staff headquarters, such as motor pools, security detachments, and the like. In the U.S. Army this organization would have been called a Headquarters Company. The IIa section handled all officer personnel matters while the IIb was responsible for enlisted personnel matters. The IIb routed requests for replacements through the IIa and was subordinate to him in all matters.

The III and IVd, Motor Pool Officer also commanded their own sections under the overall direction of the IIa.

In addition to the three major groups, divisions had special staffs with officers and sections assigned on a temporary or permanent basis. These might include a Commander of Divisional Supply Troops (subordinate to the Ib on most matters), the Senior Military Police Officer, the Commander of Projector (i.e., flame-thrower) Troops, the Gas Protection Officer and, after July 20, 1944, the National Socialist Guidance Officer.

One very important special staff officer was the Senior Artillery Commander (the ARKO or Arko). He was attached to the division on a temporary basis and was responsible for recommending the allocation of attached General Headquarters artillery units (i.e., those loaned to the division from a corps or higher headquarters) within the division. His command was also called an Arko.

When no General Headquarters artillery units were attached to the division (which was the exception, rather than the rule), the division artillery commander (Artilleriefűhrer or Arfű was responsible for all artillery matters; however, if an Arko (or Artilleriekommandanteur) was present, he normally commanded the divisional artillery forces, and the Arfű directed the division's organic artillery regiment.*

The Infantry Line Regiments. German divisions were organized in any number of ways. However, infantry units were the most numerous. The total German Army and Waffen-SS strength in 1941, for example, was 163 infantry divisions (including four light and six mountain divisions), one cavalry division, nine security divisions, fourteen motorized infantry divisions and twenty-one panzer divisions. In addition, all of the panzer divisions (except those in Africa) had at least two motorized infantry regiments (which were redesignated panzer grenadier regiments on Hitler's orders in November 1942). Because of the predominance of infantry-type units in the Wehrmacht, they will be discussed as the rule.

Early in the war, each German infantry division had three infantry regiments of three battalions each, an artillery regiment, a signal battalion, an anti-tank battalion, an engineer battalion and a reconnaissance battalion, which was changed to a füsilier battalion (or a company) in many divisions created or reorganized after 1942. Similarly, many divisions created after 1942 had only two infantry regiments, and a signal company, instead of a signal battalion.

Infantry regiments—which were renamed grenadier regiments by a Führer order in November 1942—consisted of two or three infantry battalions, an infantry howitzer company and an anti-tank company. The earlier in the war a division was formed, the more likely it was to have three

---

*In combat, the corps artillery units were commanded by Arkos. Army and Army Group artillery units were commanded by Harkos (Höherer Artilleriekommandeur).

THE GERMAN INFANTRY DIVISION, CIRCA 1939

regiments, and the more likely these regiments were to have three battalions, for a total of nine infantry battalions per division. As Hitler made known his requirement for more and more divisions, the strength of each level of command declined remarkably. After 1941, for example, the establishment level of an infantry company was reduced from 180 to 80 and, as the war dragged on, most companies were well below establishment. It's easy to see, then, why it's difficult to generalize about the strength of a German division: a 1939 division of three regiments—each with three infantry battalions consisting of companies of 180 men each—would be much stronger than a 1944 two-regiment Volksgrenadier division with only four infantry battalions in all (and these with companies of fewer than 80 men each). Besides these reductions, the divisional units—signal, anti-tank, engineer, and reconnaissance battalions—were often downgraded from battalion to company-sized units later in the war.

Infantry battalions normally consisted of three infantry companies and either a machine gun company or heavy weapons company. As late as 1944 most infantry companies had three rifle platoons and one heavy machine gun section (or an 81mm mortar section), except in Volksgrenadier divisions, where the grenadier companies had two submachinegun platoons and one rifle platoon.

The machine gun company—present in most mountain, light, and panzer grenadier divisions—included 81mm mortars and heavy machine guns. In infantry and panzer divisions, this unit was replaced by the heavy weapons company, which consisted of infantry howitzer or 120mm mortar platoons.

The first eight companies in the two-battalion regiments, or the first twelve in three-battalion regiments, were organic to the battalions (i.e., were one of the three infantry companies or the battalion's heavy weapons company). The 9th Company (or 13th Company in three-battalion regiments) was an infantry howitzer company directly under regimental control. Even in two-battalion regiments it usually bore the designation 13th Company. The equipment of this unit was varied. In Volksgrenadier divisions it included two platoons of 120mm mortars and one platoon of infantry howitzers. Infantry howitzer companies of earlier vintage divisions had more howitzer units and fewer mortar sections than divisions that were mobilized later in the war.

The 10th Company in two-battalion regiments (or 14th Company in three-battalion regiments) was the infantry anti-tank company, which was equipped with 37mm anti-tank guns or with short-range 75mm and 150mm anti-tank guns. Later they were equipped with *Panzerfäusts*, individually carried anti-tank weapons similar to the bazooka. The 14th Company in Volksgrenadier divisions was called a tank destroyer company, and was equipped solely with *Panzerfäusts*.

The Artillery Regiment. In infantry and light (or Jäger) divisions, the artillery regiments consisted of four battalions, numbered I, II, III and IV. I, II, and III battalions were equipped with towed or horse-drawn 105mm howitzers, while IV battalion had 150mm howitzers. Battalions normally consisted of three batteries of four guns each, or forty-eight guns per regiment. As with all other German military formations, the rule for this type of organization was violated with increasing frequency after 1943; many units, for example, were outfitted with captured foreign equipment.

The artillery regiments in panzer and motorized divisions were more mobile and often self-propelled. Panzer artillery regiments, however, usually had only three battalions: I and II were equipped with 105mm howitzers, and III was armed with 150mm howitzers.

Mountain artillery regiments normally consisted of four battalions. I, II, and III battalions were equipped with 75mm mountain howitzers and IV with 105mm mountain howitzers, which were lighter than normal howitzers of the same calibre.

Divisional artillery units frequently were reinforced by units from the GHQ (General Headquarters) artillery pool at corps-level or above. As already discussed, these units, as well as the organic divisional artillery regiment, were commanded by the Arko. The Arko might bring an assortment of units with him, including GHQ observation units, light, medium, heavy, or superheavy batteries or battalions, which might be horse-drawn, motorized, tractor-drawn, self-propelled, railway transported, or even fixed, in extremely rare cases. Other artillery units often found attached to the division included armored assault gun battalions, which consisted of a headquarters battery and three six-gun batteries equipped with 75mm self-propelled assault guns that were employed as if they were tanks. Flak battalions (organic to many SS panzer divisions) were occasionally attached to divisions and included three 88mm gun batteries and two 20mm gun batteries.

Divisional Units. The primary units organic to the divisional headquarters were the reconnaissance, anti-tank, engineer, and signal battalions. Divisional reconnaissance battalions were remarkably varied, even relatively early in the war. Generally speaking, however, there were two major types in 1942: those found in infantry divisions and those in motorized, light, and panzer divisions. Infantry reconnaissance battalions consisted of three companies: one mounted, one motorcycle, and one motorized (heavy weapons) company. Light, motorized, and panzer divisional reconnaissance battalions normally were completely motorized.

From 1943 onward, newly organized divisions incorporated füsilier battalions, which were organized like infantry battalions except that they were more mobile. Usually they were equipped with bicycles.

The divisional anti-tank battalions were variously equipped, but normally consisted of short-range 75mm and 150mm anti-tank guns. Later in the war they were more and more frequently equipped with hand-carried *Panzerfäusts* or even self-propelled assault guns. These guns were turretless, open-topped, tracked, and armed with a gun mounted on the hull. There usually were eighteen assault guns per battalion (and thirty-one assault guns in an assault gun brigade, which was a type of unit independent of the divisions). Many early model assault guns (i.e., 1940 or 1941 types) were mounted on Panzer Mark III chassis and might employ a low-velocity 75mm or 105mm gun or a low-velocity 105mm howitzer. These were gradually replaced by long-barrel, high-velocity 75mm guns and carried both solid (anti-tank) and high explosive shells. They continued to be mounted on the PzKw III chassis, however. These assault guns were extremely important to the German Army in World War II. Not only did they provide many divisions with excellent anti-tank protection, but they debilitated many enemy (especially Russian) armored units as well. By early 1944, for example, the assault gun arm claimed to have destroyed 20,000 enemy tanks!

Strangely, the assault gun arm was an integral part of the artillery branch, which supplied the officers and training. It was in no way subordinate to the panzer branch.

The combat engineer battalions included assault, construction, demolition, and bridging troops. They were skilled at penetrating minefields and fortified areas, as well as in delaying enemy advances when Hitler allowed his divisions to conduct timely and well-organized retreats—which occurred only rarely. The engineer battalions frequently suffered higher rates of casualties than their infantry counterparts.

Nondivisional engineer battalions were frequently attached to divisions for specific operations. Divisional engineer battalions could, on occasion, be transferred to the GHQ pool or attached to other divisions, although most corps commanders preferred to respect the unit integrity of the division whenever possible.

The division signal battalion had three constituent units: a headquarters detachment, a telephone company, and a radio company. It could, if necessary, be augmented by GHQ units, such as telegraph companies or interception units.

Divisional Support Units. Each German division had its own organic supply and transport echelons under the IIa. These units included supply companies, transport units, motor transport units, the divisional trains, repair units, and others. The variation of the German divisional supply echelons are such that generalization is impossible.

Medical units (Sanitätsabteilunge, or medical detachments) were allocated on the basis of one per division. They consisted of one or two medical companies, a field hospital, and two or three ambulance platoons. They bore the divisional auxiliary number, which was usually the same as that of the division; for example, the 304th Medical Unit belonged to the 304th Infantry Division.

Each division in the German Army, with the exception of the panzer and motorized divisions, had a veterinary company. Since the average German division had 3,000 to 6,000 horses and mules, which carried supplies, ammunition, troops, the wounded, artillery, and other important items, the significance of a good veterinary company is apparent. Table 1, for a "typical" German infantry division prior to 1943, shows the number of horse-drawn motorized vehicles, and this table may even overstate the number of motor vehicles in the typical division. The reliance that German infantry units placed on the horse has long been underestimated by historians.

Divisional Headquarters also controlled a number of what might be termed miscellaneous units, including a bakery company, a military police detachment, a slaughter unit (for animals), and a field post office unit. Other formations, such as railway repair companies, depot units, smoke units, bridging sections, and others might be attached to the division on an as-needed basis.

Panzer Divisions. The panzer divisions in the Polish and French campaigns of 1939 and 1940 possessed many more tanks than those that fought after 1940. The 1st through 5th and 10th panzer divisions consisted of two panzer regiments of two battalions each. Others (numbered 6th through 9th) had one regiment of three battalions each. The 6th, 7th, and 8th Panzers (formerly light divisions) were equipped mainly with captured Czechoslovakian tanks. The 1st, 2nd, 3rd, 4th, 5th, and 10th Panzer Divisions had to give up their second panzer regiments in the fall of 1940 to create new, smaller panzer divisions, in order to satisfy Hitler's illogical demands for more (but weaker) armored units. The number of tanks per division declined from around 320 in 1939 to 230 in 1940 and fewer than 190 in 1941. By 1943 the establishment of a panzer division required about 165 tanks (although none serving on the Eastern Front had that many), and by the end of 1944 it was reduced to 54, and the panzer regiment reduced from three to two battalions per regiment.

Table 1

THE VEHICLES OF A TYPICAL GERMAN INFANTRY DIVISION PRIOR TO 1943: HORSE VS. MOTOR

	Motor Vehicles	Horse-drawn Vehicles
Divisional Headquarters (including administrative, supply, medical, police, postal, and veterinary units)	253	245
Reconnaissance Battalion	30	3
Signal Battalion	103	7
Artillery Regiment	105	229
Anti-Tank Battalion	114	0
Engineer Battalion	87	19
Three infantry regiments (3,250 men each, and each with 683 horses, 6 small infantry guns, 2 large infantry guns, 12 anti-tank guns)	73(x3)	210(x3)
TOTALS: 17,000 men, 5,375 horses	911	1,133

A division of this size would require 53 tons of hay daily, as well as 54 tons of food, 20 tons of gasoline and diesel, 1 ton of lubricants, 10 tons of ordnance stores, and 12 tons of other stores, excluding baggage and ammunition.

After 1943, the proportion of horse-drawn vehicles per division increased as the number of motor vehicles and amount of fuel available to each division declined.

SOURCE: Deighton: p. 175

The motorized infantry strength of the panzer division also declined as the war wore on. In 1940, for example, each panzer division had a motorized infantry brigade consisting of two motorized infantry regiments of two battalions each plus a motorcycle battalion. Each battalion had some six hundred men. Gradually the strength of the battalion declined alarmingly because of casualties, and the motorized infantry brigade headquarters was phased out.

Other than these differences, the panzer division was similar in organizational structure to the German infantry division. Of course its support units were equipped with trucks or armored half-track vehicles instead of horses and were consequently more mobile than infantry support units. Most of the panzer and panzer grenadier divisions also had a motorcycle battalion not found in infantry, mountain, or jäger divisions. And, of course, there was no veterinary company in armored units.

Motorized (Panzer Grenadier) Divisions. German motorized infantry divisions were redesignated panzer grenadier divisions between November 1942 and May 1943. Originally they consisted of three motorized infantry regiments of three battalions each. In late 1940, however, they had to give up their third regiments so the High Command could form new motorized divisions, dropping the number of motorized infantry battalions per division from nine to six. Eventually—from 1941 on—they added a panzer or assault gun battalion of thirty to fifty tanks or guns each. Also, many of the line battalions traded their trucks for armored half-tracks. The support units in the panzer grenadier units were similar to those found in panzer formations.

Mountain Divisions. Mountain divisions were similar to infantry divisions except in training and in that the mountain division's equipment was lighter. Their artillery and anti-tank guns were also lighter—and of smaller caliber. They had three regiments of three battalions each. Many of these battalions had five companies: three mountain jäger, one machine gun, and one heavy weapons. Their reconnaissance units were equipped with bicycles.

Jäger (Light) Divisions. These units were similar to mountain divisions in organization and equipment, except that they only had two regiments. They were created as pursuit divisions. The exceptions were the 90th Light and 164th Light Afrika divisions, which were used, and partially equipped, for desert warfare.

Light Divisions. The original light divisions were formed beginning in 1934-36, and four (numbered 1st through 4th) were in existence when the Wehrmacht invaded Poland in 1939. They consisted of two motorized rifle regiments, a tank battalion, a reconnaissance regiment, and numerous supporting units. They proved to be too unwieldy in Poland, and in the winter of 1939-40 all four were converted into panzer units.

Security Divisions. These units were formed from 1941 on and consisted of two security (or infantry) regiments, which were also known as local defense regiments. They had no artillery and were designed to guard key towns and cities, headquarters, and other installations in Russia, and occasionally they were involved in anti-partisan operations. Most were eventually caught up in front-line fighting on the Eastern Front. The only security division found in the West was the 325th, which spent virtually its entire existence in Paris.

Miscellaneous Army Divisions. The Nazi army had an incredible number of miscellaneous or special purpose divisions, including Reserve, Replacement, Field Training, Coastal Defense, Air Landing, Fortress, Cavalry, and other divisions. They shall be discussed in turn.

Luftwaffe Units. Luftwaffe ground divisions were of three types: parachute, Luftwaffe Field, and flak. The parachute units were made up of specially trained volunteers and were excellent combat formations, although after the Battle of Crete in 1941 they were used almost exclusively as infantry divisions. The Luftwaffe Field divisions, on the other hand, were made up of drafted excess Air Force personnel who were poorly trained for the infantry role and thus did poorly in ground combat. Flak divisions were assigned to armies or army groups and served throughout the area of operations. A number of these divisions had territorial responsibilities with Germany. Since they were engaged primarily in anti-aircraft operations, they will not be discussed in this book.

The Hermann Göring Parachute Panzer and Parachute Panzer Grenadier Divisions will be discussed under their Army categories, even though they were technically Luftwaffe units.

SS Divisions. A total of forty Waffen-SS divisions were used as ground combat units during the war, even though many of these formations were not even made up of Germans. Their performance varied considerably. The most effective of these forces were the German SS panzer divisions, which were larger than their Army counterparts because each had six motorized rifle battalions per division, as compared to four in the Army panzer units. They also received the best equipment Germany could manufacture, and on a priority basis. Their officers, however, tended to be younger, less experienced, and less well trained than their Army counterparts. On the other hand, the men of the German SS divisions fought with a fanaticism not demonstrated by the average infantry division. The foreign SS divisions varied in quality from good to virtually useless.

In general, the organization of the Waffen-SS divisions was similar to the Army divisions, and they normally fought under Army command, although they were responsible to the office of the Reichsführer-SS in administrative and disciplinary matters.

SOURCES: Len Deighton, *Blitzkrieg: From the Rise of Hitler to the Fall of Dunkirk*, Alfred A. Knopf, New York, 1979: 175 (hereafter cited as "Deighton"); Gordon A. Harrison, *Cross-Channel Attack*, United States Army in World War II, European Theater of Operations, Office of the Chief of Military History, United States Government Printing Office, Washington, D.C., 1951: 240 (hereafter cited as "Harrison"); Samuel W. Mitcham, Jr., *Rommel's Last Battle: The Desert Fox and the Normandy Campaign*, Stein and Day, Briarcliff Manor, New York, 1983: 26-31 (hereafter cited as "Mitcham 1983"); O. Munzel, *Die Deutschen Gepanzer Truppen bis 1945*, Maximilian, Herford and Bonn, 1965; Albert Seaton, *The Russo-German War, 1941-45*, Praeger Publishers, New York, 1970 (hereafter cited as "Seaton"); G. Tornau and F. Korowski, *Sturmartillerie Fels in der Brandung*, Maximilian, Herford and Bonn, 1965; United States Army Military Intelligence Service, "Order of Battle of the German Army," War Department, Washington, D.C., 1942 (hereafter cited as "OB 42"); Ibid 1943 (hereafter cited as "OB 43"); Ibid 1944 (hereafter cited as "OB 44") and Ibid 1945 (hereafter cited as "OB 45").

2

The Wehrkreis System

The German Wehrkreis, or military district, had special significance for the German Army division, because it had responsibility for recruiting, drafting, inducting, and training German soldiers, as well as for mobilizing divisions and providing them with training and trained replacements. Each German division was normally associated with a single Wehrkreis. These military districts date back to 1919, when the Reichswehr functioned as the Armed Forces Command for the Weimar Republic, which had replaced the Imperial government of the Kaiser after World War I. When Hitler rose to power in 1933, he did away with the Republic, dissolved the old Reichswehr, and established the Wehrmacht. Two high commands oversaw the military expansion and later helped direct Hitler's war: the High Command of the Army (O.K.H., or Oberkommando des Heers) and later the High Command of the Armed Forces (O.K.W., or Oberkommando der Wehrmacht). Hitler, however, had the foresight to retain the Wehrkreis system, which already had written contingency plans for the substantial enlargement of the Army. At first the various Wehrkreis worked directly under O.K.H., but in 1938 the Home Army (or Replacement Army) was created to oversee and coordinate the functions of the Wehrkreis; however, it did little to change their actual operations until the fall of 1942. The Wehrkreis have not received the attention of many historians because they did their jobs so quietly, but ever so thoroughly. The Wehrkreis grew in number during the expansion program, from seven in 1932 to 19 in 1943. Although they lost some of their training missions from late 1942 until 1944, they were still the primary headquarters to which the German divisions looked for training and—more important as the war went on— replacements. The Wehrkreis were also responsible for rebuilding and refitting shattered divisions, a responsibility that also took on more importance as the war continued.

The German Army was mobilized in "waves" of divisions, a process that

continued throughout the war. This process was conducted by the
Wehrkreis, under the supervision of the Replacement Army. Table 2 shows
how this process worked for infantry divisions from 1934 until October
1944. After that point the data becomes jumbled, which is to be expected,
considering the state Nazi Germany was in by late 1944. Despite the
confusion, however, the "wave" system continued to function almost to
the end. There were at least thirty-eight mobilization waves in the 1934-45
period.

Prior to the general mobilization of June 1939, each Wehrkreis had two
components in its headquarters: a tactical component, which became a
corps headquarters upon mobilization and which went to the front, and a
second or deputy component, which remained at home to direct training
and replacement activities in the territory. This component consisted
primarily of older soldiers who were no longer able to endure the physical
hardships of field campaigns, but who were well trained and perfectly
capable of efficiently administering their territories. Table 3 reflects this
well, for it shows the Wehrkreis system as it existed in 1942, along with its
commanders and their ages. Note that the youngest commander was fifty-
eight, and the average Wehrkreis commander was in his mid-sixties, or ten
to twelve years older than a corps commander at the front. Similar condi-
tions existed in the subordinate posts. Many positions in the military
districts were held by older officers—many of them World War I veterans—
who were no longer fit for the rigors of active campaigning but who were
competent military administrators.

Table 2

GERMAN MOBILIZATION WAVES FOR INFANTRY DIVISIONS, 1934-1944

Wave	Formed	Number of divisions	Division Series	Comments
1	1934-1938	39	1-46	Peace-time army units
2	Aug. 1939	15	52-79	From reservists
3	Aug. 1939	22	199-246	Landwehr (older personnel)
4	Aug. 1939	14	251-269	From reserve units
5	Sep. 1939	11	81-98	Reservists
6	Oct. 1939	6	307-341	All disbanded, 1940
7	Dec. 1939	13	164-198	From reserve units
8	Mar. 1940	10+	351-399	Mostly older personnel
			500-level	Mostly disbanded, 1940
9	Apr. 1940	10	290-299	Mostly 1940 draft class
10	Jun. 1940	8	271-280	Disbanded, 1940
11	Sep. 1940	10	121-137	For Russian campaign
12	Oct. 1940	10	97-113	For Russian campaign
13	Dec. 1940	9	302-327	For use in occupied Western Europe
14	Jan. 1941	8	332-342	For use in occupied Western Europe
15	Apr. 1941	15	702-719	Static; for West and Balkans
16	Jul. 1941	—	—	Security regiments
17	1941-1942	9	370-389	For use in Russia
18	late 1942	8	326-348	Static; for use in West
19	Feb. 1943	10+	—	Bore numbers of divisions destroyed at Stalingrad
20	Jul. 1943	7	242-266	Static; for use in West
21	Nov. 1943	10	349-367	Employment varied
22	Dec. 1943	6	271-278	From remnants of disbanded units; used in West
23	Jan. 1944	—	—	Grenadier regiments; later absorbed by 25th Wave
24	Feb. 1944	4	42-49	From reserve divisions
25	Feb. 1944	6	72-92	For use in West
26	May 1944	4	Named	Absorbed by reformed divisions
27	Jun. 1944	5	16-189	Formed from reserve divisions
28	Jul. 1944	13	541-559	Formed from personnel on leave
29	Jul. 1944	10+	500 series	Grenadier (later Volksgrenadier)
30	Jul. 1944	—	—	Grenadier brigades
31	Aug. 1944	12	560-572	Grenadier divisions absorbed later by 32nd Wave
32+	Oct., 1944-onward			Divisions of any previous wave reformed as Volksgrenadier units; several new numbered and named divisions

Table 3

WEHRKREIS COMMANDERS IN 1942

Wehrkreis	Commander in 1942 (Age in parentheses)
I	General* Peter Weyer (63)
II	General Max Föhrenbach (70)
III	General Baron von Dalwigk zu Lichtenfels (66)
IV	General Erich Wöllwarth (70)
V	General Erwin Osswald (60)
VI	General Glokke (58)
VII	General Edmund Wachenfeld (64)
VIII	General Hans Halm (63)
IX	General Rudolf Schniewindt (64)
X	General Walter Raschick (60)
XI	General Wolfgang Muff (62)
XII	General Albrecht Steppuhn (63)
XIII	General Friedrich von Cochenhausen (63)
XVII	General Alfred Streccius (64)
XVIII	General Hubert Schaller-Kallide (60)
XX	General Max Bock (62)
General Gouvernement (Poland):	General Walter Petzel (59)

Three Wehrkreise were special-function headquarters and had no territorial responsibilities or deputy components. Wehrkreis XIV controlled the German motorized infantry divisions; Wehrkreis XV controlled the light divisions; and Wehrkreis XVI was responsible for the administration and training of Hitler's panzer divisions. When they were upgraded to Corps Headquarters in mid-1939 these Wehrkreise ceased to exist as such, and their functions were taken over by the remaining Wehrkreise.

The Replacement Army (or Home Army) was created in Berlin in 1938 to direct and coordinate the activities of the Wehrkreise, which had been directly under the High Command of the Army (O.K.H.) until that time. From its beginning until July 20, 1944, it was commanded by Colonel

---

*German general officer ranks began with major general. Divisions were commanded by major generals and lieutenant generals and, occasionally, by colonels. Wehrkreise and corps were normally commanded by full generals (three stars on the American scale). Higher headquarters were usually commanded by colonel generals and field marshals. Appendix II is a table comparing German Army, Waffen-SS and U.S. Army ranks.

General Friedrick Fromm and then by Reichsführer-SS Heinrich Himmler from July 21, 1944, until the end of the war. Colonel Count Claus von Stauffenberg, Fromm's one-eyed, one-armed chief of staff, was the officer who attempted to assassinate Adolf Hitler on July 20, but only succeeded in wounding him. The effective but weak-kneed and vacillating Fromm turned against the conspirators and, about midnight on July 20, executed von Stauffenberg, former Chief of the Army General Staff Colonel General Ludwig Beck, and three other officers. This action did not save him, however. Hitler relieved him of his command, imprisoned him, and had him executed on March 19, 1945. None of this, however, disrupted the function of the Wehrkreise, which continued to provide new divisions and to rebuild old ones until they were overrun by the Allied armies at the end of the war. Their effectiveness can be gauged by the fact that the German Army grew from 100,000 men in 1935 to more than 4,000,000 by early 1944, and had already suffered more than 2,000,000 casualties by that date. It is certainly not an exaggeration to state that, had it not been for the Wehrkreis system, the Third Reich never would have been able to keep its forces in the field for as long as it did.

Because of the close relationship that existed between each German division and its Wehrkreis, particularly early in the war, a brief description of the organization and operational history of each Wehrkreis is provided in Appendix 3. This discussion, however, may be skipped by those who are more interested in the histories of the individual divisions. Also, the home Wehrkreis of each division will be noted in subsequent chapters, because that suggests where many and possibly most of the division's personnel originated, as well as where its replacements came from. Table 4 shows the location of each Wehrkreis in 1942. Map 1 shows the location of the Wehrkreis, and their 1944 boundaries. Map 2 shows the locations of their headquarters, and Map 3 the regions of the Third Reich. Map 4 shows the location of the major battles fought by the German Army in World War II.

Table 4

THE WEHRKREISE AND THEIR TERRITORIAL RESPONSIBILITIES

Wehrkreis	Headquarters	Territorial Extent
I	Königsberg	East Prussia; extended in 1939 to include Memel and portions of northern Poland
II	Stettin	Mecklenburg and Pomerania
III	Berlin	Altmark, Neumark, and Brandenburg
IV	Dresden	Saxony and part of Thuringia; later annexed part of northern Bohemia
V	Stuttgart	Württemberg and part of Baden; extended in 1940 to include Alsace
VI	Münster	Westphalia and Rhineland; later extended into eastern Belgium
VII	Munich	Southern Bavaria
VIII	Breslau	Silesia and Sudetenland; later parts of Moravia and southwestern Poland
IX	Kassel	Hessen and part of Thuringia
X	Hamburg	Schleswig-Holstein and northern Hanover; extended in 1940 to include part of Danish Slesvig
XI	Hanover	Braunschweig, Anhalt, and most of Hanover
XII	Wiesbaden	Eifel, the Palatinate, and the Saar; part of Hessen; extended after the fall of France to include Lorraine, including the Nancy area
XIII	Nuremberg	Northern Bavaria; extended in 1938 to include part of western Bohemia
XIV	Berlin	No territorial responsibilities; ceased to exist as a Wehrkreis in 1939; later became Headquarters, XIV Panzer Corps
XV	Berlin	No territorial responsibilities; ceased to exist as a Wehrkreis in 1939; later became Headquarters, 3rd Panzer Army
XVI	Berlin	No territorial responsibilities; ceased to exist as a Wehrkreis in 1939; later became Headquarters, 4th Panzer Army
XVII	Vienna	Northern Austria; extended in 1939 to include the southern districts of Czechoslovakia
XVIII	Salzburg	Southern Austria; extended in 1941 to include the northern parts of Slovenia
XX	Danzig	The former Danzig Free State, the Polish Corridor, and the western part of East Prussia
General Gouvernement	Warsaw	Created in 1943 and included central and most of southern Poland
Bohemia and Moravia	Prague	Most of what was formerly Czechoslovakia; created in late 1942

NOTE: The territorial adjustments made by Reichsführer-SS Himmler in late 1944 are not included in this table; they were relatively minor in any event.

The division was the basic tactical unit on the battlefield; however, the divisions were directed by corps headquarters, which were, in turn, controlled by army headquarters, which were more often than not directed by army groups. Appendix IV provides a thumbnail sketch of the higher headquarters employed by the German Army and the Waffen-SS in World War II.

NOTES AND SOURCES: Fromm, a Berlin native, served in World War I in the artillery branch before joining the Reichswehr. He held a series of staff positions before becoming the Chief of the Army Department in the Reich War Ministry as a Colonel in 1933. His official title from 1938 to 1944 was Chief of Army Equipment and Commander-in-Chief, Replacement Army.

Heinrich Himmler, the Commander-in-Chief of the Replacement Army from July 21, 1944, had been in charge of the Nazi SS since before Hitler came to power in 1933. He twice directed army groups in the field: Army Group G on the Western Front in late 1944-early 1945 and Army Group Vistula on the Eastern Front in early 1945. Both times the results were disastrous. He was relieved of all his posts in late April 1945, when Hitler found out that he was attempting to negotiate with the Allies. Himmler attempted to escape in the confusion caused by the collapse of the Third Reich but was captured by the British on May 21, 1945, and two days later committed suicide by taking poison from a vial concealed in his clothing.

For the complete story of the attempt to assassinate Adolf Hitler, see Constantine FitzGibbon, *20 July,* W. W. Norton and Company, New York: 1956; James Forman, *Code Name Valkyrie: Count von Stauffenberg and the Plot to Kill Hitler,* Laurel-Leaf Library, New York: 1975; Hans-Adolf Jacobsen (ed.), *July 20, 1944,* Federal German Government Press and Information Office: 1969; Robert Manvill and Heinrich Fraenkel, *The Men Who Tried to Kill Hitler,* Coward-McCann, Inc., New York: 1964; Robert Payne, *The Life and Death of Adolf Hitler,* Random House, New York: 1973: and Erich Zimmermann and Hans Adolf Jacobsen, *Germans Against Hitler, July 20, 1944,* Federal German Government Press and Information Office, Bonn: 1960. Also see William L. Shirer, *The Rise and Fall of the Third Reich,* Simon and Schuster, New York: 1960.

Sources of the Wehrkreis system and its effects on the German war effort include Robert Goralski, *World War II Almanac, 1931-1945,* G. P. Putnam's Sons, New York: 1972; *Kriegstagebuch des Oberkommando der Wehrmacht (Wehrmachtführungsstab),* Bücher I-IV, Bernard and Graefe Verlag für Wehrwesen, Frankfurt am Main: 1961; U.S. Army Military Intelligence Division, "The German Replacement Army (Ersatzheer)," U.S. War Department, Washington, D.C.: 1945 (hereafter cited as "RA"); OB 42; OB 43; OB 45.

THE WEHRKREIS BOUNDARIES,

late 1944

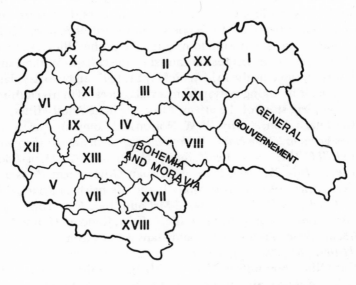

THE WEHRKREIS HEADQUARTERS, 1944

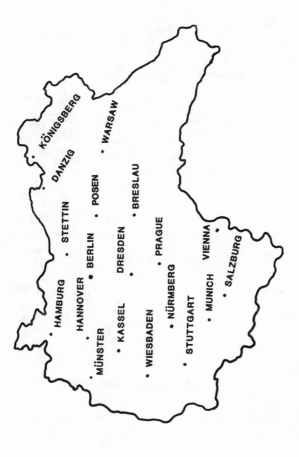

KÖNIGSBERG
DANZIG
WARSAW
STETTIN
POSEN
BERLIN
BRESLAU
HAMBURG
DRESDEN
HANNOVER
KASSEL
PRAGUE
MÜNSTER
WIESBADEN
NÜRMBERG
VIENNA
STUTTGART
MUNICH
SALZBURG

0   62   124
MILES

THE BATTLEGROUNDS, 1939–1945

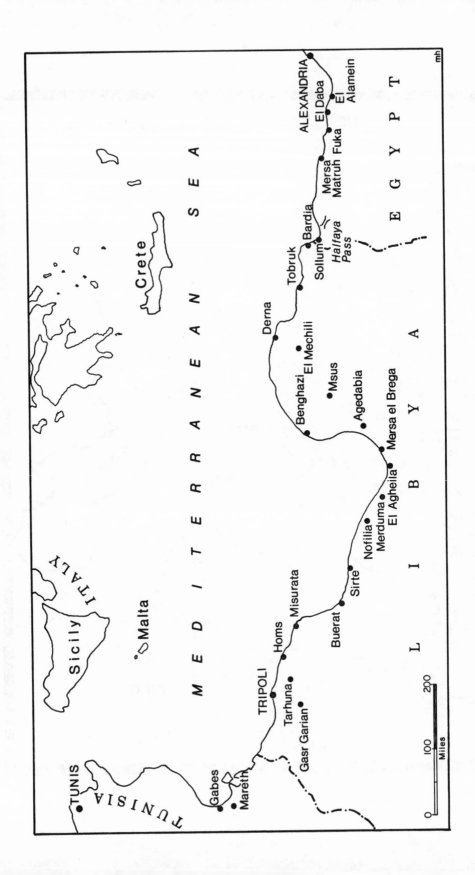

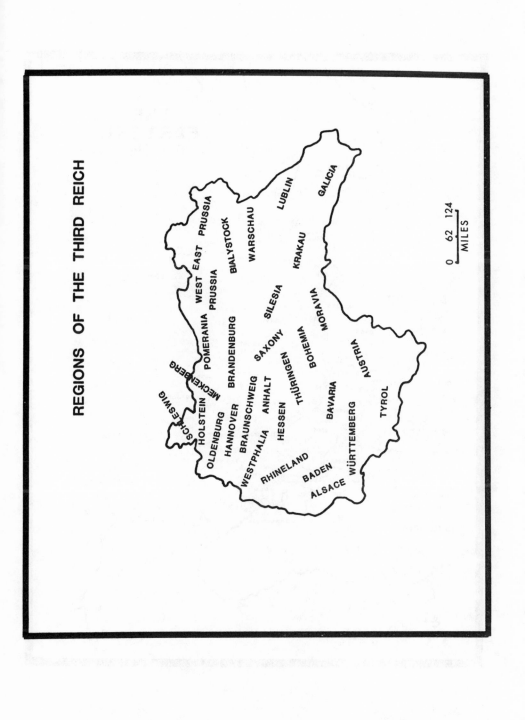

REGIONS OF THE THIRD REICH

0 62 124
MILES

SCHLESWIG
HOLSTEIN
MECKENBERG
OLDENBURG
HANNOVER
BRAUNSCHWEIG
WESTPHALIA ANHALT
HESSEN
RHINELAND
BADEN
ALSACE
WÜRTTEMBERG
POMERANIA
BRANDENBURG
WEST PRUSSIA
EAST PRUSSIA
PRUSSIA
BIALYSTOCK
WARSCHAU
LUBLIN
GALICIA
KRAKAU
SILESIA
SAXONY
THÜRINGEN
BOHEMIA
MORAVIA
BAVARIA
AUSTRIA
TYROL

THE
EASTERN
FRONT

3

The Infantry Divisions*

1st INFANTRY DIVISION

COMPOSITION: 1st Infantry Regiment, 22nd Infantry Regiment, 43rd Infantry Regiment, 1st Artillery Regiment, 1st Reconnaissance Battalion, 1st Anti-Tank Battalion, 1st Engineer Battalion, 1st Signal Battalion

HOME STATION: Königsberg, Wkr. I

This division—made up almost entirely of East Prussians—was formed by the expansion of the historic 1st Infantry Regiment in 1935, shortly after Hitler reintroduced conscription in Germany. It maintained a strong traditionalist favor and had as its divisional symbol the Hohenzollern coat of arms—the emblem of the ruling family of Imperial Germany from 1871 to 1918.

In 1939 the division invaded northern Poland as part of Army Group North. It fought well there but was only lightly engaged in the French campaign the following year.

In June 1941, the 1st Infantry Division crossed into Russia with Army Group North and was heavily engaged during the drive on Leningrad. By October 1941, its strength had been reduced by two-thirds; nevertheless, it continued to fight on the northern sector of the Russian Front, primarily as a part of the 18th Army, for more than two years. During this time, it took part in the Battle of Lake Peipus, the Battles of Lake Ladoga, and the Battle of the German Corridor (east of Leningrad), as well as the Siege of Leningrad itself. In October 1943, the 1st Infantry was attached to Army Group

*Included infantry, as well as reserve, replacement, air landing, assault, sturm, Volksgrenadier, grenadier, marine, coastal defense, security, and special purpose ("z.v.B.") divisions, as well as administrative divisional staffs and field training divisions. Those divisions that fought under more than one designation are usually listed under their last designation. Exceptions are noted in the text.

South and fought in the Battle of Krivoi Rog in the Dnieper campaign in southern Russia. Later it saw action in the Ukraine and was encircled with the 1st Panzer Army between the Bug and the Dnestr rivers in March 1944. In the subsequent breakout it formed the rear guard of the XLVI Panzer Corps and suffered heavy casualties. Later, after a period of rest and rebuilding, it was sent to the central sector, where it was one of the few divisions to escape when Army Group Center was crushed by the Soviets in June and July 1944. In October 1944, the survivors of the 1st Infantry were still with Army Group Center and ended the war fighting the Soviets in the division's home territory of East Prussia. Commanders of the East Prussian 1st Infantry Division included Lieutenant General Joachim von Kortz-fleisch (1939), Lieutenant General Philipp Kleffel (1940-42), Lieutenant General Martin Grase (1942-43), and Lieutenant General Anton von Kros-ick (late 1943-45).

NOTES AND SOURCES: Philipp Kleffel was promoted to General of Cavalry on March 1, 1942, and commanded L Corps from January 1942 until early 1944. Martin Grase, former commander of the 40th Infantry Regiment (1941), was promoted to General of Infantry on November 1, 1943, and given command of the XXVI Corps. Later he was briefly Military Governor of Belgium and Northern France (July-August 1944). Paul Carell *Scorched Earth*, Ballantine Books, New York, 1971: 242, 525 (hereafter cited as "Carell 1971"); Theodor Hartmann, *Wehrmacht Divisional Signs, 1938-45*, Almark Publishing Company, London, 1970: 9 (hereafter cited as "Hartmann"); Robert M. Kennedy, *The German Campaign in Poland (1939)*, United States Department of the Army *Pamphlet 20-255*, U.S. Army, Washington, D.C., 1956: 10B, 74 (hereafter cited as "Kennedy"); Erich von Manstein, *Lost Victories*, Henry Regnery Company, Chicago, 1958: 483-83 (hereafter cited as "Manstein"); Harrison E. Salisbury, *The 900 Days: The Siege of Leningrad*, Harper and Row, Publishers, New York, 1969: 351 (hereafter cited as "Salisbury"); OB 42: 73; and Earl F. Ziemke, *Stalingrad to Berlin: The German Defeat in the East*, U.S. Department of the Army, United States Government Printing Office, Washington, D.C., 1966: 250 (hereafter cited as "Ziemke 1966").

1st MARINE DIVISION

COMPOSITION: various *ad hoc* naval units

HOME STATION: see below

Created in 1945 by the order of Grand Admiral Karl Dönitz, the Commander-in-Chief of the German Navy, this division was turned over to Army Group Vistula by March 1, 1945 and assigned a defensive sector on the Oder River, east of Berlin. It fought its only battle in April 1945, when the Russians made their final push on the capital of the Reich. The 1st Marine was quickly destroyed in this drive.

The term "marine" in the German military of 1945 did not carry with it the connotation of elitism that it did (and does) to the American. The commander of Army Group Vistula felt that Dönitz was simply trying to impress Hitler by offering him this division—that Dönitz couldn't believe this improvised formation would help the army group in its predicament. This conclusion probably was correct: these men were trained sailors, not trained infantrymen, and were virtually useless in land battles against the Soviets.

NOTES AND SOURCES: Army Major General Wilhelm Bleckwenn, who had commanded the 708th Infantry Division as a colonel, was the commander of the 1st Marine Division, but there was little he could do to prevent the Soviets from smashing this unit. *Kriegstagebuch des Oberkommando der Wehrmacht (Wehrmachtführungsstab),* Bernard and Graefe Verlag fur Wehrwesen, Frankfurt-am-Main, 1961: Volume IV: 1898 (hereafter cited as *"Kriegstagebuch des OKW"*); Cornelius Ryan, *The Last Battle,* Popular Library, New York, 1966: 271 (hereafter cited as "Ryan").

1st LIGHT DIVISION
see 6th Panzer Division

2nd INFANTRY DIVISION
see 12th Panzer Division

2nd LIGHT DIVISION
see 7th Panzer Division

3rd INFANTRY DIVISION
see 3rd Motorized Division

3rd LIGHT DIVISION
see 8th Panzer Division

3rd MARINE DIVISION

COMPOSITION: various *ad hoc* naval formations

HOME STATION: Kiel (?)

As a weak force of naval personnel, this division was turned over to the Army by Grand Admiral Dönitz in the spring of 1945 when the Russians were at the gates of Berlin. It was assigned to Army Group Vistula and fought its only battle in front of the Nazi capital as part of von Manteuffel's 3rd Panzer Army. It was quickly destroyed by the Soviets.

SOURCES: Christopher Chant, ed., *The Marshall Cavendish Illustrated Encyclopedia of World War II*, Marshall Cavendish Corporation, New York, 1972, Volume 17: 2376 (hereafter cited as "Chant"); Ryan: 271.

4th INFANTRY DIVISION
see 14th Panzer Division

4th LIGHT DIVISION
see 9th Panzer Division

5th INFANTRY DIVISION
see 5th Jäger Division

5th LIGHT DIVISION
see 21st Panzer Division

6th INFANTRY (later VOLKSGRENADIER) DIVISION

COMPOSITION: 18th Infantry Regiment, 37th Infantry Regiment, 58th Infantry Regiment, 6th Artillery Regiment, 6th Reconnaissance Battalion, 6th Anti-Tank Battalion, 6th Engineer Battalion, 6th Signal Battalion

HOME STATION: Bielefeld, Wkr. VI

This division was created at Münster in the Reichsheer reorganization of 1921. Its personnel were mainly Westphalians but included some East Prussians and Rhinelanders. The 6th Infantry first saw action in 1940 under Major General von Biegelben in France, where it earned a reputation as an effective fighting unit. In June 1941 it took part in the invasion of Russia as part of the 9th Army, Army Group Center. The division took part in heavy fighting on the drive to Moscow but managed to cross the Volga River north of the Russian capital in late November. It was in an exposed position when the Soviet winter offensive began, holding sixteen miles of frontage when the average division supposedly could hold only six miles successfully against a determined assault. The 6th nevertheless repulsed several Soviet attacks and gave ground only gradually, while both inflicting and sustaining heavy casualties.

The 6th Infantry remained with Army Group Center for the next two and a half years. In 1942 it fought in the defensive battles on the central sector of the Russian Front and in March of the following year took part in the 9th Army's brilliant retreat from the Rzhev bulge, a maneuver that freed a dozen divisions from a very exposed position. In July 1943, under Lieutenant General Horst Grossmann (1943-44) it saw action at Kursk, as part of the XLVII Panzer Corps. Later the 6th Infantry fought in the defensive battles on the middle Dnieper. It was smashed during the Soviet summer offensive of 1944 that scattered Army Group Center. Most of the division was surrounded with the XXXV Corps and forced to surrender. The recently appointed divisional commander, Lieutenant General Hans-Walter Heyne, was among the prisoners. Enough of the 6th escaped,

however, for the High Command to recommission a skeleton 6th Volksgrenadier Division in the autumn of 1944. The rebuilt 6th—which was
never more than a battle group—was sent back to the Eastern Front and
took part in the retreat through Poland. It was in action on the Vistula in
December 1944. In the last campaign the remnants of the 6th Volksgrenadier were part of Field Marshal Ferdinand Schörner's army group, which
was surrounded by the Russians east of Prague, Czechoslovakia, in late
April and May 1945. It surrendered to the Red Army.

NOTES AND SOURCES: Hans-Walter Heyne, who was promoted to Lieutenant General effective December 1, 1943, had previously commanded the
82nd Infantry Division (1943-early 1944). Paul Carell, *Hitler Moves East,
1941-43*, Bantam Books, New York, 1966: 196, 357 (hereafter cited as
"Carell 1966"); Carell 1971: 25-26, 309, 314, 597; Kennedy: 10B; Manstein:
134; OB 42: 73; OB 43: 126.

7th INFANTRY DIVISION

COMPOSITION: 19th Infantry Regiment, 61st Infantry Regiment, 62nd
Infantry Regiment, 7th Artillery Regiment, 7th Reconnaissance Battalion,
7th Anti-Tank Battalion, 7th Engineer Battalion, 7th Signal Battalion

HOME STATION: Munich, Wkr. VII

The 7th Infantry was a Bavarian unit, formed in the Reichsheer reorganization of 1921. After 1940, the 638th Infantry Regiment, a volunteer force
of French legionnaires under Colonel Roger Labonne, was attached to the
division.
    Called "a good fighting division" by American intelligence, the 7th
Infantry was heavily engaged in southern Poland in September 1939. In the
French campaign the following year the 7th fought the British Expeditionary Force in Belgium but went into reserve after the fall of Dunkirk,
and was not subsequently engaged in the West. In 1941 it took part in the
invasion of Russia with Army Group Center and fought in the Siege of
Mogilev on the upper Dnieper. Later it was involved in the final thrust
toward Moscow and in the ensuing Russian counteroffensive that saved
Stalin's capital. The division spent 1942 on the relatively quiet central
sector and took part in the Kursk offensive, where it formed part of the
XLVI Panzer Corps. It managed to escape the near-annihilation of Army
Group Center in the summer of 1944 and conducted a fighting retreat
through Poland that fall. It finally was cut off by the last Soviet offensive,
and ended the war isolated behind Russian lines on the Hela peninsula, at

the mouth of the Vistula, where it surrendered on May 8, 1945. The 7th Infantry's divisional commanders included Major General Paul Ott (1939-40), Lieutenant General Baron Eccard von Gablenz (1940-42), Lieutenant General Hans Traut (1943), Colonel Alois Weber (1944), Lieutenant General Fritz-Georg von Rappard (1944-45), and Major General Noak (1945).

After the 199th Grenadier Regiment of the 57th Infantry Division was destroyed, the 7th Division's 19th Grenadier Regiment bore the honorary title "Infantry Regiment List," in honor of Adolf Hitler's World War I regimental commander.

NOTES AND SOURCES: Paul Ott was later promoted to General of Infantry and given command of the LII Corps (1942-43). Baron von Gablenz later commanded the 384th Infantry Division and Replacement Division Staff 404 (1942 and 1943-August 1944, respectively). He briefly commanded the XXVII Corps on the Russian Front (January 13 to April 1, 1942) and ended the war in northern Italy as commander of the 232nd Infantry Division (1945). Colonel Weber, the former commander of the 61st Grenadier Regiment of the 7th Infantry Division and a holder of the Knight's Cross with Oak Leaves, was acting divisional commander in August 1944. Carell 1966: 86, 330, 350; Carell 1971: 26; Chant, Volume 18: 2381, 2393; Hartmann: 10; Manstein: 52; OB 42: 73; OB 43: 127; OB 45: 141.

8th INFANTRY DIVISION
see 8th Jäger Division

9th INFANTRY (later VOLKSGRENADIER) DIVISION

COMPOSITION 1942): 36th Infantry Regiment, 57th Infantry Regiment, 116th Infantry Regiment, 9th Artillery Regiment, 9th Reconnaissance Battalion, 9th Anti-Tank Battalion, 9th Engineer Battalion, 9th Signal Battalion

HOME STATION: Giessen, Wkr. IX

This peacetime division was formed in 1935 and consisted of soldiers from Hessen-Nassau. Upon mobilization it was sent to the Saar Front and helped guard Germany's exposed western flank while Hitler overran Poland. It later fought well in the Battle of France, as part of Panzer Group von Kleist, and beginning in July 1941 spent three years on the southern sector of the Eastern Front. It took part in the Donets, Caucasus, Kuban, and lower Dnieper campaigns as well as the 1941 Ukraine campaign that ended with the fall of Kiev. It was down to battle group strength by October 1943. In August 1944, it was cut off and almost completely destroyed in the retreat across Rumania. Taken out of the line and rebuilt in the Ossboel-Esbjerg area of Denmark, the 9th absorbed the partially formed 584th Volksgrenadier Division and reemerged in the Ardennes offensive in late 1944 as a Volksgrenadier division; however, its former *esprit de corps* was gone. The 9th continued to fight in the West, opposing the American thrust across Luxembourg and then southern Germany, but with little success. In April 1945, the remnants of the unit (which consisted mainly of the divisional commander and his staff, since almost all of the combat units had been destroyed) were attached to the 352nd Volksgrenadier Division and defended Nuremberg as part of the XIII SS Infantry Corps. After this battle the survivors of the division surrendered to the Western Allies. The commanders of the 9th Infantry/Volksgrenadier included Lieutenant General Baron Siegmund von Schleinitz (1941-42), Major General Werner Gebb (1942), and Colonel Werner Kolb (1944-45).

NOTES AND SOURCES: The Prussian Baron von Schleinitz later commanded the 361st Infantry Division (1943-44). Major General Gebb was captured by the Russians in August 1944 and, like a great many officers taken prisoner on the Eastern Front, joined the anti-Nazi National Free Germany Committee. Colonel Kolb was a reserve officer. Carell 1966: 557; Hugh M. Cole, *The Ardennes: The Battle of the Bulge,* United States Army in World War II, European Theater of Operations, Office of the Chief of Military History, United States Government Printing Office, Washington, D.C., 1965: 641-42 (hereafter cited as "Cole 1965"); Manstein: 423, Oberkommando des Heeres (German Army High Command), Chief of the Replacement Army (Ersatz), "Frontnachweiser," 15 December 1944 (hereafter cited as "Frontnachweiser"); OB 42: 71; OB 43: 127; OB 44: 177-78; OB 45: 141-42.

10th INFANTRY DIVISION
see 10th Panzer Grenadier Division

11th INFANTRY DIVISION

COMPOSITION: 2nd Infantry Regiment, 23rd Infantry Regiment, 44th Infantry Regiment, 11th Artillery Regiment, 11th Reconnaissance Battalion, 11th Anti-Tank Battalion, 11th Engineer Battalion, 11th Signal Battalion

HOME STATION: Allenstein, Wkr. I

Formed in 1934-35 by the expansion of the 2nd Infantry Regiment of the old Reichswehr, the 11th Infantry consisted of personnel from East Prussia and the Rhineland. It participated in the Polish campaign, where it fought as part of the 3rd Army, Army Group North. After the French campaign, in which it played a minor role, the 11th was sent to the Russian Front, took part in the initial invasion of the Soviet Union in 1941 and, except for a brief period of rest and reorganization in Greece in 1943, remained in the East until the end of the war. The division took part in the sweep across the Baltic States in 1941, the Siege of Leningrad, the Battle of Zoltsy, and in the fighting north of Lake Ladoga. Later, it helped repulse the Soviet offensive south of Lake Ladoga in 1943. After rebuilding in Greece, it went back into action in northern Russia, fought in the Battle of Narva, and took part in the withdrawal from Leningrad to western Latvia. Finally it was cut off in the Courland Pocket when the Russians penetrated to the Baltic Sea in the fall of 1944 and was still there when Adolf Hitler committed suicide on April 30, 1945. A few days later, however, the division (along with the 14th Panzer Division) was evacuated from the Courland Pocket by the German Navy on the last available ships and returned home, thus avoiding Russian captivity. It was selected for evacuation by Colonel General Karl Hilpert, the Commander-in-Chief of Army Group Courland, because of its out-standing service as a "fire-fighter" division in the desperate winter battles of 1944-45, during which the Soviets made six unsuccessful attempts to crush the pocket. The 11th Infantry Division was commanded at various times by Lieutenant Generals Max Bock (1939), Herbert von Böckmann (1940), Siegfried Thomaschki (1942-43), and Karl Burdach (1943-45).

NOTES AND SOURCES: Bock was later promoted to full General and was commanding Wehrkreis XX (the Danzig-western East Prussia region) in 1942. General von Böckmann was promoted to General of Infantry and commanded L Corps on the Russian Front in 1942 and 1943. He was apparently retired by 1945. Thomaschki received a territorial command in early 1944. Karl Burdach, a former branch chief at O.K.H. (1939-42), was acting commander of the XXVII Corps in 1943. Carell 1971: 260; Kennedy: 74; Manstein: 196; Jürgen Thorwald, *Defeat in the East*, Ballantine Books, Inc., New York, 1980: 288 (hereafter cited as "Thorwald"); OB 45: 142.

12th INFANTRY (later VOLKSGRENADIER) DIVISION

COMPOSITION: 27th Infantry Regiment, 48th Infantry Regiment, 89th Infantry Regiment, 12th Artillery Regiment, 12th Reconnaissance Battalion, 12th Anti-Tank Battalion, 12th Engineer Battalion, 12th Signal Battalion

HOME STATION: Schwerin, Wkr. II

A Mecklenberg unit stationed in Pomerania prior to the start of the war, the 12th Infantry participated in almost every major campaign of the conflict. Its artillery regiment had Colonel General Werner von Fritsch, the former Commander-in-Chief of the German Army, as its honorary commander. During the Polish campaign von Fritsch, an anti-Nazi bent on suicide, joined the division, deliberately exposed himself to enemy fire, and received a fatal wound. By thus getting himself killed in action, von Fritsch satisfied his code of honor and probably spared himself a more horrible death later on, especially considering that he had once challenged Reichsführer-SS Heinrich Himmler to a duel.

The 12th Infantry Division itself, under the command of Lieutenant General Ludwig von der Leyen (1939-40), distinguished itself in Poland and later in the French campaign where, as part of II Corps, 4th Army, it beat back a French attempt to cut the "panzer corridor" and relieve the main British and French armies, which were trapped in Belgium. In 1941 the 12th invaded Russia with the 16th Army and played a part in the capture of Dvinsk. The next year, under Lieutenant General Walter von Seydlitz-Kurzbach (1941-42), the division was the main force in the relief of the II Corps trapped in the Demyansk Pocket. The division spent most of the Russian campaign in the northern sector and was successively commanded by von Seydlitz, Lieutenant General Baron Kurt-Jürgen von Lützow, and Lieutenant General Rudolf Bamber (1944), who eventually surrendered the division to the Russians in July 1944 after Army Group Center had been annihilated in the Minsk-Vitebsk encirclements. None of the combat elements of the 12th Infantry Division escaped the disaster that overtook the army group.

The 12th Infantry was rebuilt in East Prussia in the late summer and autumn of 1944 and was brought up to a strength of 14,800 men. It was also fully equipped, which was rare for a rebuilt unit in the fifth year of the war. Redesignated a Volksgrenadier division, the 12th was sent to Aachen on the Western Front in mid-September, under the command of Colonel Gerhard Engel, Hitler's former adjutant who turned out to be a capable combat commander. The 12th fought in the Ardennes as part of the I SS Panzer Corps, and American military intelligence reported that it was the best infantry division in the 6th Panzer Army. During the retreat from the Battle of the Bulge the unit formed part of the II SS Panzer Corps. It remained on the Western Front after the 6th Panzer Army went East and in February 1945 was opposing the U.S. 9th Army's advance across the Roer. By now, however, the 12th Volksgrenadier was a burned-out force, and its resistance was crumbling. It ended up in the Ruhr Pocket, where it was finally destroyed along with the rest of Army Group B, in April 1945. The division's last command, Major General König, was captured at Wuppertal on April 18, 1945.

NOTES AND SOURCES: Lieutenant General von der Leyen was later stationed at Metz as a training officer. Walter von Seydlitz-Kurzbach, who was promoted to General of Artillery in June 1942, commanded the LI Corps at Stalingrad, where he was forced to surrender in late January 1943. Baron von Lützow went on to command the XXXV Corps and was captured in the Russian summer offensive of 1944. General Bamber, the former Chief of Staff of the 21st Mountain Army (1942-43), was also captured in this offensive. Like von Seydlitz-Kurzbach and von Lützow, he joined the National Free Germany Committee. Gerhard Engel, who had been Hitler's adjutant since 1937, was promoted to Major General in late 1944. He was seriously wounded in the Battle of the Bulge but had returned to duty by February 1945. British Military Intelligence Interrogation Report CSDIC (U.K.), SRGG 1197 (c), dated 4 May 45, Air University Archives, Historical Research Center, Maxwell Air Force Base, Alabama (hereafter cited as "Air University Files"); Carell 1966: 596; Carell 1971: 288, 301; Guy Chapman, *Why France Fell: The Defeat of the French Army in 1940*, Holt, Rinehart & Winston, New York, 1968: 130 (hereafter cited as "Chapman"); Cole 1965: 81, 132; Hartmann: 10-11; Kennedy: 74; Charles B. MacDonald, *The Last Offensive*, United States Army in World War II, The European Theater of Operations, Office of the Chief of Military History, United States Government Printing Office, Washington, D.C., 1973: 27, 159; Charles B. MacDonald, *The Siegfried Line Campaign*, United States Army in World War II, The European Theater of Operations, Office of the Chief of Military History, United States Government Printing Office, Washington, D.C., 1963: 71, 87-88, 283, 410 (hereafter MacDonald's *Siegfried Line* will be cited as "MacDonald 1963" and his *Last Offensive* as "MacDonald 1973"); Hermann Teske, *Bewegungskrieg: Führungsprobleme einer Infanterie-Division im Westfeldzug, 1940*, Scharnhorst Buchkameradschaft, Heidelburg, 1955; OB 42: 74; OB 43: 128; OB 44: 178; OB 45: 142-43.

13th INFANTRY DIVISION
see 13th Panzer Division

14th INFANTRY DIVISION
see 14th Motorized Division

15th INFANTRY DIVISION

COMPOSITION: 81st Infantry Regiment, 88th Infantry Regiment, 106th Infantry Regiment, 15th Artillery Regiment, 15th Reconnaissance Battalion, 15th Anti-Tank Battalion, 15th Engineer Battalion, 15th Signal Battalion

HOME STATION: Kassel, Wkr. IX

The 15th Infantry Division was formed in 1935-36 with troops recruited from the Main-Franconia area. Later it was augmented with Austrians after that country became part of the Reich. Strangely, the division did not participate in either the Polish or French campaigns but remained in reserve except for a brief period on the Saar Front. It first saw heavy action in the Russian campaign of 1941 where the 15th took part in the Siege of Mogilev as part of Army Group Center. Later it fought in the Battle of the Yelnya Bend before being rotated back to La Rochelle, France, prior to the start of the Soviet winter offensive. The 15th Infantry remained in France until after the fall of Stalingrad, but in early February 1943, the High Command ordered the division to embark for Russia. On February 9 it was on the Atlantic coast; nine days later it was back in action on the Eastern Front, where it remained for the rest of the war. After fighting west of the Donets as part of the 4th Panzer Army, the division suffered heavy losses at the Battle of Dnepropetrovsk in the summer of 1943. It fought in the battles of the southern Ukraine and, in August 1944, was encircled west of the lower Dnestr. It broke out, but suffered such serious losses that it had to be rebuilt. Nevertheless the 15th Infantry now at battle group strength, was back in the line by October, opposing the Soviet advance through Hungary. By March 1945 it was reportedly in remnants. The next month it was surrounded—along with most of Army Group Center—in the large pocket east of Prague and was there when the war ended. Commanders of the 15th Infantry Division included Lieutenant General Walter Behschnitt (1939-41) and Lieutenant General Erich Buschenhagen (1943-44).

NOTES AND SOURCES: General Behschnitt later commanded the 254th Infantry Division in Russia and was apparently the commander of Recruiting Area Hanover I in Wehrkreis XI when the war ended. Erich Buschenhagen was promoted to General of Infantry in 1944 and given command of LII Corps. He was captured by the Russians in September 1944 and promptly joined the National Free Germany Committee. Carell 1966: 86, 92; Carell 1971: 200, 205; *Kriegstagebuch des OKW*, Volume I: 1145-46; OB 43: 128; OB 44: 179; OB 45: 144. For part of the Hungarian campaign of late 1944/early 1945, the remnants of the 27th Hungarian Light Infantry Division were under the division's command (*Kriegstage-buch des OKW*, Volume IV: 1884).

16th INFANTRY DIVISION (#1)

COMPOSITION: 60th Infantry Regiment, 64th Infantry Regiment, 79th Infantry Regiment, 16th Artillery Regiment, 16th Reconnaissance Battalion, 16th Anti-Tank Battalion, 16th Engineer Battalion, 16th Signal Battalion

HOME STATION: Rheine, Wkr. VI

This peacetime division was made up of Westphalians and Prussians. It first saw action in northern Poland in September 1939 and was later stationed on the Saar Front that winter. The 16th Infantry took part in the invasion of France in 1940 and supported the panzers in the decisive Battle of Sedan in May. After this campaign it was divided: part formed the nucleus of the 16th Panzer Division and part the base for the 16th Motorized Infantry Division.

ALSO SEE 16th PANZER DIVISION and 116th PANZER GRENADIER DIVISION

NOTES AND SOURCES: During its combat career, the original 16th Infantry Division was commanded by Lieutenant General Gotthard Heinrici (1939-40). Heinrici later spent four years on the Eastern Front, successively commanding the XLIII Corps (1941-January 1942), 4th Army (early 1942-late 1944), 1st Panzer Army (early 1945), and Army Group Vistula in the Battle of Berlin (1945). He was a devout Catholic, which made the Nazis suspicious of him, but he was also considered a master of defense. Heinrici—then a Colonel General—was relieved of his command in late April 1945, for retreating against Hitler's direct orders. *Kriegstagebuch des OKW*, Volume II: 1453; OB 45: 144. Also see Ryan.

16th INFANTRY (later VOLKSGRENADIER) DIVISION (#2)

COMPOSITION: 21st Grenadier Regiment, 223rd Grenadier Regiment, 225th Grenadier Regiment, 1316th Artillery Regiment, 16th Füsilier Battalion, 1316th Engineer Battalion, 1316th Anti-Tank Battalion, 1316th Signal Battalion

HOME STATION: Wehrkreis VIII

The second 16th Infantry Division was formed on the Western Front in July 1944, when the 16th Luftwaffe Field Division and the 158th Reserve Division were consolidated under its headquarters. The division was short on equipment and training but was well led by reserve officers. Under

Lieutenant General Ernst Haeckel it covered the northern flank of the LXIV Corps and the 19th Army on their retreat from the Bay of Biscay to Dijon, while most of the Allied forces were tied down in the Battle of Falaise; however, the division did lose two battalions to French partisans. The next month the 16th Infantry—the only division in the LXVI Corps—was trapped between the 3rd and 7th U.S. armies west of the Moselle and was smashed. Only about 1,000 of its 7,000 remaining soldiers escaped the encirclement. Later the division was reformed under its old number and reinforced with miscellaneous support troops, but it never again amounted to more than a battle group. Nevertheless it returned to the line and, still under General Haeckel, fought in southern Alsace and suffered heavy losses in Himmler's disastrous counteroffensive near Strasbourg. The remnants of the 16th Volksgrenadier (as it was redesignated in October) fought in the last campaign in southern Germany and surrendered to the Western Allies at the end of the war.

NOTES AND SOURCES: General Haeckel previously commanded the 263rd Infantry Division (1942) and the 158th Reserve Division (1942-44). Colonel Tillessen, who normally commanded the 225th Grenadier Regiment, was acting commander of the division for a brief period in 1944. Martin Blumenson, *Breakout and Pursuit,* United States Army in World War II, European Theatre of Operations, Office of the Chief of Military History, United States Government Printing Office, Washington, D.C., 1960: 561, 567 (hereafter cited as "Blumenson 1960"); Hugh M. Cole, *The Lorraine Campaign,* United States Army in World War II, European Theatre of Operations, Office of the Chief of Military History, Washington, D.C., 1950: (hereafter cited as "Cole 1950"); RA: 130; OB 45: 144.

17th INFANTRY DIVISION

COMPOSITION: 21st Infantry Regiment, 55th Infantry Regiment, 95th Infantry Regiment, 17th Artillery Regiment, 17th Reconnaissance Battalion (Bicycle), 17th Anti-Tank Battalion, 17th Engineer Battalion, 17th Signal Battalion

HOME STATION: Nuremberg, Wkr. XIII

This Bavarian division was created in the initial German military build-up of 1935 by the expansion of the 21st Infantry Regiment at Nuremberg. It fought its first battles in southern Poland and soon acquired a reputation as an effective combat unit. Later it did equally well in the invasion of France and was in the forefront of Army Group Center's last thrusts toward Moscow in the winter of 1941-42. The 17th was exhausted after the Soviet winter offensive and was sent to France to rest and rebuild in the summer of 1942. It returned to Russia in February 1943 after the fall of Stalingrad brought the German southern sector to the verge of collapse. In the spring of 1943 it took part in the battles around Kiev. After the German defeat at Kursk in July, the 17th Infantry fought on the lower Dnieper and in the southern Ukraine where it again suffered heavy casualties. Briefly taken out of the line to refit, it was defending in southern Poland in late 1944. Remnants of this veteran division were surrounded in Czechoslovakia in April 1945 and surrendered there. Commanders of the division included Major General Herbert Loch (1939-40), Lieutenant General Gustav von Zangen (1941-42), Colonel Brücker (1944), and Lieutenant General Richard Zimmer (1945).

NOTES AND SOURCES: Herbert Loch went on to command the XXVIII Corps on the Eastern Front from 1941 to 1944. From June to September 1944, he was acting commander of the 18th Army in Russia, and in 1945 he was commander of a special high command in the Eifel (i.e., the German Ardennes). He was promoted to General of Artillery in October 1941. Gustav von Zangen later commanded LXXXIV Corps in France (1942) and LXXXVII Corps, also in occupied France (1943-44). He led Army Detachment von Zangen, a rear-area command in northern Italy, in 1944 and ended the war as commander of the 15th Army on the Western Front (August 1941 to April 1945). He was promoted to General of Infantry in June 1943. Colonel Brücker was Ia of the XXIV Motorized (later Panzer) Corps on the Russian Front in 1941. Richard Zimmer, a Bavarian engineer officer, had formerly commanded the 54th Mountain Engineer Battalion. Carell 1966: 196; Kennedy: 74; *Kriegstagebuch des OKW*, Volume I: 1146; RA: 204; OB 43: 128-29; OB 45: 145.

18th INFANTRY DIVISION
see 18th Motorized Division

18th VOLKSGRENADIER DIVISION

COMPOSITION: 293rd Grenadier Regiment, 294th Grenadier Regiment, 295th Grenadier Regiment, 1818th Artillery Regiment, 18th Füsilier Battalion, 1818th Engineer Battalion, 1818th Anti-Tank Battalion, 1818th Signal Battalion

HOME STATION: Wehrkreis V

Not to be confused with the original 18th Infantry Division, which was converted into a motorized (later panzer grenadier) division and sent to the Eastern Front in 1941, this division was formed in Denmark in September

1944 chiefly from excess naval personnel transferred to the Army and members of the 571st Grenadier Division. The division also absorbed the remnants of the badly mauled 18th Luftwaffe Field Division, so all branches of the armed forces were represented in its ranks except the SS. The new Volksgrenadier division first saw combat in the West in October 1944 and was engaged in the Trier area of France the next month. In mid-December it opposed the U.S. V Corps in the Battle of the Roer River Dams, where it fought well. Later that month the 18th Volksgrenadier was assigned to the 5th Panzer Army and suffered heavy losses in the Battle of the Bulge. It was still fighting two months later, however, opposing the Allied drive on the Pruem. The remnants of the 18th Volksgrenadier finally surrendered to the Western Allies at the close of hostilities. It was commanded by Major General Hoffmann-Schönborn (1944-45).

NOTES AND SOURCES: Hoffmann-Schönborn was apparently the only commander the 18th Volksgrenadier ever had. He was an artillery officer who assumed command of the division as a Colonel but was promoted in late 1944. Prior to the formation of the 18th, he had been with the 2nd Artillery Training Regiment (probably as its commander) and had served as an inspector of assault artillery. "Frontnachweiser," 15 December 1944; *Kriegstagebuch des OKW*, Volume IV: 1891; OB 45: 145.

19th INFANTRY DIVISION
see 19th Panzer Division

19th INFANTRY (later VOLKSGRENADIER) DIVISION (#2)

COMPOSITION: 59th Grenadier Regiment, 73rd Grenadier Regiment, 74th Grenadier Regiment, 119th Artillery Regiment, 119th Füsilier Battalion, 119th Engineer Battalion, 119th Anti-Tank Battalion, 119th Signal Battalion

HOME STATION: Oksbol, Denmark, Wkr. IX

Originally designated the Division "Jutland," the 19th Infantry was formed in August 1944 at Oksbol, Denmark. It included survivors of the 19th Luftwaffe Field Division, which had been smashed on the Western Front in July. By September 1944 the 19th Infantry was with Army Group B in France and in November was conducting a fighting withdrawal across the Moselle. At that time it had a strength of 8,500, high for the German Army in the last half of 1944. In late 1944 the division absorbed the few members of the 77th Infantry Division who had not been captured or killed in Normandy, in the fall of Cherbourg, or at Dinand. It was redesignated a Volksgrenadier division at that time and sent back to the Western Front. The 19th fought in the battles in the Saar and in the retreat across southwestern Germany, where it finally surrendered at the end of the war.

NOTES AND SOURCES: The division's first leader, Lieutenant General Otto Elferdz, commanded it only briefly, when it was Headquarters, Division "Jutland," and little else. Given command of the LXXXIV Corps, he was captured near Falaise in August 1944. The 19th was later commanded by Lieutenant General Karl Wissmath, the former commander of the 199th Infantry Division (1943-44) and Colonel (subsequently Major General) Karl Britzelmayr. OB 45: 146. Also see MacDonald 1973.

20th INFANTRY DIVISION
see 20th Motorized Division

21st INFANTRY DIVISION

COMPOSITION: 3rd Infantry Regiment, 24th Infantry Regiment, 45th Infantry Regiment, 21st Artillery Regiment, 21st Reconnaissance Battalion, 21st Anti-Tank Battalion, 21st Engineer Battalion, 21st Signal Battalion

HOME STATION: Mohrungen, Wkr. 1

The 21st Infantry was created in 1935 when the 3rd Infantry Regiment "Deutsch Eylau" was expanded. In the invasion of Poland the 21st was led by Lieutenant General Hans-Kuno von Both. Later it was commanded by Lieutenant Generals Otto Sponheimer (1941), Wilhelm Bohnstedt (1941-43), Gerhard Matzky (1943-44), Priess (1944), and Major General Heinrich Götz (1945). After taking part in the French campaign the 21st crossed into Russia with Army Group North, swept through the Baltic States, and broke through the Soviet defensive positions on the Msta River, the last natural barrier before Leningrad. The division spent the next three years in northern Russia, participated in the Siege of Leningrad, fought in the Battle of Volkhov (early 1942), and in the Second Battle of Lake Ladoga in early 1943. After distinguishing itself during the retreat from Leningrad, the 21st was transferred by Army Group Center in the fall of 1944. It was smashed in the Russian invasion of East Prussia, but the survivors of the unit continued to resist—at battle group strength—until the fall of the Third Reich. The remnants of the 21st Infantry Division were still in East Prussia at the end of the war.

NOTES AND SOURCES: Hans-Kuno von Both later commanded I Corps (1940-42) and was military commander of Estonia and the Rear Area Command of Army Group North in 1943. He was promoted to General of Infantry effective January 1, 1940. Lieutenant General Bohnstedt ended the war as Inspector General of Infantry at O.K.H. He may have been promoted to General of Infantry in the last weeks of the Reich, but no record of this has been found. General Matzky had been Military Attaché to Tokyo (1940) and Chief of the Intelligence Division (O Qu IV) of the General Staff of the Army (1940-42). He was commanding XXVI Corps in East Prussia in 1945. General Götz had commanded a regiment on the Eastern Front before assuming command of the 21st. Prior to the war, the 21st Infantry Division was led by Albert Wodrig (1938), who later became a General of Artillery. Wodrig, a Prussian, later commanded XXVI Corps (1939-42) and Wehrkreis I (February 1943-1945). Carell 1966: 251, 417-21; Carell 1971: 260; Hartmann: 12; Kennedy: 74 and Map 7; RA: 20; OB 43: 129; OB 44: 180; OB 45: 146.

22nd INFANTRY (later AIR LANDING) DIVISION

COMPOSITION: 16th Infantry Regiment, 47th Infantry Regiment, 65th Infantry Regiment, 22nd Artillery Regiment, 22nd Reconnaissance Battalion, 22nd Anti-Tank Battalion, 22nd Engineer Battalion, 22nd Signal Battalion

HOME STATION: Oldenburg, Wkr. X

Originally an infantry division, the 22nd was created by the expansion of the 16th Infantry Regiment of the old Reichswehr. The personnel were from Lower Saxony. Later the division was converted into an air landing force—which in the Nazi period meant that they followed paratrooper and glider units into action in transport planes as soon as a workable airstrip could be secured. This, in turn, meant that they had lighter artillery and less heavy equipment than a standard infantry division. Elements of the 22nd were involved in the occupation of the Sudetenland in 1938. The next year the 16th Regiment of the division fought in Poland while the other two regiments were stationed on the West Wall. In the French campaign of 1940 elements of the division took part in the glider-borne assault on the key Belgian fortress of Eben Emael, while other divisional forces landed at The Hague, Rotterdam, Moerdijk, and Dordrecht. In the Dutch capital the division failed in its mission to capture the royal family, and the divisional commander, Lieutenant General Count Hans von Sponeck, was seriously wounded in the attempt. In the Russian invasion the 22nd Air Landing was equipped as a standard line unit and fought as a regular infantry force under the 11th Army, Army Group South. It was the first German division to penetrate the Dnieper line and also fought on the Pruth, Dnestr, and Bug. It took part in the initial assault on Sevastopol, where it suffered heavy losses. On June 28, 1942, combat elements of the 22nd Air Landing, along with the 24th Infantry Division, crossed a thousand-yard-wide stretch of North Bay in rubber rafts and landed in the Russian rear, east of the city. Russian resistance in Sevastopol, which had been fierce, crumbled rapidly after this surprise attack. Following the clearing of the Crimea in early July, the 22nd Air Landing was returned to Germany, once more reequipped as an air landing division, and sent to Crete where, as Field Marshal von Manstein bitterly complained, "though one of our best formations—it was to lie more or less idle for the rest of the war." Eventually the 22nd was equipped as a motorized air landing division although it was never used as such nor officially redesignated panzer grenadier. Part of the division—the 47th Grenadier Regiment—went to Tunisia in late 1942 and was captured there when the African Front collapsed in May 1943. The rest of the division remained in Crete until 1944. In autumn 1944, the High Command constructed a second 47th Grenadier Regiment and sent it to Crete. A few weeks later the 22nd was finally evacuated to the mainland, as part of the general withdrawal from the Mediterranean and lower Balkans. Assigned to the XXI Mountain Corps, it fought the Soviets and Tito's partisans in Montenegro and in the Sarajevo area and was still on the front line in northern Yugoslavia when Germany surrendered. Commanders of the 22nd Air Landing included von Sponeck (1940-42), and Lieutenant Generals Ludwig Wolff (1942), Friedrich Wilhelm Müller (1942-44), Karl-Heinrich-Georg Ferdinand Kreipe (1944), and Helmut Friebe (1945).

NOTES AND SOURCES: Count von Sponeck commanded the XLII Corps in 1942. In late December of that year he was relieved of his command for failing to obey one of Hitler's senseless hold-at-all-costs orders. He was arrested, court-martialed, imprisoned, and finally shot on the orders of Heinrich Himmler after the July 20, 1944 attempt on the Führer's life went astray. General Wolff later became Chief of the Army's Educational and Training Branch (September 1942-March 1944) and was commander of the XXXIII Corps in 1944. He was promoted to General of Infantry effective January 1, 1944. General Müller also rose to the rank of General of Infantry. He went on to command XXXIV Corps (1944), LXVIII Corps (late 1944-early 1945), and 4th Army (January-April 1945). Prior to assuming command of the 22nd Division, he had led the 105th Infantry Regiment of the 72nd Infantry Division (1939-42). General Kreipe was captured by British commandos in April 1944. General Friebe had served as commanding general of the 125th Infantry Division on the Eastern Front (1942-43) and as commander of a special anti-partisan group on the Eastern Front in 1944. Carell 1966: 291-92, 308, 505; Roger Edwards, *German Airborne*

Troops, 1939-45, Doubleday and Company, Inc., Garden City, New York, 1974: 136 (hereafter cited as "Edwards"); Hartmann: 57; Manstein: 260; OB 42: 75; OB 45: 146-47.

23rd INFANTRY DIVISION
see 26th Panzer Division

23rd INFANTRY DIVISION (#2)

COMPOSITION: 9th Grenadier Regiment, 67th Grenadier Regiment, 68th Füsilier Grenadier Regiment, 23rd Artillery Regiment, 23rd Füsilier Battalion, 23rd Anti-Tank Battalion, 23rd Engineer Battalion, 23rd Signal Battalion

HOME STATION: Potsdam, Wkr. III

The second 23rd Infantry Division was assembled at Potsdam in the fall of 1942. It adopted the regimental numbers of the original 23rd, which had been converted into the 26th Panzer Division shortly before. The 68th Regiment later received the honorary title "Füsilier," but its organization and equipment were no different from that of a standard grenadier regiment. The new division was sent into action on the Eastern Front in early 1943 and fought on the northern sector. Briefly sent to Army Group Center in late 1943, it fought in the defensive Battle of Nevel but was returned to Army Group North in February 1944 after the Russians broke the Seige of Leningrad. Later the division withdrew through Estonia, and defended Saareman Island (Ösel) in autumn 1944, against overwhelming Russian landings. It was, however, successfully evacuated by the German Navy. By October it was defending in the Courland Pocket, but in January 1945, the remnants of this veteran but depleted division were evacuated by sea to northern Germany and sent to Army Group Center in East Prussia, where it remained until the fall of Berlin. It surrendered to the Russians. Commanders of the second 23rd Infantry Division included Major General Horst von Mellenthin (1943), Major General Gurran (1943-44?), and Major General Ernest Wisselinck (1944-45).

NOTES AND SOURCES: Horst von Mellenthin, a distant relative of Frederick the Great, later commanded a corps on the Eastern Front. Major General Friedrick Wilhelm von Mellenthin, the Chief of Staff of Army Group G on the Western Front and formerly Chief of Intelligence of Panzer Army Afrika, was his brother. Major General Gurran had risen from the ranks. Ernest Wisselinck had previously been with the Officer

Training School at Dresden. *Kriegstagebuch des OKW*, Volume III: 9, 260; Volume IV: 1889; Friedrick Wilhelm von Mellenthin, *German Generals of World War II*, University of Oklahoma Press, Norman, Oklahoma, 1977: 136-38 (hereafter cited as "von Mellenthin 1977"); Seaton: 232; OB 45: 147.

24th INFANTRY DIVISION

COMPOSITION: 31st Infantry Regiment, 32nd Infantry Regiment, 102nd Infantry Regiment, 24th Reconnaissance Battalion, 24th Anti-Tank Battalion, 24th Engineer Battalion, 24th Signal Battalion

HOME STATION: Chemnitz, Wkr. IV

Created in Hitler's original military expansion of the mid-1930s, the 24th Infantry was in action from the first battle until the end of the war. It took part in the invasion of Poland as part of Army Group South. An Allied intelligence document reported that its "morale and fighting value [are] very high, to judge by the French campaign." After fighting in France, it crossed into Russia in 1941, fought its way across the Ukraine and into the Crimea with von Manstein's 11th Army, and took part in the Siege of Sevastopol for several months. With the 22nd Air Landing Division it was involved in the amphibious assault that led to the fall of the city in early July 1942. Transferred to Army Group North with the 11th Army, the division helped repulse the Russian counteroffensives in the Lake Ilmen area in the latter part of 1942. The 24th remained in the northern sector of the Eastern Front for the remainder of the war, and was part of the 18th Army when the Soviets broke the Siege of Leningrad in mid-January 1944. Unlike several other divisions, the 24th kept its composure and was later officially cited for its bravery in the withdrawal through the Baltic States. In July 1944 it held its line against the Russian summer offensive, withdrew into western Latvia at its own pace in October 1944, and ended the war in the Courland Pocket. Commanders of the 24th Infantry included Lieutenant Generals Orbricht (1939), Baron Hans von Tettau (1940-early 1944), Kurt Versock (1944), and Colonel Scholtz (1944-1945?).

NOTES AND SOURCES: Baron von Tettau was reportedly commander of Special Division Staff 604 in 1945. Carell 1966: 304, 503; Kennedy: 74 and Map 7; Manstein: 243, 260; Salisbury: 538; Seaton: 264; RA: 72; OB 42: 76; OB 43: 129; OB 44: 181; OB 45: 148; Ziemke 1966: 261.

25th INFANTRY DIVISION
see 25th Motorized Division

26th INFANTRY (later VOLKSGRENADIER) DIVISION

COMPOSITION: 39th Infantry Regiment (later 39th Füsilier Grenadier Regiment), 77th Infantry Regiment, 78th Infantry Regiment, 26th Artillery Regiment, 26th Reconnaissance Battalion, 26th Anti-Tank Battalion, 26th Engineer Battalion, 26th Signal Battalion

HOME STATION: Cologne, Wkr. VI

Raised in 1936, this division was made up mainly of Westphalian Rhinelanders, with some East Prussians. It was known as the "Dom" (Cathedral) Division, because of its divisional emblem, patterned after the Great Cathedral at Cologne (Köln). It did not take part in the invasion of Poland and was only lightly engaged in the Western campaign of 1940. The 26th got its first serious test in the Russian campaign of 1941, where it performed well. It distinguished itself when it crossed the Volga between Moscow and Leningrad and stormed Rzhev, along with the 206th Infantry Division. It was heavily engaged against the Russian winter offensive of 1941-1942. Although relatively undamaged in the defensive fighting on the central sector in 1942, the 26th again suffered heavy casualties in the Battle of Kursk, Hitler's last major offensive on the Eastern Front. It opposed the Soviet offensive after the failure of the Kursk operation and, under Lieutenant General Friedrich Höchbaum, conducted itself brilliantly in the defense of Kovel in July 1944. Although it managed to escape destruction in the Russian summer offensive that smashed Army Group Center that year, the division was finally overrun near the East Prussian border in September 1944 and had to be withdrawn from the line. It was rebuilt in October 1944 in the Warthelager Maneuver Area in western Poland, where it was fleshed out with naval and Luftwaffe personnel and recruits from Westphalia and the Rhineland formerly assigned to the 582nd Volksgrenadier Division. Redesignated a Volksgrenadier division, it was sent to the Luxembourg sector of the Western Front in November. The new VG division suffered heavy casualties in the Battle of the Bulge, where it took part in the Siege of Bastogne as part of the XLVII Panzer Corps of the 5th Panzer Army. It was transferred to the I SS Panzer Corps of the 6th Panzer Army in the latter stages of the battle. At the end of the offensive the division had a combat strength of only 1,782 men; nevertheless it remained in action and opposed the Allied drive on Pruem in February 1945. It finished the war on the Western Front. Commanders of the 26th Infantry/ Volksgrenadier Division included Lieutenant Generals Sigmund von Förster (1939-40?), Walter Weiss (1941-42), Friedrich Wiese (1942-43), John de Boer (1943-44), Höchbaum (1944), and Major General Hans Kokott (1944-45).

NOTES AND SOURCES: Förster was Rear Area Commander of Army Group South (1941-42) and had a territorial command in 1943. He was promoted to General of Infantry as of May 1, 1943, and was commanding a battle group at Odessa in April, 1944. Walter Weiss rose to the rank of Colonel General, commanding the XXVII Corps (July 1942-1944), 2nd Army (1944-early 1945), and Army Group North (March-April 1945). Friedrich Wiese was made General of Infantry effective October 1, 1943. He commanded XXXV Corps (late 1943-early 1944) and 19th Army on the Western Front (July 1944-January 1945) before being relieved of his command for his failure to retake Strasbourg. The real blame for this failure lay with Himmler. John de Boer was reportedly killed in action in 1944. Höchbaum had led the 253rd Infantry Regiment until November 1942. He commanded the 34th Infantry Division (1943-44), the 26th Infantry (1944), and then the XVIII Mountain Corps in Norway (1944-45). Prior to receiving command of the 26th Infantry, General Weiss had been Chief of Staff of I Corps in France (1940) and, after leaving the 26th, was commander of the 370th Infantry Division in Russia (1942). Carell 1966: 196, 357; Carell 1971: 305; Cole 1965: 632; MacDonald 1973: Map IV and 5-6; "Frontnachweiser," 15 December 1944; RA: 100; OB 43: 130; OB 44: 181; OB 45: 148.

27th INFANTRY DIVISION
see 17th Panzer Division

28th INFANTRY DIVISION
see 28th Jäger Division

29th INFANTRY DIVISION
see 29th Motorized Division

30th INFANTRY DIVISION

COMPOSITION: 6th Infantry Regiment, 26th Infantry Regiment, 46th Infantry Regiment, 30th Artillery Regiment, 30th Reconnaissance Battalion (Bicycle), 30th Anti-Tank Battalion, 30th Engineer Battalion, 30th Signal Battalion (Motorized)

HOME STATION: Lubeck, Wkr. X

Created by the expansion of the 6th Infantry Regiment of the old

Reichswehr in 1935, the 30th consisted of men recruited from Schleswig-Holstein in northern Germany. It was earmarked for the attack on Prague in 1938, before British Prime Minister Chamberlain gave in to Hitler's demands in the infamous Munich accords that abandoned Czechoslovakia, leaving the rump state to eventually capitulate without a fight. In 1939 the division, led by Major General von Briesen, crossed into Poland as part of Army Group South and faced probably the most massive breakout attempt launched by the Polish Army in World War II. The 30th was strained to the breaking point and only a desperate counterattack personally led by von Briesen with his last reserves turned back the Poles. Von Briesen's left arm was shattered in the fighting and had to be amputated. Shortly afterward Hitler and Colonel General Wilhelm Keitel, the Chief of the Armed Forces High Command, visited the 30th and awarded its commander the Knight's Cross, the first such award presented to a divisional commander in the war. Therefore the 30th was nicknamed the "Briesen Division." Von Briesen himself was promoted, and eventually was named Commandant of Paris (1940-42). Meanwhile, the division fought in Belgium and was with Army Group North from 1941 until the end of the war. It fought in the Battle of Dvinsk (1941) and was encircled at Demyansk with II Corps in January 1942. It was not relieved for more than a year. After it was freed in February 1943, the Briesen Division fought in the Leningrad withdrawal and in the retreat through the Baltic States. It finally surrendered in the Courland Pocket in May 1945, after the fall of Berlin. Commanders of the division included von Briesen (1939), Lieutenant Generals Franz Boehme (1940), Kurt von Tippelskirch (1940-42), Emil von Wiekede (1942-43), William Hasse (late 1943-1944), and Colonel Otto Barth (1944-45).

NOTES AND SOURCES: Of the straight-laced and physically huge von Briesen, Hitler remarked that he was what he (Hitler) imagined Prussian generals looked like when he was a child. Von Briesen retired as a General of Infantry in 1942 or 1943. Franz Boehme entered the Austrian Army in 1900 and was Chief of the General Staff of the Austrian Army at the time of the Anschluss in 1938. In October 1940, he was given command of the XVIII Mountain Corps and fought against the Russians on the Finnish sector of the Eastern Front. He was promoted to General of Mountain Troops in late 1940 or early 1941. Boehme assumed command of the 2nd Panzer Army in the Balkans in June 1944. From January 1945 until the end of the war he was Commander of the 20th Mountain Army in Norway and simultaneously Armed Forces Commander, Norway. Indicted at Nuremberg, he committed suicide on May 29, 1947. Kurt von Tippelskirch was also a Prussian who became a General of Infantry. Formerly Chief of Intelligence at O.K.H. (1940), he later served as chief German liaison officer with and advisor to the 8th Italian Army in Russia (August 1942-

early 1943), commander of the XII Corps (late 1943-44), and commander of the 4th, 1st, and 21st armies (1944-45). He briefly commanded the remnants of Army Group Vistula in late April 1945. Wilhelm Hasse, former Ia of Army Group B in France (1940) and Chief of Staff of the 18th Army (1942-43), later commanded a corps on the Eastern Front (1945). He also was promoted to General of Infantry. Colonel Barth was a regimental commander of an artillery unit on the Eastern Front before assuming command of the 30th Infantry. Carell 1966: 19, 427; Carell 1971: 288; Hartmann: 12-13; Kennedy: Map 7; Manstein: 56, 184; RA: 160; OB 43: 130-31; Plocher 1943: 414; OB 44: 182; OB 34: 149.

31st INFANTRY (later VOLKSGRENADIER) DIVISION

COMPOSITION: 12th Infantry Regiment, 17th Infantry Regiment, 82nd Infantry Regiment, 31st Artillery Regiment, 31st Reconnaissance Battalion, 31st Anti-Tank Battalion, 31st Engineer Battalion, 31st Signal Battalion

HOME STATION: Braunschweig, Wkr. XI

Recruited mainly from the Braunschweig and Brunswick areas of north-central Germany, this division fought in southern Poland in 1939. Shifted to the Western Front, it was engaged in heavy fighting in Belgium and France the following year. In 1941 it took part in the Russian invasion with the 2nd Panzer Army in the central sector as well as in Guderian's unsuccessful attempt to encircle Tula (southeast of Moscow) in late 1941. It suffered serious losses in the Russian winter offensive of 1941-42. Remaining on the defensive with Army Group Center in 1942, it fought in the Battle of Kursk in July 1943, as part of XLVI Panzer Corps, 9th Army. Later that year the 31st took part in the battles of the middle Dnieper and in the subsequent retreats through Russia. It was down to battle group strength by October. In June 1944 it faced the gigantic Russian summer offensive as part of 4th Army's XXXIX Panzer Corps and was finally overwhelmed and virtually destroyed in the fighting. Lieutenant General Ochsner, the divisional commander, was taken prisoner along with most of his men. Enough troops escaped, however, to reform the division, which was augmented with new recruits while rebuilding in Germany. Redesignated a Volksgrenadier division, the 31st returned to combat in September 1944 as part of Army Group North. It was officially commended for its conduct in the early battles of the Courland Pocket. In early 1945 it was evacuated by sea to northern Germany and fought in the Battle of Berlin with Army

Group Vistula, where it was destroyed. Divisional commanders of the 31st Infantry/Volksgrenadier included Lieutenant Generals Kaempfe (1938-40), Major General Friedrich Hossbach (1942?-43), Ochsner (1944), and Major General von Stolzmann (1945).

NOTES AND SOURCES: Rudolf Kaempfe was promoted to General of Artillery in July 1941 and was commander of Corps Command XXXV (later XXXV Corps) until he retired in 1943. Ochsner was commanding officer of the 62nd Grenadier Regiment in 1942. Hossbach, a Hessian general staff officer and former adjutant to Hitler, was an extremely strong-willed man. After leading the 31st Infantry, he directed the LVI Panzer Corps in Russia (1943-late 1944) and the 4th Army in East Prussia (January 1945). He was finally sacked for trying to break out of the East Prussian Pocket against Hitler's direct orders. Major General von Stolzmann developed a special course for snipers before rising to divisional command. Carell 1966: 111, 341; Carell 1971: 22, 26, 597; Kennedy: 71 and Map 7; OB 43: 130; OB 45: 149-50. Also see *Kriegstagebuch des OKW*, Volume IV: 1898.

32nd INFANTRY DIVISION

COMPOSITION: 4th Infantry Regiment, 94th Infantry Regiment, 96th Infantry Regiment, 32nd Artillery Regiment, 32nd Reconnaissance Battalion, 32nd Anti-Tank Battalion, 32nd Engineer Battalion, 32nd Signal Battalion

HOME STATION: Koslin, Wkr. II

Known as the "Lion Division" from its unit emblem, this division consisted mainly of Pomeranians and Prussians. Formed by the expansion of the 4th Infantry Regiment of the old Reichswehr in the mid-1930's, the Lion Division fought well throughout its career, and its effectiveness was praised in secret Allied intelligence documents. In Poland it was commanded by Lieutenant General Hermann Böhme and fought on the northern sector as part of II Corps. Transferred to the Western Front with the 4th Army, it turned back a French attempt to breach the so-called "Panzer Corridor" that extended from the German frontier to the coast of the North Sea. It remained with II Corps for the Russian invasion of 1941, fought in the Battles of Dvinsk, Lake Ilmen, and the Valdai Hills, and was tied down in the battles around Demyansk from January 1942 to February 1943. It was encircled much of this time and had to be resupplied by air. The 32nd remained on the northern sector during the defensive battles of 1943 and was briefly transferred to Army Group Center in January 1944. Hurried back to the northern sector after the Russians broke the Siege of Leningrad on January 18, the Lion Division was cited for its excellent conduct in the retreat through the Baltic States. Finally withdrawn into the Courland Pocket, it took part in the desperate battles in western Latvia in the winter of 1944-45, before being evacuated to Germany by sea in early 1945. The division was finally cut off in the Hela peninsula by the final Soviet offensive and surrendered to the Red Army on May 8, 1945. Its last commander was Lieutenant General Hans Boeckh-Behrens. Previous divisional commanders included Böhme (1939-40), Lieutenant General Ernst von Leyser (1941-42), Lieutenant General Wilhelm Wegener (1944), and Colonel George Kossmala (1944).

NOTES AND SOURCES: General Böhme later became Chief of Staff of the German Armistice Commission in France (1940-43) and commander of the 73rd Infantry Division (1943-44). He was captured by the Russians in 1944. General von Leyser went on to command the XXVI Corps in Russia (1942), and the XV and XXI Mountain Corps in Finland and Norway (1943 and 1944, respectively) as a General of Infantry. Kossmala, former commander of the 6th Infantry Regiment (1943-44), assumed command of the 272nd Infantry Division in November 1944. Hans Boeckh-Behrens had been Chief of Staff of the 16th Army in northern Russia (1942-43). Carell 1966: 376-77, 427; Carell 1971: 288; Chant, Volume 18: 2393; Chapman: 130; Alister Horne, *To Lose a Battle: France, 1940*, Little, Brown and Company, Boston, 1969: 525 (hereafter cited as "Horne"); Kennedy: 74 and Map 7; OB 42: 77; OB 43: 131; OB 44: 183; OB 45: 150.

33rd INFANTRY DIVISION
see 15th Panzer Division

34th INFANTRY DIVISION

COMPOSITION: 80th Infantry Regiment, 107th Infantry Regiment, 253rd Infantry Regiment, 34th Artillery Regiment, 34th Reconnaissance Battalion, 34th Anti-Tank Battalion, 34th Engineer Battalion, 34th Signal Battalion

HOME STATION: Heidelburg, Wkr. XII

The 34th Infantry Division was formed in 1936 from Rhinelanders and Hessians. It remained on the Western Front during the Polish campaign but fought in France the following year. In 1941 it joined in the invasion of the Soviet Union as part of Army Group Center and was heavily engaged against the Russian counterattacks of January-February 1942. The 34th Infantry fought in the defensive battles on the central sector in 1942, took part in the bitter defensive battles for Kharkov in January 1943, and distinguished itself in the third battle for that city in August 1943. It also performed well in the retreat through the northern Ukraine in the spring of 1944. After three years of more or less continuous action on the Eastern Front, however, the division was pretty well burned-out by summer. In July it was transferred to northwestern Italy, where it was part of the rear-area Army Detachment von Zangen (later the Ligurian Army), which was made up of Italian units and third-rate German formations. In October 1944, the 34th Infantry was on duty on the French-Italian frontier, guarding against a possible attempt by Eisenhower to take the German armies in Italy in the rear. The division remained with the Ligurian Army for the rest of the war and was still in northern Italy when World War II ended. It was never committed to the front-line fighting in Italy, the way it had been in Russia. Commanders of the 34th included Lieutenant Generals Max Viebahn (1937-38), Theodor Scherer (1942), Friedrich Höchbaum (1943-44), Theobald Lieb (1944), and Colonel Ferdinand Hippel (1945).

NOTES AND SOURCES: Viebahn, former Chief of Staff of Army Group 2 at Kassel, became Chief of the Operations Staff of the High Command of the Armed Forces in February 1938, but he could not get along with Wilhelm Keitel, the Chief of OKW, and was relieved after only six weeks. He held only minor staff and command appointments during World War II. Scherer, the former commander of the 281st Security Division in Russia (1941), later commanded the 87th Infantry Division (late 1942) and the 83rd Infantry Division (1943-44). He was a Bavarian. General Höchbaum previously commanded the 253rd Infantry Regiment (1942) and later led the 26th Infantry Division (1944) and the XVIII Mountain Corps in Norway and Finland (1944-45). Ferdinand Hippel succeeded Höchbaum as commander of the 253rd Infantry Regiment on November 2, 1942. Carell 1966: 414-15; Ernest F. Fisher, *Cassinò to the Alps*, United States Army in World War II, Mediterranean Theatre of Operations, Office of the Chief of Military History, United States Government Printing Office, Washington, D.C., 1977: 293, 303 (hereafter cited as "Fisher"); Hartmann: 13; Telford Taylor, *Sword and Swastika: Generals and Nazis in the Third Reich*, Quadrangle Paperbacks, Chicago, 1969: 165 (hereafter cited as "Taylor"); RA: 188; OB 43: 131; OB 45: 150-51.

35th INFANTRY (later VOLKSGRENADIER) DIVISION

COMPOSITION: 34th Infantry Regiment, 109th Infantry Regiment, 111th Infantry Regiment, 35th Artillery Regiment, 35th Reconnaissance Battalion, 35th Anti-Tank Battalion, 35th Engineer Battalion, 35th Signal Battalion

HOME STATION: Karlsruhe, Wkr. V

Formed in 1935-36, this first-wave division consisted mainly of troops from Baden and Württemberg. It was commanded by Lieutenant General Hans Reinhard (1938-40) when the war broke out. Sent to the West Wall in 1939, the 35th first saw action in Belgium in May 1940 and later fought against the British Expeditionary Force around Dunkirk. The next year it went to Russia as part of Army Group Center, where it was led by Major General Ludwig Merker. It was with Höpner's 4th Panzer Group on the drive to Moscow. When the mid-October thaw came, the men of the 35th trudged eastward through knee-deep mud. Their infantry companies were down to a strength of 30 men; nevertheless they crossed the Ruza River (October 20) and took Volokolanisk (October 27) along with 1,800 prisoners. Their supplies and ammunition were exhausted by this time so the division went over to the defensive. Stalled before the Russian capital in December, the 35th suffered heavy casualties once more against the Soviet winter offensive of 1941-42, losing more than 2,500 men—1,000 of them due to severe frostbite. Although in reality a burned-out force by then, the division remained in the line until the fall of 1942. Transferred to the southern sector in the latter part of 1942, the 35th Infantry (now under Major General Baron Rudolf von Roman) once more suffered heavy losses in the retreat across southern Russia. Returned to Army Group Center in the early spring of 1943, it took part in the Rzhev withdrawal and was heavily engaged in the defensive fighting on the central sector in the summer of 1943. Ludwig Merker—now a Lieutenant General—assumed command of the division for a second time in late 1943 or early 1944 and led what was left of it against the massive Soviet summer offensive of 1944. The 35th Infantry suffered such heavy casualties in the Battle of Bobruisk in July 1944 that it had to be taken out of the line for the first time in three years. It was rebuilt, redesignated a Volksgrenadier unit, and returned to the central sector of the Russian Front, where it fought in the Battle of Narew. Commanded by Lieutenant General Johann-Georg Richert in the last campaigns, the 35th was isolated in East Prussia in the final weeks of the war and surrendered to the Soviets shortly after Hitler's death.

NOTES AND SOURCES: General of Infantry Hans Reinhard later commanded LI Corps (1941), LXXXVIII Corps in the Netherlands (July 1942-January 1945), and Wehrkreis IV (1945). Baron von Roman was promoted to General of Infantry effective November 1, 1942, and led XXX Corps on the Eastern Front from September 1942 until 1945. Major General Ernst Meiners, the former commander of the 467th Grenadier Regiment, apparently replaced Richert in command of the 35th Volksgrenadier in the last days of the war. Carell 1966: 330; Carell 1971: 309; Hartmann: 13-14; Seaton: 188, citing H. Baumann, *Die 35 Infanterie Division im Zweiten Weltkrieg*, G. Braum, Karlsruhe, 1964: 114-17; RA: 86; OB 42: 77; OB 43: 132; OB 44: 183; OB 45: 151.

36th INFANTRY DIVISION
see 36th Panzer Grenadier Division

38th INFANTRY DIVISION

COMPOSITION: 108th Infantry Regiment, 112th Infantry Regiment, 138th Artillery Regiment, 138th Reconnaissance Battalion, 138th Anti-Tank Battalion, 138th Engineer Battalion, 138th Signal Battalion

HOME STATION: Wehrkreis III

Apparently formed in the Berlin area in late 1941 or early 1942, this division was first identified by Allied intelligence when it was transferred to the Brittany area of France in the summer of 1942. It was in the Netherlands in August, then sent into 15th Army's reserve, and finally given a sector of the Atlantic coast under 7th Army in 1943. Elements of the 38th Infantry Division were reportedly in Finland in 1942, but the division as a whole did not see combat until the spring of 1943 when it was sent to the southern sector of the Russian Front. Later that summer it was virtually destroyed in the Donets battles, and the remnants of the 38th Infantry Division were disbanded. Lieutenant General Eberhardt (1942-43) was the last commander of the division.

NOTES AND SOURCES: Eberhardt, the former commander of the 44th Motorized Infantry Regiment of the 60th Motorized Infantry Division, commanded the 38th Division from June 1942 until it was dissolved in late 1943. He later commanded the 174th Reserve Division (1944-45). Carell 1966: 183; *Kriegstagebuch des OKW*, Volume II: 1383, 1390; Volume III: 8, 732; RA: 46; OB 43: 132; OB 44: 184; OB 45: 152.

39th INFANTRY DIVISION

COMPOSITION: 113th Infantry Regiment, 114th Infantry Regiment, 139th Artillery Regiment, 139th Reconnaissance Battalion, 139th Anti-Tank Battalion, 139th Engineer Battalion, 139th Signal Battalion

HOME STATION: Wehrkreis IV

Formed in northwestern Germany in the summer of 1942, the 39th Infantry consisted mainly of Poles and other non-Germans. It was soon transferred to the Netherlands, where it performed garrison duties on the Schelde until being sent to Russia in early 1943. The division was heavily engaged on the southern sector in March, was down to battle group strength by October, and in December it suffered such heavy losses in the lower Dnieper campaign that it had to be dissolved. The 39th was never considered a first-class combat division.

SOURCES: *Kriegstagebuch des OKW,* Volume II: 1383; Volume III: 1156; RA: 100; OB 43: 132; OB 45: 152.

41st FORTRESS (later INFANTRY) DIVISION

COMPOSITION (1945): 938th Grenadier Regiment, 965th Grenadier Regiment, 733rd Grenadier Regiment, 141st Füsilier Battalion, 141st Anti-Tank Battalion, 141st Engineer Battalion, 141st Signal Battalion. The division apparently never had an organic artillery regiment.

HOME STATION: Greece; Wkr. VIII (?)

The 41st Fortress Division was formed in Greece in early 1941 and assigned the mission of guarding the Peloponnesus, that strategic isthmus connecting northern and southern Greece. Originally a two-regiment division, the 41st incorporated the 733rd Grenadier Regiment of the 133rd Fortress Division into its table of organization in September 1944. The 41st formed the rear guard of Army Group F when the Germans evacuated Greece in the fall of 1944, clashing with royalist guerrillas and the 2nd British Airborne Division during the retreat to Corinth. It was engaged in continuous small but bitter rear-guard actions as the Nazis retreated through Yugoslavia. In January 1945 it was upgraded to infantry division status and fought the regular Soviet forces between the Drava and the Sava Rivers in early 1945. The 41st Infantry was still serving on the southern sector of the Eastern Front when the war ended. Its last commander was Major General Wolfgang-Rüdiger Hauser (1944-45).

NOTES AND SOURCES: Hauser, who was promoted to Major General in late 1944, was a cavalry officer. He had formerly served on the General Staff of the Afrika Korps in 1941, as Adjutant to the Chief of the Army General Staff, and as Chief of Staff of the 14th Army in Italy (1944-45). Chant, Volume 15: 2045; OB 45: 153-54.

44th INFANTRY DIVISION "HOCH UND DEUTSCHMEISTER"

COMPOSITION (1945): 131st Grenadier Regiment, 132nd Füsilier Grenadier Regiment, 134th Grenadier Regiment, 95th Artillery Regiment, 44th Füsilier Battalion, 46th Anti-Tank Battalion, 80th Engineer Battalion, 64th Signal Battalion

HOME STATION: Vienna, Wkr. XVII

Formed in Vienna in 1938 from soldiers of the former Austrian Army, the 44th was created by the expansion of the historic 4th Viennese Regiment "Hoch und Deutschmeister." It crossed into Poland in 1939, took part in the attack on Kracow, and later in the advance across the Vistula. As part of the 6th Army in France it did less well, leading a U.S. Intelligence officer to report that its "morale [is] less high than that of the other Austrian divisions." Nevertheless it formed part of the III Motorized Corps of the 1st Panzer Group (later Army) in the initial advance into southern Russia. The Viennese division fought in the Ukraine, the Donets, and in the initial advance toward the Caucasus, until being attached to the XI Corps of the 6th Army for the drive on the Volga. In mid-November 1942, the remnants of the virtually destroyed 534th, 535th, and 536th Infantry Regiments of the recently dissolved 384th Infantry Division were attached to the 44th Division, which was cut off in Stalingrad with von Paulus's army soon after. The original 44th ceased to exist when the city fell in early February 1943.

A second 44th Infantry Division was recruited in Austria, in 1943, to replace the division destroyed at Stalingrad. It was given the honorary title "Reichsgrenadier Division Hoch und Deutschmeister." After a training period it was sent to northern Italy in August 1943, where it formed part of Field Marshal Rommel's *ad hoc* Army Group B. In December it was sent into action on the Italian Front south of Rome and remained on the front line for more than a year. It fought in the battles of the Gothic Line and launched a counterattack at Monte Battaglia in September 1944, which was described as "terrific" by the American commander. By all accounts an excellent fighting unit, the 44th was sent to the Hungarian sector of the Eastern Front in February 1945 and remained on the southern sector of the Eastern Front until the end of the war. Commanders of the Hoch und Deutschmeister Division included Lieutenant General Albrecht Schubert (1939-40), Friedrich Siebert (1941-late 1942), Lieutenant General Heinrich Deboi (late 1942-1943), Lieutenant General Dr. Franz Bayer (1943-44), and Lieutenant General von Rost (1945).

NOTES AND SOURCES: The original 44th Infantry Division consisted of the 131st, 132nd, and 134th Infantry Regiments. Its supporting units bore the same numbers in both the first and second Hoch und Deutschmeister divisions. Albrecht Schubert, a Silesian, was promoted to General of Infantry in June 1940, and later commanded XXIII Corps (1941-42), Wehrkreis XI (1943), and Wehrkreis XVII (1945). General Deboi was captured at Stalingrad. Dr. Bayer, also a Silesian, was promoted to General of Infantry in 1944. He commanded the 331st Infantry Division (1942-43) before assuming command of the 44th. He later commanded LXXX Corps on the Western Front (1945). Carell 1966: 472, 490; Fisher: 64, 82, 351; Garland and Smyth: 282-88; Hartmann: 14-15; Manstein: 52; RA: 220; OB 42: 77; OB 43: 132; OB 44: 185; OB 45: 153.

45th INFANTRY (later VOLKSGRENADIER) DIVISION

COMPOSITION: 130th Infantry Regiment, 133rd Infantry Regiment, 135th Infantry Regiment, 98th Artillery Regiment, 45th Reconnaissance Battalion, 45th Anti-Tank Battalion, 81st Engineer Battalion, 65th Signal Battalion

HOME STATION: Linz, Wkr. XVII

When Hitler annexed Austria in 1938, the 4th Austrian Division was redesignated 45th Infantry and incorporated into the Nazi Army. A year and a half later it was in action in Poland, on the right wing of Army Group South. In 1940 it participated in the French campaign and was in the initial attack on the Soviet Union in June 1941, where its reconnaissance battalion was led by Lieutenant Colonel (later Lieutenant General) Helmuth von Pannwitz, the future commander of the XV Cossack Cavalry Corps. The former Austrian Army division suffered heavy casualties in the reduction of the fortress of Brest-Litovsk in June and July 1941. Later it fought before Moscow as part of the 2nd Army and put up fierce resistance against the Soviet counteroffensive of December 1941, but was eventually forced to retreat. On December 12 Army Chief of the General Staff Halder reported the division unfit for combat for lack of supplies. The next day its main withdrawal route was cut by the Russians, and part of the division was encircled and dispersed; much of its artillery had to be abandoned because its horses starved or froze to death. The 45th nevertheless remained in the line, fought on the southern sector of the Eastern Front in 1942, and was on the central sector throughout 1943. It suffered serious casualties in the Battle of Kursk in July 1943, when Hitler's last major offensive in the East was turned back. That autumn the division fought in the defense of Sozh and in the subsequent retreats in the central sector. The 45th Infantry was largely destroyed in the Russian summer offensive of 1944, along with most of the rest of Army Group Center. The very few survivors of the 45th were used as the cadre of the 45th Volksgrenadier Division, which was formed in the Dollersheim Maneuver Area. This VG unit was in action on the Eastern Front by autumn, fought in the Battle of Warsaw in early 1945, and finally capitulated in Czechoslovakia in May 1945. The commanders of the 45th included Lieutenant General Friedrich Materna (1938-39), Major General Schlieper (1941), Major General Kühlwein (1942-43), Major General Baron Hans von Falkenstein (1943), and Major General Paul Engels (1944).

NOTES AND SOURCES: Austrian Friedrich Materna was made a General of Infantry in 1940 and went on to command the XX Corps in Russia (1941-42), and Wehrkreis XVII (late 1942-43). He was apparently retired in 1945, when he would have been 70 years of age. General Kühlwein was associated with (and possibly briefly commanded) the Brandenburg Division (1944). Baron von Falkenstein was also later associated with the Brandenburg Division. Major General Engels was captured by the Russians in July 1944 and joined the National Free Germany Committee. Carell 1966: 33, 344-45; Carell 1971: 597; Kennedy: 74 and Map 7; *Kriegstagebuch des OKW*, Volume I: 1146; Volume IV: 1876; von Mellenthin 1977: 42-43; Seaton: 224, citing Halder, *Kriegstagebuch*, Volume III: 340; RA: 220; OB 42: 78; OB 43: 133; OB 44: 185; OB 45: 154.

46th INFANTRY DIVISION

COMPOSITION: 42nd Infantry Regiment, 72nd Infantry Regiment, 97th Infantry Regiment, 114th Artillery Regiment, 46th Reconnaissance Battalion, 52nd Anti-Tank Battalion, 88th Engineer Battalion, 76th Signal Battalion

HOME STATION: Karlsbad, Wkr. XIII

Formed from Sudetenland personnel in late 1938, this division fought in Poland and in France under Major General Paul von Hase, who later became Commandant of Berlin and who was eventually executed for his part in the unsuccessful attempt to kill Hitler on July 20, 1944. Meanwhile, the division took part in the Russian campaign, attacking through the Ukraine in July 1941 and penetrating the Perekop Isthmus in the northern Crimea in September. While the bulk of the 11th Army lay siege to the naval fortress of Sevastopol on the southwestern side of the Crimean peninsula, the 46th Infantry Division, now under Lieutenant General Himer, defended the eastern approaches to the Crimea on the Kerch peninsula. In the Russian winter offensive of 1941-42 it was attacked by two full Soviet armies. Ordered to hold at all costs, General Himer and his corps commander, General Count Hans von Sponeck, decided to retreat against orders rather than to allow the division to be slaughtered. This action so infuriated Field Marshal Walther von Reichenau that he stripped the division of its banners and its honors. Hitler ordered both von Sponeck and Himer relieved of their commands. Within two weeks Field Marshal Reichenau was dead, and his successor, Field Marshal Fedor von Bock, ordered the banners returned. Officially restored to honor, the division (now under Major General Haccius) took part in the Siege of Sevastopol and in the Caucasus campaign of 1942-43, where it formed the rearguard of the XXXIX Mountain Corps in the subsequent retreat. Later it fought in the Donets, at Belgorod, in the Battle of Dnepropetrovsk (where it was seriously damaged), and in the retreat through the southern Ukraine, where it again took heavy casualties. Despite its reduced numbers, the 46th Infantry distinguished itself in the withdrawal through Transylvania. In late 1944 the division—now at regimental strength—was in action on the Slovak-Hungarian frontier. The remnants of the 46th surrendered to the Russians in Czechoslovakia in May 1945. In addition to von Hase, Haccius, and Himer, the commanders of the 46th Infantry included Major General Karl von Le Suire (1943), Lieutenant General Arthur Hauffe (1943), Lieutenant General Schneckenburger (1943), Major General Kurt Röpke (1944), and Major General Erich Reuter (1945).

NOTES AND SOURCES: Unlike Count von Sponeck, who was taken out of prison and executed on Himmler's orders after the July 20 attempt on Hitler's life failed, General Himer was not shot for retreating against orders, but his career was ruined just the same. Major General von Le Suire was soon made commander of the 117th Jäger Division in the Balkans and only directed the 46th for a short time. Arthur Hauffe was promoted to General of Infantry in 1943, briefly headed the German Army Mission to Rumania, and became commander of the XIII Corps in 1943. Erich Reuter had been with the General Branch of the Army Personnel Office in Berlin before being promoted to Major General in late 1944. Carell 1966: 297, 316-22, 482, 485; Kennedy: 74 and Map 7; Manstein: 134; RA: 204; OB 43: 133; OB 45: 154-55.

47th INFANTRY (later VOLKSGRENADIER) DIVISION

COMPOSITION: 103rd Grenadier Regiment, 104th Grenadier Regiment, 115th Grenadier Regiment, 147th Artillery Regiment, 47th Füsilier Battalion, 147th Anti-Tank Battalion, 147th Engineer Battalion, 147th Signal Battalion

HOME STATION: Probably Cologne, Wkr. VI

The 47th Infantry Division was formed in the Calais area of France from the 156th Reserve Division in February 1944. Initially engaged in Normandy, it was withdrawn before the front collapsed and thus escaped encirclement at Falaise. Later it suffered heavy losses at Mons and was forced to reform in the vicinity of Aarhus, Denmark. Redesignated a Volksgrenadier division, the 47th returned to action near Aachen, where it again suffered serious casualties. In January 1945 it went into the attack in Himmler's ill-fated offensive against Strasbourg. Later it engaged in fighting east of Aachen and in late March was opposing the American advance through the Germersheim area of Bavaria, although it was no longer a divisional-size combat force. The survivors of the 47th Volksgrenadier surrendered to the Americans at the end of the war. Its divisional commanders included Major General Karl Wahle (1944), Lieutenant General Siegfried Macholz (late 1944), and Lieutenant General Max Bork (late 1944-1945).

ALSO SEE 156th RESERVE DIVISION

NOTES AND SOURCES: Major General Wahle, former commander of the 187th Jäger Division, was captured in September 1944. Lieutenant General Macholz, former commander of the 191st Reserve Division (1943-early 1944) and the 49th Infantry Division (1944), led the 47th only briefly. Bork had previously served as Chief of Staff of the 6th Army on the Russian Front in late 1943. Carell 1971: 595-98; Chant, Volume 17: 2277, 2368; Harrison: Map VI; MacDonald 1963: 411; "Frontnachweiser," 15 December 1944; RA: 100; OB 45: 155.

48th INFANTRY (later VOLKSGRENADIER) DIVISION

COMPOSITION: 126th Grenadier Regiment, 127th Grenadier Regiment, 148th Artillery Regiment, 48th Füsilier Company, 148th Anti-Tank Battalion, 148th Engineer Battalion, 148th Signal Battalion

HOME STATION: Probably Hanover, Wkr. XI

Formed in the West Flanders area of Belgium from the 171st Reserve Division in 1944, this unit included many Poles and other non-Germans. Initially posted on the Belgian coast, the 48th was transferred to France after the collapse of the Normandy Front and first engaged the Allies in the Chartres area in August. Inexperienced in battle, inadequately trained, and not particularly loyal to the Third Reich, the 48th Infantry did not perform well in combat. It was defeated at Chartres, Metz, and later in the Siegfried Line battles. Severely damaged by Patton's 3rd Army, it finally collapsed altogether and had to be temporarily absorbed by the 559th Infantry Division in November. Reorganized in eastern Austria in early 1945, it was redesignated a Volksgrenadier division and sent to the Eastern Front. It fought as part of the 8th Army as the Russians successfully drove on Vienna and ended the war at battle group strength on the Eastern Front. Commanders of the 48th Infantry/Volksgrenadier included Colonel Arnold Scholz (October-November 1944) and Lieutenant General Casper (1944-45).

ALSO SEE 171st RESERVE DIVISION

NOTES AND SOURCES: Colonel Scholz was an acting divisional commander only. His normal position was commander of the division's 126th Grenadier Regiment. General Casper commanded the 335th Infantry Division (1942) and the 171st Reserve Division (1943) until he fell ill and had to be relieved. Blumenson 1960: 570, 584-85; Cole 1950: 48, 357, 365; Harrison: Map VI; Hartmann: 15; *Kriegstagebuch des OKW*, Volume I: 1145; Volume IV: 1904; RA: 172; OB 45: 155.

49th INFANTRY DIVISION

COMPOSITION: 148th Grenadier Regiment, 149th Grenadier Regiment, 150th Grenadier Regiment, 149th Artillery Regiment, 49th Fusilier Battalion, 149th Anti-Tank Battalion, 149th Engineer Battalion, 149th Signal Battalion

HOME STATION: Probably Braunschweig, Wkr. XI

This division was formed in the Boulogne area of France from the 191st Reserve Division in February 1944. First in combat in northern France in August 1944, the division took part in the withdrawal into the Low Countries and was smashed near the Albert Canal by Field Marshal Montgomery's soldiers. The divisional commander, Lieutenant General Siegfried Macholz, tried to reorganize his shattered units at Hasselt, but managed to assemble only 1,500 men—mostly support troops who had no anti-tank guns and only one piece of artillery: a Russian 122mm howitzer. Only one regimental headquarters—the 148th Grenadier—could be located. Soon Macholz was replaced by Lieutenant General Vollrath Lübbe, the former commander of the 462nd Volksgrenadier Division. Although at less than regimental strength, the 49th Infantry was soon back in action north of Aachen but was withdrawn after the city fell and was mercifully disbanded shortly afterward. The survivors of the division were sent to the 246th Volksgrenadier Division.

ALSO SEE 191st RESERVE DIVISION

NOTES AND SOURCES: Lieutenant General Erich Baessler was apparently in charge of the 49th Infantry when it was formed. Macholz, former commander of the 191st Reserve Division (1943-early 1944), briefly commanded the 47th Infantry Division on the Western Front in 1944. General Lübbe had commanded the 2nd Panzer Division in Russia (1943-44). Cole 1950: 192, 430; Cole 1965: 35; Harrison: Map VI; MacDonald 1963: 97-98, 282, 297, 500; RA: 172; OB 45: 156.

50th INFANTRY DIVISION

COMPOSITION: 121st Infantry Regiment, 122nd Infantry Regiment, 123rd Infantry Regiment, 150th Artillery Regiment, 150th Reconnaissance Battalion, 150th Anti-Tank Battalion, 150th Engineer Battalion, 150th Signal Battalion

HOME STATION: Wehrkreis III

Originally formed as the Küstrin Frontier Command in the Oder-Warta basin of eastern Germany, this headquarters was upgraded to infantry division status in the summer of 1939, and its frontier troops were inducted into the active army for the invasion of Poland. Lightly engaged in the Polish campaign of 1939, it fought in the French campaign and later in southern Russia, where it was involved in breaching the Perekop Isthmus in the northern Crimea and in the reduction of Sevastopol. Later, in 1942, the 50th Infantry took part in the Caucasus campaign and narrowly avoided being cut off in the Kuban bridgehead by marching across the Sea of Azov on the ice, because the land routes had been cut off or threatened by the Russians. After the retreat to the lower Dnieper, the 50th Infantry was returned to the Crimea, where, in April 1944, it faced an exact reversal of roles from that of 1941: it was defending the Perekop Isthmus against a Russian attack. Defeated, it retreated back to Sevastopol, where the divisional commander, Major General Sixt, was seriously wounded and had to be evacuated by air on May 1. Eight days later his replacement, Colonel Betz, was killed in action. In the evacuation of the Crimea by the German Navy, most of the 50th was left behind; most of these were made prisoner, except for the officers, who were brutally murdered by the Russians after they had surrendered. Only 2,800 men from the division managed to escape by sea. They were eventually transported to Germany, reformed, and sent back into action with Army Group Center. The burned-out division suffered heavy losses against the Soviet summer offensive of 1944 but was still in combat in late 1944, when it was defending a sector in East Prussia. It ended the war in this pocket. Leaders of the division included Lieutenant General Konrad Sorsche (1939-40), Lieutenant General Karl Hollidt (1941-

42), Major General Friedrich Schmidt (1942), Major General Sixt (1943-44), and Colonel Betz (1944).

NOTES AND SOURCES: Karl Hollidt, a Rhinelander, was commander of the XVII Corps on the Russian Front in 1942. In November 1942 this unit was upgraded to Army Detachment status and was renamed Army Detachment Hollidt. Eventually it was redesignated 6th Army. Hollidt was promoted to Colonel General as of September 1, 1943, and relieved of command of the 6th Army and retired in May 1944, because of his inability to halt the Russian onslaught. He was in poor health by this time. In 1945 he was recalled to service by Reichsleiter Bormann as Representative of the Gauleiter of Rhineland-Westphalia. Carell 1966: 297, 482, 503, 509; Carell 1971: 142, 538-58; Chant, Volume 7: 907; Kennedy: 74 and Map 7; Manstein 24; Hermann Plocher, *The German Air Force Versus Russia, 1943,* United States Air Force Historical Studies: Number 155, Aerospace Studies Institute, Air University, 1967; published in hardback form by Arno Press, New York, 1968: 322; RA: 46; OB 42: 78; OB 45: 156.

52nd INFANTRY (later SECURITY) DIVISION

COMPOSITION (1942): 163rd Infantry Regiment, 181st Infantry Regiment, 205th Infantry Regiment, 152nd Artillery Regiment, 152nd Reconnaissance Battalion, 152nd Anti-Tank Battalion, 152nd Engineer Battalion, 152nd Signal Battalion

HOME STATION: Kassel, Wkr. IX

Formed from reserve personnel in the summer of 1939, the 52nd was originally a three-regiment infantry division. It fought in Poland under Major General Hans-Jürgen von Armin. Elements of the 52nd took part in the invasion of Norway while other units fought in the French campaign. Sent to Russia with Army Group Center, the 52nd remained on the line for more than two years before suffering such heavy losses in the defensive Battle of Smolensk in the fall of 1943 that it had to be withdrawn. Instead of rebuilding the 52nd as an infantry division, the High Command of the Army decided to convert it into a security unit, and it was stripped of a grenadier regiment and all of its artillery. Returned to Army Group Center in early 1944, the 52nd Security never exceeded battle group strength. It was smashed by the Russian summer offensive of 1944 and had to be disbanded as a combat unit. The divisional staff, however, was transferred to Army Group North, where it controlled miscellaneous units in the Baltic States in 1944 and formed Fortress Command Libau as part of the 18th Army's reserve in 1945. Commanders of the division included von Armin (1939-

40), Lieutenant General Dr. Lothar Rendulic (1940-41), and Major General Albert Newiger (1943-44).

NOTES AND SOURCES: The Prussian Jürgen von Armin led the 17th Panzer Division in the Russian campaign for about three weeks, before he was seriously wounded in July 1941. Upon recovering, he commanded XXXIX Panzer Corps in Russia (1942) and the 5th Panzer Army in Tunisia (late 1942-1943) before succeeding Erwin Rommel as Commander-in-Chief of Army Group Afrika in March 1943. He was promoted to Colonel General on December 3, 1942, and forced to surrender in May 1943. Dr. Rendulic also became a Colonel General (on April 1, 1944). An Austrian Nazi, he got along well with Adolf Hitler. Rendulic, former Military Attache to Paris (1934-38) and Chief of Staff of XVII Corps (1938-39), distinguished himself as commander of XXXV Corps in Russia (1942-43), where he excelled in turning back Russian attacks. Later, as an army group commander, he was less successful. Meanwhile, he commanded the 2nd Panzer Army in the Balkans (summer 1943-June 1944) and the 20th Mountain Army in the retreat from Finland (late 1944). In 1945 he commanded Army Group North in East Prussia and then Army Group South, which was redesignated Army Group Ostmark, in Austria, during the last weeks of the war. Under Major General Newiger in late 1943, the 52nd Security seems to have undertaken some of the functions of a field training division. Carell 1966: 196; Carell 1971: 309; *Kriegstagebuch des OKW*, Volume III: 1888; Volume IV; 1897; Seaton: 366-67, 591; OB 45: 157. Also see Thorwald, *Defeat in the East,* and Lothar Rendulic, *Gekämpft Gesiegt Geschlagen*, Wels, München, 1957.

56th INFANTRY (later VOLKSGRENADIER) DIVISION

COMPOSITION: 171st Infantry Regiment, 192nd Infantry Regiment, 234th Infantry Regiment, 156th Artillery Regiment, 156th Reconnaissance Battalion, 156th Anti-Tank Battalion, 156th Engineer Battalion, 156th Signal Battalion

HOME STATION: Naumburg, Wkr. IV

The 56th Infantry, known as the Swords ("Schwerter") Division from its unit emblem, was formed upon mobilization in the summer of 1939. Its men were mostly Saxon reservists. It was with the 14th Army in Poland, where its primary mission seems to have been rounding up Polish stragglers. In Belgium the following year it had a much tougher task for it was involved in heavy fighting against the British Expeditionary Force. The 56th acquitted itself well. In 1941 the division was in the spearhead of

Army Group Center, crossing the Bug River on rubber rafts. The 56th took part in the advance on and retreat from Moscow and remained on the central sector of the Russian Front for the rest of the war. It suffered heavy casualties in the Battle of Kursk in July 1943 and was smashed in the Soviet summer offensive of 1944. Briefly withdrawn in the autumn of 1944, the 56th returned to Army Group Center as a Volksgrenadier division and was still fighting on the central sector (now in East Prussia) when the war ended. Its commanders included Lieutenant General Karl Kriebel (1940), Major General Karl von Oven (1941-42), and Lieutenant General Otto Lüdecke (1943-44).

NOTES AND SOURCES: Later a General of Infantry, Karl Kriebel was commander of Wehrkreis VII from early 1943 until 1945. He was a Bavarian. Karl Oven, a Prussian, was also made a General of Infantry. He commanded XLII Corps in Russia (1943-44). General Lüdecke left the 56th to command the 264th Infantry Division (1944). Carell 1966: 18; Kennedy: Map 10; RA: 72; OB 43: 134; OB 45: 157.

57th INFANTRY DIVISION

COMPOSITION: 179th Infantry Regiment, 199th Infantry Regiment, 217th Infantry Regiment, 157th Artillery Regiment, 157th Reconnaissance Battalion, 157th Anti-Tank Battalion, 157th Engineer Battalion, 157th Signal Battalion

HOME STATION: Bad Reichenhall, Wkr. VII

Created from reserve personnel in the summer of 1939, this division "distinguished itself in southern Poland and in operations on the lower Somme," to quote an Allied intelligence report. It was this Bavarian division that blunted General Charles de Gaulle's attempts to annihilate the German bridgehead at Abbeville. Despite de Gaulle's later grossly exaggerated claims of a significant success, his French 4th Armored Division was, in fact, smashed, along with another French mechanized division, at a time when France could not afford the loss. A few days later the German 18th Army took Paris, which was virtually without armored protection. After fighting in France, the 57th Infantry was sent to Russia, where it formed part of Werner Kempf's XLVIII Panzer Corps of the 1st Panzer Army in the sweep across southern Russia. The division remained on the southern sector, suffering heavy losses at the Battle of Kursk, and was encircled at Cherkassy in February 1944. It broke out but with heavy loss of equipment and life. Briefly sent to the rear to regroup, the 57th returned to the front, but this time to Army Group Center just in time for the Russian summer offensive of 1944. It was surrounded east of Minsk along with the rest of the 4th Army's XXVII Corps. Parts of the division managed to escape, but the bulk of it was destroyed. Major General Trowitz, the last divisional commander of the 57th, was among the prisoners. Soon afterward the 57th Infantry was officially disbanded. Previous divisional commanders included Lieutenant Generals Oskar Blümm (1939-41; 1942), Anton Dostler (1941-42), and Friedrich Siebert (1943).

NOTES AND SOURCES: General Blümm assumed command of Replacement Division Staff 407 on November 1, 1942, and commanded it until 1945. Anton Dostler later commanded the 163rd Infantry Division (1942-43), LXXV Corps (March-November 1944), and LXXIII Corps (1945). He was promoted to General of Infantry in August 1943. General Trowitz joined the National Free Germany Committee while in captivity. Carell 1971: 594-97; Hartmann: 15; Kennedy: 133 and Map 10; RA: 116; OB 42: 79; OB 43: 134; OB 45: 158.

58th INFANTRY DIVISION

COMPOSITION: 154th Infantry Regiment, 209th Infantry Regiment, 220th Infantry Regiment, 158th Artillery Regiment, 158th Reconnaissance Battalion, 158th Anti-Tank Battalion, 158th Engineer Battalion, 158th Signal Battalion

HOME STATION: Rendsburg, Wkr. X

Mobilized in the summer of 1939, this Lower Saxon reserve division was sent to the Saar sector in 1940 and was only slightly involved in the French campaign. It was first heavily engaged in 1941 on the northern sector of the Russian Front, where it broke through the Stalin Line, fought at Lake Peipus, and took part in the Siege of Leningrad. The next year it took part in the Battle of Volkhov (south of Leningrad) in January through March, before being switched to the Demyansk sector, where it remained for some time. During this period it was commanded by Major General Dr. Friedrich Altrichter. Switched to Army Group Center in the fall of 1943, it was hurriedly rushed back to the north in January 1944 but arrived too late to prevent the Soviets from breaking the Siege of Leningrad. It lost one-third of its men and all its heavy equipment in the withdrawal from the city. That summer the 58th returned to the central sector and was cut off in the Samland region of East Prussia in early 1945. It surrendered there in March. Commanders of this Saxon division included Altrichter (1941-42), Lieutenant General Karl von Graffen (1943), and Lieutenant General Curt Siewert (1945).

NOTES AND SOURCES: Lieutenant General Dr. Altrichter was commander of the 154th Reserve Division in 1945. Lieutenant General von Graffen was commanding Harko 316, an Army-level artillery unit, in Italy in 1945. Carell 1966: 287-88; Manstein: 196; Salisbury: 351; Ziemke 1966: 258; 262; OB 42: 79; OB 43: 135; OB 45: 158.

59th INFANTRY DIVISION

COMPOSITION: 1034th Grenadier Regiment, 1035th Grenadier Regiment, 1036th Grenadier Regiment, 159th Artillery Regiment, 59th Füsilier Battalion, 159th Anti-Tank Battalion, 159th Engineer Battalion, 159th Signal Battalion

HOME STATION: Wehrkreis II

Formed on an emergency basis in July 1944 at the Gross Born Maneuver Area, this division was in action on the Western Front by August. Its ranks were filled by troops on furlough from Norway or the Eastern Front. The commitment of such *ad hoc* divisions to combat with inadequate training (as a unit) and severe equipment shortages is indicative of the desperate situation Germany faced after the Battle of Normandy and the subsequent encirclement of the 7th and 5th Panzer armies in the Falaise Pocket in western France. The new division was commanded by Lieutenant General Walter Poppe, a veteran of the Eastern Front. The 59th fought in the Calais area and suffered heavy losses in the 15th Army's withdrawal to the North Brabant area of Holland from the French coast. By mid-September the division's total strength was 1,000 infantrymen, a few engineers, a field replacement battalion, 18 anti-tank guns, and 30 howitzers; nevertheless it fought against the elite U.S. 101st Airborne Division in Operation Market-Garden, and succeeded in delaying the advance of the British XXX Armored Corps to Arnhem, where the British 1st Airborne Division was being smashed by the II SS Panzer Corps. In October the 59th Infantry Division was in Army Group B's reserve during the Battle of the Scheldt. It took part in the retreat across the Maas and was finally taken out of the line to rest and refit in November. Despite its shortages in every department, the 59th was back on the front line in December, fighting near Aachen, in the Siegfried Line battles. In February 1945 it formed part of General Koechling's LXXXI Corps and opposed the 9th U.S. Army's attempts to cross the Roer. Eventually transferred to the 5th Panzer Army, the 59th fought against both the 1st and 3rd U.S. armies as they drove on the Rhine. At this time the division was led by Lieutenant General Hans-Kurt Hoecker. Little remained of the stubborn emergency division as the Battle of the Ruhr Pocket began, and it seems to have been dissolved (or dissolved itself) in April 1945 as German resistance in the West disintegrated and the Allies closed in on the industrial heart of the Third Reich.

NOTES AND SOURCES: Lieutenant General Poppe (1944-45) was a veteran divisional commander, having previously led the 255th Infantry Division (1943), the 217th Infantry (1943-44), and the 189th Reserve (1944). His expertise probably explains why the 59th succeeded as well as it did. Cole 1965: 613; MacDonald 1963: 125, 216-17; MacDonald 1973: 153, 189; RA: 32; OB 45: 159.

60th INFANTRY DIVISION
see 60th Panzer Grenadier Division

61st INFANTRY DIVISION

COMPOSITION: 151st Infantry Regiment, 162nd Infantry Regiment, 176th Infantry Regiment, 161st Artillery Regiment, 161st Reconnaissance Battalion, 161st Anti-Tank Battalion, 161st Engineer Battalion, 161st Signal Battalion

HOME STATION: Königsberg, Wkr. I

Formed from reservists in the summer of 1939, this East Prussian division fought in Poland under Lieutenant General Siegfried Haenicke and took part in the Siege of Warsaw. The next year it was part of Army Group B when it overran Belgium. It remained with Army Group B (which was redesignated Army Group North) for the invasion of Russia in 1941. It fought in the drive on Leningrad, took part in the Battle of the Valday Hills, opposed the Soviet winter offensive of 1941-42, and was later engaged in the Siege of Leningrad. In the winter of 1942-43 the 61st Infantry fought in the Second Battle of Lake Ladoga where it rescued the 227th Infantry Division, which had been encircled by elements of two Russian armies near Schluesselburg. It stayed in the Leningrad area throughout 1943. When the Russian winter offensive of 1944 began on January 17, the 61st was the only reserve division in the 18th Army, which was besieging the city. Committed to battle, the 61st was unable to prevent the Soviets from finally breaking the siege on January 28. Under Lieutenant General Günther Krappe, the 61st Infantry distinguished itself in the retreat through the Baltic States and was shifted to Army Group Center after the Center's disastrous defeats in June and July 1944. The division served with the XXXIX Panzer Corps in the retreat through Poland and, by

January 1945, was cut off in East Prussia, where it remained—at battle group strength—until the end of the war.

SOURCES: Carell 1966: 419; Carell 1971: 260, 265; Hartmann: 16; Kennedy: Map 10; Salisbury: 538; RA: 20; OB 44: 189; OB 45: 159.

62nd INFANTRY (later VOLKSGRENADIER) DIVISION

COMPOSITION: 164th Infantry Regiment, 183rd Infantry Regiment, 190th Infantry Regiment, 162nd Artillery Regiment, 162nd Reconnaissance Battalion, 162nd Anti-Tank Battalion, 162nd Engineer Battalion, 162nd Signal Battalion

HOME STATION: Glatz, Wkr. VIII

Made up of Silesian reservists, this division was formed upon mobilization in the summer of 1939. It fought well in Poland and France and in 1941 was on the southern sector of the Russian Front. In late 1942 it was used to stabilize the 3rd Rumanian Army, which was in the process of disintegrating under heavy Soviet attacks. Later, with Army Detachment Hollidt, the 62nd suffered heavy losses in the retreat from Stalingrad. It took part in the Kursk offensive of July 1943 and, following this reversal, was involved in the withdrawal to and from the Dnestr, where it again sustained high casualties. Withdrawn in September 1944 to refit and reorganize in the Neuhammer Maneuver Area, it was restocked with inexperienced recruits from the 583rd Volksgrenadier Division. In the fall of 1944 (probably in October), the 62nd was redesignated a Volksgrenadier division, placed under the command of Major General Friedrich Kittel (the younger brother of the defender of Metz), and transferred to the Western Front, where it fought in the Eifel battles, the Ardennes offensive, and the Battle of Monschau, where it was "virtually wiped out" by the U.S. 9th Infantry Division. Nevertheless the remnants of the 62nd were reorganized and recommitted to action as part of the 5th Panzer Army. It was finally finished off in the Ruhr Pocket, only a month before the end of the war. Its commanders, in addition to Kittel (1944-45), included Major General Walter Keiner (1939-42), Lieutenant General Rudolf Friedrich (1942), Major General Gruner (1943), and Major General Tronnier (1944).

NOTES AND SOURCES: General of Artillery Keiner was reportedly in command of the LXIX Corps in early 1944 and was Director-General of Army Ordnance in 1945. Rudolf Friedrich later commanded the 327th Infantry Division in Russia (1942-43), with limited success. Major General Tronnier was captured by the Russians in September 1944 and later joined the

National Free Germany Committee. Cole 1965: 175; Hartmann: 16-17; Kennedy: 74; Manstein: 297-98, 322, 288; MacDonald 1973: 69, 194; "Front-nachweiser," 15 December 1944; OB 42: 80; OB 43: 135; OB 45: 160.

64th INFANTRY DIVISION

COMPOSITION: 1037th Grenadier Regiment, 1038th Grenadier Regiment, 1039th Grenadier Regiment, 164th Artillery Regiment, 64th Füsilier Battalion, 164th Anti-Tank Battalion, 164th Engineer Battalion, 164th Signal Battalion

HOME STATION: Wehrkreis VI

Formed at the Wahn Maneuver Area near Cologne, this emergency unit consisted mainly of men on leave from the Eastern Front. Thrown into the line at Abbeville, France, in August 1944, it fought in the Battle of the Albert Canal and was left isolated when the 15th Army withdrew behind the Schelde. On October 2 the divisional commander, Major General Kurt Eberding, had a total of 2,350 infantrymen, plus more than 8,500 support and miscellaneous service troops, many of which were not organic to the division. Eberding hedgehogged and, despite overwhelming odds, chose to fight the entire Canadian II Corps, rather than surrender. This decision led to the month-long Battle of the Breskens Pocket, in which the 64th Infantry Division was gradually crushed. General Eberding was captured on November 2, and the fighting ended the next day. The 64th Infantry had been totally destroyed.

SOURCES: MacDonald 1963: 219, 221; Hans Speidel, *Invasion, 1944,* Paperback Library Edition, New York, 1968: 41 (hereafter cited as "Speidel"); RA: 100; OB 45: 160.

65th INFANTRY DIVISION

COMPOSITION: 145th Infantry Regiment, 146th Infantry Regiment, 147th Infantry Regiment, 165th Artillery Regiment, 165th Motorcycle Battalion, 165th Reconnaissance/Anti-Tank Battalion (combined), 165th Engineer Battalion, 165th Signal Battalion

HOME STATION: Wehrkreis XII

Originally a two-regiment division, the 65th was created in the summer of 1942 and sent to Holland in the fall. In the summer of 1943 it underwent a massive personnel exchange with the regiments of the 265th Infantry

Division, before being sent to Italy in August 1943. After crossing the border with Rommel's *ad hoc* Army Group B, it was in action in October, holding the Sangro River line against elements of Montgomery's 8th Army. In the winter fighting in southern Italy, the inexperienced 65th was mauled by the British, to the point where Lieutenant General Westphal, Chief of Staff of Army Group C, reported that "to all intents and purposes [it] no longer existed." Nevertheless the survivors of the division were reorganized and even given a third regimental headquarters—the 147th. The other two regiments were reduced from a strength of three to two infantry battalions each. In January 1944 the 65th Infantry (minus one regiment on attached duty at Genoa) was hurried back into action against the Allied landing at Anzio. A month later the division, led by Lieutenant General Dr. Georg Pfeiffer, formed part of the I Parachute Corps' attack at Anzio and remained in the line until the German front was finally broken and Rome fell. After the retreat from Anzio, the 65th withdrew to Pisato, reformed, and absorbed the personnel of the Infantry Division East Prussia, which had been trained by Wehrkreis I. Thus reinforced, the division fought in the Battles of the Gothic Line and remained on the Italian Front until the end of the war. The divisional commander in 1945 was Lieutenant General Hellmuth Pfeifer.

NOTES AND SOURCES: Lieutenant General Gustav Heistermann von Ziehlberg commanded the division in Italy until the end of November 1943, when he was seriously wounded. He later commanded the 28th Jäger Division on the Eastern Front. Lieutenant General Hans Bömers was apparently in command of the division in late 1943. General Pfeifer took over shortly afterward and led it for most of the rest of the war. Alfred Kesselring, *A Soldier's Record*. Westport, CT: Greenwood Press, 1970, p. 228; Blumenson 1969: 63-64, 206, 258; Fisher: 302 and Map III; RA: 188; OB 43: 136; OB 44: 189; OB 45: 160-61.

68th INFANTRY DIVISION

COMPOSITION: 169th Infantry Regiment, 188th Infantry Regiment, 196th Infantry Regiment, 168th Artillery Regiment, 168th Reconnaissance Battalion, 168th Anti-Tank Battalion, 168th Engineer Battalion, 168th Signal Battalion

HOME STATION: Guben, Wkr. III

Organized from second-wave reservists in the summer of 1939, the 68th Infantry fought in southern Poland under Colonel George Braum and later took part in the French campaign. The division went into Russia with Army Group South and was in Kharhov on November 14, when Braum (now a Major General) was killed when his quarters were blown up by partisans. The 68th Infantry remained on the southern sector of the Eastern Front for the rest of the war and suffered heavy losses in the initial campaign, in the withdrawal from Kiev (1943), and in the battles of the northern Ukraine (1944). It was with the 1st Panzer Army when it was encircled and broke out of the pocket east of the Dnestr. In the fall of 1944 the 68th Infantry fought in Slovakia and in southern Poland and in 1945 took part in the Silesian campaign. The division surrendered with Army Group Center (formerly South) in Czechoslovakia in May 1945. Its commanders included Lieutenant General Paul Scheuerpflug (early 1944-1945), and Lieutenant General Robert Meissner (1941-43), as well as Braum.

NOTES AND SOURCES: Meissner was an Austrian. Carell 1971: 233; Kennedy: 74 and Map 7; Manstein: 526; RA: 46; OB 42: 80; OB 44: 190; OB 45: 161; Ziemke 1966: 279-80.

69th INFANTRY DIVISION

COMPOSITION: 159th Infantry Regiment, 193rd Infantry Regiment, 236th Infantry Regiment, 169th Artillery Regiment, 169th Reconnaissance Battalion, 169th Anti-Tank Battalion, 169th Engineer Battalion, 169th Signal Battalion

HOME STATION: Wehrkreis VI

The 69th was made up of Ruhr area reservists mustered in upon mobilization in the summer of 1939. In April 1940 it landed in Norway and captured the cities of Stavanger and Bergen. Later that year it occupied the western coast of Norway from Nordfjord (100 miles north of Bergen) to Egersund. In 1941 its 193rd Infantry Regiment went to northern Finland on temporary assignment to the 210th Coastal Defense Division and did not rejoin the 69th until 1943. The parent unit, which was commanded by Lieutenant General Bruno Ortner from 1942 to 1944, was transferred to the Eastern Front in the spring of 1943. At first lightly engaged on the northern sector near Leningrad, the 69th was later involved in the retreats on the southern sector in late 1943 and 1944, before being sent to Army Group Center in autumn 1944. After the retreat through Poland, the division fought in East Prussia and was part of the 3rd Panzer Army in the Battle of Tilsit on January 19-21, 1945. Here, near where Napoleon made his famous pact with Czar Alexander, the 69th Infantry Division was virtually wiped out. The divisional commander, Lieutenant General Rein, died with his men. The remnants of the unit retreated into the fortress of Königsberg, where they also were destroyed in early April 1945.

NOTES AND SOURCES: Lieutenant General Ortner was commanding the 290th Infantry Division in the Courland Pocket at the end of the war. Chant, Volume 16: 2228; *Kriegstagebuch des OKW*, Volume III: 7, 260, 734, 1158; Volume IV: 1897; OB 42: 80; OB 43: 136; OB 44: 190; OB 45: 161-62; Ziemke 1959: 34; also see Thorwald: 89-104, for an account of the Battle of Königsberg.

70th INFANTRY DIVISION

COMPOSITION: 1018th Grenadier Regiment, 1019th Grenadier Regiment, 1020th Grenadier Regiment, 170th Artillery Regiment, 170th Füsilier Battalion, 170th Anti-Tank Battalion, 170th Engineer Battalion, 170th Signal Battalion

HOME STATION: Stuttgart, Wkr. V (?)

Nicknamed the "White Bread Division" because most of its 7,500 soldiers had stomach problems and required special diets, this division was mustered in on Walcheren Island, Holland, in 1944. Cadres of the 165th Reserve Division were also transferred to the division to assist in its training. The 70th Infantry remained on the island in the Scheldt until November 1944, when it was attacked by the British and the Canadians. The ailing soldiers fought surprisingly well, for it took Montgomery's veteran forces nine days to defeat them. The divisional commander, Lieutenant General Daser, was captured on November 9, and the fighting ended shortly thereafter. Almost all of the division's soldiers were either killed or taken prisoner.

NOTES AND SOURCES: The British Official History states General Daser surrendered on November 6, and the last resistance ended two days later. Chant, Volume 15: 2086-87; L. F. Ellis, *Victory in the West*, Volume II, *The Defeat of Germany*, Her Majesty's Stationery Office, London, 1968: 123; MacDonald 1963: 219; Speidel: 41; OB 45: 162.

71st INFANTRY DIVISION

COMPOSITION: 191st Infantry Regiment, 194th Infantry Regiment, 211th Infantry Regiment, 171st Artillery Regiment, 171st Reconnaissance Battalion, 171st Anti-Tank Battalion, 171st Engineer Battalion, 171st Signal Battalion

HOME STATION: Hildesheim, Wkr. XI

This reserve division was recruited mainly from the Hanover area and was called up for active duty in the summer of 1939. Sent to the Saar area while Hitler overran Poland, the 71st first saw action in France, where it distinguished itself at Sedan and in the advance to Verdun. Here it was led by Lieutenant General Karl Weisenberger. Sent to Russia in 1941, the division was led by Major General (later Lieutenant General) Alexander von Hartmann and formed part of the IV Infantry Corps, Army Group South. Rotated back to France to rest and refit in late 1941, it returned to Stalino in southern Russia in 1942. Assigned to the 6th Army, the 71st Infantry Division fought at Kharkhov and in the Battle of the Izyum Pocket in May, in the Battle of Voronezh in June and July, and in the Battle of the Kalach Pocket in August. It was trapped in the Stalingrad Pocket in November and was largely destroyed in the subsequent street fighting. General von Hartmann was among those killed; in the last week of the battle he reportedly deliberately exposed himself to enemy fire, preferring death to a Siberian prison camp. He was succeeded by Major General Roske, who surrendered to the Russians on January 31, 1943. Very few of its men survived Soviet captivity.

A second 71st Infantry Division was formed in Denmark in April 1943. Its commander throughout its existence was Major General (later Lieutenant General) Wilhelm Raapke. Initially sent to Istria, Slovenia, on garrison duty, the 71st crossed into northern Italy as part of the II SS Panzer Corps in the fall of 1943 and was sent to the front after the Anzio landings in January 1944. Later it took part in the Battle of Cassino. The 71st was heavily engaged for three months and had only 100 effectives left by May 18. Sent to the rear to rebuild, it went back into action in July. The 71st fought in the Battles of the Gothic Line, and suffered heavy losses in the Rimini area. Withdrawn to the Venezia-Giulia area of northern Italy to refit, it was transferred to the southern sector of the Eastern Front in late 1944 and fought in the Hungarian and Austrian campaigns. It was still in the East when the war ended.

NOTES AND SOURCES: Karl Weisenberger, a Bavarian, was promoted to General of Infantry on April 1, 1941. He later commanded XXXVI Mountain Corps (1941-44) and Wehrkreis XIII (September 1944-1945). Blumenson 1969: 361; Carell 1966: 491; Fisher: 46, 86, 278, 302; Hartmann: 17; *Kriegstagebuch des OKW*, Volume III: 1160; John Shaw et al, *Red Army Resurgent*, Time-Life Books, World War II Series, Time-Life Books, Inc., Chicago, 1979: 189 (hereafter cited as "Time-Life, Volume 20"); RA: 172; OB 43: 136-37; OB 45: 162.

72nd INFANTRY DIVISION

COMPOSITION: 105th Infantry Regiment, 124th Infantry Regiment, 266th Infantry Regiment, 172nd Artillery Regiment, 172nd Reconnaissance Battalion, 172nd Anti-Tank Battalion, 172nd Engineer Battalion, 172nd Signal Battalion

HOME STATION: Trier, Wkr. X

Originally created as the Trier Frontier Command, the 72nd was reorganized as an infantry division by incorporating two active army regiments and one reserve regiment into the former frontier unit. Most of its troops were Rhinelanders and Bavarians. Sent to the West Wall during the "Phony War" of 1939-April 1940, it was not considered a very good fighting unit in the early part of the conflict. After being lightly engaged in France, it took part in the Balkans campaign in the spring of 1941 and then crossed into Russia as a part of Army Group South. It fought in the Crimean campaign and subsequent Siege of Sevastopol, before being transferred to Army Group Center. On the central sector it took part in the winter fighting of 1942-43, in the Rzhev withdrawal, and in the Battle of Kursk. Transferred back to the southern sector, it fought in the Dnieper bend battles, in the southern Ukraine and was finally encircled at Cherkassy with the IX Infantry Corps. During the battle and eventual break-out attempt, General Stemmermann, the corps commander, personally assumed command of the division. When he was killed by an anti-tank shell, all order disappeared in the 72nd. Perhaps half of the division escaped. Reformed in the spring of 1944, it was in Poland in the summer and was officially cited for its performance in the Vistula defensive battles in August. The 72nd suffered very heavy casualties in southern Poland and was smashed as the Russians drove on Breslau and Silesia. It rallied quickly and was soon back in combat. The division ended up as part of the LVII Panzer Corps of Army Group Center, which surrendered to the Russians in Czechoslovakia. Major General Beisswanger was the division's commander in 1945; previous commanders of the 72nd Infantry included Lieutenant General Franz Mattenklott (1939-41), Lieutenant General Albert Müller-Gebhard (1942-43), and Lieutenant General Dr. Hermann Hohn (1943-early 1945).

NOTES AND SOURCES: Lieutenant General (later General of Infantry) Franz Mattenklott was in charge of Frontier Command Trier when it was reformed as the 72nd Infantry Division. He later was commander of XLII Corps on the Russian Front (1942-43) and Wehrkreis VI (June 1944-45). Lieutenant General Müller-Gebhard was commandant of Prague in 1945. Dr. Hohn was named commander of the IX Corps in April 1945. Carell 1971: 309; Chant: Volume 16: 2232; Hartmann: 18; Manstein: 34, 260; OB 43: 137; OB 45: 163.

73rd INFANTRY DIVISION

COMPOSITION: 170th Infantry Regiment, 186th Infantry Regiment, 213th Infantry Regiment, 173rd Artillery Regiment, 173rd Reconnaissance Battalion, 173rd Anti-Tank Battalion, 173rd Engineer Battalion, 173rd Signal Battalion

HOME STATION: Würzburg, Wkr. XIII

This division probably saw as much combat as any German infantry division in World War II. After being created in the initial mobilization in the summer of 1939, the 73rd was lightly engaged in Poland and France under Major General (later Lieutenant General) Bieler. Attached to Stumme's XL Motorized Corps, the 73rd swept through the Balkans and invaded Russia in July 1941. It fought in the Crimea, the subsequent Siege of Sevastopol (under the command of Lieutenant General Rudolf von Bünau), in the advance across the Don, and in the Caucasus campaign. Still under von Bünau, the division retreated into the Kuban bridgehead after the tide of the war in Russia turned against Germany and in January 1943 was heavily engaged against the Soviet amphibious landings at Novorossiysk, in which it was primarily responsible for checking the surprise Russian attack. Shortly afterward the 73rd Infantry—now at battle group strength—was pulled out of the bridgehead and sent north, where it fought at Kursk and later on the lower Dnieper, where it was led by Major General Böhme. Returned to the Crimea in early 1944, it was smashed in April and May during the retreat to Sevastopol. Part of the division escaped by sea when the fortress fell, but much of it was trapped in the city; General Böhme was captured when his tactical headquarters was overrun by the Russians. The 73rd was reformed in the summer of 1944 and reappeared in combat in September, when it helped crush the Polish Home Army in the Warsaw uprising. Later the division was sent to Army Group Center, where it held a bridgehead on the eastern bank of the Vistula until it was struck by the entire Soviet 47th Army. Under this massive attack the veteran division finally collapsed and was largely destroyed; nevertheless, the remnants of the 73rd Infantry were still in action in January 1945 opposing the Russian winter offensive in eastern Germany. The division retreated through Pomerania and fought with Army Group Vistula in the Battle of Berlin. Most of its survivors went into Russian prison camps in May 1945.

NOTES AND SOURCES: Rudolf Bünau was promoted to General of Infantry in May 1944. He commanded the XLVII Panzer Corps in Russia (1943) and the XI Corps on the Eastern Front (1944-45). He was Defense Commander of Vienna in 1945. Bünau was a Württemburger. General Böhme, former Chief of Staff of the German Artistice Commission in France

(1940-43), joined the National Free Germany Committee while a prisoner of war. Carell 1966: 296, 503, 535; Carell 1971: 172, 538-58; Hartmann: 18-19; Kennedy: 74; *Kriegstagebuch des OKW*, Volume III: 731; OB 43: 137-38; OB 44: 192; OB 45: 163-64; Ziemke 1966: 344.

75th INFANTRY DIVISION

COMPOSITION: 172nd Infantry Regiment, 202nd Infantry Regiment, 222nd Infantry Regiment, 175th Artillery Regiment, 175th Reconnaissance Battalion, 175th Anti-Tank Battalion, 175th Engineer Battalion, 175th Signal Battalion

HOME STATION: Neustrelitz, Wkr. II

Originally recruited in the Schwerin area of Prussia, this reserve division was formed upon mobilization in the summer of 1939. It served on the Saar Front (1939-40), in the French campaign (1940), and on the Eastern Front (1941-45). Initially assigned to Army Group South, it was not particularly distinguished in the early phases of the war in the East. Later it performed quite well in the Kiev withdrawal, the battles on and around the Dnestr, and the retreat across the northern Ukraine. It suffered heavy losses in the Battle of Kiev in the fall of 1943. In December 1944 it was transferred to Army Group Center at the beginning of the Soviet winter offensive of 1944-45. It was engaged in the Krakow area of Poland and ended the war in the pocket east of Prague in May 1945. Commanders of the 75th Infantry Division included Lieutenant Generals Karl Hammer (1941-42), Erich Diestel (1942), and Helmuth Beukemann 1943-45).

NOTES AND SOURCES: Lieutenant General Hammer, an Austrian, later commanded Replacement Division Staff 190 and the 190th Infantry Division (1943-45). Erich Diestel went on to command the 346th Infantry Division. RA: 32; OB 42: 81; OB 43: 138; OB 44: 192; *German Order of Battle*, 1944, Arms and Armour Press, London, 1975: D 64 (hereafter cited as "OB 44b"); OB 45: 164; Ziemke 1966: 279.

76th INFANTRY DIVISION

COMPOSITION: 178th Infantry Regiment, 203rd Infantry Regiment, 230th Infantry Regiment, 176th Artillery Regiment, 176th Reconnaissance Battalion, 176th Anti-Tank Battalion, 176th Engineer Battalion, 176th Signal Battalion

HOME STATION: Berlin, Wkr. III

Formed from Prussian reservists in the summer of 1939, this division.

first saw action in France, where it fought very well. Transferred to Poland in late 1940, it invaded Russia in 1941 and served on the southern sector from the beginning. It took part in the sweep across the Ukraine, the winter battles of 1941-42 in which Army Group South had to retreat from Rostov, the Izyum counteroffensive of May 1942, and the German victories at Voronezh and Kalack, which almost won the war on the southern sector for Germany. The 76th took part in the street fighting in Stalingrad and was encircled there in November 1942. It fought on the heavily attacked western perimeter from then until late January 1943 when it was destroyed. Lieutenant General Karl Rosenburg, the divisional commander, was among those taken prisoner when the city fell.

A second 76th Infantry Division was built in the spring of 1943 to replace the division destroyed at Stalingrad. Its unit numbers remained the same as the original 76th, except that its 230th Regiment was given the honorary title 230th Füsilier Grenadier Regiment, and its 176th Reconnaissance Battalion was replaced by the 76th Füsilier Battalion. The new division was initially based in Brittany, France, before crossing into Italy in August 1943. That autumn it was transferred to the southern sector of the Eastern Front, where it fought on the Dnieper bend, and suffered heavy losses in the Dnieper withdrawal in March 1944. Continuing in action on the Eastern Front, the 76th retreated across the Ukraine and fought in the Hungarian campaign, where it was virtually destroyed in the Battle of Oradea (October 8-12, 1944) when it and the 23rd Panzer Division defended the city for five days against the Soviet 6th Guards Tank Army. The remnants of the division were sent to Czechoslovakia, where they were surrounded with the 1st Panzer Army east of Prague at the end of April 1945. They surrendered to the Russians after Hitler committed suicide on April 30, 1945. Divisional commanders of the 76th Infantry included Lieutenant Generals Maximilian de Angelis (1941-42), Rosenburg (1942-43), Erich Abraham (1943-44), and Major General Kalkowski (1945).

NOTES AND SOURCES: General de Angelis later commanded XLIV Corps (1942-44), 6th Army (summer of 1944), and the 2nd Panzer Army (1945). He was promoted to General of Artillery in 1942. Lieutenant General Abraham was commanding the LXIII Corps in 1945. Garland and Smyth: 282-83; *Kriegstagebuch des OKW*, Volume I: 1146; Manstein: 553; von Mellenthin 1956: 225; Seaton: 494; RA: 46; OB 42: 81; OB 43: 138; OB 44: 193; OB 45: 164-65.

77th INFANTRY DIVISION

COMPOSITION: 1049th Grenadier Regiment, 1050th Grenadier Regiment, 177th Artillery Regiment, 77th Füsilier Battalion, 177th Anti-Tank Battalion, 177th Engineer Battalion, 77th Signal Battalion

HOME STATION: Wehrkreis V

Organized in the Deba Maneuver Area in Poland in the winter of 1943-44, the 77th Infantry Division included troops from previously established reinforced infantry regiments and veterans of the defunct 364th Infantry Division. Most of its men were from Württemberg. It traveled to Normandy in January and February 1944 and was on the French coast between the Cotentin and Brittany peninsulas on D-Day. Quickly engaged on the exposed left flank of the German front, it faced the bulk of two American corps that soon cut the German forces in the Cotentin in half. Isolated in the northern sector of the peninsula, the division was ordered to retire in the direction of Cherbourg. Realizing that this order was tantamount to sacrificing the unit, Major General Stegmann led his division in a breakout against Hitler's direct orders. Approximately half of the men of the 77th Infantry escaped; Stegmann, however, was killed by an American fighter-bomber, which riddled his body with 20mm shells as it strafed the column in which he was marching. His death in action probably saved him from later execution by the Nazis. Reserve Colonel Rudolf Bacherer, the senior regimental commander, assumed command of the 77th Infantry Division and completed the escape. The division had no chance to rest and recover, however, since Hitler refused to believe the major invasion in the West had come and refused to reinforce significantly Field Marshal Rommel's Army Group B with infantry units. The burned-out division therefore remained on the front lines and by late July had repulsed a number of heavy American attacks but had taken severe casualties in the process. SS General Hausser, the commander of the 7th Army, listed the division as practically destroyed; still it continued to resist until September 1944, when it was surrounded and destroyed at Dinard. Colonel Bacherer surrendered the four thousand survivors of his division at the end of this battle.

SOURCES: Blumenson 1960: 401-04, 442; Carell 1973: 186-89; Chant, Volume 12: 1668, 1671; Harrison: Map VI; RA: 86; OB 45: 165.

78th INFANTRY (later ASSAULT) DIVISION

COMPOSITION (1941): 195th Infantry Regiment, 215th Infantry Regiment, 238th Infantry Regiment, 178th Artillery Regiment, 178th Reconnaissance Battalion, 178th Anti-Tank Battalion, 178th Engineer Battalion, 178th Signal Battalion

HOME STATION: Tübingen, Wkr. V

A Württemberg division formed on mobilization from reservists, the 78th first saw action in France in 1940 and in 1941 was on the Eastern Front, where it served with Army Group Center in the initial campaign. The division distinguished itself in the battles of Bialowieza and the Yelnya bend and also fought in the Battle of Moscow and against the Soviet winter offensive of 1941-42. During that period it dropped the 238th Infantry Regiment from its table of organization and received the 14th Infantry Regiment from the 5th Infantry Division. The 78th remained on the central sector of the Russian Front and acquired such an excellent combat record that it was given the honorary title "Sturm" (Storm or Assault) division in 1942. In 1943 it took part in the Battle of Kursk and in the successful defense of Smolensk, before being crushed near Minsk in the massive Soviet summer offensive of 1944. The division's commander, Lieutenant General Hans Traut, and most of his men were captured. Reformed from experienced troops at Konstanz in September 1944, the 78th Assault Division returned to action in southern Poland in autumn and again suffered heavy casualties. The division was again largely destroyed in January 1945, when it attempted to block the Russian drive into Silesia. The remnants of this veteran division remained in action despite its losses and finally surrendered in Czechoslovakia with the rest of Army Group Center in May 1945. Commanders of the 78th Sturm Division included Lieutenant Generals Curt Gallenkamp (1940-41), Paul Völckers (1942-43), Siegfried Rasp (1944), Traut (1944), and Major General Walter Nagel (1945).

NOTES AND SOURCES: General of Artillery as of April 1, 1942, Curt Gallenkamp led XXXI Corps (1942) and LXXX Corps (1943-August 1944). Paul Völckers was promoted to General of Infantry on September 1, 1943, and commanded XXVII Corps on the Eastern Front from 1943 until he was captured by the Russians in July 1944. Both he and Traut joined the National Free Germany Committee. Siegfried Rasp was rapidly promoted. His date of rank as a Major General was November 1, 1943, and he was made a General of Infantry only about 13 months later. He commanded the 335th Infantry Division (late 1943), the 78th Sturm (1944), and was acting commander of the 19th Army on the Western Front in 1945. Walter Nagel commanded an emergency battle group under the XXX Corps on the

Eastern Front in 1943. He was Chief of Staff of the Ligurian Army in northern Italy (1944-45) before assuming command of the 78th Sturm. Carell 1966: 330, 350; Carell 1971: 26, 30, 588-97; Chant, Volume 16: 2231-32; Hartmann: 19; RA: 86; OB 42: 82; OB 43: 138; OB 45: 165-66.

79th INFANTRY (later VOLKSGRENADIER) DIVISION

COMPOSITION: 208th Infantry Regiment, 212th Infantry Regiment, 226th Infantry Regiment, 179th Artillery Regiment, 179th Reconnaissance Battalion, 179th Anti-Tank Battalion, 179th Engineer Battalion, 179th Signal Battalion

HOME STATION: Koblenz, Wkr. XII

This Rhinelander reserve division was assembled upon mobilization in the summer of 1939 and first saw action in the Saar Front against the French in 1939-40. Lightly engaged in the annihilation of the French Army in May and June 1940, it was with Army Group South in Russia in 1941 and fought its way through the Ukraine and across the Dnieper. It took part in the Battle of Kiev, where several Soviet armies were encircled and destroyed, and later opposed the Russian winter offensive of 1941-42. In 1942 the 79th Infantry fought in the Battle of Kharkov, in the encirclement of two hundred thousand Russians at Izyum, in the Battle of Voronezh, and in the encirclement at Kalack, where another Russian army was destroyed. The division was itself encircled at Stalingrad in November, 1942 and destroyed in January 1943.

A second 79th Infantry Division was created in the spring of 1943 and was quickly sent to the southern sector of the Russian Front, which had undergone crisis after crisis since November 1942. The division was initially engaged in the Kuban bridgehead in the summer of 1943 before being evacuated via the Crimea to the lower Dnieper, where it was involved in heavy fighting. At first the combat ability of the 79th was considered low, but its rating improved with experience. It took part in the retreats through the Ukraine and into Rumania in 1943 and 1944. In late August 1944 Rumania defected from the Axis, leading the 6th Army and much of Army Group South Ukraine—including the 79th Infantry—cut off. The division tried to cut its way through Russian lines with Mieth's IV Corps but was destroyed by the Red Army near the village of Chitcani on the Berlad River. General Mieth died in this battle. Only one soldier from the division made good his escape, reaching German lines in Hungary twelve days after the division was destroyed.

A third 79th Infantry Division was formed as a Volksgrenadier unit in the Thorn area of Wehrkries XX (Poland) in the fall of 1944. Most of its new recruits were transferred from the partially formed 586th Volksgrenadier Division. Transferred to the Western Front in December 1944, it was about half its authorized strength in the Battle of the Bulge, where it formed part of the LXXXV Corps of the 7th Army. In this campaign the 79th had very little artillery, but its infantrymen proved to be formidable opponents, and were highly praised by U.S. Army Intelligence. By February 1945 the division was with the LIII Corps (7th Army) in western Germany and fought in the battles of the Vianden Bulge and Bitburg. The remnants of the 276th Volksgrenadier Division were attached to the 79th near the end of the war, and the 79th VG itself was dissolved in the spring of 1945. Its survivors were absorbed by other units of the 7th Army. Commanders of the 79th Infantry/Volksgrenadier Division included Lieutenant Generals Karl Strecker (1940-early 1942), Richard von Schwerin (1942), Alexander Edler von Daniels (1942), Scherbening (1943), Friedrich Weinknecht (1943-44), and Colonel Kurt Hummel (1945).

NOTES AND SOURCES: General of Infantry Strecker later commanded XVII and XI Corps (1942). General Daniels was captured at Stalingrad. Scherbening commanded Special Administrative Division Staff 406 from 1940-42 and again from 1944 until 1945. Weinknecht was captured in Rumania in August 1944, when the second 79th Infantry Division was annihilated. Colonel Hummel, a veteran regimental commander, briefly commanded the 353rd Infantry Division on the Western Front in early 1945. Cole 1965: 535-36; *Kriegstagebuch des OKW*, Volume IV: 1901; MacDonald 1973: Map V; "Frontnachweiser," 15 December 1944; von Mellenthin 1956: 225; Seaton: 478-82; RA: 188; OB 43: 139; OB 44: 194; OB 44b: D66; OB 45: 166. Also see W. Rehm, *Jassy*, Vowinckel, Nechargemund, 1959, for a detailed description of the attempted escape of the 79th Infantry Division in the Rumanian campaign.

81st INFANTRY DIVISION

COMPOSITION: 161st Infantry Regiment, 174th Infantry Regiment, 189th Infantry Regiment, 181st Artillery Regiment, 181st Reconnaissance Battalion, 181st Anti-Tank Battalion, 181st Engineer Battalion, 181st Signal Battalion

HOME STATION: Wehrkreis VIII

Formed in Silesia in the general mobilization of 1939, the 81st Infantry first saw combat in France in 1940, when it was lightly engaged. Remaining in France on garrison duty for over a year, the division was hurriedly sent to Russia in December 1941 after the Soviet winter offensive had begun. Thrown into action on the exposed northern wing of Army Group Center as soon as it detrained, the 81st was involved in heavy defensive fighting from the outset. In January 1942 it was outflanked and encircled at Tripalevo but managed to hold out against repeated Russian attacks and was eventually rescued. The Silesian unit fought in the battles around Demyansk in November 1942 through February 1943, and, in the last two months of 1942, knocked out an amazing total of 170 Soviet tanks. Later, the 81st Infantry was rushed to Army Group North in February 1944, just after the Russians broke the Siege of Leningrad. After distinguishing itself in the retreat through the Baltic States, it was trapped in the Courland Pocket, where it remained until the end of the war. Its divisional commanders included Lieutenant General von Loeper (1941-43), Major General Schopper (1943-44), Colonel Franz Eccard von Bentivegni (late 1944-45), and Lieutenant General Christian Usinger (1945).

NOTES AND SOURCES: Lieutenant General von Loeper led the 6th Panzer Division in Poland 1939), and later commanded Panzer Replacement Division Staff 178. Colonel von Bentivegni was the head of the Counterintelligence Branch at OKH in 1944 before being sent to the Russian Front. Carell 1966: 384-85; Carell 1971: 288-89; Hartmann: 19-20; RA: 130; OB 42: 82; OB 43: 139; OB 45: 166-67.

82nd INFANTRY DIVISION

COMPOSITION: 158th Infantry Regiment, 166th Infantry Regiment, 168th Infantry Regiment, 182nd Artillery Regiment, 182nd Reconnaissance Company, 182nd Anti-Tank Battalion, 182nd Engineer Battalion, 182nd Signal Battalion

HOME STATION: Frankfurt-on-the-Main, Wkr. IX

Mobilized in the fall of 1939, this reserve division was stationed in France in 1940, was sent home on furlough during the Christmas season of 1940, and was on garrison duty in the Netherlands from early 1941 until the spring of 1942. Transferred to Army Group South in May 1942, it remained on the Russian Front for the next two years. It fought at Kursk and in the actions around Kiev before being encircled at Cherkassy in February 1944. Breaking out with heavy losses, it was in no condition to face the Soviet summer offensive of 1944, in which it was virtually destroyed by the end of July. The remnants of the 82nd Infantry were kept in the line in the Courland Pocket battles of 1944 and were disbanded in the winter of 1944-45. The survivors of the 82nd Infantry Division were distributed to other divisions in Army Group North (later Courland), where they were when the war ended. Commanders of this division included Lieutenant Generals Joseph Lehmann (1940-41), Alfred Baentsch (1942-43), and Hans-Walter Heyne (1943-44).

NOTES AND SOURCES: General Baentsch was killed in the Battle of Voronezh in 1943. General Heyne was captured by the Russians in July 1944, along with most of the division. *Kriegstagebuch des OKW*, Volume I: 1123, 1127; Volume III: 1131; RA: 144; OB 43: 139; OB 45: 167. Also see *Kriegstagebuch des OKW*, Volume III: 1877, 1888.

83rd INFANTRY DIVISION

COMPOSITION: 251st Infantry Regiment, 257th Infantry Regiment, 277th Infantry Regiment, 183rd Artillery Regiment, 183rd Reconnaissance Battalion, 183rd Anti-Tank Battalion, 183rd Engineer Battalion, 183rd Signal Battalion

HOME STATION: Hamburg, Wkr. X

The 83rd Infantry was formed in the mobilization of mid-1939 and consisted of reservists from northern Germany. It fought in Poland and France and spent Christmas of 1940 at home on furlough. It remained in France on occupation duty throughout 1941 but was hurriedly transferred to the central sector of the Russian Front at the end of the year. Here it was split into several emergency combat groups and was not fully reunited under its own divisional headquarters for six months. It fought in the defensive battles of Army Group Center in 1942 and most of 1943 and was transferred to Army Group North in autumn 1943, where it remained for the rest of the war. It took part in the Leningrad withdrawal, the Narva defensive battles, the retreat through the Baltic States, and the six battles of the Courland Pocket, in which all Soviet attempts to crush Army Group North (later Courland) were repulsed. The veteran infantry division surrendered to the Russians in May 1945. Commanders of the 83rd included Lieutenant Generals Kurt von der Chevallerie (1940) and Theodor Scherer (1942-44).

NOTES AND SOURCES: Von der Chevallerie became a General of Infantry in May 1942. He later commanded LIX Corps (1942-43) and 1st Army (May-October 1944). Scherer, a Bavarian, led a battle group at Cholm in early 1942, before assuming command of the 83rd. Both he and von der Chevallerie held the Knight's Cross with Oak Leaves. Carell 1966: 384-85; *Kriegstagebuch des OKW*, Volume II: 1362, 1369, 1375; Volume III: 6, 259, 1158; RA: 160; OB 43: 140; OB 44: 195; OB 45: 167.

84th INFANTRY DIVISION

COMPOSITION: 1051st Grenadier Regiment, 1052nd Grenadier Regiment, 1062nd Grenadier Regiment, 184th Artillery Regiment, 84th Füsilier Battalion, 184th Anti-Tank Battalion, 184th Engineer Battalion, 184th Signal Battalion

HOME STATION: Wehrkreis VI

This division was formed in Poland in February 1944, primarily from recently activated reinforced infantry regiments and the remnants of the 332nd and 355th Infantry Divisions. Initially the division had only two grenadier regiments—the 1051st and 1052nd—and was commanded by Lieutenant General Erwin Menny. By May its training was complete, and it was transported to the Rouen area of France to await the Allied invasion. Sent to Normandy in early August, it fought in the Battles of Mortain and Vire before being encircled at Falaise along with the bulk of the 5th Panzer and 7th armies. In the subsequent break-out attempt only about one infantry regiment escaped; the divisional commander was among those captured. The 84th was sent to the Somme River area in the rear of the 7th Army to reform and was reinforced with miscellaneous local defense and security units, as well as the 1062nd Grenadier Regiment. Pronounced fit for combat in September, it was attached to the II Parachute Corps, 1st Parachute Army, and fought against the U.S. 82nd Airborne Division in the Nijmegen area during Operation Market-Garden, the Allies' disastrous first attempt to breach the Rhine defenses. The 84th Infantry suffered serious casualties in the fighting and was at only battle group strength by November 1944. It remained on the front line in the northern sector of the Western Front and was fighting in the Kleve area of the Netherlands in January 1945. In late March the division was finally smashed by a series of heavy British air and ground attacks and was overrun. Many of the division's senior officers were captured along with most of the LXXXVI Corps' staff. The 84th never again appeared as an organized combat force and was apparently disbanded in the last days of the war. Its commanders included Lieutenant General Menny (1944), Colonel Fiebig (1944-45), and Colonel Siegfried Kossack (1945).

NOTES AND SOURCES: General Menny previously commanded the 18th Panzer Division in Russia (1942-43). Colonel Kossack, commander of the 1051st Grenadier Regiment and senior regimental commander in the 84th Infantry Division, replaced Colonel Fiebig as divisional commander in 1945, for reasons that are not known. Blumenson 1960: 21, 324, 552, 582; *Kriegstagebuch des OKW*, Volume III: 1890, 1900; MacDonald 1963: Map V; MacDonald 1973: 313; RA: 100; OB 45: 168.

85th INFANTRY DIVISION

COMPOSITION: 1053rd Grenadier Regiment, 1054th Grenadier Regiment, 185th Artillery Regiment, 85th Füsilier Battalion, 185th Anti-Tank Battalion, 185th Engineer Battalion, 185th Signal Battalion

HOME STATION: Wehrkreis XII

Created in February 1944 from the remnants of several disbanded units and elements of recently organized infantry regiments, the 85th Infantry Division was camped in the rear area of 15th Army in northern France on D-Day. Sent to Normandy in early August, it suffered heavy losses in the Battle of the Falaise Pocket and subsequent breakout and, by August 17, had been reduced to a total strength of one and a half infantry battalions, two pieces of field artillery, and a few miscellaneous support troops. Led by Lieutenant General Kurt Chill, the 85th took part in the withdrawal from France while simultaneously receiving reinforcements from miscellaneous Army units and the remnants of two other infantry divisions. In September it fought against Allied paratroopers in Operation Market-Garden. In October and November 1944 the division (still only at battle group strength) took part in the Battle of the Scheldt with the 15th Army in Holland. Later (still under Chill) it fought in the defensive battles near Aachen and north of Schmidt. It remained on the northern sector of the Western Front for the rest of the war.

NOTES AND SOURCES: General Chill commanded the 122nd Infantry Division in Russia (1942-43) until he was seriously wounded. Blumenson 1960: 531, 582; Chant, Volume 14: 1855; MacDonald 1963: 124, 216-17; 599; RA: 41; OB 45: 168; also see Speidel: 41.

86th INFANTRY DIVISION

COMPOSITION: 167th Infantry Regiment, 184th Infantry Regiment, 216th Infantry Regiment, 186th Artillery Regiment, 186th Reconnaissance Battalion, 186th Anti-Tank Battalion, 186th Engineer Battalion, 186th Signal Battalion

HOME STATION: Wehrkreis VI

Formed in the general mobilization of 1939, this Westphalian division first saw action in 1939 on the Saar Front, where it was lightly engaged. Later it fought in France before being attached to Army Group Center for the invasion of Russia. It fought in the Battle of Moscow under Lieutenant

General Witthöft and suffered heavy casualties. It remained on the central sector of the Eastern Front, where it took part in the defensive battles of 1942, in the Rzhev withdrawal, and in the Battle of Kursk, where it distinguished itself. The 86th Infantry was finally crushed in the Russian summer offensive of 1944. Although it was not completely wiped out, as were several other divisions in the 4th and 9th armies, the High Command decided not to rebuild the 86th, and it was dissolved in October. The 167th Infantry Regiment was converted into the 2nd Ski Jäger Regiment, and the remnants of the 186th Artillery Regiment were absorbed by the 251st Artillery Regiment of the 251st Infantry Division. Divisional commanders of the 86th Infantry included Witthöft (1940-42) and Lieutenant General Helmuth Weidling (1942-43).

NOTES AND SOURCES: Witthöft, later a General of Infantry, commanded XXVII Corps in Russia (January-September 1942) and from late 1943 until 1945 was in charge of the defensive sector of the Alps. Weidling, who was made a General of Artillery in 1944, commanded XLI Corps (October 1943-February 1944) before being named Inspector General of Flak Troops (March-August 1944). He is best known as commander of LVI Panzer Corps and the City of Berlin, which he surrendered to the Russians in May 1945, rather than escaping to safety, which he could have done. Weidling hoped that his formal capitulation would stop Russian atrocities against the civilian population of Berlin, but it did not. He died in a Soviet prison camp in the 1950s. Carell 1966: 196, 357; Carell 1971: 26, 309; OB 43: 140; OB 45: 169. Also see Ryan 1966.

87th INFANTRY DIVISION

COMPOSITION: 173rd Infantry Regiment, 185th Infantry Regiment, 187th Infantry Regiment, 187th Artillery Regiment, 187th Reconnaissance Battalion, 187th Anti-Tank Battalion, 187th Engineer Battalion, 187th Signal Battalion

HOME STATION: Wehrkreis IV

This division, which consisted mainly of Thuringian and Saxon reservists, was mobilized in the summer of 1939 and first saw combat in France as part of the XI Infantry Corps of the 6th Army. It fought very well and was given the honor of being the first German unit to enter Paris in June 1940. The next year it crossed into Russia with Army Group Center, where it fought at the Yelnya bend and against the Soviet winter offensive of 1941-42. Remaining on the central sector, it took part in the Rzhev withdrawal (March 1943), the Kursk offensive (July 1943), and the Battle of

Nevel (fall 1943). In the spring of 1944 it was transferred to Army Group North and was involved in the retreat through the Baltic States, the defense of the Narva, and the battles of the Courland Pocket. It surrendered to the Soviets in western Latvia in May 1945. Leaders of the 87th Infantry included Lieutenant General Bogislav von Studnitz (1942), Lieutenant General Theodor Scherer (briefly in 1942), Major General Gerhard Richter (1942-43), Lieutenant General Walter Hartmann (1943-44), and Major General Baron Maurtiz von Strachwitz (1945).

NOTES AND SOURCES: Theodor Scherer previously commanded the 281st Security Division (1941-42) and the 34th Infantry Division (1942). He later led the 83rd Infantry Division on the Eastern Front (1942-44). Hartmann, a Saxon, had commanded Special Administrative Division Staff 407 (1942) and was later acting commander of the XIV Panzer Corps in Italy in 1944. He went on to command I Mountain Corps (1944), VIII Corps on the Eastern Front (1944-45), and XXIV Panzer Corps in Czechoslovakia (1945). Baron von Strachwitz, a cavalry officer, had been Ia of VIII Corps in France (1940). Benoist-Mechin: 241; Carell 1966: 92, 330, 350; Carell 1971: 309; Horne: 563; RA: 72; OB 42: 83; OB 43: 140; OB 45: 169.

88th INFANTRY DIVISION

COMPOSITION: 245th Infantry Regiment, 246th Infantry Regiment, 248th Infantry Regiment, 188th Artillery Regiment, 188th Reconnaissance Battalion, 188th Anti-Tank Battalion, 188th Engineer Battalion, 188th Signal Battalion

HOME STATION: Wehrkreis VII

Made up mainly of Bavarian reservists, this division played a minor role in the Western campaign of 1940. After spending almost two years in France on occupation duties, the 88th was sent to the Russian Front in early 1942, where it fought on the southern sector in the advances and retreats of 1942-43. The division suffered heavy losses in the withdrawal from Kiev in the fall of 1943 and was surrounded with General Wilhelm Stemmerman's XI Corps at Cherkassy in February 1944. Along with the 57th Infantry Division, the 88th formed the rearguard in the breakout under Stemmerman's personal command; however, when he was killed by an anti-tank shell all order vanished. Perhaps half of the 88th Infantry escaped in the rout. The survivors were reorganized in southern Poland and were back in action by June. Again badly damaged by the Russian summer offensive of 1944, the Bavarian division rallied and was cited for its tough defense of the Vistula bend. It continued to serve on the Eastern

Front until early 1945 when it was taken out of the line and apparently disbanded in the last weeks of the war. Commanders of this division included Lieutenant Generals Friedrich Gollwitzer (1940-43), Heinrich Roth (1943), Count Georg von Rittberg (1943-44), and Christian Philipp (1945).

NOTES AND SOURCES: Gollwitzer became a General of Infantry and commander of the LIII Corps in late 1943. He was captured by the Russians in June 1944 and joined the National Free Germany Committee. Count von Rittberg was taken prisoner on the Eastern Front in January 1945. His replacement, General Philipp, was formerly commander of the 6th Mountain Division (1942-43). RA: 116; OB 42: 83; OB 43: 141; OB 45: 169-70; Ziemke 1966: 230-38.

89th INFANTRY DIVISION

COMPOSITION: 1055th Grenadier Regiment, 1056th Grenadier Regiment, 189th Artillery Regiment, 89th Füsilier Battalion, 189th Anti-Tank Battalion, 189th Engineer Battalion, 189th Signal Battalion

HOME STATION: Hamburg, Wkr. X

Known as the "Horseshoe Division" from its unit symbol, this division was created in 1944 from personnel in the reinforced infantry regiments of the Replacement Army. It trained in Norway from March to June 1944 and returned to the European mainland about the time of the Normandy invasion. Initially posted with the 15th Army in the Rouen-La Havre area, it was ordered to Normandy in late June and immediately suffered heavy losses. Near Falaise on August 8 it collapsed under the pressure of heavy British air and ground attacks and had to be taken out of the line. Reformed in the rear area of the 7th Army, it absorbed several miscellaneous units and was back in action near Aachen by September. The 89th suffered heavy casualties in these early battles of the Siegfried Line and by mid-September was a complete wreck. One of its grenadier regiments was destroyed, and the other had only 350 men, despite the fact that Colonel Roesler, the divisional commander, had already incorporated his artillerymen, engineers, and service troops into the infantry. Field Marshals von Rundstedt and Model both requested that the division be dissolved, but Hitler refused to allow it. Instead, in early November, the 89th Infantry Division was pulled out of the line. Colonel Roesler was replaced by Major General (later Lieutenant General) Walter Bruns, and the unit was rebuilt by adding Luftwaffe and Landesschützen (older) personnel. Despite these additions, the strength of the 89th during the Ardennes offensive was equal to about one battalion of infantry. Again fighting near Aachen in January 1945, the 89th Infantry faced the Allied counteroffensive that followed the Battle of the Bulge. It retreated into southern Germany in March 1945, and the few remnants of the division that survived continued to serve on the Western Front until the end of the war.

NOTES AND SOURCES: Bruns was formerly Military Attaché to Madrid (1939-41) and Commandant of Ghent (1943-44). Blumenson 1960: 324, 582; Chant, Volume 14: 1863; Cole 1965: 35; MacDonald 1963: 83, 359, 599; MacDonald 1973: Map III; Speidel: 41; RA: 160; OB 45: 170.

91st AIR LANDING DIVISION

COMPOSITION: 1057th Grenadier Regiment, 1058th Grenadier Regiment, 91st Füsilier Company, 191st Anti-Tank Battalion, 191st Engineer Battalion, 191st Signal Battalion

HOME STATION: Wehrkreis XII

Although equipped as an air landing division, the 91st served as an infantry unit throughout its short existence. Its first commander was Major General Wilhelm Falley. Formed in the Baumholder and Bitsch Maneuver Areas from replacement center personnel and men from newly created reinforced infantry regiments, the 91st was assigned the task of guarding the western coast of the Cotentin peninsula against Eisenhower's invasion. Although the Allies landed to the east, the 91st Air Landing Division was engaged against elements of the U.S. 82nd and 101st Airborne Divisions from the first day. Wilhelm Falley became involved in a fire-fight with American paratroopers near his headquarters in the pre-dawn hours of June 6 and was hit by a burst of machinegun fire; he was the first German general killed on the reopened Western Front. The 91st Division suffered tremendous casualties in the opening days of the invasion and was down to battle-group strength by the second week. Finally it became so small that it was attached to the 77th Infantry Division and later to the 243rd Infantry Division for operational purposes. The bulk of the survivors of the 91st Air Landing were killed or captured with Corps von Schlieben in the Battle of Cherbourg, but remnants of the division escaped to the south when the Americans cut LXXXIV Corps and the Cotentin in half. These units were reformed under the command of Colonel Eugen König in early July. Although the 7th Army commander, SS General Hausser, listed the division as practically destroyed in late July, the High Command chose to rebuild rather than disband it. The 91st was reinforced with two replacement battalions and sent back to the front. In early August 1944 it made a gallant stand at Rennes, denying the city to Patton's U.S. 3rd

Army for three days. Although König managed to escape with most of his little command as the city fell, Rennes was the last major battle of the division. After a brief stint on the Siegfried Line, in which it engaged in some minor skirmishing, the division was absorbed by the 344th Volksgrenadier Division.

NOTES AND SOURCES: Major General Bernhard Klosterkemper commanded the combined 91st and 243rd Divisions in Normandy in July 1944. Together they probably amounted to less than regimental strength. König, who had commanded an infantry regiment of the 251st Infantry Division on the Eastern Front (1943), was promoted to Major General in late 1944 and given command of the 272nd Volksgrenadier Division on the Western Front (1945). Blumenson 1960: 58, 358, 442; Carell 1973: 48-49; Chant, Volume 14: 1850; Harrison: Map VI; MacDonald 1963: 460; RA: 188; OB 45: 170-71.

92nd INFANTRY DIVISION

COMPOSITION: 1059th Grenadier Regiment, 1060th Grenadier Regiment, 192nd Artillery Regiment, 92nd Füsilier Battalion, 192nd Anti-Tank Battalion, 192nd Engineer Battalion, 192nd Signal Battalion

HOME STATION: Wehrkreis XVII

Activated in northern Italy in late January 1944, the 92nd was a composite of several replacement battalions. Its personnel were Austrians, Germans, and Volksdeutsche (ethnic Germans from occupied countries). Initially stationed in the Grosseto-Orbetello area as a garrison and training unit, it was sent into action in May. Colonel General Mackensen, the 14th Army commander, was far from satisfied with its performance and reported it as unfit for intensive combat. Since the Italian Front in mid-1944 was no place for untrustworthy divisions, the 92nd was dissolved shortly after the fall of Rome. Most of its personnel were incorporated into the 362nd Infantry Division. Commanders of the 92nd were Colonel Baron de La Salle von Louisenthal and Lieutenant General Werner Goeritz.

NOTES AND SOURCES: Baron von Louisenthal, former commander of the 1026th Grenadier Regiment, formed the division in early 1944 and turned it over to Goeritz, who had led the 291st Infantry Division in Russia (1942-43). Louisenthal then became senior regimental commander and took over the 1059th Grenadier Regiment. He was reportedly promoted to Major General in early 1945, but he never again exercised divisional command. Blumenson 1969: 361; Fisher: 232, 255; RA: 220; OB 45: 171.

93rd INFANTRY DIVISION

COMPOSITION (1940): 270th Infantry Regiment, 271st Infantry Regiment, 272nd Infantry Regiment, 193rd Artillery Regiment, 193rd Reconnaissance Battalion, 188th Anti-Tank Battalion, 188th Engineer Battalion, 188th Signal Battalion

HOME STATION: Berlin, Wkr. III

Consisting of Prussian reservists, this division was activated in September 1939 after the German Army crossed into Poland, setting off World War II. Sent to the Saar Front, it broke through the Maginot Line fortifications at Saarbrucken in the summer of 1940. After a brief period of garrison duty on the French coast, it was sent to Poland and invaded Russia as part of Army Group North in June 1941. The 93rd was involved in heavy fighting in the drive on Leningrad and by October was down to one-third of its authorized strength. It nevertheless remained on the front line, opposing the Soviet winter offensive of 1941-42. In autumn 1942, the 271st Infantry Regiment, which was made up primarily of S.A. (Brownshirt) volunteers, was given the honorary title "Infanterieregiment Feldhernnhalle" in recognition of its outstanding conduct in action. In the spring of 1943 the 93rd Infantry Division was taken out of the line and sent to Poland to rest and refit. In 1943, the 271st Infantry Regiment was taken from the division's table of organization and sent to France, where it formed the nucleus of the 60th Panzer Grenadier Division, which replaced a unit destroyed at Stalingrad. Meanwhile, the 93rd Infantry went back to Army Group North, which was trying desperately to maintain the Siege of Leningrad. Early in 1944 the 273rd Grenadier Regiment was added to the division, making it a three-regiment unit again. As such it fought in the Leningrad withdrawal, the retreat through the Baltic States, and in the battles of the Courland Pocket, from which it was evacuated in late 1944 or early 1945. The 93rd Infantry was shipped to Samland in East Prussia, where it was cut off and destroyed by the Soviets in March 1945. Commanders of the division included Lieutenant General Otto Tiemann (1941-43), Colonel Horst von Mellenthin (late 1943), and Major General Karl Löwrick (1944-45).

NOTES AND SOURCES: Otto Tiemann was promoted to General of Engineers in May 1944. He was commanding II Corps on the Eastern Front in 1945. Hartmann: 20; von Mellenthin 1977: 138; Salisbury: 351; OB 42: 83; OB 43: 141; OB 45: 171-72.

94th INFANTRY DIVISION

COMPOSITION: 267th Infantry Regiment, 274th Infantry Regiment, 276th Infantry Regiment, 194th Artillery Regiment, 194th Reconnaissance Battalion, 194th Anti-Tank Battalion, 194th Engineer Battalion, 194th Signal Battalion

HOME STATION: Wehrkreis IV

Composed of reservists from Saxony and the Sudetenland, this division was mobilized in September 1939, shortly after the beginning of the war. The next year it took part in the French campaign, where it was involved in the 6th Army's river crossing operation on the Somme. It took part in the invasion of Russia in 1941, including the sweep across the Ukraine, the Battle of Kiev, and the subsequent Soviet counteroffensive of the winter of 1941-42. In May 1942 it was involved in the Kharkov-Izyum fighting, in the drive across the Don, and in the Battle of Kalack, which opened the route to the Volga. In November 1942 the 94th Infantry Division was surrounded at Stalingrad, where it initially held a sector in the northeastern corner of the pocket; the divisional headquarters, however, was evacuated and attached to the XLVIII Panzer Corps of the hastily formed Army Detachment Hollidt of Army Group Don, where it controlled miscellaneous units under Lieutenant General Georg Pfeiffer (1942-43). Meanwhile, the combat troops of the division were assigned to the 24th Panzer and 16th Panzer Divisions and were captured when Stalingrad fell in early February 1943.

A second 94th Infantry Division was formed in the Lorient area of France in April 1943, under its old staff. Although incompletely trained and not ready for action, it was sent to Italy after the collapse of Mussolini's government left Germany's southern flank exposed. In August 1943 it occupied the Mount Cenis Pass and was on coastal defense duty in the Genoa area later that month. By November 1943 the division was in combat on the Bernhard Line. Although initially listed by the 10th Army's chief of staff as inexperienced and poorly trained, the 94th fought in all the major battles of the Italian campaign. It participated in the Gustav Line battles, suffered heavy casualties in the withdrawal to Rome, and took part in the defense of the Po River Valley. In the summer of 1944 it was briefly taken out of the line, withdrawn to the Udine area, and gave up most of its personnel to the 305th Infantry Division; simultaneously it received massive replacements from the Infantry Division Schlesien. The 94th Infantry returned to the front soon after and was more or less continuously engaged until the end of the war in Italy. By February 1945 the division was down to a strength of fewer than 2,600 combat effectives. Two months later it opposed the U.S. 5th Army's spring offensive and was overrun. When the XIV Panzer Corps fell back, the remnants of the 94th covered its retreat and were cut off on the south side of the Po River. On April 22 Major General Bernard Steinmetz, who had led the 94th Infantry Division for most of the Italian campaign, surrendered the remnants of his division to the Americans.

NOTES AND SOURCES: Steinmetz was Chief of Staff of the VIII Corps in 1940 and commanding officer of the reformed 274th Grenadier Regiment in 1943. Benoist-Mechin: 241; Blumenson 1969: 224; Carell 1966: 612; Fisher, 18, 46, 442, 472-74, 494; Garland and Smyth: 294; *Kriegstagebuch des OKW*, Volume III: 4; Manstein: 553; von Mellenthin 1956: 225; RA: 72; OB 42: 84; OB 43: 141; OB 45: 172.

95th INFANTRY (later VOLKSGRENADIER) DIVISION

COMPOSITION: 278th Infantry Regiment, 279th Infantry Regiment, 280th Infantry Regiment, 195th Artillery Regiment, 195th Reconnaissance Battalion, 195th Anti-Tank Battalion, 195th Engineer Battalion, 195th Signal Battalion

HOME STATION: Wehrkreis IX

The 95th Infantry Division consisted of Westphalians and Thuringian reservists who were reinducted into the army in September 1939, when the war started. It was on the Saar Front in 1939-40, where it "showed initiative and dash" in skirmishes with the French, according to Allied intelligence documents. It was on furlough at Christmas 1940 and was then sent to Poland. It was in more or less continuous action on the southern sector of the Russian Front from July 1941 until late 1942. Most of the guns of its 195th Artillery Regiment were lost when the Soviets cut into the rear of the 2nd German Army in mid-December 1941. What was left of the division continued to oppose the Soviet winter offensive of 1941-42 and was involved in the initial drives on the Volga. Transferred to Army Group Center in late 1942, it took part in the Rzhev withdrawal and later formed part of 4th Army's line west of Smolensk in the summer fighting of 1943. It suffered heavy losses in the Bryansk attack that summer. In July 1944 the 95th was the only division in the 3rd Panzer Army's reserve when the huge Russian summer offensive began. Thrown into action, it was quickly overwhelmed. Its divisional commander, Major General Michaelis, was captured and only remnants of his unit escaped. Nevertheless, the 95th was reformed as a Volksgrenadier division and sent back into action on the central sector in October. It fought at Memel, was evacuated by the German Navy to Samland and ended the war at battle group strength, opposing the Soviet invasion of East Prussia. Commanders of the 95th included Hans-

Heinrich Sixt von Armin (1940-42), Major General Eduard Aldrian (1942), Lieutenant General Edgar Röhricht (1943-44), and Michaelis.

NOTES AND SOURCES: Sixt von Armin later commanded the 113th Infantry Division and was captured at Stalingrad. Aldrian, who commanded the division on a temporary basis, later commanded the 373rd Croatian Infantry Division. Röhricht was formerly Chief of Staff of the 1st Army (1942) and was briefly acting commander of the XII Corps on the Eastern Front (1944). Carell 1971: 309, 597; Seaton: 224; OB 42: 84; OB 43: 142; OB 44b: 69. Also see *Kriegstagebuch des OKW*, Volume I: 1127; Volume IV: 1897.

96th INFANTRY DIVISION

COMPOSITION: 283rd Infantry Regiment, 284th Infantry Regiment, 287th Infantry Regiment, 196th Artillery Regiment, 196th Reconnaissance Battalion, 196th Anti-Tank Battalion, 196th Engineer Battalion, 196th Signal Battalion

HOME STATION: Wehrkreis XI

Stationed in Hanover and raised from recruits from all over north and west Germany, this division first saw combat in France in 1940. Sent East in 1941, it spent the next four years on the Russian Front. It fought at Novgorod, Lake Ilmen, and in the early stages of the Siege of Leningrad in 1941. Remaining on the northern sector through 1943, it took part in the Second Battle of Lake Ladoga, the Battle of the Volkhov, and the Battle of the German Corridor east of Leningrad. Despite its losses, the 96th Infantry remained on the line until January 1944 when it was transferred to the southern sector of the Eastern Front, where it fought in the battles of the northern Ukraine. In the summer of 1944, while part of the LIX Corps, the division was overwhelmed by the Soviet attack that eventually led to the encirclement of the 1st Panzer Army. Although there is no evidence that it was rebuilt, the remnants of the 96th were nevertheless sent back into combat. In late 1944 it was fighting the Russians in Slovakia and in 1945 was still resisting north of Vienna when the war ended. The division's commanders included Lieutenant General Erwin Vierow (1940), Lieutenant General Wolfgang Schede (1941-42), Major General Noeldechen (1942), Lieutenant General Baron Siegmund von Schleinitz (1943), and Lieutenant General Richard Wirtz (1943-44).

NOTES AND SOURCES: Vierow went on to become a General of Infantry (as of early 1941) and commanded LV Corps (1941). He was Military Commander of Northwestern France from 1943 until his capture in September

1944. Schede was commander of the 151st Reserve Division in December 1943. Richard Wirtz, former Chief Engineer of the VII Corps, was in southern France in 1944, although in what capacity is unclear. Carell 1966: 251, 261, 272, 421; Carell 1971: 242, 255, 510; *Kriegstagebuch des OKW*, Volume I: 1145; Volume III: 1158; Volume IV: 1895; Salisbury: 275; RA: 172; OB 42: 84-85; OB 43: 142; OB 45: 173.

97th INFANTRY DIVISION
see 97th Jäger Division

98th INFANTRY (later VOLKSGRENADIER) DIVISION

COMPOSITION (1942): 282nd Infantry Regiment, 289th Infantry Regiment, 290th Infantry Regiment, 198th Artillery Regiment, 198th Reconnaissance Battalion, 198th Anti-Tank Battalion, 198th Engineer Battalion, 198th Signal Battalion

HOME STATION: Wehrkreis XIII

Built with reserve personnel from Bavaria, Franconia, and the Sudetenland, the 98th Infantry was mobilized in September 1939, shortly after the outbreak of the war. After seeing action in France, the division crossed the Russian frontier with Army Group South. It was on the northern wing of von Rundstedt's army group during the Battle of Kiev in August, where it lost 78 officers and 2,300 men in the struggle for the key position of Korosten. Lieutenant General Schroeck led the unit in this battle. After the fall of Kiev the 98th was transferred to the central sector and fought in the battles around Moscow. After its six-hundred mile march through the Ukraine, it fought at Vyazma, after which it pushed on to Maloyaroslavets, only sixty miles from the Russian capital. Its supply lines were virtually cut by the mud; nevertheless the division took the important Chernishay Heights in late October, only to be thrown off again when attacked by T-34 tanks. Elements of the 289th and 290th Infantry Regiments panicked but were soon rallied. By now the 98th's infantry companies were down to twenty men each, commanded by second lieutenants and sergeants. The soldiers had not changed clothes in months and were tormented by lice and mud. On November 2, 45 miles from Moscow, the division's senior regimental commander reported it unfit for combat. Despite its poor condition, the 98th remained on the front line, opposed the Soviet winter offensive of 1941-42, and took part in the defensive battles of Army Group Center in 1942 and 1943. After fighting in the Rzhev withdrawal in March 1943, the 98th was sent back to the southern zone of the Eastern Front and served in the Kuban and Crimean campaigns, where it distinguished itself. Most of this time it was commanded by Lieutenant General Martin Gareis (1942-44), who fell seriously ill in February 1944 and was replaced by Major General (subsequently Lieutenant General) Alfred Reinhardt, who led the division for the rest of the war. Meanwhile, the 98th suffered such heavy losses in the Kuban, in the Kerch Peninsula of the Crimea, and in the retreat to Sevastopol in April and May 1944, that the 282nd Infantry Regiment had to be disbanded. Its other regiments were also shattered. The 290th Grenadier, for example, only had two hundred men left on October 29, 1943—hardly 10 percent of its June 1941 strength.

The remnants of this veteran division were evacuated from Sevastopol by the German Navy shortly before the city fell. Transferred to the Zagreb area of Yugoslavia to rest and refit in the summer of 1943, the 98th received a substantial number of poorly trained replacements from Infantry Division Schlesien and also incorporated the 117th Grenadier Regiment of the recently disbanded 111th Infantry Division into its table of organization. The 98th Infantry Division returned to combat in Italy in September 1944, where it fought at San Savino and in the Battle of the Rimini Line; however, its former combat effectiveness was gone, and the 14th Army staff rated it as unreliable. No significant reinforcements were then available for the Italian Front, however, so the 98th continued in the line. Although still in the combat zone in December, it absorbed the Grenadier Demonstration Brigade, which explains why the 117th Regiment was renamed 117th Lehr Regiment in late 1944. Apparently the raw recruits the division received in late 1943 had gained experience and skill by early 1945, for the 98th Infantry never broke under the strain of almost constant Allied pressure. In January it was fighting northeast of Bologna, and a month later (now designated a Volksgrenadier division) the 98th formed part of the LXXVI Panzer Corps in the Apennines. It fought in the Po River campaign and ended the war on the Italian Front.

NOTES AND SOURCES: General Schroeck was commanding Replacement Division Staff 192 in 1945. Gareis later recovered from his illness and commanded the 264th Infantry Division in the Balkans. Later he wrote the history of the 98th Infantry Division. Alfred Reinhardt was one of Gareis's regimental commanders in 1943. Carell 1966: 123, 151; Carell 1971: 309, 538-56; Fisher: 353, 441; *Kriegstagebuch des OKW*, Volume I: 1148; Volume III: 6; Seaton: 187-88, 429; RA: 204; OB 43: 142-43; OB 44b: D70; OB 45: 173. Also see Martin Gareis, *Kampf und Ende der Fränkish-Sudetendeustschen 98. Infanterie Division*, Gareis, Tegernsee, 1956.

100th INFANTRY DIVISION
see 100th Jäger Division

101st INFANTRY DIVISION
see 101st Jäger Division

102nd INFANTRY DIVISION

COMPOSITION (1941): 232nd Infantry Regiment, 233rd Infantry Regiment, 235th Infantry Regiment, 102nd Artillery Regiment, 102nd Reconnaissance Battalion, 102nd Anti-Tank Battalion, 102nd Engineer Battalion, 102nd Signal Battalion

HOME STATION: Wehrkreis VIII

Formed in the 12th mobilization wave in October 1940, the 102nd Infantry took part in the Russian invasion of June 1941, where it formed part of Army Group Center. In December it suffered heavy losses in the vicinity of Moscow during the Russian winter offensive of 1941-42. The next month the 102nd was encircled south of Lake Volga with the XXIII Corps, but was later rescued by the 9th Army. In February 1942 it was withdrawn to Germany to rest and refit. While there, the 235th Infantry Regiment was dissolved, and the 84th Infantry Regiment of the 8th Infantry Division was assigned to replace it. Returning to the central sector of the Russian Front in April 1942, the division took part in the Rzhev withdrawal and later fought in the Battle of Kursk as part of the XXXIX Panzer Corps. In early 1944 the 102nd apparently absorbed the remnants of the 216th Infantry Division, which had been shattered at Kursk. Meanwhile, the bulk of the 102nd Infantry escaped the disaster that overtook Army Group Center in July 1944 and continued to fight—at battle group strength—on the central sector of the Eastern Front for the rest of the war. It was in the East Prussian Pocket when the Third Reich passed into history. Commanders of the 102nd Infantry Division included Lieutenant General Johann Ansat (1941), Major General Albrecht Baler (1942), Major General Fitzlaff (1942-43), Lieutenant General Otto Hitzfeld (1943), and Lieutenant General Werner von Bercken (late 1943-45).

NOTES AND SOURCES: Baler commanded the 297th Infantry Division in 1944 and was apparently acting commander of the XXI Mountain Corps in Norway at the end of the war. Hitzfeld, who was promoted to General of Infantry in late 1944 or very early 1945, commanded the Infantry School at Döberitz (1944) and the LXVII Corps in 1944 and 1945. Carell 1966: 359,

393-94; Carell 1971: 26, 309; *Kriegstagebuch des OKW*, Volume IV: 1897; OB 43: 143; OB 45: 174.

106th INFANTRY DIVISION

COMPOSITION: 239th Infantry Regiment, 240th Infantry Regiment, 241st Infantry Regiment, 106th Artillery Regiment, 106th Reconnaissance Battalion, 106th Anti-Tank Battalion, 106th Engineer Battalion, 106th Signal Battalion

HOME STATION: Wehrkreis VI

Activated in October 1940, this division went to Russia with Army Group Center in 1941 and suffered heavy casualties in the final thrusts toward Moscow and in the subsequent Soviet counteroffensive that winter. In January 1942 the division's infantry strength was down to five hundred men, and it had hardly any of its original leaders left. Sent to northern France to rest and rebuild that spring, it did not return to the Eastern Front until the spring of 1943. The 106th fought in the Battle of Kharkov in May 1942 as part of the XLVIII Panzer Corps, 4th Panzer Army, and later advanced on the Volga with that army. It took part in the retreat from Stalingrad, the Battle of Kursk (July 1943), and the Dnieper bend campaign (fall 1943), for which it was cited for its distinguished conduct. The 106th Infantry had been reduced to battle group strength by October. In December 1943 the division suffered heavy losses northeast of Kirovograd. Caught up in the retreats on the southern sector in 1944, the 106th was encircled and destroyed at Kishinev in August 1944. A second, much-reduced 106th Infantry Division, which no doubt included some survivors of the original, was assembled at Oberheim, Germany, in early 1945. It was sent to southwestern Germany and ended the war with the XVIII SS Corps of the 19th Army on the Western Front. Lieutenant General Werner Forst (1943-44) commanded the division during much of its combat career.

NOTES AND SOURCES: Forst, former commander of the 293rd Infantry Division (1942), was later Inspector General of Artillery at OKH (June 1944 to 1945). Carell 1966: 177; Carell 1971: 39, 218, *Kriegstagebuch des OKW*, Volume I: 1147; Volume II: 1365; Volume IV: 1904; Seaton: 232; RA: 100; OB 43: 143; OB 45: 174.

110th INFANTRY DIVISION

COMPOSITION: 252nd Infantry Regiment, 254th Infantry Regiment, 255th Infantry Regiment, 120th Artillery Regiment, 110th Reconnaissance Battalion, 110th Anti-Tank Battalion, 110th Engineer Battalion, 110th Signal Battalion

HOME STATION: Oldenburg, Wkr. X

Formed in northern Germany in October 1940, the 110th Infantry was soon sent to the General Gouvernement (formerly central Poland). It was with Army Group Center in the initial attack on the Soviet Union and after a number of desperate battles penetrated to the Volga in December 1941. Pushed back by the Russian winter offensive of 1941-42, it remained on the central sector of the Eastern Front for the rest of its existence. After taking part in the defensive battles of 1942, where it suffered significant losses, it participated in the Rzhev withdrawal of March 1943 and suffered heavy losses at Bryansk in the summer of that year. Remaining in the line, it was destroyed in the Russian summer offensive of 1944. The division's commander, Lieutenant General Eberhard von Kurowski, was taken prisoner when the division was smashed.

NOTES AND SOURCES: A previous divisional commander, Lieutenant General Paul Seyffardt (1942-43), commanded the 348th Infantry Division on the Western Front and was captured at Marbaix in September 1944. Carell 1966: 196, 357; Carell 1971: 309; *Kriegstagebuch des OKW*, Volume I: 1132; RA: 160; OB 43: 143; OB 45: 175.

111th INFANTRY DIVISION

COMPOSITION: 50th Infantry Regiment, 70th Infantry Regiment, 117th Infantry Regiment, 111th Artillery Regiment, 111th Reconnaissance Battalion, 111th Anti-Tank Battalion, 111th Engineer Battalion, 111th Signal Battalion

HOME STATION: Darmstadt, Wkr. XII

This Saxon division was created in October 1940 when the 3rd and 36th Infantry Divisions were converted into two-regiment motorized units and gave up the 50th and 70th Infantry Regiments, respectively. The 117th Infantry Regiment was formed separately and incorporated into the 111th. Under Lieutenant General Stapf the division fought in the early campaigns of Army Group South in 1941, was in the Battle of Mozdok, and took part in the Caucasus campaign and subsequent withdrawal. The 111th Infantry also fought in the Kuban campaign, including the Battle of Novorossiysk, where an ambitious Soviet amphibious landing was checked. Later transferred to the Mius sector, it took heavy losses in the Battle of Taganrog and fought in the battles of the lower Dnieper, where it performed exceptionally well. Sent to the Crimea in early 1944, it was trapped when the Russians overran the peninsula. The 117th Infantry Regiment managed to escape by sea with the 50th Infantry Division, but the rest of the 111th was lost when its transport ships failed to arrive. When Sevastopol fell Major General Erich Gruner tried to surrender the division but was brutally murdered by the Russians, along with many of his men.

NOTES AND SOURCES: Promoted to General of Infantry on October 1, 1942, Otto Stapf became Commanding General of the Military Economics Staff East (1942-44) and Chief of the Armed Forces Economic Office (1944-45). Prior to taking command of the 111th, he had been Chief of the Organization Division of the General Staff (O Qu III) and Army Liaison Officer to the Commander-in-Chief of the Luftwaffe (Göring). Lieutenant General Hermann Recknagel led the division in 1942-43. Carell 1971: 142, 151, 538-39, 559-60; Hartmann: 21; RA: 172; OB 43: 144; OB 44b: D71; OB 45: 175.

112th INFANTRY DIVISION

COMPOSITION: 110th Infantry Regiment, 256th Infantry Regiment, 258th Infantry Regiment, 86th Artillery Regiment, 120th Reconnaissance Battalion, 112th Anti-Tank Battalion, 112th Engineer Battalion, 112th Signal Battalion

HOME STATION: Darmstadt, Wkr. XII

Activated in October 1940, the 112th received the 110th Infantry Regiment from the veteran 33rd Infantry Division, which was being converted into the 15th Panzer Division. The new division took part in the Russian invasion as part of Army Group Center and was involved in the battles around Moscow, where it suffered terribly from the extreme cold. Utterly unequipped for winter, the 112th Infantry reported four hundred cases of frostbite in each regiment as early as November 17. Despite its casualties the 112th Infantry fought on, opposing the 1941-42 Russian winter offensive as well as fighting in the defensive battles on the central sector in 1942 and early 1943. It suffered heavy casualties during the Kursk offensive and was caught up in the retreats after the defeat of Operation "Citadelle." The 112th was eventually surrounded at Cherkassy as part of the XLII Corps. It broke out with the remnants of two other shattered divisions but sustained ruinous casualties. The 112th was sent to Poland to regroup; however, it was in such bad condition that the High Command decided to disband it in the early spring of 1944. Leaders of the 112th Infantry Division included Major General Friedrich Mieth (1941-42) and Lieutenant General Theobald Lieb (1943).

NOTES AND SOURCES: Major General Mieth was Chief of the Operations Department (O Qu I) at OKH and had played a major role in planning Operation "Barbarossa," the German invasion of Russia. He left the 112th Infantry Division on November 24, 1942, to become Commander of Security Troops, Army Group Don. Promoted to Lieutenant General in 1943, he was leading IV Corps in August 1944, when Rumania defected and left 6th Army cut off in the eastern part of that country. General Mieth tried to break out but was unsuccessful. He died of a heart attack in the heat of battle near Jassy. His command surrendered shortly thereafter. Theobald Lieb went on to command Corps Detachment B (a temporary unit) in Russia (late 1943-44), the 34th Infantry Division (1944) and a corps in northern Italy (late 1944-45). Carell 1966: 162; Chant 1979: 96; Hartmann: 21; RA: 188; OB 43: 144; OB 45: 176; Ziemke 1966: 230-38.

113th INFANTRY DIVISION

COMPOSITION: 260th Infantry Regiment, 261st Infantry Regiment, 268th Infantry Regiment, 87th Artillery Regiment, 113th Reconnaissance Battalion, 113th Anti-Tank Battalion, 113th Engineer Battalion, 113th Signal Battalion

HOME STATION: Wehrkreis XIII

Formed in October 1940, the 113th Infantry initially remained in Germany until the winter of 1941-42, when it was sent to the Balkans to perform occupation duties. In the spring of 1942 it was transferred to the southern sector of the Russian Front, where it was led by Lieutenant General Güntzel. It was with the 6th Army in the Kharkov-Izyum, Voronezh, and Kalach battles and was surrounded with Paulus at Stalingrad in November 1942. The 113rd Infantry Division was destroyed in late January 1943. Lieutenant General Hans Heinrich Sixt von Armin was the divisional commander at the time of the surrender.

A new 113th Infantry was created in Brittany in the spring of 1943. It was sent to Army Group Center that summer but did not prove to be a particularly effective combat division. In the autumn of 1943 it suffered heavy casualties in the Dnieper withdrawal and was broken up. On October 4, 1943, one-third of the unit was attached to the 337th Infantry Division, one-third to the 18th Panzer Grenadier Division (with the XXXIX Panzer and XXVII Corps of the 4th Army, respectively), and one-third to the 256th Infantry Division of the 3rd Panzer Army. The 113th Infantry Division was officially dissolved soon after and its headquarters disbanded.

NOTES AND SOURCES: General Sixt von Armin formerly commanded the 95th Infantry Division (1940-42). Von Mellenthin 1956: 225; *Kriegstagebuch des OKW*, Volume III: 733; OB 42: 86; OB 43: 144; OB 45: 176.

120th INFANTRY DIVISION

COMPOSITION: Miscellaneous units

HOME STATION: Wehrkreis I

The 120th Infantry was created in late 1944 or early 1945 to help prevent the Russians from overrunning East Prussia. It probably never exceeded regimental strength, and was undoubtedly made up of Volksturm (a home guard army of boys and old men unfit for regular military service), and miscellaneous troops. It was in remnants by March 1, 1945, and fell into Russian captivity at the end of the war.

SOURCE: *Kriegstagebuch des OKW*, Volume IV: 1897.

121st INFANTRY DIVISION

COMPOSITION: 405th Infantry Regiment, 407th Infantry Regiment, 408th Infantry Regiment, 121st Artillery Regiment, 121st Reconnaissance Battalion, 121st Anti-Tank Battalion, 121st Engineer Battalion, 121st Signal Battalion

HOME STATION: Wehrkreis X

This division was mobilized in September 1940, attached to Army Group North in 1941, and spent the rest of the war on the northern sector of the Russian Front. It was part of von Manstein's LVI Panzer Corps in early July 1941, when it smashed the Soviet 27th Army northeast of Dvinsk. In this battle Major General Otto Lancelle, the divisional commander, was killed. The next month the 121st took part in the Battle of Mga with the 16th Army. By October it was down to 40 percent of its authorized strength but remained in action during the drive on Leningrad and the subsequent Russian attempts to break the siege of that city. By September 1942 the

121st Infantry was fighting in the Lake Ladoga sector and remained there for some time. In 1944 the division was involved in the retreat from Leningrad through the Baltic States, fought in the Battle of Pskov that June, and—at battle group strength—retreated to the western coast of Latvia in September. The burned-out division remained in the Courland Pocket until the end of the war. Commanders of the 121st included Lancelle (1940-41), Lieutenant General Martin Wandel (1942), and Colonel Ranck (1945).

NOTES AND SOURCES: General Wandel later commanded XXIV Panzer Corps (1942-43). Carell 1966: 265; *Kriegstagebuch des OKW:* Volume IV: 1877; Salisbury: 165, 275, 351; RA: 20; OB 45: 176.

122nd INFANTRY DIVISION

COMPOSITION: 409th Infantry Regiment, 411th Infantry Regiment, 414th Infantry Regiment, 122nd Artillery Regiment, 122nd Reconnaissance Battalion, 122nd Anti-Tank Battalion, 122nd Engineer Battalion, 122nd Signal Battalion

HOME STATION: Wehrkreis II

Formed in September 1940, this division consisted of personnel from Mecklenburg and Pomerania. It took part in the invasion of Russia with Army Group North and was with the I Corps in the Battles of Novgorod, Lake Ilmen, and Mga. In the early spring of 1942 it took part in the attempt to rescue II Corps (encircled at Demyansk), and on May 5 it broke the Siege of Kholm and rescued Combat Group Scherer, which had been surrounded for more than three months. In November 1942 the 122nd was again fighting in the Demyansk sector, until the II corps was finally freed in February 1943. Later that year it was committed to the Battle of Nevel with Army Group Center. Returned to Army Group North in March 1944, it was transferred to Helsinki, Finland, in July but was ordered back to the Russian Front on July 29, two days after the fall of Narva. Its departure alarmed Finnish Marshal Carl Mannerheim and was a factor in that country's defection from the Axis war effort several weeks later. Meanwhile, the 122nd Infantry retreated through Estonia and was cut off in the Courland Pocket in western Latvia by October 1944. It was still there when the war ended. Commanders of the 122nd Infantry Division included Lieutenant Generals Macholz (1941), Kurt Chill (1942-43), and Friedrich Fangohr (1944-45).

NOTES AND SOURCES: General Chill was seriously wounded in 1943. After he recovered he led the 85th Infantry Division in France, the Low Countries, and the last campaign in western Germany. Friedrich Fangohr, who was promoted to General of Infantry near the end of the war, was Ia of the 13th Infantry Division in 1939. Later he was Operations Officer of the XLI Corps (1940) and Chief of Staff of the 4th Panzer Army (1942). From May 9-23, 1945, he was Liaison Officer of the Armed Forces of the High Command to Eisenhower's headquarters. Carell 1966: 251, 256, 258, 427-31, 434-38; Carell 1971: 288; Plocher 1943: 319; Salisbury: 275; OB 42: 88; OB 44: 202; OB 45: 177; Ziemke 1959: 286; Ziemke 1966: 387.

123rd INFANTRY DIVISION

COMPOSITION: 415th Infantry Regiment, 416th Infantry Regiment, 418th Infantry Regiment, 123rd Artillery Regiment, 123rd Reconnaissance Battalion, 123rd Anti-Tank Battalion, 123rd Engineer Battalion, 123rd Signal Battalion

HOME STATION: Wehrkreis III

This Brandenburg unit was formed in September 1940, went to Russia with Army Group North in June 1941, and fought at Dvinsk and a number of other battles in the drive on Leningrad in 1941. In early January 1942, it formed the southern flank of the army group during the Russian winter offensive of 1941-42. Because of the shortage of German troops and the vastness of the territory, the division had to cover 50 miles of frontage and was badly overextended. In this exposed position it was attacked by four Soviet armies, and was crushed. The remnants of the 123rd were all but finished off at Lake Seliger on January 9, although some elements managed to escape to the Demyansk and Kholm pockets. Not freed until February 1943, the reunited and reformed division reemerged in combat later that year in the Battle of Zaporozhe on the southern sector of the Eastern Front. In February 1944 the 123rd Infantry suffered such heavy losses in the withdrawal from the lower Dnieper bend that it had to be disbanded. Lieutenant General Erwin Rauch was the last commander of the division. Most of the 416th Infantry Regiment was absorbed by the 11th Panzer Division.

NOTES AND SOURCES: Rauch later commanded the 343rd Infantry Division on the Western Front. where he was captured in September 1944. Carell 1966: 376-77, 427, 434-38; Carell 1971: 288; Manstein: 184; OB 43: 145; OB 44: 203; OB 45: 177.

125th INFANTRY DIVISION

COMPOSITION: 419th Infantry Regiment, 420th Infantry Regiment, 421st Infantry Regiment, 125th Artillery Regiment, 125th Reconnaissance Battalion, 125th Anti-Tank Battalion, 125th Engineer Battalion, 125th Signal Battalion

HOME STATION: Wehrkreis V

Made up of troops from Baden and Württemberg, the 125th Infantry was created in September 1940. It first saw action in the Balkans in the spring of 1941 as part of LI Corps, 2nd Army. Three months later it was in Russia with Army Group South and fought in the Ukraine and the Crimea. Later it took part in the capture of Rostov, the Caucasus campaign, and the Battle of Novorossiysk in the Kuban. The divisional commander and his staff—temporarily designated Command Staff for Special Purposes von Förster—served as the military administrators of the Kuban for a time in the fall of 1942, controlling parts of the 125th Infantry and 13th Panzer Divisions, as well as most of the 3rd Rumanian Mountain Division and part of the 10th Rumanian Mountain Division. Reunited in late 1942, the 125th Infantry distinguished itself in the Kuban fighting during the winter of 1942-43. Later in 1943 the division was transferred to the lower Dnieper sector by way of the Crimea and took such heavy casualties in the withdrawal from the lower Dnieper bend that it had to be disbanded. Its commanders included Lieutenant General Willi Schneckenburger (1942) and Lieutenant General von Förster (1943).

NOTES AND SOURCES: Senior regimental commander Colonel Alfred Reinhardt may have been briefly in command of the division in late 1942-early 1943. Carell 1966: 535, 559-60; Carell 1971: 156-57, 186; Hartmann: 21; *Kriegstagebuch des OKW*, Volume III: 731; RA: 86; OB 42: 88; OB 44b: D73; OB 45: 178. For a detailed description of the street fighting in the Battle of Rostov, see *Time-Life*, Volume 20: 120-21

126th INFANTRY DIVISION

COMPOSITION: 422nd Infantry Regiment, 424th Infantry Regiment, 426th Infantry Regiment, 126th Artillery Regiment, 126th Reconnaissance Battalion, 126th Anti-Tank Battalion, 126th Engineer Battalion, 126th Signal Battalion

HOME STATION: Wehrkreis VI

Formed in September 1940, this Rhinelander-Westphalian division went into battle on the northern sector of the Russian Front in June 1941 and remained there for the rest of the war. It fought at Lake Ilmen, on the Mshaga River, before Leningrad, and in the Battle of the Volkhov in early 1942. Later it took part in the relief of Demyansk in early 1943 and the withdrawal from Leningrad in early 1944, where it suffered heavy casualties. Finally pushed back to the west coast of Latvia, the division (now at regimental strength) remained isolated in the Courland Pocket until the end of the war. Its commanders included Lieutenant General Laux (1942), Major General Harry Hoppe (late 1942-43), and Major General Gotthard Fischer (1943-45).

NOTES AND SOURCES: Laux later commanded II Corps at Demyansk (1942-43). Hoppe, commander of the 424th Infantry Regiment and senior regimental commander in the 126th, moved up when Laux was promoted to corps commander in October 1942. An exceptionally brave man, Hoppe held the Knight's Cross with Oak Leaves. He was eventually promoted to Lieutenant General and later led the 278th Infantry Division in Italy (1945). Carell 1966: 20, 248, 251, 420-21; Carell 1971: 288-89; *Kriegstagebuch des OKW*, Volume IV: 1897; OB 42: 88; OB 43: 146; OB 44: 204; OB 45: 178.

129th INFANTRY DIVISION

COMPOSITION: 427th Infantry Regiment, 428th Infantry Regiment, 430th Infantry Regiment, 129th Artillery Regiment, 129th Reconnaissance Battalion, 129th Anti-Tank Battalion, 129th Engineer Battalion, 129th Signal Battalion

HOME STATION: Fulda, Wkr. IX

In September 1940, this Hessian-Thuringian division was activated. It first saw action in Russia in June of the following year. The 129th helped establish the Kalinin bridgehead on the upper Volga in October when it was part of Model's XLI Panzer Corps. Later that year it faced the Russian winter offensive as part of the 9th Army, Army Group Center. Remaining on the central sector, it took part in the defensive battles of 1942 and in the Rzhev withdrawal of early 1943. That autumn it fought in the Battle of Nevel and later escaped the Russian summer offensive of 1944, but with high casualties. In August 1944 it was defending on the Vistula, and did so well that it was officially commended; however, the 129th had suffered such heavy personnel and equipment losses during three years on the Eastern Front that it was withdrawn from the battle and disbanded as a combat division. Its headquarters, however, remained extant, and was serving as the Kommandantur of the Frische Nehrung in East Prussia in March 1945. The surviving soldiers of the 129th were distributed among the surviving divisions of Army Group Center, and most of them no doubt also fought their last battles in the East Prussian Pocket. Commanders of the 129th Infantry Division included Major General Heribert von Larisch (1941), Lieutenant General Stephan Rittau (1942), Lieutenant General Albert Praun (1942-43), and Major General Fabiunke (1943-44).

NOTES AND SOURCES: Praun, a colonel in 1941, was rapidly promoted. He was commander of the 18th Panzer Division (1942), the 129th Infantry Division (August 24, 1942 to 1943), the Chief Signal Officer of Army Group Center (1943), the commander of the 277th Infantry Division on the Western Front (1944), and finally, as General of Signal Troops, was Chief Wehrmacht Signal Officer (August 1944-45). Carell 1966: 154-55, 196; Carell 1971: 309; *Kriegstagebuch des OKW*, Volume IV: 1897; RA: 144; OB 42: 88; OB 43: 146; OB 44: 204; OB 45: 178.

131st INFANTRY DIVISION

COMPOSITION: 431st Infantry Regiment, 432nd Infantry Regiment, 434th Infantry Regiment, 131st Reconnaissance Battalion, 131st Anti-Tank Battalion, 131st Engineer Battalion, 131st Signal Battalion

HOME STATION: Wehrkreis XI

Formed in September 1940, the 131st Infantry took part in the invasion of Russia in June 1941. It remained on the Eastern Front for the next four years, fighting at Gomel, before Moscow, and in the other major battles on the central sector. It suffered heavy casualties during the Soviet winter offensive of 1941-42. After a brief period of service on the southern zone in the summer of 1943, the 131st returned to Army Group Center and subsequently was sent to a rest area in Poland after the defensive battles of late 1943. In the spring of 1944 the division was rushed back into action with the XXXII Corps and took part in the unsuccessful attempt to relieve Kovel. Later that year the 131st was smashed in the gigantic Russian summer offensive of 1944. The remnants of the now burned-out division remained on the Eastern Front until the end, fighting in the retreats through western Russia and Poland. In March 1945 it was fighting in East Prussia, with the 10th Bicycle Jäger Brigade attached, and was still in Prussia when the war ended. Its commanders included Lieutenant General Heinrich Meyer-Beurdorf (1941-43) and Major General Friedrich Weber (1944-45).

NOTES AND SOURCES: Weber, a forty-seven-year old Bavarian, had commanded the 334th Infantry Division in Tunisia in 1943. Meyer-Beurdorf had been Chief of Artillery Observation Troops at OKH before taking over the 131st. Carell 1966: 196; *Kriegstagebuch des OKW,* Volume IV: 1897; RA: 172; OB 43: 146; OB 44: 204; OB 45: 179; Ziemke 1966: 279.

132nd INFANTRY DIVISION

COMPOSITION: 436th Infantry Regiment, 437th Infantry Regiment, 438th Infantry Regiment, 132nd Artillery Regiment, 132nd Reconnaissance Battalion, 132nd Anti-Tank Battalion, 132nd Engineer Battalion, 132nd Signal Battalion

HOME STATION: Wehrkreis VII (later XII)

Originally formed in Wehrkreis VII in September 1940, this Bavarian division was later transferred to the XII Military District for replacement and training purposes. After crossing into southern Russia in 1941, the division fought in the Crimea and in the Siege of Sevastopol. It later took part in the assault that caused the fall of this giant Soviet naval fortress and was subsequently shifted to the northern sector of the Eastern Front in July 1942. It remained with the 18th Army of Army Group North for the next three years. In July 1944 the 132nd Infantry suffered heavy casualties in the Russian summer offensive and was forced into the Courland Pocket in September 1944. It was still there when the war ended. The 132nd's divisional commanders included Lieutenant Generals Rudolf Sintzenich (1940-42), Fritz Lindemann (1943), and Herbert Wagner (1945).

SOURCES: Carell 1966: 304, 503; *Kriegstagebuch des OKW:* Volume III: 1888; Manstein: 243; Salisbury: 538; RA: 188; OB 42: 89; OB 43: 146; OB 45: 89.

133rd FORTRESS DIVISION

COMPOSITION: 733rd Grenadier Regiment, 746th Grenadier Regiment, 133rd Artillery Regiment, 133rd Engineer Battalion; it is unclear what, if any, Signal, Anti-Tank or Füsilier elements this division had.

HOME STATION: Crete (?), Wkr. IV and XIII

This division was formed on the island of Crete in the eastern Mediterranean in the winter of 1943-44 when Fortress Brigade Crete was upgraded. The grenadier regiments of the 133rd had been part of the 713rd (Static) Infantry Division, which included men from the older age groups. In the spring of 1944 the 733rd Grenadier Regiment was evacuated to the mainland and incorporated into the 41st Infantry Division. In late December 1944 or January 1945, the division was dissolved as such and redesignated 133rd Fortress Area. In 1945 the elements of the division still on Crete were commanded by Colonel Barke. They surrendered to the Western Allies at the end of the war. Previous divisional commanders included Lieutenant General Dr. Ernst Kleep (1944) and Major General Wittstatt (late 1944).

NOTES AND SOURCES: Dr. Kleep had formerly been commander of the 4th Luftwaffe Field Division. Colonel Barke had commanded the 746th Grenadier Regiment on Crete (1943-44). *Kriegstagebuch des OKW*, Volume III: 1882; OB 45: 179-80.

134th INFANTRY DIVISION

COMPOSITION: 439th Infantry Regiment, 445th Infantry Regiment, 134th Artillery Regiment, 134th Reconnaissance Battalion, 134th Anti-Tank Battalion, 134th Engineer Battalion, 134th Signal Battalion

HOME STATION: Wehrkreis IV

Formed in October 1940, this division was more or less continuously engaged on the central sector of the Russian Front from June 1941 until it was destroyed in July 1944. Under Lieutenant General Hans Schlemmer it formed part of the 4th Army in the initial invasion and was with the 2nd Army in the battles around Moscow in December 1941. It suffered heavy casualties against the Russian winter offensive of 1941-42. The division lost much of its artillery when the Russians broke into the rear of the 2nd Army, and on December 12 General Halder, the Chief of the Army General Staff, reported it unfit for combat due to lack of supplies. It nevertheless remained in the line and fought in the Battle of Bryansk (1942), in the defensive battles around Gomel (1943), and at Bryansk again in the summer of 1943. It was on the front line in July 1944 when the Soviet summer offensive smashed Army Group Center. The 134th was encircled near Minsk and was destroyed there, along with the XXXV Corps and much of the 9th Army. Lieutenant General Philipp, who had replaced Schlemmer in early 1944, committed suicide rather than surrender to the Russians.

SOURCES: Carell 1966: 344; Carell 1971: 597; Hartmann: 22; Seaton: 224, citing Halder, *Kriegstagebuch*, Volume III: 340; OB 43: 147; OB 44: 205; OB 45: 180.

SPECIAL EMPLOYMENT DIVISION STAFF 136

COMPOSITION: miscellaneous non-German infantry battalions

HOME STATION: Paris (?), France

This unit was created in France in the spring of 1944 as a special field administrative staff with responsibility for helping control Eastern battalions. These units consisted mainly of Soviet prisoners-of-war who volunteered to serve in the German Army to fight Communism, to escape horrible treatment in Nazi prison camps, or both. The 136th was upgraded to a Special Employment Division that summer and was sent to Brittany, where it directed miscellaneous units in anti-Maquis operations. It was withdrawn from Brittany before the Allies cut off the peninsula and took part in the retreat to Belgium, still controlling miscellaneous formations. In September 1944 it retreated into Holland where it was taken out of the line and disbanded. The commander of Special Employment Division 136 throughout its existence was Major General Count Christoph zu Stolberg-Stolberg.

NOTES AND SOURCES: Count zu Stolberg-Stolberg formerly served as Commandant of Antwerp. He was captured by the British in September 1944. OB 45: 180.

137th INFANTRY DIVISION

COMPOSITION: 447th Infantry Regiment, 448th Infantry Regiment, 449th Infantry Regiment, 137th Artillery Regiment, 137th Reconnaissance Battalion, 137th Anti-Tank Battalion, 137th Engineer Battalion, 137th Signal Battalion

HOME STATION: Wehrkreis XVII

Created in September 1940, the 137th crossed into Russia with Army Group Center in June 1941 and remained with that army group throughout the division's existence. It fought in the Battle of the Yelnya Bend, in the final drive on Moscow, and against the 1941-42 Russian winter offensive, where it suffered heavy casualties. Later it fought at Kursk and in the battles of the central Dnieper. Badly understrength after over two years of almost continuous action, the 137th was withdrawn from combat in late 1943 and was subsequently disbanded. The survivors of the division were absorbed by the 271st Infantry Division. The 137th's commanders included

Major General Karl Dewitz gennant von Krebs (1942) and Lieutenant General Kamecke (1943).

SOURCES: Carell 1966: 92, 196; RA: 220; OB 42: 89; OB 43: 147; OB 45: 181.

DIVISION NUMBER 140 z.b.V.

COMPOSITION: 139th Jäger Brigade and 503rd Grenadier Regiment (?)

HOME STATION: see below

The 140th was a z.b.V. ("for special purposes") division created in late 1944 to control miscellaneous units during the German retreat from northern Finland. After the 20th Mountain Army's successful withdrawal, the division was stationed in the Narvik vicinity of northern Norway until the end of the war.

SOURCE: *Kriegstagebuch des OKW*, Volume IV: 1889, 1899.

141st RESERVE DIVISION

COMPOSITION (1944): 1st Reserve Grenadier Regiment, 61st Reserve Grenadier Regiment, 206th Reserve Grenadier Regiment, 1st (or 11th) Reserve Artillery Battalion, 1st Reserve Engineer Battalion

HOME STATION: Insterburg, Wkr. I

Created upon the outbreak of hostilities as Replacement Division Staff 141, this East Prussian unit had the mission of training recruits for Wehrkreis I and providing replacements for the military district's affiliated infantry divisions. It was also known as the 141st Mobilization Division. In September 1940 it was transferred to Prague with its subordinate units but returned to Germany in July 1941. In September 1942 it was redesignated a reserve division, gave up its replacement units, and was sent to Minsk in White Russia. In the latter part of 1944 it was committed to combat on the central sector of the Russian Front, which was by then in Poland. Late in 1944 the 141st Reserve was dissolved, and its men were sent to other units on the Eastern Front. Its last commander was apparently Lieutenant General Otto Schönherr (1943-44).

SOURCES: RA: 5, 20, 22; OB 45: 181.

143rd RESERVE DIVISION

COMPOSITION (1944): 68th Reserve Grenadier Regiment, 76th Reserve Grenadier Regiment, 208th Reserve Grenadier Regiment, 68th Reserve Engineer Battalion, and a reserve artillery battalion (it is unclear what signal or anti-tank elements this division had).

HOME STATION: Frankfurt-on-the-Oder, Wkr. III

Established shortly after the invasion of Poland, the 143rd was born as a replacement division staff under Wehrkreis III. In the fall of 1942 it was reorganized as a reserve division and was sent to the Luck area in northwestern Ukraine, along with its training units. Its subordinate replacement units reverted back to Wehrkreis control. In April 1943 the 143rd was reported as being in Poland and in the Ukraine by July 1943. It ceased training altogether in early 1944, however, and went into action on the Eastern Front, where it was quickly destroyed. Its commanders included Lieutenant Generals Windeck (1941-42) and Paul Stoewer (1943-44).

NOTES AND SOURCES: Windeck later commanded Replacement Division Staff 152 (1945). *Kriegstagebuch des OKW*, Volume III: 736, 1161; RA: 5; OB 43: 147; OB 45: 181.

147th FIELD TRAINING DIVISION

COMPOSITION (1943): 212th Reserve Grenadier Regiment, 268th Reserve Grenadier Regiment, 27th Reserve Engineer Battalion

HOME STATION: Augsburg, Wkr. VII

The 147th was activated as a replacement division in the Bavaria-Palatinate-Swabia region in the fall of 1939. It continued to furnish trained replacements for the VII Military District's associated infantry divisions until the spring of 1943, when it was sent to the Ukraine as a reserve division. In late 1943 it was redesignated a field training division and ended its affiliation with Wehrkreis VII. Early in 1944 it was committed to battle in Russia, where it was quickly destroyed, largely because its men were only partially trained. Its commanders included Lieutenant Generals Held (1943) and Otto Matterstock (1944).

SOURCES: *Kriegstagebuch des OKW*, Volume III: 736, 1161; RA: 116, 118; OB 43: 148; OB 45: 182.

148th INFANTRY (formerly RESERVE) DIVISION

COMPOSITION (1944): 281st Grenadier Regiment, 285th Grenadier Regiment, 286th Grenadier Regiment, 1048th Artillery Regiment, 148th Füsilier Battalion, 1048th Anti-Tank Battalion, 1048th Engineer Battalion, 1048th Signal Battalion

HOME STATION: Liegnitz, Wkr. VIII

Formed in 1939 as a replacement division staff to control replacement-training units in Silesia, this division was transferred to Metz in the Lorraine region of France in early 1941 along with its subordinate units. In autumn 1942 the 148th became a reserve division and was reorganized to include the 8th, 239th, and 252nd Reserve Grenadier Regiments, the 8th Reserve Engineer Battalion, and the 8th Reserve Signal Battalion. All these units had been transferred elsewhere or redesignated by late 1944. Meanwhile, the 148th took part in the occupation of Vichy France in November 1942, garrisoned the Toulouse area on the Mediterranean coast in early 1943, and guarded the Franco-Italian frontier later that year. From October 1943 it was stationed on the Italian Riviera. Subordinate to Army Group G in August 1944, it was upgraded to full combat status shortly thereafter. The 148th first saw action against the American invasion of southern France as a part of General Neuling's LXII Corps, 19th Army. It was in action from the first day of the campaign but with little success. Later that month it was sent to the Esterel massif and was positioned to prevent the Americans from penetrating through the French Alps and taking Kesselring's armies in Italy in the rear. Later it formed part of Army Group C and, although it was considered a second-class combat unit, was on the front line in Italy by late October. The 148th took part in the Po River Valley campaign and was fighting on the Tyrrhenian coast in early 1945. It was still in northern Italy when the war ended. The division's commanders included Lieutenant Generals Rudolf Gercke (1942), Held (1942), Hermann Böttcher (1942-early 1944), and Otto Fretter-Pico (1944-45).

NOTES AND SOURCES: Böttcher formerly commanded the 216th Infantry Division (1940) and later commanded the LXVII Reserve Corps (1944). Gercke, who led the 148th only briefly, was promoted to General of Infantry on April 1, 1942, and resumed his former post as Chief of Ground Transportation at OKH (1939-42 and 1942-45). Chant, Volume 14: 1914-21, 1928; Fisher: 303, 406; Harrison: Map VI; RA: 5, 132; OB 42: 21; OB 43: 148; OB 44b: D119; OB 45: 182.

151st RESERVE DIVISION

COMPOSITION: 21st Reserve Grenadier Regiment, 206th Reserve Grenadier Regiment, 217th Reserve Grenadier Regiment

HOME STATION: Allenstein, Wkr. I

Formed at Allenstein in 1939 as Replacement Division Staff 151, this unit was responsible for controlling replacement-training units in East Prussia. From September 1940 to July 1941 it was stationed at Budweis, Bohemia, and later in the Prague area. Returning to East Prussia for a year, it was upgraded to a reserve division in autumn 1942 and sent to Lithuania. In 1944 it ceased all training and went into action on the Eastern Front. By early 1945 it was back in East Prussia but was now operating solely as a combat infantry division, although it never formally received this designation. It was still fighting the Russians in eastern Germany when the war ended. Lieutenant General Wolfgang Schede was the commander of the 151st in 1943-44.

NOTES AND SOURCES: Schede formerly commanded the 96th Infantry Division on the Russian Front (1942-43). RA: 5, 20, 22; OB 43: 148; OB 45: 183. OB 44b lists the 228th Reserve Grenadier Regiment as part of the division in early 1944 (OB 44b: D119).

REPLACEMENT DIVISION STAFF 152

COMPOSITION: 75th Grenadier Training Regiment, 207th Grenadier Training Regiment, and other miscellaneous training units

HOME STATION: Stettin, Wkr. II

Created in Pomerania and Mecklenburg upon the outbreak of the war, the 152nd supervised replacement-training units in Wehrkreis II. In late 1941 it was transferred to Graudenz, Wehrkreis XX (formerly Poland), and remained there until late 1944. In the latter part of 1942 it lost its replacement units and gained the training elements of the 192nd Mobilization Division (Replacement Division Staff 192). The 152nd became, in fact, a field training division, although it never officially received this designation. The division was destroyed in late 1944, when the Russians overran Poland. The 152nd's divisional commanders included Lieutenant Generals Arthur Boltze (1942-43) and Windeck (1944-45).

NOTES AND SOURCES: Windeck formerly led the 143rd Reserve Division (1941-42). RA: 32, 34; OB 43: 148; OB 45: 183.

153rd FIELD TRAINING (later GRENADIER) DIVISION

COMPOSITION: 715th Field Training Regiment, 716th Field Training Regiment, 717th Field Training Regiment

HOME STATION: Potsdam, Wkr. III

The 153rd began as a replacement division in 1939 and was upgraded to reserve division status in 1942. It remained in the III Military District during this period. Sent to the Crimea in late 1942, it controlled the 23rd, 76th, and 257th Reserve Grenadier Regiments until the following spring, when it was converted into a field training unit under Lieutenant General Rene de l'Homme de Courbiere. As a field training unit it was no longer part of the Replacement Army, but came under the direct control of Army Group A and later Army Group South. In early 1944 (now designated as a grenadier division), as the Soviets neared the Crimea, the 153rd Field Training was evacuated to the lower Dnieper and became involved in combat southwest of Odessa. It remained on the line, fighting as an infantry division, and in September it was routed near Bucharest, Rumania, suffering heavy casualties in the process. Later the 153rd fought in Hungary and in December was trapped, along with the 1st and 23rd Panzer Divisions, between the Danube and Lake Balaton. The 153rd held the town of Szekesfehervar for several days but was finally overrun on December 24, 1944. Remnants of the division escaped to form a battle group of approximately regimental strength. It was still resisting as a part of the 1st Panzer Army in the Czechoslovakian Pocket when the war ended. Commanders of the 153rd included de Courbiere (1943), Lieutenant General Karl Pflaum (1943-44), and Major General Kurt Gerok (1944-45).

NOTES AND SOURCES: Lieutenant General de Courbiere formerly commanded the 213th Infantry Division (1939-41) and later commanded the 338th Infantry Division (1944). Karl Pflaum previously led the 258th Infantry Division on the Russian Front (1941-42). Chant, Volume 15: 2057; *Kriegstagebuch des OKW*, Volume I: 1146; Volume II: 1392; Volume III: 3, 731; RA: 5, 46, 72-74; OB 43: 148; OB 45: 183-84.

154th RESERVE DIVISION

COMPOSITION: 56th Reserve Grenadier Regiment, 223rd Reserve Grenadier Regiment, 255th Reserve Grenadier Regiment, 24th Reserve Artillery Battalion, 24th Reserve Engineer Battalion

HOME STATION: Dresden, Wkr. IV

Formed as Replacement Division Staff 154 shortly after the outbreak of hostilities, this unit consisted of Saxon and Sudeten Germans. Three years later it was redesignated a reserve division and sent to the Lancut area of northern Poland, where it continued to train soldiers for the IV Military District. Elements of the 154th were in combat as early as March 1944, and, after the collapse of Army Group Center in July and August 1944, the entire division was committed to battle on the central sector of the Eastern Front. It fought in White Russia, southern Poland, and, as part of 1st Panzer Army, in eastern Germany against the last Russian offensive in the spring of 1945. Most of the personnel of the 154th Reserve ended up in Soviet captivity. The last divisional commander was apparently Lieutenant General Dr. Friedrich Altricher, who had led the 154th since early 1943.

SOURCES: *Kreigstagebuch des OKW,* Volume I: 1146; Volume III: 1883; RA: 5, 72-74; OB 43: 37; OB 45: 184.

155th FIELD TRAINING DIVISION

COMPOSITION: 1227th Field Training Regiment, 1228th Field Training Regiment, 1229th Field Training Regiment

HOME STATION: Northern Italy, Wkr. V

The 155th was formed in northern Italy in December 1944 to train recruits and rear-area personnel for Army Group C. Part of its cadre came from the 20th Luftwaffe Field Division. In January 1945 elements of the division were variously reported in the Belluno, Verona, and Treviso areas of Italy. It carried on its training mission until early 1945, when it was redesignated an infantry division. It was in the process of reorganizing when the German southern front collapsed in April 1945. The men of the 155th went into Allied captivity at the end of the war.

SOURCES: *Kreigstagebuch des OKW,* Volume I: 1148; Volume IV: 1892, 1902; OB 45: 185.

156th RESERVE DIVISION

COMPOSITION: 26th Reserve Grenadier Regiment, 227th Reserve Grenadier Regiment, 254th Reserve Grenadier Regiment, 26th Reserve Artillery Regiment

HOME STATION: Cologne, Wkr. VI

Activated in September 1939 as a replacement division, the 156th initially controlled replacement and training units in Westphalia. After a tour of occupation duty in northern Poland (November 1939 to September 1940), the division returned to the VI Military District and remained there until it was upgraded to a reserve division in the fall of 1942 and was transferred to the English Channel. By late 1942 it was reported at Spa, Belgium, and in February 1943 it was located at Calais, France, but apparently was sent back to Belgium shortly afterward. By late 1943 the 156th was reportedly a full-fledged combat division, but its formal conversion to a static infantry unit did not take place until February 1944, when it was redesignated 47th Infantry Division. The 156th's commanders included Major General Noach (1942) and Lieutenant General Richard Baltzer (1942-43).

ALSO SEE 47th INFANTRY DIVISION

NOTES AND SOURCES: General Noach was retired by 1945. Baltzer had commanded the 217th Infantry Division in 1940. RA: 6, 102, 104-05; OB 42: 21; OB 43: 30; OB 45: 185.

157th RESERVE DIVISION
see 157th Mountain Division

158th RESERVE DIVISION

COMPOSITION: 18th Reserve Grenadier Regiment, 213th Reserve Grenadier Regiment, 221st Reserve Grenadier Regiment, 18th Reserve Artillery Regiment, 213th Reserve Engineer Battalion

HOME STATION: Liegnitz, Wkr. VIII

Formed as a replacement division staff upon the outbreak of the war, this unit directed replacement-training forces in Silesia until February 1941, when it was transferred to Alsace. In autumn 1942 it was upgraded to a reserve division and its replacement elements returned to Silesia and placed under other divisions. Headquartered at Strasbourg when Eisenhower landed in French North Africa in November 1942, the 158th took part in the occupation of Vichy (southern) France and remained on the Bay of Biscay near La Rochelle on occupation duty for more than a year. American intelligence reported that it was converted to a security division in early 1944, but this is almost certainly a mistake. In the summer of 1944 the soldiers of the 158th Reserve were combined with the survivors of the shattered 16th Luftwaffe Field Division to form the 16th Infantry Division and, as such, went into action in central France. The commanders of the

158th Reserve Division included Major General Schmidt-Kolbow (1942), Lieutenant General Ernst Haeckel (1943-44), and Lieutenant General Karl Pflaum (1944).

ALSO SEE 16th INFANTRY (later VOLKSGRENADIER) DIVISION (#2)

NOTES AND SOURCES: Pflaum had formerly commanded the 258th Infantry and 153rd Reserve Divisions (1941-42 and 1943-44, respectively). Both units were serving in Russia during Pflaum's tenure. RA: 5, 132; OB 42: 20; OB 43: 149; OB 45: 186.

159th INFANTRY (formerly RESERVE) DIVISION

COMPOSITION (1944): 1209th Grenadier Regiment, 1210th Grenadier Regiment, 1211th Grenadier Regiment, 1059th Artillery Regiment, 1059th Füsilier Battalion, 1059th Anti-Tank Battalion, 1059th Engineer Battalion, 1059th Signal Battalion

HOME STATION: Frankfurt-on-Main, Wkr. IX

Originally created as the 159th Replacement Division from units in Thuringia and neighboring districts in the fall of 1939, this division remained in Germany until autumn 1942, when the Home Army's replacement and training functions were divided. Renamed the 159th Reserve Division, it was sent west and took part in the occupation of Vichy France in November 1942. At that time it included the 9th, 52nd, and 251st Reserve Grenadier Regiments, the 9th Reserve Artillery Regiment, and the 15th Reserve Engineer Battalion. In early 1944 the 159th was performing garrison duties in the Arcachon area, on the Bay of Biscay coast, and was subsequently at Bordeaux, where it was stationed on D-Day. Moved into the interior of France after the Allied landings, the division was in combat by September. Soon all training functions ceased, the division was upgraded to full combat infantry status, and its subordinate elements received their 1944 designations. Meanwhile the 159th was heavily engaged in the Mulhouse area for three months (November 1944-January 1945) and held together well, despite heavy losses. In March 1945 it was part of the German 7th Army and was reported in "fairly presentable strength," although it suffered heavy losses against the American attacks in the Saar-Palatinate battles. It escaped to the east bank of the Rhine and late in March 1945 was with the XII (Provisional) Corps in southern Germany. Although burned-out by months of continuous action, it was still one of the strongest divisions in Army Group G at that time. Most of the survivors of the 159th were rounded up by the Western Allies at the end of the war.

The division's commanders included Lieutenant General Sachs (1941-42), Lieutenant General Hermann Meyer-Kabingen (1943-44), Lieutenant General Albin Nake (1944), Major General Wilhelm Dernen (late 1944), and Major General Heinz Bürcky (1945).

NOTES AND SOURCES: Sachs later commanded the LXIV Reserve Corps (1943-44). He was named General of Engineers in October 1942. Hermann Meyer-Kabingen, who was a General of Infantry in late 1944, was commander of the "Fortress" of Frankfurt-on-the-Oder on the Eastern Front in 1945. He had previously led the 197th Infantry Division (1940-42) on the Russian Front. Nake, an Austrian, had commanded Replacement Division Staff 526 (1943) and the 264th Infantry Division in the Balkans before taking over the 159th. Bürcky commanded the Officers Training School in Prague in 1943. Harrison: Map VI; MacDonald 1973: 248, 292; RA: 6, 144, 146; OB 43: 33; OB 45: 186.

160th RESERVE DIVISION

COMPOSITION: 30th Reserve Grenadier Regiment (disbanded in 1944), 58th Reserve Grenadier Regiment, 225th Reserve Grenadier Regiment, 58th Reserve Artillery Battalion, 30th Reserve Engineer Battalion

HOME STATION: Hamburg, Wkr. X

The 160th was formed as a replacement division staff by the X Military District (the Schleswig-Holstein regions of north-central Germany) to control its replacement-training units. In 1940 it was sent to Denmark and remained there until the end of the war. Initially it was stationed in Copenhagen, but was sent to the Jutland peninsula region in early 1943. It became strictly a training division in the latter part of 1942, when it gave up its replacement elements and absorbed the training battalions of the 180th and 190th Replacement Divisions. It was variously reported at the Horsens and Henne areas in the Jutland region of Denmark in 1944 and was one of the very few units in Hitler's armed forces to have a noncombat assignment in early 1945. Its commander at that time was Lieutenant General Kurt Hoffmann. Previously it had been directed by Lieutenant General Baron Horst von Uckermann (1942-September 1944).

NOTES AND SOURCES: Kurt Hoffmann had previously commanded the 715th (Static) Infantry Division (1943-44). *Kriegstagebuch des OKW*, Volume IV: 1899; RA: 6, 160; OB 43: 34; OB 44b: D121; OB 45: 187.

161st INFANTRY DIVISION

COMPOSITION: 336th Infantry Regiment, 364th Infantry Regiment, 371st Infantry Regiment, 241st Artillery Regiment, 241st Reconnaissance Company, 241st Anti-Tank Battalion, 241st Engineer Battalion, 241st Signal Battalion

HOME STATION: Wehrkreis I

This division was formed from replacement-training units in East Prussia in January 1940 and first saw action in the invasion of Russia in June 1941. It was with Army Group Center in December and suffered heavy casualties against the Russian winter offensive before Moscow. It remained in the central sector for some months afterward, before being withdrawn to northern France to rest and refit in the winter of 1942-43. Returning to action on the southern zone of the Eastern Front after the fall of Stalingrad, it again sustained heavy losses at Dnepropetrovsk in the autumn of 1943 and was reduced to battle group strength. In May of the next year it was so badly damaged in the withdrawal from the lower Dnieper Bend that it had to be disbanded. Commanders of the 161st included Major General Karl Albrecht von Groddeck (1942), Lieutenant General Recke (1942-43), and Lieutenant General Paul Drekmann (1944).

NOTES AND SOURCES: Groddeck formerly led the 244th Infantry Regiment (1941 to May 1942). Recke was reportedly captured on the Eastern Front in 1943. Drekmann had previously commanded Korps Detachment A in Greece in 1943. Carell 1966: 196; RA: 20; OB 43: 149; OB 44: 206; OB 45: 187.

162nd INFANTRY DIVISION

COMPOSITION: 303rd Infantry Regiment, 314th Infantry Regiment, 329th Infantry Regiment, 236th Artillery Regiment, 236th Reconnaissance Battalion, 236th Anti-Tank Battalion, 236th Engineer Battalion, 236th Signal Battalion

HOME STATION: Rostock, Wkr. II

This unit was originally formed by grouping a number of Pomeranian and Mecklenburger replacement-training units under the newly formed divisional headquarters in January 1940. It took part in the first campaigns in Russia and was continuously engaged from June 1941 until the first winter offensive was checked in early 1942. The 162nd suffered serious losses before Moscow in December 1941 and later served on the southern sector of the Eastern Front until the fall of 1942. Its commander at this time was Major General Professor Doctor Oscar Ritter von Niedermayer, a well-known specialist in foreign affairs. Perhaps for this reason the 162nd was selected to train Ost (Eastern) battalions, which were established by the order of the High Command in late 1941. These troops—including people from Georgia, Armenia, Azerbaijan, Kazak, Turkestan, Iran, Afghanistan, and others—all volunteered to fight in German service against Communism. After they left the 162nd these battalions (collectively called "Turks") were sent to other active divisions. The 162nd initially set up training operations in Poland but in early 1943 was transferred to Slovenia, where it simultaneously conducted training and antipartisan operations along the Ljubljana-Trieste railroad. Early in 1944 the division was transferred to Army Detachment von Zangen in northern Italy and was given the mission of guarding the Ligurian coast. By this time most of its personnel were non-Germans, and its veterans of the Russian Front had been transferred to other units. In June 1944 it was briefly committed to action on the Italian Front but was withdrawn due to its poor performance. It was again sent into action in October and was withdrawn again for the same reason. The division spent the rest of the war fighting partisans in the mountains northeast of La Spezia and later in the Tavo Valley, Italy. The 162nd surrendered to the Western Allies in 1945. Many of its personnel were turned over to the Russians after the war and disappeared. The 162nd Infantry's commanders included von Niedermayer (1941-42 and 1942-44), Lieutenant General Hermann Franke (1942), Lieutenant General Hans von Sommerfeld (1944), and Major General Ralph von Heygendorff (1945).

NOTES AND SOURCES: Sommerfeld was previously the commander of Replacement Division Staff 526. Heygendorff had been Assistant Military Attaché to Moscow prior to the war, and was commander of Administrative Headquarters Eastern Region at Radom in 1943. Carell 1966: 196, 357; Fisher: 19, 233; Hartmann: 22-23; RA: 32; OB 42: 90; OB 43: 149-50; OB 44: 207; OB 45: 188.

163rd INFANTRY DIVISION

COMPOSITION: 307th Infantry Regiment, 310th Infantry Regiment, 324th Infantry Regiment, 234th Artillery Regiment, 234th Reconnaissance Battalion, 234th Anti-Tank Battalion, 234th Engineer Battalion, 234th Signal Battalion

HOME STATION: Berlin, Wkr. III

Formed from Brandenburgers and Prussians in January 1940, the 163rd was sent to Norway three months later and suffered heavy casualties in the initial attempt to take the Norwegian capital. Most of the divisional staff and many of its men were killed when Norwegian coastal batteries sank the heavy cruiser *Blücher* south of Oslo. The division spent the next year on garrison duty in Norway and joined Mountain Corps Norway for the invasion of Russia in June 1941. Because of German diplomatic pressure, the Swedish government allowed the 163rd to go to Finland by way of Stockholm, thus causing an international incident. The 163rd fought in northern Russia and Finland for the next three years and in the winter of 1944-45 withdrew to northern Norway after destroying the Kolosyoki Nickel Works. After the Lapland retreat, the division was sent back across the Baltic and defended Kolberg, where it put up a desperate resistance. When the Russians finally stormed the city in March the 163rd was killed, almost to the last man. The division's commanders included Lieutenant Generals Erwin Engelbrecht (1940-42), Anton Dostler (1942-43), and Karl Rübel (1943-45).

NOTES AND SOURCES: Initially this division was not up to Finnish standards but adapted to fighting in the thick, depressing forests. Lieutenant General Engelbrecht, formerly the German Military Plenipotentiary in Slovakia (1939), was promoted to General of Artillery in September 1942, and commanded the XXXIII Corps from January 1943 to June 1944. In 1945 he was in charge of the Higher Command Saar. Anton Dostler, former commanding general of the 57th Infantry Division in Russia (1942), later commanded LXXV Corps (March-November 1944) and LXXIII Corps 1945). Chant, Volume 16: 2235; OB 42: 90; OB 43: 150; OB 44: 207; OB 45: 188; Ziemke 1959: 139, 304; Ziemke 1966: 399.

164th INFANTRY DIVISION
see 164th Light Afrika Division

165th RESERVE DIVISION

COMPOSITION: 205th Reserve Grenadier Regiment, 215th Reserve Grenadier Regiment, 260th Reserve Grenadier Regiment, 5th Reserve Artillery Regiment, 9th Reserve Engineer Battalion

HOME STATION: Wehrkreis V

This unit was formed as Replacement Division Staff 165 just after the invasion of Poland. During its early career it was responsible for training and replacement functions in the Württemberg-Baden region. The division was stationed in the Protectorate (formerly Czechoslovakia) from

November 1939 until September 1940, when it returned to the Third Reich. In early 1942 the 165th was transferred to the Epinal area of eastern France with only its training elements; as such it was the forerunner of the reserve division system, which was adopted throughout the army in the fall of that year. After a brief tour of duty in the Vlissingen area of the Netherlands, the division took part in the occupation of Vichy France in November 1942. It remained at Vesoul, southern France, for a time before returning to southern Holland, where it was stationed until it was disbanded in the third quarter of 1944. Its personnel were sent to various divisions on the Western Front; the divisional staff was used to form the 70th Infantry Division. The 165th's commanders included Lieutenant General Hüttmann (1942) and Lieutenant General Baron Sigmund von Schacky und Schönfeld (1943).

NOTES AND SOURCES: Baron von Schacky und Schönfeld was commander of Replacement Division Staff 413 in 1945. Harrison: Map VI; RA: 6, 88, 90; OB 42: 20; OB 43: 150; OB 45: 189.

166th RESERVE DIVISION

COMPOSITION (1944): 6th Reserve Grenadier Regiment, 69th Reserve Grenadier Regiment, 6th Reserve Artillery Battalion, 26th Reserve Engineer Battalion

HOME STATION: Bielefeld, Wkr. VI

The 166th was formed as a replacement division staff by the VI (Westphalian) Military District shortly after the war began. Other than a period of occupation duty in northern Poland (November 1939 to September 1940) when it was headquartered in Danzig, the 166th spent the first four years of the war in Germany. Transferred to Copenhagen, Denmark, in early 1943, the unit became a reserve division toward the end of the year. In early 1944 it was transferred to the Lemvig area on the Jutland peninsula and remained there until the Western Front began to disintegrate in early 1945. The 166th was thrown into battle with Army Group B and was quickly overrun by the U.S. III Corps. Remnants of the division were later encircled in the Ruhr Pocket and surrendered there in April. Although American reports indicate that the 166th was an infantry division, it apparently never received an official designation as such, although it certainly fought as one. The division's commanders included Lieutenant Generals Justin von Obernitz (1943), Helmut Castore (1943-44), and Eberhard von Fabrice (1944-45).

NOTES AND SOURCES: Lieutenant General Castore led the 329th Infantry Division in Russia (1942) and the 172nd Reserve Division in Germany

(1945). General von Fabrice commanded the 183rd Infantry Division in Russia (1942), Replacement Division Staff 172 in Germany (1942-August, 1944), and then the 166th Reserve. MacDonald 1973: 355, 360; RA: 6, 102, 105; OB 43: 30.

167th INFANTRY (later VOLKSGRENADIER) DIVISION

COMPOSITION: 315th Infantry Regiment, 331st Infantry Regiment, 339th Infantry Regiment, 238th Artillery Regiment, 238th Reconnaissance Battalion, 238th Anti-Tank Battalion, 238th Engineer Battalion, 238th Signal Battalion

HOME STATION: Wehrkreis VII

Formed from Bavarian replacement-training units in January 1940, this division saw action in France before going into Russia in 1941. It took part in the Battle of Gomel in September and was with Guderian's 2nd Panzer Army in the final thrusts toward Moscow. After helping check the Russian winter offensive, the 167th was sent to Holland to rest and refit and remained on occupation duty until early 1943, when it was sent back to the Eastern Front. As part of the 4th Panzer Army it remained in reserve until the Kursk offensive failed and the Russian counterattacks began. About three weeks later, on August 3, it was attacked northwest of Belgorod by the entire Soviet 6th Guards Army. The division was utterly shattered, being reduced "to a scattering of odds and ends" by nightfall on the first day of the offensive. Because of the critical condition on the southern sector, however, the remnants of the 167th remained in action until February 1944, when they were practically wiped out in the Cherkassy encirclement. Shortly afterwards the unit was officially disbanded. Its remnants were absorbed by the 376th Infantry Division.

A second 167th was formed in Hungary in September 1944. Designated the 167th Volksgrenadier Division, it consisted of the recruits from the partially formed 585th Volksgrenadier Division and the remnants of the 17th Luftwaffe Field Division, and some miscellaneous replacements. In November it was transferred to Slovakia to complete its training and was hurriedly sent to Belgium in December, where it took part in the latter stages of Hitler's Ardennes offensive. The division remained on the Western Front until February 1945, when it was crushed by the U.S. 3rd Army in the West Wall (Siegfried Line) battles. Two of its three regimental commanders and a large number of its men were taken prisoner. The remnants of the 167th Volksgrenadier, however, continued to resist as a part of Army Group B until it was encircled and destroyed in the Battle of the Ruhr Pocket. Commanders of the 167th Infantry/Volksgrenadier included

Major General Schartow (1942), Lieutenant General Wolf Trirenberg (1943-44), and Lieutenant General Hans-Kurt Höcker (1944-45).

NOTES AND SOURCES: Trirenberg later commanded the 347th Infantry Division on the Western Front in 1945. Höcker had previously led the 258th Infantry Division (1943) and the 17th Luftwaffe Field Division (1943-44). Carell 1966: 111, 196; Carell 1971: 71; Cole 1965: 623; MacDonald 1973: 109; "Frontnachweiser," 15 December 1944; RA: 116; OB 42: 91; OB 43: 150-51; OB 44: 208; OB 45: 190.

168th INFANTRY DIVISION

COMPOSITION: 417th Infantry Regiment, 429th Infantry Regiment, 442nd Infantry Regiment, 248th Artillery Regiment, 248th Reconnaissance Battalion, 248th Anti-Tank Battalion, 248th Engineer Battalion, 248th Signal Battalion

HOME STATION: Wehrkreis VIII

Mobilized in January 1940, the 168th included previously existing replacement-training units grouped under a new divisional headquarters. It was sent to the Eastern Front in June 1941 and remained there for the rest of the war. The 168th fought in the Belgorod (or Kursk) offensive, where it suffered heavy losses in the retreat from Kursk and in the battles west of Kiev. The division remained in the line and was with the 4th Panzer Army in the Battle of Zhitomir in December. In February 1944 the 168th Infantry was on the northern flank of Army Detachment Kempf, defending Akhtyrka (in the rear of Kharkov) against heavy Russian attacks. A few days later it was encircled near Cherkassy, where it was badly shot up and practically ceased to exist. The soldiers who managed to break out of the pocket were sent to Poland, where they were allowed to rest and the division was rebuilt; however, it never again exceeded battle group strength. A few months later the 168th was returned to southern Russia, where it served with Nehring's XXIV Panzer Corps in the withdrawals to Poland. The division fought in the battles on the Vistula in early 1945 and ended the war on the central sector of the Eastern Front. The last divisional commander was probably Lieutenant General Werner Schmidt-Hammer, who was leading it in early 1945.

NOTES AND SOURCES: Lieutenant General Dietrich Kraiss commanded the 168th Infantry in 1942. Schmidt-Hammer was commander of the 668th Infantry Regiment in 1942. Major General Holm was divisional commander in September 1944, when he was relieved for overstaying his leave.

He was sentenced to six years in prison for this offense. Air University Files SRGG 1106 (c); Hartmann: 24; *Kriegstagebuch des OKW,* Volume I: 1146; Volume IV: 1896; RA: 130; OB 43: 151; OB 45: 190.

169th INFANTRY DIVISION

COMPOSITION: 378th Infantry Regiment, 379th Infantry Regiment, 392nd Infantry Regiment, 230th Artillery Regiment, 230th Reconnaissance Battalion, 230th Anti-Tank Battalion, 230th Engineer Battalion, 230th Signal Battalion

HOME STATION: Wehrkreis IX

The 169th Infantry was created in January 1940 from already existing replacement-training units. After seeing action in France in 1940, it was sent to Finland by way of Norway in 1941, and was with the XXXVI Corps on the initial drive on Murmansk. After being repulsed here, the 169th remained in Lapland for more than two years and engaged in numerous actions against the Russians, although the strategic port of Murmansk was never taken. After Finland made a separate peace with the Soviets, the 169th Infantry took part in the retreat to Norway and was functioning as a field training division in March 1945. It was still in Norway when Berlin fell. Commanders of the division included Major General Heinrich Kirchheim (1940), Lieutenant General Hermann Tittel (1943), and Major General Radziej (1944-45).

NOTES AND SOURCES: Kirchheim, a Saxon, was a tropical warfare expert. He was sent to North Africa in 1941 and was named acting commander of the 5th Light Division of the Afrika Korps. Here he ran afoul of Erwin Rommel, who blamed him for failing to take Tobruk in May 1941. Although Kirchheim was promoted to Lieutenant General in July 1942, he never held another command and spent the rest of the war on the staff at OKH. Hermann Tittel, on the other hand, was promoted to General of Artillery in September 1943 and commanded LXX Corps (late 1943-1945). Major General Radziej had formerly been commanding officer of the 143th Mountain Infantry Regiment of the 6th Mountain Division in 1942. Carell: 1966: 454; *Kriegstagebuch des OKW:* Volume IV: 1899; OB 43: 151; OB 44: 209; OB 45: 191; Ziemke 1959: 312; Ziemke 1966: 401.

170th INFANTRY DIVISION

COMPOSITION: 391st Infantry Regiment, 399th Infantry Regiment, 401st Infantry Regiment, 240th Artillery Regiment, 240th Reconnaissance Battalion, 240th Anti-Tank Battalion, 240th Engineer Battalion, 240th Signal Battalion.

HOME STATION: Bremen, Wkr. X

Created in January 1940 from previously existing replacement-training units, the 170th first fought in Denmark three months later, when it captured Aalborg and dealt with the Danish frontier positions. The next year it was assigned to the XXX Corps, 11th Army, and took part in the advance across the Ukraine and southern Russia. In October it attacked across the Tartar trench and the Perekop Isthmus, pursued the Russians across the Crimea, and took part in the Siege of Sevastopol. In July 1942 the 170th participated in the attacks that resulted in the fall of this Soviet naval fortress. That summer, as part of von Manstein's 11th Army, the 170th Infantry was transported to the northern sector of the Eastern Front for the attack on Leningrad but was tied down in heavy defensive fighting instead. Later it faced the Russian winter offensive of 1942-43 and successfully defended a sector of the German corridor east of Leningrad against heavy Soviet attacks. The division remained with Army Group North throughout 1943 and suffered heavy losses when the Russians finally broke the Siege of Leningrad in January 1944. After the retreat through Estonia, the 170th was shifted to the central sector of the Eastern Front in July and helped check the Soviet summer offensive of 1944, although it was unable to help the major portions of the German 4th and 9th Armies, which were encircled in White Russia. The 170th Infantry, meanwhile, was returned to Army Group North and took part in the retreat through Latvia. At battle group strength now, it nevertheless fought in the several unsuccessful Russian attempts to crush the Courland Pocket. The division finally surrendered in May 1945 when the war ended. Its commanders included Lieutenant Generals Walter Wittke (1940-42), Erwin Sander (1942-43), and Walther Krause (1945).

NOTES AND SOURCES: Sander was commander of the 245th Infantry Division in the Low Countries (1943-44). Carell 1966: 32, 509; Carell 1971: 242, 249, 577-92; *Kriegstagebuch des OKW*, Volume IV: 1897; Manstein: 244, 260; Salisbury: 538; RA: 160; OB 42: 91; OB 43: 151; OB 44: 209; OB 45: 191; Ziemke 1959: 35.

171st RESERVE DIVISION

COMPOSITION: 19th Reserve Grenadier Regiment, 71st Reserve Grena-Regiment 216th Reserve Grenadier Regiment, 252nd Reserve Artillery Regiment

HOME STATION: Hanover, Wkr. XI

Initially formed as a replacement division after the invasion of Poland in 1939, the 171st remained in Hanover for the first three years of the war, conducting training and supplying replacements for the divisions affiliated with the XI Military District. In autumn of 1942 the 171st lost its replacement units and was sent to the English Channel with its training elements. Posted in the Epinal area, it was redesignated 171st Infantry Division in late 1943. It was a static unit, lacking in all categories of motorized vehicles. Early in 1944 it lost its training mission, and was renamed the 48th Infantry Division. Commanders of the 171st Reserve/Infantry included Lieutenant Generals Casper (1943) and Friedrich Fürst (1943-early 1944).

ALSO SEE 48th INFANTRY DIVISION

NOTES AND SOURCES: Casper had commanded the 335th Infantry Division on the Russian Front (1942) before being given command of the 171st Reserve. He fell ill in 1943 and had to be relieved. Later he resumed command of the 48th Infantry (formerly 171st Reserve) Division. Friedrich Fürst commanded the 14th Motorized Division in 1942-43. RA: 6, 172-74; OB 43: 152; OB 45: 192. The 31st Reserve Grenadier Regiment was reportedly attached to the division in early 1944 (OB 44b: D122).

172nd RESERVE DIVISION

COMPOSITION: 34th Infantry Replacement Training Regiment, 36th Infantry Replacement Training Regiment, 33rd Artillery Replacement Training Regiment. Possibly also included 246th Infantry Replacement Training Regiment, 79th Infantry Replacement Regiment, and 35th Artillery Replacement Training Regiment (Motorized)

HOME STATION: Mainz, Wkr. XII

The 172nd was activated in September and October 1939 as a replacement division. From November 1939 to September 1940 it was stationed in the Gneseu area of Poland (Wehrkreis XXI), where it conducted training and replacement operations. It returned to Germany in 1940 and remained there until the end of the war, still controlling replacement and training units for XII Military District. It was upgraded to reserve division status in late 1944, but it apparently never engaged in combat as a unit. Commanders of the 172nd Reserve Division included Lieutenant Generals Kurt Fischer (1939-42), Eberhard von Fabrice (July 1942 to August 1944), and Helmut Castore (August 1944-1945).

NOTES AND SOURCES: Fischer went on to become Commander of Special Administrative Division Staff 412. Fabrice, former commander of the 183rd Infantry Division in Russia (1942), later took over the 166th Reserve Division from General Castore and commanded it until the end of the war. General Castore, in addition to commanding the 166th and 172nd Reserve Divisions (1943-44 and 1944-45, respectively), had previously led the 329th Infantry Division (1942). RA: 190, 192; OB 43: 152; OB 45: 192.

173rd RESERVE DIVISION

COMPOSITION: 17th Reserve Grenadier Regiment, 73rd Reserve Grenadier Regiment, 369th Reserve Grenadier Regiment, 117th Reserve Artillery Regiment

HOME STATION: Nuremberg (Würzburg?), Wkr. XIII

Created in 1939 after the Polish campaign started, this division was initially a replacement division staff. It controlled replacement and training units in northern Bavaria until September 1943. At that time it lost its replacement units, was converted into a reserve division, and sent to Belgrade. Later it was transferred to Croatia. In early 1944, for reasons that are not apparent, it was disbanded. The 173rd's commanders included Lieutenant Generals Pflugradt (1942) and von Behr (late 1942-1944).

SOURCES: OB 44b: D122; OB 45: 192

174th RESERVE DIVISION

COMPOSITION: 24th Reserve Grenadier Regiment, 209th Reserve Grenadier Regiment, 256th Reserve Grenadier Regiment, 14th Reserve Artillery Battalion, 14th Reserve Engineer Battalion

HOME STATION: Leipzig, Wkr. IV

Mobilized as the 174th Replacement Division, this unit controlled replacement-training units in Saxony and the Sudetenland from September

1939 until the fall of 1942, although elements of the division were reported in Czechoslovakia in 1941. In the latter part of 1942 it was remustered as a reserve division in Bohemia, and its replacement units were sent home. Its training elements remained under divisional control and were sent to northern Poland in 1943. In March 1944 part of the 174th went into combat on the Russian Front, while the remaining training units were sent to an area west of Radom. Later in 1944 the entire unit went into action with Army Group Center and remained on the Eastern Front until the end of the war. Apparently it surrendered to the Soviets in East Prussia in May 1945. Its commander in January 1945 was Lieutenant General Eberhardt (1944-45).

NOTES AND SOURCES: The division had previously been commanded by Lieutenant General Konrad Guhl, who was in charge on March 31, 1942. Eberhardt had previously been commander of the 44th Infantry Regiment of the 60th Motorized Division (1940-42) and the 38th Infantry Division (June 1942-late 1943). RA: 6, 204-06; OB 42: 26; OB 43: 37; OB 45: 192.

176th INFANTRY DIVISION

COMPOSITION (December 1944): 1218th Grenadier Regiment, 1219th Grenadier Regiment, 1220th Grenadier Regiment, 1176th Artillery Regiment, 176th Füsilier Battalion, 1176th Anti-Tank Battalion, 1176th Engineer Battalion, 1176th Signal Battalion

HOME STATION: Bielefeld, Wkr. VI

The 176th was formed as a replacement division staff in the fall of 1939. From November 1939 to September 1940 it was stationed in the Danzig area (Wehrkreis XX) before returning to Germany. In 1943 it absorbed the replacement elements of the 156th and 166th Reserve Divisions when they left the Reich for France and Denmark, respectively. In return the 176th gave up its own training battalions. In 1944 the subordinate elements of the 176th were reexpanded into replacement-training units. Later that year, with the Western Front on the verge of collapse, the 176th was hurried to the Albert Canal zone in the Low Countries. In September the division had a strength of seven thousand men; however, most of these were trainees, convalescents, and semiinvalids. The division also included two Luftwaffe battalions and an "ear" battalion of men with serious hearing problems. The 176th fought in the Battle of Maastricht against Montgomery and was forced to abandon both the city and the island. It also took part in the Arnhem campaign, where it helped delay forces trying to relieve the British 1st Airborne Division. In mid-November it was in action against the U.S. 9th Army in the Siegfried Line campaign and fought holding actions in the Roer River sector. The 176th did not take part in the Battle of the Bulge but was apparently resting and rebuilding at that time. This process was not complete in early 1945 when the division was assigned to the LIII Corps. As part of Army Group B it was surrounded in the Ruhr Pocket and destroyed there. Lieutenant General Berthold Stumm (1943 to December 1944) and Colonel Christian Landau (December 1944-1945) commanded the division during its combat career.

NOTES AND SOURCES: Elements of the division were attached to a special unit in the 1st Parachute Army as of March 1, 1945, and thus escaped encirclement in the Ruhr. Colonel Landau was the commander of the 248th Artillery Regiment in the 168th Infantry Division in 1944. *Kriegstagebuch des OKW*, Volume IV: 1900; MacDonald 1963: 100, 108, 188, 519; MacDonald 1973: 353-61; RA: 100, 102-03; OB 45: 193.

REPLACEMENT DIVISION STAFF 177*

COMPOSITION: 44th Infantry Replacement Training Regiment, 131st Infantry Replacement Training Regiment, 44th Artillery Replacement Training Regiment

HOME STATION: Vienna, Wkr. XVII

The 177th was formed shortly after the invasion of **Poland began** and remained headquartered at Vienna for virtually the entire war. Elements of the division were reportedly stationed in Moravia (the eastern district of the Protectorate, as the Nazis called Czechoslovakia) in 1941, but there is no indication that these were major components. The division ceased to exist in April 1945 when the Russians overran the former Austrian capital. The 177th was not with the 6th SS Panzer Army during the defense of the city so it was no doubt dissolved before the battle began and its men incorporated into combat units of other divisions on the Eastern Front. The 177th Replacement's commanders included Major Generals Reichert (1942) and Erich Müller-Derichsweiler (1944-early 1945).

SOURCES: Peter Hoffmann, *The History of the German Resistance, 1933-1945*, Cambridge, Massachusetts, the MIT Press, 1977: 275-76 (hereafter cited as "Hoffmann"); *Kriegstagebuch des OKW*, Volume I: 1145; RA: 222; OB 42: 27; OB 45: 194.

---

*Also referred to as the 177th Replacement Division and the 177th Mobilization Division; although officially designated Replacement Division Staffs, German units of this type were frequently referred to both as Replacement Divisions and Mobilization Divisions. They were primarily involved in implementing the German draft.

180th INFANTRY DIVISION

COMPOSITION (1944): 1221st Grenadier Regiment, 1222nd Grenadier Regiment, 1223rd Grenadier Regiment, 180th Artillery Regiment, 180th Füsilier Battalion, 180th Anti-Tank Battalion, 180th Engineer Battalion, 180th Signal Battalion

HOME STATION: Verden, Wkr. X

Formed as a replacement division by the X Military District in the fall of 1939, this unit conducted replacement and training operations in north-central Germany until September 1944. At that time it was hastily sent to Holland to oppose the Allied armored-airborne assault, Operation Market-Garden. It succeeded in delaying the British XXX Armored Corps long enough to significantly contribute to the German victory at Arnhem. It remained on the northern sector of the Western Front, primarily with the 1st Parachute Army, for the rest of the war. In November 1944 it was upgraded to full infantry division status. The 180th was engaged in the Venlo area from December 1944 to January 1945. In March 1945 the division opposed the Allied drive through western Germany and fought against the British 2nd Army in the Battle of Wesel. At the end of the month it was crushed in Operation Varsity, a joint airborne-ground offensive. The division's morale was broken after this defeat. A few weeks later the remnants of the division were forced into the Ruhr Pocket, where they were destroyed. Major General Bernhard Klosterkemper was the division's commander in early 1945.

NOTES AND SOURCES: Klosterkemper, who was only in his early forties, had previously commanded the 920th Grenadier Regiment and, in Normandy, simultaneously commanded the remains of two burned-out divisions: the 243rd Infantry and the 91st Air Landing. Chant, Volume 17: 2312; MacDonald 1963: Map V; MacDonald 1973: 306-11, 315, 370; RA: 160, 162; OB 45: 195.

181st INFANTRY DIVISION

COMPOSITION (1945): 334th Füsilier Grenadier Regiment, 359th Grenadier Regiment, 363rd Grenadier Regiment, 222nd Artillery Regiment, 181st Füsilier Battalion, 222nd Anti-Tank Battalion, 222nd Engineer Battalion, 222nd Signal Battalion

HOME STATION: Wehrkreis XI

Created in January 1940 from replacement-training units in Braunschweig, Anhalt, and Hanover, this division originally consisted of the 334th, 349th, and 359th Infantry Regiments. In April 1940 it took part in the Norwegian campaign, where it was lightly engaged. It remained on occupation duty in the Dombaas area until autumn 1943 when it was transferred to the lower Adriatic coast of Yugoslavia. It left the 349th Regiment in Norway and acquired the newly formed 363rd Grenadier Regiment when it arrived in the Balkans. The division suffered heavy losses in the withdrawal from Montenegro to Sarajevo but remained in the line. It fought on the southern sector of the Eastern Front from late 1944 until the end of the war. The 181st's leaders included Major General Kurt Woytasch (1940), Lieutenant General Bayer (1942-43), and Lieutenant General Hermann Fischer (1944-45).

NOTES AND SOURCES: Fischer had formerly led the 140th Infantry Regiment of the 196th Infantry Division (1940-41). Bayer took over Replacement Division Staff 408 in late 1943. *Kriegstagebuch des OKW*, Volume I: 1145; Volume IV: 1903; RA: 172; OB 43: 153; OB 44: 210; OB 45: 195; Ziemke 1959: 33-34, 263, 330.

182nd RESERVE DIVISION

Composition: 79th Reserve Grenadier Regiment, 112th Reserve Grenadier Regiment, 342nd Reserve Grenadier Regiment, 34th Reserve Artillery Regiment

HOME STATION: Koblenz, Wkr. XII

The 182nd was formed as a replacement (mobilization) division in September and October 1939. From November 1939 to September 1940 it was stationed in the Litzmannstadt area of Poland, from which it was sent to Nancy in eastern France. In autumn 1942 its replacement units returned to Germany, and the 182nd was converted to a reserve (i.e., training) division. Following reorganization it was transferred to the Channel coast, where it headquartered at Cassel in northern France. Eventually it added the 342nd Reserve Grenadier Regiment to its table of organization. In mid-May 1944, the 182nd was still being used as a training unit. It consisted of seven poorly trained battalions, four of which were soon transferred to other divisions. There were only four guns in its four infantry gun companies. Its artillery only had two issues of ammunition, and its line units only had one issue per man. For these reasons it was not committed to heavy combat during the French campaign of 1944. The division was sent east in late 1944 and by the end of November was stationed in Slovakia. Fighting against the Russians, it sustained heavy heavy casualties in early

1945 but was still resisting—albeit at battle group strength—when the war ended. Divisional commanders of the 182nd Reserve included Lieutenant General Franz Karl (1941), Major General Karl Gümbel (1942), Major General Paul Lettow (1943), Major General Otto Schilling (1943-44), and Major General Maximilian Obst (1944-45).

NOTES AND SOURCES: Karl Franz was formerly commander of the 263rd Infantry Division in France (1940). Karl Gümbel was promoted to Lieutenant General in January 1943, and assigned to command the 348th Infantry Division. Lettow, formerly Chief Ordinance Officer of Wehrkreis VIII, was apparently retired after he left the 182nd. Major General Schilling was captured on the Western Front in October, 1944. Harrison: Map VI; *Kriegstagebuch des OKW*, Volume I: 1146; Volume IV: 1893; Friedrich Ruge, *Rommel in Normandy*, Presidio Press, San Rafael, California, 1979: 161; Speidel: 41; RA: 6, 190, 193; OB 43: 153; OB 45: 196.

183rd INFANTRY (later VOLKSGRENADIER) DIVISION

COMPOSITION: 330th Infantry Regiment, 343rd Infantry Regiment, 351st Infantry Regiment, 219th Artillery Regiment, 219th Reconnaissance Battalion, 219th Anti-Tank Battalion, 219th Engineer Battalion, 219th Signal Battalion

HOME STATION: Wehrkreis XIII

This division was formed from previously existing replacement and training units in January 1940. It took part in the Balkans campaign of 1941 and was sent to Russia later that year. The 183rd was engaged in heavy fighting in the latter stages of the advance on Moscow. It remained on the central sector until after the Rzhev withdrawal, fighting in the defensive battles of 1942 and early 1943. Transferred to the southern zone of operations, the division suffered heavy losses in the Kiev fighting that autumn and in the Northern Ukraine campaign in the spring of 1944. It was surrounded with General Hauffe's XIII Corps in the Brody Pocket in Byelorussia in July. At that time it had been so reduced by casualties that it was classified as a "cadre infantry division" and placed under General Lange's Korps Formation C, an *ad hoc* unit. The 183rd broke out of the pocket and most of its survivors escaped. Withdrawn from the combat zone after Brody, the 183rd was rebuilt at the Dollersheim Maneuver Area (Wehrkreis XVII, formerly Austria) as a Volksgrenadier unit. Most of its personnel were inexperienced, poorly trained Austrians from the 564th Grenadier Division. The fighting calibre of the 183rd declined considerably after that, although it continued to achieve creditable results. It was transferred to the Western Front that fall, where it suffered heavy losses in the battles of the Siegfried Line and at Aachen. In late November it opposed the U.S. 9th Army's Roer River offensive, where the 330th Grenadier Regiment was virtually annihilated near Geilenkirchen. The division was still opposing the U.S. 9th Army when it managed to cross the Roer in February 1945. As part of Army Group B, the 183rd Volksgrenadier was surrounded in the Ruhr Pocket in April. Divisional commander Lieutenant General Wolfgang Lange, who had commanded Korps Formation C at Brody, surrendered it to the Americans at Gummersbach later that month. The divisional commanders of the 183rd Infantry/Volksgrenadier included Lieutenant General Benighus Dippold (1940-42), Major General Eberhard von Fabrice (1942), Major General Richard Stempel (1942), Lieutenant General Dettling (1943-44), and Lieutenant General Lang (1944-45).

NOTES AND SOURCES: Dippold later commanded the 717th Infantry Division (1943) and a Special Administrative Division Staff (1944-45). Eberhard von Fabrice was promoted to Lieutenant General and commanded Replacement Division Staff 172 (July 1942-August 1944) and the 166th Reserve Division (August 1944-1945). Lieutenant General Dettling was seriously wounded on the Russian Front in the summer of 1944. After he recovered he commanded the 363rd Volksgrenadier Division on the Western Front. Carell 1966: 191; Carell 1971: 309; Hartmann: 24; MacDonald 1963: 111, 530; MacDonald 1973: 153; Seaton: 446-49; RA: 204; OB 42: 92; OB 43: 153; OB 44: 210; OB 45: 196. Also see Wolfgang Lange, *Korpsabteilung C*, Vowinckel, Neckargemünd, 1961.

187th RESERVE DIVISION
see 42nd Jäger Division

189th RESERVE (later INFANTRY) DIVISION

COMPOSITION (1944): 1212th Grenadier Regiment, 1213th Grenadier Regiment, 1214th Grenadier Regiment, 1089th Artillery Regiment, 1089th Füsilier Battalion, 1089th Anti-Tank Battalion, 1089th Engineer Battalion, 1089th Signal Battalion

HOME STATION: Kassel, Wkr. IX

This division was born as Replacement Division Staff 189 in the fall of 1939. It conducted training operations in Thuringia until the latter part of 1942, when it was upgraded to reserve division status and was sent to

France with the 15th and 214th Reserve Grenadier Regiments. It also absorbed the 28th Reserve Grenadier Regiment and the 28th Reserve Artillery Battalion from Wehrkreis VIII but lost its replacement units. In November it took part in the occupation of Vichy France and headquartered in the Clermont-Ferrand area for some time. In the spring of 1944 it was transferred to southwestern France, where it formed part of Army Group G's reserve. After D-Day the 189th Division ceased training altogether and was involved in combat in southern France by August. During the retreat to Germany it was upgraded to full field division status, although it was never considered a first-rate combat unit. By late 1944 it was fighting in southern Alsace and was in the Colmar bridgehead by January 1945. It is unclear whether or not any sizable parts of the 189th escaped the bridgehead's collapse but the division headquarters did and was sent to Oberhein to rebuild the remnants. Sometime after March 1 it returned to action in southern Germany and was still fighting against the Americans when the war ended. Commanders of the 189th Reserve/Infantry included Major General von Neindorff (1943), Lieutenant General Poppe (early 1944), Major General Count Bogislav von Schwerin (1944), Major General Degener (1944), Major General Franz Bauer (1944-45), and Colonel Eduard Zorn (1945).

NOTES AND SOURCES: Lieutenant General Poppe, formerly commander of the 255th and 217th Infantry Divisions in Russia (1942-43), later led the 59th Infantry Division on the Western Front. Degener, the former Commandant of Würzburg, led a battle group in southern France in 1944 and commanded the 189th only on a temporary basis in November 1944. Zorn, the Chief Supply Officer of 19th Army, replaced Bauer after Colmar. RA: 6, 144, 146; OB 43: 33; OB 45: 197-98. Also see MacDonald 1973.

190th INFANTRY DIVISION

COMPOSITION (1945): 1224th Grenadier Regiment, 1225th Grenadier Regiment, 1226th Grenadier Regiment

HOME STATION: Neumünster, Wkr. X

The 190th Infantry was created in the fall of 1939 as a replacement division. It operated in the Schleswig-Holstein area, controlling replacement-training units for the X Military District. In mid-September 1944 it was hastily mobilized and sent to the Western Front, where it clashed with the U.S. 82nd Airborne Division near Nijmegen. It remained on the northern flank of the Western Front and in November became one of the few units to be upgraded directly from replacement to full infantry division status, skipping the reserve division phase; however, it was still strictly a makeshift unit with very little artillery support or anti-tank protection. After spending five months in Holland (where it fought in the Goch and Venlo areas), the 190th was sent south in late March 1945 to oppose the big Allied ground/parachute offensive north of the Rhine. The division was encircled in the Ruhr Pocket with Army Group B in April and was destroyed there. Its leader in early 1945 was Lieutenant General Ernst Hammer (1944-45).

NOTES AND SOURCES: General Hammer had previously commanded the 75th Infantry Division on the Eastern Front (1941-42). MacDonald 1963: Map V; MacDonald 1973: 317, 370; RA: 160, 162; OB 43: 154; OB 45: 198.

191st RESERVE DIVISION

COMPOSITION: 31st Reserve Grenadier Regiment, 267th Reserve Grenadier Regiment, 4th Reserve Engineer Battalion

HOME STATION: Braunschweig, Wkr. XI

Established as a replacement division staff, the 191st remained in the Hanover district until the fall of 1942 when it lost its replacement mission and was sent to the English Channel with its training elements. It stayed in the Boulogne area until February 1944 when it was upgraded and redesignated 49th Infantry Division. Later it was destroyed on the Western Front. Its commanders included Major General von Dewitz gennant von Krebs (1942-43), Lieutenant General Siegfried Macholz (1943-44), and Lieutenant General Erich Baessler (early 1944).

ALSO SEE 49th INFANTRY DIVISION

NOTES AND SOURCES: Erich Baessler was reportedly in command of the division in early 1944, but this was probably only a temporary arrangement, for Lieutenant General Macholz was back in charge of the division when it was redesignated. Baessler had formerly commanded the 377th Infantry Division in Russia (1942) and the 19th Luftwaffe Field Division on occupation duty (1942-43). RA: 6, 172, 174; OB 43: 154; OB 45: 198-99.

REPLACEMENT DIVISION STAFF 192

COMPOSITION: 12th Grenadier Training Regiment, 32nd Grenadier Training Regiment

HOME STATION: Schwerin and Rostock, Wkr. II

Activated in Pomerania and Mecklenberg in the fall of 1939, the 192nd was sent to the XX Military District (Danzig/northern Poland) in the latter part of 1941. It controlled replacement and training units until the Home Army divided those functions in the fall of 1942. Then the 192nd was transferred to Gnesen, Wehrkreis XXI (formerly southern Poland), with the II Military District's replacement units. By 1944 the division was essentially a training unit. It is not certain whether the 192nd was engaged in combat when the Russians overran Poland, but apparently it was not. By January 1945 the 192nd Replacement Division had been withdrawn to Pomerania and was apparently dissolved prior to the last campaign, with its men being distributed among various combat units on the Eastern Front. Its commander in early 1945 was Lieutenant General Schroeck (1944-45).

NOTES AND SOURCES: Schroeck had formerly commanded the 98th Infantry Division in the first Russian campaign (1941). RA: 32; OB 43: 154; OB 45: 199.

REPLACEMENT DIVISION STAFF 193

COMPOSITION: 10th Infantry Replacement Training Regiment, 46th Infantry Replacement Training Regiment, 296th Infantry Replacement Training Regiment, 10th Artillery Replacement Training Regiment

HOME STATION: Regensburg, Wkr. XIII

The 193rd Replacement (or Mobilization) Division was activated after the invasion of Poland began in September 1939. It controlled replacement-training units from 1939 until the fall of 1942, training units from late 1942 to 1944, and replacement-training units again from 1944 until the end of the war. It was posted in Bohemia in 1942 and headquartered at Pilsen and later at Prague, where it remained until the Russians overran Czechoslovakia. The division itself was attached to a temporary formation, Korps Group General of Artillery Moser, and was fighting as part of Panzer Corps "Grossdeutschland" of the 4th Panzer Army when the war ended. The troops of the 193rd ended up in Russian captivity. The last commander of the 193rd Replacement Division was apparently Major General Wilhelm Behrens (1944-45).

NOTES AND SOURCES: The 10th Infantry Replacement Training Regiment was originally designated the 10th Replacement Regiment (motorized). It lost its motorized function in early 1944. Major General Paul Loehning commanded the division in 1940. He was Commandant of Hanover in Wehrkreis XI in 1945. Behrens was formerly commander of the 328th Infantry Division on the Eastern Front (1942). *Kriegstagebuch des OKW*, Volume I: 1147; RA: 204, 206, 260; OB 43: 37; OB 45: 199.

196th INFANTRY DIVISION

COMPOSITION: 340th Infantry Regiment, 345th Infantry Regiment, 362nd Infantry Regiment, 233rd Artillery Regiment, 233rd Reconnaissance Company, 233rd Anti-Tank Battalion, 233rd Engineer Battalion, 233rd Signal Battalion

HOME STATION: Bielefeld, Wkr. VI

After being formed in early 1940 the new infantry division took part in the invasions of Denmark and Norway. Elements of the 196th took Copenhagen, the Danish capital, almost without loss. By 1943 it was part of the Army of Norway's reserve. In mid-1943 the 196th Infantry was replaced in Norway by the 14th Luftwaffe Field Division; however, it left the 345th Infantry Regiment behind under the control of the 199th Infantry Division. As a two-regiment division it was sent to Russia in July 1944, where it was part of Army Group Center. It suffered heavy losses in the fighting in Byelorussia and Poland. The High Command disbanded the burned-out division in late 1944. The commanders of the 196th Infantry included Lieutenant General Richard Pellengahr (1940-43), Major General Dr. Friedrich Franek (1943), Major General von Horn (1943?-44), and Colonel Klinge (1944).

NOTES AND SOURCES: After relinquishing command of the 196th, General Pellengahr retired. General Franek went on to command the 44th and 73rd Infantry Divisions and was captured by the Soviets in the summer of 1944. Horn was relieved of his command for sending in too honest a report. Air University Files, SRGG 1106 (c); RA: 100; OB 42: 92; OB 43: 154; OB 44: 211; OB 45: 199. The 196th was absent from Army Group Center's Order of Battle as early as September 16, 1944 (*Kriegstagebuch des OKW*, Volume IV: 1874-83).

197th INFANTRY DIVISION

COMPOSITION: 321st Infantry Regiment, 332nd Infantry Regiment, 347th Infantry Regiment, 229th Artillery Regiment, 229th Reconnaissance Battalion, 229th Anti-Tank Battalion, 229th Engineer Battalion, 229th Signal Battalion

HOME STATION: Speyer, Wkr. XII

Raised in the Rhineland and Hesse from existing replacement-training units in January 1940, the 197th Infantry was sent to the central sector of the Russian Front in June 1941 and remained there throughout its career. It played a prominent role in the minor battle of encirclement at Roslavl in August, fought in the Battle of the Bialystok-Minsk Pocket and in the battles around Moscow in December 1941 and January 1942. Engaged in skirmishing and the defensive battles of Army Group Center in 1942, the 197th also took part in the Rzhev withdrawal in early 1943 and in the fighting west of Smolensk in the fall of 1943 before being destroyed in the huge Soviet offensive in the summer of 1944. The division broke up that July near Vitebsk, along with much of the 3rd Panzer Army and the bulk of the 4th Army. The last commander of the 197th Infantry Division, Colonel Hahne, is still missing and was presumably killed. Previous divisional commanders include Lieutenant Generals Hermann Meyer-Kabingen (1940-42) and Ehrenfried Boege (1943).

NOTES AND SOURCES: Meyer-Kabingen was commander of the 159th Reserve Division (1943-44) before being promoted to General of Infantry in late 1944. He fought his last battle against the Russians as Commander of Fortress Frankfurt-on-the-Oder in 1945. Boege was rapidly promoted and, as General of Infantry, took over command of XLIII Corps in the summer of 1944. Carell 1966: 66, 330, 350; Carell 1971: 309, 597; RA: 188; OB 42: 92; OB 43: 155; OB 44: 211; OB 45: 200.

198th INFANTRY DIVISION

COMPOSITION: 305th Infantry Regiment, 308th Infantry Regiment, 326th Regiment, 235th Artillery Regiment, 235th Reconnaissance Battalion, 235th Anti-Tank Battalion, 235th Engineer Battalion, 235th Signal Battalion

HOME STATION: Wehrkreis V

Mobilized in early 1940, the 198th consisted mainly of previously existing replacement-training units. It also incorporated the 33rd Infantry

Regiment, which included a large number of thirty-five to forty-five year-old men, into its organization as the 326th Infantry Regiment. The division was involved in the invasion of Denmark and helped occupy the capital of Copenhagen on April 9, 1940. It was sent to France in July of that year but did not see any action in the Western campaign. It invaded Russia as a part of Army Group South in 1941 and was in the Caucasus and Kuban campaigns of 1942-43. The division took part in the capture of Novorossiysk, a major Russian naval base on the Black Sea, in the summer of 1942, served in the rearguard of the 17th Army on the retreat back into the Kuban, and was involved in the seven-month Siege of Novorossiysk, beginning shortly after the Russian amphibious landing there in February 1943. Later that year the 198th suffered heavy losses in the Crimean withdrawal and the Battle of Tarnopol. It also fought in the Battle of Kiev in November 1943. The 198th Infantry was encircled at Cherkassy in February 1944 and, although it managed to break out and escape, it suffered heavy losses in men and equipment. Pulled out of the line in May 1944, it was reformed at Milowitz, using elements of the temporary Infantry Division Böhmen. Subsequently transferred to the French Mediterranean coast, it faced the Allied invasion of southern France in August 1944 and suffered heavy casualties once again in the withdrawal to southern Alsace. Almost continuously engaged for seven months, the 198th was part of Himmler's abortive attempt to take Strasbourg in January 1945. By the end of the month it was down to a strength of 6,891 men, about half its normal establishment. In March 1945 the division was crushed when the Colmar bridgehead was overrun; however, minor elements managed to escape across the Rhine and continued to serve on the Western Front until the end of the war a few weeks later. The 198th's divisional commanders included Major General Albert Buck (1941-42), Lieutenant General Kurt Oppenlander (1942), Major General Lüdwig Muller (1943), Lieutenant General Hans-Joachim von Horn (late 1943-1944), Major General Otto Richter (1944), and Major General Schiel (1944-45).

NOTES AND SOURCES: Lieutenant General von Horn, former Military Attaché to Helsinki (1943), was Military Attaché to Bern, Switzerland in 1945. Otto Richter was captured by the Russians in August 1944. Schiel, formerly of the General Staff's Transportation Branch, commanded the 326th Grenadier Regiment of the 198th before assuming divisional command. Carell 1966: 31, 559-60; Carell 1971: 159, 186; Chant, Volume 14: 1914; Volume 17: 2274, 2277; *Kriegstagebuch des OKW*, Volume I: 1147; Manstein: 488; OB 43: 155; OB 45: 200-01; Ziemke 1959: 61.

199th INFANTRY DIVISION

COMPOSITION (1943): 341st Infantry Regiment, 357th Infantry Regiment, 410th Infantry Regiment, 199th Artillery Regiment, 199th Reconnaissance Battalion, 199th Anti-Tank Battalion, 199th Engineer Battalion, 199th Signal Battalion

HOME STATION: Düsseldorf, Wkr. V

This division was formed in the autumn of 1939 from previously mobilized Landwehr (older age group) regiments. It was reported in Poland in September 1939 but did not take a major part in the fighting, although it may have done some mopping-up work. Apparently the 199th was judged unfit for prolonged combat, because of the age of its men; however, it was kept in existence as an occupation force. In late 1940 the division was sent to Oslo, Norway, and from the end of 1940 until May 1941 was on garrison duty in the central part of the country. During the period May to December 1941 it was in northern Norway and Finland but was not involved in combat against the Russians. Returned to Norway in late 1941, it remained on garrison duty in the Tromsö and Narvik areas of central and northern Norway for the rest of the war. Its commanders included Lieutenant Generals Hans von Kempski (1942-43), Raithel (1943), and Hellwig Luz (late 1944-45).

NOTES AND SOURCES: Hans von Kempski commanded the Rear Area of the 20th Mountain Army in Norway in 1945. Raithel was in charge of Artillery School II at Gross-Born in early 1945. Luz had served as Liquidation Officer for 6th Army (beginning in March 1943) and 6th Army and Army Group Afrika (May 1943-late 1944) before taking over the 199th Infantry. RA: 100; OB 42: 92-93; OB 43: 155; OB 45: 201.

201st SECURITY DIVISION

COMPOSITION: 406th Security Regiment, 601st Security Regiment, 466th Füsilier Company, 466th Anti-Tank Company, 466th Engineer Company, 466th Signal Company

HOME STATION: Wehrkreis IX

Created by the expansion of the 201st Security Brigade in the summer of 1942, this division was initially responsible for area-rear security in Army Group North. In September 1942 it was transferred to Army Group Center, where it protected installations and performed line of communications duties for a year. In September 1943 it was sent to the front lines. Back in the rear area by June 1944, it nevertheless suffered heavy casualties near Minsk, where the bulk of the 9th Army was destroyed. Part of the 201st Security Division escaped to the north and spent the rest of the war in the rear area of Army Group North (later Courland), in the Courland Pocket. Apparently Lieutenant General Alfred Jacobi (1942-45) commanded the 201st throughout its existence.

NOTES AND SOURCES: *Kriegstagebuch des OKW*, Volume IV: 1897; Carell 1971: 577-97; OB 43: 212; OB 45: 201

203rd SECURITY DIVISION

COMPOSITION: 613th Security Regiment, 930th Security Regiment, 931st Security Regiment (?), 203rd Füsilier Company, 203rd Anti-Tank Company, 203rd Engineer Company, 203rd Signal Company

HOME STATION: Wehrkreis III

Formed in the summer of 1942 by the expansion of the 203rd Security Brigade, this and other security divisions reflect the growing concern of the High Command for the rear areas of their eastern armies, then plagued by partisan activity. Initially assigned to Army Group Center, the 203rd was sent to the southern sector that fall and saw front-line action near Kiev in the latter part of 1943. Returned to the central zone in March 1944, it suffered heavy losses against the Soviet summer offensive three months later. Nevertheless, it continued in action on the Eastern Front until the end of the war. As late as March 1945 the 203rd was reported as in remnants but still resisting the Soviet advance through Pomerania and eastern Germany. Its commander in 1945 was Lieutenant General Pilz.

NOTES AND SOURCES: Pilz had formerly commanded the 121st Grenadier Regiment. *Kriegstagebuch des OKW*, Volume IV: 1898; RA: 46; OB 43: 213; OB 45: 202.

205th INFANTRY DIVISION

COMPOSITION: 335th Infantry Regiment, 353rd Infantry Regiment, 358th Infantry Regiment, 205th Artillery Regiment, 205th Reconnaissance Company, 205th Anti-Tank Battalion, 205th Engineer Battalion, 205th Signal Battalion

HOME STATION: Ulm, Wkr. V

This Württemberg-Baden division was activated as a Landwehr unit in the summer of 1940. Later most of its older personnel were replaced by younger men. It was on garrison duty in France in 1941 but was hurriedly sent to the Russian Front after the Soviet winter offensive began. With Army Group Center it held positions north of the Moscow-Smolensk Highway against heavy Communist attacks. The 205th remained with the 9th Army, Army Group Center, throughout 1942 and much of 1943 but was transferred to Army Group North that autumn. It proved to be an excellent defensive division in all its engagements. In Latvia in 1944 for example, it held off five Soviet Guard divisions for four days, and destroyed forty-one enemy tanks in the process. It was isolated in the Courland Pocket after the retreat through the Baltic States that fall and remained "in the pocket" for the rest of the war. Its commanders included Lieutenant General Richter (1942-43) and Lieutenant General Horst von Mellenthin (1943-44).

NOTES AND SOURCES: Richter later was given a corps-level command in Copenhagen. Mellenthin, whose brother Frederick Wilhelm was Chief of Staff of Army Group G in the West, received a corps command on the Eastern Front in 1945. Carell 1966: 385, 390; Hartmann: 24-25; von Mellenthin 1977: 140-41; RA: 86; OB 42: 93; OB 43: 156; OB 45: 202.

206th INFANTRY DIVISION

COMPOSITION: 301st Infantry Regiment, 312th Infantry Regiment, 413th Infantry Regiment, 206th Artillery Regiment, 206th Reconnaissance Company, 206th Anti-Tank Battalion, 206th Engineer Battalion, 206th Signal Battalion

HOME STATION: Gumbinnen, Wkr. I

Formed upon mobilization in 1939, this East Prussian unit initially consisted of a high portion of older (Landwehr) personnel. Later, an infusion of younger troops gave the division's soldiery a normal age distribution. It served in Poland in 1939, remained there as part of OKH's eastern reserve in 1940, and was involved in the Russian campaign from the beginning. It was led by Lieutenant General Hugo Hofl from 1939 to 1944. Along with the 26th Infantry Division, the 206th took Rzhev on the Volga River between Moscow and Leningrad in October 1941; however, the division was shattered by Russian counterattacks near Moscow from December 22, 1941, to January 4, 1942. Later that month it was briefly surrounded, along with the XXIII Corps, south of Lake Volga. It remained with Army Group Center for the rest of its existence, taking part in the defensive battles of 1942, the Rzhev withdrawal in March 1943, and the Battle of Smolensk (August 1943), among others. As part of LIII Corps, 3rd Panzer Army, the division was crushed by the massive Soviet summer offensive of 1944. Encircled at Vitebsk and ordered to stay there by Adolf Hitler himself, the divisional commander, Lieutenant General Alfons Hitter, ordered a breakout on his own responsibility. Only a few of the division's twelve thousand men managed to escape, however; General Hitter was among those taken prisoner. On July 18, 1944, the demobilization office officially declared the historic East Prussian 301st, 312th, and 413th Grenadier Regiments disbanded, and the 206th Infantry Division dead.

NOTES AND SOURCES: A few days before Hitter's breakout attempt at Vitebsk, LIII Corps also attempted to break out of the encirclement. Like the 206th Infantry, few of its men escaped. Corps commander General Gollwitzer and most of his men were captured. Carell 1966: 357, 360-62, 394; Carell 1971: 305, 309, 586, 597; Kennedy: 74; *Kriegstagebuch des OKW*, Volume I: 1122; Seaton: 438-39; OB 43: 156; OB 44: 212; OB 45: 202-03.

207th INFANTRY (later SECURITY) DIVISION

COMPOSITION (1942): 322nd Security Regiment, 374th Security Regiment, 207th Reconnaissance Company, 207th Anti-Tank Company, 207th Engineer Company, 207th Signal Company

HOME STATION: Stargard, Wkr. II

Formed as an infantry division in the summer of 1939, the 207th fought in Poland, where it attacked from Pomerania toward Danzig and played a major role in cutting the Polish corridor in the first week of the war. Not involved in the French campaign (as it was part of OKH's eastern reserve in Poland), the 207th was converted to a security division in the winter of 1940-41, and was stripped of one of its three infantry regiments and all its artillery. During the Russian campaign the division performed line of communications and security operations for Army Group North, although it did see action as a "mopping-up" unit, particularly in the Lake Ladoga area. It headquartered at Tartu, Estonia, for much of the 1941-44 period. The 207th Security was thrown into the main battle line against the Russian summer offensive of 1944 and suffered such heavy casualties that it had to be disbanded. The division's commanders were Lieutenant General Karl von Tiedemann (1939-43) and Major General Paul Hoffman (1944).

NOTES AND SOURCES: General Hoffman was commander of the 382nd Field Training Division in Russia in 1942. Following the destruction of the 207th Security, he went into retirement. Carell 1971: 260; Kennedy: 74 and Map 7; *Kriegstagebuch des OKW*, Volume I: 1122; OB 42: 114; OB 43: 114; OB 45: 203.

208th INFANTRY DIVISION

COMPOSITION: 309th Infantry Regiment, 337th Infantry Regiment, 338th Infantry Regiment, 208th Artillery Regiment, 208th Reconnaissance Company, 208th Anti-Tank Battalion, 208th Engineer Battalion, 208th Signal Battalion

HOME STATION: Cottbus, Wkr III

Formed during mobilization in June 1939, this division consisted mainly of Prussian Landwehr (ages 35-45) in the beginning. It was lightly engaged in Poland and France and remained in northern France and Belgium until December 1941. During this time it incorporated a large number of young men into its ranks, and its age structure became normal. Rushed to Russia in an emergency situation in the winter of 1941-42, it was initially split up, with one infantry regiment going to the 4th Army and the remaining two joining the 9th Army. The 208th was later reunited and remained on the Eastern Front for the rest of the war. Later it fought at Kursk and suffered heavy losses in the northern Ukraine. It was fighting in southern Poland in autumn 1944. The 208th ended the war in the pocket east of Prague in May 1945. The divisional commanders of this unit were Lieutenant Generals Moritz Andreas (1939-42), Hans-Karl von Schelle (1942-43), Karl von Schlieben (1943-44), and Hans Piekenbrock (1945).

NOTES AND SOURCES: Andreas was commander of prisoner of war camps in 1945. Schelle went on to command Korps Schelle, an *ad hoc* formation in Russia in 1943. Later that year he was acting commander of LIII Corps and commander of LII Corps. He was commanding general of the OKW Patrol Service in 1943-44 and President of the Supreme Military Court in 1945. Hans Piekenbrock was one of the most efficient members of the Abwehr (OKW's Intelligence Service) until he left it in early 1943. Carell 1966: 408-09, Kennedy: 74; RA: 46; OB 42: 92; OB 43: 156; OB 45: 203. Also see Heinz Höhne, *Canaris,* Doubleday and Company, Garden City, New York, 1979, for the story of Lieutenant General Piekenbrock's intelligence service career (hereafter cited as "Höhne 1979").

209th INFANTRY DIVISION

COMPOSITION: 304th Infantry Regiment, 394th Infantry Regiment, 414th Infantry Regiment

HOME STATION: Wehrkreis IV

Organized upon mobilization, the 209th consisted of Saxon personnel from the older age groups. It never left Germany. After the French campaign it was disbanded, except for the 414th Infantry Regiment, which was assigned to the 122nd Infantry Division.

SOURCES: *Kriegstagebuch des OKW*, Volume I: 1123; RA: 72; OB 42: 94; OB 45: 204.

210th COASTAL DEFENSE DIVISION

COMPOSITION: 388th Grenadier Regiment (attached), (?) Fortress Regiment, 210th Artillery Regiment

HOME STATION: Norway

The divisional headquarters of the 210th was created in June 1942 and sent to Norway to assume control of five fortress battalions on the Arctic coast. The 388th Infantry Regiment of the 214th Infantry Division was also attached to the 210th. It was soon sent to Lapland in northern Finland/ Russia and remained there until the Finnish capitulation. It took part in the retreat back to Norway with the XIX Mountain Corps. Posted at Trondheim in central Norway (with Fortress Brigade Lofoten attached), the 210th was still on coastal defense duty when the Third Reich fell. Its commanders included Lieutenant General Karl Wintergerst (1943-44) and Major General Kurt Ebeling (1945).

NOTES AND SOURCES: Major General Ebeling was in charge of the Thorn Artillery School (1942) and Artillery Officers' Training School III at Suippes, France (1943). *Kriegstagebuch des OKW*, Volume IV: 1899; OB 43: 158; OB 44: 214; OB 44b: D81; OB 45: 204; Ziemke 1959; 230, 245, 303; Ziemke 1966: 399.

211th INFANTRY (later VOLKSGRENADIER) DIVISION

COMPOSITION: 306th Infantry Regiment, 317th Infantry Regiment, 365th Infantry Regiment, 211th Artillery Regiment, 211th Reconnaissance Battalion, 211th Anti-Tank Battalion, 211th Engineer Battalion, 211th Signal Battalion.

HOME STATION: Wehrkreis VI

Activated upon mobilization, this division was made up of Landwehr personnel from Cologne. It was in southwestern France on occupation duty in 1941, where its personnel age structure was made normal. In January 1942 it was sent to Russia, where the Soviet winter offensive had created a major crisis. It remained with Army Group Center for two years, where it was involved in heavy fighting at Kursk, Nevel, and in White Russia in the summer of 1944. The division was pulled out of the line in late 1944 and reformed as a Volksgrenadier unit, but was back in action (at battle group strength) on the southern sector of the Eastern Front in January 1945 and was in Austria when Germany surrendered. The division's commanders included Lieutenant General Theodor Renner (1942), Lieutenant General Richard Müller (1943), Major General Dr. Gotthold Schaeler (1943), and Lieutenant General Heinrich Eckhardt (1943-45).

NOTES AND SOURCES: Schaeler became Commandant of Lille, northern France, and was captured by the Western Allies in 1944. *Kriegstagebuch des OKW,* Volume I: 1145; RA: 100; OB 42: 94; OB 43: 157; OB 45: 204.

212th INFANTRY (later VOLKSGRENADIER) DIVISION

COMPOSITION: 316th Infantry Regiment, 320th Infantry Regiment, 323rd Infantry Regiment, 212th Artillery Regiment, 212th Cyclist Company, 212th Anti-Tank Battalion, 212th Engineer Battalion, 212th Signal Battalion

HOME STATION: Munich, Wkr. VII

Initially consisting of southern Bavarians from the older age groups, this division was on the Saar Front while the bulk of the German Army overran Poland in 1939. The next year it took part in the French campaign with Army Group C. Its older personnel were largely replaced by younger men before the 212th was sent to the central sector of the Russian Front in the winter of 1941-42. In 1942 it joined Army Group North and repulsed several heavy Soviet attacks in the Second Battle of Lake Ladoga in early 1943. The division suffered heavy casualties in the retreat through Lithuania in the summer of 1944. Completely shattered, the 212th was withdrawn to Poland and rebuilt as a Volksgrenadier division with recruits from Upper Bavaria. Its new personnel were better than average for the fifth year of the war, but the rebuilt 212th still had too high a proportion of seventeen-year-olds. The division returned to action on the Western Front, fought at Trier and Echternach, and took heavy losses in the Battle of the Bulge. It lost about four thousand men in this operation in December 1944 and January 1945; the average rifle company's strength was reduced to twenty-five to thirty men. In February 1945 the 212th Volksgrenadier was smashed by the U.S. 3rd Army in the West Wall battles but remained in action to the end, resisting the Allied sweep through southern Germany at the last. The division's commanders included Lieutenant General Theodore Endres (1942-43), Major General Reymann (1943), Major General Dr. Karl Koske (1944), and Lieutenant General Franz Sensfuss (1944-45).

NOTES AND SOURCES: The 212th absorbed the 578th Grenadier Division in the winter of 1944. Dr. Koske had previously commanded the 245th Artillery Regiment. General Sensfuss was a fortress engineer and had formerly been associated with Fortress Command III. Hellmuth Reymann, who was promoted to Lieutenant General in April 1943, later commanded the 13th Luftwaffe Field Division (1943-44). Carell 1971: 280; Cole 1965: 214, 507; "Frontnachweiser," 15 December 1944; *Kriegstagebuch des OKW*, Volume I: 1147; Volume III: 1158; MacDonald 1973: 100, 105; RA: 116; OB 42: 94; OB 43: 158; OB 45: 205.

213th INFANTRY (later SECURITY) DIVISION

COMPOSITION (1942): 318th Reinforced Infantry Regiment, 254th Reinforced Infantry Regiment, 213th Cyclist Company, 213th Engineer Battalion, 213th Signal Company

HOME STATION: Glogau, Wkr. VIII

The 213th was formed as an infantry division in the Breslau area in June 1939. It played a minor role in the Polish campaign and did not see action in France. In the winter of 1940-41 it was converted into a security division, losing an infantry regiment and all of its artillery in the process. From 1941 until the summer of 1943 it performed line of communications duties in the rear areas of Army Groups South, B, Don, and South, again, in July 1943. Elements of the division were on the front lines as early as April 22, 1942 when one regiment was used to support the Italian "Celere" Infantry Division on the southern sector of the Russian Front. In the fall of 1943 the entire division was on the front line (half attached to the 75th Infantry Division and half to the 88th Infantry Division), where it fought in the Battle of Kiev. Later the 213th Security suffered very heavy losses in the Cherkassy Pocket in early 1944. It was nevertheless back in action on the central sector in July 1944, after the bulk of the 4th and 9th Armies was encircled near Minsk and Vitebsk. It remained on the Eastern Front for the rest of 1944 but was dissolved in early 1945. The 213th Security's commanders included Lieutenant Generals Rene de l'Homme de Courbiere (1939-42) and Alexander Goeschen (August 1942-1945).

NOTES AND SOURCES: Lieutenant General de Courbiere later commanded the 153rd Reserve Division (1943) and the 338th Infantry Division on the

Western Front. Goeschen, a cavalry officer, was Commandant of Bamberg, Wehrkreis XIII, in 1940. Kennedy: 74 and Map 7; *Kriegstagebuch des OKW*, Volume II: 1359-60, 1374, 1387; Volume III: 4, 258, 1156; RA: 130; OB 42: 114; OB 43: 213; OB 44: 215; OB 45: 205.

214th INFANTRY DIVISION

COMPOSITION (1940): 355th Infantry Regiment, 367th Infantry Regiment, 388th Infantry Regiment, 214th Artillery Regiment, 214th Reconnaissance Battalion, 214th Anti-Tank Battalion, 214th Engineer Battalion, 214th Signal Battalion

HOME STATION: Hanau, Wkr. IX

In June 1939 this division was mustered into service. It was made up of older personnel from the Frankfurt-on-Main area. They served on the Saar Front in 1939, and took part in the Norwegian campaign in 1940. Remaining in Scandinavia, its 388th Infantry Regiment was transferred to the 210th Coastal Defense Division in Finland in September 1941. In February 1944 this two-regiment division was sent to the Eastern Front and was with Army Group North in the retreat from Leningrad and in the Battle of the Narva. In the spring of 1944 it was transferred to Poland, where it fought as a part of Army Group North Ukraine in the autumn of 1944. It fought in the Hungarian campaign in November 1944, where it was virtually destroyed. It was disbanded in very late 1944 or early 1945. Lieutenant General Max Horn (1942-44) commanded it for much of its career.

SOURCES: *Kriegstagebuch des OKW*, Volume IV: 1875, 1886; RA: 144; OB 43: 158; OB 45: 206; Ziemke 1959: 85, 267.

215th INFANTRY DIVISION

COMPOSITION: 380th Infantry Regiment, 390th Infantry Regiment, 435th Infantry Regiment, 215th Artillery Regiment, 215th Reconnaissance Battalion, 215th Anti-Tank Battalion, 215th Engineer Battalion, 215th Signal Battalion

HOME STATION: Heilbronn, Wkr. V

Created upon mobilization in 1939, the 215th consisted of older men from Baden and Württemberg. Later its age structure was made normal by troop transfers. It played a minor part in the French campaign under Lieutenant General Baptist Kniess (1940-late 1942) and stayed in central France until the first crisis developed on the Russian Front in late 1941. It fought in the Battle of the Volkhov south of Leningrad from January to March 1942 and remained on the northern sector of the Eastern Front until the end of the war. It fought in the Siege of Leningrad, the Battle of the Narva, and was in the retreat through the Baltic States. It was cited for its conduct in the defeat of the Soviet attempts to overrun the Courland Pocket in late 1944. The 215th was still in western Latvia when the war ended. Its commander in 1945 was Lieutenant General Bruno Frankewitz (1943-45).

NOTES AND SOURCES: Kniess was named commander of the LXVI Corps on November 12, 1942, and was promoted to General of Infantry the following month. Frankewitz had previously commanded the 9th Panzer Division (early 1943). Carell 1966: 420-21, 423; Vivian Rowe, *The Great Wall of France: The Triumph of the Maginot Line*, G.P. Putnam's Sons, New York, 1967: 273, 304 (hereafter cited as "Roue"); RA: 86; OB 42: 95; OB 43: 158; OB 44: 215; OB 45: 206.

216th INFANTRY DIVISION

COMPOSITION: 348th Infantry Regiment, 396th Infantry Regiment, 398th Infantry Regiment, 216th Artillery Regiment, 216th Reconnaissance Battalion, 216th Anti-Tank Battalion, 216th Engineer Battalion, 216th Signal Battalion

HOME STATION: Hameln, Wkr. XI

Made up of Landwehr personnel from Hanover, the 216th fought in Poland and Flanders before its age structure was made normal. In late 1941 it was transferred to Russia and was disembarking from the trains at Sukhinitchi—one of 4th Army's main ammunition dumps—when it was surrounded by the Soviet 10th Army. The divisional headquarters, one and a half battalions of the 396th Infantry Regiment and one battalion of the 348th Infantry Regiment had arrived on January 3, 1942, when the battle began. With only four thousand divisional troops and one thousand supply troops and Soviet volunteers, the 216th under divisional commander Lieutenant General Baron von und zu Gilsa held the town against repeated enemy attacks. Later rescued, the division was reunited and remained with Army Group Center, fought in the defensive battles of 1942, and suffered very heavy losses at Kursk in July 1943. Again heavily engaged in the winter of 1943-44, it took so many casualties that it had to be disbanded. Its surviving personnel were absorbed by the 102nd Infantry Division. The divisional staff was reported as still in existence by the U.S. Military Intelligence in late 1944, but this is unlikely. The division's commanders included Lieutenant Generals Hermann Boettcher (1940), Baron von und zu Gilsa (1941-43), and Gimmler (1943-44).

NOTES AND SOURCES: Boettcher, a Hanoverian, went on to command the

148th Reserve Division (1942), the LXVII Reserve Corps (early 1944) and an army rear area (1945). Baron von und zu Gilsa led the elite 9th (Potsdam) Infantry Regiment in 1940 before being given command of the 216th. Promoted to General of Infantry in early 1943, he led the LXXXIX Corps in the West from mid-1943 until late 1944. Carell 1966: 411; Carell 1971: 26, 30; Seaton: 237; OB 43: 159; OB 44: 216; OB 45: 206. Also see M. Jenner, *Die 216/272 Niedersächsische Infanterie-Division*, Podzun, Bad Nauheim, 1964.

217th INFANTRY (later VOLKSGRENADIER) DIVISION

COMPOSITION: 311th Infantry Regiment, 346th Infantry Regiment, 389th Infantry Regiment, 217th Artillery Regiment, 217th Reconnaissance Battalion, 217th Anti-Tank Battalion, 217th Engineer Battalion, 217th Signal Battalion

HOME STATION: Allenstein, Wkr. I

The 217th Infantry was mobilized in June 1939 from Landwehr personnel in East Prussia. Later (probably in mid-1942) its age structure was made normal. It fought in Poland and France in 1939 and 1940, respectively, and was in the initial invasion of Russia but was mainly involved in coastal defense duties for Army Group North. Sent to the southern sector of the Eastern Front in the fall of 1943, it suffered heavy losses in the battles around Kiev. It was sent west to rebuild, redesignated a Volksgrenadier unit, and was subsequently attached to the 19th Army on the Rhone River in France. Later in 1944 it was returned to the Eastern Front and was surrounded in the Brody Pocket in White Russia in the summer of 1944. It broke out but with ruinous losses. Remaining on the line, it was overrun in December 1944 on the first day of the Soviet offensive between the Danube and Lake Balaton and casualties were so high that it had to be disbanded. Its commanders included Lieutenant Generals Richard Baltzer (1940-41) and Poppe (1943-44).

NOTES AND SOURCES: Baltzer later commanded the 156th Reserve Division. Poppe commanded four divisions in the last three years of the war: the 255th Infantry (1943), the 217th (late 1943-44), the 189th Reserve (1944) and the 59th Infantry (1944-45). Chant, Volume 14: 1914; Volume 15: 2057; Lange: 9-116; Kennedy: 74 and Map 7; Seaton: 446-49; RA: 20; OB 42: 96; OB 43: 159; OB 44: 216; OB 45: 207.

218th INFANTRY DIVISION

COMPOSITION: 323rd Infantry Regiment, 386th Infantry Regiment, 397th Infantry Regiment, 218th Artillery Regiment, 218th Reconnaissance Battalion, 218th Anti-Tank Battalion, 218th Engineer Battalion, 218th Signal Battalion

HOME STATION: Spandau, Berlin, Wkr. III

This Landwehr division was mobilized in 1939, and distinguished itself in Poland (1939) and France (1940). It was on occupation duty in Denmark in 1941, when its age structure was made normal. Sent to Russia in late 1941, it fought in all the major campaigns of Army Group North from then until the end of the war. Much of the 218th was encircled at Kholm from January 28 to May 5, 1942, before being rescued. Elements of the division, including the 218th Artillery Regiment, took part in the relief of the Kholm garrison that spring. From its arrival in Russia until the early winter of 1942-43 elements of the division were attached to a variety of other units, and the entire division was not reunited under its own headquarters until December 1943. After the Siege of Leningrad was broken in late January 1944, the 218th Infantry fought in the retreat across Estonia and was cited for distinguished conduct in the defense of the Saare Island (Ösel) in October 1944. In remnants by November, the division still fought against the Soviet attempts to crush the Courland Pocket. It ended the war there in western Latvia. Divisional commanders of this unit included Major General Baron Horst von Uckermann (1943) and Lieutenant General Viktor Lang (1942-43 and 1945).

NOTES AND SOURCES: Baron von Uckermann later commanded the 160th Reserve Division in Denmark (1943-September 1944). Viktor Lang led the 442nd Infantry Regiment from 1941 to February 14, 1942. He was promoted to Major General in July 1942 and to Lieutenant General in early 1943. Carell 1966: 435; Hartmann: 25; *Kriegstagebuch des OKW*, Volume I: 1144; Volume II: 1358, 1368-69, 1375-76, 1388-89; Volume III: 7, 260; Volume IV: 1888; James Lucas, *War on the Eastern Front, 1941-1945*, Stein and Day, New York, 1979: 197, 200; RA: 46; OB 42: 96; OB 43: 159; OB 45: 207.

221st INFANTRY (later SECURITY) DIVISION

COMPOSITION: 350th Security Regiment, 360th Security Regiment, 221st Füsilier Battalion (Cyclist), 221st Anti-Tank Company, 221st Engineer Company, 221st Signal Company

HOME STATION: Breslau, Wkr. VIII

Formed from Silesian personnel in 1939, the 221st Infantry fought in Poland in 1939. As part of the German 7th Army it may have been lightly engaged in skirmishing against the Maginot Line in the French campaign of 1940, although it was certainly not heavily engaged. After a Christmas furlough in 1940, it returned to Wehrkreis VIII and began converting into a security division, losing an infantry regiment, all of its artillery, and some of its supporting units. Initially the new security division consisted of the 350th and 375th Reinforced Infantry Regiments. Assigned to line of communications duties on the central sector of the Russian Front in 1941, elements of the division were involved in front-line combat as early as January 1942. The 221st Security fought in the retreat from Moscow and, except for the period January to April 1943, all or part of the division was on the front line from then until it was smashed at Minsk during the Russian summer offensive of 1944. The remnants of the 221st Security Division were disbanded soon after. The commanders of the division were Lieutenant Generals Johann Pflugbeil (1939-42) and Lendle (1943-44).

NOTES AND SOURCES: Although the 221st lost all its artillery during its conversion to a security division, it spent so much time on the front lines of Army Group Center that it was decided it needed its own artillery battalion, and the 221st Artillery was formed. As a rule, security divisions had no artillery whatsoever. Lieutenant General Pflugbeil was commander of the 388th Field Training Division in Russia (1942-44) and later became Commandant of Mitan, a city in Latvia in the rear area of Army Group North (1944). Kennedy: 74 and Map 7; *Kriegstagebuch des OKW*, Volume I: 1123, 1127; Volume II: 1356, 1369, 1374, 1387-88; Volume III: 7, 259, 733, 1157; Volume IV: 1888-89; RA: 130; OB 42: 114; OB 43: 214; OB 45: 208.

223rd INFANTRY DIVISION

COMPOSITION: 344th Infantry Regiment, 385th Infantry Regiment, 425th Infantry Regiment, 223rd Artillery Regiment, 223rd Reconnaissance Battalion, 223rd Anti-Tank Battalion, 223rd Engineer Battalion, 223rd Signal Battalion

HOME STATION: Dresden, Wkr. IV

Created from older personnel in 1939, the 223rd fought in France the next year and remained in southwestern France until late 1941. Sent to Army Group North in December 1941, it fought against the Soviet winter offensive of 1941-42, and in the Battle of Lake Ladoga (August-September 1942). Shifted to the southern sector in the summer of 1943, it was heavily engaged from the outset. In late 1943 it was virtually destroyed in the Battle of Kiev. Most of its survivors were incorporated into the 275th Infantry Division. Major General Christian Usinger (1942-43) was the last reported commander of the 223rd Infantry.

NOTES AND SOURCES: An artillery officer, Usinger commanded Artilleriekommand 110 (or Arko 110, a corps-level artillery command) from April 27 to October 20, 1942, when he assumed command of the 223rd as a Colonel. He was promoted to Major General on December 1, 1942. *Kriegstagebuch des OKW*, Volume II; Hartmann: 26; RA: 72; OB 42: 96; OB 43: 57, 160; OB 45: 208.

225th INFANTRY DIVISION

COMPOSITION: 333rd Infantry Regiment, 337th Infantry Regiment, 376th Infantry Regiment, 225th Artillery Regiment, 225th Reconnaissance Battalion, 225th Anti-Tank Battalion, 225th Engineer Battalion, 225th Signal Battalion

HOME STATION: Hamburg, Wkr. X

This division was formed upon mobilization in 1939 from Landwehr personnel of the Greater Hamburg area. It first saw action in 1940, when it was involved in the drive on Amsterdam. On occupation duty in France from 1940 until the end of 1941, it was one of several divisions hurriedly sent to the Russian Front in January 1942. By this time its personnel age configuration had been made normal. It was subordinated to Army Group North (later Courland) and except for a brief attachment to Army Group Center in July 1944 it remained under this headquarters until the end of the war. The division opposed the Russian winter offensive of 1941-42 and 1942-43, took part in the Siege of Leningrad, and was heavily engaged in the Battle of Demyansk (November 1942-February 1943). The 225th was involved in the retreat through the Baltic States in 1944 and fought in the Battles of the Courland Pocket (October 1944-April 1945) under Lieutenant General Ernst Walter Risse (1942-45). It ended the war in western Latvia (Courland).

NOTES AND SOURCES: Lieutenant General Hans von Basse assumed command of the 225th in 1942 and led it until September 25, 1942, when he was relieved of his command and reportedly dismissed from active duty for reasons not made clear. Possibly he ran afoul of the Nazis. Risse, a holder of the Knight's Cross with Oak Leaves and former commander of the 474th Infantry Regiment, then took over and led the 225th from then on. He was promoted to Major General in November 1942, and to Lieutenant General in early 1943. Carell 1971: 287; RA: 160; OB 43: 160; OB 45: 209. Also see *Kriegstagebuch des OKW*, Volume II.

226th INFANTRY DIVISION

COMPOSITION: 1040th Grenadier Regiment, 1041st Grenadier Regiment, 1042nd Grenadier Regiment, 226th Artillery Regiment, 226th Füsilier Battalion, 226th Anti-Tank Battalion, 226th Engineer Battalion, 226th Signal Battalion

HOME STATION: Wehrkreis VIII

The 226th was a division hastily formed in the Neuhammer Maneuver Area in the summer of 1944, just after the Normandy Front collapsed. Most of its personnel were men on furlough from the Russian Front. They were rushed to France in August and fought in the Battle of Le Havre, during which Paris's ocean port fell to the Allies. In the subsequent withdrawal northward, the division was surrounded at Dunkirk and remained there—at battle group strength—until the end of the war. The 226th Infantry was one of several units cut off in western France by the rapid Allied advances in 1944 and continued to exist in complete isolation until Germany fell.

NOTES AND SOURCES: Lieutenant General Wolfgang von Kluge was commanding the 226th in the summer of 1944 and apparently led it throughout its existence. He had previously commanded an Arko, and had led the 357th Infantry Division on the Russian Front (1944). *Kriegstagebuch des OKW*, Volume IV: 1901; RA: 130; OB 45: 209.

227th INFANTRY DIVISION

COMPOSITION: 328th Infantry Regiment, 366th Infantry Regiment, 412th Infantry Regiment, 227th Artillery Regiment, 227th Reconnaissance Battalion, 227th Anti-Tank Battalion, 227th Engineer Battalion, 227th Signal Battalion

HOME STATION: Düsseldorf, Wkr. VI

This Westphalian Landwehr division was mobilized in the summer of 1939. It fought in Belgium in 1940 and was stationed in northeastern

France from July 1940 until December 1941. Sent to Russia in early 1942, it fought on the northern sector of the Eastern Front from then until almost the end of the war. The 227th took part in the Siege of Leningrad, suffered heavy casualties in the Battle of Lake Ladoga (August-September 1942), and was encircled by the Soviet 2nd Strike and 67th armies in the next Battle of Lake Ladoga the following January. The Westphalians managed to hedgehog, rally, and break-out of the pocket—a testimony to their skill and toughness. In 1944, under Lieutenant General Wilhelm Berlin, the division sustained heavy losses in the Leningrad withdrawal and was in heavy combat in the Courland Pocket in October 1944. Well below strength but a proven combat division, the 227th Infantry was withdrawn from Russia by the German Navy and attached to the 2nd Army, Army Group Vistula. It was cut off in northeastern Germany in the last campaign in the East and surrendered to the Russians at the end of the war. The division's last leader was Major General Maximilian Wengler (late 1944-45).

NOTES AND SOURCES: Berlin was the former commander of Artillery School II (1942-43). He was reportedly leading LIV Corps at the end of the conflict. Wengler was a veteran infantry officer and regimental commander. He was promoted to Major General in late 1944. Carell 1971: 235, 250, 264; Chant, Volume 16: 2235; *Kriegstagebuch des OKW*, Volume IV: 1898; RA: 100; OB 43: 160-61; OB 45: 209-10.

228th INFANTRY DIVISION

COMPOSITION: 325th Infantry Regiment, 356th Infantry Regiment, 400th Infantry Regiment, 228th Artillery Regiment, 228th Reconnaissance Battalion, 228th Anti-Tank Battalion, 228th Engineer Battalion, 228th Signal Battalion

HOME STATION: Lötzen, Wkr. I

The 228th Infantry Division was made up of East Prussians from the older age groups. Organized in 1939, it distinguished itself in northern Poland a few months later. Its commander in this campaign was Major General Suttner. The division was in action in Russia for several weeks in 1941; however, in September it was pulled out of the line and subsequently disbanded. The reason for this action probably stemmed from the age of its soldiers.

SOURCES: Kennedy: 74 and Map 7; RA: 20; OB 42: 97; OB 43: 161; OB 45: 210.

230th COASTAL DEFENSE DIVISION

COMPOSITION: 349th Grenadier Regiment, 859th Fortress Regiment (?)

HOME STATION: Wehrkreis VIII

Formed in the summer of 1942 to control a number of miscellaneous coastal defense units under the Army of Norway, the 230th remained in the northern part of that country until the end of the war. Except for an occasional air raid, it never saw combat.

NOTES AND SOURCES: Lieutenant General Menkel, a panzer grenadier officer, was its commander in 1943 and 1944. *Kriegstagebuch des OKW*, Volume II: 1370; Volume III: 734; Volume IV: 1878; RA: 130; OB 45: 210.

231st INFANTRY DIVISION

COMPOSITION: 302nd Infantry Regiment, 319th Infantry Regiment, 342nd Infantry Regiment

HOME STATION: Wehrkreis XIII

Created upon mobilization in the summer of 1939, this division was disbanded after the fall of France the next year. Its men, who were from the older age groups, were either transferred to other units or sent home. The 231st was never involved in active campaigning.

SOURCES: *Kriegstagebuch des OKW*, Volume I: 1123; RA: 204; OB 43: 161; OB 45: 210.

232nd INFANTRY DIVISION

COMPOSITION: 1043rd Grenadier Regiment, 1044th Grenadier Regiment, 1045th Grenadier Regiment, 232nd Artillery Regiment, 232nd Füsilier Battalion, 232nd Anti-Tank Battalion, 232nd Engineer Battalion, 232nd Signal Battalion

HOME STATION: Wehrkreis IX

Organized in July 1944 in the Wildflecken Maneuver Area from older men and convalescents en route back to the Russian Front, the 232nd was intended for rear-area duties only. It was originally sent to Genoa, Italy, but was committed to combat southwest of Bologna in October and remained in action on the Italian Front for the rest of the war. By February 1945 it was defending the Apennines as part of the LI Mountain Corps, 10th Army, but was down to less than 2,600 effectives. On April 25 it was with Italian Marshal Graziani's Ligurian Army when it was cut off by the Americans. The 232nd was the only division of that army to escape; however, a week later it also surrendered, along with the rest of the remnants of Army Group C. Its commander in 1945 was Lieutenant General Eccard von Gablenz.

SOURCES: Fisher: 428, 442, 506; Hartmann: 26; RA: 144; OB 45: 210-11.

236th INFANTRY DIVISION

COMPOSITION: Various units

HOME STATION: Unknown

This unit was apparently one of those formations thrown together in the last weeks of the war from miscellaneous troop units, old men, and boys. Little is known of it, except that (according to Colonel Bauer) it formed part of the V SS Mountain Corps, 9th Army, Army Group Vistula in the last campaign. It fought in the Battle of Berlin in April and was destroyed by the Russians.

SOURCE: Chant, Volume 17: 2376.

237th INFANTRY DIVISION

COMPOSITION: 1046th Grenadier Regiment, 1047th Grenadier Regiment, 1048th Grenadier Regiment, 237th Artillery Regiment, 237th Füsilier Battalion, 237th Anti-Tank Battalion, 237th Engineer Battalion, 237th Signal Battalion.

HOME STATION: Wehrkreis XIII

This division consisted of men pulled off furlough and convalescents intercepted on their way from the hospital to the Eastern Front. Formed in Bohemia in July 1944, it was sent to Italy in September, where it was assigned line of communications duties between Pola and Trieste. The 237th apparently operated in the rear area for most of the rest of the war, although it was involved in front-line fighting in Italy in March 1945. It was transferred to the Balkans sector of the Eastern Front in the last weeks of the war and was there when the surrender came. Its commander in the last month of the war was Colonel Falkner.

NOTES AND SOURCES: Falkner was on the staff of OKH prior to being given command of the division. *Kriegstagebuch des OKW*, Volume IV: 1903; RA: 207; OB 45: 211.

239th INFANTRY DIVISION

COMPOSITION: 327th Infantry Regiment, 372nd Infantry Regiment, 444th Infantry Regiment

HOME STATION: Wehrkreis IX

The 239th was created when Nazi Germany mobilized for war in the summer of 1939. It was on the Polish-Slovakian border on September 17, 1939, but apparently did not see any fighting. It was with Army Group C during the French campaign but was only lightly engaged. Posted to the Bohemia-Moravia region of the Protectorate (formerly Czechoslovakia) in late 1940, it crossed into Russia in July 1941 and took part in the battles in the Ukraine. It was disbanded later that year, probably because of the casualties it suffered in Russia. Its commander was Lieutenant General Ferdinand Neuling (1939-41).

NOTES AND SOURCES: Neuling was named commanding general of the LXII Reserve Corps in 1942 and promoted to General of Infantry the same year. He commanded this corps until he was captured in battle on the Western Front in August 1944. Kennedy: 74 and Map 10; *Kriegstagebuch des OKW*, Volume I: 1123; RA: 130; OB 43: 161; OB 45: 212.

DIVISION STAFF 240 z.b.V.*

COMPOSITION (May 1942): 82nd Infantry Division, 167th Infantry Division, 719th Infantry Division, plus miscellaneous General Headquarters troops

HOME STATION: The Hague, The Netherlands (?)

This special purposes headquarters was formed in early 1942 to control

---

*Zur besondere Verwendung—"For Special Employment"

units under the Commander of German Troops in the Netherlands. As the reader can see from its composition, it was really a corps headquarters. In late June 1942, it was formally upgraded to corps level and redesignated LXXXVIII Corps.

SOURCE: *Kriegstagebuch des OKW*, Volume I, 1371, 1377.

242nd INFANTRY DIVISION

COMPOSITION (1944): 765th Grenadier Regiment, 917th Grenadier Regiment, 918th Grenadier Regiment, 242nd Artillery Regiment, 242nd Füsilier Battalion, 242nd Anti-Tank Battalion, 242nd Engineer Battalion, 242nd Signal Battalion

HOME STATION: Wehrkreis II

Formed in July 1943 in the Gross-Born Maneuver Area in northeastern Germany, this division initially consisted of the 917th, 918th, and 919th Grenadier Regiments. Most of its troops formerly served with depot units in Belgium. In August it was transferred to Liege, Belgium, where it performed occupation and training duties. Meanwhile, the 919th Grenadier Regiment was transferred to the 709th Infantry Division at Cherbourg. The 242nd itself was soon sent to southern France and spent the rest of its career on the Mediterranean coast. Late in 1943 it incorporated the 765th Grenadier Regiment from the 376th Infantry Division into its ranks. On August 15, 1944, American troops began the invasion of southern France, and the 242nd was soon heavily engaged. The next day Army Group G began its retreat but ordered the 242nd to stay behind and defend Toulon to the end. Eleven days later the divisional commander, Lieutenant General Johannes Baessler (1943-44), surrendered the remnants of the 242nd to the Allies. One reason the division was sacrificed was its lack of transport; it might not have been able to escape Allied armored and motorized formations even if it had been allowed to withdraw. As things worked out, it provided other elements of Army Group G with an opportunity to escape.

NOTES AND SOURCES: Baessler had commanded the 9th Panzer Division in Russia in 1942. Chant, Volume 14: 1918-21, 1928, 1945; Harrison: Map VI; Ruge: 65; RA: 32; OB 44b: D85; OB 45: 212.

243rd INFANTRY DIVISION

COMPOSITION: 920th Grenadier Regiment, 921st Grenadier Regiment, 922nd Grenadier Regiment, 243rd Artillery Regiment, 243rd Füsilier Battalion, 243rd Anti-Tank Battalion, 243rd Engineer Battalion, 243rd Signal Battalion

HOME STATION: Wehrkreis XVII

In August and September 1943 this unit was created under the command of Major General Hermann von Witzleben as Division "B" in the Döllersheim Maneuver Area in northeastern Austria. It was sent to Brittany in October but was still not up to strength on D-Day. As of January 1944, one of its three regiments was equipped with horse-drawn vehicles, one was outfitted with bicycles, and the third was motorized, but not completely formed. All of its regiments had two battalions each. The 243rd was in combat from the beginning, covering a sector on the western Cotentin peninsula. Its capable divisional commander, Lieutenant General Heinz Hellmich (who had replaced von Witzleben some weeks before), was killed by a fighter-bomber on June 16. Under almost constant ground attack and air and naval bombardment, the 243rd was down to battle group strength by June 20. Most of the division was destroyed in the Battle of Cherbourg later that month. Remnants of the division, however, managed to escape to the south, join the rest of Army Group B, and continue fighting against the American advance on St. Lô. By late July SS General Hausser, the commander of the German 7th Army, listed the division as practically destroyed. It was temporarily combined with the remnants of the 91st Air Landing Division under Colonel Bernhard Klosterkemper and fought the hedgerow battles of the western Cotentin. In August, the few survivors of the 243rd were finally pulled out of the line and sent to the Somme River-St. Quentin area to rest and rehabilitate; the division itself was disbanded and its troops sent to other commands.

NOTES AND SOURCES: Witzleben was formerly Chief of Staff of VII Corps and later chief German liaison officer with the 2nd Hungarian Army in Russia (1942), Colonel Klosterkemper, senior surviving regimental commander in the 243rd, was promoted to Major General in late 1944 and commanded the 180th Infantry Division on the Western Front in 1945. Blumenson 1960: 72-76, 442, 582; Carell 1973: 186; Chant, Volume 14: 1850; Samuel W. Mitcham, Jr., *Rommel's Last Battle: The Desert Fox and the Normandy Campaign*, Stein and Day, Briarcliff Manor, N.Y., 1983: 111-20 (hereafter cited as "Mitcham 1983"); RA: 220; OB 45: 212.

244th INFANTRY DIVISION

COMPOSITION: 932nd Grenadier Regiment, 933rd Grenadier Regiment, 934th Grenadier Regiment, 244th Artillery Regiment, 244th Füsilier Battalion, 244th Anti-Tank Battalion, 244th Engineer Battalion, 244th Signal Battalion

HOME STATION: Wehrkreis I

Activated in late 1943 (probably in Belgium), this division was soon transferred to the French Mediterranean coast, where it formed the garrison for the city of Marseilles. When the Americans landed on August 15, 1944, divisional commander Major General Schaeffer was ordered to defend the city until the end. The Siege of Marseilles began the next day and ended on August 28. The 244th was completely destroyed.

NOTES AND SOURCES: The only other commander in the 244th's history was Lieutenant General Martin Gilbert (late 1943-44). Chant, Volume 14: 1928, 1945; Harrison: Map VI: RA: 20; OB 45: 218. A British Interrogations Document lists Schaeffer as a lieutenant general (Air University Files, SRGG-1108).

245th INFANTRY DIVISION

COMPOSITION: 935th Grenadier Regiment, 936th Grenadier Regiment, 937th Grenadier Regiment, 245th Artillery Regiment, 245th Füsilier Battalion, 245th Anti-Tank Battalion, 245th Engineer Battalion, 245th Signal Battalion

HOME STATION: Wehrkreis V

Formed in Germany in August and September 1943 under the command of Lieutenant General Erwin Sander (1943-44), the 245th was a static division. Stationed near Fecamp, northern France (on the English Channel), it remained idle during the Normandy campaign but was heavily engaged as the Allies drove on the Low Countries. In September 1944 it opposed Montgomery's abortive effort to take Arnhem. From October 2 to November 8 it fought in the Battle of the Scheldt as part of the LXVII Corps, 15th Army. Briefly withdrawn to refit, it was back in action against the U.S. 3rd Army before the end of the year. Later it was engaged in northern Alsace and in OB West* reserve on March 1, 1945, and was

---

*The German abbreviation for the Commander-in-Chief, West, or his headquarters.

apparently disbanded a few days later. Its last commander was Major General Gerhard Kegler (1945).

NOTES AND SOURCES: Sander, a Prussian, had previously led the 170th Infantry Division on the Russian Front. Kegler was a former instructor at the Officers Training School at Müchen. Cole 1950: 521; Harrison: Map VI; *Kriegstagebuch des OKW,* Volume I: 1147-48; Volume IV: 1900; MacDonald 1963: 125, 216-17; RA: 86; OB 45: 213.

246th INFANTRY (later VOLKSGRENADIER) DIVISION

COMPOSITION (1941): 313th Infantry Regiment, 352nd Infantry Regiment, 404th Infantry Regiment, 246th Artillery Regiment, 246th Reconnaissance Company, 246th Anti-Tank Battalion, 246th Engineer Battalion, 246th Signal Battalion

HOME STATION: Trier, Wkr. XII

The 246th Infantry—a Hessian unit—was mobilized in late 1939 and first saw action in France in 1940, when it attacked the Maginot Line with some success. After the fall of Paris it returned to Germany, was sent back to southwestern France in the latter part of 1941, and left for the Russian Front on January 3, 1942. Prior to its departure it exchanged the 313th Infantry Regiment for the 689th Infantry Regiment of the 337th Infantry Division. The 246th fought on the central sector of the Eastern Front against the Soviet winter offensive of 1941-42 where it held back large parts of the Russian 22nd Army at Belyy on the northern flank of Army Group Center. Later it was engaged in the Battle of Smolensk in early 1943, in the Rzhev retreat, and against the huge Soviet summer offensive of 1944 in which Army Group Center was overwhelmed. The 246th Infantry, which was down to battle group strength as early as October 1943, was encircled and destroyed at Vitebsk in July 1944. The divisional commander, Major General Mueller-Buelow, was among the prisoners.

A second 246th was formed in Prague as a Volksgrenadier division in September 1944. It included former naval personnel, a few survivors of the original division, and men formerly assigned to the 565th Grenadier Division. The 246th Volksgrenadier Division included the 352nd, 404th, and 689th Grenadier Regiments, as well as the 246th Artillery Regiment and the 246th Füsilier, Anti-Tank, Engineer and Signal Battalions. It was sent into action in western France in late September. It was at nearly full strength (it had eight thousand of its authorized ten thousand soldiers) when it relieved the 116th Panzer Division at Aachen on October 7. Two weeks of heavy fighting later its commander, Colonel Gerhard Wilck, surrendered the city, a large segment of the division, and most of the garrison to the Americans. The remnants of the 246th were reformed under Colonel Peter Körte and absorbed the remnants of the defunct 49th Infantry Division, which brought its strength to 11,141. Again sent into action near Aachen in November, it was scheduled to take part in the Battle of the Bulge but was so heavily engaged in the Battle of the Huertgen Forest that the plan was cancelled. By the end of November not one of its eight infantry battalions had 100 survivors, but the U.S. units that attacked it were also decimated. Taken out of the line, the 246th Volksgrenadier incorporated a sizable number of Luftwaffe replacements into its ranks and was hurriedly thrown back into action on the Western Front due to Allied pressure. It was in action east of Monschau in January 1945 as part of the 5th Panzer Army but was sent to the 7th Army the next month after Patton's breakthrough at Pruem. By March the 246th was fighting in the Eifel area and was only one of the two divisions in 7th Army that was considered to be in reasonably good shape by 1945 standards. It ended the war on the southern sector of the Western Front. Colonel Körte was reported as killed in action in 1945, and the division's last commander was Colonel List.

NOTES AND SOURCES: Colonel Wilck, who first joined the German Army in 1916, was still alive in 1976, at the age of 80. He was living near the Rhine River at that time, pursuing his favorite hobby, gardening. Colonel List, formerly of the 138th Mountain Infantry Regiment, was in all probability senior regimental commander in the 246th when Peter Körte was killed. Carell 1966: 385, 391; Carell 1971: 309, 584-96; Cole 1965: 87; Hartmann: 26. *Kriegstagebuch des OKW*, Volume I: 1147; MacDonald 1973: 115, 198; Rowe: 273; OB 43: 162; OB 45: 213-14. Also see Charles Whiting, *Bloody Aachen*, Stein and Day Publishers, Briarcliff Manor, N.Y., 1976.

250th INFANTRY DIVISION

COMPOSITION: 262nd Infantry Regiment, 263rd Infantry Regiment, 269th Infantry Regiment, 250th Artillery Regiment, 250th Reconnaissance (later Füsilier) Battalion, 250th Anti-Tank Battalion, 250th Engineer Battalion, 250th Signal Battalion

HOME STATION: Wehrkreis XIII and Spain

This division consisted of Spanish soldiers who volunteered to fight for Germany against the communists. It was fourteen thousand strong when it was mustered in at the Grafenwöhr Maneuver Area in August 1941. Quickly sent into action at Novgorod on the northern sector of the Russian Front, the so-called "Blue Division" fought very well in all of its engagements. In the Novgorod-Leningrad-Lake Ilmen battles of late 1941-early 1942, the Spanish Fascist volunteers played a major role in turning back the Russian winter offensive in the northern sector but lost eight thousand men killed, wounded, captured, or incapacitated by frostbite. After receiving replacements from Spain, it continued in action with Army Group North and lost another three thousand-two hundred men in the Second Battle of Lake Ladoga in January and February 1943. Here its füsilier battalion lost 90 percent of its soldiers, but the division again held its positions against massive Soviet attacks. The 250th continued to serve in northern Russia until the Siege of Leningrad was broken in January 1944. At that time Spanish dictator Franco requested that the division be returned to Spain; however, about half of its veteran warriors volunteered for service in the Waffen-SS and continued to fight against the Russians until the end of the war. The Blue Division's commanders were Major General Munoz Grandes and General of Division Emilo Esteban-Infantes, both of whom were Spanish officers.

NOTES AND SOURCES: Carell 1966: 421; Carell 1971: 278-80; Chant, Volume 4: 520; Hartmann: 27; OB 43: 162; OB 44: 221; OB 45: 214; Ziemke 1966: 265. Also see Salisbury.

251st INFANTRY (later VOLKSGRENADIER) DIVISION

COMPOSITION: 451st Infantry Regiment, 459th Infantry Regiment, 471st Infantry Regiment, 251st Artillery Regiment, 251st Reconnaissance Battalion, 251st Anti-Tank Battalion, 251st Engineer Battalion, 251st Signal Battalion

HOME STATION: Hanau, Wkr. IX

The 251st was formed in the summer of 1939 from men already serving in reserve units. Except for a drive through Belgium with Army Group B in 1940, it spent its entire combat career on the Eastern Front, where it served on the central sector and was almost continuously in the line from mid-1941 until May 1945. During these years it took part in the drive on Moscow (1941), the defensive battles of 1942, the Rzhev withdrawal (1943), the Battle of Kursk (1943), and the middle Dnieper withdrawal (1943). The 251st was smashed in the Russian summer offensive of 1944 but reformed as a Volksgrenadier division in September 1944 and sent back into action in eastern Germany, where it opposed the Russian drive through Pomerania. It was part of Army Group Vistula in the Berlin campaign and ended up in Russian captivity at the end of the war. The 251st, which had earned special distinction as a defensive fighting force, was commanded by Lieutenant General Maxmilian in 1945.

NOTES AND SOURCES: Lieutenant General Hans Kratzeri commanded the 251st in 1940. He later directed Harko 303—an army-level artillery command—on the Eastern Front in 1941. Felzmann, a holder of the Knight's Cross with Oak Leaves, took over the division in 1943. Late in 1943 he was briefly acting commander of Corps Detachment I on the Eastern Front. Carell 1966: 359; Carell 1971: 309; *Kriegstagebuch des OKW*, Volume I: 1122; RA: 144; OB 42: 98; OB 43: 162; OB 44: 221; OB 45: 214.

252nd INFANTRY DIVISION

COMPOSITION (1941): 452nd Infantry Regiment, 461st Infantry Regiment, 472nd Infantry Regiment, 252nd Artillery Regiment, 252nd Reconnaissance Battalion, 252nd Anti-Tank Battalion, 252nd Engineer Battalion, 252nd Signal Battalion

HOME STATION: Neisse, Wkr. VIII

This division was formed from Silesians already serving in reserve units in 1939. It fought in Poland later that year (although only in a secondary role), on the Saar Front in 1939-40, and in France in 1940, where it distinguished itself in the successful attack on the Maginot Line. It took part in the invasion of Russia in 1941 and was more or less continuously engaged on the Eastern Front for the rest of the war. In the winter of 1941-42 it dropped the 452nd Infantry Regiment from its table of organization and received the 7th Infantry Regiment from the 28th Infantry Division. The 252nd fought at Vyazma-Bryansk, Moscow, Rzhev, Smolensk, and against the Russian summer offensive of 1944. Here it escaped after desperate fighting against vastly superior Soviet tank and mechanized formations. The High Command officially commended the division for its conduct during this operation. Later the 252nd took part in the retreat across southern Poland and ended the war in Czechoslovakia. Its commander in 1945 was Lieutenant General Walter Meizer.

NOTES AND SOURCES: Meizer, a Saxon who held the Knight's Cross with Oak Leaves, was previously commander of the 43rd Infantry Regiment (1943). Carell 1966: 140, 350; Carell 1971: 309, 583-84; Kennedy: Map 10; RA: 130; OB 43: 162-63; OB 45: 215.

253rd INFANTRY DIVISION

COMPOSITION: 453rd Infantry Regiment, 464th Infantry Regiment, 473rd Infantry Regiment, 253rd Artillery Regiment, 253rd Reconnaissance Battalion, 253rd Anti-Tank Battalion, 253rd Engineer Battalion, 253rd Signal Battalion

HOME STATION: Aachen, Wkr. VI

This Westphalian division was created in the mobilization of 1939 from men already serving in reserve units. It first saw action in France in 1940 and remained there until the spring of 1941, when it was sent to what was formerly Poland. It crossed into the Soviet Union in June 1941 and took part in the drive on Moscow. It fought against the Russian winter offensive of 1941-42, during which it was surrounded south of Lake Volga in January. Breaking out with heavy casualties, the division fought on the central sector of the Russian Front from June 1941 until May 1945 and was involved in all the major battles of the 9th Army except Kursk, when it was in 4th Army's reserve. It took part in the defeat of the Soviet fall offensive of 1943, the Dnieper withdrawal, and the retreat through the northern Ukraine and Poland. It apparently ended the war in the pocket east of Prague. The 253rd Infantry's commanders included Lieutenant Generals Schellert (1942), Kühne (1942), and Karl Becker (1943-45).

NOTES AND SOURCES: Schellert was promoted to General of Infantry in July 1943 and commanded Wehrkreis IX (headquartered in Hanover) from May 1943 to 1945. Kühne, who had commanded the 26th Infantry Division prior to 1939, was in charge of Replacement Division Staff 526 in 1945. Benoist-Mechin: 133; Carell 1966: 359, 376-77, 384-85, 394; Carell 1971: 309; *Kriegstagebuch des OKW*, Volume 1: 1127; Volume III: 733; Volume IV: 1875; RA: 130; OB 42: 98; OB 43: 163; OB 44: 222; OB 45: 215.

254th INFANTRY DIVISION

COMPOSITION: 454th Infantry Regiment, 474th Infantry Regiment, 484th Regiment, 254th Artillery Regiment, 254th Reconnaissance Battalion, 254th Anti-Tank Battalion, 254th Engineer Battalion, 254th Signal Battalion

HOME STATION: Dortmund, Wkr. VI

Raised from Rhinelanders serving in reserve units in the summer of 1939, the 254th fought in Holland, Belgium, and northern France in 1940.

Sent to Russia in 1941, it formed part of Army Group North during the drive on and Siege of Leningrad. During this period it was heavily engaged east of Leningrad and at Demyansk. It fought on the northern sector of the Eastern Front until early 1944, when it was sent to the Ukraine and took part in the subsequent retreats on the southern sector. It was resisting the Soviets in eastern Slovakia in early 1945 and ended the war in the pocket east of Prague. The 254th's commanders included Major General Friedrich Köchling (1942), Lieutenant General Walter Behschnitt (1942-43), and Lieutenant General Thielmann (1943-45).

NOTES AND SOURCES: Köchling commanded the 287th Infantry Regiment until April 10, 1942, when he took over the 254th, which he led until September 5, 1942. Behschnitt, former commander of the 15th Infantry Division (1939-40), was reportedly in charge of a recruiting area in Hanover, Wehrkreis XI, at the end of the war. Lieutenant General Thielmann had formerly commanded the 28th Engineer Battalion. Carell 1971: 287; RA: 102; OB 43: 163; OB 45: 215-16.

255th INFANTRY DIVISION

COMPOSITION: 455th Infantry Regiment, 465th Infantry Regiment, 475th Infantry Regiment, 255th Artillery Regiment, 255th Reconnaissance Battalion, 255th Anti-Tank Battalion, 255th Engineer Battalion, 255th Signal Battalion

HOME STATION: Lobau, Wkr. IV

This unit, known as the "Green Dot" division because of its unit emblem, was formed mainly from Saxon reservists, with a minority of Sudeten Germans. Organized in the summer of 1939, it first saw action in France the next year. In 1941 it took part in the drive on Moscow as part of Army Group Center, and helped check the Soviet winter offensive of 1941-42. It fought in the defensive battles on the central sector in 1942 before being transferred to the southern zone of the Eastern Front after the fall of Stalingrad. The division was part of the 4th Panzer Army during Operation Citadel, Hitler's last major offensive in the East. In the subsequent retreat through the Donets, the 255th suffered such heavy casualties that it had to be taken out of the line. It was sent to France in late 1943, where it was disbanded. Its men were scattered to various units. The commanders of the 255th Infantry included Lieutenant Generals Wetzel (1940-42) and Poppe (1943).

NOTES AND SOURCES: Wetzel was given command of V Corps in January 1942. He led it until late 1943, when he was transferred from Russia to

France, where he assumed command of the LXVI Reserve Corps. In early 1944 he was given command of Wehrkreis X, headquartered in Hamburg, a post he still held in 1945. General Poppe had previously commanded the 217th Infantry Division (1943) and later led the 189th Reserve and 59th Infantry Divisions in the West (1944 and 1944-45, respectively). Carell 1971: 17, 50; Hartmann: 28; OB 43: 1943; OB 45: 216.

256th INFANTRY DIVISION

COMPOSITION: 456th Infantry Regiment, 476th Infantry Regiment, 481st Infantry Regiment, 256th Artillery Regiment, 256th Reconnaissance Battalion, 256th Anti-Tank Battalion, 256th Engineer Battalion, 256th Signal Battalion

HOME STATION: Wehrkreis IV

Initially consisting of Saxon, Bavarian, and Sudeten reservists from Wehrkreise IV and XIII, this division was formed in the general mobilization of 1939. Its replacements came from Wehrkreis IV, so it no doubt became more and more a Saxon division as the war wore on. The 256th took part in the Dutch and Belgian campaigns of 1940 and in June 1941 invaded Russia, where it was almost continuously engaged for the next three years. In the last ten days of December 1941 it held its line near Moscow against odds of ten to one or even higher odds. A month later it was instrumental in saving the XXIII Corps, which the Soviets had surrounded. Remaining on the central sector of the Russian Front, it took part in the Rzhev withdrawal but apparently was not present at the Battle of Kursk. The 256th suffered heavy losses at the Battle of Smolensk in the autumn of 1943 and, as part of the 3rd Panzer Army, was destroyed in the Soviet summer offensive of July 1944. The divisional commander, Major General Wüstenhagen, was killed in the fighting.

A second 256th Division was created as a Volksgrenadier unit in Saxony in September 1944 with personnel from the recently formed 568th Grenadier Division, along with some veterans from the Eastern Front. Its regiments received the same numbers as the original 256th. It was first in action against the British in southern Holland in October, where it fought in the Battle of the Schelde (October 2-November 8, 1944). Later in November it was fighting in eastern France. The 256th Volksgrenadier took part in the battles in the Saar, northern Alsace, Bitche, and in the Battle of the Saar-Moselle Triangle (February 1945). Its survivors were still resisting in southern Germany when the war ended. Commanders of the 256th included Major General Folttmann (1939), Lieutenant General Kauffmann (late 1939-early 1942), Lieutenant General Paul Danhauser (early

1942-43), Wüstenhagen (1943-44), and Major General Gerhard Franz (1944-45).

NOTES AND SOURCES: Folttmann was later commander of the 164th Infantry (later Light Afrika) Division (late 1939-August 1942) and the 338th Infantry Division in France (1943). Promoted to Lieutenant General in February 1941, he was last reported by Allied intelligence as being on the Eastern Front in May 1944. Danhauser later commanded the 271st Infantry Division (late 1943-44) and was Deputy Commander of Wehrkreis XII in October 1944. Gerhard Franz was formerly Chief of Staff of the XL Panzer Corps in Russia (1942) and the Afrika Korps (1943). He was Chief of Staff of the XLII Corps in Russia (1942-43). He was relieved of his duties as Chief of Staff of the XL Panzer for a security violation in mid-1942, court-martialed, and sent to prison, along with his former commander, General of Panzer Troops Georg Stumme. Hermann Göring, who was impressed with the pair at their trial, used his influence to secure their release and subsequent reemployment in Africa, where Stumme was killed. Franz was promoted to Major General in late 1944. Carell 1966: 359-62, 400-02; Carell 1971: 309, 597; Cole 1950: 521; MacDonald 1963: 216-17; MacDonald 1973; 126; RA: 72; OB 42: 99; OB 43: 164; OB 44: 223; OB 45: 216-17.

257th INFANTRY (later VOLKSGRENADIER) DIVISION

COMPOSITION: 457th Infantry Regiment, 466th Infantry Regiment, 477th Infantry Regiment, 257th Artillery Regiment, 257th Reconnaissance Battalion, 257th Anti-Tank Battalion, 257th Engineer Battalion, 257th Signal Battalion

HOME STATION: Berlin, Wkr. III

The 257th was formed upon mobilization in 1939 and consisted of Prussians and Berliners. It was on the Saar Front in 1940 and was continuously engaged in southern Russia from June 1941 until the summer of 1942. Here it fought in the Battles of the Uman and Kiev Pockets, where hundreds of thousands of Russians were taken prisoner. In March 1942 it held Slavyansk against massive Soviet attacks. Two months later it fought in the Battle of Kharkov, where the division suffered heavy losses. After the battles of Voronezh and Kalach, during the drive to Stalingrad, the 257th was sent to France in the fall of 1942 to rest and refit. It returned to southern Russia in April 1943 and was heavily engaged at Dnepropetrovsk and in the battles on the Dnieper bend. In early 1944 it suffered heavy losses in the retreat from the Dnieper and in the encirclement near Kishinev. Rebuilt in southern Poland that autumn, it returned to action on the Western Front in December as a Volksgrenadier division, having absorbed the 587th Volksgrenadier Division. It was sent into battle in the Saar, fighting at Zweibrücken and at Bitche. The battered division was still in action on the Western Front when the war ended. Commanders of the 257th Volksgrenadier/Infantry Division included Lieutenant General Sachs (1941-42), Lieutenant General Püchler (1942-44), Lieutenant General Baron Anton von Mauchenheim gennant Bechtolsheim (1944), and Colonel Erich Seidel (1945).

NOTES AND SOURCES: Lieutenant General Püchler was appointed temporary commander of LXXIV Corps in October 1944, and by December was commanding both the LXVII and LXXXVI Corps on the northern sector of the Western Front. Baron von Bechtolsheim was formerly Ia, 6th Army under Field Marshal von Reichenau (1939-40), Commander of the 707th Infantry Division (1942), and Chief of Staff of the 1st Army in France (1942-43). Later he was in charge of Recruiting Area Regensburg, Wehrkreis XIII (1945). Colonel Seidel commanded a battle group on the Western Front in 1944. Carell 1966: 121, 472, 490, 493; "Frontnachweiser," 15 December 1944; RA: 46; OB 42: 98; OB 43: 165; OB 44: 224; OB 45: 217.

258th INFANTRY DIVISION

COMPOSITION: 458th Infantry Regiment, 478th Infantry Regiment, 479th Infantry Regiment, 258th Artillery Regiment, 258th Reconnaissance Battalion, 258th Anti-Tank Battalion, 258th Engineer Battalion, 258th Signal Battalion

HOME STATION: Rostock, Wkr. II

Created from Prussian reservists in the summer of 1939, this division was sent to the Saar later that year and took part in the assaults on the Maginot Line that helped seal the doom of French Army Group Number Three in July 1940. Sent to Russia in mid-1941, it fought at Vyazma-Bryansk and in the battles around Moscow. The 258th continued to serve with Army Group Center until late summer 1943. During the retreat from Orel, the division defended 9th Army's supply depot at Kromy against heavy odds, withstood fifteen major Soviet attacks, and frustrated the Russian attempt to seize the depot. Later in the year the Prussian division was transferred to the southern sector of the Eastern Front. It was at battle group strength by October 1943. It was routed in March 1944 during the withdrawal from the lower Dnieper bend. That August it was encircled west of the lower Dnieper and was virtually destroyed. Those few soldiers who managed to escape were sent to other units, and the 258th Infantry was disbanded.

Commanders of the division included Lieutenant General Karl Pflaum (1941-42), Lieutenant General Hans-Kurt Höcker (1943), and Major General Eugen Bleyer (1943-44). The last divisional commander, Colonel Rudolf Hielscher, was captured west of the Dnieper in 1944.

NOTES AND SOURCES: Lieutenant General Pflaum later commanded the 153rd Field Training Division in Russia (1943-44) and the 157th Reserve Division in Italy (1944). Höcker went on to command the 17th Luftwaffe Field Division in France (1943-44) and the 167th Infantry Division on the Western Front (1945). Carell 1966: 140; Carell 1971: 26; *Kriegstagebuch des OKW*, Volume III: 1155; Plocher 1943: 106; RA: 32; OB 42: 99-100; OB 44: 221; OB 45: 217.

260th INFANTRY DIVISION

COMPOSITION: 460th Infantry Regiment, 470th Infantry Regiment, 480th Infantry Regiment, 260th Artillery Regiment, 260th Reconnaissance Battalion, 260th Anti-Tank Battalion, 260th Engineer Battalion, 260th Signal Battalion

HOME STATION: Karlsruhe, Wkr.

The 260th was one of several divisions formed from men serving in reserve units in the general mobilization of 1939. Its soldiers came from the Baden and Württemberg areas. They were sent to Russia shortly after the invasion began and were heavily and almost continuously engaged from July 1941 until the Soviet winter offensive of 1941-42 finally petered out. The 260th Infantry remained with Army Group Center for the rest of its existence. It fought in the defensive battles of 1942, in the Rzhev withdrawal the next year, in the battles around Smolensk, and at Gomel. The 260th Infantry was surrounded and destroyed near Minsk in July 1944 along with the XXVII Corps and the bulk of the 4th Army. Its commander, Major General Klammt (1944), who had only recently replaced Colonel Alexander Conrady (1943?-44) in command, was among the prisoners. Previous divisional commanders included Lieutenant Generals Hans Schmidt (1940-42) and Lieutenant General Hahm (1942-43).

NOTES AND SOURCES: Schmidt became a General of Infantry in 1942 and commanded IX Corps in Russia from December 1942 until November 1943. In 1945 he was commanding troops on the Swiss border. General Hahm commanded the 389th Infantry Division on the Eastern Front from late 1943 to 1945. Carell 1966: 196; Carell 1971: 309, 597; *Kriegstagebuch des OKW*, Volume II: 1368, 1387; OB 42: 100; OB 43: 165; OB 44: 225; OB 45: 218.

262nd INFANTRY DIVISION

COMPOSITION: 462nd Infantry Regiment, 482nd Infantry Regiment, 486th Infantry Regiment, 262nd Artillery Regiment, 262nd Reconnaissance Battalion, 262nd Anti-Tank Battalion, 262nd Engineer Battalion, 262nd Signal Battalion

HOME STATION: Vienna, Wkr. XVII

This division was raised from Austrian reservists in the summer of 1939. It served on the Saar Front while Hitler overran Poland and remained there until after the fall of France in 1940. It crossed into Russia with Army Group South in June 1941 but was with the central army group by September, following the advance through the Ukraine. It fought in the Battle of Moscow and the subsequent winter retreat under heavy Soviet pressure. It took part in the relatively minor defensive actions on the central sector in 1942 and fought in July 1943 at the Battle of Kursk, where it suffered heavy casualties. Caught up in the subsquent retreats, the 262nd Infantry was listed as in remnants by October 1943 and was placed under the operational control of the 26th Infantry Division. Soon after it was returned to Austria and disbanded. Its commanders were Lieutenant Generals Edgar Theisen (1939-42) and Friedrich Karst (1942-43).

NOTES AND SOURCES: A General of Infantry as of October 1942, Theisen later commanded the LXI Reserve Corps (1943-44). He had previously been Inspector of Chemical Warfare Troops. Karst was Commandant of Brussels in 1944. Hartmann: 28; *Kriegstagebuch des OKW*, Volume III: 1157; RA: 220; OB 42: 100; OB 43: 165; OB 45: 218

263rd INFANTRY DIVISION

COMPOSITION: 463rd Infantry Regiment, 483rd Infantry Regiment, 485th Infantry Regiment, 263rd Artillery Regiment, 263rd Reconnaissance Battalion, 263rd Anti-Tank Battalion, 263rd Engineer Battalion, 263rd Signal Battalion

HOME STATION: Idar-Oberstein, Wkr. XII

Consisting of Palatinate Bavarians already serving in the reserves, this division was mobilized in mid-1939. The next year it distinguished itself in France, and fought on the central sector of the Russian Front—including the Battle of Moscow and the winter retreats of 1941-42—from June 1941 until August 1943. Transferred to Army Group North, the division took part in the retreat from Leningrad, the defense of the Narva, and the retreat through the Baltic States. Isolated in the Courland Pocket in October 1944, it held a sector of the line during the unsuccessful Soviet attempts to crush the pocket, and was still there when the war ended. Commanders of the 263rd Infantry included Lieutenant General Franz Karl (1940), Major General Ernst Haeckel (1942), and Colonel Hermann (1945).

NOTES AND SOURCES: Lieutenant General Karl was commander of Replacement Division Staff 182 in 1941. General Haeckel later commanded the 158th Reserve Division (1943-44) and the 16th Infantry Division on the Western Front (1944-45). Carell 1966: 92; RA: 188; OB 42: 100; OB 43: 165-66; OB 45: 219.

264th INFANTRY DIVISION

COMPOSITION: 891st Grenadier Regiment, 892nd Grenadier Regiment, 893rd Grenadier Regiment, 264th Artillery Regiment, 264th Füsilier Battalion, 264th Anti-Tank Battalion, 264th Engineer Battalion, 264th Signal Battalion

HOME STATION: Wehrkreis VI

Formed in Belgium in the summer of 1943, this division was not a first-class fighting unit. It was sent to Croatia in October and then to the Dalmatian coast, where it fought partisans and served on guard duty. In January 1945 the 264th was pitted against regular Soviet troops in northern Yugoslavia but was soon transferred to Denmark, where it came under the jurisdiction of the Replacement Army. It apparently remained there until the end of the war. Commanders of the 264th included Major General Wilhelm Metger (1943-44), Lieutenant General Martin Gareis (1944), Lieutenant General Albin Nake (1944), and Lieutenant General Otto Lüdecke (1944-45).

NOTES AND SOURCES: General Garies had previously commanded the 98th Infantry Division on the Russian Front (1942-44). Nake, the former commander of Replacement Division Staff 526 (1943-44), was given command of the 159th Reserve Division in the fall of 1944. Lüdecke had led the 56th Infantry Division in Russia in 1943 and through most of 1944. *Kriegstagebuch des OKW*, Volume IV: 1904; RA: 102; OB 44: 226; OB 45: 219.

265th INFANTRY DIVISION

COMPOSITION: 894th Grenadier Regiment, 895th Grenadier Regiment, 896th Grenadier Regiment, 265th Artillery Regiment, 265th Füsilier Battalion, 265th Anti-Tank Battalion, 265th Engineer **Battalion**, 265th Signal Battalion

HOME STATION: Wehrkreis XI

The 265th was formed in the summer of 1943, probably at the Bergen Maneuver Area. Its staff came from the 403rd Security Division Headquarters, which had previously served on the Russian Front. A static division, the 265th Infantry was sent to Brittany later that summer, where it exchanged personnel with the regiments of the 65th Infantry Division. Unit integrity was not a consideration in the employment of the 265th. In the fall of 1943 two of its battalions (one from the 894th and one from the 895th Grenadier Regiments) were sent to Russia; later, a battle group from the division fought in Normandy and was destroyed there. Other elements of the division were reported as fighting in the Siege of Brest, where they were also destroyed when the city fell in mid-September 1944. The bulk of the division, however, was surrounded at Lorient on the Brittany peninsula during Patton's dash to Brest. Not wishing to undergo another siege like Brest, which was costly in terms of both men and time, the Allies were content to post observation troops around the area, which the 265th held in total isolation until the end of the war. The division's commanders included Lieutenant General Walther Düvert (1943-44), Lieutenant General Russwurn (1944), and Major General Junck (1945).

NOTES AND SOURCES: Düvert had previously commanded a panzer division and had served as Chief of Staff of VI Corps. Junck had led the 74th Panzer Grenadier Regiment (1942) and had served as acting commander of the 277th Infantry Division in Normandy (July 1944). Blumenson 1960: 58, 372; Chant, Volume 14: 1861; Harrison: Map VI; RA: 172; OB 45: 219-20.

266th INFANTRY DIVISION

COMPOSITION: 897th Grenadier Regiment, 898th Grenadier Regiment, 899th Grenadier Regiment, 266th Artillery Regiment, 266th Füsilier Battalion, 266th Anti-Tank Battalion, 266th Engineer Battalion, 266th Signal Battalion

HOME STATION: Wehrkreis V

Formed in the Müsingen Maneuver Area in the summer of 1943, this static division consisted partially of veterans from the Eastern Front. Five of its battalions, however, were later filled out mainly with Eastern troops, which Admiral Ruge assessed as having "very little combat value." All the 266th's units lacked heavy weapons. It was on coastal watch duty in France from mid-1943 until the Normandy Front collapsed in August 1944. Not having enough vehicles to effect a rapid retreat, it was easy game for the U.S. 4th Armored Division as it swept up the Brittany peninsula later that month. Most of the division was captured, as was its commander, Lieutenant General Karl Sprang. Remnants of the 266th did manage to escape to Brest, where they defended against the Allied siege, and were destroyed by September 19.

NOTES AND SOURCES: Sprang, an artillery officer, had a territorial command in occupied Russia in 1942 and had commanded a battle group in Stalingrad. He was flown out before the fall of the city. Blumenson 1960: 384; Chant, Volume 14: 1861; Harrison: Map VI: Ruge; 94; RA: 86; OB 45: 220.

267th INFANTRY DIVISION

COMPOSITION: 467th Infantry Regiment, 487th Infantry Regiment, 497th Infantry Regiment, 267th Artillery Regiment, 267th Reconnaissance Battalion, 267th Anti-Tank Battalion, 267th Engineer Battalion, 267th Signal Battalion

HOME STATION: Hanover, Wkr. XI

Called the Horsehead Division because of the symbol on its unit emblem, the 267th was formed from reservists in the Hanover-Braunschweig area of Lower Saxony. It took part in the invasion of Russia in June 1941 under the command of Lieutenant General Friedrich-Karl Wachter (1941-42) and suffered heavy casualties during the advance on and retreat from Moscow. The division had lost so many horses from the cold, the lack of supplies, and lack of fodder that when it did have to retreat on December 17, 1941, it had to leave all of its artillery behind. The 267th fought in all the major battles of Army Group Center until July 1944. At that time it was encircled and destroyed, along with the XII Infantry Corps and the bulk of the 4th Army. Its last divisional commander, Lieutenant General Otto Drescher, was killed in this battle. The Horsehead Division was officially declared dissolved shortly afterwards.

NOTES AND SOURCES: Lieutenant General Wachter was later assigned to the Army Personnel Office in Berlin (1943). Carell 1966: 175; Carell 1971: 309, 597; Seaton: 210-11; OB 43: 166; OB 45: 220.

268th INFANTRY DIVISION

COMPOSITION: 468th Infantry Regiment, 488th Infantry Regiment, 499th Infantry Regiment, 268th Artillery Regiment, 268th Reconnaissance Battalion, 268th Anti-Tank Battalion, 268th Engineer Battalion, 268th Signal Battalion

HOME STATION: Munich, Wkr. VII

Formed in 1939 from reservists in the VII and XVII Military Districts, this division served on the Saar Front in 1939-40 and spent the rest of its career on the Russian Front. Here it fought at the Battle of the Yelnya Bend, before Moscow, against the Soviet winter offensive of 1941-42, in the defensive actions of 1942, and in the Rzhev withdrawal. In the summer of 1943 it suffered such heavy losses in the Battle of Kursk and the associated retreat that it was down to battle group strength by October and had to be disbanded in late 1943. Some elements of the 268th were used to form the 352nd Infantry Division, which later distinguished itself in Normandy on D-Day. The 268th's commanders included Lieutenant General Erich Staube (1939-42) and Lieutenant General Heinz Greiner (1942-43).

NOTES AND SOURCES: Staube, who was named General of Infantry to date from June 1, 1942, went on to command the XIII Corps in Russia (1942-43) and the LXXIV and LXXXVI Corps on the Western Front (late 1943-December 1944 and 1945, respectively). He was a Saxon and held the Knight's Cross with Oak Leaves. Greiner, a Bavarian who also wore the Oak Leaves on his Knight's Cross, had been a regimental commander under Staube, leading the 499th Infantry in Russia. He was given command of the 362nd Infantry Division after the 268th was disbanded and led it in Italy (1943-early 1945). Carell 1966: 196; Carell 1971: 309; Hartmann: 29; *Kriegstagebuch des OKW*, Volume III: 1157; RA: 116; OB 42: 101; OB 43: 166; OB 44: 227; OB 45: 220.

269th INFANTRY DIVISION

COMPOSITION: 469th Infantry Regiment, 489th Infantry Regiment, 490th Infantry Regiment, 269th Artillery Regiment, 269th Reconnaissance Battalion, 269th Anti-Tank Battalion, 269th Engineer Battalion, 269th Signal Battalion

HOME STATION: Delmenhorst, Wkr. X

This division was formed in the general mobilization of 1939 from men already serving in North German reserve units. In 1940 it saw action in northern France and spent the next twelve months on occupation duty in Denmark. In June 1941 it crossed into Russia with Army Group North and played a major role in the XL Panzer Corps' annihilation of the Russian III Armored Corps on the Dubysa. The division was down to 40 percent of its authorized strength by October, but still fought well in the Battle of the Volkhov, southeast of Leningrad, in early 1942. In the winter of 1942-43 the 269th was sent to Norway to rest and refit and remained on occupation duty at Bergen for more than a year and a half. In October 1944 it returned to the European mainland via Denmark and fought in the Battle of the Colmar Bridgehead on the Western Front, where it was again reduced to battle group strength. In January 1945 it was transferred to southern Poland. The 269th Infantry was in the vicinity of Dresden as the only division in 4th Panzer Army's reserve when Berlin fell. A large number of its survivors apparently managed to surrender to the Western Allies instead of to the Russians. Commanders of this veteran unit included Lieutenant General Ernst-Eberhard Hell (1940), Lieutenant General Kurt Badinski (1943), and Major General Hans Wagner (1943-45).

NOTES AND SOURCES: General of Artillery as of March 1942, Hell led the VII Corps in Russia from 1942 until August 1944, when he was captured. Kurt Badinski assumed command of the 276th Infantry Division on the Western Front in 1944 and was captured in August of that year. Both he and Hell were winners of the Knight's Cross with Oak Leaves. Hans Wagner, a veteran artillery regimental commander, apparently assumed command of the 269th while still a Colonel. Benoist-Mechin: 133; Carell 1966: 24, 421; *Kriegstagebuch des OKW*, Volume I: 1146; Volume IV: 1896; Salisbury: 351; RA: 160; OB 43: 167-68; OB 44: 228; OB 45: 221; Ziemke 1959; 261.

270th INFANTRY (later COASTAL DEFENSE) DIVISION

COMPOSITION (1944): 341st Grenadier Regiment, 856th Fortress Regiment (?)

HOME STATION: Hamburg, Wkr. X

The original 270th Infantry Division was formed in the latter part of 1939 and was dissolved after the fall of France in 1940. It apparently never had infantry regiments assigned to it and served as a sort of special administrative headquarters with miscellaneous units under its control. It never left northern Germany.

A second Headquarters, 270th Infantry Division was organized in Hamburg in 1942; however, instead of receiving infantry regiments to direct, as apparently was the original plan, the HQ was sent to central Norway, where it took charge of a variety of fortress battalions and coastal defense artillery batteries as a coastal defense unit. The 270th remained in central Norway from the summer of 1942 until the end of the war, except for a brief tour of duty in northern Finland (May to October 1944), when it guarded the rear of the 20th Mountain Army from a possible Soviet amphibious attack. The division's commanders included Lieutenant Generals Rolf Sodan (1943) and Barbänder (1944-45).

NOTES AND SOURCES: Lieutenant General Sodan was sixty-five years old and apparently living in retirement when the war ended. General Barbänder previously commanded Special Administrative Division Staff 416 in Denmark (1942-43). RA: 160; OB 44: 228; OB 45: 221.

271st INFANTRY (later VOLKSGRENADIER) DIVISION

COMPOSITION (1944): 977th Grenadier Regiment, 978th Grenadier Regiment, 979th Grenadier Regiment, 271st Artillery Regiment, 271st Füsilier Battalion, 271st Anti-Tank Battalion, 271st Engineer Battalion, 271st Signal Battalion

HOME STATION: Wehrkreis XIII

The original 271st Infantry was formed in Wehrkreis V from older age men in the early summer of 1940, when it looked as if the French campaign might be a long one. France fell in six weeks, and the 271st Infantry was dissolved that autumn. It never saw combat.

The second 271st Infantry Division began forming in west-central Germany in December 1943, under the former Headquarters, 137th Infantry Division. Many of the division's soldiers had come from the 137th, which had just been dissolved after two years of fighting on the Russian Front. The new division was soon transferred to Holland, where it completed its formation in early 1944. It was on the Mediterranean coast in early June 1944 but was still considerably understrength. Nevertheless the 271st was sent to Normandy, where it replaced the debilitated 10th SS Panzer Division in the front line near Caen on July 17. The division fought well but was encircled with much of the rest of Army Group B at Falaise and was virtually destroyed. Elements did break out; divisional commander Lieutenant General Paul Danhauser was among those who escaped. Enough remained of the original division to form a nucleus around which a Volksgrenadier division was organized in the later summer, 1944. In November the new division was sent to Czechoslovakia, and by December it was in action in Hungary and ended the war in the pocket east of Prague.

NOTES AND SOURCES: Paul Danhauser, a Bavarian who had commanded the 256th Infantry Division in Russia, led the 271st from late 1943 until

October 1944, when he was named Deputy Commander of Wehrkreis XII, headquartered at Weisbaden. The 271st absorbed the inexperienced recruits of the 576th Grenadier Division in the winter of 1944. Blumenson 1960: 225, 556; Harrison: Map VI; "Frontnachweiser," 15 December 1944; *Kriegstagebuch des OKW*, Volume I: 1146; RA: 204; OB 43: 167; OB 44b: D92; OB 45: 222.

272nd INFANTRY (later VOLKSGRENADIER) DIVISION

COMPOSITION (1944): 980th Grenadier Regiment, 981st Grenadier Regiment, 982nd Grenadier Regiment, 272nd Artillery Regiment, 272nd Füsilier Battalion, 272nd Anti-Tank Battalion, 272nd Engineer Battalion, 272nd Signal Battalion

HOME STATION: Wehrkreis III

The original 272nd Infantry Division was formed in June 1940 and disbanded two months later, after the fall of France. It consisted of older men who were called up for home service during the French campaign. As soon as the armistice with France was reached they were released back into civilian industry.

Another 272nd Infantry began to organize in Germany in December 1943 and completed its training in Belgium in early 1944. It was sent to the Lyon area of France later that year and was engaged in training at Perpignan near the Spanish frontier in June. Still badly understrength, it was nevertheless sent to the Normandy Front, where it replaced the exhausted 1st SS and 12th SS Panzer Divisions on the front line on July 13. The 272nd suffered heavy casualties in the Normandy/Falaise battles of July and August 1944 and was sent back to the III Military District to rebuild completely later that summer. This program probably took place at the Döberitz Maneuver Area, just west of Berlin. Redesignated a Volksgrenadier division, the 272nd was transferred back to the Western Front in November and fought in the Battles of the Huertgen Forest, the Bulge, and the Roer River Dams, as well as in the Eifel campaign. Burned-out after January 1945, the division was finished off in the Ruhr Pocket in April 1945. Commanders of the 272nd Infantry/Volksgrenadier included Lieutenant General Friedrich August Schack (1943-44), Colonel Eugen Kossmala (1944), and Major General Eugen König (December 1944-1945).

NOTES AND SOURCES: Lieutenant General Schack, a Silesian and holder of the Knight's Cross with Oak Leaves, was placed in command of LXXXI Corps on the Western Front in late 1944. The 272nd absorbed the 575th Grenadier Division in the fall of 1944. Colonel Kossmala, who had previously commanded the 6th Grenadier Regiment, had led the 32nd Infantry Division on the northern sector of the Eastern Front (1944). Eugen König, who, like Kossmala, wore the Oak Leaves to the Knight's Cross, had commanded a grenadier regiment in the 251st Infantry Division on the northern sector of the Russian Front. He commanded the 91st Air Landing Division in Normandy as a colonel, after General Falley was killed. Blumenson 1960: 225, 582; Chant, Volume 14: 1863; Volume 16: 2133; Harrison: Map VI; "Frontnachweiser," 15 December 1944; *Kriegstagebuch des OKW*, Volume IV: 1900; MacDonald 1963: 460, 599, 601; RA: 172; OB 42: 101; OB 43: 167; OB 45: 222.

273rd INFANTRY DIVISION

COMPOSITION: 544th Infantry Regiment, 545th Infantry Regiment, 546th Infantry Regiment

HOME STATION: Wehrkreis III

Formed from older personnel in the III Military District in the summer of 1940, the original 273rd was dissolved after the fall of France later that year.

A second 273rd was formed in the last month of the war. Apparently very much understrength, it was sent to the Eastern Front, where the remnants of the 16th Hungarian Infantry Division were attached to it, and the 273rd ended the war in Czechoslovakia.

SOURCES: "Frontnachweiser," 15 December 1944. *Kriegstagebuch des OKW*, Volume I: 1146; OB 43: 167; OB 44b: D92.

274th INFANTRY DIVISION

COMPOSITION: 862nd Grenadier Regiment, 865th Grenadier Regiment, 274th Artillery Regiment, 274th Füsilier Battalion, 274th Anti-Tank Battalion, 274th Engineer Battalion, 274th Signal Battalion

HOME STATION: Wehrkreis II

This unit was organized in Norway in the summer of 1943, from the 862nd and 865th Grenadier Regiments of the 347th and 348th Infantry Divisions, respectively. The new unit was classified as static because of its lack of motorized vehicles. It spent its entire existence guarding the coast of Norway around Drammen (autumn 1943 to July 1944) and Stavenger (July 1944 to May 1945). Small elements of the division were sent to the Western

Front in June 1944. Lieutenant General Wilhelm Russwurm commanded the division from late 1943 to 1945.

NOTES AND SOURCES: Russwurm, a signal officer, had commanded the 403rd Security Division in Russia (1942-43). Chant, Volume 13: 1704; RA: 32; OB 45: 223.

275th INFANTRY DIVISION

COMPOSITION: 983rd Grenadier Regiment, 984th Grenadier Regiment, 985th Grenadier Regiment, 275th Artillery Regiment, 275th Füsilier Battalion, 275th Anti-Tank Battalion, 275th Engineer Battalion, 275th Signal Battalion

HOME STATION: Wehrkreis IV

Formed in December 1943, the newly created unit included elements of the recently disbanded 223rd Infantry Division, which had been largely destroyed on the Eastern Front. Sent to Brittany, it was still forming in mid-February 1944, when it consisted of the divisional staff, one regimental staff, one artillery unit, two battalions of "old men," and little else. The 275th conducted training operations in Brittany until June 1944, when it replaced the exhausted Panzer Lehr Division in the line in Normandy. It was smashed in the American Cobra offensive of July 25-27, 1944, when it was subjected to repeated saturation attacks by heavy bomber groups. The survivors of Cobra suffered further severe casualties in the breakout from the Falaise pocket in August, and the division was listed as practically destroyed by SS General Hausser, commander of the 7th Army, shortly afterward. The remnants of the 275th fought at Aachen under Lieutenant General Hans Schmidt, and it was down to a strength of eight hundred men before it was taken out of the line later that month. On October 1, 1944, it absorbed the survivors of the 353rd Infantry Division, as well as some miscellaneous local defense troops. Its total strength on October 3 was five thousand men, thirteen 105mm howitzers, one 210mm howitzer and six assault guns. Thus, even after rebuilding, the 275th had only about one-third of the strength of a 1941-type division—a situation fairly typical in the German Army in the fifth year of the war. Despite its poor condition it was returned to the Aachen sector in November and fought in the Battle of the Huertgen Forest, where it was virtually destroyed. The remnants of the 275th were absorbed by the 344th Infantry Division, and the divisional staff was evacuated to Germany. In early 1945 it was stationed in the interior of the Reich and was reportedly engaged in forming a new Volksgrenadier division. However, when it reappeared in combat in Czechoslovakia in early March 1945, the 275th was listed as an infantry, not a Volksgrenadier, unit. The burned-out division was finally dissolved in the last chaotic weeks of the war, and its men probably were distributed among the various units of Army Group Center. Colonel Helmut Bechler was acting divisional commander in early 1945.

NOTES AND SOURCES: Bechler had led the 504th Grenadier Regiment of the 291st Infantry Division in 1944. Blumenson 1960: 226, 247, 273, 372, 442; Harrison: 257, Map VI; *Kriegstagebuch des OKW*, Volume IV: 1896; MacDonald 1963: 91, 99, 103, 226, 273, 330, 465; Ruge: 79; RA: 72; OB 45: 223-24.

276th INFANTRY (later VOLKSGRENADIER) DIVISION

COMPOSITION (1944): 986th Grenadier Regiment, 987th Grenadier Regiment, 988th Grenadier Regiment, 276th Artillery Regiment, 276th Füsilier Battalion, 276th Anti-Tank Battalion, 276th Engineer Battalion, 276th Signal Battalion

HOME STATION: Wehrkreis XI

One of the divisions containing older men, the original 276th Infantry was formed in the XI Military District in June 1940 and dissolved two months later, when the fall of France made its continued existence unnecessary. It never left Germany.

The second 276th Infantry Division was activated in Germany in December 1943 and was sent to Dax in southwestern France in January 1944 to complete its training. It was sent into battle in Normandy in mid-June and was virtually destroyed in the Battle of the Falaise Pocket in August. Its commander, Lieutenant General Curt Badinski, was among those taken prisoner. Reorganized in Poland as a Volksgrenadier division, the 276th returned to action in the Battle of the Bulge that December. Here it lost two thousand men and its divisional commander, Lieutenant General Kurt Moehring, who was killed. In January 1945 the division—now led by Colonel Dempwolff—was fighting north of Luxembourg. Two months later, as it opposed American attempts to cross the Rhine, the 276th had a strength of only four hundred ten men and howitzers. Finally, under the command of Colonel Werner Wagner it was smashed south of Remagen, collapsed altogether in late March, and the remnants of the 276th retreated into the Ruhr Pocket, where they were captured in April 1945.

NOTES AND SOURCES: The 276th absorbed the partially formed 580th Grenadier Division in the winter of 1944. Blumenson 1960: 551, 582;

Chant, Volume 16: 2133; Cole 1965: 228-32, 507; Harrison: Map VI; Mac-
Donald 1973: 250-51, 275, 349; "Frontnachweiser," 15 December 1944; RA:
172; OB 45: 224.

277th INFANTRY (later VOLKSGRENADIER) DIVISION

COMPOSITION (1944): 989th Grenadier Regiment, 990th Grenadier Regi-
ment, 991st Grenadier Regiment, 277th Artillery Regiment, 277th Füsilier
Battalion, 277th Anti-Tank Battalion, 277th Engineer Battalion, 277th
Signal Battalion

HOME STATION: Stuttgart, Wkr. V

The original 277th Infantry Division was formed in June 1940 and
disbanded in August of the same year. Its men—mostly from the older age
groups—were returned to the civilian economy.

The second 277th reportedly existed as a special purpose divisional staff
in Stuttgart as early as 1942, but it did not receive any standard infantry
units until December 1943, when it was organized in Westphalia as a
combat infantry division from elements of several existing and recently
disbanded divisions. Most of its replacements after the initial organization
were Austrians. In January 1944 it was transformed to Croatia and later
(under Lieutenant General Hofmann) to Narbonne in southern France.
Hofmann was replaced by Lieutenant General Albert Praum in May. Sent
to Normandy in mid-June, the 277th replaced the battered 9th SS Panzer
Division in the front line. As part of the II SS Panzer Corps, it fought well
against the British in the Battle of Caen (July 8-9) but was crushed in the
Battle of the Falaise Pocket the following month. After the battle, Colonel
Wilhelm Viebig (who had recently succeeded Praum as divisional commander) could assemble only twenty-five hundred men, and only one
thousand of these were combat troops. The 277th was sent to Hungary
where it absorbed the 374th Grenadier Division and was rebuilt as a
Volksgrenadier division. It returned to the Western Front in time to fight
in the Battle of the Bulge and was part of the XLVII Panzer Corps during
the early part of the last campaign. Viebig, who was promoted to Major
General in late 1944, was captured on the Western bank of the Rhine, when
his command post was overrun on March 9, 1945. The remnants of the
277th Infantry were trapped in the Ruhr Pocket and surrendered to the
Western Allies in April 1945.

NOTES AND SOURCES: Albert Praum commanded the 18th Panzer Division in Russia (1942), as well as the 129th Infantry Division (1942-43). He

was Chief Signals Officer for Army Group Center (1943) and led the 277th from May until August, when he was named Chief Signals Officer for OKW. Major General Junck was acting divisional commander of the 277th in July 1944—apparently Praum had fallen ill or had been wounded in early July. Junck previously led the 74th Panzer Grenadier Regiment (1942) and later commanded the 265th Infantry Division in Lorient (1945). Viebig had been commander of the 258th Grenadier Regiment in 1944. Air University Files, SRGG 1153; Blumenson 1960: 225, 551; Chant, Volume 14: 1914; Cole 1965: 83, 95-96; Harrison: Map VI; *Kriegstagebuch des OKW*, Volume IV: 1900; "Frontnachweiser," 15 December 1944; Mac-Donald 1973: 69; RA: 220; OB 42: 22; OB 45: 224-25.

278th INFANTRY DIVISION

COMPOSITION (1944): 992nd Grenadier Regiment, 993rd Grenadier Regiment, 994th Grenadier Regiment, 278th Artillery Regiment, 278th Füsilier Battalion, 278th Anti-Tank Battalion, 278th Engineer Battalion, 278th Signal Battalion

HOME STATION: Wehrkreis III

Formed in mid 1940 from Landwehr (older) reservists, the first 278th Infantry Division was dissolved after the fall of France. It never saw combat.

The second 278th was created in Belgium in late 1943 and was sent to northeastern Italy in February 1944. Here it formed part of Army Detachment von Zangen, a collection of mediocre and ill-equipped formations. By May, however, the division was on the front line opposing the British advance up the Adriatic coast. It was part of the LXXVI Panzer Corps in the battles of the Gothic Line that September and fought in every major battle in Italy after that. Most of this period it was led by Lieutenant General Harry Hoppe (1944-45). On April 22, 1945, it covered the retreat of the I Parachute Corps south of the Brenner Pass. The Corps escaped, but the bulk of the 278th was cut off and captured. Even those who got away surrendered to elements of the 5th and 7th U.S. Armies a few days later.

NOTES AND SOURCES: General Hoppe distinguished himself as the commander of the 424th Infantry Regiment (1941-42) during the advance on and siege of Leningrad. He later commanded the 126th Infantry Division (October 1942-1943). He was promoted to Lieutenant General in June 1943. Hoppe held the Knight's Cross with Oak Leaves. Fisher: 19, 278, 302, 494; Hartmann: 30; RA: 46; OB 45: 225.

280th COASTAL DEFENSE DIVISION

COMPOSITION: 3 to 5 Fortress Battalions, Miscellaneous General Head-quarters Units

HOME STATION: Norway (?)

The 280th Coastal Defense Division was formed in southern Norway in the summer of 1942. It included various fortress battalions and coastal defense artillery batteries and reportedly included the Headquarters, 280th Artillery Regiment. Its mission was to guard the coast of Norway from an invasion that never came. It remained in southern Norway, concentrated in the Stavanger area, until the end of the Third Reich. Lieutenant General von Beeren (1942-45) was the commander of the 280th.

SOURCES: *Kriegstagebuch des OKW*, Volume II: 1357; Volume III: 8, 1158; Volume IV: 1878; OB 43: 167; OB 44: 230; OB 45: 225

280th INFANTRY DIVISION

COMPOSITION: Older-age reservists

HOME STATION: Wehrkreis IV (?)

This division was formed and dissolved in Germany in 1940. Its men were mostly older reservists pressed into service during the French campaign and released from active duty during Hitler's partial demobilization of autumn 1940.

SOURCES: OB 44: 230; OB 45: 225.

281st SECURITY DIVISION

COMPOSITION: 107th Security Regiment, 368th Security Regiment, 281st Füsilier Company, 368th Anti-Tank Company, 368th Engineer Company, 281st Signal Company

HOME STATION: Wehrkreis II

Formed on the northern sector of the Russian Front in mid-1941, the 281st was encircled at Kholm on January 28, 1942. Its commander, Major General Theodor Scherer (1941-42), became commandant of the "fortress" and held it against overwhelming odds with only five thousand men until May 5, when it was relieved. Remarkably, he performed this task without artillery of any kind, although he did rely heavily on air support. The 281st Security was engaged in line of communications duties for Army Group North during the next few weeks, but its 368th Security Regiment was again in action in the battles of Demyansk from November 1942 until February 1943. Major General von Stockhausen (1942-44) led the division in these fights. The following autumn the 281st was again heavily engaged against the Russians on the northern sector of the front and was finally smashed by the Soviet summer offensive of 1944. It was disbanded at the end of the year. Contrary to its supposed rear-area mission, the 281st spent much of its time on the front line, rather than in the communications zone.

NOTES AND SOURCES: Theodor Scherer later commanded the 34th Infantry Division (August 5-November 2, 1942), the 87th Infantry Division (late 1942-1943), and the 83rd Infantry Division (1943-44). He was promoted to Lieutenant General effective November 1, 1942, and was awarded the Knight's Cross with Oak Leaves. Colonel Friedrich Wilhelm Rübesamen was acting commander of the division for part of 1944. *Kriegstagebuch des OKW*, Volume II: 1376, 1396-97; Volume III: 260; Volume IV: 1888; RA: 32; OB 43: 214; OB 45: 226.

282nd INFANTRY DIVISION

COMPOSITION: 848th Grenadier Regiment, 849th Grenadier Regiment, 850th Grenadier Regiment, 282nd Artillery Regiment, 282nd Füsilier Battalion, 282nd Anti-Tank Battalion, 282nd Engineer Battalion, 282nd Signal Battalion

HOME STATION: Wehrkreis V

Organized in France in the winter of 1942-43, the 282nd was more or less continuously engaged on the southern sector of the Russian Front from April 1943 until August 1944. It was already down to battle group strength by October 1943. The 282nd took part in the retreats from Kursk, Kiev, and the Dnieper and fought in the Battle of Kirovograd in December 1943. It finally was encircled and destroyed west of the lower Dnestr in August 1944. Its commanders included Major General Kohler (1943) and Lieutenant General Frenking (December 1943-1944).

NOTES AND SOURCES: Kohler, later a Lieutenant General, commanded the 11th Luftwaffe Field Division (late 1943-1945). Frenking was captured by the Russians in May 1944. *Kriegstagebuch des OKW*, Volume III: 1156; RA: 86; OB 44: 230; OB 45: 230.

284th SECURITY DIVISION

COMPOSITION: Two security regiments, 284th Füsilier Company, 284th Anti-Tank Company, 284th Engineer Company, 284th Signal Company.

HOME STATION: Unknown

The 284th was formed in the summer of 1942 and was involved in the rear-area operations of Army Group North until early 1944. It suffered heavy casualties in the withdrawal from Leningrad in February 1944 and was dissolved a month later.

SOURCE: OB 45: 266

285th SECURITY DIVISION

COMPOSITION: 113th Security Regiment, 322nd Security Regiment, 285th Füsilier Company, 322nd Anti-Tank Company, 322nd Engineer Company, 322nd Signal Company

HOME STATION: Wehrkreis V

This division spent most of its career on rear-area and line of communications duty for Army Group North. It was formed in Russia in late 1941, and elements were besieged in Kholm from January to May 1942, along with parts of the 281st Security Division. In the rear area for the next two years, the 285th was involved in anti-partisan operations, the Leningrad withdrawal, and opposed the Soviet summer offensive of 1944, during which it was smashed. In September 1944 the remnants of the 285th Security were under the operational control of the 20th SS Grenadier Division. It was disbanded shortly afterward. Its commander for most of its existence was Lieutenant General Gustav Adolph-Auffenberg-Komarow (1942-44).

NOTES AND SOURCES: Adolph-Auffenberg-Komarow was an Austrian. *Kriegstagebuch des OKW*, Volume IV: 1877; OB 43: 214, OB 45: 227.

286th SECURITY DIVISION

COMPOSITION: 31st Security Regiment, 61st Security Regiment, 122nd Security Regiment, 286th Füsilier Company, 286th Anti-Tank Company, 286th Engineer Company, 286th Signal Company

HOME STATION: Wehrkreis VIII

Formed in early 1942, this division served with Army Group Center throughout the war. It was used primarily in the rear area, protecting important installations and conducting anti-partisan operations. It saw front-line duty against the Russian summer offensive of 1944 and suffered heavy casualties. At battle group strength, it fought in Samland and in the East Prussian Pocket in 1945 and was in East Prussia when Berlin fell. Divisional commanders of the 286th Security included Major Generals Richert (1943) and Oschmann (1945).

The 286th was unusual for a security division in that it had three security regiments as opposed to the normal total of two per division.

SOURCES: *Kriegstagebuch des OKW*, Volume IV: 1897; OB 43: 214; OB 45: 227.

290th INFANTRY DIVISION

COMPOSITION: 501st Infantry Regiment, 502nd Infantry Regiment, 503rd Infantry Regiment, 290th Artillery Regiment, 290th Reconnaissance Battalion, 290th Anti-Tank Battalion, 290th Engineer Battalion, 290th Signal Battalion

HOME STATION: Wehrkreis X

The 290th was formed from newly trained north German personnel in March and April 1940. It fought in France a few weeks later and invaded the Soviet Union with the LVI Panzer Corps of Army Group North in June 1941. It was an effective fighting unit. The 290th Infantry spearheaded the initial attack into Russia and played a major role in the capture of Dvinsk. In August it fought in the First Battle of Lake Ilmen and was surrounded in the Demyansk Pocket in January 1942. The division's freedom of action was not restored until February 1943. Transferred to Army Group Center, it fought in the Battle of Nevel that autumn, before being returned to Army Group North. The division suffered heavy losses in the Leningrad withdrawal and was isolated in the Courland Pocket by October. Here it remained, holding off several Soviet attacks, until the end of the war. Its commanders included Lieutenant General Max Dennerlein (1940-41), Lieutenant General Baron Theodor von Wrede (1941-43), Lieutenant General Heinrichs (1944), Major General Karl Henke (late 1944), and Lieutenant General Bruno Ortner (1945).

NOTES AND SOURCES: General Dennerlein, a Bavarian, was in charge of Replacement Divisional Staff 433 at the end of the conflict. Baron von Wrede, former Military Attaché to Budapest, was reportedly Chief of the Armaments and War Production Staff in Italy in 1945. Henke was the former commander of the 770th Engineer Landing Regiment (1943) and had commanded a battle group at Kerel (1943) and Sworba (1944) on the Eastern Front. He was an acting divisional commander only. Bruno Ortner, an Austrian, had led the 69th Infantry Division in southern Russia (1943-44). Carell 1966: 21, 248, 288, 365, 375, 427; OB 42: 102; OB 43: 167-68; OB 44: 230; OB 45: 227-28.

291st INFANTRY DIVISION

COMPOSITION: 504th Infantry Regiment, 505th Infantry Regiment, 506th Infantry Regiment, 291st Artillery Regiment, 291st Reconnaissance Battalion, 291st Anti-Tank Battalion, 291st Engineer Battalion, 291st Signal Battalion

HOME STATION: Insterburg, Wkr. I

Nicknamed the Elk Division, this unit was created in April 1940 from Prussians living in the Masurian area. The 291st played a minor role in the French campaign before going to Russia in 1941. On June 22-23, the first two days of the invasion, the 291st penetrated 44 miles in the first 34 hours—an astonishing total for an infantry division. It soon loosely surrounded Riga and repulsed several desperate attempts by the Soviet garrison to break out of the city. Regimental Combat Group Lasch suffered particularly heavy casualties, but the division held its line, contained, and eventually helped destroy the Russian garrison. Later that year it took the major Soviet naval base at Liepaja after a bitter struggle. Remaining with Army Group North, the 291st fought in the Battle of Volkhov (January-March 1942) before being transferred to the Velikie Luki sector of Army Group South in early 1943. It suffered heavy losses in the retreat through the northern Ukraine and, as part of the 1st Panzer Army, was overrun in the Russian summer offensive of 1944. Although greatly reduced in numbers it remained in the line and fought in the Vistula campaign of late 1944. The 291st Infantry was finally destroyed in early 1945, when it tried unsuccessfully to block the Soviet advance into Silesia. Its commanders included Lieutenant Generals Kurt Herzog (1940-42) and Werner Goeritz (1943-44).

NOTES AND SOURCES: Kurt Herzog, a Saxon, was promoted to General of Artillery as of July 1, 1942. He commanded XXXVIII Corps from June 1942 until 1945. This unit ended the war in the Courland Pocket. General Goeritz later commanded the 92nd Infantry Division in Italy (1944). Carell 1966: 20-22, 265, 421; Carell 1971: 510; Chant, Volume 16: 2232; Hartmann: 30; OB 42: 102; OB 43: 168; OB 44: 231; OB 45: 228.

292nd INFANTRY DIVISION

COMPOSITION: 507th Infantry Regiment, 508th Infantry Regiment, 509th Infantry Regiment, 292nd Artillery Regiment, 292nd Reconnaissance Battalion, 292nd Anti-Tank Battalion, 292nd Engineer Battalion, 292nd Signal Battalion

HOME STATION: Wehrkreis II

Mobilized in April 1940, this division consisted of newly trained young men. It fought in France (1940) and on the Eastern Front (1941-45). After crossing the Bug River with Army Group Center in 1941, it fought in the Battle of the Yelnya Bend and in the subsequent drive on Moscow. It took part in the defensive actions of 1942, the Rzhev withdrawal (1943), the Battle of Kursk (where it sustained heavy casualties), in the fighting on the Sozh, and in the retreat into Poland. Down to battle group strength, it retreated through Poland and was still fighting in East Prussia when the war ended. Its commanders included Lieutenant General Dehmel (1940-41), Major General Seeger (1942-43), Lieutenant General Richard John (1943-44), and Major General Hans Gittner (1945).

NOTES AND SOURCES: General Dehmel commanded IX Corps in 1941 and, in June 1943, was Inspector of Engineers and Railway Engineers for OKH. Lieutenant General John had previously commanded the 383nd Infantry Division (1943). Hans Gittner had been Ia of XXXIX Corps (1940) and on the staff of 15th Army (1942). Carell 1966: 9; Carell 1971: 26, 37, 309; Hartmann: 30; *Kriegstagebuch des OKW*, Volume IV: 1897; RA: 32; OB 42: 168; OB 43: 168; OB 44: 231; OB 45: 228.

293rd INFANTRY DIVISION

COMPOSITION: 510th Infantry Regiment, 511th Infantry Regiment, 512th Infantry Regiment, 293rd Artillery Regiment, 293rd Reconnaissance Battalion, 293rd Anti-Tank Battalion, 293rd Engineer Battalion, 293rd Signal Battalion

HOME STATION: Berlin, Wkr. III

Organized in April 1940 from newly trained young soldiers, this unit was known as the Bear Division, because of its ties to the city of Berlin, the symbol of which is a bear. The division saw action in France in 1940 before joining Army Group Center for the Russian invasion of 1941. It fought at Moscow, Kursk, and in the Dnieper campaigns before being disbanded in early 1944 because of the heavy casualties it had suffered. Its commanders included Lieutenant General Justin von Obernitz (1942), Lieutenant General Werner Forst (1942-43), and Major General Karl Arndt (1943-44).

NOTES AND SOURCES: Werner Forst, a holder of the Knight's Cross with Oak Leaves, commanded Arko 146, a GHQ artillery unit, in 1941 and the 106th Infantry Division in occupied France (1943-44). He ended the war as Inspector of Artillery at OKH (June 1944-1945). Lieutenant General Arndt was commanding the 359th Infantry Division on the Eastern Front in 1945. Hartmann: 31; RA: 46; OB 42: 102; OB 43: 168; OB 44: 232; OB 45: 229.

294th INFANTRY DIVISION

COMPOSITION: 513th Infantry Regiment, 514th Infantry Regiment, 515th Infantry Regiment, 294th Artillery Regiment, 294th Reconnaissance Battalion, 294th Anti-Tank Battalion, 294th Engineer Battalion, 294th Signal Battalion

HOME STATION: Wehrkreis IV

Formed in April 1940 from recently trained Saxon personnel, the 294th took part in the French campaign of 1940 and in the Balkan campaign in the spring of 1941. Here it was commanded by Lieutenant General Johannes Block, who led it until 1944. The 294th crossed into southern Russia that summer and was involved in the drive on Kiev. Remaining with Army Group South, it was used to stabilize the Rumanian 3rd Army in the fall of 1942 and suffered heavy casualties when the Rumanians collapsed and set up the Stalingrad debacle. The bulk of the 8th Luftwaffe Field Division was attached to the 294th in late 1942 during the retreat from the Volga. Remaining in the line, the 294th Infantry was later encircled at Taganrog and again sustained heavy losses in the ensuing breakout after which the veteran division was again surrounded and finally smashed west of the lower Dnestr in August 1944. The remnants that escaped were attached to the 333rd Infantry Division, which absorbed them when the 294th Infantry Division was officially disbanded in late 1944.

SOURCES: Hartmann: 31; *Kriegstagebuch des OKW*, Volume II: 1393; Volume III: 4; RA: 72; OB 43: OB 44: 232; OB 45: 229.

295th INFANTRY DIVISION

COMPOSITION: 516th Infantry Regiment, 517th Infantry Regiment, 518th Infantry Regiment, 295th Artillery Regiment, 295th Reconnaissance Battalion, 295th Anti-Tank Battalion, 295th Engineer Battalion, 295th Signal Battalion

HOME STATION: Wehrkreis XI

The 295th was formed from newly trained soldiers in April 1940. It first saw combat in Russia in 1941, sweeping across the Ukraine and Donets, only to be turned back by the Russian winter offensive of 1941-42. The next year the 295th was involved in the Kharkov-Izyum battles, Voronezh, and Kalach, as well as the fighting on the Volga. The 295th Infantry was surrounded at Stalingrad in November 1942 and surrendered to the Russians in late January 1943.

A second 295th Infantry Division was organized in Norway in late 1943 and remained there the rest of the war. In the summer of 1944 it lost the 518th Grenadier Regiment, which was sent to the Lofoten Islands to form the nucleus of Fortress Brigade Lofoten. In early 1945 U.S. Intelligence reported that the 295th was preparing to leave Norway, but it apparently did not. Its commander in early 1945 was Lieutenant General Georg Dinter (late 1943-45).

NOTES AND SOURCES: Major General Dr. Otto Korfes (1942-43) surrendered the original 295th Infantry to the Soviets when Stalingrad fell. The second 295th Infantry Division's subordinate units bore the same numbers as the original. Von Mellenthin 1956: 225; RA: 172; OB 43: 169; OB 45: 229-30; Ziemke 1959: 256, 262.

296th INFANTRY DIVISION

COMPOSITION: 519th Infantry Regiment, 520th Infantry Regiment, 521st Infantry Regiment, 296th Artillery Regiment, 296th Reconnaissance Battalion, 296th Anti-Tank Battalion, 296th Engineer Battalion, 296th Signal Battalion

HOME STATION: Nuremberg, Wkr. XIII

Organized from newly trained men from northern Bavaria and the western Sudetenland, the 296th was in France in May 1940 but did not take part in any major fighting. From the summer of 1940 until the spring of 1941 it was stationed in the Dunkirk area before being transferred to Army Group Center for the invasion of Russia. It was heavily engaged in the battles around Moscow in late 1941 and early 1942, fought in the defensive battles on the central sector in 1942, in the Gomel area in 1943, and was virtually destroyed in the Soviet summer offensive of 1944. Remnants of the division, however, escaped to the north, where they were incorporated into Army Group North. A rump 296th was still holding a sector in the Courland Pocket when the war ended. Divisional commanders of the 296th Infantry included Lieutenant Generals Wilhelm Stemmermann (1941-42), Friedrich Krischer (1942-43), and Arthur Kullmer (1943-44).

NOTES AND SOURCES: Krischer, an Austrian, was commander of Arko 27 in 1942. Carell 1966: 196; *Kriegstagebuch des OKW*, Volume IV: 1897; RA: 204; OB 42: 103; OB 43: 169-70; OB 44: 233; OB 45: 230.

297th INFANTRY DIVISION

COMPOSITION: 522nd Infantry Regiment, 523rd Infantry Regiment, 524th Infantry Regiment, 297th Artillery Regiment, 297th Reconnaissance Battalion, 297th Anti-Tank Battalion, 297th Engineer Battalion, 297th Signal Battalion

HOME STATION: Vienna, Wkr. XVII

Activated in March and April 1940 the 297th first saw action in Russia with Army Group South in July 1941. It took part in the drives toward Kiev and Rostov in 1941 and opposed the Soviet winter offensive of 1941-42. In 1942, under Lieutenant General Max Pfeffer (1941-42), it was with the 6th Army in the Battle of Kharkov, in the clearing of the Izyum Pocket, in the drive across the Don, and in the Battle of Voronezh. It was subsequently encircled at Stalingrad with the 6th Army and destroyed there. Its last commander, Major General Moritz von Drebber, surrendered its remnants to the Russians. Most of the survivors later died in Russian prison camps.

A second 297th Infantry was created in Serbia in the summer of 1943, to replace the division destroyed at Stalingrad. The new 297th Infantry, however, never attained the distinguished record of the first. It was transferred in September to Albania, where it was involved in anti-partisan operations, and remained there until the following autumn, when it withdrew to Montenegro and was heavily engaged against Tito's guerrillas that fall. Later it fought against the Russians and remained on the southern sector of the Eastern Front until the end of the war. Commanders of the second 297th included Lieutenant General Albrecht Baler (1944) and Lieutenant General Otto Gullmann (1944-45).

NOTES AND SOURCES: Max Pfeffer, who was given command of the IV Corps (1942), was also trapped in Stalingrad. He was promoted to General of Artillery on January 22, 1943—less than two weeks before the city fell. General Baler, who had commanded the 102nd Infantry Division in 1942, was acting commander of the XXI Mountain Corps in Norway in 1945. General Gullmann served as Commandant of Münster before assuming command of the 297th. Carell 1966: 588; RA: 220; OB 42: 103; OB 43: 170; OB 45: 230.

298th INFANTRY DIVISION

COMPOSITION: 525th Infantry Regiment, 526th Infantry Regiment, 527th Infantry Regiment, 298th Artillery Regiment, 298th Reconnaissance Battalion, 298th Anti-Tank Battalion, 298th Engineer Battalion, 298th Signal Battalion

HOME STATION: Breslau, Wkr. VIII

Created in March and April, 1940, the 298th's soldiers were primarily newly trained Silesians. They first saw combat in southern Russia in 1941. The division fought as part of the III Panzer Corps in the Battle of Kharkov and was involved in the subsequent campaigns on the southern sector of the Eastern Front. It was with the 8th Italian Army when it collapsed during the Stalingrad encirclement and escaped only after suffering heavy casualties. During the retreat from the Volga in 1943 the division again suffered heavy losses—so much so that it had to be disbanded. Its last commander was Lieutenant General Szelinski (1942-43).

SOURCES: Carell 1966: 490, 535; *Kriegstagebuch des OKW*, Volume II: 1386, 1394; RA: 130; OB 42: 104; OB 43: 170; OB 44: 234; OB 44b: D96.

299th INFANTRY (later VOLKSGRENADIER) DIVISION

COMPOSITION: 528th Infantry Regiment, 529th Infantry Regiment, 530th Infantry Regiment, 299th Artillery Regiment, 299th Reconnaissance Battalion, 299th Anti-Tank Battalion, 299th Engineer Battalion, 299th Signal Battalion

HOME STATION: Weimar, Wkr. IX

The 299th consisted of newly inducted men from the Hesse and Thuringia regions. Activated in April 1940, it served in France in 1940 and in the initial invasion of southern Russia in July 1941. It was almost continuously engaged after that. The division was eventually transferred to Army Group North and then Center, where it fought in the Battles of Kursk and Gomel in 1943 and distinguished itself as a good combat division. On June 22, 1944, the Russians launched their massive summer offensive with 2.5 million men, and their opening attack struck the 299th Infantry; it collapsed within a few hours. Only remnants escaped, but these were withdrawn to reform the 299th Volksgrenadier Division. This formation, a mere skelton of the original 299th, took part in the Polish campaign of 1944 and continued to fight on the Eastern Front until late 1944 or very early 1945, when it was disbanded. Divisional commanders of the 299th included Lieutenant General Willi Moser (1940-late 1942) and Lieutenant General Count Ralph von Oriola (1943-1944).

NOTES AND SOURCES: The 299th was disbanded between November 26, 1944, and March 1, 1945. Willi Moser was given command of the LXXI Corps in Norway on November 1, 1942, and led it until late 1944. He was promoted to General of Artillery effective December 1, 1942. Count von Oriola later led a corps on the Western Front (late 1944) and the VI Corps on the Eastern Front (1945). Carell 1971: 26, 583; Hartmann: 32; *Kriegstagebuch des OKW*, Volume III: 8, Volume IV: 1887, 1895-1904; RA: 144; OB 43: 104; OB 44: 234; OB 44b: D96; OB 45: 231.

DIVISION 300 z.b.V.

COMPOSITION: Estonian Home Guard units

HOME STATION: Estonia and Wkr. XIII

This headquarters was created in August 1944 as a special staff to direct the mobilization of Estonian home guard regiments in the service of Nazi Germany. It was soon committed to battle on the Narva and continued to fight in the battles of the Courland Pocket until the end of the war. Many of its soldiers were later put to death by the Soviets.

SOURCES: *Kriegstagebuch des OKW*, Volume IV: 1896; OB 45: 231.

302nd INFANTRY DIVISION

COMPOSITION: 570th Infantry Regiment, 571st Infantry Regiment, 572nd Infantry Regiment, 302nd Artillery Regiment, 302nd Reconnaissance Battalion, 302nd Anti-Tank Battalion, 302nd Engineer Battalion, 302nd Signal Battalion

HOME STATION: Schwerin, Wkr. II

This division was formed in late 1940 and spent the next three years on garrison duty in Germany and France. In August 1942 it fought its first battle when the British attempted a major commando-style landing on the continent at Dieppe, France. The 302nd threw them back into the sea and inflicted heavy casualties on the landing force. From then on the 302nd was known as "the Dieppe division." Sent to southern Russia in January 1943, it was involved in the Don campaign and suffered heavy losses in the withdrawal from the lower Dnieper in March 1944. It was encircled west of the Dnieper in August 1944 and destroyed there. Its last commander, Colonel Willi Fischer, was among the prisoners. Previous divisional commanders included Lieutenant General Konrad Haase (1942), Lieutenant General Rüdiger (1943), and Major General von Bogen (1944).

NOTES AND SOURCES: Hasse was Special Disciplinary Officer of Army Group C in Italy in 1945. Major General von Bogen was captured by the Russians in July 1944, whereupon Fischer, the senior regimental commander, assumed command of the division. He had formerly directed the 302nd Artillery Regiment. RA: 32; OB 42: 104; OB 43: 171; OB 45: 231.

304th INFANTRY DIVISION

COMPOSITION: 573rd Infantry Regiment, 574th Infantry Regiment, 575th Infantry Regiment, 304th Artillery Regiment, 304th Reconnaissance Company, 304th Anti-Tank Battalion, 304th Engineer Battalion, 304th Signal Company

HOME STATION: Wehrkreis IV

Formed in late 1940, this division was transferred to Belgium shortly afterward, and remained there for two years. In December 1942 it was rushed to the Eastern Front, where the southern sector was on the verge of collapse. It saw its first action in the Donets, where it behaved badly. The next month, as Army Group Don retreated from Stalingrad, panic again broke out in the ranks of the 304th. Despite its unreliability, the division continued to serve on the southern sector and suffered heavy losses at Taganrog and in the withdrawal to the lower Dnieper bend (March 1944). It fought in the Ukraine and in southern Poland in 1944 and ended the war on the Eastern Front, probably in the huge pocket east of Prague. Its divisional commanders included Major General Ernst Sieler (1942?-43), Lieutenant General Heinrich Krampft (1943-44), and Sieler again (1945).

NOTES AND SOURCES: Ernst Sieler was promoted to Lieutenant General on July 1, 1943. He served on the Supreme Military Court. Carell 1971: 128-29; Manstein: 392; RA: 72; OB 42: 104; OB 43: 171; OB 44: 235; OB 45: 232.

305th INFANTRY DIVISION

COMPOSITION: 576th Infantry Regiment, 577th Infantry Regiment, 578th Infantry Regiment, 305th Artillery Regiment, 305th Reconnaissance Company, 305th Anti-Tank Battalion, 305th Engineer Battalion, 305th Signal Company

HOME STATION: Konstanz, Wkr. V

The original 305th Infantry Division was formed in late 1940 and remained in Germany until mid-1941. Posted to western France, it was sent to the southern sector of the Russian Front in May 1942. It fought with 6th Army at Kharkov, Izyum, Voronezh, Kalach and Stalingrad, where it was surrounded and destroyed in January 1943.

A second 305th was created in France in May 1943 and sent to Nice on the Mediterranean, where it helped replace the unreliable Italian 4th Army. The new division's subordinate units bore the same numbers as the old. It entered Italy with Rommel's Army Group B in late summer 1943 and, in the latter part of 1943, was sent into battle in southern Italy. It suffered many casualties south of Rome and in January 1944 received a considerable number of replacements from the 94th Infantry Division. The 305th returned to action soon after but that summer was withdrawn to northern Italy to rest and refit. It was back on the front line in autumn and was engaged in the Rimini-Cesena area in October. It was fighting west of Bologna in January 1945 and ended the war on the Italian Front. Its leaders included Lieutenant General Friedrich Wilhelm Bruno Hauck (1943-44) and Colonel Friedrich Trompeter (late 1944-45).

NOTES AND SOURCES: Hauck assumed acting command of the LXXVI

Panzer Corps in Italy in December 1944. Colonel Trompeter, his senior regimental commander, moved up to divisional commander. Blumenson 1969: 315; Fisher: 18, 302; Garland and Smyth: 290-93; RA: 86; OB 42: 104; OB 43: 171; OB 44: 236; OB 45: 233.

306th INFANTRY DIVISION

COMPOSITION: 579th Infantry Regiment, 580th Infantry Regiment, 581st Infantry Regiment, 306th Artillery Regiment, 306th Reconnaissance Company, 306th Anti-Tank Battalion, 306th Engineer Battalion, 306th Signal Company

HOME STATION: Wehrkreis VI

Formed in late 1940, the 306th was sent to Belgium a year later and was transferred to southern Russia in December 1942. It fought in the Stalingrad relief campaign and opposed the Soviet drive on Rostov as a part of Army Group Don. It suffered heavy losses in the Battle of Taranrog (December 1942), and the Dnieper bend withdrawal (March 1944), and was reported at battle group strength as early as October 1943. In August and September 1944, the 306th suffered such heavy losses in the Dnestr withdrawal that it had to be disbanded. Its last commander was apparently Lieutenant General Karl-Erik Koehler (1943-44).

NOTES AND SOURCES: Koehler was Chief of Staff of the Replacement Army prior to taking over the 306th. He was in Norway in 1945, reportedly serving as commander of the XXXIII Corps. *Kriegstagebuch des OKW*, Volume III: 1158; Manstein: 322; RA: 102; OB 43: 172; OB 45: 233.

307th INFANTRY DIVISION

COMPOSITION: Various older sources

HOME STATION: Wehrkreis V

This division consisted of men from older age groups called up in the fall of 1939. After France fell, Hitler mistakenly concluded that the war was as good as won, so he ordered the 307th and its sister divisions disbanded in the autumn of 1940.

SOURCE: OB 45: 233.

309th INFANTRY DIVISION

COMPOSITION: Various reservists

HOME STATION: Unknown

Formed from older-age reservists in the latter part of 1939, this division was dissolved after the fall of France in the summer of 1940.

SOURCE: OB 45: 233.

310th INFANTRY DIVISION

COMPOSITION: Older-age reservists

HOME STATION: Unknown

The 310th was activated in autumn 1939. It consisted of men from the older-age groups. Unlike its sister divisions, part of the 310th was involved in combat in 1940, when it took part in the invasion of Norway. After the French surrendered, the division was demobilized, and most of its men were sent home.

SOURCES: OB 45: 234; Ziemke 1959: 50.

311th INFANTRY DIVISION

COMPOSITION: 247th Infantry Regiment, 249th Infantry Regiment, 250th Infantry Regiment

HOME STATION: Wehrkreis I

Created in East Prussia in the winter of 1939-40, the 311th was made up mostly of older men. It never left Germany. Its regiments were disbanded in 1940 after the French campaign. The Headquarters was converted to an administrative command and was sent to Warsaw, where it was still functioning in 1943 under Lieutenant General Albrecht Brand (1940-43).

NOTES AND SOURCES: Lieutenant General Brand was placed in charge of the Königsberg fortifications in 1943. *Kriegstagebuch des OKW*, Volume I: 1123; RA: 20; OB 42: 105; OB 43: 172; OB 45: 234.

317th INFANTRY DIVISION

COMPOSITION: Various older units

HOME STATION: Wehrkreis XIII

The 317th was mobilized in the sixth induction wave in the fall of 1939. Like the other units mobilized at this time, it was made up of older reservists. After France fell in June 1940, Hitler felt that he no longer needed units like the 317th, so he demobilized it and several other divisions. Many of the division's former soldiers returned to civilian life.

SOURCE: OB 45: 234.

319th INFANTRY DIVISION

COMPOSITION: 582nd Infantry Regiment, 583rd Infantry Regiment, 584th Infantry Regiment, 319th Artillery Regiment, 319th Reconnaissance Company, 319th Anti-Tank Battalion, 319th Engineer Battalion, 319th Signal Company

HOME STATION: Wehrkreis IX

In November 1940 this division was organized and took over the defense of the English Channel Islands of Guernsey, Jersey, Alderney, Sark, Herm, and Jethou the following summer. It was also responsible for the city of St. Malo and a sector of the French coast in 1941. In 1943 and 1944 Hitler was so convinced that the Allies would have to take the Channel Islands before they could land in France that he reinforced the 319th to the incredible strength of 40,000 men, making it the largest division in the German Army during World War II. Eisenhower bypassed the Channel Islands when he landed on the Normandy coast and isolated the 319th Infantry, which remained isolated until the end of the war. Elements of the division were transferred back to the continent before the Normandy Front collapsed and fought in the Cotentin peninsula battles of mid-1944. The main body of the division, however, surrendered at 7:14 A.M. on May 9, 1945, seven hours after the official end of the war—having hardly fired a shot in anger during its five years' existence. The commanders of the Channel Island division included Lieutenant Generals Erich Müller (1942-43) and Count Rudolf von Schmettow (1944-45).

NOTES AND SOURCES: Müller was reportedly in command of the 353rd Infantry Division in the autumn of 1944. Count von Schmettow, a Silesian, had previously been Commandant of Breslau. Harrison: 130-31; Hartmann: 32; RA: 144; OB 43: 172; OB 44: 237; OB 45: 234.

320th INFANTRY (later VOLKSGRENADIER) DIVISION

COMPOSITION: 585th Infantry Regiment, 586th Infantry Regiment, 587th Infantry Regiment, 320th Artillery Regiment, 320th Reconnaissance Company, 320th Anti-Tank Battalion, 320th Engineer Battalion, 320th Signal Company

HOME STATION: Wehrkreis VIII

The 320th Infantry was formed in late 1940 and was sent to Belgium a year later. In January 1942 it was transferred to Brittany and moved to northeastern France in April. In early 1943 it was sent to the southern sector of the Eastern Front and first saw action in the Battle of Kharkov in February, where it was used to help stabilize the shattered 2nd Hungarian Army. In July it fought in Operation Citadel, Hitler's last major offensive in the East. Later the 320th took part in the retreats on the southern zone, and was down to battle group strength by October 1943. In January 1944 it was officially cited for its conduct in the Battle of Kirovograd, but in August it was encircled west of the lower Dnieper and suffered such heavy losses that it had to be withdrawn from the front to reform. In late 1944 the 320th, now designated a Volksgrenadier division, returned to combat in southern Poland. It surrendered, along with the 1st Panzer Army, in the Czechoslovakian Pocket in May 1945. Its divisional commanders included Lieutenant General Karl Maderholz (1941-42), Lieutenant General Georg Postel (1943-44), and Major General von Kiliani (1944?-1945).

NOTES AND SOURCES: Karl Maderholz later commanded Replacement Division Staffs 410 (1943) and 467 (late 1943-44). Postel briefly commanded XXX Corps before being captured by the Russians in July 1944. The 320th absorbed the partially formed 588th Volksgrenadier Division in the winter of 1944. Carell 1971: 197; Hartmann: 34; "Frontnachweiser," 15 December 1944; *Kriegstagebuch des OKW*, Volume III: 1156; RA: 130; OB 43: 172; OB 44: 238; OB 45: 234-35.

321st INFANTRY DIVISION

COMPOSITION: 588th Infantry Regiment, 589th Infantry Regiment, 590th Infantry Regiment, 321st Artillery Regiment, 321st Reconnaissance Company, 321st Anti-Tank Battalion, 321st Engineer Battalion, 321st Signal Company

HOME STATION: Wehrkreis XI

Activated in late 1940, the 321st was posted at Abbeville, northeastern

France, in April 1941. In December 1942 it was sent to Russia and was heavily engaged as part of Army Group Center the following spring. By October 1943 the division had practically ceased to exist as a separate entity; part of it was attached to the 110th Infantry Division and part to the 211th Infantry Division. In December 1943 the division was formally disbanded; some of its men were transferred to France to form the 352nd Infantry Division at St. Lô. The remainder of its soldiers were absorbed by other divisions on the Eastern Front.

SOURCES: *Kriegstagebuch des OKW,* Volume III: 1157; RA: 172; OB 43: 172; OB 45: 235.

323rd INFANTRY DIVISION

COMPOSITION: 591st Infantry Regiment, 592nd Infantry Regiment, 593rd Infantry Regiment, 323nd Artillery Regiment, 323rd Reconnaissance Company, 323rd Anti-Tank Battalion, 323rd Engineer Battalion, 323rd Signal Company

HOME STATION: Wehrkreis XIII

The 323rd Infantry Division was created in late 1940 and spent several months in northwestern France in late 1941 and early 1942. In May 1942 it was sent to the southern sector of the Eastern Front and served there for a year, compiling a respectable combat record in heavy defensive fighting. It suffered such heavy casualties in the Russian winter offensive of 1942-43 that it was in remnants by April 1943 and was placed under the operational control of the 26th Infantry Division of Army Group Center by July. Sent back to the southern sector in the fall of 1943, it sustained such heavy losses in the retreat from Kiev that it was decided to disband it, and its men were sent to other units on the Russian Front. The 323rd Infantry's last commander was apparently Lieutenant General Johann Bergen, who led it in 1942 and 1943.

NOTES AND SOURCES: Bergen later commanded the 390th Field Training Division (1944-45). *Kriegstagebuch des OKW,* Volume III: 259, 733; OB 43: 173; OB 44: 238; OB 45: 235.

325th SECURITY DIVISION

COMPOSITION (1943): 1st Security Regiment, 5th Security Regiment, 6th Security Regiment, 190th Security Regiment, 325th Artillery Regiment, 325th Füsilier Company, 325th Anti-Tank Battalion, 325th Engineer Battalion, 325th Signal Battalion

HOME STATION: Paris, France

This unit was organized under the Military Governor of France in May 1943 to occupy Paris and control all Army local defense troops and security forces in the French capital. As such, it was the only security division serving on the Western Front in World War II. In August 1944 the division was placed under the 1st Army, Army Group B for the defense of the city. At that time it had a strength of 25,000 to 30,000 men, but very few of them were combat troops. Although Hitler ordered it to destroy Paris, the 325th did not do so, because the city's commandant, General Dietrich von Choltitz, and divisional commander Lieutenant General Baron Wilhelm von Boineburg-Lengsfeld, deliberately withheld the necessary orders. Most of the men of the 325th Security escaped from Paris before it fell. The division, however, had lost its reason for existing. Its soldiers were distributed among other divisions that had suffered heavy losses in the Normandy fighting. The 325th Security was dissolved in August 1944. Baron von Boineburg-Lengsfeld commanded it throughout its existence.

NOTES AND SOURCES: "No soldier had more miraculous good luck in surviving the war than the Thuringian Lieutenant General Hans Wilhelm Freiherr von Boineburg-Lengsfeld," Brett-Smith wrote. The Baron commanded the 23rd Panzer Division in Russia (1941-42) but was relieved of his command for the same security violation that earned General of Panzer Troops Georg Stumme and his chief of staff prison terms. Once, on the Russian Front, von Boineburg-Lengsfeld was run over by a tank and survived, although he suffered from many broken bones. He was deeply involved in the plot to overthrow the Nazi regime and on July 20, 1944 arrested virtually every S.S. man, Gestapo agent and Security Policeman in Paris, only to have to release them that night. Remarkably, his role in the plot was not detected, although his immediate superior, General of Infantry Heinrich von Stülpnagel, the Commandant of Paris, was arrested and eventually executed by the Gestapo. In April 1945 he was brought before a military court to answer charges that he surrendered Paris without a fight. Baron von Boineburg-Lengsfeld managed to get the trial postponed. He then hopped into a car, drove to Erfurt, and surrendered to the advancing Americans. Blumenson 1960: 592-93; Richard Brett-Smith, *Hitler's Generals*, Presidio Press, San Rafael, California, 1976: 181-82 (hereafter cited as

"Brett-Smith"); OB 45: 236. Also see Pierre Galante, *Operation Valkyrie: The German Generals' Plot Against Hitler*, Harper and Row, New York: 1981.

326th INFANTRY (later VOLKSGRENADIER) DIVISION

COMPOSITION: 751st Grenadier Regiment, 752nd Grenadier Regiment, 753rd Grenadier Regiment, 326th Artillery Regiment, 326th Füsilier Battalion, 326th Anti-Tank Battalion, 326th Engineer Battalion, 326th Signal Battalion

HOME STATION: Wehrkreis VI

Organized in late 1942, the 326th Infantry Division was hurriedly attached to Army Detachment Felber and took part in the occupation of Vichy France in November 1942 following the Allied landings in French North Africa earlier that month. After a brief period of occupation duty on the French Mediterranean coast, it was stationed in the Narbonne area from April 1943 until January 1944 and then sent to northern France. On July 22, 1944, it relieved the 2nd Panzer Division on the front line in Normandy but because of its inexperience it was overrun by the British at Caumont later that month. In August it was trapped in the Falaise Pocket, where elements of the division broke out, but the unit as a whole was smashed. In late August it was collecting its stragglers in the St. Quentin-Somme River area, but was soon sent to a safer region, Hungary, where it was rebuilt as a Volksgrenadier division. The 326th reappeared on the Western Front in the Roer River battles in mid-December, where it helped hold the Hellenthaler Wald against the U.S. V Corps. Later it fought in the Ardennes offensive and was defending in the Eifel area south of St. Vith in January 1945. The following month the 326th was smashed in the Second Battle of the Schnee Eifel, where the Americans described it as "dazed" and "disorganized." By March it was in "tiny remnants," retreating along with the LIII Corps of the German 7th Army. The remnants of the 326th Volksgrenadier ended up in the Ruhr Pocket. The division's commanders included Lieutenant General Viktor von Drabich-Waechter (1944) and Major General Dr. Erwin Kaschner (1945).

NOTES AND SOURCES: Dr. Kaschner had previously commanded the 486th Grenadier Regiment of the 262nd Infantry Division on the Eastern Front in 1943. The division absorbed the recently created 579th Grenadier Division in the winter of 1944. Blumenson 1960: 225, 294-95, 324, 422-42, 582; Chant, Volume 16; 2133; Cole 1965: 87; *Kriegstagebuch des OKW*, Volume II: 1398; "Frontnachweiser," 15 December 1944; MacDonald 1963: 599; MacDonald 1973: 87, 89, 204; RA: 102; OB 43: 173; OB 44: 239; OB 45: 236.

327th INFANTRY DIVISION

COMPOSITION: 595th Infantry Regiment, 596th Infantry Regiment, 597th Infantry Regiment,, 327th Artillery Regiment, 327th Reconnaissance Company, 327th Anti-Tank Battalion, 327th Engineer Battalion, 327th Signal Company

HOME STATION: Wehrkreis XVII

The 327th was formed in Austria in late 1940 and sent to eastern France in the fall of 1941. It spent 1942 at LaRochelle in southwestern France and took part in the occupation of Vichy France in November 1942. In the spring of 1943 it was sent to the central sector of the Russian Front and, after the German defeat at Kursk, was transferred to the southern sector. Fighting in the Ukraine, it suffered such heavy losses in the retreat from Kiev that it had to be disbanded and its survivors were absorbed by the 377th Infantry Division. Divisional commanders of the 327th Infantry included Lieutenant General Wilhelm Rupprecht (1942), Major General Theodor Fischer (1942), and Lieutenant General Rudolf Friedrich (1942-43).

NOTES AND SOURCES: Rupprecht, the former Commandant of Regensburg, Wehrkreis XIII, later commanded the 18th Luftwaffe Field Division in France (1943-44). Fischer, who only reached general rank in August 1942, had just given up leadership of the 338th Infantry Regiment and was an acting divisional commander only. Rudolf Friedrich relinquished command of the 62nd Infantry Division on the Russian Front on October 30, 1942, and assumed command of the 327th on the same day. Hartmann: 34; *Kriegstagebuch des OKW*, Volume III: 733, 1157; RA: 220; OB 43: 173; OB 44b: D99; OB 45: 236-37.

328th INFANTRY DIVISION

COMPOSITION: 547th Infantry Regiment, 548th Infantry Regiment, 549th Infantry Regiment, 328th Artillery Regiment, 328th Reconnaissance Company, 328th Anti-Tank Battalion, 328th Engineer Battalion, 328th Signal Company

HOME STATION: Wehrkreis IX

Shortly after being mobilized in late 1941, this unit was sent to Army Group Center on the Eastern Front, where it was divided into three parts. Each infantry regiment was assigned to a different corps in the 3rd Panzer and 9th Armies of Army Group Center during the Soviet winter offensive of 1941-42. It was not reunited until July or August 1942, but after that was again broken up in the defensive battles of 1942-43. By November 1942 one of its regiments had been returned to the West, where it took part in the occupation of Vichy France. By December 12 half of the division was in the south of France and half in Russia. On New Year's Day 1943 only one regiment remained in the Soviet Union, and by the spring of 1943 the 328th had again been reunited. It returned to Russia in the late summer of 1943 and was employed on the southern sector this time. The division fought at Kursk and was largely destroyed in the retreats following the failure of Operation Citadel; the remnants of the 328th were absorbed by the 353rd Infantry Division. Commanders of the division included Major General Wilhelm Behrens (1942) and Lieutenant General Joachim von Treschow (1942-43).

NOTES AND SOURCES: Behrens was later commander of Replacement Division Staff 193 (1945). Treschow later commanded the 18th Luftwaffe Field Division in France (1944) and LXIII Corps (late 1944-45). *Kriegstagebuch des OKW*, Volume II: 1362, 1368, 1381, 1388, 1390, 1395, 1398; Volume III: 6, 8, 732, 1156; OB 43: 174; OB 44: 240; OB 45: 237.

329th INFANTRY DIVISION

COMPOSITION: 551st Infantry Regiment, 552nd Infantry Regiment, 553rd Infantry Regiment, 329th Artillery Regiment, 329th Reconnaissance Company, 329th Anti-Tank Battalion, 329th Engineer Battalion, 329th Signal Company

HOME STATION: Wehrkreis VI

Known as the "Hammer Division" because of its unit symbol, this formation was created in late 1941, and spent almost its entire combat career with Army Group North (later Courland) in Russia. In March and April 1942 it helped reestablish contact with the II Corps, trapped in the Demyansk encirclement. The 329th continued to fight in the desperate battles around Demyansk until the II Corps made good its escape in February 1943. In January 1942 the 553rd Infantry Regiment was encircled at Kholm and was not rescued until the following spring. The division itself continued to serve on the northern sector, except for a brief period in early 1944 when it was attached to Army Group Center for the Battle of Nevel. Returning to the northern sector, the 329th fought in the withdrawal to Courland and was officially cited for distinguished conduct in the retreat through eastern Latvia. It was still in the Courland Pocket when the war ended. Its commanders included Major General Helmut Castore (1942), Lieutenant General Dr. Johannes Mayer (1944-45), and Colonel Werner Schulze (1945).

NOTES AND SOURCES: General Castore later commanded the 166th Reserve Division (1943-August 1944) and the 172nd Reserve Division (1944-45). Dr. Mayer, a Silesian, held the Knight's Cross with Oak Leaves and Swords. Colonel Schulze, a Saxon, commanded a grenadier regiment for two years before assuming divisional command. He held the Knight's Cross with Oak Leaves. Carell 1966: 427-38; Carell 1971: 288; RA: 102; OB 43: 174; OB 45: 237.

330th INFANTRY DIVISION

COMPOSITION: 554th Infantry Regiment, 555th Infantry Regiment, 556th Regiment, 330th Artillery Regiment, 330th Motorcycle Battalion, 330th Anti-Tank Battalion, 330th Engineer Battalion, 330th Signal Battalion

HOME STATION: Wehrkreis V

Organized in late 1941, the 330th Infantry was in battle shortly afterwards because of the crisis on the Eastern Front. In January 1942 it held its positions at Demidov, just north of the Moscow-Smolensk Motor Highway, against strong elements of the 4th Soviet Strike Army. The 330th continued to serve in Russia (mostly under 9th Army) in the heavy defensive fighting of 1942 and 1943. By October 1943 the division was at battle group strength and had ceased to function as a separate combat entity. Part of the unit was attached to the 35th Infantry Division and part to the 78th Sturm Division, both of 4th Army. In late 1943 or very early 1944 it was dissolved when Army Group Center consolidated a number of understrength divisions. The 330th's commanders included Lieutenant Generals Karl Graf (1942) and Count Edwin von Rothkirck und Trach (1942-43).

NOTES AND SOURCES: Rothkirck und Trach, the former commander of the Breslau Fortifications and Commandant of Lwow (1941), later commanded the German lines-of-communications area in White Russia (1943-44) and LIII Corps (1944-45). He was a Silesian. Carell 1966: 385, 390; *Kriegstagebuch des OKW*, Volume III: 1157; OB 42: 106-07; OB 43: 174; OB 45: 238.

331st INFANTRY DIVISION

COMPOSITION: 557th Infantry Regiment, 558th Infantry Regiment, 559th Infantry Regiment, 331st Artillery Regiment, 331st Reconnaissance Company, 331st Anti-Tank Battalion, 331st Engineer Battalion, 331st Signal Company

HOME STATION: Wehrkreis XVII

Formed in eastern Austria in late 1941, the 331st was sent to Army Group Center in early 1942. Later it was shifted to Army Group North. It fought on the Russian Front for two years, where it suffered heavy losses in the defensive fighting of 1942-43. It was reformed in Germany at the Wahn Maneuver Area, where it incorporated the partially trained members of Infantry Division Wahn into its ranks. Transferred to Calais, the 331st returned to action in the withdrawal through France. On August 28, while defending south of Paris, it was attacked by the U.S. 1st Army, and "just melted away." The survivors of the 331st were regrouped and sent to Holland, where they fought on the northern sector of the Western Front until the end of the war. Commanders of this division included Lieutenant General Fritz Hengen (1941), Lieutenant General Dr. Bayer (1942-43), Major General Heinz Furbach (1944), Major General Karl Rheim (1944), and Major General Steinmüller (1945).

NOTES AND SOURCES: Hengen ended the war as commanding general of Recruiting Area Chemnitz, Wehrkreis IV. Dr. Bayer went on to command the 44th Infantry Division in Italy (1943-44) and the LXXX Corps on the Western Front. He was promoted to General of Infantry in 1944. Heinz Furbach led the 432nd Grenadier Regiment of the 44th Infantry Division in 1943. Major General Steinmüller had been commander of a grenadier regiment on the Eastern Front. Blumenson 1960: 575-79; Harrison: 235, Map VI; RA: 220; OB 43: 174-75; OB 44: 241; OB 45: 238.

332nd INFANTRY DIVISION

COMPOSITION: 676th Infantry Regiment, 677th Infantry Regiment, 687th Infantry Regiment, 332nd Artillery Regiment, 332nd Reconnaissance Company, 332nd Anti-Tank Battalion, 332nd Engineer Battalion, 332nd Signal Company

HOME STATION: Wehrkreis VIII

This Silesian unit was created in January 1941 and was posted in

Normandy in August. It remained in France until February 1943, when it was ordered to the southern sector of the Russian Front following the end of resistance in Stalingrad. En route, however, the 332nd was diverted to the 2nd Army on the southern flank of Army Group Center, which had come under heavy attack. After helping repulse the Soviet winter offensive of 1942-43 the 332nd Infantry fought in the Kursk offensive and was smashed on August 3, 1943, in the Third Battle of Kharkov. Continuing in action, what was left of the division was surrounded in February 1944 at Cherkassy, when about half of its survivors were lost, along with all its heavy equipment. The 332nd was pulled out of the line and dissolved shortly thereafter.

SOURCES: Carell 1971: 17, 50; Manstein: 431; RA: 130; OB 43: 175; OB 45: 238; Ziemke 1966: 149

333rd INFANTRY DIVISION

COMPOSITION: 679th Infantry Regiment, 680th Infantry Regiment, 681st Infantry Regiment, 333rd Artillery Regiment, 333rd Motorcycle Company, 333rd Anti-Tank Battalion, 333rd Engineer Battalion, 333rd Signal Company

HOME STATION: Wehrkreis III

Formed in January 1941, this division was largely made up of Poles. It was sent to southwestern France in May and then to Brittany the following year. In early 1943 it was transferred to the southern sector of the Russian Front, where it fought in the Donets battles as a part of 1st Panzer Army; however, by autumn it had suffered so many casualties that it had to be disbanded.

SOURCES: *Kriegstagebuch des OKW*, Volume III: 8, 258, 732, 1156; RA: 46; OB 42: 106; OB 43: 175; OB 44b: D101; OB 45: 239.

334th INFANTRY DIVISION

COMPOSITION: 754th Motorized Infantry Regiment, 755th Motorized Infantry Regiment, 756th Motorized Infantry Regiment, 334th Artillery Regiment, 334th Mobile Battalion (a combined Reconnaissance/Anti-Tank unit), 334th Engineer Battalion, 334th Signal Company

HOME STATION: Wehrkreis XIII

This division was formed in the fall of 1942 as a composite division; its

754th, 755th, and 756th Infantry Regiments were raised in the XIII, XVII, and XVIII Military Districts, respectively. It was sent to North Africa in December 1942 shortly after its creation. The 334th Division fought well in the battles of the Tunisian Bridgehead but was destroyed when Army Group Afrika collapsed in May 1943.

The 334th Infantry Division was remustered in southern France in July and August 1943. Unlike the original 334th, all three of its regiments came from Wehrkreis XIII. The new division was transferred to Italy in November 1943, where it fought in all the subsequent campaigns of Army Group C. By May 1944 it was down to battle group strength but remained on the front line despite its casualties and shortages in personnel. The 334th suffered heavy losses in the battles of the Gothic Line and in September 1944 bore the brunt of the Allied push through the Futa Pass. The next month it was still in action, fighting on the Florence-Bologna Road as a part of XIV Panzer Corps. Finally, in December, it was shifted to the relatively inactive Adriatic sector but was not substantially reinforced or rebuilt. In February 1945 the division was back in the center of action in the defense of Bologna; however, it now numbered fewer than twenty-six hundred effectives. The 334th was finally destroyed on April 23, 1945, along with the rest of the LI Mountain Corps, in the last Allied offensive on the Italian Front. Commanders of the 334th included Major General Friedrich Weber (1942-43), Lieutenant General Heinz Ziegler (1943), Major General Heinrich-Hermann von Hülsen (1943), and Lieutenant General Helmuth Boehlke (1944-45).

NOTES AND SOURCES: Friedrich Weber, a Bavarian, later commanded the 131st Infantry Division on the Eastern Front (1944-45). Lieutenant General Ziegler, formerly on the staff of the Home Army (1942), was Chief of Staff of the XLII Corps in 1940. Later he was Chief of Staff of the 5th Panzer Army (1942-43), acting commander of the 334th (1943), and acting commander of the Afrika Korps (1943), all in Tunisia. Heinrich-Hermann von Hülsen was taken prisoner when Tunisia fell in May 1943—the same month he received his promotion to Major General of Panzer Grenadiers. General Boehlke had formerly commanded the 134th Grenadier Regiment of the 44th Infantry Division "Hoch und Deutschmeister" in Italy (1943). He rose from the rank of Colonel to Lieutenant General in less than two years. Fisher: 18, 194, 268, 302, 442, 495-96; Hartmann: 35; RA: 204; OB 43: 173; OB 45: 239.

335th INFANTRY DIVISION

COMPOSITION: 682nd Infantry Regiment, 683rd Infantry Regiment, 684th Infantry Regiment, 335th Artillery Regiment, 335th Reconnaissance Company, 335th Anti-Tank Battalion, 335th Engineer Battalion, 335th Signal Company

HOME STATION: Wehrkreis V

The 335th consisted mainly of Poles in German service. It was formed in Germany in January 1941 and was sent to northern France in the summer of 1941. Transferred to Brittany the following March, the 335th took part in the occupation of Vichy France in November 1942. It was sent to southern Russia in early 1943 and was almost continuously in action for the next year and a half. It fought at Kursk, in the subsequent retreats through the Donets, and in the Dnieper bend battles. The 335th was destroyed at Kishinev, west of the Dnieper, in August 1944. Its commanders included Lieutenant General Casper (1942 and 1944) and Lieutenant General Siegfried Rasp (1943).

NOTES AND SOURCES: Casper commanded the 171st Reserve Division in 1943 before he reported ill and was relieved. Upon recovering he apparently returned to command the 335th. He later commanded the 48th Infantry Division on the Eastern Front (1944-45). Siegfried Rasp advanced rapidly from the rank of Colonel in October 1943, to General of Infantry in late 1944. He led the 78th Sturm Division in Russia (1944) and was commander of the 19th Army on the Western Front in 1945. Like General Manteuffel, he bypassed the corps level of command altogether. Hartmann: 35; RA: 86; OB 43: 176; OB 44: 243; OB 44b: D102; OB 45: 240.

336th INFANTRY DIVISION

COMPOSITION: 685th Infantry Regiment, 686th Infantry Regiment, 687th Infantry Regiment, 336th Artillery Regiment, 336th Reconnaissance Company, 336th Anti-Tank Battalion, 336th Engineer Battalion, 336th Signal Company

HOME STATION: Rheine, Wkr. IV

This Saxon unit was built around cadres from the 256th Infantry Division in January 1941. It was posted to Normandy shortly thereafter and was transferred to Brittany in March 1942. Sent to Russia in May 1942, it suffered severe losses in the Battle of Taganrog, was with the XL Panzer Corps in the Second Battle of Kharkov (1942), and served with Army

Detachment Hollidt in the unsuccessful attempt to relieve Stalingrad. Its commander in these campaigns was Lieutenant General Walter Lucht. In 1943 the 336th was sent to the Crimea, where it faced the Soviet spring offensive of 1944. It bore the brunt of the Russian attack on the Perekop Isthmus that April; most of the division was lost when the XLIX Mountain Corps finally gave way. Major General Rolf Hagemann, the divisional commander, was seriously wounded in the fighting and had to be evacuated by airplane. Most of his division was not so lucky: it retreated into Sevastopol, where it was captured when the city fell. Only a few of its soldiers managed to reach the evacuation points and escape by sea before the Russians captured them. The 336th was never rebuilt.

NOTES AND SOURCES: Walter Lucht commanded Arko 44 and Harko 310 (two GHQ artillery units) in 1941 and 1942, respectively. From late 1943 until 1945 he led LXVI Corps. Lucht was promoted to General of Artillery in October 1943. Hagemann, a holder of the Knight's Cross with Oak Leaves, had led I Battalion, 139th Mountain Infantry Regiment (1939-40). Carell 1966: 649; Carell 1971: 538-39; Manstein: 319, 388; RA: 72; OB 43: 176; OB 44: 243; OB 45: 240.

337th INFANTRY (later VOLKSGRENADIER) DIVISION

COMPOSITION (1941): 688th Infantry Regiment, 689th Infantry Regiment, 690th Infantry Regiment, 337th Artillery Regiment, 337th Reconnaissance Company, 337th Anti-Tank Battalion, 337th Engineer Battalion, 337th Signal Company-

HOME STATION: Wehrkreis VII

Created in January 1941, this division was on garrison duty in central France from August 1941 until late 1942. During this period it gave up the 689th Infantry Regiment and received the 313th Infantry Regiment from the 246th Infantry Division. In late 1942 the division was transferred to the central sector of the Russian Front and remained there until July 1944, when it was decimated in the Russian summer offensive. The division's leader, Lieutenant General Otto Schünemann, became commander of the XXXIX Panzer Corps when General Martinez was killed. Schünemann himself was killed a few days later, and only remnants of his former division escaped. The remains of the 337th were reformed in Germany as a Volksgrenadier unit, absorbing the partially trained recruits of the 570th Grenadier Division. The 337th Volksgrenadier fought in Poland and East Prussia at very much reduced strength. It was dissolved in late 1944 or very early 1945.

NOTES AND SOURCES: The exact date the 337th ceased to exist is uncertain, but it was dropped from the Order of Battle of the Wehrmacht between November 26, 1944, and March 1, 1945. Carell 1971: 309, 596-97; "Front-nachweiser," 15 December 1944; *Kriegstagebuch des OKW,* Volume IV: 1886; RA: 116; OB 43: 176; OB 45: 241.

338th INFANTRY DIVISION

COMPOSITION: 757th Grenadier Regiment, 758th Grenadier Regiment, 759th Grenadier Regiment, 338th Artillery Regiment, 338th Füsilier Battalion, 338th Anti-Tank Battalion, 338th Engineer Battalion, 338th Signal Battalion

HOME STATION: Wehrkreis II

This static division was formed in France in late 1942, as a Wehrkreis II affiliate. Veteran divisional commander Lieutenant General Folttmann was its first leader (1942-44). The division garrisoned a sector of the French Mediterranean coast west of Marseilles until the Allies landed in August. The 338th lacked enough transportation to evacuate all its men, even after it commandeered all available French vehicles; it thus suffered considerable losses in the retreat to the German frontier, mostly in terms of men captured. In September it was essentially rebuilt from miscellaneous troops and sent into action in southern Alsace. Here General Folttmann was fatally wounded in the Battle of Belfort Gap in November. He was replaced by thirty-nine-year-old Colonel Wolf Ewert. The 338th suffered heavy casualties at Mulhouse but remained in action and was even sent to the Roer sector, where it fought in the Battle of the Linnich Bridgehead and other Rhineland battles. The remnants of the veteran division were forced into the Ruhr Pocket in April 1945 and were destroyed there. The last reported commander of the 338th was Colonel Rudolf von Oppen (December 1944-1945).

NOTES AND SOURCES: Lieutenant General Folttmann had previously commanded the 256th Infantry Division (1939) and was leading the 164th Infantry (later Light Afrika) Division in late 1939. Colonel Hafner was reportedly acting as divisional commander of the 338th in October 1944— Folttmann may have been on leave or acting as a corps commander. Hafner later commanded the 716th Infantry Division on the Western Front (1945). Colonel Ewert was soon superseded in divisional command by Colonel von Oppen, who had previously led a brigade in southern France. Blumenson 1960: 570, 585; Chant, Volume 14: 1914; Harrison: Map VI; Hartmann: 35-38; MacDonald 1973: 167, 370; RA: 32; OB 45: 241.

339th INFANTRY DIVISION

COMPOSITION: 691st Infantry Regiment, 692nd Infantry Regiment, 693rd Infantry Regiment, 339th Artillery Regiment, 339th Reconnaissance Company, 339th Anti-Tank Battalion, 339th Engineer Battalion, 339th Signal Company

HOME STATION: Jena, Wkr. IX

The 339th Infantry Division was mobilized at Jena in January 1941 and was almost immediately sent to central France, where it remained until late 1941. Transferred to Army Group Center on the Russian Front, the 339th took part in several battles from December 1941 until late 1943, including Moscow, the subsequent retreats, and the defensive battles of 1942-43. Already greatly reduced by casualties, the 339th was sent to the southern sector in late 1943. It was attached to Lange's Korps Formation C as a "cadre infantry division," indicating that it was below battle group strength. In July 1944 it was surrounded in the Brody Pocket in Byelorussia. It broke out but was no longer an effective combat unit. The High Command ordered it disbanded, and its survivors were assigned to the 363rd Infantry Division.

SOURCES: *Kriegstagebuch des OKW*, Volume II: 1361-62; Volume III: 1157; Seaton: 449; OB 43: 176; OB 45: 241-42; also see Lange.

340th INFANTRY (later VOLKSGRENADIER) DIVISION

COMPOSITION: 694th Infantry Regiment, 695th Infantry Regiment, 696th Infantry Regiment, 340th Artillery Regiment, 340th Reconnaissance Company, 340th Anti-Tank Battalion, 340th Engineer Battalion, 340th Signal Company

HOME STATION: Königsberg, Wkr. I

Mustered in at the East Prussian capital in January 1941, this division was stationed in the Hamburg district (Wehrkreis X) until mid-1941, when it was transferred to the Calais area of France. One year later it was moved again, this time to the southern sector of the Russian Front. The 340th fought in a number of bitter engagements and suffered particularly heavy losses in the withdrawal from Kiev in the autumn of 1943. In early February 1944, when the 340th Division held the extreme left flank of Army Group South against a Soviet offensive, it had a strength of three infantry and two artillery battalions. Four months later it was encircled east of

Lwow and was largely destroyed. The remnants that escaped formed the cadre for a reconstituted 340th, which was designated a Volksgrenadier unit in September 1944. Its ranks were filled by the wholesale absorption of recruits from the partially formed 572nd Grenadier Division. This new force first saw action on the Western Front in November. It fought in the battles east of Aachen before being attached to the I SS Panzer Corps in the latter stages of the Battle of the Bulge, where it took heavy casualties from American counterattacks. In March 1945 the division was with the XIII SS Corps, retreating toward the interior of southern Germany, in "tiny remnants," according to the U.S. Army's Official History. It was dissolved in the last days of the war and its few remaining men incorporated into other shattered formations, probably in the XIII SS Corps. The commanders of the 340th Infantry/Volksgrenadier Division included Lieutenant General Friedrich Wilhelm von Neumann (1941), Lieutenant General Butze (1942-44), and Colonel Theodor Tolsdorf (1944-45).

NOTES AND SOURCES: General Neumann later directed the 712th Infantry Division (1943-44) and LXXXVIII Corps (1945), both on the Western Front. Colonel Tolsdorf was only thirty-six years old in 1945 and was considered to be very brave. He held the Knight's Cross with Oak Leaves and Swords. Tolsdorf had commanded the 22nd Füsilier Regiment in 1943. Like his division, he was from East Prussia. *Kriegstagebuch des OKW*, Volume I: 1131, 1138; Volume IV: 1147; MacDonald 1963: 559 and Map VII; MacDonald 1973: 34, 201, 204; OB 42: 108; OB 43: 176-77; OB 45: 242; Ziemke 1966: 247.

341st INFANTRY DIVISION

COMPOSITION: 638th Infantry Regiment, 639th Infantry Regiment, 640th Infantry Regiment

HOME STATION: Wehrkreis I (?)

Mobilized upon the outbreak of hostilities, this division was in existence only a few months. It was dissolved in the partial demobilization following the fall of France. The 341st never left Germany.

SOURCE: OB 45: 242.

342nd INFANTRY DIVISION

COMPOSITION: 697th Infantry Regiment, 698th Infantry Regiment, 699th Infantry Regiment, 342nd Artillery Regiment, 342nd Reconnaissance Company, 342nd Anti-Tank Battalion, 342nd Engineer Battalion, 342nd Signal Company

HOME STATION: Kaiserslautern, Wkr. XII

Activated in January 1941, the 342nd first saw combat in mopping-up operations in Yugoslavia the following winter. In February 1942 it was sent to Army Group Center, where it fought in the Rzhev withdrawal and in the Battle of Kursk, among others. It distinguished itself against the Russians and was twice officially cited for its conduct in the summer of 1944. Later that year the division was sent to Army Group North Ukraine and fought in Hungary, and by March 1945 it was down to battle group strength. The 342nd remained in action on the Eastern Front until the fall of the Third Reich, ending the war in eastern Germany. Its commanders included Major General Baron Albrecht von Digeon von Monteton (1942), Major General Kurt Hoffmann (1942), Major General Hans Roth (1942), and Lieutenant General Albrecht Baier (1943).

NOTES AND SOURCES: Baron von Digeon von Monteton was promoted to Lieutenant General in 1943 and was commanding the 391st Field Training Division in 1945. Major General Roth was named Commandant of Cologne in February 1943, and still held the post in 1945. Kurt Hoffmann, who was promoted to Lieutenant General in 1943, later commanded the 715th Infantry Division in Italy (1943-44) and the 160th Reserve Division in Denmark (1945). Carell 1971: 309; *Kriegstagebuch des OKW*, Volume IV: 1875, 1896; RA: 188; OB 42: 108; OB 43: 177; OB 45: 242.

343rd INFANTRY DIVISION

COMPOSITION: 851st Grenadier Regiment, 852nd Grenadier Regiment, 343rd Artillery Regiment, 343rd Füsilier Battalion, 343rd Anti-Tank Battalion, 343rd Engineer Battalion, 343rd Signal Battalion

HOME STATION: Wehrkreis XIII

The 343rd was mustered in at the Grafenwöhr Maneuver Area in southwestern Germany in October 1942. It was a static division, which meant it had very little organic transportation and was short on all forms of equipment. Early the next spring it was sent to France, where it guarded a sector of the Atlantic coast near Brest. In mid-August 1944, when the Allies broke through the Normandy Front, the 343rd formed part of the German garrison in the Siege of Brest. The survivors of the division surrendered when the city fell on September 19, 1944. The last divisional commander was Lieutenant General Josef Rauch, who was taken prisoner at Brest. Major General Hermann Kruse (1943-44) previously commanded the 343rd.

NOTES AND SOURCES: Rauch had previously commanded the 123rd Infantry Division on the Russian Front (1943-44). Blumenson 1960: 639; Harrison: Map VI; RA: 204; OB 45: 243.

344th INFANTRY (later VOLKSGRENADIER) DIVISION

COMPOSITION: 854th Grenadier Regiment, 855th Grenadier Regiment, 344th Artillery Regiment, 344th Füsilier Battalion, 344th Anti-Tank Battalion, 344th Engineer Battalion, 344th Signal Battalion

HOME STATION: Wehrkreis V

Created in October 1942 this division was initially assigned to occupation duty near Bordeaux in early 1943. In the fall of that year it was ordered to defend a sector of the Bay of Biscay from Arcachon to Hendaye against a possible Allied invasion. In the summer of 1944 the 344th saw its first action and suffered heavy losses in the Battle of Normandy. In late August it was covering the retreat of the 5th Panzer Army when it was attacked by large elements of the U.S. 1st Army. The 344th "just melted away," to quote the U.S. Army's Official History, but later rallied and was combined with the battered Panzer Lehr Division to form a temporary battle group. Finally taken out of the line that fall, the survivors were lumped together with miscellaneous troops and remnants of the 275th Infantry and 91st Air Landing Divisions to form the 344th Volksgrenadier Division. In November 1944 it fought in the Battle of the Huertgen Forest and again suffered heavy casualties. Early in 1945 it was sent to the Eastern Front and ended the war at battle group strength with Army Group Center in Czechoslovakia. Commanders of the division included Lieutenant General Eugen-Felix Schwalbe (1943-44), Major General Erich Walther (1944), and Colonel Goltzsch (1944-45?).

NOTES AND SOURCES: The 344th Infantry Division initially included the 832nd Grenadier Regiment. Lieutenant General Schwalbe was in command of the 719th Infantry Division on the Western Front in late 1944. Erich Walther, the former commander of the 4th Parachute Regiment

(1943-44), was a holder of the Knight's Cross with Oak Leaves. He was commander of the 2nd Hermann Göring Panzer Grenadier Division in East Prussia in 1945. Colonel Goltzsch was probably commander of the 344th Volksgrenadier until the surrender, but this is uncertain. Blumenson 1960: 576-77, 579; MacDonald 1963; 437, 460; RA: 86; OB 43: 177; OB 45: 243.

346th INFANTRY DIVISION

COMPOSITION: 857th Grenadier Regiment, 858th Grenadier Regiment, 346th Artillery Regiment, 346th Füsilier Battalion, 346th Anti-Tank Battalion, 346th Engineer Battalion, 346th Signal Battalion

HOME STATION: Wehrkreis IX

This two-regiment, static infantry division was formed in autumn 1942 and sent to France the next year. It was on duty in the St. Malo sector of Brittany until the spring of 1944, when it was transferred to Le Havre on the north bank of the Seine. Its commander at this time was Lieutenant General Erich Diester (1942?-44). It was quickly thrown into the Normandy fighting, where it took part in the Battle of Caen against the British. By June 13 its companies had only thirty-five to sixty men left apiece. On July 15, only six of the division's anti-tank weapons were still operational. The remnants of the 346th Infantry were in the Battle of the Falaise Pocket, where much of Army Group B was encircled and forced to break out with heavy casualties. The 346th retreated across France and Belgium and was fighting in the Dordrecht area of Holland that fall, and in October and November it was with the LXVII Infantry Corps in the Battle of the Scheldt. Its strength at this time was twenty-four hundred men and thirty-eight 105mm howitzers. On October 11 General Diestel was replaced by Major General Walter Steinmueller. The 346th remained in action in the Netherlands until the end of the war; however, it seems to have been assigned to relatively inactive sectors from November 1944 on, because it was considered burned-out after the Battle of the Scheldt.

NOTES AND SOURCES: A 1945 U.S. intelligence report indicates that Steinmueller's replacement of Diestel was only temporary and that Diestel may have returned to command the 346th in 1945; this seems unlikely, however. Diestel had formerly commanded the 75th Infantry Division in 1942. Blumenson 1960: 121; Harrison: Map VI; *Kriegstagebuch des OKW*, Volume IV: 1900; MacDonald 1963: 216-17, 220; MacDonald 1973: Map XII; Ruge: 184, 225; RA: 144; OB 45: 242.

347th INFANTRY DIVISION

COMPOSITION (1942): 860th Grenadier Regiment, 861st Grenadier Regiment, 862nd Grenadier Regiment, 347th Artillery Regiment, 347th Füsilier Battalion, 347th Anti-Tank Battalion, 347th Engineer Battalion, 347th Signal Battalion

NOTES AND SOURCES: Wehrkreis II

Originally a three-regiment static unit, the 347th Infantry was mobilized in October 1942 and sent to Holland soon after. It was reduced to two infantry regiments in 1943, when the 862nd Grenadier was transferred to the 274th Infantry Division. The remainder of the 347th occupied a sector of the Dutch coast opposite Amsterdam until the summer of 1944, when it was sent into battle on the Normandy Front. The unit suffered heavy losses in the subsequent retreat and was rebuilt by the incorporation of miscellaneous troops into its ranks. The 880th Grenadier Regiment was also assigned to the division. In September 1944 the 347th was back in action in the Siegfried Line battles but was later transferred to the Saar sector and was fighting near Saarlautern by January 1945 under the command of Lieutenant General Wolf Trierenberg (1944-45). The division remained on the Western Front until the end of the war. Its last commander was Lieutenant General Siry, who was captured at Friedrichsrode on April 10, 1945.

NOTES AND SOURCES: Wolf Trierenberg, a Bavarian, had commanded the 167th Infantry Division on the southern sector of the Russian Front in 1943. Air University File (SRGG 1192 [c]): Cole 1950: 506; Harrison: Map VI; Hartmann; 38; *Kriegstagebuch des OKW*, Volume II: 1390; MacDonald 1963: 83; Ruge: 184, 225; Speidel: 41; RA: 32; OB 43: 178; OB 45: 244.

348th INFANTRY DIVISION

COMPOSITION (1942): 863rd Grenadier Regiment, 864th Grenadier Regiment, 865th Grenadier Regiment, 348th Artillery Regiment, 348th Füsilier Battalion, 348th Anti-Tank Battalion, 348th Engineer Battalion, 348th Signal Battalion

HOME STATION: Wehrkreis XII

Another three-regiment static division, the 348th Infantry was formed in October 1942, given to 15th Army, and sent to the Dieppe area of France in November 1942. In 1943 it gave up the 865th Grenadier Regiment, which was combined with the 862nd Grenadier Regiment of the 347th Infantry Division to form the 274th Infantry Division. Meanwhile, the 348th continued to guard the Channel coast until the autumn of 1944, when the Allied armies broke through the Normandy Front, crossed the Seine, and attacked the German 15th Army in the rear. The 348th Infantry suffered such heavy losses in the subsequent fighting retreat that it had to be disbanded. Commanders of the division included Lieutenant Generals Karl Gumbel (1943) and Paul Seyffardt (1944), who was captured at Marbaix during the retreat toward Germany.

NOTES AND SOURCES: Karl Gumbel previously commanded the 182nd Reserve Division. General Seyffardt had led the 110th Infantry Division in Russia in 1942. Blumenson 1960: 597-98; Harrison: Map VI; RA: 188; OB 45: 244.

349th INFANTRY (later VOLKSGRENADIER) DIVISION

COMPOSITION: 911th Grenadier Regiment, 912th Grenadier Regiment, 913th Grenadier Regiment, 349th Artillery Regiment, 349th Füsilier Battalion, 349th Anti-Tank Battalion, 349th Engineer Battalion, 349th Signal Battalion

HOME STATION: Wehrkreis I

This unit was formed in October 1943 and was initially assigned to the Calais area of France. In April 1944, however, it was transferred to the Russian Front, where it arrived just in time to be overrun by the massive Soviet summer offensive. The 349th was encircled at Brody in Byelorussia in July, along with the rest of General Hauffe's XIII Corps. Divisional commander Lieutenant General Otto Lasch (1943-September 1944) led it in a successful breakout attempt, but with heavy losses. Sent to the rear, the 349th was reformed as a Volksgrenadier division in August and September 1944 and sent back to the Eastern Front. It was fighting in East Prussia in early 1945 and continued in action there until the end of the war. Its commander in the last days was Major General Karl Koetz (1944-45).

NOTES AND SOURCES: Most of XIII Corps was captured at Brody and General Hauffe was killed. Lasch was named acting commander of the LXIV Corps in late 1944 and later was in charge of the defense of Königsberg. The 349th absorbed the 567th Grenadier Division in September 1944. Koetz, who was only thirty-seven years old in 1945, had previously commanded a grenadier regiment on the Eastern Front. Both men held the Knight's Cross with Oak Leaves. "Frontnachweiser," 15 December 1944. Seaton: 446-49; RA: 20; OB 45: 245.

351st INFANTRY DIVISION

COMPOSITION: 641st Infantry Regiment, 642nd Infantry Regiment, 643rd Infantry Regiment

HOME STATION: Wehrkreis XVII

This division was formed in eastern Austria in May 1940 and was dissolved later that year, after the fall of France. It never left Germany.

SOURCES: RA: 220; OB 45: 245.

352nd INFANTRY (later VOLKSGRENADIER) DIVISION

COMPOSITION: 914th Grenadier Regiment, 915th Grenadier Regiment, 916th Grenadier Regiment, 352nd Artillery Regiment, 352nd Füsilier Battalion, 352nd Anti-Tank Battalion, 352nd Engineer Battalion, 352nd Signal Battalion

HOME STATION: Wehrkreis XI

Formed from elements of the 268th and 321st Infantry Divisions in October and November 1943, this non-static division was assigned a sector of the eastern Cotentin peninsula in January 1944. On June 6 it was struck by the Allied invasion. Pounded by fierce aerial bombardments and the big guns of the Allied navies, it was attacked by three British and Canadian infantry divisions and two armored brigades, as well as American units. By June 7 it was down to battle group strength; however, the 352nd was directly responsible for denying the vital city of Caen to Field Marshal Montgomery on D-Day and thus delayed the collapse of the entire Western Front for several weeks. The survivors of June 6 remained in the line, and by August the division had so few men left that it was temporarily absorbed by the 2nd Panzer Division. It was reconstituted as a separate division in August, and was rebuilt as a Volksgrenadier unit in the Schleswig-Holstein area of northern Germany. Returned to action on the Western Front, the 352nd fought in the Eifel battles, in the Ardennes offensive, and in the Rhineland operations south of Remagen. The Division surrendered to the Western Allies at the end of the war. Its commanders included Major General Eberhard Schuckmann (1943?-44), Lieutenant General Krauss (1944), Major General Erich Schmidt (1944), and Major General Bazing (1945).

NOTES AND SOURCES: Krauss was in command on D-Day. Schuckmann formerly directed the 387th Infantry Division on the Russian Front (1943).

A familiar scene to soldiers world-wide—foot-sore infantry. These troops are being treated by a medic in the Polish campaign, 1939.

(above) A German medical unit evacuates wounded to the Fatherland from Poland, 1939. In the early years of the war, each combat division had two ambulance companies. Even in nonmotorized divisions, these units were motorized, for obvious reasons.

(below) Adolf Hitler greets Wehrmacht troops at the October 5, 1939, parade celebrating victory over Poland. At this time, Erwin Rommel commanded the Führer Guard Battalion.

(above) German machine-gun team preparing for action on the French border, 1939–40.

(below) Wehrmacht infantrymen cross a river under fire in France, 1940. A French artillery shell has just exploded in the background.

(above) Members of the 7th Air Division with Adolf Hitler, who has just decorated them with Knight's Crosses, Belgium, 1940. These men have just taken the fortress of Eben Emael by glider-borne assault. Later they served on the Eastern Front. The 7th Air Division formed the cadre for the first German parachute divisions and were members of the Luftwaffe, not the Army.

(below) Signal troops lay a telephone line on the Western Front, 1940. Each German combat division in the early years of the war had a signal battalion; later in the war many had only a signal company.

(above) Colonel General (later Field Marshal) von Reichenau listens to a report from divisional commander Lieutenant General Dietrich, Western Front, 1940. A ruthless pro-Nazi, von Reichenau died in a plane crash in January 1942. An architect of German rearmament, he distinguished himself as an army commander in Poland, France, and Russia.

(below) Tanks of Rommel's 7th Panzer Division in action in France, 1940. These light tanks typified the equipment found in the original light divisions, which were redesignated 6th, 7th, 8th, and 9th Panzer Divisions during the winter of 1939–40. These units were later equipped with more modern panzers.

(above) German horses being off-loaded in Norway, 1940. Typically, Hitler used his less-mobile divisions of older troops for occupation duties, freeing more mobile units for front line service. Luftwaffe Field Divisions were also used as occupation troops when possible, after their relative uselessness as combat units had been proven.

(below) A heavy field piece being prepared for movement on the African Front, 1941.

(above) A German half-track with a section of infantry, probably photographed in the Balkans, 1941. Few German infantry divisions were so luxuriously equipped.

(below) A dispatch rider for the Leibstandarte Adolf Hitler (later 1st SS Panzer) Division in the Balkan campaign, 1941.

A tired, dirty private soldier in the Balkans, 1941.

A tank belonging to the 1st SS Panzer Division, Balkan campaign, 1941. The streams here, one observer noted, were easier to negotiate than the roads.

(above) A formation of Afrika Korps Panzer Grenadiers, August 19, 1941.

(left) Erwin Rommel, then a Colonel General, congratulates General Ludwig Crüwell on his birthday in March 1942. Rommel's success as commander of German forces in North Africa led to his appointment as commander of Army Group B in late 1943.

(above) A Russian highway, 1941. The appalling Soviet road network was that country's salvation in 1941, for it significantly delayed the German advance and gave Stalin and Zhukov time to prepare a counterattack from the gates of Moscow in December of that year.

(below) Divisional supply troops behind the Russian Front, winter of 1941–42. For most of Hitler's divisions, the horse carried or pulled more supplies, ammunition, and artillery than did motorized vehicles and was more important.

(left) German infantry prepares to move out on a trench line on the Russian Front, 1942.

(right) A forward observer and his radio operator on the Russian Front, 1942. The radio operator is wearing the Iron Cross, First Class, and the ribbon of the Iron Cross, Second Class. These men belonged to the 29th Motorized Infantry Division, which was all but wiped out at Stalingrad.

(below) A German artillery piece in action on the Russian Front.

(above) Heavy artillery in action on the Russian Front. Note the flight of the projectile at upper left. Although almost all German combat divisions had their own organic artillery regiments, corps headquarters and above supplied the divisions with much of their artillery on an attached basis.

(below) A convoy of the 100th Jäger Division, pursuing the Soviets, summer 1942. The divisional emblem can be seen on the truck at left. The 100th Jäger met its end in the Battle of Stalingrad, January 1943.

(above) A Soviet city after the Wehrmacht passed through.

(below) The huge fortress guns at Sevastopol, being inspected by men of the German 11th Army. Led by Field Marshal Erich von Manstein, the troops of that army overran the Soviet naval fortress in July 1942, after a long siege.

(left) SS Lieutenant General Fegelein, Commander of the SS Cavalry Brigade on the Russian Front (1941–42) and the 8th SS Cavalry Division in the Balkans (1942–43). Later he became Himmler's liaison officer at Führer Headquarters and married the sister of Eva Braun, Hitler's mistress. Hitler had him shot for desertion in the last days of the war.

(right) Theodor Eicke, one of the original concentration camp commanders, was director of operations at Dachau as early as 1933. An extremely brutal man, he led the 3rd SS Panzer Division on the Russian Front, where it committed numerous atrocities. He was killed in action on the Eastern Front in February 1943.

(below) Lieutenant General Boldenstern, commander of the 29th Motorized Infantry Division, is being decorated with the Knight's Cross by General of Panzer Troops Lemelsen, commander of the XLVII Panzer Corps, Russian Front, summer of 1942. Lemelsen had been commander of the 29th Motorized Infantry Division himself, during the Polish campaign. He later commanded the 10th and 14th armies on the Italian Front.

The swastika goes up in Stalingrad, 1942. When it finally came down in early February 1943, the 6th Army had been destroyed and some of Hitler's best divisions annihilated.

(left) Major General Munoz Grandes, the commander of the Spanish Blue Division, being decorated with the Iron Cross on the Northern Sector of the Russian Front. This unit, also known as the 250th Infantry Division, consisted of Spanish volunteers, most of whom were Fascists and all of whom were anti-Communist. When Spanish dictator Franco ordered the division home, approximately half of its personnel volunteered to join the SS instead.

(below) Ski troops move up to the front, Russia, 1942 or 1943. Later, a ski division was formed (the 1st Ski Jäger Division), but it did not distinguish itself and the experiment was not repeated.

(above) A panzer unit advances toward contact during the Battle of Kursk, July 1943. The panzer units suffered such heavy losses in this, the greatest tank battle of the war, that some of them never fully recovered.

(below) Members of the 8th Panzer Regiment, 15th Panzer Division, prepares to move out. As part of the Afrika Korps, the 15th Panzer distinguished itself in numerous battles before being destroyed in Tunisia in May 1943.

(left) A flame-thrower team of the Grossdeutschland Panzer Division on the Russian Front. Members of this elite unit were drawn from all over Germany; all were volunteers. Many authors incorrectly refer to Grossdeutschland as an SS division.

(right) A mortar crew in action on the Russian Front, probably summer 1943.

(below) An infantry fire team moving into the attack during street fighting in Stalingrad, 1942. The battle lasted from September 1942 to February 1943. In the end, more than twenty of Hitler's divisions were destroyed.

(above) A German soldier examines the graves of some of his compatriots who died in the Battle of Normandy.
(below) Field Marshal Rommel and Lieutenant General Hans Speidel in the field, France, 1944. Speidel was Rommel's chief of staff until the Desert Fox was wounded on July 17, 1944. The tanks in the background are of Czech manufacture and were captured by the Germans in 1938. The troops in black uniforms belong to the Army panzer corps and probably are members of the 21st Panzer Division, which was equipped with many captured vehicles.

(above) The spoils of battle, Western Front, 1944. *(Bundesarchiv)*
(below) Some of Rommel's infantrymen eat in the hedgerows of
Normandy, 1944. Supplying even the basic needs of soldiers such
as these became a monumental task as the battle wore on.
(Bundesarchiv)

(left) A German artilleryman scans the skies for enemy aircraft, France, 1944. The Allied fighter-bombers were greatly feared in Normandy and killed or severely wounded several German generals, including Erwin Rommel. *(Bundesarchiv)*

(below) German gunners train their rocket launcher on Allied positions. *(Bundesarchiv)*

(right) Splattered with mud and dirt, Lieutenant General Karl Wilhelm von Schlieben, the captured commander of Fortress Cherbourg, awaits the arrival of the American commander, Major General J. Lawton Collins, June 27, 1944.

(bottom) This photo, taken after the Battle of Argentan on August 20, 1944, shows signs of the German disintegration after the Battle of Normandy was lost.

(above) Field Marshal Gerd von Rundstedt with U.S. Lieutenant General Alexander Patch, May 5, 1945. Von Rundstedt had been restored to command of OB West in September 1944, only to be relieved again in March 1945, after American troops captured the bridge at Remagen.

(below) German infantrymen take boots from dead Americans during the Battle of the Bulge, December 1944. By the end of the fifth year of the war, Hitler's divisions were experiencing shortages of all classes of supplies and of manpower.

Colonel General Alfred Jodl, at the time he formally surrendered Germany to the Allies, May 1945. Jodl, Chief Operations Officer of OKW, was hanged as a war criminal in 1946.

Bazing had previously been Chief Engineer Officer of the 20th Mountain Army in Lapland on the Eastern Front (1942) and of Army Group F in the Balkans (1943-44). The 352nd absorbed the recruits of the newly formed 581st Grenadier Division in the fall of 1944. Blumenson 1960: 247, 442, 570; Chant, Volume 14: 1850; Volume 16: 2133; Cole 1965; 214; Harrison: 334, Map VI; "Frontnachweiser," 15 December 1944; MacDonald 1973: 286; RA: 172; OB 45: 245. For a detailed description of the 352nd on D-Day, see Paul Carell, *Invasion: They're Coming,* Bantam Books, New York: 1973 (hereafter cited as "Carell 1973").

353rd INFANTRY DIVISION

COMPOSITION: 941st Grenadier Regiment, 942nd Grenadier Regiment, 943rd Grenadier Regiment, 353rd Artillery Regiment, 353rd Füsilier Battalion, 353rd Anti-Tank Battalion, 353rd Engineer Battalion, 353rd Signal Battalion

HOME STATION: Wehrkreis II

Cadres from the veteran 328th Infantry Division were used to form this division in October 1943. The 353rd was in Brittany by late 1943, and was engaged in the Normandy fighting in June 1944. In late July, elements of the much-reduced 353rd attempted to halt the decisive American breakthrough but without success. The 353rd was almost constantly in action for several weeks; in August it was surrounded near Falaise and broke out of the huge pocket with the II Parachute Corps. Perhaps half of the survivors of the division escaped capture. Because of Allied pressure, the 353rd was allowed only a brief respite. It was back at the front in September, controlling a miscellaneous assortment of five local security battalions, an infantry replacement-training regiment, and a Luftwaffe Field unit of battalion strength. With this composite force it fought in the early battles of the Siegfried Line campaign, but on October 1 the division was absorbed by the 275th Infantry Division. The divisional headquarters, however, was not disbanded but went to Germany to take charge of new forces assembling in Luxembourg. In late November the new division under the old HQ again returned to action in the Aachen area, and was fighting south of Düren in January 1945. The 353rd fought in the Roer River battles and was with the LVIII Panzer Corps in the Battle of Cologne in March. By the time it escaped it was again a burned-out shell and its survivors finally surrendered to the Western Allies at the end of the war. The 353rd Infantry's commanders included Lieutenant General Paul Mahlmann (1944), Lieutenant General Erich Müller (1944), Colonel Thieme (1944-45), and Colonel Kurt Hummel (1945).

NOTES AND SOURCES: Lieutenant General Erich Müller, former commander of the 319th Infantry Division, was reportedly commander of the 353rd for a brief period in the fall of 1944 but was soon replaced by Colonel Thieme, the commander of the 943rd Grenadier Regiment and senior regimental commander in the division. Why the change was made is not known. Blumenson 1960: 247; 547; MacDonald 1963: 70, 330, 583, Map IV; MacDonald 1973: 161, 191; Speidel: 42; RA: 32; OB 45: 246.

355th INFANTRY DIVISION

COMPOSITION: 866th Grenadier Regiment, 867th Grenadier Regiment, 868th Grenadier Regiment, 355th Artillery Regiment, 355th Füsilier Battalion, 355th Anti-Tank Battalion, 355th Engineer Battalion, 355th Signal Battalion

HOME STATION: Wehrkreis V

Formed in France in February 1943, this division first saw combat in southern Russia in August of that year. In late 1943 it had suffered such heavy losses during the retreats following Kursk that it had to be disbanded; its survivors were absorbed by the 364th Infantry Division.

SOURCES: RA: 86; OB 45: 246.

356th INFANTRY DIVISION

COMPOSITION: 869th Grenadier Regiment, 870th Grenadier Regiment, 871st Grenadier Regiment, 356th Artillery Regiment, 356th Füsilier Battalion, 356th Anti-Tank Battalion, 356th Engineer Battalion, 356th Signal Battalion

HOME STATION: Wehrkreis IX

This division was created in France in early 1943 from reserve companies and subsequently functioned as a training division until October 1943, when it was transferred to the Italian Front. Not considered a first-rate fighting unit, the 356th performed coastal defense duties and conducted antipartisan operations in the Genoa area until May 1944. At this time the crisis at Anzio forced Field Marshal Kesselring to commit the division to the front line. The 356th Infantry spent the next six months at the front, before being sent to Hungary in January 1945. By April 1945 it was in remnants but was still in combat as part of the I SS Panzer Corps, 6th SS Panzer Army, in the Battle of Vienna and in the Austrian campaign. The survivors of the division fell into Soviet hands at the end of the war. Commanders of the unit included Lieutenant General Faulenbach (1943-44), Colonel Kleinhenz (1944), and Colonel von Saldern (1945).

NOTES AND SOURCES: Faulenbach was commander from August 1943 to October 1944. Colonel von Saldern was commander of the 869th Grenadier Regiment in 1944 and, as senior regimental commander, was acting divisional commander in 1945. Fisher: 19, 302, 419; Harrison: 38-39; RA: 144; OB 45: 246-47.

357th INFANTRY DIVISION

COMPOSITION: 944th Grenadier Regiment, 945th Grenadier Regiment, 946th Grenadier Regiment, 357th Artillery Regiment, 357th Füsilier Battalion, 357th Anti-Tank Battalion, 357th Engineer Battalion, 357th Signal Battalion

HOME STATION: Wehrkreis XVII

The 357th Infantry Division was activated in the Radom area of Poland in October and November 1943. It was attached to Army Group Center in early 1944 and was heavily engaged at Tarnopol and in the retreat across the northern Ukraine and southern Poland. In December 1944 it was shifted to the Hungarian sector, where it was subjected to heavy Soviet attacks. Later it joined Panzer Corps Feldherrnhalle and ended the war fighting the Russians in southeastern Germany. Its commanders included Lieutenant General Wolfgang von Kluge (1944) and Major General Rintelen (1945).

NOTES AND SOURCES: Kluge, former commander of Arko 107, was transferred to the 226th Infantry Division, which was surrounded at Dunkirk in the summer of 1944, and remained there until the end of the war. *Kriegstagebuch des OKW*, Volume I: 1145; Manstein: 526; Seaton: 498; OB 45: 247.

358th INFANTRY DIVISION

COMPOSITION: 644th Infantry Regiment, 645th Infantry Regiment, 646th Infantry Regiment

HOME STATION: Wehrkreis VIII

A Landwehr division consisting of older men, this unit was activated in early 1940 and was sent to Flanders just after Belgium and northern France were conquered. It was disbanded after the French surrender in July 1940 and was never involved in combat.

SOURCES: *Kriegstagebuch des OKW,* Volume 1: 1124; RA: 130; OB 42: 108; OB 43: 178; OB 45: 247.

359th INFANTRY DIVISION

COMPOSITION: 947th Grenadier Regiment, 948th Grenadier Regiment, 949th Grenadier Regiment, 359th Artillery Regiment, 359th Füsilier Battalion, 359th Anti-Tank Battalion, 359th Engineer Battalion, 359th Signal Battalion

HOME STATION: Wehrkreis III

In October 1943 this division was mobilized in Poland and was sent to the 4th Panzer Army in southern Russia in early 1944. It helped defend Tarnopol against heavy Soviet attacks and later fought in southern Poland and Slovakia. It was at battle group strength by February 1945. The 359th remained on the Eastern Front until the end of the Third Reich, surrendering in Czechoslovakia in early May 1945. Its commander in 1945 was Lieutenant General Karl Arndt (1944-45).

NOTES AND SOURCES: General Arndt previously commanded the 293rd Infantry Division on the Russian Front (1943-early 1944). *Kriegstagebuch des OKW,* Volume I: 1146; Volume IV: 1896; Manstein: 526; OB 45: 247.

361st INFANTRY (later VOLKSGRENADIER) DIVISION

COMPOSITION: 951st Grenadier Regiment, 952nd Grenadier Regiment, 953rd Grenadier Regiment, 361st Artillery Regiment, 361st Füsilier Battalion, 361st Anti-Tank Battalion, 361st Engineer Battalion, 361st Signal Battalion

HOME STATION: Wehrkreis VI

Organized in Denmark in October and November 1943, this division was sent to the Russian Front in March 1944. It was badly damaged in the summer of 1944, when it was smashed along with the rest of Army Group Center. The division was encircled at Brody in Byelorussia with Hauffe's XIII Corps. Elements of the 361st managed to break out, but most of the division—including its commander, Major General Gerhardt Lindemann—was captured. After retreating into Poland, the remnants of the 361st were withdrawn from the line and sent to Germany to rebuild. The unit incorporated the 569th Grenadier Division and other (smaller) formations into its ranks and by the fall of 1944 had completed its training. The newly designated Volksgrenadier division fought in the Arnhem battles on the Western Front before being transferred to the Saar sector. After fighting in eastern France the 361st was posted to the Vosges Mountains, where it absorbed elements of the 553rd Infantry Division before being absorbed itself by the 559th Infantry Division in January 1945. Its commander at that time was Colonel Alfred Philippi (1944-45). Previous commanders included Lindemann and Baron Siegmund von Schleinitz (1943-44).

NOTES AND SOURCES: Major General Lindemann, a holder of the Knight's Cross with Oak Leaves, was erroneously reported as killed in action by the German press. Baron von Schleinitz, a Prussian, had commanded the 9th Infantry Division in Russia before taking over the 361st. Cole 1950: 311-12; Harrison: 235; *Kriegstagebuch des OKW*, Volume IV: 1891; Seaton: 446-49; RA: 102; OB 45: 248.

362nd INFANTRY DIVISION

COMPOSITION: 954th Grenadier Regiment, 955th Grenadier Regiment, 956th Grenadier Regiment, 362nd Artillery Regiment, 362nd Füsilier Battalion, 362nd Anti-Tank Battalion, 362nd Engineer Battalion, 362nd Signal Battalion

HOME STATION: Wehrkreis VII

This division was formed in the Rimini area of northern Italy in October and November 1943 and remained in Italy throughout its career, fighting in all the major campaigns on that front. It first saw action in the Anzio sector in January 1944 and was overrun four months later when the Allies broke out of the bridgehead. Virtually destroyed at Cisterna near Rome in June, the division was rebuilt that summer when it absorbed the 1059th and 1060th Grenadier Regiments of the defunct 92nd Infantry Division. The 362nd returned to action in the Gothic Line and was engaged at Bologna in December 1944. The division was finally shattered in the last Allied offensive in Italy. On April 23, 1945, it was encircled and forced to surrender. Its commanders included Lieutenant General Heinz Greiner (1944-45) and Major General Friedrich von Schellwitz (1945).

NOTES AND SOURCES: Lieutenant General Greiner, a Bavarian, had previously commanded the 499th Infantry Regiment of the 268th Infantry

Division (1941) and then the division itself in Russia (1942-43). He held the Knight's Cross with Oak Leaves. Blumenson 1969: 361; Fisher: 166, 302, 494, Map III; RA: 116; OB 45: 248.

363rd INFANTRY (later VOLKSGRENADIER) DIVISION

COMPOSITION: 957th Grenadier Regiment, 958th Grenadier Regiment, 959th Grenadier Regiment, 363rd Artillery Regiment, 363rd Füsilier Battalion, 363rd Anti-Tank Battalion, 363rd Engineer Battalion, 363rd Signal Battalion

HOME STATION: Wehrkreis IX

Organized in October and November 1943 from elements of the 339rd Infantry Division and smaller units, the 363rd trained in Poland before being sent to the Jutland peninsula of Denmark in May 1944. From there it was again transferred in June, this time to Belgium. The next month it first appeared in combat in Normandy, where it was surrounded at Falaise in August. Only 2,500 of its men escaped in the subsequent breakout. These were sent to St. Quentin on the Somme River for a rest, before being sent on to Germany to reform as a Volksgrenadier division. In late September 1944 the 363rd was back in combat, fighting the U.S. 101st Airborne Division near Nijmegen and later the British in the Arnhem area of Holland. In late November the division was shifted to the Roer River area and opposed the U.S. 9th Army in the Roer River-Siegfried Line battles. In March 1945 the remnants of the 363rd were part of the 5th Panzer Army, still resisting in the vicinity of Cologne. It was destroyed in the Ruhr Pocket in April. Lieutenant General Augustus Dettling was the commander of the 363rd in 1944 and 1945.

NOTES AND SOURCES: General Dettling had previously led the 183rd Infantry Division on the Russian Front. Wounded in August 1944, he was nevertheless soon back in command of the unit. The division absorbed the 566th Grenadier Division in the fall of 1944. Blumenson 1960: 296, 552, 582; "Frontnachweiser," 15 December 1944; MacDonald 1963: 201-02, 572-73; MacDonald 1973: 155, 190; RA: 144; OB 45: 249.

364th INFANTRY DIVISION

COMPOSITION: 971st Grenadier Regiment, 972nd Grenadier Regiment, 973rd Grenadier Regiment, 364th Artillery Regiment, 364th Füsilier Battalion, 364th Anti-Tank Battalion, 364th Engineer Battalion, 364th Signal Battalion

HOME STATION: Wehrkreis V (?)

Formed in Poland in October and November 1943, this division consisted mainly of the survivors of the 355th Infantry Division. In early 1944 the 364th was disbanded and most of its personnel were transferred to the 77th Infantry Division.

SOURCES: RA: 86; OB 45: 249.

365th INFANTRY DIVISION

COMPOSITION: 647th Infantry Regiment, 648th Infantry Regiment, 649th Infantry Regiment

HOME STATION: Wehrkreis V

This division was made up of Landwehr personnel—trained reserve soldiers in the thirty-five to forty-five-year-old age group. It was organized in March 1940 and disbanded after the fall of France. The Headquarters was not dissolved but was sent to Lwow, Poland, as Administrative Area Command ("Oberfeldkommandatur") 365 in late 1940. Its commander in 1942 was Lieutenant General Buettel.

SOURCES: RA: 86; OB 42: 30, 102; OB 45: 249

367th INFANTRY DIVISION

COMPOSITION: 974th Grenadier Regiment, 975th Grenadier Regiment, 976th Grenadier Regiment, 367th Artillery Regiment, 367 Füsilier Battalion, 367th Anti-Tank Battalion, 367th Engineer Battalion, 367th Signal Battalion

HOME STATION: Wehrkreis VII

Formed in October and November 1943, this division was sent to Croatia in December and on to the Russian Front under Major General Zwade

(1943-44) in early 1944. It was with the II SS Panzer Corps in March and helped rescue the 1st Panzer Army, which had been surrounded in Galicia. The 367th later fought in Poland and East Prussia and was destroyed in the Battle of Königsberg in March 1945.

SOURCES: Carell 1971: 523; *Kriegstagebuch des OKW*, Volume IV: 1876, 1897; RA: 116; OB 45: 250; Ziemke 1966: 280.

369th INFANTRY DIVISION

COMPOSITION: 369th Grenadier Regiment, 370th Grenadier Regiment, 369th Artillery Regiment, 369th Füsilier Battalion, 369th Anti-Tank Battalion, 369th Engineer Battalion, 369th Signal Battalion

HOME STATION: Stockerau, Wkr. XVII

The 369th, nicknamed the "Devil's Division," consisted mainly of Croatians. Its forerunner, the 369th Croatian Infantry Regiment, had been attached to the 100th Jäger Division and had been destroyed with it at Stalingrad. The new division—staffed by German officers and N.C.O.'s and led by German Major General Fritz Niedholdt (1943-44)—was formed in early 1943. It served mainly in Crotia, protecting the Axis lines of communications and constantly fighting Tito's guerrillas and later fighting against the Russians. It also suffered heavy desertions. The 369th was down to battle group strength by early 1945 but was still operating on the Balkans sector of the Eastern Front when the war ended. Unlike its predecessor, the 369th Division was an unstable and relatively poor combat unit.

SOURCES: Hartmann: 39; *Kriegstagebuch des OKW*, Volume IV: 1903; RA: 220; OB 43: 178; OB 45: 250.

370th INFANTRY DIVISION

COMPOSITION: 666th Infantry Regiment, 667th Infantry Regiment, 668th Infantry Regiment, 370th Artillery Regiment, 370th Reconnaissance Company, 370th Anti-Tank Battalion, 370th Engineer Battalion, 370th Signal Company

HOME STATION: Wehrkreis VIII

The 370th was formed in France in May 1942 and was sent to the Russian Front almost as soon as its organization was complete. It fought in the

Caucasus campaign and in the Kuban Bridgehead before being sent to the lower Dnieper in autumn 1943. The following May it suffered heavy losses in the Dnieper withdrawal, took part in the retreat through the Ukraine, and in August 1944 was encircled and destroyed at Kishinev, Rumania, with the IV Corps of the 6th Army. The commanders of the 370th were Lieutenant General Walther Weiss (1942), Lieutenant General Fritz Becker (1943), Major General Johannes Niehoff (1944), and Major General Count von Hülsen (1944).

NOTES AND SOURCES: Walther Weiss, former Chief of Staff of I Corps (1940), became Commander of XXVII Corps in late 1942. He later led the 2nd Army on the Eastern Front (June 1943-1945) and became a Colonel General (February 1944). Count von Hülsen was captured at Kishinev, along with the rest of the division. Seaton: 481-84; RA: 130; OB 43: 178; OB 45: 250-51.

371st INFANTRY DIVISION

COMPOSITION: 669th Infantry Regiment, 670th Infantry Regiment, 671st Infantry Regiment, 371st Artillery Regiment, 371st Reconnaissance Company, 371st Anti-Tank Battalion, 371st Engineer Battalion, 371st Signal Company

HOME STATION: Wehrkreis VI

The 371st Infantry Division completed its training in France in May 1942 and joined the 6th Army on the Eastern Front that summer. With this army it penetrated across the Don and to the Volga in heavy fighting. Involved in the street fighting in Stalingrad, it was encircled with 6th Army in November 1942 and destroyed when the city fell in January 1943.

A second 371st Infantry was formed in Germany to replace the division destroyed at Stalingrad. It completed its organization in May 1943 and was sent to Italy and Slovenia in November 1943 and then to Croatia in December. A month later it was transferred to the Russian Front and remained there until the end of the war, fighting in the Ukraine, southern Poland, and southeastern Germany. It ended the war in the pocket east of Prague. The last commander of the 371st was apparently Lieutenant General Hermann Johannes Neihoff (1944-45).

NOTES AND SOURCES: Neihoff previously led the 370th Infantry Division in Russia (1944) and was in command of the 371st in January 1945. *Kriegstagebuch des OKW,* Volume I: 1146; Volume IV: 1875, 1896; von Mellenthin 1956: 225; RA: 102; OB 43: 179; OB 45: 251.

372nd INFANTRY DIVISION

COMPOSITION: 650th Infantry Regiment, 651st Infantry Regiment, 652nd Regiment

HOME STATION: Wehrkreis IV

Organized from Landwehr (older) personnel in May 1940, the 372nd was dissolved after the fall of France. In August 1940 its staff became Administrative Area Command ("Oberfeldkommandatur") 372 and was sent to Kielce, Poland, where it came under the supervision of the General Gouvernement.

SOURCES: RA: 72; OB 42: 30, 108; OB 45: 251.

373rd INFANTRY DIVISION

COMPOSITION: 383rd Grenadier Regiment, 384th Grenadier Regiment, 373rd Artillery Regiment, 373rd Füsilier Battalion, 373rd Anti-Tank Battalion, 373rd Engineer Battalion, 373rd Signal Battalion

HOME STATION: Stockerau, Wkr. XVII

A Croatian division led by German cadres, this force was organized in early 1943 and spent most of its career fighting Tito's guerrillas in Yugoslavia. It was a fourth-rate combat unit that suffered excessive rates of desertion throughout its existence. The 373rd saw action against the Russians in the last few months of the war. Its commanders included Lieutenant Generals Zellner (1943-44) and Eduard Aldrian (1945).

NOTES AND SOURCES: Zellner was formerly Chief of Staff of Wehrkreis XVII (1941). Aldrian had served as acting commander of the 95th Infantry Division (1942). Hartmann: 39; *Kriegstagebuch des OKW*, Volume I: 1145; RA: 220; OB 45: 251-52.

376th INFANTRY DIVISION

COMPOSITION: 672nd Infantry Regiment, 673rd Infantry Regiment, 766th Infantry Regiment, 376th Artillery Regiment, 376th Reconnaissance Company, 376th Anti-Tank Battalion, 376th Engineer Battalion, 376th Signal Company

HOME STATION: Wehrkreis VII

Formed in May 1942, this division first saw action in the drive on

Stalingrad. Surrounded in the city, its commander—Lieutenant General Alexander Edler von Daniels—surrendered it to the Russians without 6th Army's approval in late January 1943. Almost all of its men died in the Battle of Stalingrad or later in Siberian prison camps.

The second 376th Infantry Division was created in Holland in 1943. Later that year it was sent to Russia, where it fought in the Dnieper and Dnestr campaigns and in the Battle of Kirovograd. The 376th was encircled during the Rumanian withdrawal and destroyed, along with the rest of IV Corps and most of the rebuilt 6th Army. The commanders of this division included von Daniels (1942-43) and Major General Schwarz (1943-44).

NOTES AND SOURCES: Daniels had commanded the 79th Infantry Division in 1942. He joined the National Free Germany Committee after being captured. Major General Schwarz was captured in Rumania. Hartmann: 39; Seaton: 481-84; OB 43: 179; OB 45: 252.

377th INFANTRY DIVISION

COMPOSITION: 768th Infantry Regiment, 769th Infantry Regiment, 770th Infantry Regiment, 377th Artillery Regiment, 377th Reconnaissance Company, 377th Anti-Tank Battalion, 377th Engineer Battalion, 377th Signal Company

HOME STATION: Wehrkreis IX

Created in the spring of 1942, this division was sent to the southern—and later the central—sector of the Russian Front. It suffered heavy casualties in the Stalingrad campaign and the subsequent retreats and defensive battles. By July 1943 the remnants of the 377th were under the operational control of the 340th Infantry Division. Remaining in action, it absorbed the remnants of the 327th Infantry Division in early 1944 to help fill out its own depleted ranks. Later that spring it was largely destroyed by the Soviets during the retreat across central Russia, and its survivors were absorbed by other units in Army Group Center.

NOTES AND SOURCES: Lieutenant General Erich Baessler, later commander of the 19th Luftwaffe Field Division (1942-43) and the 191st Reserve Division (1944), led the 377th for most of 1942. *Kriegstagebuch des OKW:* Volume III: 733; RA: 144; OB 43: 179; OB 45: 252.

379th INFANTRY DIVISION

COMPOSITION: 656th Infantry Regiment, 651st Infantry Regiment, 658 Infantry Regiment

HOME STATION: Wehrkreis IX

Created in late 1939, this unit was a line-of-communications division, made up of older reservists. In late 1940 its personnel were sent home, and its headquarters became Administrative Area Command 379, located in Lublin, Poland.

SOURCES: RA: 144; OB 42: 30, 108; OB 45: 253.

380th INFANTRY DIVISION

COMPOSITION: 656th Infantry Regiment, 657th Infantry Regiment, 658th Infantry Regiment.

HOME STATION: Wehrkreis III (?)

One of the units formed from older men, the 380th Infantry was mobilized in March 1940 and disbanded later that year, after the defeat of France. It was not involved in combat.

SOURCES: OB 42: 108; OB 45: 253.

381st FIELD TRAINING DIVISION

COMPOSITION: 615th Field Training Regiment, 616th Field Training Regiment, 617th Field Training Regiment

HOME STATION: Wehrkreis XVIII

The 381st was formed in Russia, behind the front, in the fall of 1942, and was considered to be solely the property of Army Group A. Field Training Divisions—unlike other divisions—were not transferred between army groups except in extremely rare cases but, rather, remained under a single army group HQ throughout their existence. The 381st was engaged in training personnel in the rear areas of southern Russia until early 1944, when it was disbanded and its men sent to combat divisions. Major General Helmut Eisenstuck (1942-44) commanded the 381st Field Training Division.

NOTES AND SOURCES: Major General Eisenstuck was reported in Gironde, France, in the summer of 1944. What he was doing there is unclear. He apparently never received another divisional or higher command. *Kriegstagebuch des OKW*, Volume II: 1385; OB 45: 254.

382nd FIELD TRAINING DIVISION

COMPOSITION: 618th Field Training Regiment, 619th Field Training Regiment, 620th Field Training Regiment

HOME STATION: Wehrkreis IX

Formed in the rear area of the Eastern Front, the 382nd was the property of Army Group B during the Stalingrad campaign. It conducted training of soldiers en route to other units in Russia and possibly took part in some antipartisan operations. It existed from the fall of 1942 until early 1943 and was dissolved about the same time that Headquarters, Army Group B, ceased to exist in early February 1943.

NOTES AND SOURCES: Divisional commander Major General Paul Hoffmann apparently retired immediately upon relinquishing command of the 382nd. *Kriegstagebuch des OKW*, Volume II: 1385; Volume III: 5; Seaton: 347; OB 45: 254.

383rd INFANTRY DIVISION

COMPOSITION: 531st Infantry Regiment, 532nd Infantry Regiment, 533rd Infantry Regiment, 383rd Artillery Regiment, 383rd Reconnaissance Company, 383rd Anti-Tank Battalion, 383rd Engineer Battalion, 383rd Signal Company

HOME STATION: Wehrkreis I

The 383rd Infantry was organized in the winter of 1941-42. It trained at the Stablack Maneuver Area in East Prussia and was sent to the Eastern Front in June 1942. Initially with Army Group South, then B, and finally Center, the division was continuously and often heavily engaged throughout its existence. It fought in the early stages of the Stalingrad advance and against the massive but unsuccessful attacks the Soviets hurled at the 2nd Army in early 1943. The 383rd was destroyed, along with most of the rest of Army Group Center, in the Russian summer offensive of 1944. Its commanders included Lieutenant General Richard John (1942-early 1943) and Lieutenant General Edmund Hoffmeister (1943-44).

NOTES AND SOURCES: General John later commanded the 292nd Infantry Division (1943-44). Hoffmeister was briefly in command of the XLI Panzer Corps before he was also captured in the Russian summer offensive of 1944. *Kriegstagebuch des OKW*, Volume II: 1379, 1387; Volume III: 259; OB 45: 254. See Seaton for the story of the Russian attacks on 2nd Army in early 1943.

384th INFANTRY DIVISION

COMPOSITION: 534th Infantry Regiment, 535th Infantry Regiment, 536th Infantry Regiment, 384th Artillery Regiment, 384th Reconnaissance Company, 384th Anti-Tank Battalion, 384th Engineer Battalion, 384th Signal Company

HOME STATION: Wehrkreis IV

Formed in the winter of 1941-42, the 384th was sent to the southern sector of the Russian Front in May 1942. It fought in the Battle of Kharkov as part of the III Panzer Corps, 1st Panzer Army, before departing for the Stalingrad area. Here its combat units were surrounded in the Russian offensive of November 1942 but headquarters of the 384th were located to the west of the main Soviet thrust and thus escaped encirclement. Half of the division's combat troops were attached to the 44th Infantry Division and the other half to the 376th Infantry Division, both of which were destroyed, along with the rest of the 6th Army, in January 1943. Meanwhile, the divisional HQ controlled miscellaneous formations and combat groups under the 4th Panzer Army and later Group Meith (later IV Corps) of Army Detachment Hollidt.

After Stalingrad fell the divisional headquarters was sent to northern France, where it began forming a new division with its old regimental numbers. In late 1943 the 384th Infantry returned to southern Russia and was involved in the Dnieper bend battles. It was encircled at Kishinev, west of the lower Dnestr, and was destroyed there in autumn 1944.

SOURCES: Carell 1966: 490; Hartmann: 14, *Kriegstagebuch des OKW*, Volume II: 1393; Volume III: 4; OB 43: 180; OB 45: 254.

385th INFANTRY DIVISION

COMPOSITION: 537th Infantry Regiment, 538th Infantry Regiment, 539th Infantry Regiment, 385th Artillery Regiment, 385th Reconnaissance Company, 385th Anti-Tank Battalion, 385th Engineer Battalion, 385th Signal Company

HOME STATION: Wehrkreis VI

Activated in the winter of 1941-42 at Bergen, Wehrkreis XI, this division was sent to Russia in early spring 1942. It never fought as a united division. One-third of it was sent to Army Group North, and the rest went to 2nd Army, on the southern flank of Army Group Center. The units on the northern sector of the Eastern Front were under the direct control of L Corps but were eventually attached to the 24th Infantry Division. The southern elements were sent to the aid of the 8th Italian Army when it collapsed during the encirclement of Stalingrad. These elements suffered heavy losses in the retreat from the Volga and Don. The Army High Command decided to disband the 385th in the spring of 1943 as a result of these casualties. The division's last commander was Major General Eberhard Schuckmann (1942?-43).

NOTES AND SOURCES: General Schuckmann later commanded the 352nd Infantry Division in France prior to D-Day. The third of the division with Army Group North was probably absorbed by units on the northern sector of the Eastern Front, but this is not certain. *Kriegstagebuch des OKW,* Volume II: 1358, 1367, 1370, 1389; Volume III: 5, 258; RA: 102; OB 43: 180; OB 45: 254.

386th INFANTRY DIVISION

COMPOSITION: 659th Infantry Regiment, 660th Infantry Regiment, 661st Infantry Regiment

HOME STATION: Wehrkreis VI

The 386th Infantry made up of older reservists, was one of the units that were created in the first half of 1940. It remained in Germany while the first-line Wehrmacht divisions overran France and was disbanded late in 1940.

SOURCES: RA: 102; OB 42: 109; OB 43: 180; OB 44b: D109; OB 45: 254.

387th INFANTRY DIVISION

COMPOSITION: 541st Infantry Regiment, 542nd Infantry Regiment, 543rd Infantry Regiment, 387th Artillery Regiment, 387th Reconnaissance Company, 387th Anti-Tank Battalion, 387th Engineer Battalion, 387th Signal Company

HOME STATION: Wehrkreis VII

Nicknamed the "Rheingold Division," this force was created in early 1942 and sent to the southern sector of the Russian Front shortly afterward. It was continuously and frequently heavily engaged in fighting on the Eastern Front from the summer of 1942 until May 1944. The 387th was assigned to support the 8th Italian Army during the Stalingrad campaign and suffered heavy losses when that formation collapsed in late 1942. It also sustained severe casualties in the withdrawal from the lower Dnieper in 1944. Considered burned-out, the 387th was withdrawn from the line in the early summer of 1944 and disbanded.

SOURCES: *Kriegstagebuch des OKW:* Volume II: 1394; RA: 116; OB 43: 181; OB 45: 255

388th FIELD TRAINING DIVISION

COMPOSITION: 638th Field Training Regiment, 639th Field Training Regiment, 640th Field Training Regiment

HOME STATION: Wehrkreis I

Formed in the rear area (communications zone) of Army Group North on the northern sector of the Russian Front in late 1942, the 388th engaged in training men for Army Group North (16th and 18th armies). It retreated into the Courland Pocket after the Soviets broke the Siege of Leningrad and was still there at the end of the war. The division was redesignated Field Training Division "Nord" in 1944 and Field Training Division "Kurland" in 1945 when Army Group's North name was changed to Army Group Courland. Its commander for most of its existence was Lieutenant General Johannes Pflugbeil (1942-44).

SOURCES: *Kriegstagebuch des OKW,* Volume II: 1389; Volume III: 1158; Volume IV: 1877, 1897, OB 45: 255.

389th INFANTRY DIVISION

COMPOSITION: 544th Infantry Regiment, 545th Infantry Regiment, 546th Infantry Regiment, 389th Artillery Regiment, 389th Reconnaissance Company, 389th Anti-Tank Battalion, 389th Engineer Battalion, 389th Signal Company

HOME STATION: Wehrkreis XII

Organized from Hessian troops in the winter of 1941-42, this division was initially commanded by Lieutenant General Erwin Jaenecke, the future commander of the 17th Army in Crimea. The 389th fought on the southern sector of the Russian Front during the drive across the Don and the Volga, and in the Siege of Stalingrad. It was encircled in Stalingrad when the Soviets turned the tables on 6th Army in November 1942 and surrendered to the Russians in late January 1943. Its last commander, Major General Martin Lattman, was among the prisoners.

A second 389th Infantry Division was formed in France in the summer of 1943. Like its predecessor, this division was sent to the southern sector of the Russian Front. It first saw action in October 1943, and in February 1944 it was surrounded at Cherkassy, where only two hundred of its men managed to escape. These survivors were temporarily assigned to the 57th Infantry Division; however, the 389th was resurrected in the rear area of Army Group Center shortly thereafter. It was soon transferred to Army Group North and was isolated in the Courland Pocket in the fall of 1944. The 389th Infantry, however, was brought back to Germany by sea. It was cut off east of Berlin in the final campaign and surrendered to the Russians. Its divisional commanders included Jaenecke (1942), Lattmann (1942-43), Colonel (later Major General) Paul Herbert Forster (1943-44), and Lieutenant General Hahn (1945).

NOTES AND SOURCES: Jaenecke, an engineer officer, was formerly Chief of Staff to the Inspector of Fortifications (1938-39) and Chief Supply Officer to OB West (1941). After commanding the 389th Infantry, he led the IV Corps during the Battle of Stalingrad but was ordered out just days before the fortress fell. He then commanded LXXXVI Corps in the West (1943), before being given command of the 17th Army in Crimea. Promoted to Colonel General in February 1944, he was relieved because of his repeated insistence to Field Marshal von Kleist and to Adolf Hitler that the Crimea should be evacuated. His advice was ignored and 17th Army was destroyed in May 1944. In January 1945 Jaenecke was discharged from the Army for writing Hitler a letter spelling out Germany's adverse position. Martin Lattmann was promoted to Major General effective January 1, 1943, only four weeks before the fall of Stalingrad. His brother, Colonel Hans Lattmann, also an artillery officer, was Chief of Artillery for Army Group B during the Normandy campaign. Colonel Kurt Kruse was apparently in charge of the division briefly during its reformation period in France in 1943. Later, as a Major General, Kruse commanded Harko 317, which was in charge of General Headquarters artillery units for the 14th Army in Italy in 1945. General Hahn had previously commanded the 260th Infantry Division in Russia (1942-43). Carell 1966: 490, 615-16; Hartmann: 42; Mitcham 1983: 31, 136, 174; Plocher 1943: 323; RA: 188; OB 43: 181; OB 45: 255; Ziemke 1966: 234. For the full story of Colonel General Jaenecke's efforts to evacuate the Crimea and the subsequent destruction of 17th Army at Sevastopol, see Carell 1971 and Brett-Smith.

390th FIELD TRAINING (later SECURITY) DIVISION

COMPOSITION: 635th Field Training Regiment, 636th Field Training Regiment, 637th Field Training Regiment

HOME STATION: Wehrkreis XI

This unit was created in the rear area of Army Group Center in Russia early in the winter of 1942-43. It was caught up in the disaster that overtook the army group in the summer of 1944, was hurriedly committed to combat, and suffered heavy losses. Its 637th Regiment was converted into the 566th Security Regiment and lost to the division. The 390th itself was converted to a security division under 3rd Panzer Army in the latter part of 1944 but was disbanded in early 1945. Its last commander was Lieutenant General Johann Bergen (1944-45).

NOTES AND SOURCES: Bergen had previously commanded the 323rd Infantry Division on the southern sector of the Russian Front (1942-43). *Kriegstagebuch des OKW*, Volume II: 1387; Volume IV: 1876; RA: 172; OB 45: 256.

391st FIELD TRAINING (later SECURITY) DIVISION

COMPOSITION: 718th Field Training Regiment, 719th Field Training Regiment, 720th Field Training Regiment

HOME STATION: Wehrkreis XII

The 391st Field Training Division was created in the winter of 1942-43, under the headquarters of Army Group Center. Its 719th Regiment was formerly an infantry unit in the 206th Infantry Division. The 391st was smashed in the summer of 1944 when the Russians overwhelmed Army Group Center. Later that year the 719th and 720th Field Training Regiments were converted into the 312th and 565th Security Regiments, respectively. The divisional headquarters was returned to Germany and became Division Staff 391 z.b.V. ("For Special Purposes"). In March 1945 it was controlling miscellaneous combat formations under V SS Mountain Corps, 9th Army, Army Group Vistula and it was destroyed in the Battle of Berlin. Its last commander was Lieutenant General Baron Albrecht von Digeon von Monteton (1944-45).

NOTES AND SOURCES: Baron von Digeon von Monteton had led the 342nd Infantry Division in Russia in 1942. *Kriegstagebuch des OKW*, Volume IV: 1898; RA: 188; OB 45: 256.

392nd INFANTRY DIVISION

COMPOSITION: 845th Grenadier Regiment, 846th Grenadier Regiment, 847th Grenadier Regiment, 392nd Artillery Regiment, 392nd Füsilier Battalion, 392nd Anti-Tank Battalion, 392nd Engineer Battalion, 392nd Signal Battalion

HOME STATION: Wehrkreis XVII

This division consisted of Croatian soldiers led by German cadres. It was formed in Croatia in the fall of 1943, transferred to Austria for training, and returned to Crotia in 1944. It behaved better than the other German-Croatian divisions and was even cited for distinguished action against the partisans in Yugoslavia, later fighting the Soviets when they overran the Balkans. The 392nd ended the war on the southern sector of the Eastern Front. Its commander in 1945 was Lieutenant General Johann Mickl (early 1944 to 1945).

NOTES AND SOURCES: Johann Mickl, an Austrian who held the Knight's Cross with Oak Leaves, was of the panzer branch. He had led the 155th Panzer Grenadier Regiment of the 90th Light Division in Africa (1941) and a panzer grenadier brigade on the Eastern Front (1942). Hartmann: 39; RA: 220; OB 45: 256.

393rd INFANTRY DIVISION

COMPOSITION: 662nd Infantry Regiment, 663rd Infantry Regiment, 664th Infantry Regiment

HOME STATION: Wehrkreis VI

This line-of-communications division was made up of older troops. It was activated in late 1939 and disbanded in late 1940. Its headquarters was converted into Administrative Area Headquarters 393 and was sent to Warsaw. In October 1942 it was reportedly at Piaseczno, Poland, under the command of Major General Kurt Sieglin.

SOURCES: RA: 102; OB 42: 30, 110; OB 45: 257.

395th INFANTRY DIVISION

COMPOSITION: 674th Infantry Regiment, 675th Infantry Regiment

HOME STATION: Wehrkreis I

An East Prussian Landwehr division, this unit was organized in the winter of 1939-40 and dissolved after the fall of France. It never left East Prussia and never saw combat. The divisional headquarters was converted into Administrative Area Headquarters 395.

SOURCES: *Kriegstagebuch des OKW*, Volume I: 1123, 1125; OB 43: 180; OB 44b: D110; OB 45: 257.

399th INFANTRY DIVISION

COMPOSITION: 662nd Infantry Regiment, 663rd Infantry Regiment, 664th Infantry Regiment

HOME STATION: Wehrkreis I

Like the 395th Infantry Division, the 399th was created in the winter of 1939-40, from older reservists. It also never left East Prussia and its reason for existence was mainly to guard against a surprise Russian invasion of eastern Germany and Poland while the main German armies were busy in France in 1940—an event that never happened. The 399th's regiments were dissolved in late 1940; however, its Headquarters was sent to eastern Poland as Administrative Area Command 399.

SOURCES: *Kriegstagebuch des OKW*, Volume I: 1123, 1125; OB 43: 191; OB 45: 257.

SPECIAL DIVISION STAFF 400

COMPOSITION: Unknown

HOME STATION: See below

Little is known about this unit. It was formed from Administrative Area Headquarters 400 in Poland in 1944 and was sent to the Eastern Front to control miscellaneous formations. It was disbanded by October 1944.

SOURCE: OB 45: 257.

REPLACEMENT DIVISION STAFF 401

COMPOSITION: 161st Infantry Replacement Regiment, 228th Infantry Replacement Regiment

HOME STATION: Konigsberg, Wkr. I

The 401st began its career as Special Administrative Division Staff 401 in the winter of 1939-40. As such, it controlled local defense and other General Headquarters troops in East Prussia until the fall of 1942. At that time the 141st and 151st Replacement Divisions were upgraded to reserve divisions and sent to Russia. The 401st was in turn upgraded to a replacement division and took over the replacement battalions of the departing units; as such, it was primarily responsible for implementing the German draft. In late 1944, as the Russians crossed into East Prussia, the 401st Replacement was sent into combat with its subordinate units. Its men remained on the Eastern Front until the end of the war; the 401st itself may have been upgraded to full infantry division status in the last weeks of the Third Reich, but this is by no means certain. Its divisional commanders included Lieutenant General von Diringshofen (1942-44) and Major General Ruff (1945).

SOURCES: RA: 22-23; OB 43: 181; OB 44b: D128; OB 45: 258.

402nd INFANTRY DIVISION

COMPOSITION: 258th Infantry Replacement Regiment and 522nd Infantry Replacement Regiment; probably also included the 2nd Artillery Replacement Training Regiment, 2nd Anti-Tank Replacement Training Battalion, 2nd Engineer Replacement Training Battalion, 2nd Construction Engineer Replacement Training Battalion, 2nd Signal Replacement Training Battalion

HOME STATION: Stettin, Wkr. II

Organized in late 1939, the 402nd was originally a special administrative division staff used to control General Headquarters and miscellaneous troops in the II Military District. In the fall of 1942 it was upgraded to a replacement division when Wehrkreis II lost the 152nd and 192nd Replacement Divisions. The 402nd continued to provide training and replacement services until early 1945, when Pomerania was invaded by the Russians. The division was pressed into front line fighting and took part in the Siege of Kolberg (now Kolobrzeg) in February and March 1945. It fought very well, but when the city fell the soldiers of the division were killed almost to a man. The division's commander in January 1945 (about the time it became an infantry division) was Lieutenant General Richard Stenzel (1944-45).

NOTES AND SOURCES: General Stenzel formerly commanded an Artillery Replacement Regimental Staff in Wehrkreis XVII (Austria). Kolobrzeg is located in present-day Poland. Chant, Volume 16: 2235; RA: 34-35; OB 42: 18; OB 43: 26; OB 45: 258.

403rd SECURITY DIVISION

COMPOSITION: 177th Security Regiment, 406th Security Regiment, 403rd Reconnaissance Company, 403rd Anti-Tank Company, 403rd Engineer Company, 403rd Signal Company

HOME STATION: Berlin, Wkr. III

Originally created as Special Administrative Division Staff 403, this unit spent the first two years of the war supervising local defense and General Headquarters troops in the III Military District. In late 1941 it was reorganized as a security division and was behind the central sector of the Russian Front in November 1941. Later employed behind Army Group South, the 403rd was disbanded in early 1943 after providing the staff for the 265th Infantry Division. Its combat soldiers were apparently used to help reform the 79th and 384th Infantry Divisions. The 403rd Security was never committed to the main battle area as a combat unit, but elements were periodically assigned to front-line corps and sent into the fighting. The division's last commander was Lieutenant General Wilhelm Russwurm (1942-43).

NOTES AND SOURCES: Russwurm later commanded the 274th Infantry Division in Norway (late 1943-1945). *Kriegstagebuch des OKW*, Volume II: 1367, 1369, 1374; OB 42: 19; OB 43: 215; OB 44b: D117; OB 45: 258.

REPLACEMENT DIVISION STAFF 404

COMPOSITION: 524th Infantry Replacement Training Regiment, 544th Infantry Replacement Training Regiment, 554th Infantry Replacement Training Regiment. Probably also included the 4th Artillery Replacement Training Regiment (Motorized)

HOME STATION: Dresden, Wkr. IV

The 404th was formed as a special administrative divisional staff in the winter of 1939-40. It became a replacement division in autumn 1942 when the 154th and 174th Replacement Divisions of Wehrkreis IV were upgraded to reserve divisions and sent to Poland. In the latter part of 1944, after the 154th and 174th were fully committed to battle on the Eastern Front, the 404th expanded some of its existing replacement units into replacement-training units. The division was committed to combat when the Soviets overran the IV Military District in the spring of 1945.

NOTES AND SOURCES: The 544th and 554th Infantry Replacement Training Regiments also operated in Wehrkreis IV, but it is unclear whether one or both of them were controlled by the 404th or Replacement Division Staff 464, which was headquartered at Chemnitz. *Kriegstagebuch des OKW*, Volume I: 1147; RA: 72-81; OB 43: 28, 182; OB 45: 259.

REPLACEMENT DIVISION STAFF 405

COMPOSITION: 5th Infantry Replacement Training Regiment, 35th Infantry Replacement Training Regiment, 78th Infantry Replacement Training Regiment

NOTES AND SOURCES: Stuttgart, Wkr. V

Created to control local defense units and Wehrkreis V headquarters troops, this unit functioned as a special administrative divisional staff from late 1939 until early 1942. Reorganized as a replacement division staff, it was transferred to Strasbourg, where it controlled replacement training units in Alsace until the German defenses in Normandy collapsed. In September 1944 the unit was in charge of fortification work in the Vosges. Later it retreated to Oberkirch, where it worked on the Rhine defenses in addition to carrying out its regular duties. It was committed to combat as part of LXIV Corps, 19th Army in early 1945 and fought in western Germany in the last campaign of the war. Its commanders included Lieutenant Generals Otto Tscherning (1943) and Seeger (1944?-45).

NOTES AND SOURCES: At the end of the war the 405th (known officially as Division Number 405) was the only division in the newly formed 24th Army. General Seeger commanded the 292nd Infantry Division in Russia (1941-42). *Kriegstagebuch des OKW*, Volume I: 1147; RA: 88-89; OB 42: 20; OB 43: 182; OB 45: 259.

406th INFANTRY DIVISION

COMPOSITION: 211th Infantry Replacement Training Regiment, 426th Infantry Replacement Training Regiment, 536th Infantry Replacement Training Regiment, 6th Artillery Replacement Training Regiment, 6th Anti-Tank Replacement Training Battalion, 6th Construction Engineer Replacement Training Battalion, 1st Field Raiding Replacement Training Battalion (?)

HOME STATION: Munster, Wkr. VI

This Westphalian divisional staff spent most of the war as a special administrative divisional HQ, directing Wehrkreis headquarters troops and local defense units in the VI Military District. In September 1944 it was sent to Geldern, western Germany, where it apparently engaged in training attached local defense battalions. The 406th was redesignated an infantry division at this time. The crisis on the Western Front forced a premature end to the training process, and in October 1944 the 406th was sent to Arnhem, where it held a section of the West Wall. A month later it was virtually destroyed near Gross-Beck. The Headquarters was returned to Germany, where it again became a special administrative staff. The 406th was back on the front lines again in January 1945, however, directing miscellaneous formations of marginal value. It was trapped and destroyed in the Wesel Pocket west of the Rhine in March 1945. Its commander throughout most of its career was Lieutenant General Scherbening (1940-42 and 1944-45).

NOTES AND SOURCES: Scherbening commanded the 79th Infantry Division in 1943. MacDonald 1973: Maps VII and VIII; OB 43: 30; OB 45: 259.

REPLACEMENT DIVISION STAFF 407

COMPOSITION: 307th Infantry Regiment Training Regiment (?), 527th Infantry Replacement Training Regiment, 27th Artillery Replacement Training Regiment (?)

HOME STATION: Munich (later Augsburg), Wkr. VII

Initially created as a special administrative divisional staff, this unit directed Wehrkreis headquarters units and local defense forces until early 1943, when it became a full-fledged replacement division. The next year, as the German reserve and field training divisions were sent into combat, the 407th assumed a training mission as well. In early 1945 the division was engaged in constructing defensive positions in southern Germany and, in April, was ordered to hold Augsburg at all costs. The divisional commander, Major General Franz Fehn, refused to blow up the city's bridges or engage in futile house-to-house fighting. He evacuated all military hospitals and gave several hundred tons of stockpiled rations to the civilian population shortly before the Americans arrived. Fehn surrendered his command to the U.S. 3rd Infantry Division. Previous divisional commanders included Lieutenant Generals Oskar Blümm (1939-41 and November 1, 1942, to 1945) and Walter Hartmann (1942).

NOTES AND SOURCES: Oskar Blümm led the 57th Infantry Division in Russia for most of 1942. Hartmann later commanded the 87th Infantry Division (1943-44) and was acting commander of the XIV Panzer Corps (June 1944), and commander of the I Mountain Corps (1944), VIII Corps (1944) and XXIV Panzer Corps on the Russian Front (1945). He was promoted to General of Artillery in the summer of 1944. He was a Saxon and held the Knight's Cross with Oak Leaves. MacDonald 1973: 435-36; RA: 118; OB 43: 182; OB 45: 260.

REPLACEMENT DIVISION STAFF 408

COMPOSITION (1945): Local Defense, Replacement, and Replacement Training Units in Breslau

HOME STATION: Breslau, Wkr. VIII

Originally formed as a special administrative divisional staff under

Wehrkreis VIII, the 408th was converted to a replacement division in the fall of 1942, when the training and replacement functions of the Home Army were directed. In the summer of 1944 the division began training operations as well. The 408th itself was sent into the battle zone in early 1945 when the Russians invaded Silesia and besieged Breslau. Whether the division was committed to action as a unit or was divided among the combat forces in the city is not clear. In any event its survivors went into Soviet captivity when the city fell.

NOTES AND SOURCES: In late 1943 the division's commander was Lieutenant General Bayer, the former leader of the 181st Infantry Division (1942-43). RA: 132; OB 43: 182; OB 45: 260.

REPLACEMENT DIVISION STAFF 409

COMPOSITION (1943): 519th Infantry Replacement Training Regiment, 529th Infantry Replacement Training Regiment, 572nd Infantry Replacement Training Regiment; probably also included the 15th Motorized Artillery Replacement Training Regiment, 3rd Reconnaissance Replacement Training Battalion, 9th Anti-Tank Replacement Training Battalion, 9th Engineer Replacement Training Battalion, and the 9th or 40th Signal Replacement Training Battalion

HOME STATION: Kassel, Wkr. IX

In the winter of 1939-40 this divisional staff was formed as a special administrative divisional staff to control headquarters and local defense troops in Wehrkreis IX. In the fall of 1942 it received the replacement elements of the 159th and 189th Reserve Divisions when they went to France. After these divisions were committed to battle on the Western Front, the 409th assumed their training duties as well. Elements of the 409th were sent to the front in the last days of the war, but they did not see heavy fighting. The division's commanders included Major General Hans Ehrenberg (1940-44) and Lieutenant General Albert Zehler (1944-45).

NOTES AND SOURCES: Zehler, an Austrian, previously commanded Harko 304. RA: 146-47; OB 43: 33; OB 45: 260.

SPECIAL ADMINISTRATIVE DIVISION STAFF 410

COMPOSITION (1945): 154th Infantry Replacement Training Battalion, 220th Infantry Replacement Training Battalion, 377th Infantry Replacement Training Battalion, 490th Infantry Replacement Training Battalion

HOME STATION: Hamburg, Wkr. X

Created in late 1939 as a special administrative divisional staff, the 410th controlled local defense and headquarters troops in Hamburg until September 1944. At that time the 180th and 190th Reserve Divisions were taken from Wehrkreis control and hurriedly thrown into the battles against the British XXX Corps and assorted Allied airborne units. The 410th took charge of the units these divisions left behind and conducted replacement and training operations in northern Germany until the end of the war. There is no record indicating that it was ever formally upgraded to replacement division status, although that was its real function by late 1944. The division's commanders included Lieutenant Generals Karl Maderholz (1943), Adolf Poetter (1943-44?), and Josef Braumer (1945).

NOTES AND SOURCES: Karl Maderholz commanded the 320th Infantry Division in Russia (1942-43) and later commanded Replacement Division Staff 467 in Munich (late 1943-44). General Braumer formerly directed the 187th Reserve Division (later 42nd Jäger) (1942-43). He was an Austrian. OB 43: 34; OB 45: 261.

SPECIAL ADMINISTRATIVE DIVISION STAFF 411

COMPOSITION: 111th Infantry Replacement Training Regiment and miscellaneous GHQ units

HOME STATION: Hanover, Wkr. XI

The 411th was formed by Wehrkreis XI in late 1939 to control its headquarters and local defense troops. It was still conducting this duty in late 1943 and apparently continued to do so until the end of the war. It assumed command of some replacement training battalions in late 1944. Major General Gero von Gersdorff commanded the 411th from early 1943 to 1945.

NOTES AND SOURCES: Gersdorff had been Chief of Staff of Wehrkreis XI in 1942. OB 43: 35; OB 45: 261

SPECIAL ADMINISTRATIVE DIVISION STAFF 412

COMPOSITION: Varying attached units

HOME STATION: Wiesbaden, Wkr. XII

The 412th directed headquarters units and local defense formations in the XII Military District from its creation in late 1939 until it was disbanded in 1943. Its last reported commander was Lieutenant General Kurt Fischer (1942-43).

NOTES AND SOURCES: Fischer, who was 68 in 1945, previously commanded Replacement Division Staff 172 (1939-42). OB 42: 26; OB 43: 36; OB 45: 261.

REPLACEMENT DIVISION STAFF 413

COMPOSITION: 113th Infantry Replacement Training Regiment, 17th Artillery Replacement Training Regiment

HOME STATION: Nuremberg, Wkr. XIII

Activated as a special administrative divisional staff in the spring of 1940, the 413th was reorganized as a replacement division in September 1943 when the 173rd Replacement Division was upgraded to reserve division status and sent to Croatia. In 1944 the 413th expanded its subordinate elements into replacement-training units and operated in this role until the Allies approached Nuremberg. The 413th was then thrown into battle and was still resisting when the war ended. Commanders of the division included Major General Heinrich Thoma (1942), Major General Meyerhoffer (1943-45), and Lieutenant General Baron Sigmund von Schacky und Schönfeld (1945).

NOTES AND SOURCES: Thoma later commanded Special Administrative Division Staff 432 in Silesia (1942-45). Meyerhoffer was Chief of Staff of Wehrkreis XIII (headquartered at Nuremberg) in 1945. Baron von Schacky und Schönfeld had previously commanded the 165th Reserve Division in occupied France (1942-44). The 231st Reserve Grenadier Regiment apparently was attached to the 413th for a time after the departure of the 173rd Division. The 231st had been dissolved by late 1944. *Kriegstagebuch des OKW*, Volume I: 1147; Volume II: 1462; RA: 206; OB 43: 37; OB 45: 261.

416th INFANTRY DIVISION

COMPOSITION: 712th Grenadier Regiment, 713th Grenadier Regiment, 714th Grenadier Regiment, 416th Artillery Regiment, 416th Füsilier Battalion, 416th Anti-Tank Battalion, 416th Engineer Battalion, 416th Signal Battalion

HOME STATION: Wehrkreis X

The 416th began its career as a special purpose divisional staff in late 1941. That winter it was in the Silkeborg area of Denmark, controlling the 930th and 931st Infantry Regiments. In the summer of 1942 it was reorganized as a full-fledged infantry division, with the composition shown above. The 416th consisted mainly of older soldiers, with an average age of thirty-eight and was nicknamed the "Whipped Cream Division," because of the special diets many of its men required. In early September 1944 it was earmarked for the seizure and occupation of the Aland Islands in the Baltic Sea, south of the Gulf of Bothnia, between Finland and Sweden; however, the orders were cancelled by Hitler, who decided that the 416th could not be spared. The following month it was committed to battle on the Western Front. At that time it had 8,500 men, but very little artillery. In November it withdrew across eastern France, under heavy pressure from the U.S. Army Air Force. The 416th fought in the Merzig area of the Saar, in the so-called Saar-Moselle triangle, in the West Wall battles, and was continuously engaged from November 1944 to February 1945. Its men took part in the retreat across Germany and surrendered to the Western Allies at the end of the war. The 416th's commanders included Lieutenant Generals Barbänder (1942-43) and Kurt Pflieger (1944-45).

NOTES AND SOURCES: Barbänder went on to command the 270th Coastal Defense Division in Norway (1944-45). Cole 1950: 384, 387-88; MacDonald 1973: 118; RA: 160; OB 43: 183; OB 44b: D110; OB 45: 262; Ziemke 1966: 268, 391.

SPECIAL ADMINISTRATIVE DIVISION STAFF 417

COMPOSITION: 172nd Infantry Replacement Training Regiment, 174th Infantry Replacement Training Regiment

HOME STATION: Vienna, Wkr. XVII

The 417th was formed in late 1939 or early 1940 under XVII Military

District. It supervised the operation of local defense and headquarters troops in the Wehrkreis until early 1945, when it was disbanded. Its soldiers were no doubt incorporated into units of the 6th SS Panzer Army for the defense of Vienna in April 1945. Its commanders included Lieutenant Generals Rudolf Wanger (1942-44) and Adalbert Mikulicz (1944-45).

SOURCES: Hoffmann: 466; OB 43: 38; OB 45: 262.

REPLACEMENT DIVISION STAFF 418

PROBABLE COMPOSITION, 1944: 136th Mountain Infantry Replacement Training Regiment, 137th Mountain Infantry Replacement Training Regiment, 138th Mountain Infantry Replacement Training Regiment, 139th Mountain Infantry Replacement Training Regiment, 112th Mountain Artillery Replacement Training Regiment, 48th Anti-Tank Replacement Training Battalion, 82nd Mountain Engineer Replacement Training Battalion

HOME STATION: Salzburg, Wkr. XVIII

This unit was created in the fall of 1943 when the 188th Reserve Division was sent to northern Italy. In late 1944 its subordinate units expanded training units to units with combined replacement-training missions. The 418th was still in Salzburg when the war ended. Its commander in 1945 was Major General Max Jais.

NOTES AND SOURCES: As the only replacement division in Wehrkreis XVIII, the 418th probably controlled all the Wehrkreis XVIII replacement training units (see "Probable Composition"), although a few of these may have come directly under Wehrkreis control. Major General Jais had been commandant of Klagenfurt, Wehrkreis XVIII (northern Austria), in 1943. OB 43: 183; OB 45: 262.

REPLACEMENT DIVISION STAFF 421

COMPOSITION: Various attached recruiting and mobilization units

HOME STATION: Wehrkreis I

Originally formed as a z.b.V. ("for special purposes") divisional staff in East Prussia in 1940, the 421st was involved in training various attached units until the latter part of 1943 or early 1944 when it was disbanded. The reason why is not revealed by the records.

NOTES AND SOURCES: Lieutenant General Paul Gerhardt, who was Commander of Recruiting Area Allenstein (1939-45), a subdivision of I Military District, was simultaneously commander of Special Administrative Division Staff 421, presumably throughout most of its existence. Major General Janssen reportedly commanded Replacement Division Staff 421 in 1942. RA: 20-23; OB 43: 24, 183.

SPECIAL ADMINISTRATIVE DIVISION STAFF 428

COMPOSITION: Varying attached local defense and occupation units

HOME STATION: Graudenz, Wkr. XX

The 428th was formed in the winter of 1939-40 to control and support headquarters and local defense troops in West Prussia. Much of this area had been taken from Poland in September 1939 and contained many Polish nationals. The 429th was dissolved between September 1942 and April 1943, and its troop units were placed under the command of other headquarters.

SOURCES: OB 42: 28; OB 43: 184; OB 45: 263.

SPECIAL ADMINISTRATIVE DIVISION STAFF 429

COMPOSITION: Varying security and occupation troops

HOME STATION: Posen, Wkr. XXI

This divisional staff was formed in the winter of 1939-40 to support General Headquarters and security units in what was formerly western and southern Poland. It also engaged in occupation duties. Lieutenant General Schartow supervised the division in 1943. The 429th was dissolved in very late 1943, or more probably, early 1944.

SOURCES: OB 42: 28; OB 43: 40; OB 45: 263.

SPECIAL ADMINISTRATIVE DIVISION STAFF 430

COMPOSITION: Varying attached units

HOME STATION: Gnesen, Wkr. XXI

Another special administrative divisional staff, the 430th was formed in western Poland in the winter of 1939-40 to control miscellaneous occupation and local defense troops, as well as to support Wehrkreis headquarters units. It was disbanded in 1943 or shortly before.

SOURCES: OB 42: 28; OB 45: 263.

SPECIAL ADMINISTRATIVE
(later REPLACEMENT) DIVISION STAFF 431

COMPOSITION: One or more local defense regiments; miscellaneous GHQ units

HOME STATION: Litzmannstadt, Wkr. XXI

Originally formed to control local defense, security, occupation, and General Headquarters troops in western Poland, the 431st came into existence in 1940. Later it was transferred to Lodz, Poland, to supervise occupation forces and to train miscellaneous attached units. It was redesignated a replacement division in 1943 and was dissolved in late 1943 or early 1944. Its commanders included Lieutenant General Otto von Schwerin (1943).

SOURCES: OB 42: 28; OB 43: 40; OB 45: 263.

SPECIAL ADMINISTRATIVE
(later REPLACEMENT) DIVISION STAFF 432

COMPOSITION: 370th Infantry Replacement Training Regiment, 528th Infantry Replacement Training Regiment

HOME STATION: Kattowitz, Wkr. VIII, with a branch Headquarters at Neisse

Originally organized as a special administrative divisional staff in the spring of 1940, the 432nd was reorganized in autumn 1942, when the Home Army divided the replacement and training missions of Wehrkreis VIII. It took charge of replacement units in Silesia and in 1944 expanded them into replacement-training units when the 148th and 158th Reserve Divisions gave up their training functions. The 432nd was still engaged in these operations in early 1945, when the Soviets invaded Silesia. In September 1944 elements of the divisional staff were involved in collecting infantrymen from disorganized units at Königshutte, Upper Silesia. This indicates that the 432nd probably was committed to the battles in Silesia as a combat unit in the spring of 1945, but this is not certain. Its divisional commander was Lieutenant General Heinrich Thoma (August, 1942-1945).

NOTES AND SOURCES: Thoma was a Bavarian and a member of the Mountain Troops branch. He had led the 85th Mountain Infantry Regiment and held the Knight's Cross. He had previously commanded Special Administrative Division Staff 413 at Nuremberg (1942). *Kriegstagebuch des OKW*, Volume II: 1462; RA: 132; OB 43: 184; OB 45: 264.

REPLACEMENT DIVISION STAFF 433 (MOTORIZED)

COMPOSITION: 533rd Infantry Replacement Training Regiment, 543rd Infantry Replacement Training Regiment, 168th Artillery Replacement Training Regiment

HOME STATION: Frankfurt-on-the Oder, Wkr. III

The 433rd was established when the 233rd Motorized Replacement Division was upgraded to a reserve panzer division and sent to Denmark in late 1943. The 433rd took over the replacement units formerly belonging to the 233rd. The new division directed panzer and panzer grenadier replacement units until January 1945, when the Russians threatened the German capital. The 433rd was then sent into battle on the Eastern Front along with all the other miscellaneous formations Hitler could muster. The division's commander at that time was Lieutenant General Max Dennerlein (1945). The survivors of the 433rd were still serving in eastern Germany when Berlin fell.

NOTES AND SOURCES: Dennerlein, a Bavarian engineer officer, previously commanded the 290th Infantry Division on the Russian Front (1941-42). OB 45: 264.

SPECIAL ADMINISTRATIVE DIVISION STAFF 438 (later SPECIAL PURPOSE DIVISION) (z.b.V.)

COMPOSITION: 18th Local Defense Regiment, 184th Local Defense Regiment

HOME STATION: Klagenfurt, Wkr. XVIII

Originally created as a special administrative divisional staff in 1943, the

438th became a z.b.V. ("for special purposes") unit later that year, when it became responsible for antipartisan operations in the southeastern part of the XVIII Military District. This area had been part of Yugoslavia until it was overrun by the German Army in 1941. In late 1944 the division was still performing this mission; however, it was no doubt committed to battle on the Eastern Front in 1945, as the Russians closed in on Vienna. Lieutenant General Ferdinand Noeldechen was commanding the 438th in January 1945.

NOTES AND SOURCES: Noeldechen, an artillery officer, reportedly commanded a Saxon infantry division on the Eastern Front (1942-43). OB 45: 264.

440th ASSAULT DIVISION (ASSAULT DIVISION RHODES)

COMPOSITION (Sept., 1944): 939th Fortress Brigade (Rhodes), 967th Fortress Brigade (Cos), 938th Fortress Brigade (Leros)

HOME STATION: Rhodes

This division was formed on the island of Rhodes (in the Aegean Sea, off the coast of Greece) in 1943 from Assault Brigade Rhodes. Its infantry components where from the 440th Grenadier Regiment of the 164th Light Afrika Division (or at least those elements that had escaped the German collapse in North Africa), and its service personnel came from the remnants of the 999th Infantry Division (Penal), which had been destroyed in Tunisia in May 1943. The 440th remained in Rhodes until September 1944, when it evacuated the island during the general withdrawal from the Aegean Sea and the southern Balkans. The division was in combat against the Russians on the southern sector of the Eastern Front by October, and was disbanded in December 1944. Its men went to other units fighting on the Russian Front. Lieutenant General Ulrich Werner Kleeman commanded the division in 1943 and 1944.

NOTES AND SOURCES: Kleeman was commander of the 3rd Motorized Infantry Brigade of the 3rd Panzer Division in France and Russia (1940-42) and was later commander of the 90th Light Division in Libya and Egypt from April 1942 until he was seriously wounded near Alma Halfa Ridge in September. He took over the 440th upon his recovery and ended the war as commander of the IV Panzer Corps. Kleeman was from Baden and held the Knight's Cross with Oak Leaves. OB 45: 285; also see Mitcham 1982 and Paul Carell, *Foxes of the Desert*, E.P. Dutton, New York: 1960 (hereafter cited as "Carell 1960"); *Kriegstagebuch des OKW*. Volume IV: 1882.

441st COASTAL DEFENSE DIVISION

COMPOSITION: Various fortress battalions and coastal defense batteries

HOME STATION: Hanover, Wkr. XI

American military intelligence reported that this division was "possibly created" in 1944 for special but unspecified purposes. It was disbanded shortly afterward. Why the Germans would organize a coastal defense division in the land-locked province of Hanover is a mystery, unless it had a combined coastal defense/anti-aircraft artillery training mission.

SOURCE: OB 45: 265.

442nd SECURITY (later SPECIAL ADMINISTRATIVE) DIVISION

COMPOSITION (1941): Two security regiments and smaller support units

HOME STATION: Wehrkreis VIII

The 442nd was formed in early 1940 and was sent to the Eastern Front in 1941, where it served as a line-of-communications division for Army Group Center. It gave up its security units in 1943 and was transferred to Germany as a special administrative divisional staff. Its whereabouts in 1945 is unknown; however, it was reportedly still in existence and under the command of Lieutenant General zu und von Bornemann in January.

SOURCES: RA: 130; OB 42: 115; OB 43: 213; OB 45: 265.

444th SECURITY DIVISION

COMPOSITION: 45th Security Regiment, 602nd Security Regiment, 444th Reconnaissance Company, 444th Anti-Tank Company, 444th Engineer Company, 444th Signal Company

HOME STATION: Wehrkreis XII

Formed in early 1940, the 444th consisted of two reinforced infantry regiments but with no artillery. Stationed in France in the second half of 1940 as a special purposes division, the 444th was sent to Russia in 1941 and served in the communications zone of the southern sector until 1944, when it was dissolved. This was probably a result of the casualties it suffered in the front-line fighting of 1943-44. Its commander in 1943 was Lieutenant General Auleb and Lieutenant General Ritter von Nolo reportedly commanded the division in 1944.

SOURCES: *Kreigstagebuch des OKW*, Volume I: 1127; RA: 188; OB 43: 215; OB 45: 265.

454th SECURITY DIVISION

COMPOSITION: 57th Security Regiment, 375th Security Regiment, 454th Reconnaissance Company, 454th Anti-Tank Company, 454th Engineer Company, 454th Signal Company

HOME STATION: Wehrkreis VIII

This division was formed in 1940 and was serving in the rear area of Army Group South in Russia in 1941. As such it guarded key installations and conducted antipartisan operations in the Ukraine and nearby regions from 1941 until the end of 1943. In early 1944 it was attached to the XIII Corps of the 4th Panzer Army and was given the responsibility of defending Rovno, an important railroad junction west of Kiev. The 45th Division held the city from January 6 to February 2, 1944, against regular Soviet forces, but was finally forced to retreat. In July 1944 it was again in the front line, opposing the Russian summer offensive. It was encircled and virtually destroyed with XIII Corps at Brody in Byelorussia. Divisional commander Major General Nedtwig was among the prisoners. After this battle, the burned-out remains of the 454th Security were withdrawn from the line and disbanded. Previous commanders of the 454th included Lieutenant General Hellmuth Koch (1942-44).

SOURCES: *Kriegstagebuch des OKW*, Volume I: 1127, Seaton: 446-49; OB 43: 215; OB 45: 265; Ziemke 1966: 246.

455th SECURITY DIVISION

COMPOSITION: Two security regiments and smaller support units

HOME STATION: Unknown

The 455th Security was activated in 1940 and was briefly in the rear area of Army Group South in Russia in 1941. It was disbanded in 1942, for unknown reasons.

SOURCES: OB 43: 215; OB 45: 266.

REPLACEMENT DIVISION STAFF 461

COMPOSITION: 11th Infantry Replacement Training Regiment, 491st Infantry Replacement Training Regiment, 521st Infantry Replacement Regiment (?)

HOME STATION: Bialystok, Wkr. I

In the winter of 1941-42 this division's headquarters was organized as Special Purpose Division Bialystok. It controlled miscellaneous formations in what was formerly eastern Poland until autumn 1942, at which time it took over several replacement battalions and some training units in the I Military District. It also had the mission of establishing raiding detachments for special missions, mainly on the Russian Front. In the latter part of 1944, as the Soviets overran Poland, the 461st was transferred from the southeastern part of the Wehrkreis to Osterode, on the western edge. What part the division played in the battles for East Prussia is not known; however, since it is not listed in the Wehrmacht's Order of Battle for April 1945, it is almost certain that it was disbanded and its subordinate units transferred to combat divisions in the last weeks of the war. The 461st's commanders included Lieutenant General Hans Erich Nolte (1941-44) and Major General Richard zu und von Wenk (1945).

NOTES AND SOURCES: General Nolte, who was sixty-three in 1945, reportedly retired upon giving up command of the 461st. RA: 22-23; OB 43: 184; OB 45: 266.

462nd VOLKSGRENADIER DIVISION

COMPOSITION: 1215th Grenadier Regiment, 1216th Grenadier Regiment, 1217th Grenadier Regiment, 1462nd Artillery Regiment, 462nd Füsilier Battalion, 1462nd Anti-Tank Battalion, 1462nd Engineer Battalion, 1462nd Signal Battalion

HOME STATION: Metz, Wkr. XII

The 462nd was created in Lorraine, France, as a replacement unit in the fall of 1942. It assumed command of the replacement units formerly belonging to the 182nd Reserve Division, then on its way to the English Channel. Filled out from miscellaneous school and fortress units, it was sent into battle in August 1944 after the German front in Normandy collapsed. The following month it was upgraded to full combat division status, and was redesignated a Volksgrenadier unit. On November 1 the 1216th Grenadier Regiment was transferred to the nearby 19th Volksgrenadier Division and to fill the gap the 1010th Security Regiment was extracted from the 1217th Grenadier Regiment and reorganized. From early November until November 28, 1944, the 462nd defended Metz, its old home station, against vastly superior elements of Patton's U.S. 3rd Army. The division had only seven thousand men when the battle began and lacked heavy weapons; however, its student units included some of the best young soldiers in Nazi Germany. The ranks of one regiment at Metz, for example, were made up almost entirely of second lieutenants who had won battlefield commissions, mainly on the Eastern Front. During the siege the divisional commander, Lieutenant General Vollrath Lübbe, suffered a stroke and had to be relieved on November 14. He was replaced by Major General Heinrich Kittel, a tough veteran who had successfully defended fortresses on the Russian Front. A week later he was seriously wounded in front-line fighting. Finally, after a heroic defense, the 462nd was overwhelmed and the fortress fell on November 28. General Kittel was captured in a field hospital and only about eleven hundred men from the 462nd Volksgrenadier escaped the fall of fortress Metz; almost all of these were wounded men who had been evacuated earlier. The division was officially disbanded shortly afterward.

NOTES AND SOURCES: Colonel Joachim Wagner, former commander of the N.C.O. School in Wehrkreis XII, commanded the division in early 1944. Lübbe later recovered sufficiently from his stroke to command the 49th Infantry Division (1944-45). Chant, Volume 15: 2095; Cole 1950; 48, 125, 430, 446-47; RA: 188, 190-91; OB 45: 266. Anthony Kemp, *The Unknown Battle: Metz, 1944:* Stein and Day/*Publishers*, Briarcliff Manor, N.Y. 1981.

REPLACEMENT DIVISION STAFF 463

COMPOSITION: 293rd Infantry Replacement Training Regiment, 523rd Infantry Replacement Regiment, 23rd Artillery Replacement Training Regiment (Motorized)

HOME STATION: Potsdam, Wkr. III

In the reorganization of the Replacement Army in the fall of 1942, the 143rd and 153rd Replacement Divisions were sent to Russia as field training and reserve divisions, respectively. The 463rd was created to control the replacement units they left behind. In 1944 it was expanded to include replacement-training units. The 463rd was involved in the last campaign on the Eastern Front, which ended in the fall of Berlin. Its commander in early 1945 was Lieutenant General Habenicht.

NOTES AND SOURCES: Habenicht, when a Major General, had commanded Field Replacement Division E, a temporary unit, in 1941. OB 45: 267.

REPLACEMENT DIVISION STAFF 464

COMPOSITION: 534th Infantry Replacement Training Regiment, 24th Artillery Replacement Training Regiment

HOME STATION: Chemnitz, Wkr. IV

This division was created by IV Military District when the 154th and 174th Replacement Divisions were upgraded to reserve division status in late 1942. The 464th took over the replacement units that they left behind. In late 1944 the division expanded its subordinate elements into replacement-training units. Its men were sent into action on the Eastern Front, fighting as infantry and defending Prague as part of the 4th Panzer Army. The remnants of the 545th Volksgrenadier Division were attached to the 464th for this last battle. The 464th was surrounded, along with the bulk of Army Group Center, in the huge pocket east of Prague in April 1945 and surrendered to the Russians at the end of the war.

SOURCES: *Kriegstagebuch des OKW*, Volume I: 1147; RA: 72-74; OB 45: 267.

REPLACEMENT DIVISION STAFF 465

COMPOSITION: 515th Infantry Replacement Training Regiment, 525th Infantry Replacement Training Regiment, 25th Artillery Replacement Training Regiment

HOME STATION: Ludwigsburg, Wkr. V

Created in early 1942, the new division assumed command of the replacement units the 165th Reserve Division left behind when it went to France. In early 1943 the 465th was transferred to the Epinal area of eastern France but returned to Ludwigsburg the next year. In autumn 1944 it was expanded to include replacement-training units. It was still conducting these functions in 1945 when the Western Allies overran Württemberg and Baden, and the 465th Replacement Division ceased to exist.

NOTES AND SOURCES: Major General Gottfried von Erdmannsdorff, the former Commandant of Erfurt, commanded the 465th in 1943. He was later captured on the Eastern Front (January 1944). RA: 72-74, 88, 90; OB 45: 267.

REPLACEMENT DIVISION STAFF 467

COMPOSITION: 517th Infantry Replacement Training Regiment, 527th Infantry Replacement Training Regiment, 537th Mountain Infantry Replacement Training Regiment (?), 79th Mountain Artillery Replacement Training Regiment (?)

HOME STATION: Munich, Wkr. VII

After beginning its career as Special Administrative Division Staff 467, the unit was upgraded to a replacement division in autumn 1942 when the replacement and training functions of the 157th Reserve Division were divided. In autumn 1944 the subordinate units of the 467th became replacement-training units again. It was still conducting these missions in the Bavaria-Palatinate-Swabia region when the Western Allies overran southern Germany in the early spring of 1945. The divisional commander of the 467th for most of its existence was Lieutenant General Karl Graf (1939-45).

NOTES AND SOURCES: General Graf, a Bavarian, had retired from the Army in 1936, but was recalled to active duty to command the 467th. He briefly commanded the 330th Infantry Division (1942). Lieutenant General Karl Maderholz, former commander of the 320th Infantry Division (1942) and Replacement Division Staff 410 (1943), was in command of the 467th in late 1943, almost certainly on a temporary basis. RA: 118; OB 43: 184; OB 45: 267.

REPLACEMENT DIVISION STAFF 471

COMPOSITION: 515th Infantry Replacement Regiment, 561st Infantry Replacement Regiment, 571st Infantry Replacement Regiment, and apparently also the 19th Artillery Replacement and the 31st Artillery Replacement Regiments

HOME STATION: Hanover, Wkr. XI

The 471st was organized in the fall of 1942, to take over the replacement functions of the 171st and 191st Reserve Divisions, which had been sent to the English Channel area. When these units were committed to the fighting on the Western Front, the 471st assumed their training missions as well, and its subordinate units became replacement-training units. The 471st ceased operations when Hanover was overrun in the spring of 1945. Its commander in early 1945 was Lieutenant General Erich Dennecke (1944-45).

NOTES AND SOURCES: Dennecke, who was sixty years old in 1945, had been acting commander of the LXIX Reserve Corps in late 1943. RA: 174-78; OB 45: 268.

REPLACEMENT DIVISION STAFF 487

COMPOSITION: 262nd Infantry Replacement Training Regiment, 587th Infantry Replacement Training Regiment

HOME STATION: Linz, Wkr. XVII

Created in autumn 1942, this unit supplied replacements from northern Austria until its facilities were overrun by the Russians in the spring of 1945. It was probably expanded to include training functions in 1944. Its commander in 1945 was Major General Gustav Wagner.

NOTES AND SOURCES: Linz, the home station of the 487th, was considered by Hitler to be his home city. General Wagner had previously commanded the III Battalion of the 44th Infantry Regiment. Later he commanded a regiment of his own (1942). RA: 222-23; OB 45: 268.

526th FRONTIER GUARD (later REPLACEMENT) DIVISION

COMPOSITION: 211th Infantry Replacement Training Regiment, 253rd Infantry Replacement Training Regiment, 416th Infantry Replacement Training Regiment, 536th Infantry Replacement Training Regiment

HOME STATION: Aachen, Wkr. VI

Formed in 1939 or 1940, this division controlled miscellaneous formations on the German western border and later in Belgium until autumn 1942, when it became a replacement division. In 1944 it began conducting training operations as well. In August 1944 it was sent to the Western Front with its combat elements, while its "reserve" staff returned to Germany to continue its replacement and training missions, thus effectively splitting the division in two. After fighting in the Battle of Aachen, the 526th's combat units were absorbed by other divisions, and the main headquarters resumed its previous missions. The unit was still operating when the Allies overran western Germany. Its commanders included Lieutenant Generals Hans von Sommerfeld (1942-43), Albin Nake (1943-44), and Fritz Kuehne (1945).

NOTES AND SOURCES: Lieutenant General von Sommerfeld later commanded the 162nd Infantry Division in Italy (1944). Lieutenant General Nake subsequently led the 264th Infantry and 159th Reserve Divisions in 1944. Cole 1950: 587; RA: 103; OB 43: 30, 185; OB 45: 268.

537th FRONTIER GUARD DIVISION

COMPOSITION: Various frontier guard units

HOME STATION: Innsbruck, Wkr. XVIII

Created in 1939 to control miscellaneous units on the southern frontier of the Third Reich, the 537th guarded the German-Swiss border area until 1943, when it was disbanded.

SOURCES: OB 43: 185; OB 45: 268.

538th FRONTIER GUARD DIVISION

COMPOSITION: Various frontier guard units

HOME STATION: Klagenfurt, Wkr. XVIII

Along with the 537th Frontier Guard Division, the 538th patrolled the southern border of what was formerly Austria from 1939 until 1943, when it was disbanded.

SOURCES: OB 43: 185; OB 45: 269.

539th FRONTIER GUARD DIVISION
(later SPECIAL ADMINISTRATIVE DIVISION STAFF)

PROBABLE COMPOSITION: 14th Local Defense Replacement and Training Battalion, 50th Local Defense Replacement and Training Battalion

HOME STATION: Prague, Wkr. Bohemia and Moravia

The 539th was formed in 1939 or 1940 to control miscellaneous frontier guard and local defense units in Bohemia. In October 1942 it was redesignated a special administrative divisional staff and took over the few replacement-training battalions in Wehrkreis Bohemia and Moravia. It was still in operation in 1945 when the Russians overran Czechoslovakia. Its commanders included Lieutenant Generals Dr. Richard Speich (1943-44) and Wilhelm Thomas (1944-45?).

SOURCES: Hoffmann: 463; RA: 262; OB 43: 185; OB 45: 269.

540th FRONTIER GUARD DIVISION
(later SPECIAL ADMINISTRATIVE DIVISION STAFF)

COMPOSITION: Various local defense and attached units

HOME STATION: Brünn, Wkr. Bohemia and Moravia

Formed in 1939 or early 1940, the 540th controlled frontier guard and other local defense troops in the Moravia area of the Protectorate (formerly Czechoslovakia) until October 1942. At that time it was redesignated a special administrative divisional staff and directed local defense and General Headquarters troops until Moravia was overrun by the Soviets in the spring of 1945. Its divisional commanders included Lieutenant General Karl Tarbuk von Sensenhorst (1942-44) and Lieutenant General Benignus Dippold (1944-45).

NOTES AND SOURCES: Tarbuk von Sensenhorst retired in 1944. Dippold had led the 183rd and 717th Infantry Divisions in Russia and the Balkans, respectively (1940-42) and 1943, respectively), before taking over command of the 540th. OB 43: 185; OB 45: 269.

541st GRENADIER (later VOLKSGRENADIER) DIVISION

COMPOSITION: 1073rd Grenadier Regiment, 1074th Grenadier Regiment, 1075th Grenadier Regiment, 1541st Artillery Regiment, 1541st Füsilier Battalion, 1541st Anti-Tank Battalion, 1541st Engineer Battalion, 1541st Signal Battalion

HOME STATION: Wehrkreis XI

This unit was organized and trained as a grenadier division in the summer of 1944. In July 1944 it was sent to the central sector of the Russian Front, where the battered Army Group Center had retreated after the 4th and 9th armies had been smashed by the Soviet summer offensive. The

541st, which was redesignated a Volksgrenadier division in the summer of 1944, fought in Poland and was forced into the East Prussian Pocket in late 1944. It remained in action there against repeated Russian attacks for the rest of the war. It was down to battle group strength by February 1945.

SOURCES: *Kriegstagebuch des OKW*, Volume IV: 1897; RA: 172; OB 45: 269

542nd GRENADIER (later VOLKSGRENADIER) DIVISION

COMPOSITION: 1076th Grenadier Regiment, 1077th Grenadier Regiment, 1078th Grenadier Regiment, 1542nd Artillery Regiment, 1542 Füsilier Battalion, 1542nd Anti-Tank Battalion, 1542nd Engineer Battalion, 1542nd Signal Battalion

HOME STATION: Wehrkreis I

Originally formed in East Prussia as a grenadier unit, the 542nd was upgraded to Volksgrenadier status and sent to Army Group Center in the summer of 1944. It fought in Poland and eastern Germany and was still opposing Russian attacks in its home area of East Prussia when the war ended.

SOURCES: RA: 20; OB 45: 270.

543rd GRENADIER DIVISION

COMPOSITION: 1079th Grenadier Regiment, 1080th Grenadier Regiment, 1081st Grenadier Regiment, 1543rd Artillery Regiment, 543rd Füsilier Battalion, 1543rd Anti-Tank Battalion, 1543rd Engineer Battalion, 1543rd Signal Battalion

HOME STATION: Wehrkreis V

In July 1944 this division was formed in the Württemberg-Baden-Alsace region in the German Army's 29th mobilization wave. Later that summer it was disbanded, and its men were used to rebuild other divisions depleted in the fighting.

SOURCE: OB 45: 270.

544th GRENADIER (later VOLKSGRENADIER) DIVISION

COMPOSITION: 1082nd Grenadier Regiment, 1083rd Grenadier Regiment, 1084th Grenadier Regiment, 1544th Artillery Regiment, 1544th Füsilier Battalion, 1544th Anti-Tank Battalion, 1544th Engineer Battalion, 1544th Signal Battalion

HOME STATION: Wehrkreis VIII

Activated in July 1944, this grenadier unit was upgraded in late summer 1944 and sent to the reeling Army Group Center on the Eastern Front. It suffered heavy casualties in Poland and East Prussia in 1944-45 and was down to battle group strength by March 1, 1945. The 544th was still fighting in East Prussia when the war ended.

SOURCES: *Kriegstagebuch des OKW*, Volume IV: 1897; OB 45: 270.

545th GRENADIER (later VOLKSGRENADIER) DIVISION

COMPOSITION: 1085th Grenadier Regiment, 1086th Grenadier Regiment, 1087th Grenadier Regiment, 1545 Artillery Regiment, 545th Füsilier Battalion, 1545th Anti-Tank Battalion, 1545th Engineer Battalion, 1545th Signal Battalion

HOME STATION: Wehrkreis XII

One of the several 29th wave divisions, the 545th was formed in July 1944. Later that summer it was upgraded to a Volksgrenadier division and sent to Army Group Center on the Eastern Front. It ended the war in East Prussia, having been reduced by casualties to below regimental strength by early 1945.

SOURCES: *Kriegstagebuch des OKW*, Volume I: 1146; OB 45: 271

546th GRENADIER DIVISION

COMPOSITION: 1088th Grenadier Regiment, 1089th Grenadier Regiment, 1090th Grenadier Regiment, 1546th Artillery Regiment, 546th (?) Füsilier Battalion, 1546 Anti-Tank Battalion, 1546th Engineer Battalion, 1546th Signal Battalion

HOME STATION: Unknown

Mobilized in July 1944, this unit was disbanded later that summer. Its personnel were used to rebuild units shattered earlier that year.

SOURCE: OB 45: 271.

547th GRENADIER (later VOLKSGRENADIER) DIVISION

COMPOSITION: 1091st Grenadier Regiment, 1092nd Grenadier Regiment, 1093rd Grenadier Regiment, 1547th Artillery Regiment, 547th Füsilier Battalion, 1547th Anti-Tank Battalion, 1547th Engineer Battalion, 1547th Signal Battalion

HOME STATION: Wehrkreis X

Originally a grenadier unit, the 547th completed its organization in July 1944 and was soon in action on the central sector of the Eastern Front, which had recently collapsed. It took part in the retreat through Poland and ended the war cut off in the Danzig area with the 2nd Army.

SOURCES: *Kriegstagebuch des OKW*, Volume IV: 1898; OB 45: 271. Also see Seaton: 524.

548th GRENADIER (later VOLKSGRENADIER) DIVISION

COMPOSITION: 1094th Grenadier Regiment, 1095th Grenadier Regiment, 1096th Grenadier Regiment, 1548th Artillery Regiment, 548th Füsilier Battalion, 1548th Anti-Tank Battalion, 1548th Engineer Battalion, 1548th Signal Battalion

HOME STATION: Wehrkreis IV

The 548th was formed, like the other divisions of its series, in July 1944. It was redesignated a Volksgrenadier unit and sent to the central sector of the Eastern Front, where it fought in Poland and East Prussia before surrendering to the Russians in May 1945.

SOURCE: OB 45: 272.

549th GRENADIER (later VOLKSGRENADIER) DIVISION

COMPOSITION: 1098th Grenadier Regiment, 1099th Grenadier Regiment, 1549th Artillery Regiment, 549th Füsilier Battalion, 1549th Anti-Tank Battalion, 1549th Engineer Battalion, 1549th Signal Battalion

HOME STATION: Wehrkreis II

The 549th was formed in the Mecklenburg-Pomerania region of northeastern Germany in July 1944. Soon after it was upgraded to Volksgrenadier status and transferred to Army Group Center on the Eastern Front. It fought in Poland and East Prussia from autumn 1944 until the end of the war. It was in remnants by February 1945.

SOURCES: *Kriegstagebuch des OKW*, Volume IV: 1898; RA: 32; OB 45: 272.

550th GRENADIER DIVISION

COMPOSITION: 1110th Grenadier Regiment, 1111th Grenadier Regiment, 1112th Grenadier Regiment, 1550th Artillery Regiment, 550th Füsilier Battalion, 1550th Anti-Tank Battalion, 1550th Engineer Battalion, 1550th Signal Battalion

HOME STATION: Wehrkreis II

Organized in July 1944, the 550th Grenadier was dissolved later that summer. Its men were used to rebuild older divisions that had been burned out in the campaigns of 1944.

SOURCE: OB 45: 272.

551st GRENADIER (later VOLKSGRENADIER) DIVISION

COMPOSITION: 1113rd Grenadier Regiment, 1114th Grenadier Regiment, 1115th Grenadier Regiment, 1551st Artillery Regiment, 1551st Füsilier Battalion, 1551st Anti-Tank Battalion, 1551st Engineer Battalion, 1551st Signal Battalion

HOME STATION: Wehrkreis II

Formed at the Thorn Maneuver Area in Wehrkreis XX, the 551st was redesignated a Volksgrenadier division and sent to Army Group Center in the summer of 1944. It fought in Poland and was later attached to the 3rd Panzer Army. In early 1945 the 551st was cut off in the Samland-Danzig area and ended the war there.

SOURCES: *Kriegstagebuch des OKW*, Volume IV: 1897; RA: 32; OB 45: 273.

552nd GRENADIER (later VOLKSGRENADIER) DIVISION

COMPOSITION: 1116th Grenadier Regiment, 1117th Grenadier Regiment, 1118th Grenadier Regiment, 1552nd Artillery Regiment, 552nd Füsilier Battalion, 1552nd Anti-Tank Battalion, 1552nd Engineer Battalion, 1552nd Signal Battalion

HOME STATION: Wehrkreis V

This division was created in the 29th wave in July 1944, redesignated a Volksgrenadier division, and sent to the central sector of the Russian Front. It was apparently dissolved soon after, for there is no mention of it in the War Diary of the High Command of the Armed Forces.

SOURCES: OB 45: 273; also see *Kriegstagebuch des OKW*, Volume IV.

553rd GRENADIER (later VOLKSGRENADIER) DIVISION

COMPOSITION (1944): 1119th Grenadier Regiment, 1120th Grenadier Regiment, 1121st Grenadier Regiment, 1553rd Artillery Regiment, 553rd Füsilier Battalion, 1553rd Anti-Tank Battalion, 1553rd Engineer Battalion, 1553rd Signal Battalion

HOME STATION: Wehrkreis V

Mustered in at the Münsingen Maneuver Area, Wehrkreis V, the 553rd was upgraded to Volksgrenadier status soon after and sent to the Western Front, where it was in action near Nancy, France, in early September 1944. In mid-November it defended the Saverne Gap in the Vosges Mountains against the U.S. 7th Army and held it up for several days. Eventually, however, the 553rd was overwhelmed. Its commander, Major General Johannes Bruhn, was captured, and the road to Strasbourg was opened for the Americans. The remnants of the division were absorbed by the 361st Infantry Division. Meanwhile, the headquarters of the 553rd was sent to the Karlsruhe area and given charge of miscellaneous combat units. In early January 1945, it took part in Himmler's Operation "Northwind," aimed at retaking Strasbourg. The rebuilt division did well and even succeeded in reaching the outskirts of the city before being turned back. Taken out of the line, the 553rd Volksgrenadier was the only division in Army Group G's reserve in March 1945. It ended the war on the southern sector of the Western Front. The division's commanders included Lieutenant General Julius Braun (early 1944-September 1944), Bruhn (1944), Colonel Erich Löhr (1944), and Major General Hüter (1945).

NOTES AND SOURCES: Braun was commanding the 4th Mountain Division in early 1944, before taking over the 553rd. Colonel Löhr was court-martialed in 1945, probably on Himmler's orders, because of his failure to take Strasbourg. Hüter was previously on the staff of the Inspector of Armaments of Wehrkreis VIII. Chant, Volume 16: 2111, 2274; Volume 17: 2277; Cole 1950: 49, 288; RA: 172; OB 45: 273.

554th INFANTRY DIVISION

COMPOSITION: 621st Infantry Regiment, 622nd Infantry Regiment, 623rd Infantry Regiment

HOME STATION: Wehrkreis V

The 554th was formed in early 1940 as a positional ("Stellungs") division. As part of the 7th Army, it faced the French across the Maginot Line on a quiet sector of the front. It was disbanded in August 1940 in the partial demobilization following the fall of France.

SOURCES: *Kriegstagebuch des OKW*, Volume I: 1123; RA: 86; OB 43: 185; OB 45: 274.

555th INFANTRY DIVISION

COMPOSITION: 624th Infantry Regiment, 625th Infantry Regiment, 626th Infantry Regiment, 627th Infantry Regiment

HOME STATION: Wehrkreis VI

Formed as a Stellungs (positional) division in early 1940, the 555th was part of 7th Army on the Siegfried Line. It was disbanded shortly after the fall of France. The 555th was unusual because it had four infantry regiments.

SOURCES: *Kriegstagebuch des OKW*, Volume I: 1123; OB 43: 185; OB 45: 274.

556th INFANTRY DIVISION

COMPOSITION: 628th Infantry Regiment, 629th Infantry Regiment, 630th Infantry Regiment

HOME STATION: Wehrkreis XII

Like Hitler's other positional divisions, the 556th was created in early 1940 and disbanded in August of that same year. It served on the Siegfried Line in 1940. Most of its personnel were from older men (thirty-five and over) and returned to the civilian labor force inside the Reich.

SOURCES: *Kriegstagebuch des OKW*, Volume I: 1123; RA: 188; OB 43: 186; OB 45: 274.

557th INFANTRY DIVISION

COMPOSITION: 632nd Infantry Regiment, 633rd Infantry Regiment, 634rd Infantry Regiment

HOME STATION: Wehrkreis IV

The 557th was created in the Saxony-Thuringia region as a positional division in early 1940. It served as part of the 7th Army, Army Group C, opposite the French Maginot Line. It was dissolved on Hitler's orders after the French surrendered in June 1940.

SOURCES: OB 43: 186; OB 44b: D111, OB 45: 274.

558th GRENADIER (later VOLKSGRENADIER) DIVISION

COMPOSITION: 1122nd Grenadier Regiment, 1123rd Grenadier Regiment, 1124th Grenadier Regiment, 1558th Artillery Regiment, 558th Füsilier Battalion, 1558th Anti-Tank Battalion, 1558th Engineer Battalion, 1558th Signal Battalion

HOME STATION: Wehrkreis XIII

This division was organized as a grenadier division in July 1944. Later that summer it was redesignated a Volksgrenadier unit and sent to the central sector of the Eastern Front, where it fought in the Polish campaign of 1944-45. It ended the war, in remnants, with the 4th Army in East Prussia.

NOTES AND SOURCES: On March 29, 1945, the entire 4th Army had only 2,530 German combat effectives, 2,830 wounded soldiers, and 3,300 auxiliaries, mainly Russians. *Kriegstagebuch des OKW*, Volume IV: 1897; Thorwald: 96; OB 45: 274.

559th GRENADIER (later VOLKSGRENADIER) DIVISION

COMPOSITION: 1125th Grenadier Regiment, 1126th Grenadier Regiment, 1127th Grenadier Regiment, 1559th Artillery Regiment, 559th Füsilier Battalion, 1159th Anti-Tank Company, 1559th Engineer Battalion, 1559th Signal Battalion

HOME STATION: Wehrkreis IX

Formed in the summer of 1944, the 559th was originally a grenadier division; however, unlike most of the 1944 grenadier units, this one had a high proportion of young veterans. Upgraded to Volksgrenadier status, it was fighting the Americans in the Nancy area of eastern France in September. The 559th was heavily engaged in the Saar area and in northern Alsace in late 1944 and was pretty well burned-out by New Year's Day 1945. In January, however, it absorbed the remnants of the 361st Infantry Division and continued to fight in the West Wall battles. In late March 1945 the division was holding part of the southern sector of the German line on the Western Front, when it was cut off and destroyed on the western bank of the Rhine. Its commander was Major General Baron Kurt von Mühlen (1944-45).

NOTES AND SOURCES: Baron von Mühlen formerly commanded the 75th Jäger Regiment of the 5th Jäger Division on the Eastern Front (1942-43). Cole 1950: 245, 249, 473; MacDonald 1973: 243, 286; RA: 144; OB 45: 275.

560th GRENADIER (later VOLKSGRENADIER) DIVISION

COMPOSITION: 1128th Grenadier Regiment, 1129th Grenadier Regiment, 1130th Grenadier Regiment, 1560th Artillery Regiment, 560th Füsilier Battalion, 1560th Anti-Tank Battalion, 1560th Engineer Battalion, 1560th Signal Battalion

HOME STATION: Wehrkreis X

Originally a grenadier unit, the 560th was formed from miscellaneous units and Luftwaffe personnel stationed in Norway and Denmark in August 1944. Initially headquartered in the Moss area of southern Norway, the 560th was upgraded by the High Command and earmarked for the Eastern Front; however, Hitler countermanded that order and transferred it to Denmark instead. The division first saw combat in the Battle of the Bulge in December 1944, where it was commanded by Colonel Rudolf Langhaüser and formed part of the LVIII Panzer Corps, 5th Panzer Army. The following January it was with the II SS Panzer Corps and fought in the Eifel area, near St. Vith. The next month it was part of Army Group B's reserve but was committed to the Battle of Echternach against the U.S. 3rd Army after the collapse of the 212th Volksgrenadier Division. It was finally destroyed in the Ruhr Pocket in April. Its last commander was Colonel Langhaüser (1944-45).

NOTES AND SOURCES: Langhaüser commanded the 1130th Grenadier Regiment of the 560th in 1944, before rising to divisional command. Chant, Volume 16: 2133; Cole 1965: 195-96; MacDonald 1973: 26, 105; RA: 160; OB 45: 275; 9th U.S. Air Force Interrogation Report, 30 Jan 45, Air University Files.

561st GRENADIER (later VOLKSGRENADIER) DIVISION

COMPOSITION: 1141st Grenadier Regiment, 1142nd Grenadier Regiment, 1143rd Grenadier Regiment, 1561st Artillery Regiment, 561st Füsilier Battalion, 1561st Engineer Battalion, 1561st Anti-Tank Battalion, 1561st Signal Battalion

HOME STATION: Unknown

Organized in August 1944, this unit was almost immediately redesignated a Volksgrenadier formation and sent to Army Group Center on the Eastern Front. It fought in the Vistula and East Prussian campaigns, and was destroyed at Königsberg in March 1945.

NOTES AND SOURCES: Colonel Walter Gorn, former commando of the Krampnitz Panzer School, was named Commander of the 561st on July 21, 1944. He was involved in the plot to assassinate Hitler. Hoffmann: 434; *Kriegstagebuch des OKW*, Volume IV: 1897; OB 45: 275.

562nd GRENADIER (later VOLKSGRENADIER) DIVISION

COMPOSITION: 1144th Grenadier Regiment, 1145th Grenadier Regiment, 1146th Grenadier Regiment, 1562nd Artillery Regiment, 562nd Füsilier Battalion, 1562nd Anti-Tank Battalion, 1562nd Engineer Battalion, 1562nd Signal Battalion

HOME STATION: Wehrkreis I (?)

Created in August 1944, this unit was upgraded to Volksgrenadier status that autumn and was sent to Army Group Center on the Eastern Front. It fought in Poland and ended the war in remnants, cut off in East Prussia with the 4th Army. It was dissolved in April 1945, and its survivors surrendered to the Soviets early the following month.

SOURCES: *Kreigstagebuch des OKW*, Volume IV: 1897; OB 45: 276.

563rd GRENADIER (later VOLKSGRENADIER) DIVISION

COMPOSITION: 1147th Grenadier Regiment, 1148th Grenadier Regiment, 1149th Grenadier Regiment, 1563rd Artillery Regiment, 563rd Füsilier Battalion, 1563rd Anti-Tank Battalion, 1563rd Engineer Battalion, 1563rd Signal Battalion

HOME STATION: Wehrkreis III

The 563rd was formed in Germany in August 1944 and was soon sent to the central sector of the Eastern Front as a Volksgrenadier unit. In September it was transferred from Poland to Army Group North, and in late 1944 it was isolated in the Courland Pocket, where it was when the war ended.

SOURCE: OB 45: 276.

564th GRENADIER DIVISION

COMPOSITION: 1150th Grenadier Regiment, 1151st Grenadier Regiment, 1152nd Grenadier Regiment, 1564th Artillery Regiment, 564th Füsilier Battalion, 1564th Anti-Tank Battalion, 1564th Engineer Battalion, 1564th Signal Battalion

HOME STATION: Wehrkreis XVII

This unit was organized in Austria in the late summer 1944 and was absorbed by the 183rd Infantry Division soon after. Most of its men ended up in the Ruhr Pocket in April 1945.

SOURCES: RA: 220; OB 45: 276.

565th GRENADIER DIVISION

COMPOSITION: 1153rd Grenadier Regiment, 1154th Grenadier Regiment, 1155th Grenadier Regiment, 1565th Artillery Regiment, 565th Füsilier Battalion, 1565th Anti-Tank Battalion, 1565th Engineer Battalion, 1565th Signal Battalion

HOME STATION: Wehrkreis XIII

The division was activated in Bohemia in September 1944 and disbanded soon after. Its personnel were absorbed by the 246th Infantry Division and fought on the Western Front until the end of the war.

SOURCES: RA: 204; OB 45: 277.

566th GRENADIER DIVISION

COMPOSITION: 1156th Grenadier Regiment, 1157th Grenadier Regiment, 1158th Grenadier Regiment, 1566th Artillery Regiment, 566th Füsilier Battalion, 1566th Anti-Tank Battalion, 1566th Engineer Battalion, 1566th Signal Battalion

HOME STATION: Wehrkreis IX (?)

Created in the 31st mobilization wave in September 1944, this unit was disbanded soon after. Its soldiers were used to reconstitute other units.

SOURCE: OB 45: 277.

567th GRENADIER DIVISION

COMPOSITION: 1159th Grenadier Regiment, 1160th Grenadier Regiment, 1161st Grenadier Regiment, 1567th Artillery Regiment, 567th Füsilier Battalion, 1567th Anti-Tank Battalion, 1567th Engineer Battalion, 1567th Signal Battalion

HOME STATION: Wehrkreis XIII

Created in the 31st mobilization wave of September 1944, this unit's men were used for forming divisions in the 32nd wave. The division itself was dissolved almost as soon as it was established.

SOURCES: "Frontnachweiser," 15 December 1944; OB 45: 277.

568th GRENADIER DIVISION

COMPOSITION: 1162nd Grenadier Regiment, 1163rd Grenadier Regiment, 1164th Grenadier Regiment, 1568th Artillery Regiment, 568th Füsilier Battalion, 1568th Anti-Tank Battalion, 1568th Engineer Battalion, 1568th Signal Battalion

HOME STATION: Wehrkreis IV

Activated in September 1944, the 568th existed only briefly. It was disbanded later that year and its men absorbed by the 256th Infantry Division, which had been badly hurt in the Battle of the Scheldt. The newly designated 256th Volksgrenadier Division was returned to the Western Front.

SOURCES: RA: 72; OB 45: 277.

569th GRENADIER DIVISION

COMPOSITION: 1165th Grenadier Regiment, 1166th Grenadier Regiment, 1167th Grenadier Regiment, 1569th Artillery Regiment, 569th Füsilier Battalion, 1569th Anti-Tank Battalion, 1569th Engineer Battalion, 1569th Signal Battalion

HOME STATION: Wehrkreis VI

Formed in September 1944, the 569th was absorbed by the 361st Infantry Division later that year. Its men subsequently served on the Western Front.

SOURCES: RA: 102; OB 45: 278.

570th GRENADIER DIVISION

COMPOSITION: 1168th Grenadier Regiment, 1169th Grenadier Regiment, 1170th Grenadier Regiment, 1570th Artillery Regiment, 570th Füsilier Battalion, 1570th Anti-Tank Battalion, 1570th Engineer Battalion, 1570th Signal Company

HOME STATION: Wehrkreis II (?)

Organized in September 1944, the 570th Grenadier was dissolved soon after. Its men were transferred to the 337th Volksgrenadier Division, which was then in the process of rebuilding.

SOURCES: *Kriegstagebuch des OKW.* Volume IV: 1883; "Frontnachweiser," 15 December 1944: OB 45: 278.

571st GRENADIER DIVISION

COMPOSITION: 1171st Grenadier Regiment, 1172nd Grenadier Regiment, 1173rd Grenadier Regiment, 1571st Artillery Regiment, 1571st Reconnaissance Company, 1571st Anti-Tank Battalion, 1571st Engineer Battalion, 1582nd Signal Company

HOME STATION: Wehrkreis V

The 571st was mobilized in September 1944 and dissolved soon after. Its men were incorporated into the 18th Infantry (subsequently Volksgrenadier) Division, and sent to the Western Front.

NOTES AND SOURCES: The 571st was apparently initially formed directly under the Headquarters, Replacement Army. It presumably came under Wehrkreis V when it was decided that it would be absorbed by the 18th Volksgrenadier. *Kriegstagebuch des OKW*, Volume IV: 1883; "Frontnachweiser," 15 December 1944; OB 45: 278. Also see 18th INFANTRY (later VOLKSGRENADIER) DIVISION

572nd GRENADIER DIVISION

COMPOSITION: 1174th Grenadier Regiment, 1175th Grenadier Regiment, 1176th Grenadier Regiment, 1572nd Artillery Regiment, 1572nd Reconnaissance Company, 1572nd Anti-Tank Battalion, 1572nd Engineer Battalion, 1572nd Signal Company

HOME STATION: Wehrkreis II

Organized in September 1944 this division's troops were used to form the 340th Volksgrenadier Division, a unit reconstituted from the 340th Infantry, which had been smashed at the Battle of Lwow, Poland, on the Eastern Front. The new 340th was sent to the Aachen sector of the Western Front.

SOURCES: "Frontnachweiser," 15 December 1944; OB 45: 242, 278. Also see 340th INFANTRY (later VOLKSGRENADIER) DIVISION.

573rd GRENADIER DIVISION

COMPOSITION: 1177th Grenadier Regiment, 1178th Grenadier Regiment, 1179th Grenadier Regiment, 1573rd Artillery Regiment, 1573rd Reconnaissance Company, 1573rd Anti-Tank Battalion, 1573rd Engineer Battalion, 1573rd Signal Company

HOME STATION: Wehrkreis VIII

Another of the partially formed "32nd Wave" divisions, this unit was absorbed by the rebuilding 708th Volksgrenadier Division in September 1944. It never saw action as a unit.

SOURCES: *Kriegstagebuch des OKW,* Volume IV: 1883; "Frontnachweiser," 15 December 1944. Also see OB 45 and RA, and 708th INFANTRY (later VOLKSGRENADIER) DIVISION.

574th GRENADIER DIVISION

COMPOSITION: 1180th Grenadier Regiment, 1181st Grenadier Regiment, 1182nd Grenadier Regiment, 1182nd Artillery Regiment, 1182nd Anti-Tank Battalion, 1182nd Engineer Battalion, 1182nd Signal Company

HOME STATION: Stuttgart (?), Wkr. V

The 574th Grenadier was partially formed in September 1944 but was absorbed in November by the rebuilding 277th Volksgrenadier Division, which had previously been decimated by casualties. The 574th never saw combat under the designations mentioned above.

SOURCES: *Kriegstagebuch des OKW*, Volume IV: 1883; "Frontnachweiser," 15 December 1944; RA; OB: 45. Also see 277th INFANTRY (later VOLKSGRENADIER) DIVISION.

575th GRENADIER DIVISION

COMPOSITION: 1183rd Grenadier Regiment, 1184th Grenadier Regiment, 1185th Grenadier Regiment, 1575th Artillery Regiment, 1575th Reconnaissance Company, 1575th Anti-Tank Battalion, 1575th Engineer Battalion, 1575th Signal Company

HOME STATION: Wehrkreis III

This division—like a dozen others—was partially formed in September 1944. The Replacement Army discontinued this process and used the soldiers assigned to the 575th as replacements for the rebuilding 272nd Volksgrenadier Division in October or November 1944.

SOURCES: *Kreigstagebuch des OKW*, Volume IV: 1883; "Frontnachweiser," 15 December 1944; RA; OB 45. Also see 272nd INFANTRY (later VOLKSGRENADIER) DIVISION.

576th GRENADIER DIVISION

COMPOSITION: 1186th Grenadier Regiment, 1187th Grenadier Regiment, 1188th Grenadier Regiment, 1576th Artillery Regiment, 1576th Reconnaissance Company, 1576th Anti-Tank Battalion, 1576th Engineer Battalion, 1576th Signal Company

HOME STATION: Wehrkreis XIII

Partially formed in the autumn of 1944, the 576th Grenadier was dissolved soon after. Its troops were used as replacements for the 271st Volksgrenadier Division.

SOURCES: *Kriegstagebuch des OKW*, Volume IV: 1883; "Frontnachweiser," 15 December 1944. Also see 271st INFANTRY (later VOLKSGRENADIER) DIVISION.

577th GRENADIER DIVISION

COMPOSITION: 1189th Grenadier Regiment, 1190th Grenadier Regiment, 1191st Grenadier Regiment, 1577th Artillery Regiment, 1577th Reconnaissance Company, 1577th Anti-Tank Battalion, 1577th Engineer Battalion, 1577th Signal Company

HOME STATION: Cologne (?), Wkr. VI

This division never got out of the organizational stages. Prior to the completion of this process, its draftees were transferred to the 47th Infantry Division, which was rebuilding as a Volksgrenadier division in the winter of 1944. The headquarters of the 577th Grenadier was disbanded.

SOURCES: *Kriegstagebuch des OKW,* Volume IV: 1883; "Frontnachweiser," 15 December 1944. Also see RA and OB 45, and 47th INFANTRY (later VOLKSGRENADIER) DIVISION.

578th GRENADIER DIVISION

COMPOSITION: 1192nd Grenadier Regiment, 1193rd Grenadier Regiment, 1194th Grenadier Regiment, 1578th Artillery Regiment, 1578th Reconnaissance Company, 1578th Anti-Tank Battalion, 1578th Engineer Battalion, 1578th Signal Company

HOME STATION: Munich (?), Wkr. VII

This division was in the process of organizing in mid-September 1944. Instead of allowing it to complete its training, however, the Home Army broke up the 581st and sent its men to the rebuilding 212th Volksgrenadier Division, where they were used as replacements.

SOURCES: *Kriegstagebuch des OKW,* Volume IV: 1883; "Frontnachweiser," 15 December 1944. Also see 212th INFANTRY (later VOLKSGRENADIER) DIVISION.

579th GRENADIER DIVISION

COMPOSITION: 1195th Grenadier Regiment, 1196th Grenadier Regiment, 1197th Grenadier Regiment, 1579th Artillery Regiment, 1579th Reconnaissance Company, 1579th Anti-Tank Battalion, 1579th Engineer Battalion, 1579th Signal Company

HOME STATION: Wehrkreis VI

Partially formed in the fall of 1944, the 579th Grenadier Division was used to rebuild the veteran combat units of the 326th Volksgrenadier (formerly Infantry) Division, which had been smashed in the summer of 1944.

SOURCES: *Kriegstagebuch des OKW*, Volume IV: 1883; "Frontnach-weiser," 15 December 1944; also see RA and OB 45, and 326th INFANTRY (later VOLKSGRENADIER) DIVISION.

580th GRENADIER DIVISION

COMPOSITION: 1198th Grenadier Regiment, 1199th Grenadier Regiment, 1200th Grenadier Regiment, 1580th Artillery Regiment, 1580th Reconnaissance Company, 1580th Anti-Tank Battalion, 1580th Engineer Battalion, 1580th Signal Company

HOME STATION: Wehrkreis XI

Formed in the late fall of 1944, it was soon disbanded and—like the other 32nd Wave divisions—was used to fill out the ranks of previously decimated units. Its soldiers were transferred to the rebuilding 276th Volksgrenadier (formerly Infantry) Division.

SOURCES: *Kriegstagebuch des OKW*, Volume IV: 1883; "Frontnach-weiser," 15 December 1944; RA; OB 45. Also see 276th INFANTRY (later VOLKSGRENADIER) DIVISION.

581st GRENADIER DIVISION

COMPOSITION: 1203rd Grenadier Regiment, 1204th Grenadier Regiment, 1205th Grenadier Regiment, 1581st Artillery Regiment, 1581st Reconnaissance Company, 1581st Anti-Tank Battalion, 1581st Engineer Battalion, 1581st Signal Company

HOME STATION: Wehrkreis XI

Created in the 32nd mobilization wave, the 581st Grenadier was not permitted to complete its training. Its regiments were absorbed by the 352nd Volksgrenadier (formerly Infantry) Division, which had been virtually destroyed on D-Day.

SOURCES: *Kriegstagebuch des OKW*, Volume IV: 1883; "Frontnachweiser," 15 December 1944; also see RA: OB 45. Also see 352nd INFANTRY (later VOLKSGRENADIER) DIVISION.

582nd VOLKSGRENADIER DIVISION

COMPOSITION: 1206th Grenadier Regiment, 1207th Grenadier Regiment, 1208th Grenadier Regiment, 1582nd Artillery Regiment, 1582nd Reconnaissance Company, 1582nd Anti-Tank Battalion, 1582nd Engineer Battalion, 1582nd Signal Company

HOME STATION: Wehrkreis VI

This unit, like its sister divisions, never got out of the organizational stages. It was disbanded in November 1944, and its men were used to help rebuild the 26th Volksgrenadier Division, which had previously been smashed on the Eastern Front.

SOURCES: *Kriegstagebuch des OKW*, Volume IV: 1883; "Frontnachweiser," 15 December 1944; RA; OB 45. Also see 26th INFANTRY (later VOLKSGRENADIER) DIVISION.

583rd VOLKSGRENADIER DIVISION

COMPOSITION: never fully formed

HOME STATION: Wehrkreis VIII

Shortly after its activation was authorized in September 1944, the 583rd was disbanded. Its soldiers were used as replacements for the 62nd Volksgrenadier (formerly Infantry) Division, which had been decimated on the Eastern Front.

SOURCES: *Kriegstagebuch des OKW*, Volume IV: 1883; "Frontnachweiser," 15 December 1944. Also see 62nd INFANTRY (later VOLKSGRENADIER) DIVISION.

584th VOLKSGRENADIER DIVISION

COMPOSITION: never fully formed

HOME STATION: Wehrkreis IX

Authorized in September 1944, the 584th was in the early organizational stages when the Replacement Army decided to use it to rebuild decimated 9th Infantry (later Volksgrenadier) Division, which had been almost completely destroyed by the Soviets in Rumania. The new 9th was sent to the Western Front. The 584th's divisional headquarters was disbanded soon after.

SOURCE: *Kriegstagebuch des OKW*, Volume IV: 1883; "Frontnachweiser," 15 December 1944. Also see 9th INFANTRY (later VOLKSGRENADIER) DIVISION.

585th VOLKSGRENADIER DIVISION

COMPOSITION: never fully formed

HOME STATION: Wehrkreis VII

The 585th was partially organized in September 1944 and then used as a replacement pool for the 167th Volksgrenadier Division, which was then in the process of organizing.

SOURCE: *Kriegstagebuch des OKW*, Volume IV: 1883; "Frontnachweiser," 15 December 1944. Also see 167th INFANTRY (later VOLKSGRENADIER) DIVISION.

586th VOLKSGRENADIER DIVISION

COMPOSITION: never fully formed

HOME STATION: Wehrkreis XII

This "peoples' grenadier" division existed for only a short time in the fall of 1944. It was used to furnish troops to the 79th Volksgrenadier Division, which was then forming in the Thorn area of Poland (Wehrkreis XX).

SOURCE: *Kriegstagebuch des OKW*, Volume IV: 1883; "Frontnachweiser," 15 December 1944; OB 45: 166. Also see 79th INFANTRY (later VOLKSGRENADIER) DIVISION.

587th VOLKSGRENADIER DIVISION

COMPOSITION: never fully formed

HOME STATION: Wehrkreis III

The 587th was never fully formed. It was dissolved in late 1944, and its men sent to the 257th Volksgrenadier (formerly Infantry) Division, then rebuilding in Poland.

SOURCE: *Kriegstagebuch des OKW*, Volume IV: 1883; "Frontnachweiser," 15 December 1944; OB 45: 216-17. Also see 257th INFANTRY (later VOLKSGRENADIER) DIVISION.

588th VOLKSGRENADIER DIVISION

COMPOSITION: never fully formed

HOME STATION: Wehrkreis VIII

This unit was created in September 1944 and disbanded that winter. Its men were transferred as replacements to the 320th Infantry Division, which was rebuilding as a Volksgrenadier unit in Poland, following the disastrous losses it had suffered in Russia in the autumn of 1944.

SOURCE: *Kriegstagebuch des OKW*, Volume IV: 1883; "Frontnachweiser," 15 December 1944; OB 45: 234-35. Also see 320th VOLKSGRENADIER DIVISION.

SPECIAL DIVISION STAFF 601

COMPOSITION: Miscellaneous units

HOME STATION: Prague (?)

Formed in late summer 1944, this headquarters was used to control miscellaneous units on the southern sector of the Eastern Front. It ended the war in the pocket east of Prague.

SOURCES: *Kriegstagebuch des OKW*, Volume IV: 1896; OB 45: 278.

SPECIAL DIVISION STAFF 602

COMPOSITION: Miscellaneous Units

HOME STATION: Prague (?)

Like its sister divisions, the 601st and 603rd, this headquarters controlled miscellaneous units on the southern sector of the Eastern Front from late summer 1944 until the end of the war. It was trapped east of Prague with the rest of Army Group Center.

SOURCES: *Kriegstagebuch des OKW*, Volume IV: 1896; OB 45: 278.

SPECIAL DIVISION STAFF 603

COMPOSITION: Miscellaneous GHQ troops

HOME STATION: Unknown

Organized in late summer 1944, the 603rd controlled miscellaneous GHQ units on the southern sector of the Russian Front until at least March 1945 and probably until the end of the war.

SOURCES: *Kriegstagebuch des OKW*, Volume IV: 1896; OB 45: 279.

SPECIAL DIVISION STAFF 604

COMPOSITION: Miscellaneous units from the Netherlands

HOME STATION: Wehrkreis XI

Also known as Division von Tettau, this headquarters was formed in September 1944 when Operation Market Garden was in full swing. It was commanded by Lieutenant General Hans von Tettau, the Director of Operations and Training of the Armed Forces Netherlands, and consisted of miscellaneous German combat units. The 604th was sent into battle at Arnhem against the British 1st Airborne Division, on the western flank of the II SS Panzer Corps' battle line, and fought well. The British parachute division suffered more than 50 percent casualties and had to be disbanded after Arnhem. The 604th later fought in the Utrecht vicinity, and was reportedly sent to the Eastern Front in early 1945. It had been dissolved by March 1945, however.

NOTES AND SOURCES: Lieutenant General von Tettau had previously commanded the 24th Infantry Division (1940-44). MacDonald 1963; Map V; OB 45: 279. Also see Ellis, Volume II: 29-55.

SPECIAL DIVISION STAFF 606

COMPOSITION: Miscellaneous units

HOME STATION: Wehrkreis V

Originally created as Division Rässler in late summer 1944, the 606th controlled miscellaneous units in the Netherlands until the end of the war. Its commander was Lieutenant General Rudolf Rässler.

NOTES AND SOURCES: Rässler, a cavalry officer, had once been training officer at Aachen, Wehrkreis VI. OB 45: 279.

SPECIAL DIVISION STAFF 607

COMPOSITION: Miscellaneous units

HOME STATION: Wehrkreis I (?)

The 607th was created by Army Group North (previously Center) in early 1945 to serve as Fortress Command Pillau under Army Detachment Samland in East Prussia. It was destroyed in March 1945, when Pillau fell to the Russians.

SOURCE: *Kriegstagebuch des OKW*, Volume IV: 1897.

SPECIAL DIVISION STAFF 608

COMPOSITION: Varying attached units

HOME STATION: Unknown

This staff was formed by Army Group A in late 1944, probably to control GHQ units and/or to collect stragglers initially, for it served directly under Army Group Headquarters at first. By March 1945, however, it was being used as a combat division under XL Panzer Corps, 4th Panzer Army, Army Group Center, on the Eastern Front. The 35th SS Police Division was under the operational control of the 608th in the last campaign. It ended the war on the Eastern Front, near Dresden.

SOURCE: *Kriegstagebuch des OKW*, Volume IV: 1896.

609th INFANTRY DIVISION

COMPOSITION: Miscellaneous units

HOME STATION: Dresden, Wkr. IV

This unit was formed in Dresden in early 1945 from stragglers, Volkssturm, and rear-area SS men. Sent to Breslau in February, it was soon surrounded in the Silesian capital. Despite its hopeless position, the 609th defended Breslau in bitter house-to-house fighting in a most creditable manner. It was still fighting in the ruins of the city, even after the fall of Berlin. It surrendered to the Soviets in May 1945.

SOURCE: Chant: 192.

SPECIAL DIVISION STAFF 610

COMPOSITION: Miscellaneous units

HOME STATION: Berlin (?), Wkr III

This unit was organized in the rear area of Army Group Vistula in early 1945 and apparently controlled General Headquarters units and miscellaneous formations. It fought in the Berlin campaign—the last of the war.

SOURCE: *Kriegstagebuch des OKW*, Volume IV: 1898.

SPECIAL DIVISION STAFF 613

COMPOSITION: Miscellaneous units

HOME STATION: Narvik (?), Norway

Organized in early 1945 after the German evacuation of Finland and much of Lapland, this unit controlled miscellaneous formations in Norway as part of 20th Mountain Army's reserve. It never saw combat.

SOURCE: *Kriegstagebuch des OKW*, Volume IV: 1899.

SPECIAL DIVISION STAFF 614

COMPOSITION: Miscellaneous occupation units

HOME STATION: Denmark

The 614th Special Division Staff was organized in early 1945 to direct the German occupation forces in northern Jutland (i.e., the Danish peninsula). It was still there when the war ended.

SOURCE: *Kriegstagebuch des OKW*, Volume IV: 1899.

SPECIAL DIVISION STAFF 615

COMPOSITION: Miscellaneous combat units

HOME STATION: Unknown

This headquarters was organized in early 1945 to control miscellaneous combat units attached to the 4th Panzer Army on the Eastern Front. It was still resisting in the Dresden area when the war ended.

SOURCES: *Kriegstagebuch des OKW*, Volume I: 1146; Volume IV: 1896.

702nd INFANTRY DIVISION

COMPOSITION: 722nd Infantry Regiment, 742nd Infantry Regiment, 662nd Artillery Battalion, 702nd Anti-Tank Company (?), 702nd Engineer Company, 702nd Signal Company

HOME STATION: Wehrkreis II

Formed from older personnel in April 1941, the 702nd was sent to southern Norway the following month. By the end of June it was in northern Norway, and in September 1944 it was transferred to Trondheim, in the central part of the country. A static division, the 702nd remained on garrison and coastal watch duty until the end of the war. Its last commander was Lieutenant General Karl Edelmann (1945). Prior to that it had been led by Lieutenant General Otto Schmidt (1943-44). For at least part of 1942, its 742nd Infantry Regiment was attached to the 181st Infantry Division.

NOTES AND SOURCES: Edelmann had been a branch chief at OKH (1939-43). RA: 32; OB 42: 110; OB 43: 187; OB 45: 279.

704th INFANTRY DIVISION
see 104th Jäger Division

707th INFANTRY DIVISION

COMPOSITION: 727th Infantry Regiment, 747th Infantry Regiment, 657th Artillery Battalion, 707th Engineer Company, 707th Signal Company

HOME STATION: Wehrkreis VII

In April 1941 this division was mustered in. Like all the 700-series units, its was both static and considerably smaller than the normal German infantry division and was well understrength in artillery and support troops. The 707th was sent to the Eastern Front and was performing line-of-communications duties for Army Group Center in October. The following autumn it was transferred to the southern sector but returned to Army Group Center shortly afterward. In the summer of 1943 it was fighting on the front line near Bryansk. In June 1944 it was one of only two divisions in 9th Army's reserve when the massive Soviet summer offensive hit Army Group Center. Quickly committed, the 707th was soon smashed.

Major General Gier, the divisional commander, was taken prisoner along with most of his men. The remnants of the little division were officially disbanded soon after. Previous commanders of the 707th included Major General Baron Anton von Mauchenheim gennant Bechtolsheim (1942), Major General Schefold (1943), and Lieutenant General Rudolf Busich (late 1943).

NOTES AND SOURCES: Baron von Mauchenheim was formerly Ia, 6th Army (1939-40). Later he served as Chief of Staff, 1st Army (1942-43), Commander of the 257th Infantry Division on the Russian Front (1944), and Commander, Recruiting Area Regensburg, Wehrkreis XIII (1945). He was promoted to Lieutenant General in 1943. *Kriegstagebuch des OKW,* Volume III: 1157; OB 42: 110-11; OB 43: 187; OB 45: 280.

708th INFANTRY (later VOLKSGRENADIER) DIVISION

COMPOSITION (1945): 728th Grenadier Regiment, 748th Grenadier Regiment, 760th Grenadier Regiment, 1708th Artillery Regiment, 708th Füsilier Battalion, 708th Anti-Tank Battalion, 708th Engineer Battalion, 708th Signal Battalion

HOME STATION: Wehrkreis VIII

Formed in the Strasbourg area from Landeschützen personnel, the 708th originally consisted of only two infantry regiments—the 728th and 748th—an artillery battalion and the 708th Engineer and Signal Companies. In November 1941 this static division was posted to central and southwestern France and later served in Brittany. In autumn 1943 it was sent to Russia, where it served in the rear area of Army Group Center, fighting partisans. The 708th returned to western France in February 1944, and that summer it was transferred from the Garonne River estuary north of Bordeaux to Normandy. Rated as a poor-quality fighting unit, it was largely destroyed by the French 2nd Armored Division, which overran it near Falaise on August 9. The remnants were sent to Slovakia, where the 708th was hastily rebuilt as a three-regiment division with normal supporting units. The 708th absorbed the 573rd Grenadier Division in the fall of 1944. Returned to the Western Front in November, it suffered heavy losses south of Strasbourg and was disbanded in early 1945. Its commanders included Lieutenant General Hermann Wilck (1942-44) and Colonel Wilhelm Bleckwenn (1944-45).

NOTES AND SOURCES: In the last weeks of the war, Colonel Bleckwenn was promoted to Major General and given command of the 1st Marine

Division, a collection of excess naval personnel with very little ground combat training. It was destroyed in the Battle of Berlin. Blumenson 1960: 422, 498, 566; Chant, Volume 14: 1855, 1864; "Frontnachweiser," 15 December 1944; Harrison: Map VI; RA: 130; OB 43: 187; OB 45: 280.

709th INFANTRY DIVISION

COMPOSITION (1943): 729th Infantry Regiment, 739th Infantry Regiment, 709th Artillery Battalion, 709th Engineer Battalion, 709th Signal Company

HOME STATION: Wehrkreis IX

This understrength static division was formed from older men in April 1941 and sent to Brittany, France, on garrison duty in November. In the spring of 1943 it was transferred to Cherbourg and served as the city garrison. While there, it received the 919th Grenadier Regiment from the 242nd Infantry Division, but its personnel remained overage: the average soldier in the 709th was thirty-six years old in 1944. The 709th nevertheless fought credibly from D-Day until the fall of Cherbourg, where its remnants were destroyed. The divisional commander, Lieutenant General Karl-Wilhelm von Schlieben (1943-44), surrendered the city on June 30, 1944.

NOTES AND SOURCES: General von Schlieben had previously led the 18th Panzer Division in Russia. Major General Eckhard Geyso, former commander of the Döberitz Maneuver Area (1942-43), was reportedly acting commander of the 709th before the arrival of Schlieben. Harrison: Map VI, 147; RA: 144; OB 42: 111; OB 43: 186; OB 45: 281. For the story of the fall of Cherbourg, see Carell 1973 and Mitcham 1983.

710th INFANTRY DIVISION

COMPOSITION: 730th Infantry Regiment, 740th Infantry Regiment, 710th Artillery Battalion, 710th Engineer Company, 710th Signal Company

HOME STATION: Wehrkreis X

Formed in April 1941 as an undersized static division from Landesschützen (older) personnel, the 710th was posted to Oslo, Norway, where it replaced the younger, full-strength and better-equipped 163rd Infantry Division. The 710th Infantry later performed occupation duties at Kristiansand, Norway, and in Denmark. In December 1944 it was sent to the Adriatic sector of the Italian Front to free more experienced units for service in the East. It was withdrawn north of Venice in January 1945 and sent to the I SS Panzer Corps of the 6th SS Panzer Army in Hungary, where it fought against the Russians in the battles and retreats through western Hungary and in the Battle of Vienna. It was still resisting in Austria when the war ended. Commanders of the 710th included Lieutenant Generals Theodor Petsch (1941-late 1944) and Licht (1944-1945).

NOTES AND SOURCES: General Licht previously commanded a regiment of the 17th Panzer Division in Russia (1941-42), the 17th Panzer itself (early 1943), and the 21st Luftwaffe Field Division (1943-44). Fisher: 420; RA: 160; OB 42: 111; OB 43: 187; OB 45: 281; Ziemke 1959: 139.

711th INFANTRY DIVISION

COMPOSITION (1943): 731st Infantry Regiment, 744th Infantry Regiment, 711th Artillery Battalion, 711th Engineer Company, 711st Signal Company

HOME STATION: Wehrkreis XI

The 711th Infantry was formed from older troops in April 1941 and sent to northeastern France in August. In December 1941 the static unit was posted to Rouen, and in the spring of 1944 it was moved to the Deauville area, in the 15th Army's zone south of the Seine, where it headquartered at Pont L'Eveque. It fought in Normandy, where it suffered heavy casualties and was withdrawn to Holland to rebuild. Reconstituted south of Rotterdam, the 763rd Grenadier Regiment was added to the division, and its strength was brought up to three battalions of German and two battalions of Eastern troops. In October and November the 716th fought in the Battle of the Scheldt, and it was defending a sector near Gorinchem in December, when it was transferred to the Eastern Front. At only battle group strength, the division was surrounded in the pocket east of Prague and surrendered to the Russians in May 1945. The commander of the 711th during its combat career was Lieutenant General Josef Reichert (late 1943-1945).

NOTES AND SOURCES: Reichert, a Bavarian, had command of the 714th Infantry Division (later redesignated 114th Jäger) in the Balkans (1942-43). The division was reportedly briefly under the command of Major General Deutsch for part of 1944. Deutsch had previously commanded the 715th Infantry Division in occupied France (1943). Harrison: Map VI; Hartmann: 42; MacDonald 1963: 216-17, 220; OB 43: 187-88; OB 45: 281-82.

712th INFANTRY DIVISION

COMPOSITION: 732nd Infantry Regiment, 745th Infantry Regiment, 652nd Artillery Battalion, 712th Engineer Company, 712th Signal Company

HOME STATION: Wehrkreis XII

Organized as a static division in April 1941, the 712th was sent to northeastern France in August and to Normandy the following January. In the spring of 1942 it was posted to a sector of the Belgian-Dutch coast near Zeebrugge and remained there until autumn 1944, when the British and Americans arrived. Under Lieutenant General Friedrich-Wilhelm Neumann (1943-44) it fought against Operation Market-Garden in September and attacked and delayed British relief columns heading for Arnhem. It later opposed the British 32nd Guards (Tank) Brigade in the Battle of Oss, took part in the withdrawal across the Maas in October, and fought in the Heusden area that winter. In January 1945 the remnants of the 712th were sent to the Eastern Front, where they fought in the Battle of Berlin in April and where they were destroyed.

NOTES AND SOURCES: General Neumann formerly commanded the 340th Infantry Division (1941) and was named commander of the LXXXVIII Corps in Holland in 1945. Chant, Volume 17: 2376, MacDonald 1963: Map V; OB 43: 188; OB 45: 282.

713th INFANTRY DIVISION

COMPOSITION: 733rd Infantry Regiment, 746th Regiment, 713th Artillery Battalion, 713th Engineer Company, 713th Signal Company

HOME STATION: Wehrkreis XIII

This static division—made up of Landesschützen personnel—was created in April 1941. By autumn part of the division was in southern Greece and the rest in Crete, where they remained until late 1943 when the 713th was disbanded. Its regiments were transferred to the 133rd Fortress Division, which was forming in Crete at that time.

SOURCES: RA: 204; OB 43: 188; OB 45: 282.

714th INFANTRY DIVISION
see 114th Jäger Division

715th INFANTRY DIVISION

COMPOSITION (1942): 715th Infantry Regiment, 735th Infantry Regiment, 715th Artillery Battalion, 715th Reconnaissance Company, 715th Engineer Battalion, 715th Signal Company

HOME STATION: Wehrkreis V

The 715th (Static) Infantry Division was activated in April 1941, and sent to southwestern France that fall. In late summer 1943 it took over the Cannes-Nice sector on the Mediterranean coast when elements of the Italian 4th Army returned home. In January 1944 the 715th was sent to Italy following the Anzio landings and fought there until June, suffering heavy losses when the Allies broke out of the beachhead and took Rome. Sent to the rear, the 715th was rebuilt, largely from troops of the reinforced 1028th Grenadier Regiment. The division fought in the Gothic Line battles in September and was transferred to the Adriatic sector soon after. In early 1945 it was sent to the 1st Panzer Army on the Eastern Front and surrendered in Czechoslovakia. Its commanders included Major General Deutsch (1943), Lieutenant General Kurt Hoffmann (1943-44), Lieutenant General Greiner (1944), Lieutenant General Hans Georg Hildebrandt (1944), and Major General von Rohr (1945).

NOTES AND SOURCES: Major General Deutsch was reportedly briefly acting commander of the 711th Infantry Division (1944). He later led the 22nd Flak Division (1944) and the 16th Flak Division (1945). Kurt Hoffmann was commander of the 160th Reserve Division in Denmark in 1945. Hans Georg Hildebrandt had served with the Afrika Korps and briefly commanded the 21st Panzer Division in Tunisia in early 1943. He was reportedly still in Italy with Army Group C in 1945. Blumenson 1969: 361, 419-21; Fisher: Map III; Garland and Smyth: 294; Hartmann: 42-43; RA: 86; OB 42: 112; OB 43: 188; OB 45: 283.

716th INFANTRY DIVISION

COMPOSITION: 726th Infantry Regiment, 736th Infantry Regiment, 716th Artillery Battalion, 716th Reconnaissance Company, 716th Engineer Battalion, 716th Signal Company

HOME STATION: Wehrkreis VI

Formed from older personnel, the 716th was mustered in in April 1941 and sent to the Caen area of Normandy in May. It remained in the area until D-Day, when it was smashed by the British 2nd Army. It did, however, help prevent Montgomery from taking Caen on June 6 and thus allowed Field Marshal Rommel time to bottle up the Allies in hedgerow country for weeks. The 716th was withdrawn to Perpignan on the Mediterranean coast for refitting, but it was caught up in the battle for southern France instead. After suffering heavy losses at Chalon-sur-Saone, the 716th was withdrawn to Alsace and reformed again from miscellaneous troops. At the start of 1945, however, it had only 4,546 men. The 716th Infantry was virtually destroyed in the Colmar bridgehead later that month. Remnants of the division managed to escape, however, and were still fighting in southern Germany at the end of the war. The division's commanders included Lieutenant General Wilhelm Richter (1943-late 1944) and Colonel Hafner (late 1944-45).

NOTES AND SOURCES: Colonel Hafner was commander of the 736th Grenadier Regiment of the 716th in 1944 and senior regimental commander of the division. He reportedly served briefly as acting commander of the 338th Infantry Division in France in October, 1944. Chant, Volume 14: 1914; Volume 17: 2274; Harrison: Map VI; *Kriegstagebuch des OKW*, Volume I: 1147; RA: 102; OB 42: 112; OB 43: 189; OB 45: 283.

717th INFANTRY DIVISION
see 117th Jäger Division

718th INFANTRY DIVISION
see 118th Jäger Division

719th INFANTRY DIVISION

COMPOSITION: 723rd Infantry Regiment, 743rd Infantry Regiment, 719th Artillery Battalion, 719th Engineer Company, 719th Signal Company

HOME STATION: Wehrkreis III

This over-age, static unit was created in April 1941 and sent to Brittany in the winter of 1941-42 as an occupational division. It was posted to the Dordrecht area of Holland in late 1942, where it remained until being sent into action against the British on the Dutch-Belgian frontier in the summer of 1944. Despite the age of its troops, the 719th fought very well at Tilburg and in the Battle of the Scheldt, where it was badly cut up. Reformed at Dordrecht, the division was sent to Saarbrucken in the 1st Army's zone, where the staff referred to its artillery as "the Artillery Museum of Europe," so old and diverse were its guns. The rebuilt 719th was committed to the battles in the Saar and ended the war in southwestern Germany as part of the XVIII SS Corps, 19th Army. Its commanders included Lieutenant Generals Erich Höcker (1943-44), Karl Sievers (August-October 1944), Eugen-Felix Schwalbe (late 1944), and Major General Heinz Gäde (1945).

NOTES AND SOURCES: Erich Höcker, who was sixty-one in 1944, apparently retired from the Army in that year. He had previously been Landwehr Training Officer at Oppeln. Karl Sievers had commanded the 16th Luftwaffe Field Division (1943-44), which was twice routed near Caen in the Normandy campaign and dissolved soon after. Schwalbe had led the 344th Infantry Division in France (1943-44). Gäde had been Military Attaché to Sofia (Bulgaria), 1943-44. Cole 1950: 553; Harrison: Map VI; MacDonald 1963: 123, 219; Speidel: 41; OB 43: 189; OB 45: 284.

999th INFANTRY DIVISION (PENAL)
see 999th Light Afrika Division

RESERVE DIVISION "BÄRWALDE"

COMPOSITION: Miscellaneous units

HOME STATION: Berlin (?)

Reserve Division "Bärwalde" was a hastily assembled collection of old men, Hitler Youth, and miscellaneous rear area troops who were mostly unfit for combat duty. It was rushed to Army Group Vistula in early 1945 for the defense of Berlin. Most of it seems to have made good its escape from the Russians in April and May 1945.

SOURCE: *Kriegstagebuch des OKW*, Volume IV: 1898. Also see Ryan.

INFANTRY DIVISION "BERLIN"

COMPOSITION: Miscellaneous units

HOME STATION: Berlin, Wkr. III

Thrown together from miscellaneous troops, old men, and boys, this unit probably never exceeded regimental strength. It fought only one battle, and that was before Berlin in April 1945, where it was destroyed.

SOURCE: *Kriegstagebuch des OKW*, Volume IV: 1898.

FÜHRER BEGLEIT DIVISION

COMPOSITION: Various Führer Guard units

HOME STATION: Berlin, Wkr. III

Unlike most of the German divisions created in 1945, this was a good combat formation. Its cadre unit, the Führer Begleit Brigade (the Führer's Escort Brigade) had fought well in the Battle of the Bulge. The division was sent to Czechoslovakia in 1945 and ended the war in the pocket east of Prague. Its commander was Major General Otto-Ernst Remer (1945).

NOTES AND SOURCES: Remer, a veteran of the Eastern Front, had commanded the Guard Battalion "Grossdeutschland" in Berlin (1944) and took over the Führer Escort Brigade when it was created on August 1, 1944. Remer assumed command of the Führer Begleit Division on January 31, 1945. General Remer had been a favorite of Hitler's since July 20, 1944, when he played a major role in suppressing the Count von Stauffenberg's *coup.* He was promoted to Major General that day. *Kriegstagebuch des OKW,* Volume IV: 1896. Also see Hoffmann: 412-39; 479, 503.

FÜHRER GRENADIER DIVISION

COMPOSITION: Various attached combat units

HOME STATION: Berlin, Wkr. III

Organized in early 1945, this division had about one-quarter of the tank strength remaining to the depleted Army Group Vistula. When Hitler sent it and the 25th Panzer Division south in early April, that Army Group lost half of its panzers on the eve of the Battle of Berlin. The Führer Grenadier Division fought in the Battle of Vienna and ended the war in Austria, fighting the Russians as part of Dietrich's 6th SS Panzer Army. It was commanded by Major General Hellmuth Mader.

SOURCES: *Kriegstagebuch des OKW,* Volume I: 1145; Ziemke 1966: 455, 469.

RESERVE DIVISION "POMERANIA"

COMPOSITION: Miscellaneous units

HOME STATION: Wehrkreis II

Organized in early 1945, this division was the main unit in General Raus's newly activated 11th Army, which was charged with the defense of Pomerania. Colonel Seaton described the division as "a motley force of engineers, Luftwaffe ground staff, naval survey units, and Volksturm battalions, without artillery, anti-tank guns, signal equipment, or supply services, in some cases without regimental or battalion commanders . . ." After examining the situation, Raus reported back to Hitler that he doubted if Pomerania could be held. The reserve division took part in the retreat through Pomerania and was with the 3rd Panzer Army in the Battle of Berlin, which ended the war.

SOURCES: *Kriegstagebuch des OKW,* Volume IV: 1898; Seaton: 540.

POLICE DIVISION "SILESIA"

COMPOSITION: Miscellaneous police units

HOME STATION: Wehrkreis VIII (?)

This division was made up of police units and miscellaneous formations from Silesia. Created in 1945, it was destroyed in the last campaign of the war. It never reached divisional strength and was totally unsuited for ground combat against the Russians.

SOURCE: *Kriegstagebuch des OKW*, Volume IV: 1898

4

The Jäger and Light Divisions*

1st SKI JÄGER DIVISION

COMPOSITION: 1st Ski Jäger Regiment, 2nd Ski Jäger Regiment, ? Engineer Battalion, 152nd Signal Battalion, Anti-Tank Battalion (?), Füsilier Battalion (?)

HOME STATION: Wehrkreis VIII

Formed as the 1st Ski Brigade in October 1943, this unit was converted to a division in Lower Bavaria in the summer of 1944. The 2nd Ski Regiment was created from the former 167th Grenadier Regiment of the old 86th Infantry Division, which had been smashed in Russia. Following the completion of its training, the division was sent to the badly mauled Army Group Center in the summer of 1944, and it was involved in the retreat to the Vistula. In October it was transferred to Slovakia but returned to southern Poland in December and fought on the Eastern Front until the end of the war. It surrendered to the Russians in Czechoslovakia in May 1945. The 1st Ski Jäger Division never earned any special distinction; as a result, no second ski division was ever created. Its commanders included Lieutenant General Gustav Hundt (1944-45) and Colonel Steets (1945).

NOTES AND SOURCES: Steets was the Ia (Operations Officer) of the 20th Mountain Army in Finland in 1943. *Kriegstagebuch des OKW*, Volume I: 1146; RA: 204; OB 45: 313.

---

*The original German Light Divisions, numbered 1st, 2nd, 3rd, and 4th, were converted into panzer divisions in the winter of 1939-40. See 6th, 7th, 8th, and 9th Panzer Divisions, respectively.

5th JÄGER DIVISION

COMPOSITION (1943): 56th Jäger Regiment, 75th Jäger Regiment, 5th Motorized Artillery Regiment, 5th Bicycle Battalion, 5th Anti-Tank Battalion, 5th Motorized Engineer Battalion, 5th Motorized Signal Battalion

HOME STATION: Konstantz, Wkr. V

Originally the 5th Infantry Division, this unit was formed at Stuttgart in the mid-1930s. Its soldiers were recruited from Baden and Württemberg, and were originally divided into three infantry regiments.

The 5th Infantry did not take part in the Polish campaign of 1939 and was only lightly engaged in the invasion of France the following year. In 1941, however, it took part in the Russian campaign and was involved in bitter fighting in the Vyasma sector. In December it was sent to France to rest and refit and to be converted into a Jäger division. In this reorganization it lost its third regiment (the 14th Infantry), which was apparently dissolved. The 5th Jäger was equipped as a pursuit division, with an organizational structure similar to a mountain division, except with more vehicles. It returned to Russia in February 1942 and was attached to Army Group North, where it remained for some time. In March and April 1942, it was part of Combat Group von Seydlitz and helped break the Russian encirclement of the II Corps at Demyansk. Later, in the winter of 1942-43, as part of the X Corps, 16th Army, it fought in the battles around Staraya Russa. After the collapse of Army Group Center, the 5th Jäger was sent west to aid in the defense of Poland and, later, eastern Germany. It fought its last battle in front of the Nazi capital and was destroyed there in April 1945. Commanders of the 5th Jäger included Lieutenant Generals Wilhelm Fahrmbacher (1939-40), Karl Allmendinger (1940-43), Helmuth Thumm (1943-44), and Friedrich Sixt (1944-45).

NOTES AND SOURCES: Fahrmbacher was promoted to General of Artillery in November 1940 and commanded the XXV Corps in Western France (1941-45). For a brief period in June 1944, he was acting commander of the LXXXIV Corps in the Battle of Normandy. Fahrmbacher was isolated in Lorient, France, behind Allied lines, for the last nine months of the war. General of Infantry as of April 1943, Karl Allmendinger led V Corps in Russia (1943-May, 1944) before being named commander of the 17th Army in the last days of the Crimean campaign. He held no further command after being relieved of this post in September. Helmuth Thumm was promoted to General of Infantry in late 1944 and led LXIV Corps on the Western Front from December 1944 on. Friedrich Sixt formerly served as Chief of Staff of the 7th Army in France (1943) and commander of the 50th

Infantry Division in Russia (1944). Carell 1966: 427-34; Carell 1971: 288; Kennedy: 10B; RA: 72; OB 42: 68; OB 43: 195; OB 45: 313; Ziemke 1966: 477.

8th JÄGER DIVISION

COMPOSITION: 38th Jäger Regiment, 84th Jäger Regiment, 8th Artillery Regiment, 8th Bicycle Battalion, 8th Anti-Tank Battalion, 8th Engineer Battalion, 8th Signal Battalion

HOME STATION: Neisse, Wkr. VIII

The 8th Jäger was formed from Silesian personnel as the 8th Infantry Division shortly after conscription was reintroduced in Germany in March 1935. It initially included the 28th, 38th, and 84th Infantry Regiments. The 8th Infantry fought well in Poland, where it broke through strong enemy frontier fortifications in eastern Upper Silesia. Later it took part in the advance on Kracow. The next year it fought well in France. It was sent to Russia in 1941 and suffered heavy losses in the initial campaign. The division was returned to France in the fall of 1942 and converted into a Jäger division, losing its 28th Infantry Regiment in the process. Returned to Russia in early 1942, the 8th fought in the Demyansk relief operations in the northern sector until II Corps was freed in February 1943. The divisional commander of the 8th Jäger—Lieutenant General Gustav Höhne —directed the operation that finally restored freedom of movement to the corps. The division continued to fight on the northern sector until after the retreat from Leningrad began. In March 1944 it was sent to the southern sector and fought in the retreats through the Ukraine and the Carpathians. What remained of the 8th Jäger was surrounded in Czechoslovakia in April 1945 and surrendered to the Russians in May. Commanders of the 8th Infantry/Jäger Division included Lieutenant Generals Rudolf Koch-Erpach (1935-40), Höhne (1941-43), and Friedrich-Jobst Volckamer von Kirchensitten-Back (1943-44).

NOTES AND SOURCES: Koch-Erpach was later commander of Wehrkreis VIII, headquartered at Breslau (early 1942-1945). He was promoted to General of Cavalry in late 1940. Höhne, a General of Infantry as of the spring of 1943, went on to direct LIV Corps (1943), VIII Corps (late 1943-44) and LXXXIX Corps on the Western Front (1945). Benoist-Mechin: 133; Carell 1966: 427-34; Carell 1971: 288; *Kriegstagebuch des OKW*, Volume I: 1146; Volume IV: 1895; Manstein: 52; RA: 130; OB 42: 68; OB 43: 195; OB 45: 272, 314.

28th JÄGER DIVISION

COMPOSITION: 49th Jäger Regiment, 83rd Jäger Regiment, 28th Artillery Regiment, 28th Bicycle Battalion, 28th Anti-Tank Battalion, 28th Engineer Battalion, 28th Signal Battalion

HOME STATION: Breslau, Wkr. VIII

Formed in the peacetime army as the 28th Infantry Division, it initially included the 7th, 49th and 83rd Infantry Regiments. The men were mainly Silesians, with some Volksdeutsche from Poland intermixed. The 28th fought well in the invasion of Poland, took part in the Western campaign of 1940, and in 1941 struck into Russia with Army Group Center. In November the 28th Division was transferred to France, where it was converted into a Jäger division. Its 7th Infantry Regiment was reassigned to the 252nd Infantry Division. Early in 1942 the "new" 28th reappeared on the Eastern Front, this time on the southern sector, and fought on the Kerch peninsula and in the final assault on the naval fortress of Sevastopol in the Crimea. Transferred to the northern sector with von Manstein's 11th Army, the Jäger troops were earmarked for attachment to Finland, but they were held up by order of Field Marshal Georg von Küchler, who committed them to action with his Army Group North near Demyansk in late 1942. In January and February 1943, the 28th fought in the Second Battle of Lake Ladoga and remained in the northern zone until mid-1944. In July 1944, the division was attached to Group von Saucken and tried to prevent the encirclement of the bulk of the 4th Army near Minsk, but failed. Assigned to the tactically bankrupt Army Group Center, the 28th Jäger suffered heavy losses in the retreat into Poland, where it took part in the fighting near the old Brest-Litovsk fortress in the Polish marchland. The remnants of the division, less than a thousand men, ended the war in the East Prussian pocket. Lieutenant General Gustav Heistermann von Ziehlberg (late 1944-45), who was leading the division in January 1945, was apparently its last commander. Previous leaders of the 28th Infantry/Jäger included Lieutenant General Hans von Obstfelder (1936-40), Lieutenant General Hans Sinnhuber (1941-42), Major General Hubertus Lamey (1944), and Lieutenant General Hans Speth (1944).

NOTES AND SOURCES: General von Obstfelder was promoted to General of Infantry effective June 1, 1940. He led XXIX Corps in Russia (1940-43), LXXXVI Corps on the Western Front (late 1943-December 1944), and 1st Army in France and western Germany (December 1944-February 1945). He ended the war as commander of the 19th Army in southwestern Germany (March-May 1945). A Saxon, von Obstfelder held the Knight's Cross with Oak Leaves and Swords. Hans Sinnhuber, General of Artillery as of

October 1943, commanded LXXXII Corps (1943-September 1944). Hubertus Lamey, former Ia of the 27th Infantry Division, went on to command the 118th Jäger Division (1945). Hans Speth, former Chief of Staff of the 18th Army (1943), was later Commandant of the War Academy (1945). Heistermann von Ziehlberg was the ex-commander of the 65th Infantry Division (1943). Carell 1966: 482, 484, 503, 509; Carell 1971: 260, 287, 591-94; Kennedy: 74 and Map 7; *Kriegstagebuch des OKW*, Volume IV: 1897; Manstein: 244; Salisbury: 538; RA: 130; OB 42: 68; OB 43: 196; OB 45: 314.

42nd JÄGER DIVISION

COMPOSITION: 25th Jäger Regiment, 40th Jäger Regiment, 142nd Artillery Regiment, 142nd Füsilier Battalion, 142nd Anti-Tank Battalion, 142nd Engineer Battalion, 142nd Signal Battalion

HOME STATION: Wehrkreis XVII

This division was set up as Replacement Division Staff 187 in 1938, following the annexation of Austria. Its troops were mainly Austrian and Volksdeutsche. Upon the reorganization of the Replacement Army in the fall of 1942, the 187th was upgraded to reserve division status and transferred to Croatia as a training unit under Home Army control. It was converted into the 187th Jäger Division in the winter of 1943-44, and was redesignated the 42nd Jäger Division in March 1944. That same month it took part in the occupation of Hungary but was back in northern Yugoslavia by May. Shortly afterward it was transferred to Genoa, northern Italy, and was in combat in the Gothic Line campaign of September 1944. It fought well there, as it did in the Battle of Bologna (December 1944) and in the final campaign in Italy. By March 1945 it had a strength of less than twenty-six hundred men; nevertheless it served on until the capitulation of the German forces in Italy in April 1945. Commanders of the 42nd Jäger included Lieutenant General Josef Brauner (1944) and Major General Walter Jost (1945).

NOTES AND SOURCES: Jost was Chief of the Central Office at OKW in late 1943. Fisher: 411, 442, 462-66; RA: 220-23; OB 45: 315.

90th LIGHT DIVISION
see 90th Panzer Grenadier Division

97th JÄGER DIVISION

COMPOSITION (1942): 204th Jäger Regiment, 207th Jäger Regiment, 81st Artillery Regiment, 97th Reconnaissance Battalion, 97th Anti-Tank Battalion, 97th Engineer Battalion, 97th Signal Battalion

HOME STATION: Wehrkreis VII

Organized in December 1940, the 9th Jäger crossed into southern Russia in 1941 and fought in the Ukraine and Donets campaigns of that year. It was involved in repulsing the Soviet winter offensive of 1941-42 and took part in the Caucasus campaign of 1942-43, and in the subsequent retreat. It also fought in the Battle of Kursk (July 1943), where it suffered heavy casualties. Transferred to the lower Dnieper that autumn, it fought very well in the retreats through the Ukraine and was officially cited for bravery. The 97th Jäger—now much reduced by heavy fighting—was routed in March 1944 by the rapidly advancing Russians but continued to resist on the front line for the rest of the war. It was transferred to the Slovakian sector in October 1944 and ended the war in the huge pocket east of Prague in May 1945. Commanders of the division included Lieutenant General Maximilian Fretter-Pico (1940-41), Major General Blumentritt (1943), Lieutenant General Rupp (1943), Lieutenant General Ludwig Müller (1943), and Lieutenant General Friedrich Karl Rabe von Pappenheim (late 1943-1945).

NOTES AND SOURCES: Fretter-Pico, former Chief of Staff of XXV Corps (1938-39), later commanded XXX Corps (1942-44) and 6th Army (1944-45), both on the Eastern Front. He was relieved of his command in early 1945 for his failure to stem the Russian tide. He was promoted to General of Artillery in June 1942. Müller, former Chief of Staff of XXIV Corps, commanded the 101st Jäger and 198th Infantry Divisions (1942 and 1943, respectively). He commanded the 97th Jäger for a brief period in the latter part of 1943. Müller was captured on the Russian Front in July 1944 and joined the National Free Germany Committee. He had been promoted to General of Infantry shortly before. Rabe von Pappenheim was the German Military Attaché to Budapest (1939-43). Carell 1971: 159; Hartmann: 43; RA: 116; OB 42: 69; OB 43: 197; OB 45: 315.

99th JÄGER DIVISION
see 7th Mountain Division

100th JÄGER DIVISION

COMPOSITION: 54th Jäger Regiment, 227th Jäger Regiment, 83rd Artillery Regiment, 100th Reconnaissance Battalion, 100th Anti-Tank Battalion, 100th Engineer Battalion, 100th Signal Battalion

HOME STATION: Vienna, Wkr. XVII

This division was formed in Vienna in December 1940. The 54th Jäger Regiment formerly had been an infantry regiment under the 54th Infantry Division. The 369th Reinforced (Croatian) Infantry Regiment was attached to the 100th Jäger in 1941 and remained with it until it was destroyed at Stalingrad. The division itself first saw action in southern Russia with the 17th Army in 1941 and was involved in the sweep to Odessa. It opposed the Russian winter offensive of 1941-42, fought in the Battle of Kharkov (May 1942), the encirclement and Battle of Staryyoskol, the advance across the Don, the drive to the Volga, and in the street fighting in Stalingrad (1942). It was with 6th Army when it was encircled in November 1942 and was destroyed when Stalingrad fell in January 1943.

A second 100th Jäger Division was created in the Belgrade area in May 1943. That summer it was transferred to Albania **and was** rushed to the southern sector of the Eastern Front in March 1944. **Here it** joined the II SS Panzer Corps and helped rescue the 1st Panzer **Army, which** was encircled between the Bug and the Dnestr. Subsequently **transferred** to Army Group Center, it took part in the withdrawal from **Russia** and the battles in southern Poland in the fall of 1944. It was fighting the Soviets in Czechoslovakia when the war ended. Commanders of the 100th Jäger included Lieutenant Generals Sann (1941-43) and Willibald Utz (1944-45).

NOTES AND SOURCES: Sann was captured at Stalingrad. Utz commanded the 100th Mountain Infantry Regiment of the 5th Mountain Division. Carell 1966: 490, 495, 523; Carell 1971: 523; Hartmann: 46-47; RA: 200; OB 42: 69; OB 43: 197; OB 45: 315-16.

101st JÄGER DIVISION

COMPOSITION: 228th Jäger Regiment, 229th Jäger Regiment, 85th Artillery Regiment, 101st Reconnaissance Battalion, 101st Anti-Tank Battalion, 101st Engineer Battalion, 101st Signal Battalion

HOME STATION: Wehrkreis V

This Baden-Württemberg unit was created in December 1940, fought in the drive across the Ukraine and southern Russia in 1941, and in the winter battles of 1941-42. In 1942-43 it took part in the Battle of Kharkov, the Caucasus campaign, and the retreat into the Kuban, during which it suffered heavy casualties, fighting off partisans and regular Soviet troops. Evacuated across the Kerch Straits, it was transferred to the lower Dnieper in the latter part of 1943. In March 1944 it was surrounded with the 1st Panzer Army and formed the rear guard of the XLVI Panzer Corps in the subsequent breakout. Cited for its conduct in the retreat across the northern Ukraine, the 101st Jäger was withdrawn to Slovakia in the fall of 1944. Sent south in early 1945, it fought in the retreats through Hungary and into Austria. It ended the war at battle group strength on the southern sector of the Eastern Front. Commanders of the 101st included Lieutenant General Erich Marcks (1941), Lieutenant General Ludwig Müller (1942), Lieutenant General Emil Vogel (1942-mid-1944), and Major General Assman (1944-45).

NOTES AND SOURCES: Erich Marcks was formerly Chief of the General Staff of the 18th Army and helped plan Operation Barbarossa in the winter of 1940-41. He lost a leg on the Eastern Front. Upon recovering he assumed command of the LXXXIV Corps in Normandy, which bore the brunt of the fighting on D-Day. He was killed by an Allied fighter-bomber near St. Lô on June 12, 1944. Müller, former Chief of Staff of XXIV Corps, later commanded the 198th Infantry and 97th Jäger Divisions, before being captured on the Russian Front in July 1944. Vogel was commander of the XXXVI Mountain Corps in 1945. Carell 1966: 488-89; Carell 1971: 159, 525; *Kriegstagebuch des OKW*, Volume I: 1145; Plocher 1941: 295; RA: 96; OB 42: 69; OB 43: 197; OB 45: 316.

104th JÄGER (formerly 704th INFANTRY) DIVISION

COMPOSITION: 724th Jäger Regiment, 734th Jäger Regiment, 654th Artillery Regiment, 104th Reconnaissance Battalion, 104th Anti-Tank Battalion, 104th Engineer Battalion, 104th Signal Battalion

HOME STATION: Wehrkreis IV

Formed as the 704th Infantry Division in April 1941, this unit initially included the 724th and 734th Infantry Regiments, the 654th Artillery Regiment, the 704th Reconnaissance and Signal Companies, and the 704th Engineer Battalion. In May 1941 it was sent to Serbia, where it performed occupation duties in the Belgrade area until May 1943. In April 1943 the division was converted into a light division and redesignated 104th Jäger. Its signal and reconnaissance units were expanded and its anti-tank battalion added at this time. By June, the new Jäger division was stationed in the Epirus area of western Greece and remained there until the rapidly advancing Soviet armies threatened to take Army Group F and the Balkans in the rear. The 104th Jäger withdrew through Yugoslavia and was involved in heavy combat with Tito's partisans. It continued to fight on the southern sector of the Eastern Front until the end of the war. Commanders of the 704th Infantry/104th Jäger included Major General Borowski (1941-42), Lieutenant General Hans Juppe (1942-43), and Lieutenant General Hartwig von Ludwiger (1943-45).

NOTES AND SOURCES: Major General Borowski, who was in his sixties, retired in the fall of 1942. Hans Juppe was formerly Chief of the Communications Branch of the High Command of the Armed Forces. He was Army Inspector of the Croat Wehrmacht, 1941-42. General von Ludwiger, a Silesian who held the Knight's Cross with Oak Leaves, was commander of the 704th Infantry when it was converted into a Jäger division. Colonel Steyrer was acting commander of the division in May 1944. RA: 72; OB 42: 110; OB 43: 186; OB 45: 316.

114th JÄGER (formerly 714th INFANTRY) DIVISION

COMPOSITION: 721st Jäger Regiment, 741st Jäger Regiment, 661st Artillery Regiment, 114th Reconnaissance Battalion, 114th Anti-Tank Battalion, 114th Engineer Battalion, 114th Signal Battalion

HOME STATION: Wehrkreis I

Originally the 714th Infantry Division—a two-regiment, static unit—

the 114th consisted mainly of Poles, Czechs, and Volksdeutsche. It was sent to Yugoslavia in November 1941 and took part in numerous anti-partisan operations from then until December 1943. Meanwhile, it was upgraded to a Jäger division in early 1943 and given the number 114th. In January 1944 it was transferred to the Fiume area of Italy, and in February it was thrown into action against the Allied beachhead at Anzio. Later it took part in the Anzio counterattack, the retreat from the Gustav Line, the battles of the Gothic Line, and the Battle of Bologna. It fought well, but was down to a strength of only 984 effectives by March 1945. The remnants of the division—which now amounted to less than a battalion in terms of real combat strength—were destroyed near the Po River, along with the LI Mountain Corps on April 23, 1945. Commanders of the 714th/114th included Lieutenant General Friedrich Stahl (1942-43), Major General Bourquin (1943-44), and Major General Hans Ehlert (1944-45).

NOTES AND SOURCES: Stahl was later Commandant of Warsaw (1943-44). Ehlert was previously Ia of the 269th Infantry Division (1940), on the staff of the Afrika Korps (1941), and Chief of Staff of Fortress Crete (1943?-44). Blumenson 1969: 313, 361, 419-21; Chant, Volume 11: 1511; Fisher: 18, 302, 442, 455-56; Hartmann: 47; RA: 20; OB 42: 112; OB 43: 188; OB 45: 317.

117th JÄGER (formerly 717th INFANTRY) DIVISION

COMPOSITION: 737th Jäger Regiment, 749th Jäger Regiment, 670th Artillery Regiment, 117th Reconnaissance Battalion, 117th Anti-Tank Battalion, 117th Engineer Battalion, 117th Signal Battalion

HOME STATION: Wehrkreis I

Formed as the 717th (Static) Infantry Division in April 1941, this unit was sent to Yugoslavia, where it conducted antipartisan operations until the spring of 1943. At that time it was converted to a Jäger unit and was sent to Greece, where it guarded the Peloponnesus until the summer of 1944. It took part in the withdrawal through the Balkans and suffered heavy losses against Tito's partisans in September. In 1945 it fought against the Russians and was in transit to the 6th SS Panzer Army in Austria when Berlin fell. Commanders of the 717th/117th included Lieutenant General Dr. Walter Hinghofer (1942), Lieutenant General Benighus Dippold (1943), Lieutenant General Karl von LeSuire (1943-44), Major General Dr. Fritz Benicke (1944), and Lieutenant General August Wittmann (1945).

NOTES AND SOURCES: Dippold, former commander of the 183rd Infantry

Division (1940-42), later directed Special Administrative Division Staff 540 (1944-45). Karl von LeSuire was Ia of the 30th Infantry Division (1940) and Chief of Staff of the XIX Mountain Corps in Finland (1943) before taking over the 117th Jäger. He later commanded the 46th Infantry Division (1944) and ended the war as commander of the XXIV Panzer Corps in Czechoslovakia (1945). He was promoted to General of Mountain Troops in late 1944. Dr. Benicke was commander of the 25th Panzer Grenadier Regiment in 1943. Wittmann was the former leader of the 3rd Mountain Division in Lapland and southern Russia (1942-44). *Kriegstagebuch des OKW*, Volume I: 1145; Volume III: 261; Volume IV: 1903; OB 43: 188; OB 45: 317.

118th JÄGER (formerly 718th INFANTRY) DIVISION

COMPOSITION: 738th Jäger Regiment, 750th Jäger Regiment, 668th Artillery Regiment, 118th Reconnaissance Battalion, 118th Anti-Tank Battalion, 118th Engineer Battalion, 118th Signal Battalion

HOME STATION: Wehrkreis XVIII

Raised in western Austria in April 1941, this unit was originally a static division, as were all German divisions in the 700 series. From 1941 until 1943, when it bore the designation 718th Infantry, it had only an engineer and signal company in its support troops, with no organic anti-tank or reconnaissance forces. Sent to Serbia in the summer of 1941, it conducted antipartisan operations and was on occupation duty for two years. Upgraded to Jäger status in the spring of 1943, it was sent to Herzegovina and remained there until the summer of 1944, when it was sent to guard the Dalmatian coast against possible Allied landings from the Adriatic. In early 1945 it was sent to the Eastern Front and fought in southern Germany until the end of the war. Its commanders included Lieutenant General Hans Johann Fortner (1942-43), Major General Josef Kübler (1944), Colonel Rudolf von Gertler (1944), and Major General Hubertus Lamey (1945).

NOTES AND SOURCES: Gertler was an acting commander only. From 1943 to 1945 he was C.O. of the 668th Artillery Regiment of the 118th Jäger. Lamey had previously commanded the 28th Jäger Division (1944). *Kriegstagebuch des OKW*, Volume I: 1134, 1145; Volume II: 1357; Volume III: 261, 735; Volume IV: 1895; OB 43: 189; OB 45: 318.

164th LIGHT AFRIKA DIVISION

COMPOSITION: 125th Panzer Grenadier Regiment, 382nd Panzer Grenadier Regiment, 433rd Panzer Grenadier Regiment, 220th Artillery Regiment, 220th Reconnaissance Battalion, 220th Anti-Tank Battalion, 220th Engineer Battalion, 220th Signal Battalion

HOME STATION: Wehrkreis XII

This unit was formed in January 1940 at the Königsbrück Maneuver Area, Wehrkreis IV, as the 164th Infantry Demonstration Division. At that time it included the 382nd, 433rd, and 440th Infantry Regiments. It remained in reserve during the French campaign but fought in Greece during the Balkan campaign of 1941 and remained there, on occupation duty at Salonika, for a year. During that period the 440th Infantry Regiment was detached from the division to form Grenadier Regiment Rhodes. In the spring of 1942 the 164th was transferred to Crete and received the 125th Infantry Regiment, which had previously been a frontier unit stationed at Saarbrücken. It had also seen action during the French campaign. In the summer of 1942 the division was transferred to North Africa. It fought extremely well (mainly against the Australians) in the defensive actions around El Alamein from July through early November 1942. The 382nd Infantry Regiment—without vehicles—arrived at the front on July 10, 1942, just in time to save the Headquarters of Panzer Army Afrika from the British and Australians. It had been threatened because the Italian Sabratha Division collapsed, and Allied infantrymen were within 3,000 yards of the HQ when the 382nd arrived. Such incidents were fairly common on the North African Front in 1942. Finally crushed, the remnants of the 164th Light retreated a thousand miles across Egypt and Libya into Tunisia, where they were finally destroyed when Army Group Afrika collapsed. Commanders of the 164th Infantry Demonstration/Light Afrika Division included Major General Folttmann (1940) and Lieutenant General Karl-Hans Lungerhausen (1942-43).

NOTES AND SOURCES: The regiments of the 164th were designated panzer grenadier in late 1942. General Folttmann, former commander of the 256th Infantry Division (1939), later commanded the 338th Infantry Division (1942-44) on the Western Front. He was killed at Belfort Gap in November 1944. Lieutenant General Karl-Hans Lungerhausen escaped the collapse in Tunisia and went on to command the 90th Panzer Grenadier Division in Italy (1943-44). He was engaged in forming Italian units for Army Group C when the war ended. A Silesian, Lungerhausen was promoted to Lieutenant General effective September 1, 1943. I.S.O. Playfair, *The Mediterranean and Middle East*, Volume III, *British Fortunes Reach Their Lowest*

Ebb, His Majesty's Stationery Office, London, 1960: 246 (hereafter cited as "Playfair"); Erwin Rommel, *The Rommel Papers* (B.H. Liddell Hart, ed.), Harcourt, Brace and Company, New York, 1953: 313 (hereafter cited as "Rommel"); OB 45: 318.

999th LIGHT AFRIKA DIVISION

COMPOSITION: 961st Afrika Rifle Regiment, 962nd Afrika Rifle Regiment, 963rd Afrika Rifle Regiment, 999th Artillery Regiment, 999th Reconnaissance Battalion, 999th Anti-Tank Battalion, 999th Engineer Battalion, 999th Signal Battalion

HOME STATION: Heuberg and Baden, Wkr. V

This penal unit was formed near Antwerp in October 1942, as Afrika Brigade 999. It consisted of both political prisoners and real criminals pressed into the military service of the Third Reich. Upgraded to divisional status in March 1943, it was also known as the 999th Infantry Division (Penal). Its 961st and 962nd Rifle Regiments and many of its divisional support troops were sent to Tunisia in March 1943 and were captured there when Army Group Afrika surrendered in May. The 963rd Infantry Regiment and some of the support units had not yet been sent from staging areas in Italy to Tunisia when the end came, so they were diverted to Greece and either became fortress units or were absorbed into Assault Division Rhodes. The division's replacement headquarters at Heuberg and Baden continued to train criminal and political prisoners for military service, but the division *per se* was disbanded. In its brief combat career, the 999th fought well against the French, British, and Americans.

NOTES AND SOURCES: The telephone exchange at Scotland Yard in London was (is?) 999; this is reportedly why the Germans adopted 999 as the number for their penal units. Major General Kurt Thomas, the former commandant of Führer Headquarters, initially commanded the 999th in Africa, but escaped the Tunisian debacle. Promoted to lieutenant general on October 1, 1943, he was reportedly killed later on the Eastern Front. OB 45: 284. Also see Paul Carell, *The Foxes of the Desert*, E.P. Dutton, New York, 1960, for a detailed description of the last battles in North Africa, in which the 999th was involved (hereafter cited as "Carell 1960").

5

The Mountain Divisions

1st MOUNTAIN DIVISION

COMPOSITION: 98th Mountain Infantry Regiment, 99th Mountain Infantry Regiment, 79th Mountain Artillery Regiment, 54th Cyclist Battalion, 54th Anti-Tank Battalion, 54th Mountain Engineer Battalion, 54th Mountain Signal Battalion

HOME STATION: Garmisch, Wkr. VII

This unit, consisting mainly of Bavarians with some Austrians intermixed, was part of Hitler's expanded peacetime army. Its third regiment, the 100th Mountain Infantry, was reassigned to the 5th Mountain Division in 1940. Under the command of Major General Ludwig Kübler, it took part in the Polish campaign as part of the 14th Army and saw action in the Carpathians, where it distinguished itself by capturing the Dukla Pass. Later it played a minor role in the French and Balkan campaigns. In 1941 the division crossed into Russia and, as part of Army Group South, took part in the Battles of the Uman Pocket, Kiev, Stalino, and the Dnieper crossings. By May 1942 it was with the III Panzer Corps and fought in the Battle of Kharkov. Later it was at the spearhead of von Kleist's Caucasus campaign. After the disaster of Stalingrad, Kleist's Army Group A was forced to retreat, and the 1st Mountain Division was involved in the first of a long series of withdrawals and rear-guard actions on the road back to Germany. In March 1943, the division was withdrawn from the front and sent to northern Greece, where it was rebuilt and engaged in antipartisan operations. Later it was reported on the Greco-Albanian frontier, and subsequently in western Serbia and Montenegro. The division was still fighting south of Belgrade in October 1944. The 1st Mountain Division ended the war as part of Army Group South, fighting the Russians in central Styria. It ended up in Soviet captivity. Divisional commanders of the 1st Mountain included Kübler (1937-39), Major General Hubert Lanz (1942-43), Major General Kress (1943), Lieutenant General Walter Stettner, Ritter von Grabenhofen (1943-44), and Lieutenant General Josef Kübler (1945).

NOTES AND SOURCES: Ludwig Kübler, a Bavarian, was promoted to General of Mountain Troops in August 1940 and briefly commanded a corps. He was commanding general of 4th Army before Moscow from December 1941 until January 20, 1942, when he was relieved of his command at his own request. This had the effect of permanently denying him further advancement. He was later in charge of the Rear Area Command of Army Group Center (1943) and the Adriatic Coastal Defense (1944-45). Hubert Lanz, former commander of the 100th Mountain Infantry Regiment (1935) when it was part of the 1st Mountain Infantry Division, was Chief of Staff of the XVIII Mountain Corps in 1940. Later he became commander of Army Detachment Lanz in Russia (1943) and XXII Mountain Corps in the Balkans and on the Eastern Front (September 1943-1945). He was promoted to General of Mountain Troops in 1943. Lanz briefly served as Acting Commander, Army Group A (June-July 1943), while Field Marshal von Kleist was on leave. Lieutenant General Ritter von Stettner successively commanded the I Battalion of the 98th Mountain Infantry Regiment and the 99th Mountain Infantry Regiment, both of the 1st Mountain Division, before receiving the command of the division itself. He was killed in action near Belgrade on October 18, 1944. Josef Kübler was the former Operations Officer (Ia) of the 12th Army (1940) and commander of the 118th Jäger Division (early 1943-late 1944). Carell 1966: 121, 293, 495, 560; Kennedy: 74 and Map 7; Manstein: 33; Plocher 1943: 327; OB 42: 70; OB 43: 210; OB 44: 292; OB 45: 318, 583; Ziemke 1966: 376. For the story of the German mountain troops in World War II, as well as excellent detailed descriptions of some of their battles, see James Lucas, *Alpine Elite: German Mountain Troops in World War II*, Jane's Publishing Company, Inc., New York: 1980 (hereafter cited as "Lucas").

2nd MOUNTAIN DIVISION

COMPOSITION: 136th Mountain Infantry Regiment, 137th Mountain Infantry Regiment, 111th Mountain Artillery Regiment, 67th Cyclist Battalion, 47th Anti-Tank Battalion, 82nd Mountain Engineer Battalion, 67th Mountain Signal Battalion

HOME STATION: Innsbruck, Wkr. XVIII

Consisting primarily of Tyrolean Austrians, the 2nd Mountain Division was part of the peacetime army after the *Anschluss* made Austria a part of the Third Reich. Initially it was one of the best fighting units in the German Army. It fought in Poland in 1939 as part of Army Group South, and the next year it invaded Norway with the XXI Combat Group (later HQ, Army of Norway). From May 5 to June 13 it traveled across a roadless wilderness, from Trondheim to Narvik, to rescue the 3rd Mountain Division, then besieged by a British corps in northern Norway. In June 1941 the division advanced on Murmansk with Mountain Corps Norway but was stopped short by Russian counterattacks and the impossible terrain. In 1942 the 2nd Mountain campaigned in Lapland, as part of Schörner's XIX Mountain Corps, and continued to fight on the Arctic sector of the Eastern Front until Finland concluded a separate peace with Russia in late 1944. On the retreat back to Norway the 2nd Mountain was mauled and badly shaken by the Russian winter offensive of 1944-45. After the withdrawal from northern Finland the division was returned to the European mainland, where its two regiments were rebuilt from personnel taken from supply and other noncombat units. It joined the LXXXII Corps of Army Group G on the Western Front and in February 1945 was back in action in the Battle of the Saar-Moselle Triangle; however, the division's best soldiers were dead or captured, and its former elitism gone. The remnants of the 2nd Mountain Division ended the war in Württemberg, southern Germany, and surrendered to the Western Allies. The commanders of the 2nd Mountain included Lieutenant General Valentin Feurstein (1938-41), Major General Ernest Schlemmer (1941-42), Lieutenant General Ritter Georg von Hengl (1942-43), and Major General Hans Degan (1944-45).

NOTES AND SOURCES: A native of Bregenz, Austria, Valentin Feurstein was in the Austrian Army until 1938, when that country was annexed by Nazi Germany and he assumed command of the 2nd Mountain Division. Later he commanded the LXII Corps (1941-42), LXX Corps (1942), and LI Mountain Corps (1943-44), before being named commander of the Alpine Front (1945). He was promoted to General of Mountain Troops in 1941. Schlemmer—former commander of the 137th Mountain Infantry and 136th Mountain Infantry Replacement Regiments—later commanded the 188th Infantry Division and Special Administrative Division Staff 418. In 1945 he was commanding Axis troops in Milan, Italy. Ritter von Hengl, former commander of the 137th Mountain Infantry Regiment, later served as commander of the XIX Mountain Corps (1943) and the LIX Corps (1944). In 1945 he was Chief National Socialist Guidance Officer at OKH, a post he had held since May 1944. Hans Degen, a Bavarian who had served with mountain units in World War I, was Ia of the 2nd Mountain Division (1938), Ia of the 1st Mountain Division (1939-40), Chief of Staff of VI Corps (1941), Chief of Staff of XIX Mountain Corps (1944), and commander of the 2nd Mountain Division. He was badly wounded in the last weeks of the war. Hartmann: 47, 49; Kennedy: 74; Lucas: 206, 241-43, 246-47; MacDonald 1973: 153; Ziemke 1959: 95-97, 326-27; Ziemke 1966: 304, 312; OB 42: 70; OB 43: 210.

3rd MOUNTAIN DIVISION

COMPOSITION: 138th Mountain Infantry Regiment, 139th Mountain Infantry Regiment, 112th Mountain Artillery Regiment, 68th Cyclist Battalion, 48th Anti-Tank Battalion, 83rd Mountain Engineer Battalion, 68th Mountain Signal Battalion

HOME STATION: Graz, Wkr. XVIII

This unit was formed from the 5th and 7th Divisions of the Austrian Army after that country was annexed by Germany in 1938. It was almost constantly engaged throughout World War II, except for a period of occupation duty in Norway in 1940-41. Its original commander, Major General Eduard Dietl, led the division in the invasion of Poland, where it formed part of the XVIII Corps, 14th Army, Army Group South. The next year, 1940, the division performed its greatest feat of arms when its 138th Mountain Infantry Regiment took Trondheim and the rest of the division seized Narvik, the strategically vital port in northern Norway. A British Expeditionary Force, hoping to deprive Hitler of his strategic iron ore, which had to be shipped to Germany via Narvik, counterattacked Dietl's isolated force and at one point succeeded in retaking the city in heavy fighting. The battle lasted from April 9 until mid-June, but was finally won by the mountaineers, but not before Dietl seriously discussed marching his troops into internment in Sweden. For his performance Dietl was awarded command of Mountain Corps Norway, of which the 3rd Mountain Division became a part. From Narvik the division marched into northern Finland, took part in the invasion of Russia in June 1941, and advanced on Murmansk, the strategic Soviet port on the Arctic Ocean. Finally repulsed by fierce Soviet counterattacks and virtually impassable terrain, the division was engaged in prolonged skirmishing and patrolling north of the Arctic Circle for more than a year. Sent to Army Group North in August 1942, the 3rd Mountain was soon sent to the southern sector of the Eastern Front, which was threatening to collapse following the disaster on the Volga. It was part of Army Detachment Hollidt in late 1942, and it took part in the effort to relieve Stalingrad but failed. Later the 3rd Mountain suffered heavy casualties on the southern sector of the Eastern Front in 1943 and 1944, especially in Rumania, where it was attacked by Russians in the front and by Rumanians from behind; nevertheless, the remnants of the division continued to resist and were fighting the Soviets in Upper Silesia when the war ended. Its commanders included Lieutenant Generals Dietl (1938-40), Hans Kreysing (1942-43), August Wittmann (1943-44), and Paul Klatt (1945).

NOTES AND SOURCES: The 139th Mountain Infantry Regiment and I Battalion, 112th Mountain Artillery Regiment were left in Norway when the division went to Russia in 1942 and became the 139th Infantry Brigade under the control of the 20th Mountain Army in Lapland and Finland. Eduard Dietl—a Bavarian with Nazi sympathies, whom Hitler both liked and respected—later commanded the 20th Mountain Army (1942-44). He was idealized by the Nazi propaganda machine. Dietl was promoted to Colonel General effective June 1, 1942, and was killed in an airplane crash while on a visit to Austria in the summer of 1944. Hans Kreysing was promoted to General of Mountain Troops in 1943 and commanded the XVII Mountain Corps in Russia (1943-44). He had formerly commanded the 3rd Mountain Infantry Regiment (1942). August Wittmann was commander of the 117th Jäger Division on the Eastern Front in 1945. Paul Klatt commanded the 138th Mountain Infantry Regiment of the division from 1941 to 1943. Carell 1966: 450-51; Carell 1971: 123; Kennedy: 74 and Map 7; Lucas: 207, 242; Manstein: 319, 392; Seaton; 476; RA: 234; OB 42: 70; OB 43: 210; Ziemke 1959: 33, 234, 326.

4th MOUNTAIN DIVISION

COMPOSITION: 13th Mountain Infantry Regiment, 91st Mountain Infantry Regiment, 94th Mountain Artillery Regiment, 94th Motorcycle Battalion, 94th Anti-Tank Battalion, 94th Mountain Engineer Battalion, 94th Mountain Signal Battalion

HOME STATION: Wehrkreis IV

The fourth German mountain division was formed in the autumn of 1940 from southern German recruits and cadres supplied by the 25th and 27th Infantry Regiments. It first saw action in the Balkans campaign of 1941, where it fought in Greece. Later that year it invaded Russia as part of Army Group South and suffered heavy casualties in the initial advances toward the Volga. It spent much of 1942 fighting the Soviets on the Kerch peninsula of the Crimea, east of Sevastopol. Later, the division took part in the Caucasus campaign and was engaged in heavy fighting at Novorossiysk, where the Germans contained the Russian amphibious landings on the Kuban. By early 1944 the 4th Mountain had been shifted northward and fought in the Battles of the Dnieper Bend, where Field Marshal von Manstein commended it for its part in smashing the 1st Soviet Tank Army.

The 4th Mountain Division continued to fight on the Russian Front as the German forces retreated across southern Russia, Rumania, Hungary, and into Austria. The division ended the war at battle group strength on the southern sector of the Eastern Front. Lieutenant General Friedrich Breith (1944-45) was its last reported commander. Previous commanders included Lieutenant Generals Karl Eglseer (1940-42), Hermann Kress (1943), and Julius Braun (1944).

NOTES AND SOURCES: Karl Eglseer, who had spent 30 years in the Austrian Army, briefly commanded the 714th Infantry Division in 1942, before being named commander of the XVIII Mountain Corps. A General of Mountain Troops at the time of his death, he was killed in an airplane crash in 1944. Julius Braun was given command of the 553rd Volksgrenadier Division in 1944 and was captured on the Eastern Front in September of that year. General Breith had previously directed Arko 127 (1941) and Artillery School I (1942-43). Carell 1971: 187; Hartmann: 49; Lucas: 207, 242; Manstein: 509; OB 42: 71; OB 43: 211.

5th MOUNTAIN DIVISION

COMPOSITION (1943): 85th Mountain Infantry Regiment, 100th Mountain Infantry Regiment, 95th Mountain Artillery Regiment, 95th Motorcycle Battalion, 95th Anti-Tank Battalion, 95th Mountain Engineer Battalion, 95th Mountain Signal Battalion

NOTES AND SOURCES: Salzburg, Wkr. XVIII

The 5th Mountain Division was formed under Major General Julius "Papa" Ringel in the autumn of 1940 from the 100th Mountain Infantry Regiment of the 1st Mountain Division and elements of the 10th Infantry Division. Its personnel were mainly Bavarians, with some Austrians added. After a training period in the Alps, it first saw action in the Balkans campaign of 1944, where it helped crack the Metaxas Line and took part in the subsequent sweep through Greece. A few weeks later it was part of General Student's mixed paratrooper mountaineer task force, which defeated the British army on Crete. The 5th Mountain's timely relief of the paratroopers late on the second day of the Battle of Maleme was the turning point of the campaign. The division remained on the island for a time and Ringel—now a Lieutenant General—assumed command of the island. From September 1941 to early 1942 the division was on occupation duty in Norway; however, after things began to go wrong in Russia, the 5th Mountain was sent to Army Group North and from January to March 1942 it helped check Russian counteroffensives between Lake Ladoga and Novgorod. Later it took part in the Siege of Leningrad, operated on the Finnish Front for a time, and then returned to the Leningrad sector, where it helped maintain the siege in mid-1943. In December, the division was withdrawn from the Eastern Front and sent to Italy, where it relieved the 305th Infantry Division just prior to the First Battle of Cassino in January 1944. Later that month it was fighting against the Allied landing forces in the vicinity of Anzio. The 5th Mountain spent the rest of the war in Italy, and participated in the battles of the Gustav and Gothic Lines (where it distinguished itself), as well as Army Group C's retreat up the peninsula. It surrendered to the Allies near the Po River in late April 1945. Commanders of the 5th Mountain Division included Ringel (1940-44) and Major General Schrank (1945).

NOTES AND SOURCES: Ringel, who served in the Austrian Army from 1909 to 1938, was Ia of the 268th Infantry Division (1938), commander of the 266th Infantry Regiment (1939), and briefly commander of the 3rd Mountain Division in 1940. He later led the LXIX Corps (1944) and (as General of Mountain Troops) Corps Ringel, a miscellaneous collection of soldiers fighting the Russians in southern Austria in 1945. He was an outstanding divisional and corps commander. Like many mountain officers, Major General Schrank was previously associated with the 1st Mountain Division. Blumenson 1969: 376; Carell 1966: 421; Carell 1971: 242; Fisher: 18, 302; Hartmann: 49-50; Lucas: 208, 245-46; Salisbury: 539; OB 42: 71; OB 43: 211; Ziemke 1959: 209, 218.

6th MOUNTAIN DIVISION

COMPOSITION: 141st Mountain Infantry Regiment, 143rd Mountain Infantry Regiment, 118th Mountain Artillery Regiment, 1057th Mountain Motorcycle Battalion, 157th Anti-Tank Battalion, 91st Mountain Engineer Battalion, 96th Mountain Signal Battalion

HOME STATION: Klagenfurt, Wkr. XVIII

The 6th Mountain was formed in the winter of 1939-40 and was in action in France a few months later. It was engaged in occupation duties in Poland in late 1940 and early 1941, before being transferred south. During the Balkans campaign it took part in the drive on Salonika, capturing Athens in coordination with the 2nd Panzer Division. It was also lightly engaged in the invasion of Crete. In October 1941 it was transferred to Norway, where it formed the northern wing of Mountain Corps Norway on the drive for Murmansk. During this operation it was commanded by Major General Ferdinand Schörner, who later became infamous as

Hitler's most brutal Field Marshal. The 6th Mountain remained in action on the Arctic sector of the Eastern Front until Finland renounced its alliance with Germany in late 1944. It was with the XIX Mountain Corps, 20th Mountain Army, during the retreat across Lapland and was still in Norway in May 1945, when the war ended. It surrendered to the British. Commanders of the 6th Mountain Division included Schörner (1940-42), Lieutenant General Philipp Christian (1942-44), and Major General Max Pemsel (1944-April 2, 1945).

NOTES AND SOURCES: The 6th Mountain Division was formed from cadres from the 139th Mountain Infantry Regiment, 3rd Mountain Division. Artillery cadres were provided by the 113th Artillery Regiment, I Battalion, 752nd Artillery Regiment, and III Battalion, 112th Artillery Regiment. Ferdinand Schörner commanded the XIX Mountain Corps on the Finnish sector of the Eastern Front (1942-43), before being sent to the center of the fighting. Although he had no tank training, he commanded XL Panzer Corps in the Dnieper fighting (late 1943-February 1944), and did a superb job of holding and then evacuating the Nikopol Pocket against vastly superior Soviet forces. On February 18, 1944, he was appointed Chief of the National Socialist Leadership Corps at OKH, but in March was named Commander-in-Chief of Army Group South Ukraine (formerly Army Group A). Later he commanded Army Group North (July 24, 1944-January 1945) and Army Group A (later Center) from January 1945 until late April 1945. He was promoted to Field Marshal on April 5, 1945, and, on April 29, 1945, was named Commander-in-Chief of the Army by Adolf Hitler on the day before Hitler committed suicide. Schörner abandoned his command during the last week of the war and fled to Austria, where he surrendered to the Americans. Turned over to the Russians, he was sentenced to twenty-five years imprisonment, but only served nine of them. He returned to Munich after his release and died in the 1970s. Philipp Christian commanded the 88th Infantry Division on the Eastern Front in 1945. Max Pemsel had served as Chief of Staff of the 7th Army in France before falling into Hitler's bad graces after the German collapse in Normandy. On April 2, 1945, he was summoned to Berlin to take charge of the defense of the doomed capital of the Reich, but bad weather delayed his arrival until April 12, by which time another commander had been appointed—much to Pemsel's relief. Colonel General Jodl, Chief of Operations at OKW, named him Chief of Staff of Marshal Graziani's Ligurian Army in northern Italy, and Pemsel got out of Berlin as quickly as he could. Brett-Smith: 202-05; Carell 1966: 456-57, 459-60; Lucas: 208-09; von Mellenthin 1977: 176; Ryan 1966: 375-76; RA: 234; OB 42: 71; OB 43: 211-12; Ziemke 1959: Map 22.

7th MOUNTAIN DIVISION

COMPOSITION: 144th Mountain Infantry Regiment, 206th Mountain Infantry Regiment, 82nd Mountain Artillery Regiment, 99th Motorcycle Battalion, 99th Anti-Tank Battalion, 99th Mountain Engineer Battalion, 99th Mountain Signal Battalion

HOME STATION: Wehrkreis XIII

Originally formed as the 99th Jäger Division in December 1940, this division initially included the 206th and 218th Jäger Regiments. The 218th Jäger, however, was disbanded when the unit was reorganized as a mountain division in the winter of 1941-42. Meanwhile, as the 99th Jäger, the division fought as part of Army Group South on the Russian Front in 1941, before returning to Germany to reorganize. In the spring of 1942 it was sent to Finland and remained there until the Finns renounced their military alliance with the Nazis in late 1944. In the subsequent retreat from Lapland the 7th Mountain formed part of the XVIII Mountain Corps, 20th Mountain Army. After arriving in Norway, the High Command ordered the division to return to Europe; however, the war ended before it could disembark. The division surrendered to the British at Trondheim in May 1945.

NOTES AND SOURCES: The division's 99th Replacement Battalion was converted into a ski unit in September 1943 and lost to the division. Lieutenant General August Krakau, former commander of the 85th Mountain Infantry Regiment (1941-42), led the 7th Mountain for most of its combat career (1942-44). Lucas: 209; RA: 204; OB 42: 71; OB 43: 212; Ziemke 1959: 209, 293, 312; Ziemke 1966: 401.

8th MOUNTAIN DIVISION

COMPOSITION: 142nd Mountain Infantry Regiment, 144th Mountain Infantry Regiment, 124th Mountain Artillery Regiment, (?) Bicycle Battalion, (?) Anti-Tank Battalion, (?) Mountain Engineer Battalion, (?) Mountain Signal Battalion

HOME STATION: Wehrkreis XVIII

Formed in Norway in 1942, this division served in Finland, the Russian zone of Lapland, and in Norway for the first two years of its history. It never particularly distinguished itself, and, according to U.S. Intelligence sources, never reached full strength. In late 1944 and early 1945 it was transferred from the northern theater of operations to Italy, and saw action in the Po River Valley in the last campaign in that country. Although it reported a strength of only three thousand men in 1945, the 8th Mountain was the largest combat unit in the German 10th Army at that time—an indication of the operational bankruptcy the Germans had reached in Italy by the spring of 1945. The 8th Mountain surrendered in northern Italy in late April 1945.

SOURCES: Fisher: 442; RA: 234; OB 43: 212; OB 45: 322.

9th MOUNTAIN DIVISION

COMPOSITION (Northern Group): 139th Mountain Infantry Regiment, 140th Mountain Infantry Regiment. (Southern Group): see below

HOME STATIONS: Norway and Dachstein, Wkr. XVII

In the last confusing days of the war, the German High Command accidentally gave the number "9" to two different mountain divisions. The first 9th Mountain Division (which received its designation after the retreat through Finland) consisted of a battle group in Norway that was led by Major General Kräutler. It surrendered to the British in May 1945. The second 9th Mountain Division was made up of Combat Group Semmering. This unit consisted of forces guarding the Semmering Pass in eastern Austria and included men from the Mountain Artillery School at Dachstein, the SS Mountain Replacement Battalion at Leoben, and ground crews from the Boelcke fighter squadron of the Luftwaffe. It fought against the Russians in the last months of the war but did not receive the designation 9th Mountain Division until twelve days before the conflict ended.

SOURCE: Lucas: 209-10.

157th RESERVE MOUNTAIN DIVISION
see 8th Mountain Division

188th RESERVE MOUNTAIN (later MOUNTAIN) DIVISION

COMPOSITION (1943): 136th Reserve Mountain Regiment, 137th Reserve Mountain Regiment, 139th Reserve Mountain Regiment, I Battalion, 112th Reserve Mountain Artillery Regiment, 83rd (?) Reserve Mountain Engineer Battalion

HOME STATION: Salzburg, Wkr. XVIII

As most of the other reserve divisions, the 188th was created as a replacement division staff in the fall of 1939. It spent the next three years training and supplying replacement personnel for divisions associated with the XVIII Military District in northern Austria. Almost all of its subordinate elements were mountain units. In early 1943 the division was stationed at Marburg in Slovenia. In the fall of 1943 it was sent to the Merano area of northern Italy with its mountain training regiments and was upgraded to reserve division status. The 188th was subordinate to Army Group C's Army Detachment von Zangen, a collection of second- and third-rate divisions in northern Italy. In early 1944 it was in the Istrian peninsula area, conducting antiguerrilla operations in the army group's communications zone. In late 1944 it was upgraded to full mountain division status, was sent to the Balkans, and took part in the last campaign as a regular combat division. Its commander at that time was sixty-seven-year-old Lieutenant General Wilhelm von Hösslin (1943-45). It ended the war on the southern sector of the Eastern Front.

SOURCES: *Kriegstagebuch des OKW*, Volume IV: 1903; RA: 6; OB 43: 153; OB 45: 197.

6

The Panzer Divisions

1st PANZER DIVISION

COMPOSITION (1943): 1st Panzer Regiment, 1st Panzer Grenadier Regiment, 113th Panzer Grenadier Regiment, 73rd Panzer Artillery Regiment, 1st Motorcycle Battalion, 4th Panzer Reconnaissance Battalion, 37 Anti-Tank Battalion, 37th Panzer Engineer Battalion, 37th Panzer Signal Battalion

HOME STATION: Weimar, Wkr. IX

Formed on October 15, 1935, this division initially included the 1st and 2nd Panzer Regiments and the 1st Panzer Grenadier Regiment. The division consisted mainly of Saxons and Thuringians with draftees from other parts of Germany. Its first commander was Lieutenant General Baron Maximilian von Weichs, who later became a Field Marshal. The 1st Panzer took part in the occupation of Prague and Austria in 1938 and the Polish campaign of 1939, when it rolled from the frontier to the suburbs of Warsaw in just eight days. Sent to the west that winter, it attacked across Luxembourg and southern Belgium in May 1940 and fought in the Battle of Sedan, the drive across France, and in the Battle of Dunkirk, before turning south and helping finish off the doomed French Republic. After this campaign, the 2nd Panzer Regiment was transferred to the newly formed 16th Panzer Division, and the 113th Panzer Grenadier Regiment was incorporated into the 1st Panzer Division. In the Russian campaign of 1941 the division formed part of Army Group North's 4th Panzer Group (later Army), and took part in the annihilation of the Soviet III Armored Corps at Dubysa in June. The 1st Panzer was seriously depleted by casualties, and by August 16 had only forty-four serviceable tanks; nevertheless it took part in the drive on Moscow, opposed the Russian winter offensive, and in 1942 fought in several defensive battles on the central sector of the

Eastern Front. Greatly reduced by losses, the 1st Panzer was withdrawn for resting and refitting in early 1943. Initially it was sent to France but spent that spring in Greece. In late summer 1943 it returned to the Russian Front, fighting on the southern sector as part of the XLVIII and later III Panzer Corps of the 1st Panzer Army. It took part in the Battle of the Kiev Salient and the counteroffensive west of Kiev (November-December 1943), as well as spearheading the attempt to rescue the XI and XLII Corps, which were surrounded at Cherkassy in February 1944. It could not penetrate the last six miles to the pocket but was still successful in saving half the trapped Germans. The next month the 1st Panzer rescued the 96th and 291st Infantry Divisions from the Soviet spring offensive of 1944. The division fought in the battles of the Dnieper Bend, the north Ukraine, and eastern Poland in 1944. Retreating behind the Vistula, it was transferred to Hungary and was cited for its counterattack against the Russians at Debrecen. Most of the division was trapped and destroyed at Szekesfehervar, Hungary, in December 1944, when the 6th Army collapsed; despite its losses, however, the remnants of the 1st Panzer Division continued fighting on the southern sector of the Eastern Front until the end of the war. Commanders of the division included von Weichs (1935-37), Lieutenant General Rudolf Schmidt (1938-39), Lieutenant General Friedrich Kirchner (1940-41), Lieutenant General Eugen Walter Krüger (1942-43), Major General Koll (1944), Major General Werner Marcks (1944), and Colonel Thunert (1945).

NOTES AND SOURCES: Baron von Weichs, a Bavarian cavalry officer, commanded the 18th Cavalry Regiment (1928) and the 2nd Cavalry Division at Weimar (1933) before assuming command of the 1st Panzer Division. In 1937 he took over command of the XIII Military District and XIII Corps at Nuremberg and rose to the command of the 2nd Army in 1940. He led this force in France, Yugoslavia, and Russia until he fell ill during the Battle of Moscow in December 1941. In January 1942 he was briefly Commander-in-Chief of Army Group South, following the death of Field Marshal von Reichenau on January 17. From July 1942 to February 1943 he was Commander-in-Chief of Army Group B on the Russian Front and was involved in the Stalingrad disaster. Placed in reserve for a period, Baron von Weichs was re-employed in August 1943 as Commander-in-Chief, Southeast (i.e., the Balkans) and, as such, commanded Army Group F during the retreat from southeastern Europe. He was retired on Hitler's orders on March 25, 1945: the Führer had always mistrusted von Weichs because of his strong Catholic leanings. The Baron's promotion to Field Marshal was dated July 19, 1940. His friend and successor as commander of the 1st Panzer Division was Rudolf Schmidt, who rose to the rank of Colonel General. He commanded the XXXIX Motorized (later Panzer) Corps in France and Russia (1940-41), was acting commander of the 2nd

Army during the Battle of Moscow (once again replacing von Weichs), and was commander of the 2nd Panzer Army on the Russian Front from December 26, 1941, to July 10, 1943. Although popular with Hitler, he was critical of the Nazi regime and was relieved of his command two days before the Battle of Kursk began, because some of his letters containing anti-Nazi statements fell into the Führer's hands after the Gestapo arrested Schmidt's brother on an unrelated matter. Friedrich Kirchner became a General of Panzer Troops in early 1942 and commanded the XLI Panzer Corps (late 1941) and the LVII Panzer Corps (early 1942-1945). Walter Krüger also became a General of Panzer Troops (from May 1944). He served as acting commander of the LXVIII Corps (October 1943) and commander of the LVIII Panzer Corps (1944-45). Werner Marcks, a veteran of the Afrika Korps, had led the 104th Panzer Grenadier Regiment of the 21st Panzer Division (1941-42) and was acting commander of the 90th Light Division in Libya in July 1942. Colonel Thunet was previously Chief of Staff of the LVIII Reserve Panzer (subsequently Panzer) Corps in 1943. Benoist-Mechin: 68; Carell 1966: 24, 79, 336, 398; Chant 1979: 102; Chant, Volume 15: 2057; Chapman: 347-48; Paul Joseph Goebbels, *The Goebbels Diaries* (edited and translated by Louis P. Lochner), originally published by Doubleday and Company, Inc., Garden City, New York: 1948; Universal-Award House, Inc., edition, New York, 1971: 414; Hartmann: 60-61; Kennedy: 74; MacDonald 1963: 300; Manstein: 488, 526; Seaton: 360, 367; RA: 144; OB 42: 55; OB 43: 198; OB 45: 286; Ziemke 1966: 225-38. For a detailed description of the Balkans campaign, see U.S. Department of the Army Pamphlet 20-260, *The German Campaign in the Balkans (Spring 1941)*, United States Department of the Army, Washington, D.C.: 1953.

2nd PANZER DIVISION

COMPOSITION (1943): 3rd Panzer Regiment, 2nd Panzer Grenadier Regiment, 304th Panzer Grenadier Regiment, 74th Panzer Artillery Regiment, 2nd Motorcycle Battalion, 5th Panzer Reconnaissance Battalion, 38th Anti-Tank Battalion, 38th Panzer Engineer Battalion, 38th Panzer Signal Battalion

HOME STATION: Würzburg, Wkr. XIII; later Vienna, Wkr. XVIII

Formed in 1935, this division initially included the 3rd and 4th Panzer Regiments and the 2nd Panzer Grenadier Regiment. In 1938 it was transferred to Vienna after the annexation of Austria. By the start of the war, most of the men of the division were Austrians. The 2nd Panzer suffered heavy losses in central Poland in 1939 and took part in the French campaign of 1940, where it formed part of Guderian's XIX Motorized Corps. It captured Abbeville on the English Channel in May, thus isolating the main Allied armies in the Dunkirk Pocket and sealing the doom of France. In late 1940 the division gave up the 4th Panzer Regiment plus other cadres to the newly authorized 13th Panzer Division and added the 304th Panzer Grenadier Regiment to its table of organization. The reorganized 2nd Panzer took part in the Balkans campaign and took Athens along with the 6th Mountain Division. It crossed into Russia in 1941 as part of the XLI Panzer Corps. Elements of the unit managed to reach as far as Khimki, a small river port five miles from Moscow, and certain elements even reported being able to see the Kremlin itself, before they were thrown back by the start of the Soviet winter offensive of 1941-42. Remaining on the central sector, the battered division took part in the defensive fighting of 1942, the Rzhev withdrawal, the Battle of Kursk, and the middle Dnieper battles of the winter of 1943-44, where it suffered heavy casualties. Withdrawn to France to rest and refit, the 2nd Panzer was thrown into the Battle of Normandy in June 1944. It took part in the unsuccessful counterattack at Mortain in August and, with only twenty-five tanks left, was surrounded at Falaise in August. Breaking out with losses, it was reformed at Wittlich in the Eifel area of western Germany, where it temporarily absorbed the remnants of the 352nd Infantry Division. It was sent back into combat in the Ardennes offensive, where it again suffered heavy casualties. In the last campaign the 2nd Panzer was fighting against the Americans in 1945 and was down to a strength of only four tanks, three assault guns, and two hundred men. The survivors of the old division were grouped with Panzer Brigade Thüringen and ended the war defending Fulda in April 1945. Its commanders included Major General Heinz Guderian (October 1935-1938), Lieutenant General Rudolf Veiel (1938-41), Lieutenant General Baron Hans-Karl von Esebeck (1942), Lieutenant General Vollrath Lübbe (1943), Lieutenant General Baron Heinrich von Lüttwitz (late 1943-1944), Major General Schoenfeld (late 1944), Major General Meimad von Lauchert (1944-45), and Major General Heinz Kokott (1945).

NOTES AND SOURCES: Heinz Guderian—the father of the Blitzkrieg—was Germany's leading advocate of mobile, armored warfare before World War II and greatly influenced Hitler in that direction. In 1938 he was given command of the XVI Corps and, in 1939, the XIX Motorized Corps. He distinguished himself in Poland (1939), France (1940), and in the early stages of the Russian campaign (1941), where he commanded the 2nd Panzer Group. Relieved by Hitler for the German failure before Moscow, he held no further commands but was Inspector General of Panzer Troops (1943-44) and Chief of the General Staff of the Army (July 1944-March 1945), a job for which he was unsuited. The outspoken Colonel General Guderian was again relieved by Hitler after a bitter argument in March

1945 and surrendered to the Western Allies in northern Italy the next month. Rudolf Veiel, a Württemberger, was promoted to General of Panzer Troops in the spring of 1942. After leading a panzer corps in Russia (1941-42), he became commander of Wehrkreis V (late 1943-45). Baron von Esebeck commanded the 6th Motorized Infantry Brigade of the 6th Panzer Division in France (1940) before assuming command of the 15th Panzer Division in North Africa. He was wounded in the Siege of Tobruk in 1941 and, upon his recovery, was placed in charge of the 2nd Panzer. He subsequently commanded the XLVI Panzer Corps (late 1942-early 1943) and the LVIII Panzer Corps (1943-44), and was acting commander of Wehrkreis XVII in Vienna in mid-1944. Esebeck was arrested in connection with the July 20, 1944, attempt on Hitler's life, and spent the rest of the war in prison. Baron von Lüttwitz, former commander of the 20th Panzer Division in Russia (1943), later commanded the XLVII Panzer Corps on the Western Front (1944-45), where he directed German forces in the Siege of Bastogne (December 1944). Schoenfeld previously commanded the 29th Panzer Grenadier Regiment of the 3rd Panzer Grenadier Division. General von Lauchert was formerly commanding officer of the 15th Panzer Regiment, 11th Panzer Division (1943-44). Blumenson 1960: 295, 422, 505, 549; Blumenson 1969: 42; Carell 1966: 180, 336; Carell 1971: 26-37, 309; Chant, Volume 14: 1859-61; Chant 1979: 96; Chapman: 347-48; Cole 1965: 177-80; Heinz Guderian, *Panzer Leader*, Ballantine Books, Inc. (by arrangement with E. P. Dutton and Company, Inc., New York, 1957), New York, 1967: 25-29; Harrison: Map VI; Kennedy: 74, Map 7; MacDonald 1973: 93, 257, 259; Manstein: 482-83; von Mellenthin 1977: 199; Speidel: 42; RA: 220; OB 42: 55; OB 43: 199; OB 45: 286-87. Guderian also wrote the book *Achtung! Panzer!* (published in 1937) which outlined his basic concepts of armored warfare and was considered revolutionary at the time.

3rd PANZER DIVISION

COMPOSITION (1943): 6th Panzer Regiment, 3rd Panzer Grenadier Regiment, 394th Panzer Grenadier Regiment, 75th Panzer Artillery Regiment, 3rd Motorcycle Battalion, 327th (?) Panzer Reconnaissance Battalion, 327th (?) Anti-Tank Battalion, 39th Panzer Engineer Battalion, 39th Panzer Signal Battalion

HOME STATION: Berlin, Wkr. III

Known as the "Bear Division" from its emblem, the Berlin Bear, the 3rd Panzer Division was activated at the Wünsdorf Maneuver Area on October 15, 1935. At that time it included the 5th and 6th Panzer and 3rd Panzer Grenadier Regiments. Its personnel were mainly Prussians. The 3rd

Panzer took part in the *Anschluss* and then the Polish campaign of 1939, where it formed part of Guderian's XIX Corps, attacking from Pomerania to Thorn in northern Poland, and then southeast to Brest-Litovsk. The 3rd also distinguished itself in France in 1940 as part of Höpner's XVI Motorized Corps. It fought in the Battle of the Albert Canal and in the battles south of Brussels, as well as the pursuit after the fall of Dunkirk, which ended in the capitulation of France. In late 1940 the division supplied the 5th Panzer Regiment to the 5th Light (later 21st Panzer) Division, and received the 394th Panzer Grenadier Regiment in exchange. Like the other panzer divisions that were similarly reduced in the winter of 1940-41, the Bear Division lost about half its tank strength. The 3rd Panzer invaded Russia on June 22, 1941, and seized the Koden Bridge on the frontier by a *coup de main*. Under future Field Marshal Walter Model, it took part in the Battle of the Bialystok-Minsk Pocket and the Dnieper River crossings, before being sent to the southern sector, where it helped trap several Russian armies, comprising 667,000 men, in the Kiev area. During the Soviet winter offensive of 1941-42 it acted as a "fire brigade" and in March 1942 held Kharkov against massive Soviet attacks. With the 4th Panzer Army, the division took part in the Caucasus campaign and suffered heavy losses in the battles around Mozdok. It escaped from the Kuban by crossing the Sea of Azov over the ice after Rostov was threatened in January 1943. It fought in the Battle of Kursk in July and suffered heavy losses in the Kharkov battles of autumn 1943. Remaining in the line despite its casualties, the 3rd Panzer fought in the Dnieper campaign (where it again distinguished itself), at Kiev, and in the retreat through the Ukraine. It fought its way out of encirclement in Rumania, took part in the Hungarian campaign, and ended the war on the southern sector of the Eastern Front. Its commanders included Lieutenant General Fessman (1935-36), Lieutenant General Baron Leo Geyr von Schweppenburg (1937-39), Lieutenant General Georg Stumme (1940), Model (1941), Lieutenant General Hermann Breith (1942-43), Major General Fritz Bayerlein (1943), Lieutenant General Franz Westhoven (1943-44), Lieutenant General Denkert (1944), Major General Hecker (1944-45?), and Lieutenant General Phillips (1945).

NOTES AND SOURCES: The 3rd Panzer was one of the three original panzer divisions in the German Army. Baron Geyr von Schweppenburg, former German Military Attache' to London, Brussels, and The Hague (1937-39), was an anti-Nazi from Württemberg. He led the XXIV Panzer Corps (1940-42), the XL Panzer Corps (1942), and the LVIII Panzer Corps (1942-43) before being named Inspector General of Panzer Troops in 1943. He was appointed commander of Panzer Group West (later 5th Panzer Army) in the latter part of 1943 and led it in the opening days of the Normandy campaign. He was severely wounded by Allied bombers on June 9, 1944, and his chief of staff was killed. Recovering from his wounds in late June, he returned to Normandy, only to be relieved of his command on Hitler's orders in early July. He was never again employed. After the war, von Schweppenburg became a military historian. For the details of Stumme's career, see 7th Panzer Division. Walter Model, a Field Marshal as of March 1, 1944, distinguished himself in Russia as an extremely energetic commander and excellent tactician. He commanded 9th Army (1942-January 1944), Army Group North (January-March 1944), Army Group North Ukraine (April-June 1944), and Army Group Center (June-August 1944). Sent to the West, he was less successful. Briefly Commander-in-Chief of OB West (i.e., C-in-C of the Western Front) in August 1944, he was commander of Army Group B from September 1944 until it was destroyed in the Ruhr Pocket in April 1945. Model himself committed suicide in a wooded area near Düsseldorf rather than surrender and for years lay in an unmarked grave. Hermann Breith left the 3rd Panzer in late 1942 to take charge of the III Panzer Corps, which he led on the Eastern Front until the end of the war. Fritz Bayerlein, Guderian's former Ia in France and Russia, had served as Chief of Staff of the Afrika Korps (1941-42) and Chief of Staff of Panzer Army Afrika (1942-43). In 1944 he became commander of the Panzer Lehr Division, which he led on the Western Front from D-Day until almost the end of the war. He commanded the LIII Corps in the Battle of the Ruhr Pocket, where he was taken prisoner. Major General Hecker had been Chief Engineer Officer of Panzer Army Afrika in 1942 and distinguished himself in the capture of Bir Hacheim, where he was wounded. In early 1944 he was commander of the 20th Panzer Division. Before assuming command of the 3rd Panzer, Lieutenant General Philipps was associated with the weapons and equipment manufacturing office of the OKH Ordnance Department. Benoist-Mechin: 241; Carell 1966: 9, 474, 488, 491, 512, 546-50; Carell 1971: 19, 48, 142; Chapman: 347-48; Hartmann: 61-62; Manstein: 488, 525; RA: 46; OB 42: 55, 199; OB 45: 287. Also see Brett-Smith: 176-78, for an account of von Schweppenburg's career.

4th PANZER DIVISION

COMPOSITION (1943): 35th Panzer Regiment, 12th Panzer Grenadier Regiment, 33rd Panzer Grenadier Regiment, 103rd Panzer Artillery Regiment, 34th Motorcycle Battalion, 7th Panzer Reconnaissance Battalion, 49th Anti-Tank Battalion, 79th Panzer Engineer Battalion, 79th Panzer Signal Battalion

HOME STATION: Würzburg, Wkr. XIII

This peacetime division was formed in 1938 and consisted mainly of

Bavarians, with draftees from other parts of Germany. Initially it included the 35th and 36th Panzer and 12th Panzer Grenadier Regiments. In the summer of 1939 it received the 33rd Panzer Grenadier Regiment from the 13th Motorized Division. In the Polish campaign it distinguished itself by penetrating from Germany to the outskirts of Warsaw in just eight days, although it could not take the city and lost about half its tanks in the attempt. The next year it spearheaded the invasion of Holland, took part in the Dunkirk campaign, and helped finish off France in June 1940. That winter it lost the 36th Panzer Regiment plus some cadres to the 14th Panzer (formerly 4th Infantry) Division. As part of Army Group Center, the 4th Panzer crossed into Russia in 1941 and fought at Minsk, Bryansk, Vyazma, and other bitterly contested points on the road to Moscow. In December 1941 it attempted to encircle the strategic city of Tula, southeast of Moscow, but failed, suffering heavy losses in the attempt. Remaining on the central sector of the Russian Front until 1944, it fought in the Kursk and Dnieper campaigns and tried unsuccessfully to check the Soviet summer offensive of 1944. In November 1944 it was isolated in the Courland Pocket but was evacuated by sea to northern Germany in early 1945. Now in remnants, the 4th Panzer took part in the Berlin campaign of 1945—the last of the war. Its divisional commanders included Lieutenant General Georg-Hans Reinhardt (1938-39), Major General Joachim Stevers (1939-40), Major General Baron von Langermann-Erlenkamp (1941), Lieutenant General Hans Eberbach (1942-43), Lieutenant General Erich Schneider (1943), Lieutenant General Dietrich von Saucken (1943-44), and Major General Clemens Betzel (1945).

NOTES AND SOURCES: Reinhardt rose to the rank of Colonel General. He commanded the XLI Motorized (subsequently Panzer) Corps in France and Russia (1940-41) and the 3rd Panzer Army from late 1941 until the fall of 1944. Named commander of Army Group Center in late 1944, Hitler relieved him of his command because Reinhardt demanded permission to abandon East Prussia in order to avoid being isolated there in early 1945. General Stever was retired by 1945. Major General Baron von Langermann-Erlenkamp commanded the 29th Motorized Infantry Division in France in 1940. Hans Eberbach replaced Geyr von Schweppenburg as commander of Panzer Group West (which was then upgraded to 5th Panzer Army). Eberbach—now a General of Panzer Troops—held this post from July 5 to August 21, 1944, when he was named commander of the 7th Army. He held his new command only ten days. He was captured on August 31, 1944, during the German retreat from France. Erich Schneider, an artillery officer with an advanced engineering degree, had formerly served in the Ballistics Branch. In 1945 he was the Head of the Experimental and Testing Group of the Army Ordnance Office. Dietrich von Saucken, who held the Knight's Cross with Oak Leaves and Swords, was a cavalry officer.

He led a panzer corps on the Oder in early 1945, before being named commander of the 2nd Army in East Prussia (March-May 1945). Saucken was an extremely capable commander. Major General Betzel had previously led the 103rd Panzer Artillery Regiment of the 4th Panzer Division (1942-43). Benoist-Mechin: 241; Carell 1966: 69, 79, 80, 136-37; Carell 1971: 35, 591-94; Chant, Volume 2: 217; Volume 14: 1931; Chapman: 347-48; Manstein: 487, 538; OB 42: 56; OB 43: 199-200; OB 45: 288.

5th PANZER DIVISION

COMPOSITION (1943): 31st Panzer Regiment, 13th Panzer Grenadier Regiment, 14th Panzer Grenadier Regiment, 116th Panzer Artillery Regiment, 55th Motorcycle Battalion, 8th Panzer Reconnaissance Battalion, 53rd Anti-Tank Battalion, 89th Panzer Engineer Battalion, 85th Panzer Signal Battalion

HOME STATION: Oppeln, Wkr. VIII

Originally a peacetime division, the 5th Panzer fought well throughout its existence and was six times cited for distinguished conduct in combat on the Eastern Front. Organized in November 1938 after the annexation of the Sudetenland, the division's troops were mainly Silesians and Sudeten Germans. Initially consisting of the 15th and 31st Panzer and 14th Panzer Grenadier Regiments, the division played a minor and "inconspicuous" role in the Polish campaign of 1939 and a "prominent" part in the French campaign of 1940, according to Allied intelligence evaluations. Late in 1940 it supplied the 15th Panzer Regiment plus other cadre troops to the newly forming 11th Panzer Division. In 1941 the 5th Panzer was involved in the Balkans campaign, fighting in both Yugoslavia and Greece, including a sharp battle with (and victory over) the 2nd New Zealand Division at Molos. Crossing into Russia with Army Group Center, the 5th Panzer took part in heavy fighting all the way to the gates of Moscow. Remaining on the central sector, it faced the Soviet winter offensive of 1941-42, fought in the defensive battles of 1942, the Rzhev withdrawal, and suffered heavy losses in the unsuccessful Kursk offensive. Later in 1943 it fought in the battles on the middle Dnieper and in the summer of 1944 it counterattacked against the massive Russian offensive, inflicting considerable casualties on the Soviets. The 5th Panzer was unable to turn the tide and save the trapped elements of the 4th and 9th armies, and, with the remnants of Army Group Center, it took part in the retreats across White Russia, Poland, and into East Prussia. It was still fighting there when the war ended. Commanders of this division included Lieutenant Generals Heinrich von Vietinghoff gennant Scheel (1938-39), Hartlieb gennant Walsporn (1940), Joachim

Lemelsen (1940), Gustav Fehn (1941-42), Eduard Metz (1942-43), and Karl Decker (1944-45).

NOTES AND SOURCES: Heinrich von Vietinghoff was a tough, solid East Prussian soldier—highly capable but not brilliant. He later led XIII Corps in France (1940), XLVI Panzer Corps in the Balkans and Russia (1941-42), 9th Army in Russia (September-December 1942), and 15th Army in France (late 1942-September 1943) before being sent to Italy. He fought his most famous battles here as commander of the 10th Army (September 1943-January 1945) or acting Commander-in-Chief of Army Group C (October-December 1944). He was named commander of Army Group Courland in January 1945 but returned to Italy as Commander-in-Chief—this time on a permanent basis—in March 1945. Two months later he surrendered to the Allies. He was promoted to Colonel General in September 1943. General von Vietinghoff is best known for his very skillful retreats before the Americans and British in Italy (1943-44). Joachim Lemelsen, former commander of the 29th Motorized Infantry Division (1938-39), later led XLVII Panzer Corps in Russia (1942-43), was acting commander of the 10th Army in Italy (October-December), and commanded 14th Army in Italy (1945). He was promoted to General of Panzer Troops in 1940. Gustav Fehn was given command of the XL Panzer Corps in Russia in late 1942 and the Afrika Korps in Libya in December of that year. Early in 1943 he was seriously wounded and evacuated to Germany. Upon recovering, he successively commanded XXI Mountain Corps (late 1943-mid-1944) and XV Mountain Corps (1944-45). His promotion to General of Panzer Troops dates from November 1, 1942. General Decker commanded the 3rd Panzer Regiment in Russia (1941-42) prior to commanding the 3rd Panzer Division. Benoist-Mechin: 304; Carell 1966: 175, 330; Carell 1971: 309, 591-92; Chant 1979: 53; Kennedy: 74; von Mellenthin 1977: 176-77; RA: 130; OB 42: 56; OB 43: 200; OB 45: 288.

6th PANZER DIVISION

COMPOSITION (1943): 11th Panzer Regiment, 4th Panzer Grenadier Regiment, 114th Panzer Grenadier Regiment, 76th Panzer Artillery Regiment, 6th Motorcycle Battalion, (?) Panzer Reconnaissance Battalion, 41st Anti-Tank Battalion, 57th Panzer Engineer Battalion, 82nd Panzer Signal Battalion

HOME STATION: Wüppertal, Wkr. VI

Created as the 1st Light Division, this unit was composed of Westphalians and Rhinelanders. It initially contained the 4th Mechanized Cavalry

Regiment and the 65th Panzer Battalion. It fought in southern Poland in 1939 and was converted to a panzer division that winter, after the High Command pronounced its light division experiment a failure. Sent to France in 1940, it was smaller than the panzer divisions created earlier and was equipped with light, Czech-made tanks; nevertheless, it performed creditably in the West. Sent to Russia in 1941, it broke through the Stalin Line and was involved on the drive to and early Siege of Leningrad. Transferred to Army Group Center, it suffered such heavy losses in the Soviet winter offensive of 1941-42 that it had to be sent back to France to rest and refit. While out of the line, the division gave up its inferior Czech tanks and was re-equipped with excellent Mark III (PzKw III) tanks, armed with long-barreled 50mm guns. After Stalingrad was surrounded, the 6th Panzer was rushed back to the Soviet Union, where it tried to relieve the 6th Army, but was halted at Bolwassiljewka, thirty miles south of the city. After the retreat from the Volga, the 6th Panzer Division fought at Kursk, in the Dnieper battles, and in the northern Ukraine, where it was encircled, but broke out. Withdrawn from the line to refit, the 6th was hastily sent to the central sector of the Eastern Front shortly after the Russians surrounded the bulk of the 4th and 9th armies. Later, the now burned-out division was sent to Hungary, where it fought in the battles around Budapest. It ended the war on the southern sector of the Eastern Front. Commanders of the 6th Panzer Division included Major General von Loeper (1939), Lieutenant General Franz Werner Kempf (1940), Lieutenant General Landgraf (1941), Lieutenant General Erhard Raus (Nov. 1941-1942), Major General von Huenersdorff (1943), Major General Walter Denkert (1943), and Lieutenant General Baron Rudolf von Waldenfels (1943-45).

NOTES AND SOURCES: Erich Höpner commanded the unit in 1938, when it was still the 1st Light Division. Höpner went on to command the XVI Motorized Corps in Poland and France, and the 4th Panzer Group (subsequently Army) in Russia (1941). Höpner was promoted to Colonel General in 1941. He was relieved of his command for ordering an unauthorized retreat in January 1942. He played an active role in the attempt to kill Hitler on July 20, 1944, and was executed soon after. Werner Kempf, an East Prussian who was promoted to General of Panzer Troops in April 1941, led XVIII Panzer Corps in Russia (1941-early 1943), and Army Detachment Kempf (subsequently 8th Army) until mid-1943, when he fell afoul of Hitler and was relieved. In late 1944 he was in charge of German troops in the Vosges Mountainers on the French frontier. He had commanded Panzer Division "Kempf" (later 10th Panzer Division) in the Polish campaign. General Raus, an Austrian, was Chief of Staff of XVII Corps (1939), Commander of the 243rd Infantry Regiment (1940), and, briefly, Commander of the 6th Rifle Brigade (1941) before assuming command of the 6th Panzer. He was promoted to General of Panzer Troops in 1943 and Colonel General in August 1944. He commanded II Corps (1943), XLVII Panzer Corps (1943), 4th Army (as acting CG) (late 1943-May 1944), 1st Panzer Army (1944), and 3rd Panzer Army in eastern Germany (1945). He was acting commander of Army Group North Ukraine in the summer of 1944. Major General von Huenersdorff was shot in the head at Kursk on July 14, 1943, and died three days later. He was a young man, and his wife served as his nurse while he lay dying. Major General Denkert, a former Commander of the Guard at Führer Headquarters, apparently served briefly as acting commander of the 19th Panzer Division (June 1944). He was commander of the 3rd Panzer Grenadier Division in 1945. Colonel Max Sperling was acting commander of the 6th Panzer Division in August 1944. Carell 1966: 23-24, 236, 267; Carell 1971: 66, 81-83, 123, 530; Chapman: 347; Clark: 266; Harrison: 141; Hartmann: 63-64; Kennedy: 74, 133, Map 7; Manstein: 389, 499; Seaton: 327; RA: 100; OB 42: 56; OB 43: 200; OB 45: 289.

7th PANZER DIVISION

COMPOSITION (1941): 25th Panzer Regiment, 6th Panzer Grenadier Regiment, 7th Panzer Grenadier Regiment, 78th Panzer Artillery Regiment, 7th Motorcycle Battalion, 37th Panzer Reconnaissance Battalion, 42nd Anti-Tank Battalion, 58th Panzer Engineer Battalion, 83rd Panzer Signal Battalion

HOME STATION: Gera, Wkr. IX

Formed at Gera in 1938 as the 2nd Light Division, its men came from Thuringia, which was not noted for the fighting qualities of its soldiery; nevertheless, the 7th Panzer turned out to be an outstanding combat unit. It initially included the 66th Panzer Battalion and the 6th and 7th Mechanized Cavalry Regiments, as well as a reconnaissance regiment. It took part in the invasion of Poland, was converted to a panzer division in the winter of 1939-40, and placed under the command of Major General Erwin Rommel, who would become the "Desert Fox." Equipped mainly with captured and inferior Czech tanks, the 7th Panzer smashed its way through Belgium and France, repulsed the major Allied counterattack of the campaign at Arras, and cut off the escape of major French and British forces at Cherbourg. It was engaged in occupation duties in the Bordeaux region until being sent east in the spring of 1941. It crossed into Russia in June and fought in the battles of the Minsk Pocket, the Dnieper crossings, Smolensk, and Moscow. It suffered such heavy losses in the winter fighting that it was sent back to France in May 1942 to rest and refit. In November of that year it took part in the occupation of Vichy France. Sent to the southern sector of the Russian Front after the fall of Stalingrad, the 7th Panzer defended against heavy Soviet attacks aimed at Rostov in early 1943. Later it fought in the Battle of Kharkov. After being repulsed in the Kursk offensive, the 7th Panzer fought in the battles around Kiev and Zhitomir, where it was twice cited for distinguished conduct. In November, the division took heavy casualties in the Kiev withdrawal and fought in the Tarnopol area until March 1944, when it was overrun and the 1st Panzer Army encircled. The remnants of the division broke out, but not a single tank survived the operation. Down to battle group size, the 7th nevertheless fought on and opposed the Russian summer offensive of 1944 as a part of Army Group Center. Escaping disaster, it was again officially cited for distinguished conduct in August 1944 for its action in the Battle of Raseiniai in Lithuania. It was heavily engaged when the Russian winter offensive of 1944-45 hit the Vistula and was trapped in Danzig as part of Army Group North in early 1945. Evacuated by sea, but without any vehicles or tanks, the 7th Panzer took part in the Battle of Berlin in April 1945. Some of its men managed to escape to Allied lines and surrender to the Anglo-Americans. Commanders of the 2nd Light/7th Panzer included Lieutenant General Georg Stumme (1939-40), Rommel (1940-early 1941), Baron von Stroke (1942), Major General Baron Hans von Funck (1942-43), Lieutenant General Adalbert Schulz (1943), Lieutenant General Hasso Eccard von Manteuffel (1944), and Lieutenant General Dr. Karl Mauss (1944-45).

NOTES AND SOURCES: Georg Stumme was promoted to General of Panzer Troops in 1941 and led the Panzer Corps in the Balkans and Russia (1941-42). He was court-martialed and imprisoned for a security violation in 1942 but was then pardoned and made acting commander of Panzer Army Afrika in Egypt, after Erwin Rommel reported sick. Stumme died of a heart attack on October 23, 1942, while in action against an Australian attack. Erwin Rommel's brilliant career is well known. He commanded the famous Afrika Korps (1941), Panzer Group Afrika (1941-42), Panzer Army Afrika (1942-43), Army Group Afrika (1943), and Army Group B in northern Italy and then France (1943-44). He won incredible victories against overwhelming odds in Africa, and conducted a brilliant defensive campaign in Normandy in 1944. He committed suicide on October 14, 1944, after the Gestapo and Hitler discovered that he was in sympathy with the conspirators of July 20. In exchange for his suicide, the Nazis agreed to spare his family. Hitler kept his end of the bargain. Frau Rommel died in the 1970s and his only child, Manfred, was mayor of Stuttgart, West Germany, in 1983. Baron von Funck, former Military Attache' to Madrid during the Spanish Civil War (1936-39), led the 5th Panzer Regiment (1939-early 1940) and, ironically, was initially selected over Erwin Rommel to be chief German commander in North Africa but was passed over because he took a pessimistic view of the situation there and did not want the post. Funck subsequently led the 7th Panzer Division and the XLVII Panzer Corps on the Eastern and Western Fronts (1944). A General of Panzer Troops, Baron von Funck was reported killed in action in August 1944. General Schulz was killed in action on the Eastern Front in late 1943. Hasso Eccard von Manteuffel, a nephew of Baron von Stroke, briefly succeeded his uncle in divisional command (1944). He also briefly commanded a division in Tunisia (1943). Von Manteuffel was commander of the Grossdeutschland Panzer Division (1944) before being elevated directly from divisional to army command in August 1944 and led the 5th Panzer Army on the Western Front (1944-45) and the 3rd Panzer Army in the East (1945). A Prussian, von Manteuffel held the Knight's Cross with Oak Leaves, Swords, and Diamonds. He was only forty-eight years old in 1945. The young General of Panzer Troops had also commanded the 3rd Panzer Grenadier Regiment of the 3rd Panzer Division in Russia in 1941. Dr. Karl Mauss, who was also rapidly promoted, led the 25th Panzer Grenadier Regiment of the 7th Panzer Division in Russia (1943). He was a holder of the Knight's Cross with Oak Leaves and Swords. Carell 1966: 80, 334, 623; Carell 1971: 39, 66, 208, 510; Chapman: 347; Kennedy: 74 and Map 10; Manstein: 298-99; von Mellenthin 1977: 211; Plocher 1943: 335; OB 42: 57; OB 43: 201; OB 34: 289-90. For a description of von Manteuffel's career, see John S. D. Eisenhower, *The Bitter Woods*, G. P. Putnam's Sons, New York, 1969. For the story of the 7th Panzer's campaign in France, see Rommel and Desmond Young, *Rommel: The Desert Fox*, Harper and Row, Publishers, New York: 1965 (hereafter cited as "Young"). Also see Samuel W. Mitcham, Jr., *Triumphant Fox: Erwin Rommel and the Rise of the Afrika Korps*, Stein and Day Publishers, Briarcliff Manor, New York, 1984. For Rommel's career, see Young; Mitcham 1982 and 1983; and David Irving, *The Trail of the Fox*, E. P. Dutton, New York: 1977.

8th PANZER DIVISION

COMPOSITION: 10th Panzer Regiment, 8th Panzer Grenadier Regiment, 28th Panzer Grenadier Regiment, 80th Panzer Artillery Regiment, 8th Motorcycle Battalion, 59th Panzer Reconnaissance Battalion, 43rd Anti-Tank Battalion, 59th Panzer Engineer Battalion, 59th Panzer Signal Battalion

HOME STATION: Cottbus, Wkr. III

This unit was formed in 1938 as the 3rd Light Division. At the time it included the 67th Panzer Battalion, the 8th and 9th Mechanized Cavalry Regiments, and a reconnaissance regiment. It fought in Poland in 1939 and in the winter of 1939-40 was converted to a panzer division. Equipped mainly with inferior Czech tanks, the division was part of Reinhardt's XLI Motorized Corps in France and suffered heavy losses in the Battles of the Meuse Crossings. The next year it took part in the Balkans campaign, where it was lightly engaged. In June 1941 it invaded Russia as part of von Manstein's LVI Panzer Corps and was heavily engaged in the drive on Leningrad, fighting in the battles of Dvinsk, Luga, Lake Ilmen, and Novgorod. The next year it fought in the defensive battles of Army Group Center and was transferred to the southern sector after the Kursk attacks failed. That autumn it sustained heavy losses in the withdrawal from Kiev. It was more or less continuously in combat in 1944, fighting in the northern Ukraine, in southern Poland, and in Slovakia. The 8th Panzer was sent to Hungary in December and retreated to Austria in 1945. It ended the war on the southern sector of the Eastern Front. Commanders of the 8th Panzer Division included Lieutenant General Adolf Kuntzen (1939-40), Lieutenant General Erich Brandenberger (1941-43), Lieutenant General Sebastian Fichtner (1943), and Major General Gottfried Frolich (late 1943-1945).

NOTES AND SOURCES: Kuntzen later commanded LVII Panzer and LXXXI Corps (late 1941-42 and 1942-September 1944, respectively). He was promoted to General of Panzer Troops in July 1941. Brandenberger was commander of XXIX Corps in Russia (1943-44) and the 7th Army on the Western Front (October 1944-1945). He was made a General of Artillery in August, 1943. Carell 1966: 21-22; Chapman: 347-48; Kennedy: 74 and Map 7; Manstein: 182; von Mellenthin 1977: 214; Salisbury: 95; RA: 46; OB 42: 57; OB 43: 201; OB 45: 290-91.

9th PANZER DIVISION

COMPOSITION (1942): 33rd Panzer Regiment, 10th Panzer Grenadier Regiment, 11th Panzer Grenadier Regiment, 102nd Panzer Artillery Regiment, 9th Motorcycle Battalion, 9th Panzer Reconnaissance Battalion, 50th Anti-Tank Battalion, 86th Panzer Engineer Battalion, 81st Panzer Signal Battalion

HOME STATION: Vienna, Wkr. XVII

In 1938, after Germany annexed Austria, Hitler formed the 4th Light Division in Vienna. It initially included the 33rd Panzer Battalion and the 10th and 11th Mechanized Cavalry Regiments. The division took part in the invasion of Poland in 1939. That winter it was converted to an armored division and redesignated 9th Panzer. It fought in the Western campaign of

1940, in which it played a major role in knocking the Netherlands out of the war in six days. After Dunkirk it was part of Panzer Group Guderian in the pursuit operations that finished off France. It covered more ground than any other division in the Western campaign. The next year the 9th Panzer took part in the blitzkrieg through the Balkans, fighting in both Greece and Yugoslavia. As part of Army Group South, the division swept through the Ukraine and was involved in the encirclement of Kiev. It remained on the southern sector, facing the Soviet winter offensive of 1941-42 and taking part in the offensive that resulted in Stalingrad. The following year the 9th Panzer was transferred to Army Group Center, where it was engaged in the Battle of Kursk and the subsequent retreats. Returning to the southern sector, it was in heavy combat in the Dnieper battles and by January 1944 was down to a strength of thirteen tanks. Its infantry and artillery units were also very much reduced. Sent to Nimes in southern France to rebuild, it absorbed the 155th Reserve Panzer Division and engaged in training for a time. Eventually it was posted to an area on the Rhone River northwest of Marseilles, and by the time the Allies landed it had a strength of 12,768 men. The 9th was soon sent to Avignon, and in early August was rushed to the disintegrating 7th Army in Normandy, just in time to be encircled at Falaise. It broke out of the pocket, with ruinous losses, and by late August had a strength of only one infantry and one artillery battalion, with perhaps a dozen operative tanks. Remaining in the line, it took part in the Battle of Aachen and other Siegfried Line fighting, where it lost another thousand men: about two-thirds of its remaining combat strength. It was sent into Army Group B's reserve around the end of September and rehabilitated once more, receiving 11,000 replacements and 178 armored vehicles, at least 22 of which were late-model PzKw VI "Tiger" tanks. Soon it was back at the front, fighting in the Geilenkirchen-Aachen sector. It launched a spoiling attack against U.S. Forces in the Peel Marshes in November, before going into OKW Reserve. In December the 9th Panzer played a prominent role in the Battle of the Bulge but suffered heavy losses when Hitler refused to allow a timely retreat. Despite repeated heavy casualties, the division's morale never flagged. It distinguished itself once more in the Eifel fighting of early 1945 and again in the Battle of the Erft River in February, when it was down to a strength of twenty-nine tanks and sixteen assault guns. Still, in late February, it launched a spirited but unsuccessful counterattack against the U.S. bridgehead on the Rhine at Remagen. By this time it had only six hundred men and fifteen tanks left. On March 5, 1945, the 9th Panzer was attacked by strong Allied forces and finally collapsed; its commander, Major General Baron Harald Gustav von Elverfeldt, was killed in action. The remnants of the once-proud division were forced into the Ruhr Pocket, where they surrendered in April. The last commander of the division probably was Colonel Dingler, its senior regimental commander. Previous commanders included Lieutenant General Walter Raschick (1936-37), Lieutenant General Dr. Alfred Ritter von Hubicki (1938-41), Lieutenant General Bruno von Frankewitz (1942-43), Major General Erwin Jolasse (late 1943-August, 1944), Lieutenant General Walter Scheller (1944), and Baron von Elverfeldt (1944-45).

NOTES AND SOURCES: General Raschick later directed the Eifel Frontier Command (1938-39) and Wehrkreis X, headquartered at Hamburg (1942-44). He retired as a General of Infantry in May 1944. Dr. Hubicki, an Austrian, led the LXXXIX Corps in France (1942-43) before becoming Chief of the German Military Mission to Slovakia in 1944. He became a General of Panzer Troops in 1942. Bruno von Frankewitz later commanded the 215th Infantry Division on the northern sector of the Eastern Front (1943-45). Baron von Elverfeldt was previously Ia of the XV Corps (1939), Chief of Staff of the 9th Army in Russia (1942), and an instructor at the War Academy in Berlin (1944). Blumenson 1960: 422, 501; Carell 1966: 125; Carell 1971: 26-34; Chant, Volume 14: 1855; Volume 16: 2133; Chapman: 347-48; Harrison: 240, 244, Map VI; Kennedy: 74, Map 7; MacDonald 1963; 69, 74, 95, 242-44, 567; MacDonald 1973: 34, 163, 191, 221, 370; Manstein: 52; von Mellenthin 1977: 155; OB 42: 57-58; OB 43: 202; OB 45: 291; Ziemke 1966: 241.

10th PANZER DIVISION

COMPOSITION (1942): 7th Panzer Regiment, 69th Panzer Grenadier Regiment, 86th Panzer Grenadier Regiment, 90th Panzer Artillery Regiment, 10th Motorcycle Battalion, 90th Panzer Reconnaissance Battalion, 90th Anti-Tank Battalion, 90th Panzer Engineer Battalion, 90th Signal Battalion

HOME STATION: Stuttgart, Wkr. V

This division was formed in the summer of 1939 as a composite unit, made up of a number of previously established active duty formations from throughout Germany. Some of these were transferred from the 20th and 29th Motorized Infantry Divisions. The 10th Panzer began forming in Prague but was thrown into the Polish campaign of 1939 before this process was completed, and for that reason it was in reserve during much of the operations. That winter it completed its organization and was designated 10th Panzer. The division played a vital role in the French campaign. As part of Guderian's XIX Motorized Corps it broke through the French lines at Sedan and penetrated all the way to the English Channel. After being involved in the mopping-up operations in the West, the 10th Panzer was sent to Russia in June 1941 and fought in the battles of the Minsk

Pocket and Smolensk. It was heavily engaged against the Russian winter offensive of 1941-42 and held Rzhev against repeated attacks. The division suffered such heavy losses that it was sent to the Amiens area of France in May 1942 to rest and rebuild. Still there when the Allies landed in North Africa, the division took part in the occupation of Vichy France in November 1942 and was then rushed to Tunisia as fast as transport became available. Elements of the division were primarily responsible for Eisenhower's failure to take Tunis in 1942; however, when the Axis front collapsed in May 1943, the division was trapped. Its commanders included Major General Ferdinand Schaal (1939-41), Lieutenant General Wolfgang Fischer (1941-43), and Lieutenant General Baron Friedrich von Broich (1943).

NOTES AND SOURCES: Schaal was named commander of the Afrika Korps in September 1941; however, he had been in Libya less than a month before he fell ill and had to be returned to Europe. Promoted to General of Panzer Troops effective October 1, 1941, Schaal was commander of the LVI Panzer Corps in Russia (late 1941-42) and later was Military Plenipotentiary and Commander of Wehrkreis Böhmen and Mähren (1943-44). He was in charge of maintenance on the Western Front in 1944 and 1945. Wolfgang Fischer distinguished himself in Tunisia before being killed in action in February 1943, when his command car hit a mine. Baron von Broich, former commander of the 24th Motorized Infantry Brigade (1941-42), was captured when Tunisia fell in May 1943. Benoist-Mechin: 68; Carell 1966: 80; Chant, Volume 16: 2232; Chapman: 347-48; Kennedy: 74 and Map 7; Manstein: 34, 488; OB 42: 58; OB 45: 292. Also see W.G.F. Jackson, *The Battle for North Africa*, 1940-43, Mason Charter, New York: 1975, for a more detailed description of the 10th Panzer's campaign in Tunisia.

11th PANZER DIVISION

COMPOSITION (1943): 15th Panzer Regiment, 110th Panzer Grenadier Regiment, 111th Panzer Grenadier Regiment, 119th Panzer Artillery Regiment, 61st Motorcycle Battalion, 231st Panzer Reconnaissance Battalion, 231st Anti-Tank Battalion, 231st Panzer Engineer Battalion, 341st Panzer Signal Battalion

HOME STATION: Görlitz, Wkr. VIII

The 11th Panzer—a Silesian unit—was formed from the 11th Motorized Infantry Brigade (which had fought in France) and the 15th Panzer Regiment of the 5th Panzer Division. It first saw action in the Balkans in April

1941 and captured Belgrade. It crossed into Russia with Army Group South, fought at Kiev, and was sent to Army Group Center for the Battle of Moscow. In the drive on Stalingrad, it was not encircled, although it did suffer heavy losses from the Soviet winter offensive of 1942-43, in the Stalingrad relief effort, and in the subsequent retreats. The 11th Panzer played a major role in halting the Russians east of Rostov and thus kept the escape route of Army Group A opened. The division fought at Kursk and suffered heavy losses at Krivog Rog in the fall of 1943. It was surrounded, along with several other divisions, at Cherkassy in February 1944. It broke out, but with such appalling loses in life and equipment that it had to be almost completely rebuilt. It absorbed the remnants of the 416th Grenadier Regiment of the 123rd Infantry Division (which had also been smashed on the Eastern Front) and was sent to the Libourne area of southern France, where it absorbed the personnel of the 273rd Reserve Panzer Division. The 11th Panzer remained in the West and was stationed at Toulouse for a time. In July 1944, it conducted delaying operations up the Rhone Valley against the Allied forces that had landed in southern France. It fought in Alsace, took part in the defense of the Belfort Gap, and in the subsequent withdrawal to the Saar, before being sent to the Ardennes in December 1944. By the time the Battle of the Bulge began, the division had only thirty-five hundred men left, and only eight hundred of these were infantry. After the failure of this, Hitler's last offensive in the West, the 11th Panzer Division was reinforced and sent into the Battle of the Saar-Moselle Triangle and again suffered serious losses. The following month it tried to overrun the U.S. Bridgehead at Remagen but was down to a strength of four thousand men, twenty-five tanks, and eighteen pieces of artillery, and was repulsed; nevertheless, it was one of the strongest panzer divisions left on the Western Front. Kesselring ordered it transferred to Army Group G on the southern sector of the front in March, so it escaped encirclement in the Ruhr Pocket and fought until the end of the war. The remnants of this veteran combat division, which had distinguished itself in a dozen battles, surrendered to the U.S. 3rd Army on May 4, 1945. Commanders of the 11th Panzer included Lieutenant Generals Ludwig Crüwell (1941), Gunther Angern (1941-42), Hermann Balck (1942), Helmuth von der Chevallerie (1943), and Wend von Wietersheim (1943-45).

NOTES AND SOURCES: Ludwig Crüwell, an excellent tactical commander, had previously led the 2nd Motorized Infantry Division (1939-40), and did a fine job in the French campaign. Later he was promoted to General of Panzer Troops, and led the Afrika Korps in a brilliant manner during Operation Crusader. Had Rommel listened to his advice, it is unlikely the British would have managed to break the Siege of Tobruk in December 1941. Rommel named him Deputy Commander of Panzer Army Afrika in early 1942. He was captured when the British shot down his airplane over the Gazala Line in May 1942. He did not see Germany again until 1948. General Angern later commanded the 16th Panzer Division in Russia (1942). Hermann Balck distinguished himself as commander of the 1st Panzer Grenadier Regiment in France in 1940 and later as commander of the XLVIII Panzer Corps on the southern sector of the Russian Front (late 1942-1944). He was awarded the Knight's Cross with Oak Leaves, Swords and Diamonds and was promoted to General of Panzer Troops. Briefly he commanded both the XLVIII and XL Panzer Corps and in August 1944 was commander of the 4th Panzer Army. Sent to the West, he served as Commander-in-Chief of Army Group G (October-December 1944), and ended the war as commander of the 6th Army on the Eastern Front. Helmuth von der Chevallerie, former Chief of Staff of the I Corps, later commanded the 273rd Reserve Panzer Division (1943-44). Ironically, his old command absorbed his new one. Wend von Wietersheim, a veteran panzer grenadier regimental commander, held the Knight's Cross with Oak Leaves and Swords. Blumenson 1960: 535; Carell 1966: 118, 330, 649; Carell 1971: 47, 123; Clark: 261; Cole 1950: 217, 237, 450, 527; Harrison: 244, Map VI; Hartmann: 64; MacDonald 1973: 118, 126, 142, 221, 345, 467; Manstein: 389, 526; von Mellenthin 1977: 183; OB 42: 58; OB 43: 202; OB 45: 292.

12th PANZER DIVISION

COMPOSITION: 29th Panzer Regiment, 5th Panzer Grenadier Regiment, 25th Panzer Grenadier Regiment, 2nd Panzer Artillery Regiment, 22nd Motorcycle Battalion, 2nd Panzer Reconnaissance Battalion, 2nd Anti-Tank Battalion, 32nd Panzer Engineer Battalion, 2nd Panzer Signal Battalion

HOME STATION: Stettin, Wkr. II

The 2nd Infantry Division—the forerunner of the 12th Panzer—was created at Stettin in the Reichsheer organization of 1921. Its personnel were Prussians. In 1934-35 it was reorganized to include the 5th, 25th, and 92nd Infantry Regiments, and in 1936-37 it was again reformed, this time as a motorized infantry division. In the summer of 1939 its 92nd Motorized Infantry Regiment was attached to the 60th Motorized Infantry Division, a separation that was made permanent in 1940. Meanwhile, the 2nd Motorized fought in northern Poland and in France, where it was part of Wietersheim's XIV Corps. In the fall of 1940 it was reorganized as a panzer division. The following year it fought in Russia, taking part in the Minsk encirclement, the crossing of the Dnieper, and the Battle of Smolensk, as well as the Battle of Mga on the northern sector. Hit hard by the Soviet winter offensive of 1941-42, it was withdrawn to Estonia to rest and refit. Soon back in action, the 12th Panzer took part in the battles south of Leningrad in 1942, before being sent to the central sector of the front. It fought at Kursk in July 1943 and later in the battles of the middle Dnieper and Dneister. Transferred back to Army Group North in January 1944, it arrived too late to prevent the Soviets from breaking the Siege of Leningrad, but it did distinguish itself in the retreat across the Baltic States. That summer it tried to prevent the encirclement of the 4th and 9th armies, but it failed and was driven into the Courland Pocket in September. Early in 1945 it was withdrawn to northern Germany by sea and ended the war at battle group strength, fighting in East Prussia. Commanders of the 2nd Infantry/11th Panzer Division included Lieutenant General Fedor von Bock (1931-34), Lieutenant General Bader (1939), Lieutenant General Ludwig Crüwell (1940), Lieutenant General Josef Harpe (1940-42), Lieutenant General Walter Wessel (1942-43), and Major General Baron Erpo von Bodenhausen (1943-45).

NOTES AND SOURCES: Fedor von Bock was looked upon as one of Hitler's top generals in the first half of the war. He had won the *Pour le Merite* in the First World War. He was Chief of Staff of Wehrkreis III (1920-23), commander of the 1st Cavalry Division (1928-29?) and the 1st Infantry Division (1930) before being named leader of the 2nd Infantry in 1931. He was simultaneously commander of Wehrkreis II (1931-34). Bock commanded Army Group 3 at Dresden (1935-38), Army Group 1 in Berlin (1939), Army Group North in the Polish campaign (1939), Army Group B in France and the Low Countries (1940), and Army Group Center on the Russian Front in 1941, until Hitler relieved him of his command on December 19, 1941, for his failure to capture Moscow and his persistent desire to retreat. He was recalled to high command on January 19, 1942, following the death of Field Marshal von Reichenau. A Field Marshal since July 19, 1940, von Bock was again sacked by Hitler on July 15, 1942, and saw no further active service. He was killed in an air raid near Kiel on May 2, 1945—two days after Hitler himself had committed suicide. For Crüwell's career, see notes for the 11th Panzer Division. He was 64. Josef Harpe previously led the 3rd Panzer Regiment (1935) and was Chief of Staff of the 1st Panzer Brigade. Later he commanded this unit (1939-40). Later he led XLI Panzer Corps (1942-43), 9th Army (late 1943-44), 4th Panzer Army (1944), Army Group North Ukraine (June-August 1944), and Army Group A (from September 1944). He was relieved of command on January 17, 1945. Baron von Bodenhausen was cited for his distinguished leadership in 1944. Carell 1966: 26, 69, 80; Carell 1971: 591-94; Kennedy: 10B, 74, Map 7; Manstein: 131-32, 538; Salisbury, 275; OB 42: 58-59; OB 43: 208; OB 45: 293-94; Ziemke 1966: 258.

13th PANZER DIVISION

COMPOSITION (1943): 4th Panzer Regiment, 66th Panzer Grenadier Regiment, 93rd Panzer Grenadier Regiment, 13th Panzer Artillery Regiment, 43rd Motorcycle Battalion, 13th Panzer Reconnaissance Battalion, 13th Anti-Tank Battalion, 13th Panzer Engineer Battalion, 13th Panzer Signal Battalion

HOME STATION: Magdeburg, Wkr. XI

The 13th Panzer was initially formed as the 13th Infantry Division in 1935-36 and included the 33rd, 66th, and 93rd Infantry Regiments. In the winter of 1936-37 it was converted to a motorized infantry unit and in the summer of 1939 gave up the 33rd Infantry Regiment to the 4th Panzer Division. The 13th Motorized Infantry—now a two-regiment unit—took part in the conquests of Poland and France, distinguished itself in both campaigns, and was converted into a panzer division in the autumn of 1940. It spent the winter of 1940-41 in Rumania and crossed into Russia with Army Group South in 1941. The division was very heavily engaged, almost from the beginning. It fought in the drive on and encirclement of Kiev, in the Battle of the Chernigovka Pocket, and in the capture of Rostov. By November 1941, its divisional commander and two of its regimental commanders were suffering from nervous exhaustion. After helping halt the Soviet winter offensive of 1941-42, the 13th Panzer took part in von Kleist's drive on the Caucasus oilfields in 1942. Most of the division escaped isolation in the Kuban before the Russians retook Rostov, although part of it was cut off and had to be evacuated later via the Crimea. Reunited under the command of the resurrected 6th Army, the 13th Panzer fought in the lower Dnieper battles and suffered heavy losses when the Rumanians defected in September 1944. The division had only forty tanks left when the battle began and lost almost all of them. Withdrawn to reform in October, the 13th was back in action on the southern sector of the Eastern Front in November; large parts of the division were encircled at Budapest in December, but the remnants fought on in Austria and were still resisting the Russians when the war ended. Commanders of the 13th Panzer Division included Lieutenant General Otto (1939), Lieutenant General Traugott Herr (1942-43), Major General Hauser (1943), Major General Hans Mikosch (1943-44), and Major General Schmidhuber (1945).

NOTES AND SOURCES: Traugott Herr, former commander of the 13th Motorized Infantry Brigade (1940-41), later commanded the LXXVI Panzer Corps in Italy (1944-45). A General of Panzer Troops from September 1943, he was acting commander of the 14th Army in Italy (December 1944). Major General Hauser was seriously wounded in late 1943. Hans Mikosch had made himself a reputation as commander of the combat engineer battalion that reduced the strategic Belgian fortress of Eben Emael in 1940. He was directing an engineer construction staff in East Prussia in 1945. Benoist-Mechin: 133; Carell 1966: 300-01, 533; Carell 1971: 153, 537; Chant, Volume 15: 2057; Chapman: 347-48; Kennedy: 74; Manstein: 398; Seaton: 197-98 (citing Franz Halder, *Kriegstagebuch*, Volume III: 319), 483, 500; RA: 172; OB 42: 59; OB 43: 201-03; OB 44: 283; OB 45: 294.

14th PANZER DIVISION

COMPOSITION (1943): 36th Panzer Grenadier Regiment, 108th Panzer Grenadier Regiment, 4th Panzer Artillery Regiment, 64th Motorcycle Battalion, 40th Panzer Reconnaissance Battalion, 4th Anti-Tank Battalion, 13th Panzer Engineer Battalion, 13th Panzer Signal Battalion

HOME STATION: Dresden, Wkr. IV

Formed at Dresden as the 4th Infantry Division in the Reichswehr organization of 1921, this division included the 52nd, 103rd, and 108th Infantry Regiments by 1935. It fought well in Poland and in the French campaign of 1940, where it followed up the decisive tank breakthrough at Sedan. In August and September of that year it was reorganized as the 14th Panzer Division, receiving the 36th Panzer Regiment from the 4th Panzer Division but giving up the 52nd Motorized Infantry Regiment to the 18th Panzer Division. The following spring it was involved in the Balkans campaign and took part in the Russian invasion later that year. The 14th Panzer fought in the drive across the Ukraine, the Battle of Kiev, the Chernigovka Pocket, and in other battles on the southern sector, where it suffered serious losses. After the Russian winter offensive of 1941-42 had been checked, the division fought in the drive across the Don and to the Volga. It was surrounded with the 6th Army in Stalingrad in November 1942 and was destroyed there in January 1943.

The 14th Panzer Division was resurrected in Brittany, France, in the summer of 1943 and returned to southern Russia in time to take part in the Battle of Kiev that autumn. In more or less continuous retreat after that, it fought in the Dnieper battles and suffered such heavy losses in the withdrawal from that river that it had to be rebuilt in the summer of 1944. That September it was sent to the northern sector of the front and was soon isolated in the Courland Pocket. After Berlin fell, the 14th Panzer (along with the 11th Infantry Division) was returned to Germany on the last available shipping before Army Group Courland capitulated, and thus it escaped Russian captivity. These two units were selected because they had been the "firefighters" of the army group when the Russians tried unsuccessfully to crush the pocket several times in the winter of 1944-45. Commanders of the 4th Infantry/14th Panzer Division included Major General Hansen (1939), Major General Friedrich Kühn (1942), Major General Heim (1942), and Lieutenant General Martin Unrein (late 1943-1945).

NOTES AND SOURCES: Hansen commanded the division in Poland, before it was converted into a panzer unit. Heim, former Chief of Staff of the 6th Army (1941-42), was named commander of the XLVIII Panzer Corps on November 1, 1942. The corps was a mechanical disaster. Ordered to prevent the encirclement of Stalingrad, most of Heim's tanks broke down almost immediately, and the corps itself barely escaped encirclement. An enraged Hitler ordered Heim arrested on November 26. He was subsequently court-martialed and imprisoned. Eventually released, Heim was commandant of Boulogne and surrendered it to the Canadians in September 1944. Carell 1966: 301, 490, 495, 564, 599; Kennedy: 10B, 74; *Kriegstagebuch des OKW,* Volume II: 1453; Manstein: 482, 487; von Mellenthin 1956; 225; Thorwald: 288; RA: 72; OB 42: 59; OB 43: 204; OB 45: 295.

15th PANZER DIVISION

COMPOSITION: 8th Panzer Regiment, 115th Panzer Grenadier Regiment, 33rd Panzer Artillery Regiment, 33rd Panzer Reconnaissance Battalion, 33rd Anti-Tank Battalion, 33rd Panzer Engineer Battalion, 33rd Panzer Signal Battalion

HOME STATION: Kaiserslautern, Wkr. XII

This unit was formed in 1935-36 as the 33rd Infantry Division of the peacetime army. It initially included the 104th, 110th, and 115th Infantry regiments. It fought in France in 1940 and was reorganized as the 15th Panzer in the fall of 1940, receiving the 8th Panzer Regiment but giving up the 110th Infantry Regiment to the 112th Infantry Division. Its horses were transferred to Wehrkreis IX and were incorporated into the 129th Infantry Division. In the spring of 1941 it was sent to Libya to form one of the two divisions of Erwin Rommel's Afrika Korps. That summer it gave up the 104th Panzer Grenadier Regiment to the 5th Light Division, which was reorganizing as the 21st Panzer Division. The 15th Panzer fought in all the campaigns on the North African Front except the first: it arrived too late to be on hand when Rommel captured Benghazi in April 1941. The division took part in the unsuccessful attacks on Tobruk in April and May

1941, helped defeat the British relief attempts aimed at Tobruk that summer (Operations *Brevity* and *Battleaxe*), and was severely mauled in heavy fighting in Operation *Crusader* (November 18-December 7, 1941). Down to a handful of tanks, it retreated into Libya. Reinforced by shipments of panzers from Europe in January 1942, the 15th Panzer fought in Rommel's Second Cyrenaican campaign and helped retake Benghazi. Later in 1942 it was involved in the battles of the Gazala Line, the capture of Tobruk, and the invasion of Egypt. It was checked and virtually destroyed in the El Alamein battles. By the time Rommel retreated in early November 1942, the 8th Panzer Regiment had lost all of its tanks and its regimental commander was dead; the 33rd Panzer Artillery Regiment had only seven guns left. The 15th Panzer retreated through Egypt, Libya, and into Tunisia. There it turned to attack again, at the Kasserine Pass. Finally checked, the division was destroyed in the final collapse in North Africa in May 1943. Its commanders included Major General von Prittwitz (1941), Major General Hans-Karl von Esebeck (1941), Major General Walter Neumann-Silkow (1941), Major General Gustav von Vaerst (1942), Colonel Eduard Crasemann (1942), and Lieutenant General Willibald Borowietz (1943).

NOTES AND SOURCES: General von Prittwitz was killed in action by an anti-tank shell near Tobruk in early May 1941. Major General von Esebeck, former commander of the 6th Motorized Infantry Brigade (6th Panzer Division) in the French campaign, was wounded by a shell splinter near Tobruk that summer. For details of his subsequent career, see Notes, 2nd Panzer Division. Major General Walter Neumann-Silkow, whose mother was Scottish, was killed in action on December 7, 1941. Major General von Vaerst was wounded in late May 1942, and did not return to action until August 25. At the Battle of Alma Halfa Ridge he was acting commander of the Afrika Korps, and his division was commanded by Colonel Eduard Crasemann, commander of the 33rd Panzer Artillery Regiment (1941-43) and later—as Major General—of the 26th Panzer Division on the Italian Front. Vaerst himself was promoted to General of Panzer Troops in March 1943 and led the 5th Panzer Army in Tunisia until it surrendered on May 12, 1943. Lieutenant General Borowietz, the former Chief Engineer Officer of Panzer Army Afrika (1942-43), lost his sanity and committed suicide while in captivity. See Carell 1960; Irving 1977; Jackson; von Mellenthin 1956; Mitcham, 1982 and 1984; and Young. Also see OB 43: 204 and OB 44b: B5.

16th PANZER DIVISION

COMPOSITION: 2nd Panzer Regiment, 64th Panzer Grenadier Regiment, 79th Panzer Grenadier Regiment, 16th Panzer Artillery Regiment, 16th Motorcycle Battalion, 16th Panzer Reconnaissance Battalion, 16th Anti-Tank Battalion, 16th Panzer Engineer Battalion, 16th Panzer Signal Battalion

HOME STATION: Munster, Wkr. VI

Formed in 1935-36 as the 16th Infantry Division, this unit was made up mainly of Westphalians, with some East Prussians interspersed. It initially included the 60th, 64th, and 79th Infantry Regiments. It was in the Saar in 1939 and thus missed the Polish campaign, but the division did well in France the following year. It was present at Sedan, supporting the German armor. That summer it was converted into a panzer division, receiving the 2nd Panzer Regiment from the 1st Panzer Division and supplying the 60th Infantry Regiment (now motorized) to the 16th Motorized Infantry Division, which was then being formed. The new panzer division was in action on the southern sector of the Russian Front from July 1941. It was almost continuously engaged, fighting in the Ukraine campaign, the Battle of Kiev, the Donets battles, against the Russian winter offensive of 1941-42, and in the drive across the Don and to the Volga. It was surrounded with 6th Army at Stalingrad and destroyed there in January 1943.

A second 16th Panzer Division was formed in the spring of 1943 and sent to the Taranto sector of Italy in June. Shifted to Salerno just before U.S. General Clark's invasion of Italy, the 16th Panzer at first absorbed the full weight of the invasion and inflicted heavy casualties on the Allied landing forces, but it lost two-thirds of its own tank strength in the heavy fighting. It continued in the line and fought delaying actions north of Naples until late 1943, when it was returned to the Eastern Front just in time to take part in the counteroffensive against Kiev. The 16th Panzer suffered heavy losses at Kiev and in the withdrawal across the northern Ukraine. It also tried unsuccessfully to relieve the pocket at Cherkassy. In the fall of 1944 the 16th Panzer was engaged west of the Vistula. It fought in the retreat through Poland and ended the war at battle group strength in the Czechoslovakian Pocket. Commanders of the division included Lieutenant General Siegfried Henrici (1941), Lieutenant General von Angern (1942), Lieutenant General Hans Hube (1942), Lieutenant General Count Gerhart von Schwerin (1943), Major General Rudolf Sieckenius (1943), Major General Back (1944), and Major General Dietrich von Muller (1944-45).

NOTES AND SOURCES: Siegfried Henrici was promoted to General of Panzer Troops on or about January 1, 1943, and led the XL Panzer Corps on the Eastern Front from the summer of 1943 until 1945. Gunther von Angern was previously commander of the 11th Panzer Division (1941-42). Hans Hube, who had lost an arm in the First World War, commanded the XIV Panzer Corps in Stalingrad until he was flown out of the pocket on Hitler's orders. He later commanded the German forces in the Sicilian campaign (1943) and the 1st Panzer Army in Russia (November 1943-1944). He was killed in an airplane crash in April 1944. Count von Schwerin-Krosigk later led the 116th Panzer Division on the Western Front (1944) and ended the war in Italy. Rudolf Sieckenius was previously commander of the 2nd Panzer Regiment of the 16th Panzer Division (1941-42). Blumenson 1969: 86; Carell 1966: 488, 586; Hartmann: 66; Manstein: 515; von Mellenthin 1956: 225; RA: 100; OB 42: 60; OB 43: 205; OB 45: 295; Ziemke 1966: 225.

17th PANZER DIVISION

COMPOSITION: 39th Panzer Regiment, 40th Panzer Grenadier Regiment, 63rd Panzer Grenadier Regiment, 27th Panzer Artillery Regiment, 17th Motorcycle Battalion, 27th Panzer Reconnaissance Battalion, 27th Anti-Tank Battalion, 27th Panzer Engineer Battalion, 27th Panzer Signal Battalion

HOME STATION: Augsburg, Wkr. VII

The 27th Infantry Division—forerunner of the 17th Panzer—was created in 1935 and 1936 and initially included the 40th, 63rd, and 91st Infantry Regiments. Its personnel were Swabians who fought extremely well in Poland and France. The division was converted to the 17th Panzer in the fall of 1940; at the same time it gave up its 91st Regiment to the 4th Mountain Division. In June 1941 it struck into Russia with Army Group Center, fighting at Brest-Litovsk, the Minsk encirclement, in the Dnieper crossings, at Smolensk, and in the Battle of Moscow. It destroyed one hundred Russian tanks in a single day—July 9, 1941—at Orsha, during the Dnieper crossing operations. Transferred to the southern sector of the front in 1942, it took part in the attempt to relieve Stalingrad but was itself encircled and had to fight its way out. By Christmas Eve 1942, the 17th was down to a strength of eight tanks and one anti-tank gun. Later it fought at Kursk (July 1943) and in the subsequent retreats from the Donets, the Dnieper bend, and the northern Ukraine. In March 1944 it was encircled with the 1st Panzer Army but again broke out. In September 1944 it was still resisting west of the Vistula. It opposed the Russian drive east of the river in the winter of 1944-45 and ended the war in the pocket east of Prague. Commanders of the 27th Infantry/17th Panzer Division included

Lieutenant General Bergmann (1939-40), Lieutenant General Jürgen von Armin (1940-41), Major General Ritter von Weber (1941), Lieutenant General Wilhelm Ritter von Thoma (1941-42), Lieutenant General Fridolin von Senger und Etterlin (late 1942-1943), Lieutenant General Licht (1943), Major General Karl-Friedrich von der Meden (spring 1943-spring 1944), Lieutenant General Hans Tröger (1944), Major General Rudolf Henrici (late 1944), and Colonel Albert Brux (1945).

NOTES AND SOURCES: Lieutenant General Bergmann commanded the 6th Infantry Division in France (1940) and was later killed on the Eastern Front. Jürgen von Armin was wounded in action on June 26, 1941, and replaced by Ritter von Weber. Armin was promoted to General of Panzer Troops on October 1, 1941, and returned to active duty on November 11 as commander of the XL Panzer Corps (1941-42). He became commander of the 5th Panzer Army in Tunisia on December 3, 1942 and—as a Colonel General—took over Army Group Afrika from Erwin Rommel on March 9, 1943. Two months later he was forced to surrender to the Allies. Ritter von Weber was wounded in the Battle of Smolensk on July 18, 1941, and died a few days later. He was replaced by von Thoma (1941-42), who had commanded the German panzer forces in the Spanish Civil War with great distinction. Thoma was wounded seventeen times in his career, which ended shortly after he was appointed commander of the Afrika Korps in October 1942. He was captured by the British at El Alamein on November 4, 1942. General von Senger, a veteran cavalry officer, formerly served with the 3rd Cavalry Regiment and the 1st Cavalry Division, about which service he later wrote a book. He was a German delegate to the Italian-French Armistice Commission (1941-42) before assuming command of the 17th Panzer in late 1942. He was briefly Wehrmacht Commander in Sicily (1943) before taking over the XIV Panzer Corps, which he led very well for the rest of the war. He was promoted to General of Panzer Troops effective January 1, 1943. Lieutenant General Licht had commanded a regiment in the 17th Panzer Division in Russia (1941). General Tröger was captured by the Russians in 1944. Major General Henrici was apparently an acting divisional commander only and he was in charge of Arko 126 in 1945. Colonel Brux became prisoner of the Soviets in January. The author was unable to determine who the last commander of the 17th Panzer Division was. Carell 1966: 42, 80, 344, 651; Carell 1971: 89, 525; Guderian: 131, 140, 144; Hartmann: 68; Kennedy: 74, Map 7; *Kriegstagebuch des OKW*, Volume I: 1146; Manstein: 134, 498-99, 515; Seaton: 330-31; RA: 116; OB 42: 60; OB 43: 205; OB 44: 285; OB 45: 296; Ziemke 1966: 225.

18th PANZER DIVISION

COMPOSITION: 18th Panzer Regiment, 52nd Panzer Grenadier Regiment, 101st Panzer Grenadier Regiment, 88th Panzer Artillery Regiment, 18th Motorcycle Battalion, 88th Panzer Reconnaissance Battalion, 88th Anti-Tank Battalion, 209th Panzer Engineer Battalion, 88th Panzer Signal Battalion

HOME STATION: Wehrkreis IV

The 18th Panzer was formed in the fall of 1940 as a result of Hitler's decision to create new armored divisions by weakening older panzer and motorized divisions. The 18th Panzer received the 52nd Motorized Infantry Regiment from the 4th Infantry Division and the 101st Motorized from the 14th Infantry Division. The new unit first saw action in Russia, crossing the Bug in underwater tanks originally designed for Operation Sea Lion (the invasion of Britain). It spent the rest of 1941 fighting in a number of battles, including the Minsk encirclement, the Dnieper crossings, Smolensk, and Moscow, all on the central sector of the Russian Front. It was also involved in the operations against Kiev in 1941 and opposed the Soviet winter offensive of 1941-42 near the Soviet capital. In the summer of 1942 it was sent to the southern sector of the Eastern Front, where it took part in the initial advances on Stalingrad, but it was soon returned to Army Group Center, with which it fought in the defensive battles of 1942-43. In autumn 1943 the 18th was fighting around Kiev, and in November it suffered such heavy losses in the counteroffensive west of Kiev that it had to be disbanded. Commanders of the 18th Panzer included Lieutenant General Streich (1941), Lieutenant General Walter Nehring (1941-42), Major General Albert Praun (1942), Lieutenant General Erwin Menny (1942-43), Major General Karl Wilhelm von Schlieben (1943), and Lieutenant General Baron Karl von Thungen-Rossback (1943).

NOTES AND SOURCES: Streich had commanded the 5th Light (subsequently 21st Panzer) Division in Libya in 1941, before being relieved of his command by Erwin Rommel. Guderian, under whom he served in Russia, also had a low opinion of him. General Nehring, a former member of Guderian's staff in France (1940), later commanded the Afrika Korps (1942), until he was seriously wounded by an Allied fighter-bomber on the night of August 31-September 1, 1942, during the advance on Alma Halfa Ridge. Returning to duty in November, he was commander of the newly formed XC Corps during the initial American drive on Tunis, whose capture he prevented. From February 1943 to April 1945 he was commander of the XXIV Panzer Corps on the Eastern Front. In the last days of the war he led the 1st Panzer Army in Czechoslovakia. He was still alive in the early 1970s, living as a retired General of Panzer Troops. Albert Praun later became a General of Signal Troops. He commanded the 129th Infantry Division (1942-43), was Chief Signal Officer of Army Group Center (1943-44), led the 277th Infantry Division (May-August 1944), and served as Chief Signal Officer of the Wehrmacht (1944-45). Erwin Menny later led the 84th Infantry Division on the Western Front until he was captured in August 1944. Karl Wilhelm von Schlieben directed the 709th Infantry Division (1943-44) and Korps von Schlieben in Normandy. He surrendered the "fortress" of Cherbourg to the Americans in late June 1944. Baron von Thungen-Rossback was in charge of Recruiting Area Berlin I in 1945. Carell 1966: 14-15, 68-69, 80, 196; Carell 1971: 26; RA: 72; OB 42: 61; OB 43: 206; OB 45: 297. For the detailed story of the Rommel-Streich feud, see Irving 1977.

19th PANZER DIVISION

COMPOSITION (1943): 27th Panzer Regiment, 73rd Panzer Grenadier Regiment, 74th Panzer Grenadier Regiment, 19th Panzer Artillery Regiment, 19th Motorcycle Battalion, 19th Panzer Reconnaissance Battalion, 19th Anti-Tank Battalion, 19th Panzer Engineer Battalion, 19th Panzer Signal Battalion

HOME STATION: Hanover, Wkr. XI

This division was formed as the 19th Infantry in the military expansion of 1935-36 and initially included the 59th, 73rd, and 74th Infantry Regiments. It fought in the Polish campaign of 1939 (where it suffered heavy losses at Bzurs in southern Poland) and in Belgium, against the British Expeditionary Force. In the fall of 1940 it was reorganized as a panzer division, adding the 27th Panzer Regiment and giving up the 59th Infantry Regiment to the 20th Panzer Division. Sent to Russia in 1941, it fought in the Bialystok and Minsk encirclements and in the Battle of Moscow. It remained on the central sector in the defensive battles of 1942 and was sent to the critical southern sector in late 1942. In January 1943 it escaped to Army Group Don after the 8th Italian Army, which it had been supporting, collapsed. The division took part in the Kursk offensive of July 1943 and suffered heavy casualties there and in the subsequent retreats. It was fighting near Kiev in December 1943 and was heavily engaged in the withdrawal through the northern Ukraine in March 1944. Rushed north after Army Group Center was crushed, the 19th and two other panzer divisions surprised and destroyed the III Soviet Tank Corps north of Warsaw and thus halted the Russian summer offensive of 1944. It was cited for this action. In autumn 1944 the 19th Panzer was resisting west of the

Vistula. Now at battle group strength, the division retreated into Czechoslovakia and ended the war in the pocket east of Prague. Its commanders included Lieutenant General Schwentes (1939), Lieutenant General Otto von Knobelsdorff (1940-42), Lieutenant General Postel (1942-43), Lieutenant General Gustav Schmidt (1944), and Major General Hans Källner (1943 and 1944-45).

NOTES AND SOURCES: Von Knobelsdorff later commanded XLVIII Panzer Corps (1943-44) and XL Panzer Corps (1944), both on the Eastern Front, and the 1st Army on the Western Front (September-December 1944). He was relieved of his command for his outspoken opposition to Hitler's plan to strip his sector of armor for the Ardennes offensive. Källner, commander of the 73rd Panzer Grenadier Regiment (1941-42) and the 19th Panzer Grenadier Brigade (73rd and 74th Panzer Grenadier Regiments and 19th Motorcycle Battalion, 19th Panzer Division) (1942-43), was only promoted to Colonel on March 1, 1942. His first tour as commander of the 19th Panzer was apparently as an acting commander only. Benoist-Mechin: 133; Carell 1966: 67, 151; Carell 1971: 39, 66; Kennedy: 74, Map 7; Manstein: 397; von Mellenthin 1977: 208; RA: 172; OB 42: 61; OB 43: 206; OB 44: 286; OB 45: 297; Ziemke 1966: 340.

20th PANZER DIVISION

COMPOSITION (1943): 21st Panzer Regiment, 59th Panzer Grenadier Regiment, 112th Panzer Grenadier Regiment, 92nd Panzer Artillery Regiment, 20th Motorcycle Battalion, 92nd Panzer Reconnaissance Battalion, 92nd Anti-Tank Battalion, 92nd Panzer Engineer Battalion, 92nd Panzer Signal Battalion

HOME STATION: Gotha, Wkr. IX

Formed in autumn 1940, when Hitler weakened the existing panzer divisions, this Hessian unit received the 59th Panzer Grenadier Regiment from the 19th Infantry Division. It first saw action on the central sector of the Eastern Front, took part in the Minsk encirclement and the Battle of Smolensk, penetrated to the western Dvina, and took Ulla on July 9. In late August it fought in the Battle of Mga and took the city, which was a major junction on the Moscow-Leningrad Railroad. Later that year it suffered heavy losses both at Vitebsk and Moscow. It remained on the central front from 1942 to 1944, taking part in the defensive battles of 1942 and the Kursk offensive. In June 1944 it was encircled by the massive Soviet offensive and had to fight its way out, with ruinous losses. Transferred to Army Group South Ukraine (a supposedly quiet sector), the 20th Panzer again suffered heavy casualties when the Rumanians defected and the front collapsed. In November 1944 the division (or what was left of it) was in East Prussia and the following month was transferred to the Hungarian sector. After fighting in Austria, the burned-out division was sent to Czechoslovakia, where it ended the war surrounded east of Prague in May 1945. Divisional commanders of the 20th Panzer included Lieutenant General Horst Stumpff (1941-42), Lieutenant General Baron Heinrich von Lüttwitz (1943), Major General Hecker (late 1943?-1944), and Lieutenant General Mortimer von Kessel (1944-45).

NOTES AND SOURCES: Baron von Lüttwitz later commanded the 2nd Panzer Division (late 1943-September 1944) and XLVII Panzer Corps (September 1944-45) on the Western Front. Here he directed the besieging forces at Bastogne (December 1944). For Hecker's story, see notes, 3rd Panzer Division. Mortimer von Kessel was formerly associated with OKH's Personnel Office. Carell 1966: 42, 78, 80; Carell 1971: 22, 24, 278, 580; OB 43: 206-07; OB 44: 286; OB 45: 298.

21st PANZER DIVISION

COMPOSITION (Africa): 5th Panzer Regiment, 104th Panzer Grenadier Regiment, 155th Panzer Artillery Regiment, 3rd Reconnaissance Battalion, 39th Anti-Tank Battalion, 200th Panzer Engineer Battalion, 200th Panzer Signal Battalion

HOME STATION: Berlin, Wkr. III

Formed as the 5th Light Division in late 1940, it received the 5th Panzer Regiment from the 3rd Panzer Division. Sent to North Africa in April-May 1941, it joined the famous Afrika Korps, took part in the drive to Egypt and fought in the unsuccessful efforts to take Tobruk. That summer it received the 104th Panzer Grenadier Regiment from the 15th Panzer Division and was redesignated 21st Panzer. It fought in the Battleaxe and Crusader campaigns (where it lost most of its tanks), the retreat from Cyrenaica in 1941 and subsequent counterattack which retook Benghazi. It then again showed its excellent fighting abilities in overrunning the Gazala Line, in the capture of Tobruk, and in the sweep into Egypt. Checked at El Alamein and Alam Halfa Ridge, it was virtually destroyed in the Second Battle of El Alamein in October and November 1942, having only twelve tanks left when the order came to retreat. Withdrawing across Libya, it did not panic and turned to help administer the U.S. Army a notable defeat at Kasserine Pass. It was finally destroyed in the fall of Tunisia in May 1943.

A second 21st Panzer Division was formed in Normandy in mid-1943. It included a number of Afrika Korps veterans but was equipped with unreliable light tanks, mostly of foreign manufacture. It was the only panzer division in France to be rated as unfit for service on the Eastern Front. The composition of the second 21st Panzer Division included the 22nd Panzer Regiment, the 125th and 192nd Panzer Grenadier Regiments, the 21st Panzer Reconnaissance Battalion, the 220th Panzer Engineer Battalion, the 200th Panzer Signal Battalion, and the 305th Army Anti-Aircraft Battalion. It was the only panzer division to counterattack the Allies on D-Day (although it struck hours later than it should have) and many of its second-rate tanks were destroyed by the British. Although its panzer regiment was smashed, its grenadiers fought doggedly in front of Caen for weeks. At battle group strength, the 21st Panzer nevertheless saved the 326th Infantry Division from being overrun by the British in late July. After the retreat through France, it was assigned to Army Group G, where it served as a "fire brigade" on the southern sector of the Western Front. In January 1945 the 21st was involved on the drive on Strasbourg, before being sent to the Eastern Front in February. It ended the war on the southern sector. Commanders of the 5th Light/21st Panzer included Lieutenant General Streich (1940-41), Major General Johannes von Ravenstein (1941), Major General Georg von Bismarck (1942), Major General von Randow (1942-43?), Major General Hans Georg Hildebrandt (early 1943), Major General Baron Kurt von Liebenstein (1943), Major General von Hülsen (1943), Lieutenant General Edgar Feuchtinger (1943-45), and Major General Marcks (1945).

NOTES AND SOURCES: Lieutenant General Streich and General Erwin Rommel had a mutual distaste for one another, which led to Rommel's relieving Streich of his command for his failure to take Tobruk in May 1941. Streich later commanded the 18th Panzer Division in Russia (1941), again without distinction. Von Ravenstein was captured by the New Zealanders on November 28, 1941, during the Crusader battles. Georg von Bismarck distinguished himself in the capture of Tobruk (June 1942). He was killed near Alma Halfa Ridge on September 1, 1942. Randow led the division at El Alamein. Hildebrandt escaped the fall of Tunisia and later commanded the 715th Infantry Division (1944). He was reportedly still serving in Italy in 1945. Baron von Liebenstein surrendered the remnants of the 21st Panzer Division to the Allies in May 1943. Feuchtinger, who helped with the Nazi Party's Nuremberg rallies prior to the start of the war, was a favorite of Adolf Hitler. He worked with the Führer's secret weapons program before assuming command of the 21st Panzer. He was a poor field commander, to judge from his performance during the Normandy campaign. Blumenson 1960: 324; Chant, Volume 17: 2277; Cole 1950: 553; Hartmann: 66-67; OB 45: 298. Also see Carell 1970 and Mitcham, 1982 and 1983.

22nd PANZER DIVISION

COMPOSITION: 204th Panzer Regiment, 129th Panzer Grenadier Regiment, 140th Panzer Grenadier Regiment, 140th Panzer Artillery Regiment, 24th Motorcycle Battalion, 140th Anti-Tank Battalion, 140th Panzer Engineer Battalion, 140th Panzer Signal Battalion

HOME STATION: Wehrkreis XII

The 22nd Panzer Division started forming in France in October 1940 but was not completely trained until autumn 1941. Sent to the Crimea on the Eastern Front in 1942, this green unit was mauled in the Battle of Parpach on March 20. Two months later, however, it broke through the Soviet 10th Army on the Kerch peninsula and sealed the fate of ten Red Army divisions. It fought at Rostov in July, and in November 1942 it attempted unsuccessfully to prevent the encirclement of the 6th Army. It was part of XLVIII Panzer Corps at this time. By December 1942, as it retreated on the Don, the 22nd Panzer had only ninety-six tanks left, and most of these were not up to standards mechanically; in fact, Field Marshal von Manstein called the division "a complete wreck." It was probably on his recommendation that the 22nd Panzer was disbanded in January 1943. Its 129th Panzer Grenadier Regiment was later incorporated into the 15th Panzer Grenadier Regiment. Major General Wilhelm von Apell (1942-43) led the division throughout its active combat career.

SOURCES: Carell 1966: 482, 486, 535, 620-21, 650; Manstein: 322, 389; OB 42: 62; OB 45: 207, 299.

23rd PANZER DIVISION

COMPOSITION: 201st Panzer Regiment, 126th Panzer Grenadier Regiment, 128th Panzer Grenadier Regiment, 128th Panzer Artillery Regiment, 128th Motorcycle Battalion, 128th Panzer Reconnaissance Battalion, 128th Panzer Engineer Battalion, 128th Panzer Signal Battalion

HOME STATION: Wehrkreis V

In October 1940, the 23rd Panzer Division began forming in France. Its training was completed in autumn 1941, and the following spring it was sent to the Russian Front. It fought in the fierce battles for Kharkov and Terek that spring and narrowly escaped encirclement near Stalingrad that November. It took part in the 4th Panzer Army's attempt to relieve the city but was unsuccessful. By January 1943, it was down to twenty tanks. Placed in the new 6th Army's reserve in the spring of 1943, the 23rd Panzer was involved in the Mius withdrawal that summer and was heavily engaged in the battles of the Dnieper Bend in autumn. In February 1944 it was cited for its conduct in the fighting west of the river, where it was encircled in March. Breaking out with heavy losses, the 23rd Panzer was at battle group strength thereafter. It fought in Poland in the fall of 1944 and was transferred to Hungary after the disaster in Rumania. It led 8th Army's counterattack on Nyiregyhaza (October 23-29, 1944) and took the town, destroying or causing the abandonment of about six hundred Soviet tanks—a major German victory for the fifth year of the war. The 23rd Panzer also took part in the counterattack west of Debrecen and was again cited for distinguished conduct in the battles around Puszta. A large part of the division was trapped in the medieval town of Szekesfehervar, when the 6th Army's front in Hungary collapsed, and was destroyed there. The remnants of the 23rd Panzer Division were still fighting in Austria when the war ended. Commanders of the division included Lieutenant General Baron Wilhelm von Boineburg-Lengsfeld (1941-42), Major General Erwin Mack (1942), Lieutenant General Nikolaus von Vormann (1943-44), Major General Kraeber (1944), and Major General Josef von Radowitz (1945).

NOTES AND SOURCES: Baron von Boineburg-Lengsfeld was relieved of his command for a security violation—the same violation that brought General of Panzer Troops Georg Stumme and his chief of staff prison terms. For details of the Baron's career, see notes, 325th Security Division. Vormann was acting commander of XLVIII Panzer Corps (late 1943-March 1944) and commander of the 9th Army (late 1944). As a colonel, Kraeber was commander of Panzer Training School I (1943). Josef von Radowitz was previously commander of the 28th Panzer Grenadier Regiment, 8th Panzer Division (1944). Carell 1966: 491, 512, 550; Chant, Volume 15: 2057; Clark: 266; Hartmann: 68; *Kriegstagebuch des OKW*, Volume III: 258; Manstein: 330; Seaton: 494; RA: 72; OB 42: 62-63; OB 45: 299.

24th PANZER DIVISION

COMPOSITION (1945): 24th Panzer Regiment, 21st Panzer Grenadier Regiment, 26th Panzer Grenadier Regiment, 89th Panzer Artillery Regiment, 24th Panzer Reconnaissance Battalion, 40th Anti-Tank Battalion, 40th Panzer Engineer Battalion, 86th Panzer Signal Battalion, 283rd Army Anti-Aircraft Battalion

HOME STATION: Frankfurt-on-the-Oder, Wkr. III

Originally this was the 1st Cavalry Division of the German Army—the only cavalry division it had when the war broke out. The division was created in 1921, in the Reichsheer reorganization following the defeat of the Second Reich in World War I. It fought in Poland as a brigade and in the Western campaign of 1940. This division also did very well in Russia in 1941, fighting at the Dnieper crossings and at Smolensk, and protecting the southern flank of Guderian's 2nd Panzer Army from Russian attacks out of the Pripet marshes. It was transferred back to eastern France in the winter of 1941 and converted to a panzer unit. The 1st Cavalry Division's colors were retired in February 1942: an event that was considered historic. Meanwhile, the 24th Panzer returned to Russia, was attached to the 6th Army for the summer offensive of 1942 and was encircled and destroyed at Stalingrad in early 1943.

A new 24th Panzer was organized in Normandy in March-April, 1943. Sent to northern Italy in August, it was transferred to the Russian Front as winter approached. It fought in the Battle of Kiev in November, where it suffered heavy casualties. In February 1944 the 24th participated in the Cherkassy relief operation, for which it was officially cited. The following month it again sustained heavy losses in the withdrawal from the lower Dnieper bend. By July 1944 the remains of the division were fighting in southern Poland. Transferred to the Hungarian sector, the 24th Panzer took part in the counterattack west of Debrecen and took heavy casualties in the unsuccessful defense of Kecskemet. Sent north again, the 24th Panzer Division ended the war fighting Russians in East Prussia. Commanders of the 1st Cavalry/24th Panzer Division included Lieutenant General Kurt Feldt (1940-41), Major General Bruno Ritter von Hauenschild (1942), Lieutenant General Arno von Lenski (late 1942-1943), Lieutenant General Reichsfreiherr (Reichsbaron) Maximillian von Edelsheim (1943-late 1944), and Major General Gustav-Adolf von Nostitz-Wallwitz (1945).

NOTES AND SOURCES: Feldt, former commander of the 1st Cavalry Brigade (1939), was later Military Commander of Southwestern France (March 1943-July 1944) and Corps Feldt (1945). Ritter von Hauenschild was later Chief Motor Transport Officer at OKH (1943-44) and Commandant of the Berlin Defense Area (early 1945). He had been promoted to Lieutenant General in early 1944. Arno von Lenski surrendered the survivors of the 24th Panzer Division to the Russians at Stalingrad on February 2, 1943, along with parts of the 389th Infantry Division. Reichsfreiherr von Edelsheim was commanding the XLVIII Panzer Corps in 1945. Von Nostitz-Wallwitz was commander of the divisional artillery regiment in 1944. Carell 1966: 83, 521, 585; Hartmann: 69-70; Kennedy: 10B, 69, Map 7; Manstein: 139, 143, 487, 525; von Mellenthin 1956: 225; Seaton: 336; OB 42: 63; OB 45: 300.

25th PANZER DIVISION

COMPOSITION: 25th Panzer Regiment, 146th Panzer Grenadier Regiment, 147th Panzer Grenadier Regiment, 91st Panzer Artillery Regiment, 8th Motorcycle Battalion, 87th Anti-Tank Battalion, 87th Panzer Engineer Battalion, 87th Panzer Signal Battalion

HOME STATION: Wehrkreis VI

The 25th Panzer was formed in Norway in early 1942 for a possible invasion of Sweden. A full panzer division was not considered necessary to accomplish this task, so the 25th Panzer was well below strength until August 1943, when it was transferred to northern France. Soon it was on its way to Russia, where it fought on the central and southern sectors for two and a half years, with only one major respite. It suffered heavy losses—largely due to inexperience—in the Kiev battles of October and November 1943 and again took heavy casualties in the withdrawal across the northern Ukraine in March 1944. Sent to Denmark to reform in April, the 25th Panzer helped defend the Vistula in Poland and was engaged in the defense of Warsaw in January 1945. It retreated across Pomerania in March, and in April 1945 it was sent to Vienna, along with the Führer Grenadier Division. The move cost Army Group Vistula half its armor on the eve of the Battle of Berlin and its armor was weak already. The 25th Panzer, for example, was a mere battle group by this time. It fought in the losing Battle of Vienna and ended the war in Austria. Its divisional commanders included Major General Tröger (1942?-43), Lieutenant General Haarde (1943), Lieutenant General Adolf von Schell (1943-44), and Major General Paul Schurmann (1944-45?).

NOTES AND SOURCES: Lieutenant General von Schell previously served as Commissioner of Transportation under the Four-Year Plan (1938-42) and as Inspector of Army Motorization (1940-43). Chant, Volume 17: 2277; Hartmann: 70-71; Manstein: 488; von Mellenthin 1977: 207-08; RA: 100; OB 43: 208; OB 45: 301; Ziemke 1966: 469.

26th PANZER DIVISION

COMPOSITION (1943): 202nd Panzer Regiment, 9th Panzer Grenadier Regiment, 67th Panzer Grenadier Regiment, 23rd Panzer Artillery Regiment, 23rd Motorcycle Battalion, 23rd Anti-Tank Battalion, 23rd Panzer Engineer Battalion, 23rd Panzer Signal Battalion

HOME STATION: Potsdam, Wkr. III

A "first-wave" unit from the Brandenburg/Berlin area, this division originally bore the title 23rd Infantry Division and was formed by the expansion of cadres of the historic 9th Infantry ("Potsdam") Regiment in 1934-35, adopting much of the tradition of the old Imperial Guards. During World War II, it lived up to its ancestor unit's reputation as a fine combat unit. The 23rd Infantry was lightly engaged in Poland, fought in France in 1940, and invaded Russia in 1941. It crossed the Dnieper with the 2nd Panzer Army on the central sector and fought at Smolensk. It took part in the Siege of Mogilev on the Dnieper from July 20-26, where it lost more than one thousand men. The 26th Panzer pushed on to the gates of Moscow, suffering heavy casualties along the way. By January 1942 it had barely one thousand infantrymen left, and its nine infantry battalions were consolidated into three because of casualties. The divisional artillery was down to one 50mm anti-tank gun and three howitzers. It was surrounded south of Fedorovka by the Soviet winter offensive of 1941-42. Relieved, the 23rd Infantry remained on the central sector until summer 1942, when it was sent to Brittany, France, to reform as the 26th Panzer Division. The new unit trained in France for about a year before being sent to Italy in July 1943. It remained on this front for the rest of the war, fighting in the Anzio counterattacks, the battles of the Gustav Line, and in the retreat up the peninsula to the Gothic Line. Meanwhile, it absorbed the 1027th Reinforced Grenadier Regiment. In November the division was cited for distinguished action between the Apennines and the Adriatic. It defended a sector of the Adriatic in early 1945 and fought its last battle south of the Po River in April. Stopped by one of Hitler's senseless orders, the 26th Panzer (and the bulk of the LXXVI Panzer Corps) were unable to retreat behind the Po River. Caught between the Po and the Apennines, it was destroyed by the Allied armies. Only a few men managed to swim across the Po and escape. The division lost all of its tanks and vehicles and virtually ceased to exist. Commanders of the 23rd Infantry/26th Panzer Division included Major General Count Erich von Brockdorff-Ahlefeld (1939-40), Major General Hellmich (1941), Major General Baron Smilo von Lüttwitz (1943-44), and Major General Eduard Crasemann (1945).

NOTES AND SOURCES: Count von Brockdorff was promoted to Lieutenant General and later to General of Infantry. He commanded II Corps from 1940 to 1942, and conducted a classic defense in the Demyansk Pocket on the northern sector of the Russian Front during the winter of 1941-42. He was in poor health in early 1942 and had to be relieved. The author has been able to find no record of his death, but he held no commands after 1942. Baron von Lüttwitz was promoted to General of Panzer Troops and briefly commanded the 9th Army on the Eastern Front before being relieved of his command by Field Marshal Schorner on January 17, 1945, apparently for his failure to hold Warsaw. Eduard Crasemann was commander of the 33rd Panzer Artillery Regiment, 15th Panzer Division in

North Africa (1941-43). He was acting commander of the 15th Panzer Division at Alma Halfa Ridge (September 1942). In 1944 he directed an artillery command (an Arko) in Finland. Blumenson 1969: 289, 419; Carell 1966: 80, 85-86, 181, 184; Fisher: 19, 82, 302, 498; Garland and Smyth: 75; Kennedy: 74; RA: 46; OB 43: 208; OB 45: 147, 301. Also see Seaton: 232.

27th PANZER DIVISION

COMPOSITION: (?) Panzer Regiment, 140th Panzer Grenadier Regiment, 127th Panzer Artillery Regiment, 127th Anti-Tank Battalion, 127th Panzer Engineer Battalion, 127th Panzer Signal Battalion

HOME STATION: See below

The 27th Panzer Division was apparently formed in two echelons—part of the divisional base (including the artillery regiment) was formed in France in the summer and autumn of 1942 and then was sent to Voronezh, Russia, in the rear area of the 2nd Army. Here it was joined by Brigade Michalik—which mainly consisted of the 140th Panzer Grenadier Regiment (formerly of the 22nd Panzer Division)—to form the 27th Panzer Division. The 127th Panzer Engineer Battalion was trapped and destroyed at Stalingrad and never joined the rest of the unit. The new division fought on the Don and in the retreat from Stalingrad, and apparently was broken up over the whole southern sector; parts, for example, were attached to the Italian 8th Army. In any event the division was disbanded after the Soviet winter offensive of 1942-43 had been stopped. Most of its equipment and survivors were evidently absorbed by the 7th Panzer Division.

SOURCES: *Kriegstagebuch des OKW*, Volume II: 1387, 1394; OB 43: 209; OB 45: 302.

116th PANZER (formerly 16th PANZER GRENADIER) DIVISION

COMPOSITION (1943): 116th Panzer Battalion, 60th Panzer Grenadier Regiment, 156th Panzer Grenadier Regiment, 146th Motorized Artillery Regiment, 59th Motorcycle Battalion, 116th (formerly 341st) Panzer Reconnaissance Battalion, 146th Anti-Tank Battalion, 146th Motorized Engineer Battalion, 228th Motorized Signal Battalion

HOME STATION: Rheine, Wkr. VI

The 16th Motorized (later Panzer Grenadier) Division was created in the late summer of 1940, when the 16th Infantry Division was divided. It received the 60th Infantry Regiment from the 16th Infantry and its other units from the VI Military District. It fought in the Balkans and the Ukraine in 1941, helping to break the Stalin Line in June. The division remained on the southern sector in 1942, fighting in the Caucasus before being shifted north to cover the large gap between the 1st and 4th Panzer armies in the vast wilderness south of Stalingrad. The recon battalion penetrated to within twenty miles of Astrakhan, the furthest eastward advance of any German unit during the entire war. The 16th Panzer Grenadier fought against the Russians in the winter of 1942-43, before being transferred to the newly reconstituted 6th Army in the spring of 1943. It did not take part in the Battle of Kursk but did fight in the retreat to the Mius, suffering heavy casualties in the fighting around Zaporozhe. The following spring it bore very heavy losses in the withdrawal from the lower Dnieper, and the remnants of the 16th Panzer Grenadier Division were then transported to France, where they were merged with the much larger 179th Reserve Panzer Division to form the 116th Panzer Division.

The new division was on the north bank of the Seine on D-Day but was not committed to action until late July. It fought in the counterattack at Mortain in August but was unable to halt the American breakout later that month. The 116th was encircled at Falaise and broke out with heavy losses. The Greyhound Division—as the 116th Panzer was nicknamed—was down to six hundred men, twelve tanks, and no artillery by August 21, 1944. In mid-September it was in action at Aachen when its divisional commander, Lieutenant General Count Gerhard von Schwerin-Krosigk, was relieved of his command by Hitler for ordering an unauthorized retreat from the city. Hitler's decision led to bloody street fighting in Aachen, but seems to have been the tactically correct one this time, for it significantly delayed the American advance into western Germany. Meanwhile, the 116th Panzer was withdrawn to the Düsseldorf area to reform in September and October 1944 and was reinforced to a strength of 11,500 men, but still had a total of only forty-one tanks. The division was sent to Cologne in November. It spearheaded the southern prong of Hitler's Ardennes offensive in December 1944 and suffered heavy casualties. Withdrawn to Kleve in January 1945, the 116th Panzer was in action in the Netherlands in February, trying unsuccessfully to halt the British and Canadian advance on Germany. Shifted south in the spring, it was encircled and destroyed in the Battle of the Ruhr Pocket. Commanders of the 16th Infantry/16th Motorized/116th Panzer Division included Major General von Hoenitke (1939), Lieutenant General Henrici (1941-42), Count von Schwerin (January 1943-1944), Colonel Heinrich Voigtsberger (September 1944), and Major General Siegfried von Waldenburg (1944-45).

NOTES AND SOURCES: Count von Schwerin, a veteran of the Afrika Korps

(1941), held the Knight's Cross with Oak **Leaves and S**words. Colonel Voigtsberger was an acting commander only. **In 1945 he w**as back in his regular slot: commander of the 60th Panzer Grenadier Regiment. Major General von Waldenburg had previously served as Military Attaché to Rome (1943) and then on the staff of LXXX Corps, apparently as Ia (late 1943). Blumenson 1960: 296, 505, 539-49, 577, 579; Carell 1966: 119, 521, 550-56; Carell 1971: 134; Chant, Volume 14: 1859-61; Volume 16: 2133; Cole 1965: 195; Harrison: Map VI; Hartmann: 71-72; Kennedy: 74, Map 7; MacDonald 1963: 82, 282, 284; MacDonald 1973: 140, 357, 370; Speidel: 42; RA: 100; OB 42: 64; OB 43: 191-92, 205; OB 45: 302.

(130th) PANZER LEHR DIVISION

COMPOSITION: 130th Panzer Regiment, 901st Panzer Grenadier Regiment, 902nd Panzer Grenadier Regiment, 130th Panzer Artillery Regiment, 130th Panzer Reconnaissance Battalion, 130th Anti-Tank Battalion, 130th Panzer Engineer Battalion, 130th Panzer Signal Battalion, 311th Army Anti-Aircraft Battalion

HOME STATION: Wehrkreis III

The Panzer Lehr was formed from the Demonstration (Lehr) units of panzer training schools at Potsdam and in the Bergen Maneuver Area in Wehrkreis XI. It was especially designed to repel the Western Allies' invasion of 1944. Sent to eastern France in early 1944, it was transferred to Budapest, Hungary, where it incorporated the 901st Infantry Lehr Regiment into its organization. This regiment had been operating as an independent unit in the Balkans. The new division was camped in the Orleans, France, area in May 1944 and in the LeMans area in early June. When the Allied invasion came, the Panzer Lehr Division was one of the strongest divisions in the German Army, with one hundred nine tanks, forty assault guns, and six hundred and twelve half-tracked vehicles—double the normal panzer division's component of half-tracks. The division was rushed to Normandy and thrown into the Battle of Caen, where it helped halt Montgomery's advance, but at a terrible cost. On June 25 it had only sixty-six tanks left, and by July 25 its combined tank/assault gun total stood at fifty—or 22 percent of its original two hundred and thirty. Sent to oppose the American advance from St. Lô, it was struck by sixteen hundred U.S. heavy and medium bombers on July 25. Two days later the divisional commander reported Panzer Lehr as "finally annihilated." In early August its remnants were temporarily absorbed by the 2nd SS Panzer Division, under which it fought at Falaise. In September, when it was assigned to the 1st Army as an independent formation, the division's strength was one panzer grenadier battalion, six 105mm howitzers, one engineer company, five tanks, a reconnaissance platoon and a two hundred-man special battalion formed from stragglers. It fought in the early Siegfried Line battles with LXXXI Corps, before being rebuilt by the 6th Panzer Army at Paderborn, Wehrkreis VI. It received seventy-two new tanks and hundreds of replacement soldiers, mostly of indifferent quality. It was quickly returned to the 1st Army, then fighting in the Saar sector, in November 1944 and helped prevent Army Group G from collapsing under Patton's heavy attacks. Once again sent north in December, it was committed to the Battle of the Bulge, where Panzer Lehr besieged Bastogne as part of the XLVII Panzer Corps but failed to take the town. After the defeat of the Ardennes offensive, Panzer Lehr fought in the Battle of the Maas Line in the Netherlands (March 1945) but could not prevent the British and Canadians from breaking through the position. The division attempted to eradicate the American bridgehead at Remagen in early March but failed. In this battle the Lehr had only three hundred men and fifteen tanks left. The burned-out division retreated into the Ruhr Pocket in April 1945, and at the end of this battle surrendered to the U.S. 99th Infantry Division. Lieutenant General Fritz Bayerlein commanded Panzer Lehr throughout its existence, except for the Battle of the Ruhr Pocket. Here he commanded LIII Corps, of which the remnants of Panzer Lehr were a part.

NOTES AND SOURCES: Fritz Bayerlein, an old friend of Field Marshal Erwin Rommel, served as an enlisted man in World War I. Rejoining the Army after he was unable to find civilian employment in the early days of the Weimar Republic, he secured a commission in the 1920s and joined the General Staff. He was Operations Officer (Ia) of Guderian's 2nd Panzer Group in Russia (1941), Chief of Staff of the Afrika Korps (1941-42), Chief of Staff of Panzer Army Afrika (1942), acting commander of the Afrika Korps (1942), and Chief of Staff of the 1st German-Italian Panzer Army in Tunisia (1942-43). Wounded in the last days of the war in North Africa, he was evacuated to Europe. Upon recovery, he commanded the 3rd Panzer Division in Russia (1943), before being given command of Panzer Lehr. Blumenson 1960: 273, 422; Cole 1950: 464-65, 469; Cole 1965: 37, 473; Harrison: 234, 334; Hartmann: 72-73; MacDonald 1963: Map III, 42; MacDonald 1973: 140, 221, 346, 370; OB 45: 302-03. For the story of the destruction of Panzer Lehr in the Normandy campaign, see Carell 1973.

155th RESERVE PANZER (formerly REPLACEMENT) DIVISION

COMPOSITION: 7th Reserve Panzer Battalion, 5th Reserve Panzer Grenadier Regiment, 25th Reserve Motorized Grenadier Regiment, 260th Reserve Artillery Battalion, 7th Reserve Panzer Anti-Tank Battalion, 5th Reserve Panzer Reconnaissance Battalion, 19th Reserve Panzer Engineer Battalion

HOME STATION: Ulm, Wkr. V

This division was activated on September 1, 1939, as Replacement Division Staff 155 (Motorized). In November it was transferred to Prague but returned to Wehrkreis V in September 1940. In late 1943 it was redesignated a reserve panzer division and sent to Remnes in northwestern France with the motorized and panzer training units of the V Military District. By March 1944 the division had only sixty tanks (PzKw III's and IV's). Admiral Ruge, Rommel's naval advisor, noted that the loss of trained personnel, which the 155th supplied to other armored units, had severely retarded the division's combat readiness. In May 1944 the 155th Reserve Panzer was absorbed by the 9th Panzer Division. Its last commander was Lieutenant General Max Fremerey (late 1943-44).

NOTES AND SOURCES: Max Fremerey, a cavalry officer, had previously commanded the 29th Motorized Infantry Division on the Russian Front (1942). He later commanded the 233rd Reserve Panzer Division in Jutland (1945). Ruge: 96; RA: 6, 88; OB 43: 148; OB 45: 184.

PANZER REPLACEMENT DIVISION STAFF 178

COMPOSITION (1945): 85th Panzer Grenadier Replacement Training Regiment, 128th Motorized Replacement Training Regiment

HOME STATION: Liegnitz, Wkr. VIII

Created in 1939 as Motorized Replacement Division Staff 178, it was used to control motorized training and replacement units in Silesia. It never left VIII Military District. In autumn 1942 it retained both its training and replacement functions, despite the fact that almost all of the other replacement divisions in the Home Army gave up their training formations. The 178th was redesignated a panzer replacement division staff in the summer of 1943, and was destroyed when the Soviets overran Silesia in 1945. Its commander in early 1945 was Lieutenant General von Loeper (1944-45).

SOURCES: RA: 132-33; OB 43: 152; OB 45: 194.

179th RESERVE PANZER DIVISION

COMPOSITION: 1st Reserve Panzer Battalion, 81st Reserve Panzer Grenadier Regiment, 29th Reserve Motorized Grenadier Regiment, 29th Reserve Panzer Artillery Battalion, 1st Reserve Panzer Reconnaissance Battalion, 1st Reserve Anti-Tank Battalion (?), 1st Reserve Panzer Engineer Battalion (?), 1st Reserve Panzer Signal Battalion (?)

HOME STATION: Weimar, Wkr. IX

This unit was originally created as Replacement Division Staff 179, to control replacement training units in the IX Military District. Formed in 1939 just after the outbreak of the war, it was reorganized as the 179th Reserve Panzer in late 1943 and sent to the Laval area of western France. By late January 1944, the division could only deploy one panzer company, one combat-ready foot battalion, and one coastal defense battalion. It lacked anti-tank weapons, communications equipment, and even transport for its artillery. In May 1944 it was combined with the 16th Panzer Grenadier Division to form the 116th Panzer Division.

SOURCES: Hartmann: 71; Ruge: 62; RA: 146; OB 43: 33; OB 45: 194.

233rd RESERVE PANZER DIVISION

COMPOSITION: 5th Reserve Panzer Battalion, 83rd Reserve Panzer Grenadier Regiment, 3rd Reserve Motorized Grenadier Regiment, 59th Reserve Artillery Battalion, 3rd Reserve Panzer Reconnaissance Battalion, 3rd Reserve Anti-Tank Battalion, 3rd Reserve Panzer Engineer Battalion, 3rd Reserve Panzer Signal Battalion (?)

HOME STATION: Frankfurt-on-the-Oder, Wkr. III

Established in 1939 after the invasion of Poland to control motorized replacement and training units in the III Military District, it was reorganized as a reserve panzer unit in late 1943 and sent to central Jutland. It remained in Denmark, headquartered at Horsens, training panzer crews and motorized troops, until the end of the war. It apparently never saw combat. Commanders of the 233rd Reserve Panzer included Lieutenant General Heinrich Wosch (early 1944), Major General Kurt Cuno (1944), and Lieutenant General Max Fremerey (1944-45).

NOTES AND SOURCES: General Cuno was commander of the 3rd Panzer Grenadier Division in Italy in October 1944. General Fremerey previously commanded the 29th Motorized Infantry Division in Russia (1942) and the 155th Reserve Panzer Division in France (1943-44). RA: 6; OB 43: 26, 161; OB 45: 211.

273rd RESERVE PANZER DIVISION

COMPOSITION: 35th Reserve Panzer Battalion, 40th Reserve Panzer Grenadier Battalion, 20th Reserve Motorized Grenadier Battalion, 41st Reserve Motorized Grenadier Battalion, 167th Reserve Artillery Battalion, 10th Reserve Anti-Tank Battalion, 46th Reserve Engineer Battalion

HOME STATION: Wehrkreis XIII

The 273rd was formed in late 1943 to control motorized and panzer training units and to train mobile troops from Wehrkreis XIII, VII, and others. It was the only German reserve division not derived from a replacement division staff. It existed only about seven months, being absorbed by the 11th Panzer Division in May 1944. Its commander was Lieutenant General Helmuth von der Chevallerie (1943-44).

NOTES AND SOURCES: General von der Chevallerie had formerly led the 11th Panzer Division (1943). Hartmann: 64; RA: 6, 118; OB 45: 223.

PANZER DIVISION "CLAUSEWITZ"

COMPOSITION: Various sources

HOME STATION: See below

This *ad hoc* division was raised mainly from boys in the Hitler Youth in 1945. In the last days of the war it attempted to rescue Berlin, which had been surrounded by the Soviets. It penetrated to within twenty miles of the Führerbunker but was unable to relieve the city. Retreating to the west, it attacked the U.S. 1st Army in an attempt to prevent the encirclement of German forces in the Harz Mountains. It raised considerable havoc in the Allied rear but was ultimately encircled and finally destroyed by the U.S. 5th Armored Division near Braunschweig in April 1945. The young men and boys of this division still believed in Hitler and Nazism and had high morale despite their hopeless situation. They added the last touch of *elan* to the Nazi war effort.

SOURCES: Chant, Volume 17: 2357-2361; Ziemke 1966: 491.

PANZER DIVISION "FELDHERRNHALLE" (2)

COMPOSITION: Various sources

HOME STATION: See below

This unit was formed in very early 1945, probably from cadres of the Panzer Grenadier Division "Feldherrnhale" (60th Panzer Grenadier Division). Very much understrength, the new division formed part of Panzer Korps "Feldherrnhalle" of the 8th Army, Army Group South, in Austria. It was still there when the war ended.

SOURCE: *Kriegstagebuch des OKW*, Volume I: 1146.

PANZER DIVISION "GROSSDEUTSCHLAND"

COMPOSITION: Grossdeutschland Panzer Regiment, Grossdeutschland Panzer Grenadier Regiment, Grossdeutschland Füsilier Regiment, Grossdeutschland Artillery Regiment, Grossdeutschland Panzer Reconnaissance Battalion, Grossdeutschland Anti-Tank Battalion, Grossdeutschland Panzer Engineer Battalion, Grossdeutschland Panzer Signal Battalion, Grossdeutschland Panzer Army Anti-Aircraft Battalion, Grossdeutschland Assault Gun Battalion

HOME STATION: Berlin, Wkr. III

This division was formed in May 1942 from the elite Infantry Regiment "Grossdeutschland," which had served in France, the Balkans, and Russia. Its soldiers were specially selected volunteers from all over Germany. Its unofficial title was, in fact, "the Bodyguard of the German People." Grossdeutschland (or "G.D.") fought exceptionally well throughout the war. At first a panzer grenadier unit, it was redesignated a panzer division in the winter of 1943-44. Initially sent to the southern sector in June 1942, it was shifted to the central sector in September and back to the south after Stalingrad was surrounded. It was heavily and continuously in combat during the Russian winter offensive of 1942-43. In March 1943 it helped retake Kharkov and Belgorod and fought at Kursk in July. Grossdeutschland was heavily engaged in the Kharkov battles of late 1943, in the Donets basin withdrawal, and in the Dnieper bend fighting (1944). After being in heavy fighting in Bessarabia in the spring of 1944, it was rushed northward after the collapse of Army Group Center. In August 1944 it was defending East Prussia, a mission it continued until the end of the war. Elements were cut off in Memel in 1945 and evacuated to Germany via sea; some of these troops ended up on the northern sector of the Western Front. Commanders of the Grossdeutschland Division included Major General Count von Schwerin (1940-41), Major General Wilhelm-Hunold von Stockhausen (1941), Lieutenant General Hermann Balck (January-May 1943), Lieutenant General Walter Hoernlein (1943), Lieutenant General Hasso-Eccard von Manteuffel (1944), and Major General Karl Lorenz (1944-45).

Three independent units that were extensions of the Grossdeutschland Division were the Führer Escort Battalion, the Führer Grenadier Battalion, and the Brandenburg Panzer Grenadier Division.

NOTES AND SOURCES: For General Balck's career, see notes, 11th Panzer Division. Walter Hoernlein, who commanded Grossdeutschland both as a regiment (1941-42) and as a division (1943), was commanding the LXXXII Corps in 1945. Von Manteuffel, who held the Knight's Cross with Oak Leaves, Swords, and Diamonds, had previously commanded the 7th Panzer Division on the Eastern Front (1943). Bypassing the corps level altogether, he was commander of the 5th Panzer Army on the Western Front (1944-45) and the 3rd Panzer Army in the East (1945). General Lorenz was the former commander of the Grossdeutschland Panzer Grenadier Regiment (1943-44). Carell 1966: 521, 542; Carell 1971: 17, 199; Chapman: 347-48; Hartmann: 52-53; von Mellenthin 1977: 206; RA: 46; OB 43: 195; OB 45: 303-04.

(1st) PARACHUTE PANZER DIVISION "HERMANN GÖRING"

COMPOSITION: Hermann Göring Panzer Regiment, 1st Hermann Göring Panzer Grenadier Regiment, 2nd Hermann Göring Panzer Grenadier Regiment, 1st Hermann Göring Panzer Artillery Regiment, 1st Hermann Göring Anti-Aircraft Regiment, 1st Hermann Göring Panzer Reconnaissance Battalion, 1st Hermann Göring Anti-Tank Battalion, 1st Hermann Göring Panzer Engineer Battalion, 1st Hermann Göring Panzer Signal Battalion

HOME STATION: Thorn [Wkr. XX]

This unit, which was actually part of the Luftwaffe, was an all-volunteer force into which foreigners and Volksdeutsche were not accepted. Its designation as a parachute division was honorary only. It was formed in occupied France as a regiment, expanded to a brigade in the summer of 1942, and was enlarged to divisional size in Belgium in January 1943. Elements of the division were hurriedly sent to Tunisia in early 1943 and were destroyed when Army Group Afrika collapsed in May. Meanwhile, the rest of the division was assembled in Italy for shipment to Africa but was committed to the defense of Sicily instead. The Hermann Göring

Division was reconstituted while in Italy and fought in all the major battles on the Italian Front until May 1944, when it was placed in OKW Reserve at Leghorn, northern Italy, en route to France. At that moment the Allies started their Gustav Line offensive against Cassino and broke out of the Anzio beachhead. The Hermann Göring rushed into the counterattack, temporarily slowing the Allied advance on Rome, and allowed a large segment of the 14th Army to escape. After the fall of Rome, the division was sent to the Russian Front and in August halted the Russian summer offensive north of Warsaw (along with the 5th SS and 19th Panzer Divisions) by destroying the Soviet III Armored Corps. The parachute-panzer division remained on the central sector of the Eastern Front during the retreat into East Prussia and remained there until the end of the war. It was nearly annihilated in the fighting for that province. Commanders of the first Hermann Göring Division included Lieutenant General Paul Conrath (1943-44) and Major General Wilhelm Schmalz (1944-45).

NOTES AND SOURCES: A second Hermann Göring Division, the 2nd Hermann Göring Parachute Panzer Grenadier Division, was created in 1945. Paul Conrath was Inspector General of Parachute Troops in 1945. Wilhelm Schmalz, who transferred from the Army to the Luftwaffe in 1944, was named commander of Panzer Corps "Hermann Göring" in East Prussia in early 1945. Blumenson 1969: Map II, 419-21; Edwards: 142; Fisher: 39, 169-71; Garland and Smyth: 51, 81; OB 45: 304-05; Ziemke 1966: 340.

PANZER DIVISION "HOLSTEIN"

COMPOSITION: Various miscellaneous units and troops

HOME STATION: Wehrkreis X

This *ad hoc* division was formed in northern Germany near the end of the war and was sent to Army Group Vistula. It had few tanks and was well below divisional strength. It opposed the Russian drive on Berlin and dissolved itself after Hitler's death.

SOURCE: *Kriegstagebuch des OKW*, Volume IV: 1898.

PANZER DIVISION "MÜNCHBERG"

COMPOSITION: 1st Münchberg Panzer Grenadier Regiment, 2nd Münchberg Panzer Grenadier Regiment, Panzer Artillery Regiment "Münchberg" (?)

HOME STATION: Wkr. IV (?)

Formed in the last weeks of the war, this unit was part of Army Group Vistula and fought in the Battle of Berlin. In the April 23-May 3, 1945, period it was involved in street fighting in the suburbs and city. A panzer unit in name only, Münchberg had only a handful of tanks and barely enough vehicles to transport its wounded; nevertheless, it fought well, largely because of the toughness and personal example of its commander, Major General Mummert, who was wounded on May 1 and disappeared in the fighting on May 3. Münchberg broke up on May 4, and its men tried to make their way to the west to surrender to the British and Americans. Only a few made good their escape, however, and most fell into Russian captivity.

SOURCES: Chant, Volume 17: 2376; Thorwald: 206-43.

PANZER DIVISION "NORWAY"

COMPOSITION: Panzer Battalion "Norway," Panzer Grenadier Regiment "Norway," plus miscellaneous motorized units

HOME STATION: Oslo, Norway

This unit was formed in Norway in late 1943 to deter Swedish adherence to the Allies. It was about regimental strength and had forty-seven PzKw III tanks that had been left behind when the 25th Panzer Division was transferred to Russia. All its tanks had unsatisfactory transmissions. The division never saw combat. Its commanders included Colonels Roth (1943) and Maetschke (1945).

SOURCES: *Kriegstagebuch des OKW*, Volume IV: 1878; Ziemke 1959; 267.

7

The Motorized and Panzer Grenadier Divisions

2nd MOTORIZED INFANTRY DIVISION
see 12th Panzer Division

3rd PANZER GRENADIER DIVISION

COMPOSITION (1944): 103rd Panzer Battalion, 8th Motorized Grenadier Regiment, 29th Motorized Grenadier Regiment, 3rd Motorized Artillery Regiment, 103rd Panzer Reconnaissance Battalion, 3rd Anti-Tank Battalion, 3rd Motorized Engineer Battalion, 3rd Motorized Signal Battalion

HOME STATION: Frankfurt-on-the Oder, Wkr. III

Originally the 3rd Infantry Division of the peacetime army, this unit was formed in Hitler's initial military expansion by the enlargement of the 8th Infantry Regiment of the old Reichswehr. It included the 8th, 29th, and 50th Infantry Regiments. The 3rd fought in northern Poland in 1939 and in France in 1940. It was reorganized in the fall of 1940, was fully motorized, and had to give up its 50th Infantry Regiment to the 111th Infantry Division. It crossed into Russia in 1941 as part of Army Group North and took part in the initial drive on Leningrad. Shifted south late in the year, it was involved in the final thrusts on Moscow and opposed the Russian winter offensive of 1941-42. The next summer it was sent to Army Group South, took part in the advance across the Don, and was encircled at Stalingrad in November. It surrendered to the Russians in February 1943.

A second 3rd Motorized (now designated Panzer Grenadier) Division was formed in southwestern France in the spring of 1943, by absorbing most of the 386th Motorized Division, a mediocre formation, into a newly formed divisional table of organization. The reborn 3rd Panzer Grenadier, however, performed well in combat. Sent to Italy in June, it opposed the Allied landings at Salerno in September, fought in the Battles of Cassino and the Bernhard Line, opposed the Allied beachhead at Anzio in January 1944, and took part in the retreat to Rome in May and June 1944. Withdrawn to Florence in late June, it was transferred to the Western Front in August and was initially engaged southeast of Paris. The 3rd Panzer Division took part in the withdrawal from France, the evacuation of Nancy, and was resisting near Metz, covering the Saar industrial area, in September 1944. Two months later it had been rebuilt to a strength of twelve thousand men, thirty-one 75mm anti-tank guns, and thirty-eight artillery pieces, making it a considerable combat force for the fifth year of the war. Sent to Aachen in November, it both suffered and inflicted severe casualties in the battle for that city. Withdrawn briefly to the interior of Germany for rest and reorganization, it was back in action in the Ardennes in December 1944 and fought in the Eifel battles of January 1945. Defending in the vicinity of Cologne in March 1945, it was trapped and destroyed in the Ruhr Pocket in April 1945. Commanders of the 3rd Motorized/Panzer Grenadier Division included Lieutenant General Fritz-Hubert Gräser (1941), Lieutenant General Curt Jahn (1941-42), Lieutenant General Helmuth Schlömer (1942-43), Lieutenant General Fritz Hubert (1943), Gräser again (1943-44), Major General Kurt Cuno (1944), and Major General Walter Denkert (1944-45).

NOTES AND SOURCES: General Gräser was promoted and named commander of the XLVIII Panzer Corps on the Eastern Front in the summer of 1944. Curt Jahn commanded the Artillery School at Jüterbog (near Berlin) in 1939-40. In 1944 he was in charge of a special purposes artillery command in Italy. While in the Stalingrad pocket, Schlömer was named commander of the remnants of the XIV Panzer Corps (early 1943). Cuno was probably a temporary commander only, holding the divisional command of the 3rd Panzer Grenadier only briefly in the fall of 1944. He had previously commanded the 233rd Reserve Panzer Division. Walter Denkert had previously served as Commander of the Guard at Führer Headquarters. Cole 1950: 60, 193; Cole 1965: 83: Fisher: Map III; Garland and Smyth: 203; Hartmann: 54; MacDonald 1963: 284, 290, 410; MacDonald 1973: 70, 190, 353, 370; RA: 46; OB 44: 263; OB 45: 305.

10th PANZER GRENADIER DIVISION

COMPOSITION (early 1943): 20th Panzer Grenadier Regiment, 41st Panzer Grenadier Regiment, 10th Motorized Artillery Regiment, 40th Motorcycle Battalion, 10th Panzer Reconnaissance Battalion, 10th Anti-Tank Battalion, 10th Motorized Engineer Battalion, 10th Motorized Signal Battalion; the 110th Panzer Battalion was added later

HOME STATION: Regensburg, Wkr. XIII

The 10th was originally formed as an infantry division by the expansion of the 20th Infantry Regiment of the old Reichswehr. Its men came from northern Bavaria and the western Sudetenland, and it initially included the 20th, 41st, and 85th Infantry Regiments. It fought in southern Poland in September 1939 and in France in 1940. That autumn the 10th was reformed as a motorized division and gave up its 85th Infantry Regiment to the 5th Mountain Division. It took part in the Balkans campaign of 1941 and invaded Russia with Army Group Center on June 22. The division fought at Smolensk, the Dnieper crossings, Kiev, Moscow, and other important battles in 1941, suffering heavy casualties in the process. After the Soviet winter offensive of 1941-42 was halted, the 10th Motorized remained on the central sector during the defensive actions of 1942 and took part in the unsuccessful Kursk offensive of July 1943. Sent to the southern sector, the 10th (now redesignated Panzer Grenadier) suffered heavy losses in the Battle of Kiev in the fall of 1943. By January 1944 it had only thirty-seven hundred men and was defending ten miles of frontage. It retreated through the Ukraine and suffered such heavy losses in the Dnestr withdrawal in August 1944 that it had to be withdrawn for rest and reorganization. Later that year it returned to the Eastern Front; now, however, it was only at battle group strength. Only the 20th Panzer Grenadier Regiment was still extant, as the 110th Panzer Battalion and 41st Panzer Grenadier Regiment had been disbanded due to casualties. The remnants of the 10th Panzer Grenadier Division surrendered to the Soviets in Czechoslovakia at the end of the war. Commanders of the 10th included Lieutenant General von Cochenhausen (1939), Major General von Loeper (1941), Lieutenant General August Schmidt (1942-late 1944), Colonel Alexander Vial (late 1944-early 1945), and Major General Kossmann (1945).

NOTES AND SOURCES: Colonel Vial was captured by the Russians in January 1945. Carell 1966: 80, 557; Hartmann: 55; Kennedy: 74; Seaton: 415, 483; RA: 204; OB 42: 64; OB 43: 191; OB 44: 264; OB 45: 306.

14th PANZER GRENADIER DIVISION

COMPOSITION: 11th Panzer Grenadier Regiment, 53rd Panzer Grenadier Regiment, 14th Motorized Artillery Regiment, 14th Panzer Reconnaissance Battalion, 14th Anti-Tank Battalion, 14th Motorized Engineer Battalion, 14th Motorized Signal Battalion

HOME STATION: Leipzig, Wkr. IV

Created as an infantry division in Hitler's enlarged peacetime army, this Saxon unit took part in the invasions of Poland and France "without winning special distinction," according to U.S. Military intelligence. Nevertheless, it was converted into a motorized infantry division in the fall of 1940, losing its third infantry regiment in the process. Sent to Russia in 1941, it was on the Eastern Front from the first day of the invasion until the fall of Berlin. It was part of Army Group Center (later North) from beginning to end. In 1941 the 14th Motorized was prominent in the Battle of Vitebsk, the battles of encirclement at Vyazma-Bryansk, and the drive on Moscow. In late October 1941 it helped establish the Kalinin bridgehead on the upper Volga, between Moscow and Leningrad. The division spent 1942 in the Rzhev sector and played a part in the withdrawal from the Rzhev salient in 1943. It was the only division in the reserve of the 4th Army when Army Group Center was smashed in July 1944; as such, it escaped total destruction but was reduced to battle group strength nevertheless. The remnants of the 14th Panzer Grenadier continued to fight on the central sector of the Eastern Front in Poland and eastern Germany until the end. It surrendered to the Soviets in East Prussia in May 1945. Lieutenant General Hermann Flörke (1943-45) was apparently the last commander of the depleted division.

NOTES AND SOURCES: Lieutenant General Friedrich Fürst, former commander of the 14th Panzer Grenadier (1942-43), became the commander of the 171st Reserve Division in mid-1943. Carell 1966: 141, 154-55; Carell 1971: 309, 570; RA: 72; OB 42: 64; OB 44: 264; OB 45: 143.

15th PANZER GRENADIER DIVISION

COMPOSITION (1944): 115th Panzer Battalion, 104th Panzer Grenadier Regiment, 115th Panzer Grenadier Regiment, 33rd Motorized Artillery Regiment, 115th Panzer Reconnaissance Battalion, 33rd Anti-Tank Battalion, 33rd Motorized Engineer Battalion, 33rd Motorized Signal Battalion

HOME STATION: Kaiserslautern, Wkr. XII

This unit was formed in Sicily from the remnants of the 15th Panzer Division, which escaped destruction in Tunisia; the temporary Division "Sizilien" (a collection of miscellaneous units); and the 129th Panzer Grenadier Regiment of the defunct 22nd Panzer Division from the Russian Front. The 129th was later absorbed by the 115th Panzer Grenadier Regiment. Although not completely trained or equipped, it fought in Sicily with some credit and was highly praised by General von Senger (commander of the XIV Panzer Corps) for its conduct at Salerno in September 1943. From October until March 1944 the 15th Panzer Grenadier fought in the Cassino area, before being placed in reserve. It took part in the retreat from Rome and the withdrawal to the Gothic Line. Sent to southern France in September 1944, it was split up and scattered in 1st Army's makeshift effort to slow the Allied advance. The next month it was finally pulled out of the line—after over a year of almost continuous action—and rebuilt under the direction of the XLVII Panzer Corps. By the first of November it had a strength of thirteen thousand men, but only seven tanks. In November it fought in the Battle of the Peel Marshes and the Siegfried Line battles around Aachen and Geilenkirchen. In December the division took part in the Siege of Bastogne. After this defeat it retreated to the Kleve area and was involved in the Battle of the Maas Line in the Netherlands in February 1945. Unable to prevent the British-Canadian breakthrough, the survivors of the 3rd Panzer Grenadier were retreating across northern Germany when the war ended. Commanders of the division included Lieutenant General Eberhard Rodt (1943-44), Major General Ernst Gunther Baade (late 1943), Karl-Theodor Simon (November 1944), Colonel Hans-Joachim Deckert (November-December 1944), and Colonel Wolfgang Maucke (December 1944-1945).

NOTES AND SOURCES: Major General Baade, who had distinguished himself in North Africa and Sicily, was apparently an acting divisional commander only, for Rodt returned to command soon after and led the 3rd until the fall of 1944. Baade later commanded the 90th Panzer Grenadier Division in Italy and was promoted to Lieutenant General. He was killed on the last day of the war. Colonel Simon was also an acting commander.

In 1945 he was back at his permanent assignment: commander of the division's 33rd Motorized Artillery Regiment. Colonel Maucke was formerly commander of the 115th Panzer Grenadier Regiment, 15th Panzer Grenadier Division (1944). Blumenson 1969: 323-24, Map II; Cole 1950: 48-49, 96, 475; Cole 1965: 473-74; Fisher: 18; Garland and Smyth: 51; MacDonald 1963: 243, 567; MacDonald 1973: 140; RA: 188; OB 45: 306-07.

16th PANZER GRENADIER DIVISION
see 116th Panzer Division

18th PANZER GRENADIER DIVISION

COMPOSITION (1944): 118th Panzer Battalion, 30th Panzer Grenadier Regiment, 51st Panzer Grenadier Regiment, 18th Motorized Artillery Regiment, 118th Panzer Reconnaissance Battalion, 118th Anti-Tank Battalion, 118th Motorized Engineer Battalion, 118th Motorized Signal Battalion

HOME STATION: Liegnitz, Wkr. VIII

This unit began its career in 1935-36 as the original 18th Infantry Division—not to be confused with the 18th Volksgrenadier Division, which was formed in 1944. It initially included the 30th, 51st, and 54th Infantry Regiments. It fought in Poland in 1939 and the Western campaign of 1940. That fall it gave up the 54th Infantry Regiment and was motorized. Committed to the Russian Front in 1941 as part of Hoth's 3rd Panzer Group, it fought in the Bialystok and Minsk encirclements, the Dnieper crossings, and the Battle of Smolensk. It was badly mauled in the Soviet winter offensive of 1941-42, losing nine thousand men and dropping to a strength of seven hundred forty-one combat effectives by December 22. Soon after it was put into reserve behind the northern sector of the front. In March 1942, however, it was back in the line and took part in the rescue of II Corps at Demyansk. Remaining on the northern sector in the defensive battles of 1942 and 1943, the 18th Panzer Grenadier fought around Demyansk and at Staraya Russa. That autumn it was sent to Army Group Center and fought in the unsuccessful defense of Smolensk that fall. In the spring of 1944 it was officially cited for distinguished action in the central Dnieper fighting. The 18th Panzer Grenadier was virtually destroyed in the Russian summer offensive of 1944. Encircled at Minsk with the XII Corps of the 4th Army, divisional commander Lieutenant General Zutavern committed suicide rather than surrender to the Russians. The tiny remnants of the burned-out division that escaped Minsk retreated to

East Prussia and fought in the Battle of Berlin in the last days of the war. Commanders of the division included Lieutenant General Erich von Manstein (1938), Major General Cranz (1939-40?), Major General Friedrich Herrlein (1941), Lieutenant General Werner von Erdmaunsdorf (1941-43), and Lieutenant General Zutavern (1944).

NOTES AND SOURCES: Von Manstein—later a Field Marshal—is considered by many to have been the foremost strategist and military commander in World War II. After commanding the 18th Infantry he was Chief of Staff of Army Group South in Poland (1939), devised the plan that subsequently led to the fall of France while serving as Chief of Staff of Army Group A (1940), and commanded XXXVIII Corps during the mopping up of French resistance in 1940. Later he commanded LVI Panzer Corps (1941), 11th Army (1941-42), Army Group Don (1942-43), and Army Group South (1943-44), all on the Russian Front. Hitler retired him in March 1944. Von Manstein's son, Lieutenant Gero von Manstein, was a member of the 18th when he was killed in action in October 1942. Major General Herrlein fell seriously ill in December 1941 and had to be replaced. Later he recovered and became Chief Intelligence Officer of the General Staff (1942-43). In 1945 he was commanding the LV Corps. Herrlein was promoted to General of Infantry in February 1944. General von Erdmaunsdorf was later given an administrative post in the Dresden area. Carell: 1966: 67, 80, 286, 373-74, 427-34; Carell 1971: 300, 597; Chant, Volume 18: 2381; Cole 1965: 143; Kennedy: 74, Map 7; Manstein: 21, 269; MacDonald 1963: 599; von Mellenthin 1977: 24; Seaton: 575; RA: 116; OB 42: 64-65; OB 43: 192; OB 45: 308.

20th PANZER GRENADIER DIVISION

COMPOSITION (1944): 120th Panzer Battalion, 76th Panzer Grenadier Regiment, 90th Panzer Grenadier Regiment, 20th Motorized Artillery Regiment, 120th Panzer Reconnaissance Battalion, 20th Anti-Tank Battalion, 20th Motorized Engineer Battalion, 20th Motorized Signal Battalion

HOME STATION: Hamburg, Wkr. X

Created in 1935-36 as the 20th Infantry Division, it initially included the 69th, 76th, and 90th Infantry Regiments. Most of its troops were recruited from the Hamburg area. In 1937-38 it was motorized and received the designation "motorized infantry division." It was earmarked for the attack on Prague in 1938 but did not see combat there because of the Munich agreement between Hitler and Chamberlain. On September 1, 1939, it experienced its first action when it struck into the Danzig corridor of Poland. It fought well in Poland and took part in the conquest of France, where it traveled great distances but saw little shooting. On the Eastern Front in 1941 it fought with Army Group Center at Smolensk, the Dnieper crossings, and at Minsk, before being sent to the northern sector, where it fought its way across the Dvina River and spearheaded the 16th Army's drive on Oreshek, on the road to Leningrad. The 20th, redesignated a panzer grenadier unit in the fall of 1942, remained on the northern sector until the spring of 1943, when it was sent to Army Group Center and fought in the defensive battle of Velikie Luki. Transferred south that autumn, the 20th suffered heavy losses in the Battle of Kiev and the subsequent retreat in November 1943. It was again mauled in the Russian summer offensive of 1944. Subsequently engaged in southern Poland, the 20th Panzer Grenadier was ordered to Berlin in March 1945. Upon receiving these orders, divisional commander Major General Scholz committed suicide. The remnants of the division defended Seelow Heights in the Third Reich's last stand and were destroyed there. Commanders of the division included Lieutenant General Mauriz Wiktorin zu Hainburg (1939-40), Lieutenant General Hans Zorn (1941-42), Lieutenant General Erich Jaschke (1942-43), Lieutenant General Fries (1944), Lieutenant General Georg Jauer (1943-44), and Scholz (1944-45).

NOTES AND SOURCES: Wiktorin zu Hainburg, an Austrian, was promoted to General of Infantry in late 1940. He later led XXVIII Corps (1941-42) and was commander of Wehrkreis XIII (May 1942-September 1944). He apparently retired at the end of that assignment (he was 61 in 1944). General of Infantry Zorn, who was promoted to that rank effective June 1, 1942, later led XL Panzer Corps (1942), XXXII Corps (1942), and XLVI Panzer Corps (1942-43). General Zorn was killed by a Russian aircraft in a rear-guard action on August 2, 1943. Erich Jaschke, a West Prussian, was also promoted to General of Infantry. He led XIII Corps (1943) and LV Corps (1943), and was later Chief Infantry Officer of the Army General Staff (1944?-45). In 1938-39 he had been Chief of Staff of the Inspectorate of Infantry. General Jauer, an artillery officer, went on to command XLVIII Panzer Corps (late 1944) and the Panzer Corps "Grossdeutschland" (late 1944-45), both on the Eastern Front. Benoist-Mechin: 290; Carell 1966: 76, 80, 265, 421; Hartmann: 55-56; Kennedy: 74, Map 7; Plocher 1943: 104; Salisbury: 308-09; OB 42: 65; OB 43: 192; OB 45: 308-09.

25th PANZER GRENADIER DIVISION

COMPOSITION: 125th Panzer Battalion, 35th Panzer Grenadier Regiment, 119th Panzer Grenadier Regiment, 25th Motorized Artillery Regiment, 25th Panzer Reconnaissance Battalion, 25th Anti-Tank Battalion, 25th Motorized Engineer Battalion, 25th Motorized Signal Battalion

HOME STATION: Ludwigsburg, Wkr. V

The 25th was formed in 1934-35 as an infantry division by the expansion of the 13th Infantry Regiment of the old Reichswehr. It initially included the 13th, 35th, and 119th Infantry Regiments. The 25th Infantry was lightly engaged in Poland in 1939 and France in 1940. That autumn it was reorganized as a motorized unit, and its 13th Regiment was transferred to the 6th Mountain Division. It was sent to the Russian Front in June 1941 and served on the central sector for the next three years. It fought in the 2nd Panzer Group's battles of encirclement at Minsk, Kiev, and Moscow. It took heavy casualties at Kursk and fought at Smolensk in the fall of 1943. In the summer of 1944 the 25th Panzer Grenadier suffered heavy losses in the encirclement east of Minsk, escaping only because it was part of Army Group Center's mobile reserve when the offensive began. Withdrawn to the Grafenwöhr Maneuver Area in Wehrkreis XIII for refitting, the division was sent to the Western Front after the German collapse in France. That fall it was engaged at Püttlingen, north of Saarbrücken. Meanwhile, it absorbed the 107th Panzer Brigade. Elements of the rebuilt division unsuccessfully opposed the United States advance on Metz in November. The 25th Panzer Grenadier was holding the Bitche sector in December 1944 during the Battle of the Bulge. After the defeat of the Ardennes offensive it was sent to the East, where it defended a sector north of Berlin during the last Russian offensive; most of its survivors, however, managed to escape to surrender to the English and Americans. The commanders of this division included Lieutenant General Christian Hansen (1939), Lieutenant General Erich Clossner (1940), Lieutenant General Siegfried Heinrici (1942), Lieutenant General Anton Grasser (1942-43), and Colonel Arnold Burmeister (1944-45).

NOTES AND SOURCES: Clossner was later commander of LIII Corps (1942-43). Christian Hansen was promoted to General of Artillery in early 1940. He commanded X Corps (1940-44) and 16th Army (February-September 1944), both on the Eastern Front. Anton Grasser, former commander of the 119th Infantry Regiment (1940), was later promoted to General of Infantry and commanded Army Detachment Narva on the northern sector of the Russian Front (late 1944). Carell 1966: 196; Chant, Volume 13: 1777; Volume 18: 2381; Cole 1950: 390, 471; OB 42: 65; OB 43: 193; OB 45: 309; Ziemke 1966: 487.

29th PANZER GRENADIER DIVISION

COMPOSITION (1944): 129th Panzer Battalion, 15th Panzer Grenadier Regiment, 71st Panzer Grenadier Regiment, 29th Motorized Artillery Regiment, 129th Panzer Reconnaissance Battalion, 29th Anti-Tank Battalion, 29th Motorized Engineer Battalion, 29th Motorized Signal Battalion

HOME STATION: Erfurt, Wkr. IX

Formed in 1934-35 by the expansion of the 15th Infantry Regiment of the old Reichswehr, it initially included the 15th, 71st, and 86th Infantry Regiments. Its personnel were mainly from Thuringia, with draftees from other parts of Germany. It became a motorized unit in 1937-38 and gave up the 86th Motorized Infantry Regiment to the 10th Panzer Division in the summer of 1939. The division fought hard in Poland and distinguished itself in the German drive to the English Channel in 1940. The "Falcon Division," as it was nicknamed, performed in an outstanding manner in all of its battles. Crossing into Russia in 1941, it fought in the Bialystok and Minsk encirclements, in the Dnieper crossings, at Smolensk, Kharkov, the Don crossings, and at Stalingrad, where it was itself surrounded in November 1942 and destroyed in late January 1943. Even as late as January 12, 1943, when it was in its death throes, the 29th, together with the 3rd Motorized Infantry Division, repulsed ten to twelve Soviet divisions and knocked out one hundred tanks, all in a single day.

A second 29th—this one a panzer grenadier division—was formed in the spring of 1943 in southwestern France. The new unit absorbed the bulk of the 345th Reserve Panzer Grenadier Division. It fought in Sicily in July 1943 and took part in all the major campaigns in Italy, including Salerno, Anzio, and the Po River campaign in 1945. On April 24 of that year it (and the rest of the LXXVI Panzer Corps) was caught by the British 8th Army between the Po and the Apennine Mountains and was destroyed. Only a few survivors of the division managed to reach the Po River and swim across it to safety. Even these were rounded up in the next few days, but the division itself ceased to exist as of April 24. Commanders of the 29th Motorized Infantry/Panzer Grenadier Division included Lieutenant General Joachim Lemelsen (1939), Major General Baron Willibald von Langermann und Erlenkamp (1940), Major General Walter von Boltenstern (1941-42), Major General Fremerey (1942), Major General Hans Georg von Leyser (1942-43), Major General Walter Fries (1943), and Major General Fritz Polack (1944?-45).

NOTES AND SOURCES: After commanding the 29th Motorized, Joachim Lemelsen led the XLVII Panzer Corps on the central sector of the Russian Front (1941). He was named acting commander of the 10th Army in Italy

(November-December 1943) and was named commander of the 14th Army in Italy after General von Mackensen was relieved of his command in June 1944. Later, in October 1944, he was again named commander of the 10th Army and on February 17, 1945, was appointed commander of the 14th Army for the second time. He was promoted to General of Panzer Troops in 1940 or early 1941. Baron von Langermann und Erlenkamp later led the 4th Panzer Division (1941) and the XXIV Panzer Corps (1942), both on the Eastern Front. He was promoted to General of Panzer Troops as of June 1, 1942. Walter von Boltenstern was promoted to Lieutenant General in August 1942. He was commanding Panzer Replacement Division Staff 179 in late 1943 and apparently was Commandant of Warsaw for a period in 1944. General Fremerey later led the 155th and 233rd Reserve Panzer Divisions (1943-44 and 1944-45, respectively). General Fries, former commander of the 15th Motorized Infantry Regiment of the 29th Motorized Infantry Division (1941-42), led the 29th Panzer Grenadier from June 1943 to August 1944. He was reportedly briefly commander of the 20th Panzer Grenadier Division. Fries held the Knight's Cross with Oak Leaves and Swords. General Leyser surrendered the remnants of the original 29th Division to the Soviets when Stalingrad fell. Benoist-Mechin: 133; Blumenson 1969: 289, 419-21; Carell 1966: 41-42, 67, 80, 512-13, 629; Chapman: 347-48; Fisher: 302, 498; Garland and Smyth: 74, 284; Kennedy: 74, Map 7; Manstein: 355-56; RA: 144; OB 42: 65; OB 43: 193; OB 45: 309-10.

36th PANZER GRENADIER (later INFANTRY and VOLKSGRENADIER) DIVISION

COMPOSITION (1942): 87th Motorized Infantry Regiment, 118th Motorized Infantry Regiment, 36th Motorized Artillery Regiment, 36th Panzer Reconnaissance Battalion, 36th Anti-Tank Battalion, 36th Motorized Engineer Battalion, 36th Motorized Signal Battalion

HOME STATION: Wiesbaden, Wkr. XII

Formed in 1935-36 as the 36th Infantry Division of the peacetime Army, the troops of this unit were mainly Bavarians from the Palatinate. Initially it included the 70th, 87th, and 118th Infantry Regiments. Remaining on the Western frontier in 1939, the 36th fought well in the French campaign of 1940. That autumn it was converted to a motorized infantry division and gave up the 70th Infantry Regiment to the 111th Infantry Division. It fought its way through the Baltic States in 1941 and was especially heavily engaged at Kalinin, where it helped establish a bridgehead on the upper Volga in late October. Later it stormed the last Leningrad fortifications on Duderhof Hill, before being halted by the order of Adolf Hitler, who thought Leningrad would fall without costly street fighting. The division also suffered heavy casualties against the Russian winter offensive of 1941-42. Transferred to Army Group Center, it fought in the defensive battles around Rzhev in the summer of 1942 and again took heavy losses. In July 1943 it fought in the bitterly contested Battle of Kursk. Reduced to battle group strength, it took part in the retreats of 1943-44 on the central sector. By October 1943 the 36th Panzer Grenadier was in remnants and under the operational control of the much-reduced 268th Infantry Division. In May 1944 it was finally reformed into a two-regiment infantry division. As such it was encircled at Berezina in June. The 36th broke out but with heavy casualties. The next month it was smashed by the massive Soviet summer offensive. Many of its men, including divisional commander Major General Conrady, were taken prisoner. The surviving remnants of the 36th were returned to Germany and reformed at the Baumholder Maneuver Area as a three-regiment Volksgrenadier division (the 165th Grenadier Regiment being added). Some of its units were still partially motorized, however, and were sent to the Western Front in September to oppose Patton's advance through France. The division was badly mauled in the battles in eastern France and Luxembourg in late 1944 but was still reckoned a good combat division. In January 1945 it took part in Himmler's abortive attempt to retake Strasbourg. The 36th Volksgrenadier fought in the retreat through the Saar and southern Germany, where it was when the war ended. Commanders of the 36th Infantry/Motorized Infantry/Panzer Grenadier/Infantry/Volksgrenadier Division included Lieutenant General Georg Lindemann (1937-40), Lieutenant General Ottenbacher (1941), Lieutenant General Hans Gollnik (1942-43), Conrady (1944), and Major General August Welln (1944-45).

NOTES AND SOURCES: Georg Lindemann, a senior cavalry officer, was promoted to Colonel General in mid-1942. He led L Corps in Russia (1941-early 1942), 18th Army in the Leningrad sector (early 1942-May 1944), and Army Group North (May-August 1944). He was relieved of his command by Hitler for refusing to launch a useless attack. In 1945 he returned to active duty as Commander-in-Chief, Denmark. General Gollnick later commanded XLVI Panzer Corps (late 1943-1944) and the fortress of Memel (November 1944). He ended the war as a corps commander on the Eastern Front. Gollink was a Pomeranian. He was promoted to General of Infantry in October 1943. Carell 1966: 154-59, 230, 267; Carell 1971: 230, 309, 578, 597; Chant, Volume 17: 2277; Cole 1950: 50, 365, 482, 526; MacDonald 1963; 64; RA: 188; OB 42: 65-66; OB 43: 194; OB 45: 151-52.

60th PANZER GRENADIER DIVISION "FELDHERRNHALLE"

COMPOSITION (1944): 160th Panzer Battalion, 120th Panzer Grenadier Regiment "Feldherrnhalle," 271st Füsilier Regiment "Feldherrnhalle," 160th Motorized Artillery Regiment, 160th Panzer Reconnaissance Battalion, 160th Anti-Tank Battalion, 160th Motorized Engineer Battalion, 160th Motorized Signal Battalion

HOME STATION: Danzig, Wkr. XX

The 60th Panzer Grenadier (originally a non-motorized infantry division) was organized from the Danzig Heimwehr (Home Army) and the S.A. (Brownshirt) Brigade Eberhardt—a German combat force smuggled into Danzig before the war. These units took part in the struggle for the Free City of Danzig, the Westerplatte, the Hela peninsula, and surrounding areas of Poland in September 1939. The new infantry division, which included the 242nd, 243rd, and 244th Infantry Divisions in 1939, was formed in September, after northern Poland had been cleared. It fought in France in 1940, after which it was reorganized as a motorized division in the fall of 1940. It dropped its previous regimental numbers and received the 12th Motorized Infantry Regiment (formerly of the 2nd Motorized Infantry Division) and the Headquarters, 120th Motorized Infantry Regiment. After helping overrun Yugoslavia, it fought on the southern zone of the Russian Front in 1941 and 1942, during the advance through the Ukraine and the Donets Basin. It fought in the Battles of Kiev, Rostov, and Kharkov, and the drive to the Volga. It was surrounded at Stalingrad with the 6th Army and was destroyed there in January 1943.

A second 60th Motorized (now referred to as Panzer Grenadier) Division was created in southern France in the summer of 1943. It was built around the 271st Infantry Regiment "Feldherrnhalle," which had previously served with the 93rd Infantry Division in Russia. The division received the honorary title "Feldherrnhalle" because it contained a high number of Brownshirt volunteers. In August 1943 it was sent to southern France during the period of vacillation of the post-Mussolini Italian government, while the Italian 4th Army evacuated the area and returned home. Ultimately the new mobile division was posted to the Greco-Turkish frontier region, and then was sent to the Eastern Front in the fall of 1943. It fought against the massive Soviet summer offensive of 1944 that annihilated Army Group Center. The division was smashed and almost trapped east of the Dnieper. Divisional commander Major General von Steinkeller was among those captured. In October it was fighting in Hungary, where much of it was surrounded and destroyed during the siege of Budapest. Remnants of the Feldherrnhalle Division, however, were still fighting on the Eastern Front when the war ended. Commanders of this veteran division included Lieutenant General Eberhardt (1939-40), Major General Arenstorff (1941), Lieutenant General Otto Kohlermann (1942 and early 1943-early 1944), Major General von Steinkeller (1944), and Major General Günther Pape (1944-45).

NOTES AND SOURCES: Arenstorff was reportedly missing in action on the Eastern Front in 1944. General Pape was only thirty-eight years old in 1945. Carell 1966: 490, 590; Carell 1971: 575-76, 597; Chant, Volume 15: 2054, 2057; Volume 17: 2376; Garland and Smyth: 294; Harrison: 148; Hartmann: 57-58; von Mellenthin 1956: 225; Seaton: 500; RA: 244; OB 42: 66; OB 43: 194; OB 45: 310-11.

90th PANZER GRENADIER (formerly LIGHT) DIVISION

COMPOSITION (1944): 190th Panzer Battalion, 200th Motorized Grenadier Regiment, 361st Motorized Grenadier Regiment, 190th Motorized Artillery Regiment, 190th Panzer Reconnaissance Battalion, 190th Anti-Tank Battalion, 190th Motorized Engineer Battalion, 190th Motorized Signal Battalion

HOME STATION: Wehrkreis III

This division was formed in Libya in late 1941 as the Afrika Division z.b.V. ("for special purposes"), but it was soon redesignated 90th Light Division. It initially included the 155th, 200th, and 361st Motorized Infantry (later Panzer Grenadier) Regiments, which were not fully motorized until the spring of 1942. The 190th Motorized Artillery Regiment, the 580th Panzer Reconnaissance Battalion, and the 900th Motorized Engineer Battalion were also part of its table of organization. The 90th Light took part in the Siege of Tobruk (1941), where it helped stabilize Italian infantry units and fought well against both the Tobruk garrison and elements of the British 8th Army, which finally succeeded in relieving Tobruk after three weeks of bitter fighting during Operation Crusader (November-December 1941). The division was involved in the retreat from Cyrenaica, the recapture of Benghazi (January 1942), the three-week Battle of the Gazala Line (May-June 1942), the storming of Tobruk (June 1942), the drive into Egypt, the Battle of Mersa Matruh (June 26-27, 1942), and the battles of El Alamein. By June 27 it had only sixteen hundred men left; nevertheless, except for a brief moment of panic in the First Battle of El Alamein, it fought extremely well throughout the Desert War and was as feared and respected as the Afrika Korps, of which it was not a part. After Panzer Army Afrika was crushed in the Second Battle of El Alamein (October 23-November 4, 1942), the 90th Light formed Rommel's rearguard and retreated through Egypt, Libya, and Tunisia, where it was finally destroyed in May 1943, when the German front in North Africa finally collapsed.

The second 90th—this one designated panzer grenadier—was formed in June 1943 from miscellaneous units in Sardinia and was briefly known as "Division Sardinia." That fall it was withdrawn to Corsica and then to northern Italy. That winter it was sent to the front and was engaged near Cassino. From then on it fought in all the major campaigns of the Italian Front, including the Anzio counterattack, the retreat from Rome, the battles of the Caesar and Gothic lines, and the Battle of the Po River. Finally burned out by almost constant combat, the 90th Panzer Grenadier was virtually destroyed near Bologna in April 1945. The commanders of the 90th Light/Panzer Grenadier included Major **General** Summermann (1941), Major General Richard Veith (1942), **Colonel** Werner Marcks (1942), Major General Ulrich Kleeman (1942**), Major** General Count Theodor von Sponeck (1942-43), Lieutenant **General Count** Gerhard von Schwerin (1944), and Lieutenant General Ernst **Baade (1944-45).**

NOTES AND SOURCES: The 361st Motorized Infantry Regiment of the 90th Light Division contained a high portion of veterans of the French Foreign Legion. Major General Summermann was killed in the Cyrenaican retreat on December 15, 1941, near Gazala. Major General Veith was wounded in the Battle of the Gazala Line, May 1942. He later became a special disciplinary officer with Army Group North in Russia. Marcks was an acting divisional commander at Tobruk. Kleeman was wounded near Alma Halfa Ridge in September 1942. Later he led Assault Division Rhodes (1943-September 1944) in the Balkans and IV Panzer Corps (1945) on the Eastern Front. He had commanded the 3rd Motorized Infantry Brigade of the 3rd Panzer Division prior to taking over the 90th Light. Count von Sponeck, who performed brilliantly in the retreat from Egypt and Libya (1942-43), was captured when Tunisia fell in May 1943. General von Schwerin commanded the 116th Panzer Grenadier Division on the Western Front in 1944. General Baade, a veteran of the Afrika Korps, distinguished himself while directing the ferrying operations across the Straits of Messina during the German evacuation of Sicily. He was a brilliant, unorthodox, and highly decorated commander who was killed in an Allied bombing raid on the last day of the war. Fisher: 167, 471, 476; Ronald Lewin, *Rommel as a Military Commander*, Ballantine Books, New York, 1970: 12; RA: 46; OB 45: 311. Also see Carell 1960, Irving 1977, Mitcham, 1982 and von Mellenthin 1956.

345th RESERVE PANZER GRENADIER DIVISION

COMPOSITION: 345th Reserve Panzer Battalion, 148th Reserve Panzer Grenadier Regiment, 152nd Reserve Grenadier Regiment

HOME STATION: Wehrkreis IX

The 345th was formed in the latter part of 1942 and was sent to southern France. In the summer of 1943 it was absorbed by the 29th Panzer Grenadier Division, which was resurrected in mid-1943 to replace a division destroyed at Stalingrad.

SOURCES: Blumenson 1969: 289; RA: 144; OB 45: 311.

386th MOTORIZED INFANTRY DIVISION

COMPOSITION: 386th Reserve Panzer Battalion, 149th Motorized Infantry Regiment, 153rd Motorized Infantry Regiment

HOME STATION: Wehrkreis III

This division was formed in October 1942 and absorbed by the 3rd Panzer Grenadier Division in the summer of 1943, to replace a division destroyed at Stalingrad. It was stationed in southern France at the time. The 386th Motorized was considered a mediocre unit.

NOTES AND SOURCES: The commander of the 386th Motorized was Major General Kurt Jesser (1942?-43). He was later commander of the 74th Security Brigade in southern France (1944) and was reportedly killed in action on the Western Front later that year. Blumenson 1969: 289; RA: 46; OB 45: 312.

BRANDENBURG DIVISION (later PANZER GRENADIER DIVISION "BRANDENBURG")

COMPOSITION (1943): 1st Brandenburg Panzer Grenadier Regiment, 2nd Brandenburg Panzer Grenadier Regiment, 3rd Brandenburg Panzer Grenadier Regiment, 4th Brandenburg Panzer Grenadier Regiment, 5th Brandenburg Panzer Grenadier Regiment, a parachute company and other special units, including some with foreign language skills

HOME STATION: Berlin, Wkr. III

This division began its career on October 25, 1939, as the 800th

Construction Training Company. It was made up of commando units that performed well in Poland and was directly under the Abwehr—the German Armed Forces Military Intelligence Department. On January 10, 1940, it was redesignated the Bau-Lehr-Battalion z.b.V. 800 (800th Construction Training Battalion—for Special Utilization). It was steadily expanded to a regiment and finally a division. Elements of the "Brandenburgers" fought in practically every major campaign from 1940 to 1943, including the Balkans, Italy, North Africa, Russia, and France (1940), where it particularly distinguished itself. In the Western campaign of 1940 75 percent of the then battalion won Iron Crosses—probably the highest percentage ever achieved by any German unit during the entire war. Elements of the division also earned special distinction by disguising themselves as wounded Russians and seizing the critical Dvina River bridge at Daugavpils, behind Soviet lines, on June 26, 1941. They then turned back repeated Soviet counterattacks until they were relieved by the LVI Panzer Corps. In autumn 1942 the special units were upgraded to divisional status. However, as the Abwehr's influence at Führer Headquarters declined, the Brandenburgers came increasingly under the control of OKW, which used it as a regular line unit. By early 1943 only the 5th Brandenburg Regiment "Kurfürst" was employed in commando-style missions. Posted to the Balkans in late 1943, the special functions of the division and affiliated units were taken over by the new SS Raiding Detachments (Jagdverbände) in the fall of 1944. In October of that year it was reformed in Vienna as a panzer grenadier division and transferred to the Eastern Front. It ended the war at battle group strength with the 4th Panzer Army, resisting the last Russian advance in the vicinity of Dresden. The division's commanders included Colonel Paul Haehling von Lanzenauer (1942-43), Colonel Erwin Lahousen (1943), and Major General Alexander von Pfuhlstein (1943-44).

NOTES AND SOURCES: Haehling von Lanzenauer fell ill in March 1943 and had to be relieved. Lahousen was an acting commander only. Later promoted to major general, he was an Abwehr Section Chief. Major General von Pfuhlstein was arrested for his part in the July 20, 1944, attempt to assassinate Adolf Hitler. His guilt could not be definitely established, however, so he was not hanged, but he was demoted to the rank of private. He had previously served ten days confinement for striking an SS colonel with his fist after that officer questioned the courage of the Brandenburg Division. Von Pfuhlstein was apparently replaced as divisional commander by Lieutenant General Kühlwein, the former commander of the 45th Infantry Division on the Eastern Front (1942-43). Heinz Höhne, *Canaris*, Doubleday and Company, Inc., Garden City, New York, 1979: 377, 415, 467, 497; Hoffmann: 275-76; *Kriegstagebuch des OKW*, Volume III: 1160, Volume IV: 1896; Seaton: 103; OB 45: 103. Also see Carell 1960, for the story of the Brandenburg units in North Africa.

PANZER GRENADIER DIVISION "FELDHERRNHALLE"
see 60th Panzer Grenadier Division

PANZER GRENADIER DIVISION "GROSSDEUTSCHLAND"

PROBABLE COMPOSITION: 2nd "Grossdeutschland" Panzer Grenadier Regiment, 2nd "Grossdeutschland" Fusilier Regiment

HOME STATION: Berlin, Wkr. III

This unit was organized in late 1944 and was associated with its more famous predecessor, Panzer Division "Grossdeutschland." It probably never exceeded regimental strength. The new unit fought in eastern Germany and Poland before being sent to East Prussia, where it was decimated in January 1945. Remnants of the division, however, were still fighting in East Prussia with Panzer Corps "Hermann Göring" at the end of the war.

SOURCES: *Kriegstagebuch des OKW*, Volume IV: 1887, 1897.

(2nd) PARACHUTE PANZER GRENADIER DIVISION "HERMANN GÖRING"

PROBABLE COMPOSITION: 2nd Hermann Göring Panzer Grenadier Regiment, 3rd Hermann Göring Panzer Grenadier Regiment, 2nd Hermann Göring Motorized Artillery Regiment, 2nd Hermann Göring Reconnaissance Battalion, 2nd Hermann Göring Anti-Tank Battalion, 2nd Hermann Göring Engineer Battalion, 2nd Hermann Göring Signal Battalion

HOME STATION: See below

This unit, which never reached full strength, was created as the sister unit of the (1st) Parachute Panzer Division "Hermann Göring." In both cases the term "parachute" was honorary. The "H.G." Panzer Grenadier Division was assigned to the new Parachute Panzer Corps "Hermann Göring" and was smashed in East Prussia in early 1945. It was later transferred south and ended the war in the pocket east of Prague. Its commander was Major General Erich Walther.

NOTES AND SOURCES: This division was probably created from Parachute Replacement and Training Brigade "Hermann Göring." which was headquartered at the Thorn Maneuver Area in Poland. Walther had previously commanded the 4th Parachute Regiment (1943-44) and the 344th Infantry Division on the Western Front (1944). He held the Knight's Cross with Oak Leaves. *Kriegstagebuch des OKW*, Volume I: 1147; Volume IV: 1897; RA: 252; OB 45: 639.

PANZER GRENADIER DIVISION "KURMARK"

PROBABLE COMPOSITION: (?) Panzer Battalion, Panzer Grenadier Regiment "Kurmark"

HOME STATION: See below

Another *ad hoc* division formed in the last days of the war, Kurmark probably never exceeded regimental strength and was a panzer grenadier division in name only. It fought in the Battle of Berlin and was destroyed when the front collapsed in April 1945.

SOURCES: Chant, Volume 17: 2376; *Kriegstagebuch des OKW*, Volume IV: 1898

8

The Parachute Divisions

1st PARACHUTE DIVISION

COMPOSITION: 1st Parachute Regiment, 3rd Parachute Regiment, 4th Parachute Regiment, 1st Parachute Artillery Regiment, 1st Parachute Anti-Aircraft Artillery Regiment, 1st Parachute Anti-Tank Battalion, 1st Parachute Engineer Battalion, 1st Parachute Signal Battalion

This unit was formed in Russia in autumn 1942 from the old 7th Air Division, the original German paratroop force. Its first commander was Major General Richard Heidrich, a veteran of France, Crete, and the Siege of Leningrad. In March 1943, the division was withdrawn from the Eastern Front and sent to southern France, where it completed its formation and engaged in training until after the German collapse in Africa. In July it was sent to Sicily, where it delayed the Allied drive on the Catania Plain and later fought a violent battle at the Primasole Bridge against British paratroopers. After being evacuated to Italy, the 1st Parachute spent the rest of the war in a long retreat up the Italian peninsula. At the time of the Allied landings at Salerno, the division was in action against Montgomery's 8th Army at Foggia, on the heel of the Italian boot. The division fought its most famous battle at Cassino in early 1944, where it held its positions despite massive American ground and air attacks, including aerial bombardments of the heaviest kind. General von Vietinghoff, the commander of the 10th Army, later commented that "No troops but the 1st Parachute Division could have held Cassino." After the fall of Rome in June 1944, the greatly reduced division was shifted to the Adriatic sector and later suffered heavy casualties in the withdrawal to Bologna. In 1945 Lieutenant General Heidrich was promoted to the command of the I Parachute Corps, which was also serving in Italy. He was replaced as divisional commander by Major General Karl-Lothar Schultz, who surrendered the 1st Parachute to the Allies after the German front in northern Italy finally collapsed in the spring of 1945.

ALSO SEE 7th AIR DIVISION

NOTES AND SOURCES: Heidrich, a former Free Corps veteran, commanded the 3rd Parachute Regiment of the 7th Air Division in France and Russia (1940-42). Schultz was the commander of the 1st Parachute Regiment under Heidrich (1943-44). Both men held the Knight's Cross with Oak Leaves and Swords. Blumenson 1969: 67, 448; Chant, Volume 17: 2277; Edwards: 135-37; Fisher: 18.

2nd PARACHUTE DIVISION

COMPOSITION: 2nd Parachute Regiment, 6th Parachute Regiment, 7th Parachute Regiment, 2nd Parachute Artillery Regiment, 2nd Parachute Anti-Tank Battalion, 2nd Parachute Engineer Battalion (?), 2nd Parachute Signal Battalion, 2nd Parachute Anti-Aircraft Battalion, 2nd Parachute Machine Gun Battalion

This unit first saw action as the 2nd Parachute Brigade on the North African Front. In November 1942 it was on the southern flank of Panzer Army Afrika, when Field Marshal Rommel's famous Afrika Korps was all but destroyed at El Alamein. Because of a shortage of vehicles and fuel, Rommel was forced to abandon the brigade (and the Italian X Infantry Corps, which it was supporting) to its fate. The Italians surrendered but Major General Hermann Bernard Ramcke, commander of the parachute brigade, carried out a brilliant ambush, captured a British transport column, and managed to rejoin the remnants of Rommel's army in one of the most daring feats of arms the Germans executed during World War II. The brigade was evacuated from North Africa before the Axis collapse and formed the nucleus around which the 2nd Parachute Division was created in the spring of 1943. The new division also included the 2nd Parachute Regiment, which had been part of the veteran 7th Air Division before that unit was disbanded in 1943.

Initially stationed in Brittany, the new parachute division was sent south in the summer of 1943 and took part in the occupation of Rome after the Badoglio government tried to defect to the Allies later that year. In the latter part of 1943 the 2nd Parachute was transferred to the Russian Front, where its 6th Parachute Regiment was almost wiped out. Down to a strength of thirty-two hundred men by January 1944, the division was still holding thirteen miles of frontage. It was finally withdrawn from combat that May and sent to Wahn, Germany, to refit and rebuild, and was then returned to Brittany, minus the 6th Parachute Regiment, which was attached to the 91st Air Landing Division in Normandy. After the collapse of the German front in Normandy, Ramcke (now a lieutenant general) assumed command of the fortress of Brest and forced the U.S. 3rd Army to lay siege to the city. The battle lasted from mid-August until September 19, 1944. Ramcke, Colonel von der Mosel (his chief of staff), and their men put up a fierce resistance and seriously disrupted Patton's timetable. On Hitler's orders Nazi Germany's highest decoration—the Knight's Cross with Oak Leaves, Swords, and Diamonds—was parachuted into the fortress and awarded to Ramcke. Finally, however, the division's supplies ran out, the fortress was overrun, and the 2nd Parachute Division was destroyed. Ramcke and most of his men spent the rest of the war in prison camps.

After the original 2nd Parachute Division was destroyed at Brest, a second division of that name was formed in Germany and Holland. Although not as distinguished as its predecessor, the new 2nd Parachute fought well against the British and the Americans in operations around Arnhem, in the Reichswald battles, and in the Battles of the Rhine Crossings. As late as March 1945 it was on the northern sector of the Western Front with LXIII Corps, 1st Parachute Army, Army Group H. In April, however, it was shifted south and was trapped, along with the bulk of Field Marshal Model's Army Group B, in the Ruhr Pocket, and was destroyed there.

NOTES AND SOURCES: As senior regimental commander, Colonel Hans Kroh, a holder of the Knight's Cross with Oak Leaves and Swords, assumed command of the 2nd Parachute Division when Ramcke became commander of Fortress Brest. It was Kroh who surrendered the division to the Americans. This native of Berlin had previously served as Ia of the 7th Air Division (1940), battalion commander in the 2nd Parachute Regiment (1941-43), and as commander of the 2nd Parachute Regiment (1943-44). After World War II, Kroh commanded the 1st Air Landing Division in the peacetime West German Army (mid-1950's). He died in 1967. Commanders of the rebuilt 2nd Parachute Division included Lieutenant General Gustav Wilke (1944) and Lieutenant General Walther Lackner (1944). Wilke later led the 5th Parachute division (1944) and Lackner commanded the 6th Parachute Division (1945). Blumenson 1960: 639; Chant, Volume 14: 1861; Edwards: 137, 156; Garland and Smyth: 286; Seaton: 415; Vormann: 29.

3rd PARACHUTE DIVISION

COMPOSITION: 5th Parachute Regiment, 8th Parachute Regiment, 9th Parachute Regiment, 3rd Parachute Artillery Regiment, 3rd Parachute Anti-Tank Battalion, 3rd Parachute Engineer Battalion, 3rd Parachute Signal Battalion, 3rd Heavy Mortar Unit (Parachute)

Formed in the Reims area of France during the latter part of 1943, this division had a cadre from the 1st Parachute Regiment of the 1st Parachute Division. It was commanded for most of its existence by Major General Richard Schimpf. When it completed its training the division was at full strength, and had over seventeen thousand men. Like almost all German parachute units created after 1941, it never saw airborne operations but fought as an infantry division. Initially stationed in Brittany in 1944, the 3rd Parachute was soon committed to the Normandy fighting, where it suffered heavy casualties resisting the American advance through the hedgerows to St. Lô. By July 11, 1944, it was down to 35 percent of its former strength. After the front collapsed in late July, the division was surrounded in the Falaise Pocket in August, where most of its survivors were captured. Schimpf, now a Lieutenant General, was seriously wounded in the breakout but was carried out of the pocket by his men. Lieutenant General Eugen Meindl, the commander of the II Parachute Corps, assumed personal command of the 3rd Parachute after Schimpf fell and was himself severely wounded in the breakout. Despite its reduced numbers, the tough division stayed in action, mainly because Army Group B had nothing left but burned-out units with which to fight the Allies. In September 1944, the 3rd Parachute, now "almost insignificant in numbers," was surrounded in the Mons Pocket but again broke out. It was finally sent to the rear and was rebuilt at Oldenzaal, Holland, mainly from personnel released from Luftwaffe ground support units; nevertheless, the division performed creditably in the Ardennes offensive, where it was part of the I SS Panzer Corps, 6th Panzer Army. It did, however, suffer more casualties than it should have; this was because of the inexperience of its soldiers. After the Battle of the Bulge, the 3rd Parachute Division was transferred to the 5th Panzer Army and was engaged in delaying the Allied drive west of the Rhine in early 1945. There, near Eifel, as part of the LXXIV Corps, the division fell victim to one of Hitler's "hold-at-all-costs" orders and was not allowed to withdraw behind the Rhine when it still had time to do so. Most of the division, including General Schimpf, was captured. The survivors of the disintegrating division escaped into the Ruhr Pocket, where the 3rd Parachute was encircled for a fourth and final time. Its remnants surrendered to the Allies in April 1945.

NOTES AND SOURCES: Schmipf, a Bavarian, was Chief of Staff of Luftgau

VIII (the Air Force equivalent of a Wehrkreis) in 1943. Lieutenant General Wadehn, later commander of the 8th Parachute Division (1945), commanded the 3rd Parachute while Schimpf recovered from his Falaise wounds. Blumenson 1960: 543, 582, 683; Chant, Volume 16: 2133; Edwards: 137-38; Harrison: Map VI; MacDonald 1973: 193, 223.

4th PARACHUTE DIVISION

COMPOSITION: 10th Parachute Regiment, 11th Parachute Regiment, 12th Parachute Regiment, 4th Parachute Artillery Regiment, 4th Parachute Anti-Tank Battalion, 4th Parachute Engineer Battalion, 4th Parachute Signal Battalion, 4th Parachute Anti-Aircraft Battalion

The 4th Parachute Division was formed at Perugia, Italy, from cadres furnished by the 2nd Parachute Division and two Italian parachute divisions: "Folgore" and "Nembo." It was commanded by Major General Heinrich Trettner throughout its existence. The division first saw action in January 1944 against the American beachhead at Anzio, where it formed part of General Schlemm's I Parachute Corps. The 4th Parachute was more or less continuously engaged on the Italian Front for the next sixteen months and fought in the battles north of Florence, at Rimini, Bologna, and in the struggle for the Gothic Line. In 1945, while still part of the I Parachute Corps, it fought its last battle at Verona, where it was finally surrounded and forced to surrender to the American forces on April 26.

NOTES AND SOURCES: Trettner was Chief of Staff of the XI Air Corps in 1943 and assumed command of the 4th Parachute toward the end of that same year. Blumenson 1969: 419-21; Edwards: 138; Fisher: Map III, 302, 501-02.

5th PARACHUTE DIVISION

COMPOSITION: 13th Parachute Regiment, 14th Parachute Regiment, 15th Parachute Regiment, 5th Parachute Artillery Regiment, 5th Parachute Anti-Aircraft Regiment, 5th Parachute Anti-Tank Battalion, 5th Parachute Engineer Battalion, 5th Parachute Signal Battalion, 5th Parachute Heavy Mortar Unit

In March 1943 the 5th Parachute Division was formed at Reims from the Demonstration Battalion (Lehr-battalion) of the XI Air Corps and was posted in Normandy under the command of Major General Gustav Wilke. In June 1944 it was heavily engaged in the Normandy fighting and was later trapped in the Falaise Pocket when the German front collapsed. In late July, SS General Paul Hausser, the commander of the 7th Army, listed the division as practically destroyed. Since the divisional headquarters had been lost at Falaise, the remnants of the 5th Parachute were placed under the command of the 275th Infantry Division.

Sometime later the Luftwaffe decided to rebuild the 5th Parachute from excess ground personnel, thus making it little more than a Luftwaffe Field division, and an understrength one at that. In addition to its poorly trained personnel, the division was plagued by internal friction, because its staff officers were appointed by Colonel General Kurt Student and were very hostile to divisional commander Colonel (later Major General) Ludwig Heilmann, who disliked Student. Despite its problems, the 5th Parachute fought in the West Wall battles as part of Army Group G in southern Germany and was later assigned to the LXXXV Corps, 7th Army, Army Group B, for the Ardennes offensive, during which it took part in the Siege of Bastogne. It seems to have performed well here but by February 1945, when it fought at the Battle of Pruem just west of the Rhine, it was down to battle group strength. A month later, as part of the 15th Army, it was trapped with its back to the Rhine and was almost totally destroyed. General Heilmann was among those taken prisoner. Some stragglers from the division did manage to escape to the Ruhr Pocket, where they were rounded up a few weeks later.

NOTES AND SOURCES: Gustav Wilke briefly commanded the 2nd Parachute Division in 1944. General Heilmann was a former company commander in the 21st Infantry Regiment in Poland and France (1939 and 1940, respectively), before transferring from the Army to the Luftwaffe. He led a battalion of the 3rd Parachute Regiment (1941-43) and the regiment itself (1943-44), before rising to divisional command. He held the Knight's Cross with Oak Leaves and Swords. "King" Ludwig, as he was nicknamed, died in 1959. Blumenson 1960: 422, 442; Cole 1965: 208-13; Edwards: 138, 154; Harrison: 71; MacDonald 1963: Map III; MacDonald 1973: 86.

6th PARACHUTE DIVISION

COMPOSITION: 16th Parachute Regiment, 17th Parachute Regiment, 18th Parachute Regiment, 6th Parachute Artillery Regiment, 6th Parachute Artillery Regiment, 6th Parachute Anti-Tank Battalion, 6th Parachute Engineer Battalion, 6th Parachute Signal Battalion, 6th Parachute Anti-Aircraft Battalion, 6th Parachute Heavy Mortar Unit

Formed at Amiens in northern France in June 1944, the 6th Parachute was in action on the Normandy Front within a month. It suffered heavy casualties when the front collapsed and was sent to the rear to reorganize. Meanwhile, it lost the 16th Parachute Regiment, which was transferred to the Hermann Göring Panzer Corps, and other elements of the division formed cadres for the organization of the 7th Parachute Division. As part of the 5th Panzer Army, the remnants of the 6th Parachute Division attempted to halt the Allied drive on Paris, but without success. By September 1944, when the division fought in the Battle of the Mons Pocket, it had a combat strength of only two infantry battalions; nevertheless, it remained on the front line, taking part in the Arnhem operation and in the battles for Holland and the Rhineland. In late March 1945, it was part of the II Parachute Corps, 1st Parachute Army, and was trying to contain the British bridgehead over the Rhine. When the war ended, Lieutenant General Hermann Plocher surrendered the survivors of the 6th Parachute to the Canadians near Zutphen. Although not as distinguished as some of the other German airborne units, the 6th Parachute had been in action almost continuously since its formation and had performed creditably. Commanders of the 6th included Lieutenant Generals Rüdiger von Heyking (1944), Walther Lackner (1944), and Plocher (1944-45).

NOTES AND SOURCES: General Rüdiger von Heyking was captured at Mons. Lackner had previously commanded the 2nd Parachute Division (1944). Plocher, who was commissioned in 1922 in the same regiment as Erwin Rommel and his future chief of staff, Hans Speidel, became a pilot in 1925 and joined the Luftwaffe as a captain in 1935. He served in Spain (1936-38) and was Chief of Staff of the Condor Legion (1937-38). Plocher later served as Chief of Staff of the V Air Corps in France and Russia (1940-42) and Chief of Staff of Luftwaffe Command East (later 6th Air Fleet) (1942-43). He directed the formation of the 19th Luftwaffe Field Division (1943), led the 4th Air Division (1943), and was Chief of Staff of the 3rd Air Fleet on the Western Front (October 1943 to July 1944). He later wrote three books on German Air Force operations in Russia for the United States Air Force Historical Division (see the Bibliography). Blumenson 1960: 576-77, 683; Edwards: 139; MacDonald 1973: Map XII; and Hermann Plocher, *The German Air Force Versus Russia, 1941,* United States Air Force Historical Studies: Number 154, Aerospace Studies Institute, Air University, 1966. Published in hardcover by Arno Press, New York: 1968.

7th AIR DIVISION

COMPOSITION: 1st Parachute Regiment, 2nd Parachute Regiment, 3rd Parachute Regiment

As the original German parachute division, the 7th Air was established in 1938 and was still not completely formed when the war broke out in 1939. Its 3rd Parachute Regiment, for example, was not formed until 1940, after the fall of France. Under the overall command of Major General (later Colonel General) Kurt Student (1938-40), the father of the German parachute forces, the 7th Air was not originally designed to fight as a division. For example, in the Danish and Norwegian campaigns, individual companies parachuted behind enemy lines to seize vital installations and were later relieved by Army ground units. In the first hours of the campaign in the Low Countries, elements of the division's glider forces took the key Belgian fortress of Eban Emael, while other parachute units seized the vital Albert Canal bridges. To the north, other divisional units were committed behind Dutch lines, preventing the Dutch from blowing up critical bridges before German panzer and motorized units could cross them. They played a key role in the capture of Rotterdam and the elimination of the Dutch Army in only six days. The paratroopers proved the worth of airborne soldiers in this campaign and in a very real sense were the fathers of modern airborne warfare. As a result of these successes, Hitler decided to expand his parachute arm; this program included enlarging the 7th Air Division by establishing the 3rd Parachute Regiment, as well as divisional engineer, machine-gun, anti-aircraft, and motorcycle units. During this expansion the division was commanded by Major General Putziger, since General Student had been critically wounded at Rotterdam.

In 1941 the 7th Air was back in action again during the Greek campaign, during which the 2nd Parachute Regiment captured the Corinth Canal Bridge by parachute assault. Later, the entire division was employed in the invasion of Crete, where it played the major role in defeating the Allied Expeditionary Force under New Zealand's General Freyberg; however, its casualties were so appallingly high that Hitler overreacted, as he frequently did, and declared that he would never again use airborne troops on a massive scale. As a result, after a brilliant beginning, the German parachute arm was relegated to the role of fighting as regular infantry for the rest of the war. All future major airborne operations in World War II were conducted by the Allies. Meanwhile, the survivors of the division were sent to the Russian Front in 1941, where they fought at Rzhev, Mius, and in the Siege of Leningrad. In February 1943, the division was in southern Russia, defending the Dnepropetrovsk-Stalino rail line as a part of Army Group Don. A month later it was pulled out of the line, sent to southern France, and disbanded. Most of its men were transferred to the newly formed 1st Parachute Division, although some formed cadres for other parachute units. The last divisional commander of the 7th Air was Lieutenant General Petersen.

NOTES AND SOURCES: Kurt Student, a World War I airplane pilot, was running a glider instruction course as a Reichswehr captain as early as 1924. He commanded the XI Air Corps (1940-43) and directed the invasion of Crete. He prepared and planned the invasion of Malta in 1942, but this operation was cancelled by Hitler. Later he directed the 1st Parachute Army (1944) and Army Group H (1944-45), both in the Netherlands. In February 1945 he was replaced in army group command by Colonel General Blaskowitz and reassumed command of the 1st Parachute Army. In the last days of the war he was named commander of Army Group Vistula, which had by then virtually ceased to exist. He surrendered to the British in May 1945. Major General Süssmann commanded the 7th Air at Crete and was killed there. General Petersen was given command of the IV Luftwaffe Corps on the southern sector of the Russian Front in 1943, but, since this formation only consisted of Luftwaffe Field divisions, it performed miserably. Later, this HQ was redesignated XC Corps and served on the Western Front. Petersen was promoted to General of Fliers in 1943. Brett-Smith: 145-47; Edwards: 135, 145-50; Ziemke 1966: 87.

7th PARACHUTE DIVISION

COMPOSITION: 19th Parachute Regiment, 20th Parachute Regiment, 21st Parachute Regiment, 7th Parachute Artillery Regiment, 7th Parachute Anti-Tank Battalion, 7th Parachute Engineer Battalion, 7th Parachute Signal Battalion

Created in September 1944 as Parachute Division Erdmann, this hastily organized unit was in action within days, attacking the British Market-Garden corridor, as their XXX Armored Corps tried to relieve the British 1st Airborne Division at Arnhem. By delaying the relief force, the division rendered significant aid to the II SS Panzer Corps, which annihilated the Allies' first foothold across the Rhine before it could be reinforced. After this distinguished beginning the emergency unit was upgraded to full parachute division status and in October was augmented with elite personnel from parachute and Waffen-SS schools, as well as combat groups from the 6th Parachute Division. This reorganization took place at Venlo in lower Holland. Lieutenant General Wolfgang Erdmann remained in command of the 7th Parachute, Army Group H, throughout its existence.

The new division opposed the British on the northern sector of the Western Front for eight months. In February 1945 it again faced the XXX Armored Corps and destroyed a large number of its tanks in the Battle of Kappeln. Later, the 7th Parachute opposed Montgomery's Rhine crossings and subsequent drive across northwest Germany, but with less success. When the war ended, Erdmann surrendered his veterans to the British near Oldenburg. Despite its hasty creation, the division had shown itself to be an excellent combat unit and proved that Nazi Germany was still capable of putting together solid fighting formations, even in the fifth year of the war.

NOTES AND SOURCES: Wolfgang Erdmann was formerly associated with the Luftwaffe's Organizational Branch. He was Chief of Staff of the 1st Parachute Army in 1944, a post he left to assume command of Parachute Division Erdmann. Edwards: 139; MacDonald 1973: Map XII.

8th PARACHUTE DIVISION

COMPOSITION: 22nd Parachute Regiment, 23rd Parachute Regiment (never fully formed), 24th Parachute Regiment, 8th Parachute Artillery Regiment (?), 8th Parachute Anti-Tank Battalion (?), 8th Parachute Engineer Battalion, 8th Parachute Signal Battalion

The 8th Parachute Division was formed in the Cologne-Wahn area of western Germany in December 1944, after the Allies had already established footholds in German territory. Created too late to fight in the Battle of the Bulge, the 8th Parachute was part of Meindl's II Parachute Corps in the Reichswald battles in northwestern Germany, where it fought well. The division, which apparently never exceeded regimental strength, took part in the defensive battles against Field Marshal Montgomery's 21st Army Group until it was decisively defeated south of Bremen in April 1945. Later that month Lieutenant General Wadehn, the only commander the division ever had, surrendered it to the Allies.

NOTES AND SOURCES: Wadehn had previously commanded the 3rd Parachute Division (late (1944). Edwards: 139; MacDonald 1973: Map XII.

9th PARACHUTE DIVISION

COMPOSITION: 25th Parachute Regiment, 26th Parachute Regiment, 27th Parachute Regiment (never fully formed), 9th Parachute Artillery Regiment, 9th Parachute Anti-Tank Unit, 9th Parachute Engineer Unit, 9th Parachute Signal Unit, 9th Parachute Heavy Mortar Unit

Formed from assorted Luftwaffe ground units, this division was an airborne force in name only, although it did have some paratroopers in it. The 9th was committed to action in two parts: the first battle group of two battalions fought under Major General Niehoff at Breslau, where it was finally destroyed after a bitter siege. Resistance in Breslau, in fact, continued even after Berlin fell. The second group, under divisional commander Major General Bruno Brauer, fought on the Oder and in Pomerania before being virtually annihilated as the Russians drove on Berlin.

NOTES AND SOURCES: General Brauer had been one of the first German paratroopers in the 1930s, and was named commander of the 1st Parachute

Regiment in 1938. He led the regiment in Holland (1940) and Crete (1941), distinguishing himself in both campaigns. Afterward he commanded the German occupation forces in Crete, before falling into disfavor with Hitler and being sent into retirement. He was unemployed until 1945, when he was reactivated to command the 9th Parachute. After the war the Soviets turned him over to the Greeks, who executed him for alleged war crimes committed in Crete. The evidence is difficult to evaluate in his case. Edwards: 140, 153; Seaton: 575.

10th PARACHUTE DIVISION

COMPOSITION: 28th Parachute Regiment, 29th Parachute Regiment, 30th Parachute Regiment, 10th Parachute Artillery Regiment (never completely formed), 10th Parachute Engineer Battalion, 10th Parachute Signal Battalion

This unit was formed in the Krems-Melk area of Austria in March 1945 from detachments of the 1st and 4th Parachute Divisions and miscellaneous troops. In fact it was a division in name only, for it never reached more than battle-group strength. Under Major General von Hofmann, its only commander, the 10th Parachute fought the Russians in the Danube Valley before being transferred to Czechoslovakia in the last days of the war. It surrendered along with the 1st Panzer Army in May 1945 and went into Soviet captivity.

SOURCE: Edwards: 140.

9

The Luftwaffe Field Divisions

1st LUFTWAFFE FIELD DIVISION

COMPOSITION: 1st Field Infantry Regiment, 2nd Field Infantry Regiment, 1st Field Artillery Regiment, 1st Field Füsilier Company, 1st Field Anti-Tank Battalion, 1st Field Engineer Battalion, 1st Field Signal Company, 1st Field Flak Battalion

In 1942, Hitler authorized the formation of the Luftwaffe Field divisions from excess air force ground personnel, because Reichsmarschall Hermann Göring personally appealed to him not to release his men to the Army where their "fine National Socialist attitudes" would be contaminated. This was a horrible mistake on Hitler's part, for it led to the commitment of well over a dozen inadequately trained Luftwaffe ground divisions to combat, mainly on the Eastern Front, and cost thousands of men their lives. The 1st Luftwaffe Field Division completed its training in early 1943 and was sent to Army Group North on the Eastern Front. Not heavily engaged in 1943, the 1st Field saw its first major fighting in the withdrawal from Leningrad in January 1944, during which it suffered such heavy losses that it had to be disbanded. Like most of the other Luftwaffe ground divisions, it proved itself utterly inadequate to face the enemy in infantry-style combat. The 1st Luftwaffe Field Division was commanded by Major General Petrauscke (1943-44?).

SOURCE: OB 45: 326.

2nd LUFTWAFFE FIELD DIVISION

COMPOSITION: 3rd Field Infantry Regiment, 4th Field Infantry Regiment, 2nd Field Artillery Regiment, 2nd Field Füsilier Company, 2nd Field Anti-Tank Battalion, 2nd Field Engineer Battalion, 2nd Field Signal Company, 2nd Field Flak Battalion

Formed in 1942-43, the 2nd Field Division was sent to Army Group Center in late 1943. Apparently it did not please the army group commander, Field Marshal Ernst Busch, for he succeeded in getting the division disbanded in early 1944. What happened to the men of this division is not clear; it is fairly certain, however, that they remained on the central sector of the Russian Front, and most of them probably were captured when the Russians smashed Army Group Center in July and August 1944.

NOTES AND SOURCES: Busch, an ardent Nazi, no doubt won a battle of influence at Führer Headquarters, or else the 2nd Field would not have been disbanded. OB 45: 326.

3rd LUFTWAFFE FIELD DIVISION

COMPOSITION: 5th Field Infantry Regiment, 6th Field Infantry Regiment, 3rd Field Artillery Regiment, 3rd Field Füsilier Company, 3rd Field Anti-Tank Battalion, 3rd Field Engineer Battalion, 3rd Field Signal Company, 3rd Field Flak Battalion

Like most of the other Luftwaffe Field divisions, the 3rd was formed in 1942-43. Like its sister division, the 2nd Luftwaffe Field, it was sent to Army Group Center in late 1943 and was disbanded in 1944, before the Russians began their gigantic summer offensive. Its personnel remained on the Eastern Front.

SOURCE: OB 45: 326.

4th LUFTWAFFE FIELD DIVISION

COMPOSITION: 7th Field Infantry Regiment, 8th Field Infantry Regiment, 4th Field Artillery Regiment, 4th Field Füsilier Company, 4th Field Anti-Tank Battalion, 4th Field Engineer Battalion, 4th Field Signal Company, 4th Field Flak Battalion

Like the 2nd and 3rd Luftwaffe Field Divisions, the 4th was formed in

1942-43 and sent to Army Group Center. Unlike the 2nd and 3rd Field, it was still in existence in July 1944, when the Soviet summer offensive virtually destroyed Army Group Center. Along with most of the rest of the 3rd Panzer Army's LIII Corps, the 4th Field Division was surrounded and destroyed at Vitebsk. Its commander, Lieutenant General Pistorius, was among those killed in this battle.

NOTES AND SOURCES: A previous divisional commander, Lieutenant General Dr. Ernst Klepp (late 1943), later commanded the 133rd Fortress Division on Crete (1944). Carell 1971: 584-96; OB 45: 326.

5th LUFTWAFFE FIELD DIVISION

COMPOSITION: 9th Field Infantry Regiment, 10th Field Infantry Regiment, 5th Field Artillery Regiment, 5th Field Füsilier Company, 5th Field Anti-Tank Battalion, 5th Field Engineer Battalion, 5th Field Signal Company, 5th Field Flak Battalion

Authorized in 1942 and completely assembled by early 1943, the 5th Luftwaffe Field Division was sent to the southern sector of the Russian Front. It was soon smashed by the Russians in the last phases of their winter offensive of 1942-43 and was subsequently disbanded.

SOURCE: OB 45: 327.

6th LUFTWAFFE FIELD DIVISION

COMPOSITION: 11th Field Infantry Regiment, 12th Field Infantry Regiment, 6th Field Artillery Regiment, 6th Field Füsilier Company, 6th Field Anti-Tank Battalion, 6th Field Engineer Battalion, 6th Field Signal Company, 6th Field Anti-Aircraft Battalion

The 6th Field Division was created in the winter of 1942-43, and, along with the 4th Luftwaffe Field Division, was sent to Army Group Center, which attached it to LIII Corps, 3rd Panzer Army. The division was encircled and destroyed at Vitebsk. Lieutenant General Rudolf Peschel (1943-44), the divisional commander, was killed in the fighting.

NOTES AND SOURCES: A previous divisional commander, Lieutenant General Rüdiger von Heyking, later led the 6th Parachute Division in France and was captured at Mons (September 1944). Carell 1971: 584-96; OB 45: 327.

7th LUFTWAFFE FIELD DIVISION

COMPOSITION: 13th Field Infantry Regiment, 14th Field Infantry Regiment, 7th Field Artillery Regiment, 7th Field Füsilier Company, 7th Field Anti-Tank Battalion, 7th Field Engineer Battalion, 7th Field Signal Company, 7th Field Anti-Aircraft Battalion

Formed in late 1942, the 7th Field was perhaps the first of the Luftwaffe ground divisions to see action. It was sent to Army Group Don, which was then engaged in the Stalingrad relief campaign and was trying to fend off massive Russian attacks at the same time. The army group attached the division to newly created Army Detachment Hollidt, which was desperately trying to hold the Upper Chir River line. The 7th Field did not provide General Hollidt much help and was badly mauled in the fighting; however, unlike most Air Force infantry units, it did not collapse completely. It was nevertheless disbanded in May 1943 and its personnel absorbed by the 15th Luftwaffe Field Division.

SOURCES: Manstein: 319; OB 45: 327.

8th LUFTWAFFE FIELD DIVISION

COMPOSITION: 15th Field Infantry Regiment, 16th Field Infantry Regiment, 8th Field Artillery Regiment, 8th Field Füsilier Company, 8th Field Anti-Tank Battalion, 8th Field Engineer Battalion, 8th Field Signal Company, 8th Field Anti-Aircraft Battalion

Formed in 1942, the 8th Luftwaffe Field Division was sent to Army Detachment Hollidt, along with the 7th Luftwaffe Field Division. After fighting on the Upper Chir in the winter of 1942-43, it had to be taken out of the line and was disbanded in the summer of 1943.

SOURCES: Manstein: 319; OB 45: 327-28.

9th LUFTWAFFE FIELD DIVISION

COMPOSITION: 17th Field Infantry Regiment, 18th Field Infantry Regiment, 9th Field Artillery Regiment, 9th Field Füsilier Company, 9th Field Anti-Tank Battalion, 9th Field Engineer Battalion, 9th Field Signal Company, 9th Field Anti-Aircraft Battalion

After being formed in late 1942, the 9th Field arrived on the northern sector of the Russian Front in January 1943. It was first heavily engaged in the retreat from Leningrad in February 1944 and suffered such heavy casualties that it had to be disbanded.

SOURCE: OB 45: 328

10th LUFTWAFFE FIELD DIVISION

COMPOSITION: 19th Field Infantry Regiment, 20th Field Infantry Regiment, 10th Field Artillery Regiment, 10th Field Füsilier Company, 10th Field Anti-Tank Battalion, 10th Field Engineer Battalion, 10th Field Signal Company, 10th Field Anti-Aircraft Battalion

Created in 1942, this Air Force ground division was sent to Army Group North in January 1943 and was part of the 18th Army when the Russians broke the Siege of Leningrad in January 1944. The massive Soviet assaults that broke the siege began on January 14; by January 17, the 10th Luftwaffe Field Division was smashed. It suffered further losses in the initial retreats through the Baltic area of the Soviet Union to the Narva and was disbanded shortly thereafter.

SOURCES: OB 45: 328; Ziemke 1966: 234, 253.

11th LUFTWAFFE FIELD DIVISION

COMPOSITION: 21st Field Infantry Regiment, 22nd Field Infantry Regiment, 11th Field Artillery Regiment, 11th Field Füsilier Company, 11th Field Anti-Tank Battalion, 11th Field Engineer Battalion, 11th Field Signal Company, 11th Field Anti-Aircraft Battalion

Authorized in 1942, the 11th Field Division finished its training in early 1943 and was sent to the Aegean Islands off of the coast of Greece as an occupation force. In February 1944 it was transferred to the Megara area of Greece, where it remained until August and no doubt took part in antipartisan operations. In September 1944 it retreated through southern Yugoslavia as part of the general withdrawal from the Balkans. It fought Tito's guerrillas in the Drava-Sava area in the fall of 1944 and was still on the southern sector of the Eastern Front in early 1945. It was never dissolved and was still in the East when the war ended. Its commander in early 1945 was Lieutenant General Kohler (late 1943-45).

NOTES AND SOURCES: Luftwaffe Lieutenant General Karl Drum commanded the 11th Field in 1943. Drum, former Chief of the Inspectorate of Air Reconnaissance Forces and Operations in the Air Ministry, was a specialist in army-air force coordination. He briefly served as Commander-in-Chief of Wehrmacht Forces in Holland before assuming command of the 11th. Later he was promoted to General der Flieger and was Commander of Luftwaffe Administrative Area, Western France. After the war he worked on historical studies for the U.S. Air Force at Karlsruhe, West Germany. Kohler had previously commanded the 282nd Infantry Division in Russia (1943). He transferred to the Luftwaffe in 1943. Most, but not all, Luftwaffe Field divisional commanders were members of the Luftwaffe. *Kriegstagebuch des OKW*, Volume IV: 1903; Plocher 1942: 416; OB 45: 328.

12th LUFTWAFFE FIELD DIVISION

COMPOSITION: 23rd Field Infantry Regiment, 24th Field Infantry Regiment, 12th Field Artillery Regiment, 12th Field Füsilier Company, 12th Field Anti-Tank Battalion, 12th Field Engineer Battalion, 12th Field Signal Company, 12th Field Anti-Aircraft Battalion

Created in 1942-43, the 12th Field was posted to Army Group North in 1943 and took heavy casualties in the withdrawal from Leningrad. It apparently received significant replacements from Luftwaffe Field divisions that were disbanded in early 1944. In any event the 12th Field was still in action in October 1944, when it took part in the retreat to western Latvia. It took part in the Battles of the Courland Pocket in the winter of 1944-45, when the Soviets tried unsuccessfully to crush Army Group North (later Courland). It was still in existence when the 18th Army surrendered to the Soviets at the end of the war. Its commander in 1945 was Major General Gottfried Weber (late 1943-45).

SOURCES: *Kriegstagebuch des OKW*, Volume IV: 1897; OB 45: 329.

13th LUFTWAFFE FIELD DIVISION

COMPOSITION: 25th Field Infantry Regiment, 26th Field Infantry Regiment, 13th Field Artillery Regiment, 13th Field Füsilier Company, 13th Field Anti-Tank Battalion, 13th Field Engineer Battalion, 13th Field Signal Company, 13th Field Anti-Aircraft Battalion

Formed in 1942, this division was stationed at the Gross-Born Maneuver Area in Pomerania in early 1943 before being sent to the northern sector of the Russian Front. It was crushed when the Russians broke the Siege of Leningrad and had to be disbanded. Its commanders included Lieutenant General Hellmuth Reymann (1943-44).

SOURCE: OB 45: 329.

14th LUFTWAFFE FIELD DIVISION

COMPOSITION: 27th Field Infantry Regiment, 28th Field Infantry Regiment, 14th Field Artillery Regiment, 14th Field Füsilier Company, 14th Field Anti-Tank Battalion, 14th Field Engineer Battalion, 14th Field Signal Company, 14th Field Anti-Aircraft Battalion

This division was formed in 1942 and early 1943, although it was not finished with its training nor even fully equipped before its first elements were sent to Norway to replace the 196th Infantry Division, which was on its way to the Russian Front. Initially posted in the Mo area, the 14th Field was later transferred to the Jutland peninsula in Denmark, where it underwent an extensive change in personnel in the summer of 1944. Returning to Norway in mid-1944, it was posted in the Nordland area and remained in Norway until the end of the war. The 14th was never involved in ground combat. Its commander in early 1945 was Lieutenant General Gunther Lohmann (1944-45).

SOURCES: OB 45: 329; Ziemke 1959: 262.

15th LUFTWAFFE FIELD DIVISION

COMPOSITION: 29th Field Infantry Regiment, 30th Field Infantry Regiment, 15th Field Artillery Regiment, 15th Field Füsilier Company, 15th Field Anti-Tank Battalion, 15th Field Engineer Battalion, 15th Field Signal Company, 15th Field Anti-Aircraft Battalion

Authorized in 1942, this division was not fully **formed in** late 1942 when it was sent to Army Group Don in southern **Russia. According** to Field Marshal von Manstein, it "disintegrated during its first few days in action." Taken out of the line, it absorbed the survivors of the 7th Luftwaffe Field Division and was sent back to the fighting, despite its deficiencies. The fact that von Manstein had to rely on Air Force infantry divisions evidences how desperate the situation on the southern sector of the Russian Front had grown by 1943. In autumn 1943, the 15th Field fought at Taganrog and again sustained heavy losses. Shortly afterward, it was disbanded, and its personnel were assigned to various infantry divisions, except for the anti-tank battalion, which was transferred intact to a panzer division. Lieutenant General Willibald Spang was the commander of the 15th Field.

SOURCES: Manstein: 318-19; OB 45: 330.

16th LUFTWAFFE FIELD DIVISION

COMPOSITION: 31st Field Infantry Regiment, 32nd Field Infantry Regiment, 45th Field Infantry Regiment, 16th Field Artillery Regiment, 16th Field Füsilier Company, 16th Field Anti-Tank Battalion, 16th Field Engineer Battalion, 16th Field Signal Company, 16th Field Anti-Aircraft Battalion

Originally a two-regiment Field division, the 16th was formed in 1942-43 and stationed in the Hague-Haarlem area of Holland. In June 1944, it created the 45th Field Infantry Regiment by reducing its other infantry regiments to two battalions each. At that time it was on garrison duty in Amsterdam as part of the Armed Forces Netherlands. In late June it was sent to Normandy and on July 2 replaced the Panzer Lehr Division on the front line of Army Group B. The very next day the British launched a major offensive on Caen and immediately overran the 16th Field, which lost 75 percent of its men within hours. The survivors were eventually collected and attached to the 21st Panzer Division. Later they were withdrawn from the line and consolidated with the 158th Reserve Division to form the 16th Infantry Division, which continued to serve on the Western Front until the end of the war. Lieutenant General Karl Sievers (1943-44) was the commander of the 16th Luftwaffe Field Division.

NOTES AND SOURCES: Unlike many Luftwaffe Field divisional commanders, Sievers was an Army officer. Later in 1944 he was given command of the 719th Infantry Division. Blumenson 1960: 561; Carell 1973: 238; Harrison: Map VI; Speidel: 41; OB 45: 330.

17th LUFTWAFFE FIELD DIVISION

COMPOSITION: 33rd Field Infantry Regiment, 34th Field Infantry Regiment, 17th Field Artillery Regiment, 17th Field Füsilier Company, 17th Field Anti-Tank Battalion, 17th Field Engineer Battalion, 17th Field Signal Company, 17th Field Anti-Aircraft Battalion

Originally assembled and trained in Pomerania, the 17th Field was posted as a static infantry division on the French Atlantic coast. In the spring of 1944 it was camped near the Seine River east of Le Havre as part of the 15th Army. After the Normandy Front collapsed, it helped defend Paris as a part of the 5th Panzer Army. On August 28 it was attacked by a much superior force from the U.S. 1st Army, and was virtually destroyed. Soon after, it was officially dissolved, and its survivors were absorbed by the 167th Infantry Division. The 17th Luftwaffe Field was led by Lieutenant General Hans-Kurt Höcker (1943-44).

NOTES AND SOURCES: Höcker, an Army officer, had previously commanded the 258th Infantry Division on the Eastern Front (1943) and later led the 167th Infantry Division in the West (1945). Blumenson 1960: 575-76, 579; Cole 1965: 623; Harrison: Map VI; OB 45: 330.

18th LUFTWAFFE FIELD DIVISION

COMPOSITION: 35th Field Infantry Regiment, 36th Field Infantry Regiment, 47th Field Infantry Regiment, 18th Field Artillery Regiment, 18th Field Füsilier Company, 18th Field Anti-Tank Battalion, 18th Field Engineer Battalion, 18th Field Signal Company, 18th Field Anti-Aircraft Battalion

This division was created in France, probably in the Rochefort area, and served in northern France and Belgium throughout its existence. In 1943 it was on duty in the Calais and Dunkirk areas of the North Sea, as part of the 15th Army. In the spring of 1944 its third regiment, the 47th Infantry, was formed from the third battalions of the 35th and 36th Field Infantry Regiments. The division first saw action in August 1944, when it took part in the defense of Paris as a part of the 5th Panzer Army. A month later, after it took part in the retreat to Belgium, the 18th Field was trapped in the Mons Pocket. Badly understrength when the battle began, it had practically ceased to exist by the time it was over. Only about three hundred men succeeded in breaking out of the trap. Later in September it was dissolved, and its few remaining men joined the 18th Volksgrenadier Division. Its divisional commanders were Major General Reinshagen (1943), Lieutenant General Wilhelm Rupprecht (1943-44), and Lieutenant General Joachim von Treschow (1944).

NOTES AND SOURCES: Reinshagen was an Air Force officer. Rupprecht was formerly commandant of Regensberg (Wehrkreis XIII) and later directed the 327th Infantry Division on the Russian Front (1942). Joachim von Treschow previously led the 328th Infantry Division in Russia (1942-43) and was given command of the LXIII Corps in late 1944. Blumenson 1960: 575-76, 683; Harrison: Map VI; Speidel: 41; OB 45: 331.

19th LUFTWAFFE FIELD DIVISION

COMPOSITION: 37th Field Infantry Regiment, 38th Field Infantry Regiment, 46th Field Infantry Regiment, 19th Field Artillery Regiment, 19th Field Füsilier Company, 19th Field Anti-Tank Battalion, 19th Field Engineer Battalion, 19th Field Signal Company, 19th Field Anti-Aircraft Battalion

The 19th Luftwaffe Field Division finished its initial organization in the Munich area in March 1943 and arrived in Normandy the following month. From June through December it served in Holland, garrisoning the Walcheren. In January 1944 the 19th was posted in the Ghent-Bruges area of Belgium and went to the Thielt area in the spring. While there it reorganized and added the 46th Field Infantry Regiment to its table of organization by reducing its other infantry regiments to two battalions each. In June, when the Italian Front threatened to collapse under severe Allied pounding, the division was transferred to Italy, where it first saw combat later in that month. The 19th proved to be an inadequate infantry division, as evidenced by its heavy casualties. The remnants of the division were sent to Denmark, inducted into the Army, and assigned to the newly formed 19th Volksgrenadier Division, which fought on the Western Front for the rest of the war.

NOTES AND SOURCES: The 19th Luftwaffe Field was initially formed under Luftwaffe Major General Hermann Plocher, who was the former Chief of Staff of the Condor Legion in Spain (1937-38), Chief of Plans and Mobilization on the Luftwaffe General Staff (1938-39), and Chief of Staff of the V Air Corps (later Luftwaffe Command East and 6th Air Fleet) (1940-43). He later led the Luftwaffe's 4th Air Division (1943), was Chief of Staff of the 3rd Air Fleet in France (1944), and the 6th Parachute Division on the Western Front (1944-45). Army Major General Erich Baessler led the 19th Luftwaffe Field in 1943. He had previously commanded the 377th Infantry Division on the Russian Front (1942). Promoted to Lieutenant General effective January 1, 1944, he was given command of the 191st Reserve Division on the French coast. Harrison: Map VI; Plocher 1941: xiii-xiv.

20th LUFTWAFFE FIELD DIVISION

COMPOSITION: 39th Field Infantry Regiment, 40th Field Infantry Regiment, 20th Field Artillery Regiment, 20th Field Füsilier Company, 20th Field Anti-Tank Battalion, 20th Field Engineer Battalion, 20th Field Signal Company, 20th Field Anti-Aircraft Battalion

After completing its formation in 1943, the 20th Field remained in

Germany until August, when it was transferred to Denmark. In June 1944
it was moved again, this time to a combat zone in Italy where it suffered
heavy losses. By October it was so small that it was tactically subordinated
to the 26th Panzer Division. Pulled out of the line in November, the 20th
Field was stationed at Treviso, Italy, where it was dissolved in early 1945.
The survivors of the division probably were assigned to the 155th Field
Training Division. The last commander of the 20th Luftwaffe Field
Division was Major General Erich Fronhöfer (1944-45). Its previous
commander, Colonel Voelcker (1944) was reportedly captured on the Ital-
ian Front in November, 1944.

NOTES AND SOURCES: Erich Fronhöfer commanded a panzer regiment in
1940 and was previously a tactics instructor at Wünsdorf. Colonel
Voelcker was a panzer grenadier officer. OB 45: 331-32.

21st LUFTWAFFE FIELD DIVISION

COMPOSITION: 41st Field Infantry Regiment, 42nd Field Infantry Regi-
ment, 21st Field Artillery Regiment, 21st Field Füsilier Company, 21st
Field Anti-Tank Battalion, 21st Field Engineer Battalion, 21st Field Signal
Company, 21st Field Anti-Aircraft Battalion

Formed in 1943, this division was in combat on the northern sector of the
Russian Front in the winter of 1943-44 and suffered heavy losses in the
retreat from Leningrad. It was heavily engaged in the Lake Ilmen area in
February 1944, but it held together and was still in action when Army
Group North withdrew to the Latvian coast in October. It finished the war
in the Courland Pocket.

NOTES AND SOURCES: Army Lieutenant General Licht, who led the
division in 1943 and 1944, commanded the 710th Infantry Division in Italy
and on the Eastern Front (1944-45). OB 45: 332.

22nd LUFTWAFFE FIELD DIVISION

COMPOSITION: 43rd Field Infantry Regiment, 44th Field Infantry Regi-
ment, 22nd Field Artillery Regiment, 22nd Field Füsilier Company, 22nd
Field Anti-Tank Battalion, 22nd Field Engineer Battalion, 22nd Field
Signal Company, 22nd Field Anti-Aircraft Battalion

Formation of this division was started in 1943 but never completed. Why
it was stillborn is not clear; however, the poor combat record of the earlier
Luftwaffe infantry divisions probably had a great deal to do with it.

NOTES AND SOURCES: The only commander this division had was Luft-waffe Major General Robert Fuchs. A former bomber group commander in the Condor Legion in Spain and in the 153rd Bomber Wing, he led the 26th Fighter Wing (1939) and the 33rd Fighter Regiment (1942) prior to taking over the 22nd Field. He later commanded the Luftwaffe's 1st Air Division on the Eastern Front (December 1943 to 1945). Plocher 1943: 108, 320; OB 45: 332.

10

The SS Divisions

SS VERFÜGUNGS DIVISION

COMPOSITION: SS "Deutschland" Regiment, SS "Germania" Regiment, SS "Der Führer" Regiment, and other, smaller SS units.

HOME STATION: Various SS posts

This, one of the first Waffen-SS (or Armed SS) divisions, was formed in late 1939 as the SS began its first steps in infringing into the Army's sphere as the principal military force of the German nation. The division did well in the French campaign of 1940 but was dissolved soon after, in order that its veterans could be used to form other SS divisions. Most of the men of the Verfügungs (Decree) Division went to the 2nd SS Panzer Division "Das Reich," which was formed that winter, while others formed cadres around which the 5th SS Panzer Division "Viking" was formed.

NOTES: The commander of the Verfüngungs division was SS Lieutenant General Paul Hausser, who later led II SS Panzer Corps in Russia and the West (1943-44) and the 7th Army on the Western Front until he was severely wounded in the fall of 1944. Later he briefly commanded Army Group G. Hausser had already retired from the Army as a lieutenant general before joining the SS.

1st SS PANZER DIVISION
"LEIBSTANDARTE ADOLF HITLER"

COMPOSITION (1945): 1st SS Panzer Regiment, 1st SS Panzer Grenadier Regiment, 2nd SS Panzer Grenadier Regiment, 1st SS Panzer Artillery Regiment, 1st SS Panzer Reconnaissance Battalion, 1st SS Anti-Tank Battalion, 1st SS Panzer Engineer Battalion, 1st SS Panzer Signal Battalion, 1st SS Anti-Aircraft Battalion, 1st SS Projector Battalion

HOME STATION: Berlin

Formed from SS volunteers in 1934 as a bodyguard unit for Adolf Hitler, the 1st SS served as an independent motorized regiment in Poland and France before being expanded to a full motorized infantry division in early 1941. It took part in the Balkans campaign of 1941 and crossed into southern Russia with Army Group South in July 1941. It advanced along the Black Sea coast in August, took part in the opening phases of the Crimean campaign, and was devastated in the Battle of Rostov during the Soviet winter offensive of 1941-42. After seeing some action in the summer of 1942, the Leibstandarte (Personal Standard or Flag) was pulled out of the line and sent to northern France in August, where it rested, and was refitted, reinforced, and was redesignated an SS panzer grenadier unit. While the 1st SS was refitting, the Allies landed in French North Africa, so the Leibstandarte took part in the occupation of Vichy France in response. Returned to the Eastern Front in the spring of 1943, the division took part in the Kursk offensive and suffered heavy casualties in the Battle of Kharkov (1943) before being transferred to northern Italy. While there it was upgraded to an SS panzer division and helped disarm the Italian Army after the Fascist regime collapsed, but it did not see any fighting. Returning to southern Russia in the autumn, the 1st SS was involved in heavy combat west of Kiev, at Tarnopol, and in the Dnieper battles. It unsuccessfully tried to prevent the encirclement of the 1st Panzer Army in 1944. The division was itself surrounded at Skala in the spring of that year and suffered ruinous losses in the ensuing breakout. Transferred to northern Belgium to be rebuilt again, the Leibstandarte was reinforced to a strength of 21,386 men. It fought in the Caen sector during the Battle of Normandy, was involved in the unsuccessful German counterattack at Mortain, and was surrounded at Falaise. Before it broke out of this pocket the 1st SS Panzer was reduced to an armored strength of only thirty tanks. Withdrawn to northwestern Germany, the veteran SS division was rebuilt once more before being placed in reserve behind the Aachen front. It fought in the Ardennes counteroffensive and subsequent withdrawal before being sent to Hungary, where it fought in the unsuccessful Lake Balaton counterattack. Hitler, displeased with the failure of one of the Leibstandarte's attacks, ordered it to remove the Adolf Hitler cuffband from the uniforms of its troops. The division responded by sending him a pile of their medals—in a latrine bucket. The survivors of the division retreated into Austria in 1945 and fought in the Battle of Vienna. It ended the war on the southern sector of the Eastern Front. Commanders of the Leibstandarte included SS Lieutenant General Otto "Sepp" Dietrich (1934-43), SS Major General Theodor Wisch (1944), SS Lieutenant General Hermann Priess (1944-45?), and SS Major General Wilhelm Mohnke (1945).

NOTES AND SOURCES: Dietrich, a long-time Nazi and great personal friend of Adolf Hitler, was prominent in the Blood Purge of 1934, when hundreds of S.A. "Brownshirt" leaders and other enemies of the regime were murdered. After commanding the 1st SS Panzer, he led the I SS Panzer Corps (1943-44) and the 6th Panzer Army (later 6th SS Panzer Army) (1944-45). Although he rose to the rank of SS Colonel General, he was not considered a brilliant commander. Theodor Wisch, a holder of the Knight's Cross with Oak Leaves and Swords, was seriously wounded on the Western Front in 1944. He was only 38 years old in 1945. Priess was former commander of the 3rd SS Panzer Division (1943-44) and led the I SS Panzer Corps on the Eastern Front in 1945. Wilhelm Mohnke had previously been the commander of the 26th SS Panzer Grenadier Regiment of the 12th SS Panzer Division in 1944. Blumenson 1960: 190, 505, 570; Carell 1966: 294-95, 297, 542, 623; Carell 1971: 17, 510-11; Chant, Volume 14: 1858-61; Volume 17: 2372; Cole 1965: 260; Harrison: 240, Map VI: John Keegan, *Waffen SS: The Asphalt Soldiers*, Ballantine Books, Inc., New York, 1970: 76, 82; Kennedy: Map 7; Manstein: 209-10, 482; Charles W. Snydor, Jr., *Soldiers of Destruction: The SS Death's Head Division, 1933-1945*, Princeton University Press, Princeton, New Jersey, 1977: 275-76 (hereafter cited as "Snydor"). Speidel: 42; OB 43: 216; OB 44: 325; OB 45: 336-37; Ziemke 1966: 225.

2nd SS PANZER DIVISION "DAS REICH"

COMPOSITION: 2nd SS Panzer Regiment, 3rd SS Panzer Grenadier Regiment "Deutschland," 4th SS Panzer Grenadier Regiment "Der Führer," 2nd SS Panzer Artillery Regiment, 2nd SS Panzer Reconniassance Battalion, 2nd SS Anti-Tank Battalion, 2nd SS Engineer Battalion, 2nd SS Panzer Signal Battalion, 2nd SS Anti-Aircraft Battalion, 2nd SS Projector Battalion

HOME STATION: "Deutschland" Regiment: Munich
"Der Führer" Regiment: Vienna.

The 2nd SS Division was formed in the winter of 1940-41 from two

regiments of the old SS Verfügungs Division and the SS Motorcycle
regiment "Langemarck," which was made up of Germans and Germanic
volunteers. Initially designated an SS panzer grenadier division, it first saw
action in the Balkans campaign, and later in 1941 it took part in the
invasion of the Soviet Union, fighting in the battles of the Dnieper crossings, Smolensk, Kiev, and the Battle of Moscow. It lost almost ten thousand
men in the winter campaign: 60 percent of its combat strength. Sent to
France in the summer of 1942 to rest and refit, Das Reich was converted to a
panzer division and took part in the occupation of Vichy France in
November. Returned to the Russian Front soon after, it fought at Kharkov
in March 1943, at Kursk in July, and at Kiev in November, where it suffered
heavy casualties. Transferred to the Toulouse area of southwestern France
in February 1944, it was ordered to Normandy when the Allies landed. On
route to the front in June, it committed a famous atrocity at Tulle, where
its men hanged ninety-five Frenchmen, and at Oradour, where it killed
more than four hundred men, women, and children, in reprisal for the
murder of Major Helmut Kampfe, commander of the division's reconnaissance battalion. In the Normandy campaign it was used as a "fire brigade," being divided into several combat groups and fighting on various
sectors of the front. In this battle its commander, SS Lieutenant General
Heinz Lammerding, was wounded and his replacement, SS Colonel
Tychesen, was killed. After taking part in the counterattack at Mortain, the
division was surrounded with the bulk of Army Group B at Falaise. The
2nd SS Panzer broke out, but by August 21 it had a strength of only four
hundred fifty men, fifteen tanks, and six guns. By September it was down to
its last three tanks. After a brief rebuilding period in northwestern Germany, the greatly reduced Das Reich Division was in reserve near Aachen,
took part in the Ardennes offensive, and was subsequently sent to Hungary, where it took part in the 6th SS Panzer Army's Lake Balaton offensive: Hitler's last major attack in the war. The division was still in action
on the Eastern Front at the end of the war. Commanders of the 2nd SS
Panzer included SS Lieutenant General Willi Bittrich (1942), SS Lieutenant General Walter Krüger (1943-44), Lammerding (1944), Tychensen
(1944), and SS Colonel Karl Kreutz (1944-45?).

NOTES AND SOURCES: Willi Bittrich, an Air Force officer who transferred
to the SS in order to gain more rapid promotions, later commanded the 8th
SS Cavalry Division (1942-43), the 9th SS Panzer Division (1943-June
1944), and the II SS Panzer Corps (June 1944-1945). He is best known for
destroying the British 1st Airborne Division's bridgehead at Arnhem in
September 1944. He was promoted to Obergruppenführer (General of SS)
in August 1944. Krüger, formerly commander of the 4th SS Panzer Grenadier Division on the Russian Front (1941), later led the VI SS Panzer Corps
on the Eastern Front (1945). He held the Knight's Cross with Oak Leaves

and Swords. Lammerding was formerly Operations Officer of the 3rd SS Panzer Division and of von dem Back-Zelewski's antipartisan forces on and behind the Eastern Front, 1941-43. He was on wounded leave from July to December 1944 and was later Chief of Staff of Army Group Vistula during Himmler's tenure as commander (1945). Tychensen, whose face had been mutilated by wounds, previously led the 4th SS Panzer Grenadier Regiment of the Das Reich Division. Colonel Kreutz, 36 years old, was apparently an acting commander. His permanent assignment was commander, 2nd SS Panzer Artillery Regiment. Blumenson 1960: 275, 422, 554, 577; Blumenson 1969: 42; Carell 1966: 80, 90, 623; Carell 1971: 17, 525; Chant, Volume 14: 1859-61; Volume 17: 2372; Cole 1965: 583; Keegan: 76, 82, 91; Manstein: 488; MacDonald 1973: 27; George Stein, *Waffen SS*, Cornell University, New York, 1966: 176-68 (hereafter cited as "Stein"); OB 43: 216-17; OB 44: 325; OB 45: 337. For the story of the division's atrocities in France in June, 1944, see Max Hasting's excellent book, *Das Reich* (New York: Holt, Rinehart and Winston, 1981).

3rd SS PANZER DIVISION "TOTENKOPF"

COMPOSITION (1943): 3rd SS Panzer Regiment, 5th SS Panzer Grenadier Regiment "Thule," 6th SS Panzer Grenadier Regiment "Theodor Eicke," 3rd SS Panzer Artillery Regiment, 3rd SS Panzer Reconnaissance Battalion, 3rd SS Anti-Tank Battalion, 3rd SS Panzer Engineer Battalion, 3rd SS Panzer Signal Battalion, 3rd SS Anti-Aircraft Battalion, 3rd SS Projector Battalion

HOME STATION: Berlin (Oranienburg)

The "Totenkopf," or Death's Head Division, was created as an SS motorized division in October 1939. Probably the most brutal German division to serve in World War II, most of its men had previously served as concentration camp guards at Dachau, Sachsenhausen, or Buchenwald. Its men fought well in France and Flanders in 1940, although elements of the division did show signs of panic when struck by the British counterattack at Arras in May. Totenkopf was not well-led initially, but this situation improved as the SS officers gained practical experience. The division murdered a number of Allied prisoners during the Flanders campaign and committed at least one atrocity against the British. After the French capitulation, the 3rd SS was assigned to occupation duties in the Bay of Biscay area, until being sent to Poland to prepare for the invasion of Russia in the spring of 1941. Totenkopf fought on the northern sector of the Eastern Front from June 1941 to October 1942. It suffered such heavy losses in the initial advance on Leningrad that its 2nd SS Totenkopf Motorized Infantry

Regiment (as it was then called) had to be dissolved in July 1941. Later surrounded in the Battle of the Demyansk Pocket in the winter of 1941-42, it distinguished itself in the heavy fighting, although it suffered tremendous losses. Of the 17,265 men who crossed into Russia with "Totenkopf," 12,625 were casualties by March 20, 1942. Of these, only 5,029 had been replaced. Nevertheless, fighting with fanatical bravery, it remained in the line, playing a decisive role in keeping the sole supply route to II Corps at Demyansk open against repeated Russian attacks. By September 1942 its infantry and artillery regiments, reconnaissance, engineer, and anti-tank battalions had all suffered an average of 80 percent casualties, and the division was at less than regimental strength. Finally in October 1942 it was sent to France, where it was rebuilt as an SS panzer division. After taking part in the occupation of Vichy France in November 1942, it briefly served on guard duty on the Mediterranean coast, before being returned to Russia in February 1943. Upon its return to the Eastern Front, its commander and founder, SS General Theodor Eicke, was killed when his reconnaissance plane was shot down by the Russians on February 28. The 3rd SS Panzer Division spent the rest of its career on the Eastern Front, serving as a fire brigade and fighting as Kharkov, Kursk (where it lost 50 percent of its tanks and vehicles), and the Dnieper campaign, where it again suffered heavy casualties. It helped slow the Russian spring offensive of 1944 west of Kirovograd and was transferred to Army Group Center in July 1944, after the 4th and 9th armies collapsed. Despite its reduced numbers, Totenkopf participated in the defense of Warsaw and once again took heavy losses. Transferred to Hungary in December, 1944, it took part in the unsuccessful counterattack west of Budapest and ended the war in Austria. In May 1945, the 3rd SS surrendered to the Americans, who promptly turned them over to the Russians. Many of the former members of the division disappeared while in Soviet captivity. Commanders of the division included SS General Theodor Eicke (1939-43), SS Lieutenant General Max Simon (1943), SS Lieutenant General Hermann Priess (1943-44) and SS Major General Helmuth Becker (1945).

NOTES AND SOURCES: A native of Alsace-Lorraine, Eicke was in charge of antiespionage services for I. G. Farben prior to the Nazi rise to power in 1933. He was commandant of the Dachau concentration camp (1933-34) and was named Inspector of Concentration Camps and SS Guard Formations in 1934, a post he held until assuming command of the Totenkopf division on November 14, 1939. Eicke, one of the toughest and most ruthless Nazis, played an important role in the suppression of the Brownshirts during the Night of the Long Knives in 1934. He was seriously wounded in July 1941, and temporarily replaced in divisional command by SS Colonel Matthias Kleinheisterkamp (July 1941) and SS Major General Georg Keppler (July-September 1941), who had led the "Der Führer" Regiment (later the 4th SS Panzer Grenadier Regiment) in France. SS

Lieutenant General Max Simon was acting divisional commander from July to October 1942 and permanent divisional commander from the time of Eicke's death until October 1943, when he assumed command of the 16th SS Panzer Grenadier Division. He later commanded the XIII SS Corps on the Western Front (1945). Hermann Priess was named commander of the 1st SS Panzer Division in July 1944, and commanded the I SS Panzer Corps in 1945. He held the Knights Cross with Oak Leaves and Swords. Hellmuth Becker, former commander of the 3rd SS Panzer Regiment (1943) was executed by the Russians without trial in 1945. Carell 1966: 237-46, 623; Carell 1971: 17, 218; Cole 1950: 48; Keegan: 64-65, 76, 82, 91; Charles W. Snydor: 35, 165-66, 168, 222, 243-45, 250, 290, 311; Robert Wistrich, *Who's Who in Nazi Germany*, Macmillan Publishing Company, New York, 1982: 63-65; OB 43: 217; OB 44: 326; OB 45: 338; Ziemke 1966: 284.

4th SS PANZER GRENADIER DIVISION "POLIZEI"

COMPOSITION (1945): 4th SS Panzer Battalion, 7th SS Panzer Grenadier Regiment, 8th SS Panzer Grenadier Regiment, 4th SS Panzer Artillery Regiment, 4th SS Panzer Reconnaissance Battalion, 4th SS Anti-Tank Battalion, 4th SS Panzer Engineer Battalion, 4th SS Signal Battalion, 4th SS Anti-Aircraft Battalion

HOME STATION: See below

The SS Police Division was formed from members of the German police in October 1939. It initially consisted of the 1st, 2nd, and 3rd Police Infantry Regiments. After finishing training in February 1940, the division fought in the French campaign and took part in the invasion of Russia in June 1941. It never distinguished itself in combat to the degree its brother German Waffen-SS divisions did, although it performed creditably. It fought in all the major battles of Army Group North from June 1941 to May 1943, including Lake Ilmen, Volkhov, and Lake Ladoga, where it suffered heavy casualties. The 4th SS performed security duties in the Protectorate (formerly Czechoslovakia) and Poland in the spring of 1943, before being transferred to Greece that summer. By September 1944 the unit was in Serbia, fighting Tito's partisans, before returning to action against the Russians in Hungary in November. The 4th SS took part in the Battle of Berlin as part of Army Group Vistula and was dissolved soon after; some of its men probably managed to escape the Russians and surrender to the British and Americans at the end of the war, but most ended up in Soviet POW camps. The commanders of the Police Division included SS Lieutenant General Karl von Pfeffer-Wildenbruch (1939-40), SS Lieutenant General Walter Krüger (1941), SS Lieutenant General Friedrich Jeckeln (1942), SS Lieutenant General Alfred Wünnenberg

(1942-43), SS Major General Fritz Schmedes (1943-44), SS Colonel Helmut Dörner (late 1944), and SS Colonel Walter Harzer (1945).

NOTES AND SOURCES: Most of the commanders of the 4th SS held rank in both the German Police and the Waffen-SS; General von Pfeffer-Wildenbruch, for example, was chief of an important element of the German Order Police. As a General of Waffen-SS, he later distinguished himself as the commander of the IX SS Mountain Corps and commander of the German and Hungarian forces surrounded in Budapest (late 1944-45). He was captured by the Russians in February 1945, after a heroic but hopeless siege. Walter Krüger, General of Waffen-SS from June 21, 1944, later led the 2nd SS Panzer Division in Russia (1943-early 1944) and the VI SS Panzer Corps (1945). Alfred Wünnenberg, a General of Waffen-SS and Police, was acting Chief of the Order Police and Chief of the Main Depot of Order Police in 1945. Helmut Dörner, age thirty-six, was an SS-Police officer and held temporary divisional command only. He led the 8th SS Panzer Grenadier Regiment (1944-45) and wore the Knights Cross with Oak Leaves and Swords. He was advanced to the rank of Oberführer (an SS rank roughly equal to junior Major General) on January 30, 1945. Walter Harzer was previously Ia of the 9th SS Panzer Division (1944) and acting commander of that division (September 1944). Carell 1966: 250, 421; Carell 1971: 279; Keegan: 66; Seaton: 491; OB 43: 218; OB 45: 338-39; Ziemke 1966: 477.

5th SS PANZER DIVISION "VIKING"

COMPOSITION (1945): 5th SS Panzer Regiment, 9th SS Panzer Grenadier Regiment "Germania," 10th SS Panzer Grenadier Regiment "Westland," 5th SS Panzer Artillery Regiment, 5th SS Panzer Reconnaissance Battalion, 5th SS Anti-Tank Battalion, 5th SS Panzer Engineer Battalion, 5th SS Panzer Signal Battalion, 5th SS Anti-Aircraft Battalion, 5th SS Projector Battalion

HOME STATION: Hamburg and Klagenfurt

The 5th SS Division was formed from the "Germania" Regiment of the SS Verfügungs Division and two regiments of Scandinavian, Dutch, and Flemish volunteers. Subsequent replacements were drawn from Volksdeutsche from the Balkans and from German volunteers, giving the unit a real international character (as well as a real language problem) by the end of the war. Nevertheless it fought well in all of its engagements. As the "Germania" Standarte (Regiment) it took part in the French campaign, where its commander, SS Colonel Felix Steiner, distinguished himself. Remustered as a panzer grenadier division in December 1940, "Viking" served on the southern sector of the Russian Front, eventually ending up in the Caucasus. It fought at Kursk in July 1943, where it suffered heavy losses. Briefly withdrawn from the line, the 5th SS was converted to a panzer division in October 1943. It participated in the Cherkassy encirclement in February 1944, escaping only after suffering heavy casualties. Sent to Poland in April, it again sustained heavy losses in the battles around Warsaw that autumn. Transferred to Hungary, it took part in the unsuccessful attempt to relieve Budapest in December and was largely destroyed in the Battle of Vienna in April 1945. Its commanders included Steiner (1940-43), SS Lieutenant General Herbert Gille (1943-44), and SS Colonel Rudolf (or Joachim) Mühlenkamp (1945).

NOTES AND SOURCES: Steiner was promoted to General of Waffen-SS in 1944 and led the III SS Panzer Corps (1944) and the 11th SS Army (1945). He held the Knight's Cross with Oak Leaves and Swords. Herbert Gille, former commander of the 5th SS Panzer Artillery Regiment, also became a General of Waffen-SS. He was later commander of the IV SS Panzer Corps (1945). Although unquestionably brave—he was awarded the Knight's Cross with Oak Leaves, Swords, and Diamonds—Gille was a poor corps commander and narrowly avoided being relieved of his command in early 1945. Colonel Mühlenkamp was only thirty-five years old in 1945. Carell 1966: 533, 546, 552; Carell 1971: 89; Keegan: 68, 91; OB 43: 217; OB 44: 327, OB 45: 339; Ziemke 1966: 340. For an excellent personal history of a young SS man, as well as the story of the battles of the Viking Division, see Peter Neumann, *The Black March*, Bantam Books, New York, 1960.

6th SS MOUNTAIN DIVISION "NORD"

COMPOSITION: 11th SS Mountain Infantry Regiment "Reinhard Heydrich," 12th SS Mountain Infantry Regiment "Michael Gesimar," 6th SS Mountain Artillery Regiment, 6th SS Mountain Reconnaissance Battalion, 6th SS Anti-Tank Battalion, 6th SS Mountain Engineer Battalion, 6th SS Mountain Signal Battalion, 6th SS Anti-Aircraft Battalion. The 506th SS Panzer Grenadier Battalion was reportedly attached to the division in 1945.

HOME STATION: Austria

Raised in Austria as an SS Regiment in late 1940, "North" was first upgraded to a brigade and then became a division in April 1941. It included many Volksdeutsche mountaineers. In June 1941 it was sent to Finland, from whence it struck into Russia with the Army of Norway in the unsuccessful drive on Murmansk. It behaved badly at first, a fact partially attributable to the dark, depressing Finnish forests. The 6th SS nevertheless remained in northern Russia and was continuously engaged until autumn 1944. It took part in the retreat from Lapland to Norway and in mid-November 1944 embarked from Oslo, bound for Denmark. By December it was fighting on the Western Front, in the Saar sector. Cut off on the wrong (western) side of the Rhine River by the rapid Allied advance of March 1945, the division—now six thousand strong—put up a spirited resistance. It took U.S. forces several days to run it to earth. The divisional commander, SS Lieutenant General Karl Heinrich Brenner (late 1944-45) was captured on April 2, ending organized resistance by the 6th SS. Previous divisional commanders included SS Lieutenant Generals Georg Keppler (1942), Matthias Kleinheisterkamp (1943), Lothar Debes (1944), and Friedrich-Wilhelm Krüger (1944).

NOTES AND SOURCES: Keppler, Kleinheisterkamp, and Krüger all became Generals of Waffen-SS, and the latter became a General of Police as well. Georg Keppler was later Territorial Commander of Waffen-SS in Bohemia and Moravia (1943-44) and commander of the I SS Panzer Corps (1944). Kleinheisterkamp was also commander of an SS corps in 1944. Lothar Debes was commander of the 10th SS Panzer Division in 1944. Krüger was in charge of SS Police in Poland in 1943 and commander of the V SS Mountain Corps in 1945. Karl Heinrich Brenner, a Lieutenant General of Police as well as of Waffen-SS, was Inspector of Police in Wehrkreis XVIII (northern Austria) in 1942. Carell 1966: 454; Keegan: 156; MacDonald 1973: 250, 349-50; OB 43: 217-18; OB 44: 327; OB 45: 340; Ziemke 1966: 159-60, 222-23, 292-93, 312.

7th SS VOLUNTEER MOUNTAIN DIVISION "PRINZ EUGEN"

COMPOSITION: 13th SS Mountain Infantry Regiment "Artur Phelps," 14th SS Mountain Infantry Regiment "Skanderberg," 7th SS Mountain Artillery Regiment, 7th SS Mountain Reconnaissance Battalion, 7th SS Anti-Tank Battalion, 7th SS Mountain Engineer Battalion, 7th SS Mountain Signal Battalion, 7th SS Anti-Aircraft Battalion

HOME STATION: Serbia

The 7th SS Mountain Division was formed in northern Serbia in the spring of 1942. Its troops were Volksdeutsche (ethnic Germans) from Hungary, Rumania, and Yugoslavia. The following spring the 7th SS was transferred to Bosnia and the Dalmatian coast, where it operated against partisans. In October 1944 it was shifted to the Belgrade area to cover the eastern flank of the German withdrawal through Yugoslavia, where it suffered heavy losses. These casualties were made good near the end of the year when some of the more reliable elements of the disbanded 21st SS Mountain Division "Skanderberg" or "Albanian #1" were absorbed by the 7th SS. At this time the 14th SS Mountain Infantry Regiment was given the honorary title "Skanderberg." The division ended the war in the Balkans as part of Army Group F. It fell into Russian captivity at the end of the conflict. Its commanders included SS Lieutenant General Artur Phelps (1942-43), SS Major General Reichsritter Carl von Oberkamp (1944), and SS Major General Otto Kumm (1945).

NOTES AND SOURCES: Oberkamp was later with the Headquarters of the V SS Corps (1944). Otto Kumm, who was only thirty-six years old in 1945, previously led the 4th SS Panzer Grenadier Regiment of the Das Reich (2nd SS) Panzer Division in Russia (1943). Keegen: 100, 158; Stein: 170, 200, 204, 221, 274; OB 43: 218; OB 44: 328; OB 45: 340.

8th SS CAVALRY DIVISION "FLORIAN GEYER"

COMPOSITION (1943): 15th SS Cavalry Regiment, 16th SS Cavalry Regiment, 17th SS Cavalry Regiment, 18th SS Cavalry Regiment, 8th SS Artillery Regiment, 8th SS Panzer Reconnaissance Battalion, 8th SS Anti-Tank Battalion, 8th SS Engineer Batallion, 8th SS Signal Battalion, 8th SS Anti-Aircraft Battalion

HOME STATION: Debica, General Gouvernement

Originally formed as an SS Cavalry brigade in late 1941, this unit first saw action against the Russian winter offensive of 1941-42 and remained in more or less continuous contact until autumn 1942, when it was upgraded to divisional status. The 8th SS was soon back in the line and fought on the southern and central sectors of the Eastern Front until late 1943, when it was transferred to the Brod area of Yugoslavia. By April 1944 it was in Hungary and in September was sent into action in Transylvania, after the German front in Rumania collapsed. The 8th SS Cavalry was encircled in Budapest with the IX SS Mountain Corps in December 1944, and, after a bitter resistance, it was destroyed by the Russians in early 1945. Of the estimated thirty-five thousand Axis soldiers surrounded in the Hungarian capital, only about seven hundred succeeded in breaking out and making their way back to German lines. Commanders of the division included SS Major General Willi Bittrich (1942-43), SS Lieutenant General Hermann Fegelein (1943-44), and SS Major General Joachim Rumohr (1944-45).

NOTES AND SOURCES: For the story of Bittrich's career, see notes, 2nd SS Panzer Division. Hermann Fegelein, a former groom whom Shirer described as "quite illiterate," led the unit when it was known simply as the SS Cavalry Brigade. He commanded it on the Russian Front (late 1941-May 1942). Later he commanded a battle group on the Eastern Front (1942-43), before being named to command of the 8th SS. Later he was promoted to General of Waffen-SS and became Himmler's SS Liaison Officer at Führer Headquarters (1944-45). He solidified his position in the Third Reich by marrying Gretl Braun, the sister of Hitler's mistress, Eva Braun. On April 26, 1945, during the Battle of Berlin, he deserted, but Hitler noticed his absence and sent an SS party to find him. They captured him in civilian clothes on the afternoon of April 27, and two days later he was executed on Hitler's orders, only one day before the Führer himself committed suicide. Eva Braun made no attempt to save him. He was thirty-nine years old at the time of his death. His brother Waldemar, age thirty-three, was commanding a regiment in the 8th SS Cavalry Division during the Siege of Budapest. SS Major General Rumohr, who was only thirty-five years of age in 1945, had previously commanded an SS artillery regiment and held the Knight's Cross with Oak Leaves. Keegan: 156; Seaton: 419-20; OB 43: 218; OB 44: 328; OB 45: 341. For Fegelein's story, see William L. Shirer, *The Rise and Fall of the Third Reich*, Simon and Schuster, New York, 1960: 1114, 1121-22.

9th SS PANZER DIVISION "HOHENSTAUFEN"

COMPOSITION: 9th SS Panzer Regiment, 19th SS Panzer Grenadier Regiment, 20th SS Panzer Grenadier Regiment, 9th SS Panzer Artillery Regiment, 9th SS Panzer Reconnaissance Battalion, 9th SS Anti-Tank Battalion, 9th SS Engineer Battalion, 9th SS Panzer Signal Battalion, 9th SS Anti-Aircraft Battalion, 9th SS Projector Battalion

HOME STATION: See below

The formation of this division was authorized by Hitler in December 1942, and it was organized in northeastern France early the next year. It spent that summer training in the Amiens area, before being sent to the Mediterranean coast area of France in February 1944. Hohenstaufen was hastily sent into combat on the Eastern Front in March 1944, where it took part in the Tarnopol counteroffensive that saved the 1st Panzer Army. Soon after it was shifted to Poland to prevent a possible Russian advance through that sector. The 9th SS was quickly returned to France in June and was soon heavily engaged in the Normandy fighting. It suffered heavy losses in the battles west of Caen (against the British), in the Montain counterattack (against the Americans), and in the Falaise breakout. Although it had inflicted severe losses on the Allies, it was down to a strength of four hundred sixty men, twenty guns, and twenty to twenty-five tanks by August 21. Transferred to the rear at Arnhem, the 9th SS, with its sister division, the 10th SS Panzer, was in an ideal position to counter the British 1st Airborne Division's parachute assault on Arnhem in September 1944. Under the command of the II SS Panzer Corps, they virtually destroyed the elite Allied paratrooper unit. After resting and refitting in the Arnhem vicinity, the Hohenstaufen Division took part in the Battle of the Bulge and was sent to Hungary in February 1945. It ended the war fighting in Austria on the southern sector of the Eastern Front. The division's commanders included SS Lieutenant General Willi Bittrich (1943-44), SS Colonel Mueller (1944), and SS Colonel Sylvester Stadler (1944-45).

NOTES AND SOURCES: For Bittrich's career, see notes, 2nd SS Panzer Division "Das Reich." Bittrich was named commander of the II SS Panzer Corps on June 29, 1944, and commanded that unit at Arnhem. He was replaced as commander of the 9th SS by Colonel Mueller, former commander of the 20th SS Panzer Grenadier Regiment (1943?-44). Mueller was killed in action on July 14, 1944, and replaced by SS Colonel Stadler, who was until then commanding officer of the 4th SS Panzer Grenadier Regiment, 2nd SS Panzer Division (1942-44). Stadler was thirty-five years old in 1945. SS Colonel Walter Harzer (age 32), the division's operations officer, was acting commander of the 9th SS Panzer Division in September 1944. He later commanded the 4th SS Panzer Grenadier Division "Police" (1945). Blumenson 1960: 190, 577; Carell 1971: 523; Carell 1973: 209-10; Chant, Volume 14: 1811; Keegan: 90-91; Hastings: 215; *Kriegstagebuch des OKW*, Volume I: 1146; Mitcham 1983: 128-29; Stein: 218; OB 44: 329; OB 45: 341.

10th SS PANZER DIVISION "FRUNDSBERG"

COMPOSITION: 10th SS Panzer Regiment, 21st SS Panzer Grenadier Regiment, 22nd SS Panzer Grenadier Regiment, 10th SS Panzer Artillery Regiment, 10th SS Panzer Reconnaissance Battalion, 10th SS Anti-Tank Battalion, 10th SS Panzer Engineer Battalion, 10th SS Panzer Signal Battalion, 10th SS Anti-Aircraft Battalion, 10th SS Projector Battalion

HOME STATION: See below

Formed in southwestern France in the winter of 1942-43, the 10th SS was the sister division of the 9th SS Panzer. At first designated SS Panzer Division "Karl der Grosse" (Karl the Great), it was transferred to southeastern France in the summer of 1943 and by autumn was in Normandy. In October it was remustered as a panzer division. Hastily sent to the

Eastern Front in March 1944, "Frundsberg" took part in the Tarnopol offensive that saved the 1st Panzer Army. By April, the 10th SS was in Poland as part of the reserve, and in June it returned to France. The Frundsberg Division was badly hurt in the Normandy fighting and subsequent encirclement at Falaise. By August 21 its strength had been reduced to that of a weak infantry battalion, and all of its tanks had been destroyed; nevertheless, the division took part in the withdrawal from France. Sent to Arnhem to regroup, the 10th SS helped destroy the British 1st Airborne Division in September. Later that month the 10th SS Panzer was part of Colonel General Student's 1st Parachute Army in the Albert Canal-Siegfried Line battles. Shifted back to Germany, the division was transferred to the Aachen area in November and then to the Saar, replacing the 9th Panzer Division, which was earmarked for the Battle of the Bulge. The Frundsberg Division did not fight in the Ardennes offensive but took part in the unsuccessful attempt to take Strasbourg in January 1945. The survivors of the 10th SS Panzer Division were returned to the Eastern Front in February and were defending east of Berlin until late March, when they were transferred from Army Group Vistula to Army Group Center. The division fought its last battles in eastern Germany and Czechoslovakia in April and May 1945. Its commanders included SS Lieutenant General Karl von Treuenfeld (1943?-44), SS Lieutenant General Lothar Debes (1944), SS Colonel Otto Paetsch (1944), and SS Major General Heinz Harmel (1944-45).

NOTES AND SOURCES: SS General von Treuenfeld was seriously wounded in the Tarnopol battles in 1944. Lothar Debes's tenure as commander of the 10th SS was apparently very brief. He had previously commanded the 6th SS Mountain Division. SS Colonel Paetsch was acting commander of the 10th SS Panzer in November 1944. Soon after he returned to his normal assignment as commander of the 10th SS Panzer Regiment. Heinz Harmel, former commander of the 3rd SS Panzer Grenadier Regiment of the 2nd SS Panzer Division (1943-June 1944), led the Frundsberg Division from June 1944 until 1945, except for the period when SS Colonel Paetsch was acting commander. Harmel held the Knight's Cross with Oak Leaves and Swords. Blumenson 1960: 190, 539, 577; Carell 1971: 523, 529; Chant, Volume 14: 1859-61; Volume 17: 2277, 2372; Keegan: 90-91; MacDonald 1963: 110, 548, 567; Stein: 218-19; OB 45: 342; Ziemke 1966: 469.

11th SS VOLUNTEER PANZER
GRENADIER DIVISION "NORDLAND"

COMPOSITION: 11th SS Panzer Battalion "Hermann von Salza," 23rd SS Panzer Grenadier Regiment "Norge," 24th SS Panzer Grenadier Regiment "Danemark," 11th SS Panzer Artillery Regiment, 11th SS Panzer Reconnaissance Battalion, 11th SS Anti-Tank Battalion, 11th SS Panzer Engineer Battalion, 11th SS Signal Battalion, 11th SS Anti-Aircraft Battalion

HOME STATION: See below

The 11th SS was formed in 1943 by the merger of three Germanic legions: "Niederlande," or Netherlands (sixteen hundred men), "Dänemark," or Denmark (seven hundred men), and "Norwegen," or Norway (six hundred men). Its ranks were rounded out by Volksdeutsche volunteers from the Balkans and by transfers from the "Nordland" Regiment of the 5th SS Panzer Division "Viking." In the autumn of 1943 it was in northern Crotia, apparently engaged in training, but in January 1944 it was transferred to Army Group North, which was unsuccessfully trying to prevent the Russians from breaking the Siege of Leningrad. The 11th SS took part in the retreat across the old Baltic states region and suffered heavy casualties in the Narva area. From September 18-22, 1944, "Nordland" force-marched 250 miles in four days from the Narva area to Riga, arriving just in time to prevent a major Russian breakthrough and save the 18th Army and Army Detachment Narva from encirclement and annihilation. It withdrew into the Courland Pocket in October 1944 but was returned to Germany via ship in early 1945. In April 1945 it took part in the Battle of Berlin, where it was destroyed. The commanders of the 11th SS included SS Major General Fritz Scholz (1944), SS Major General Joachim Ziegler (1945), and SS Colonel Gustav Krukenberg (1945).

NOTES AND SOURCES: Ziegler formerly commanded the 4th SS Panzer Grenadier Brigade "Niederlande" (1944), which was later upgraded to the 34th SS Panzer Grenadier Division. He was relieved of his command by General Weidling, commander of the LVI Panzer Corps, on April 28, 1945. Weidling was dissatisfied with his performance during the Battle of Berlin. SS Colonel Krukenberg, the division's last commander, led it less than a week. Chant, Volume 18: 2381; Keegan: 96, 129, 157; Seaton: 581; Stein: 162-63, 208; OB 45: 342; Ziemke 1966: 406, 487.

12th SS PANZER DIVISION "HITLER JUGEND"

COMPOSITION: 12th SS Panzer Regiment, 25th SS Panzer Grenadier Regiment, 26th SS Panzer Grenadier Regiment, 12th SS Panzer Artillery Regiment, 12th SS Panzer Reconnaissance Battalion, 12th SS Anti-Tank Battalion, 12th SS Panzer Engineer Battalion, 12th SS Panzer Signal Battalion, 12th SS Anti-Aircraft Battalion, 12th SS Projector Battalion

HOME STATION: See below

As its name implies this unit was formed mainly from Hitler Youth members, and was recruited from military fitness camps of that organization. Its training cadres were supplied by the 1st SS Panzer Division. The average age of the soldiers of the 12th SS in 1943 was seventeen. Activated on June 24, 1943, the 12th spent the next year in Belgium, where it served primarily as a training unit for other SS divisions. In April 1944 it was sent to France and was rushed to the threatened Normandy sector on June 6, where it helped contain, but could not defeat, the D-Day invasion. Remaining on the line for almost a month, the young men of the Hitler Youth Division fought with fanatical dedication to the Nazi cause; 90 percent of them were casualties before the campaign was over. Despite its losses, the 12th SS fought with great skill and courage, inflicting heavy casualties on their British and Canadian opponents. On July 4, for example, the one hundred fifty survivors of the 25th SS Panzer Grenadier Regiment, supported by the divisional reserve (two or three tanks and one 88mm antiaircraft gun) repulsed the entire Canadian 8th Infantry Brigade, two battalions of the British 78th Armored Division, and associated Allied support units in the Battle of the Carpiquet Airfield. The 12th SS evacuated Caen on July 15, but on August 8 they saved the day at Falaise by preventing a British breakthrough. Eventually encircled, the Hitler Youth Division broke out, but by August 21 it had only three hundred men and ten tanks left, and all its artillery had been lost or destroyed. By October, the 12th SS Panzer was temporarily defunct; its few survivors were in Aachen, fighting the Americans as Combat Group Diefenthal of the 1st SS Panzer Division. Withdrawn and hastily rebuilt, the unit fought in the Ardennes, where it was at battle group size. In February 1945 it took part in the Lake Balaton offensive in Hungary, and in April it was part of the 6th SS Panzer Army in the Battle of Vienna. It ended the war on the southern sector of the Eastern Front. Commanders of the Hitler Jugend included SS Lieutenant General Witt (1944), SS Major General Kurt "Panzer" Meyer (1944), SS Major General Kraemer (1944), and SS Colonel Hugo Kraas (1944-45).

NOTES AND SOURCES: Fritz Witt was killed in Normandy by Allied naval gunfire on June 16, 1944. He had commanded a regimental battle group in the 1st SS Panzer Division in Russia (1943-44) before assuming command of the 12th SS Panzer. "Panzer" Meyer, veteran commander of the 1st SS Panzer Reconnaissance Battalion of the Leibstandarte Adolf Hitler (1941) and the 25th SS Panzer Grenadier Regiment of the 12th SS Panzer Division (1943-44), held the Knight's Cross with Oak Leaves and Swords. As senior regimental commander in the 12th SS, he took over the division when Witt died and was the youngest divisional commander in the German armed forces at the time. He was captured in September 1944, during the retreat across France. Even after the war, Meyer was a tremendous admirer of Adolf Hitler. SS Major General Kraemer, a former member of the Army General Staff and former Chief of Staff of the I SS Panzer Corps (1944), was acting commander of the division in November 1944. He was later Chief of Staff of the 6th SS Panzer Army (1945). Hugo Kraas was commander of the 2nd SS Panzer Grenadier Regiment of the 1st SS Panzer Division in 1944, when he was named commander of the Hitler Jugend Division. Blumenson 1960: 190, 539-40, 577; Carell 1973: 177; Chant, Volume 14: 1863, Volume 17: 2372; Harrison: Map VI; Keegan: 91; MacDonald 1963: 300; MacDonald 1973: 34; Mitcham 1983: 142; OB 44: 329; OB 45: 343.

13th SS MOUNTAIN DIVISION "HANDSCHAR" (Kroatische #1)

COMPOSITION: 27th SS Mountain Infantry Regiment, 28th SS Mountain Infantry Regiment, 13th SS Mountain Artillery Regiment, 13th SS Mountain Reconnaissance Battalion, 13th SS Anti-Tank Battalion, 13th SS Mountain Engineer Battalion, 13th SS Mountain Signal Battalion, 13th SS Anti-Aircraft Battalion

HOME STATION: Croatia

Probably the worst combat unit in the Waffen-SS, the 13th was formed in the spring of 1943 as the Bosnian-Herzegovinian or "B.H." Division. It initially consisted of Bosnian Moslems and Croat volunteers, operating under cadres of the 7th SS Mountain Division "Prinz Eugen." When volunteers lagged, Christian members of the Croatian National Army were forced to join the new SS division.

The 13th SS had many of the old trappings of the Muslim regiments of the former Austrian Army, including the fez and regimental imams, who led prayers. Sent to south-central France in mid-1943 to train, the division promptly mutinied. The rebellion was quelled internally but the unit, which steadfastly refused to operate its own area, had to be returned to Yugoslavia, after brief stays in lower Silesia and Austria in late 1943. Back in the Balkans, it largely confined itself to massacring defenseless Christian villagers and establishing record desertion rates. In October 1944, during the retreat from the Balkans, the 2nd Panzer Army disarmed the well-equipped but unreliable division and took its arms and supplies for German troops. Himmler finally committed it to combat on the Eastern Front in late 1944, but it performed so poorly in Hungary that he withdrew it and disbanded it in early 1945. Commanders of the miserable 13th included SS Lieutenant General Sauberzweig (1943-44) and SS Major General Hampel (1944-45).

NOTES AND SOURCES: Gruppenführer Sauberzweig later commanded the IX SS Corps (1944). Keegan: 104-05, 157; OB 44: 331; OB 45: 343; Ziemke 1966: 378.

14th SS GRENADIER DIVISION (Galizische #1)

COMPOSITION: 29th SS Grenadier Regiment, 30th SS Grenadier Regiment, 31st SS Grenadier Regiment, 14th SS Artillery Regiment, 14th SS Füsilier Battalion, 14th SS Anti-Tank Battalion, 14th SS Engineer Battalion, 14th SS Signal Battalion, 14th SS Anti-Aircraft Battalion (?)

HOME STATION: Ukrainian Galicia

Formed from Ukrainian volunteers with German and Austrian officers and N.C.O.s, the 14th SS was organized and trained in Galicia, beginning in April 1943. In March 1944 it was sent into action on the central sector of the Russian Front, where it was trapped in the Brody-Tarnow Pocket in the Soviet summer offensive in July. Only three thousand of the division's fourteen thousand men managed to break out. The remnants of the unit were sent to Slovakia and then to Germany for reforming and were returned to the Eastern Front (then in southern Poland) in late 1944. By March the burned-out division was fighting in Slovakia. It fell into Soviet captivity at the end of the war, and most of its men were subsequently killed. SS Major General Fritz Freitag was the divisional commander in late 1944-1945.

NOTES AND SOURCES: The 14th SS Grenadier was described by Colonel Seaton as well equipped but poorly trained and inexperienced. Freitag came to the 14th SS from the 4th SS Panzer Grenadier Division, where he was a regimental commander (1943). Keegan: 157; Seaton: 447; OB 45: 344.

15th SS GRENADIER DIVISION (Lettische #1)

COMPOSITION: 32nd SS Grenadier Regiment, 33rd SS Grenadier Regiment, 34th SS Grenadier Regiment, 15th SS Artillery Regiment, 15th SS Füsilier Battalion, 15th SS Anti-Tank Company, 15th SS Engineer Battalion, 15th SS Signal Battalion, 15th SS Anti-Aircraft Battalion

HOME STATION: Latvia

This division consisted almost exclusively of Latvian volunteers and police battalions, with a few German officers and N.C.O.s added. It was formed in August 1943 and was soon in action with Army Group North, fighting in all its major campaigns from late 1943 until January 1945, including the retreat through the Baltic States and the first battles of the Courland Pocket. Evacuated by sea to Germany, the remnants of this unit took part in the defense of Pomerania, where it suffered heavy casualties. It was finished off in the Battle of Berlin. Many of its survivors were later executed by the Soviets. Commanders of the 15th SS included SS Lieutenant General Count Carl-Friedrich von Püchler-Burghaus (1943-44), and SS Colonel Nikolaus Heilmann (1945).

SOURCES: Keegan: 104-05, 129, 157; Stein: 179; OB 44: 331; OB 45: 344.

16th SS PANZER GRENADIER DIVISION "REICHSFÜHRER SS"

COMPOSITION: 16th SS Panzer Battalion, 35th SS Panzer Grenadier Regiment, 36th SS Panzer Grenadier Regiment, 16th SS Panzer Artillery Regiment, 16th SS Panzer Reconnaissance Battalion, 16th SS Anti-Tank Battalion, 16th SS Engineer Battalion, 16th SS Signal Battalion, 16th SS Anti-Aircraft Battalion

HOME STATION: See below

This division was formed in Slovenia in October 1943 by expanding the Reichsführer SS Assault Brigade, which had been engaged in Corsica. It consisted of German and Volksdeutsche troops. By January 1943 elements of the 16th SS had returned to the Mediterranean sector, and these were committed to the Anzio fighting in February 1944; other units were involved in the occupation of Hungary in March. By May the entire division had been sent to Germany and was reunited as part of the OKW reserve. It was sent back to Italy in June, after the Allies successfully attacked the Gustav Line and took Rome. The division was continuously engaged on the Italian Front until December, fighting in the Gothic Line and the battles around Bologna. In December 1944 it was transferred to the Hungarian sector and spent the rest of the war on the southern sector of the Eastern Front. It fought its last battle at Vienna in April 1945. The division's last commander was thirty-four-year-old SS Major General Otto Baum, who was leading it in early 1945. Previous commanders included SS Lieutenant General Max Simon (1944).

NOTES AND SOURCES: Max Simon led the 3rd SS Panzer Division "Totenkopf" on the Eastern Front (1943) and later commanded the XIII SS Corps in the West (1945). Otto Baum, a holder of the Knight's Cross with Oak Leaves, Diamonds, and Swords, was one of the most highly decorated men in Nazi Germany. He had commanded a battalion in the 3rd SS Panzer Division during the Battle of the Demyansk Pocket (1941-42) and a panzer grenadier regiment in the 3rd SS (1943). He led the 17th SS Panzer Grenadier Division on the Western Front for a brief time in 1944. Blumenson 1969; 313, 344-45; Fisher: 80, 302, 321, 382, 420; Keegan: 157; Snydor: 489-90; Stein: 184; OB 45: 344-45.

17th SS PANZER GRENADIER DIVISION "GÖTZ VON BERLICHINGEN"

COMPOSITION: 17th SS Panzer Battalion, 37th SS Panzer Grenadier Regiment, 38th SS Panzer Grenadier Regiment, 17th SS Panzer Artillery Regiment, 17th SS Reconnaissance Battalion, 17th SS Anti-Tank Battalion, 17th SS Engineer Battalion, 17th SS Signal Battalion, 17th SS Anti-Aircraft Battalion

HOME STATION: See below

This elite division, named for a German robber baron of the Middle Ages, was formed in western France in October 1943. It included Germans, Volksdeutsche, Belgians, and Rumanians. By June 6, 1944, it was stationed southwest of Tours in southwestern France as part of OKW's reserve. It was quickly rushed to Normandy and on June 11 was counterattacking at Carentan against the U.S. 82nd and 101st Airborne Divisions. Remaining in the line, it defended in the St. Lô sector against heavy odds and in late July was reported by 7th Army commander SS Colonel General Hausser as practically destroyed. In early August the remnants of the 17th SS were temporarily absorbed by the 2nd SS Panzer Division. Withdrawn from the combat zone soon after, it rebuilt and refitted at Chartres in eastern France, absorbing the 49th and 51st SS Panzer Grenadier Brigades, which had been transferred from Denmark and intended for use in forming the new 26th and 27th SS Panzer Grenadier Divisions. By November, when it was thrown into the Battle of Metz, the 17th SS had almost sixteen thousand men; however, it only had four tanks and six assault guns, and lacked mobile equipment of all kinds. Moreover, its replacements were of marginal quality, and its former elitism was gone. The 17th SS was mauled at Metz, and on December 4, 1944, had a strength of only four thousand men, of which only seventeen hundred were infantry effectives. After Metz fell, the remnants of the 17th SS fought in the Saar battles. Still west of the Rhine on March 22, 1945, it collapsed under repeated Allied attacks. Nevertheless, the surviving fragments of the division fought in the unsuccessful defense of Nuremberg in April. It surrendered to the Western Allies at the end of the war. Divisional commanders of the Götz von Berlichingen included SS Lieutenant General Werner Ostendorff (1944), SS Colonel Eduard Deisenhofer (1944), SS Major General Otto Baum (1944), SS Colonel Hans Lingner (1944-45), and SS Colonel Fritz Klingenberg (1945).

NOTES AND SOURCES: Werner Ostendorff, former Chief of Staff of the II SS Panzer Corps in Russia (1942-43), was seriously wounded in 1944. SS Colonel Deisenhofer, previously commander of the 21st SS Panzer Grenadier Regiment, 10th SS Panzer Division, led the 17th SS Division only briefly. Hans Lingner, an SS officer since 1935, was captured in January 1945. Franz Klingenberg, an SS officer since 1934, was the commander of the SS Cadet School at Bad Tolz in 1944. Blumenson 1960: 422, 442, 570; Carell 1973: 145-46; Cole 1950: 48-49, 422-23, 526-27; Harrison: 244, Map VI; Keegan: 91; MacDonald 1973: 263, 412, 415, 423; OB 45: 345. For the story of Otto Baum's career, see Notes, 16th SS Panzer Grenadier Division.

18th SS VOLUNTEER PANZER GRENADIER DIVISION "HORST WESSEL"

COMPOSITION: 18th SS Panzer Battalion, 39th SS Panzer Grenadier Regiment, 40th SS Panzer Grenadier Regiment, 18th SS Panzer Artillery Regiment, 18th SS Panzer Reconnaissance Battalion, 18th SS Anti-Tank Battalion, 18th SS Engineer Battalion, 18th SS Signal Battalion, 18th SS Anti-Aircraft Battalion

HOME STATION: See below

The 18th SS Division was formed in Hungary in the spring of 1944 by expanding the 1st SS Motorized Infantry Brigade, which had been fighting on the Eastern Front since 1942. The new division, which consisted mainly of Volksdeutsche (ethnic Germans from outside the Reich), was named after the subject of the Nazi Party Anthem. Unlike many so-called panzer grenadier units in the fifth year of the war, it was properly equipped. In July 1944 it was sent to Army Group Center and helped stem the tide of the Soviet summer offensive. Later it fought in southern Poland and Slovakia, then ended the war in the pocket east of Prague. Its commander in 1945 was SS Colonel Wilhelm Trabandt (1944-45).

NOTES AND SOURCES: Trabandt was commander of the 1st SS Motorized Infantry Brigade in 1943. Keegan: 100; OB 45: 345.

19th SS GRENADIER DIVISION (Lettische #2)

COMPOSITION: 42nd SS Grenadier Regiment, 43rd SS Grenadier Regiment, 44th SS Grenadier Regiment, 19th SS Artillery Regiment, 19th SS Füsilier Battalion, 19th SS Anti-Tank Company, 19th SS Engineer Battalion, 19th SS Signal Battalion, 19th SS Anti-Aircraft Battalion

HOME STATION: Latvia

This division was formed in the Soviet Union behind the lines of Army Group North in March 1944. Its parent unit was the 2nd Latvian SS Volunteer Brigade, which had been involved in combat on the Eastern Front since late 1943. The division—which reached full strength—was involved in heavy fighting in the retreat from Leningrad and through the Baltic States. It suffered heavy casualties before retiring into the Courland Pocket, where it was when Germany surrendered. Most of the surviving Latvians were subsequently executed by the Soviets. The 19th SS Grenadier Division's commander in early 1945 was SS Lieutenant General Bruno Streckenbach (1944-45).

NOTES AND SOURCES: Streckenbach was formerly Deputy Chief of Security Police and the SS Security Service (1942) and head of the SS Administrative and Personnel Department (1942-43). Keegan: 103-04, 157; Stein: 178; OB 45: 346.

20th SS GRENADIER DIVISION (Estnische #1)

COMPOSITION: 45th SS Grenadier Regiment, 46th SS Grenadier Regiment, 47th (?) SS Grenadier Regiment, 20th SS Artillery Regiment, 20th SS Füsilier Battalion, 20th SS Anti-Tank Company, 20th SS Engineer Battalion, 20th SS Signal Battalion, 20th SS Anti-Aircraft Battalion

HOME STATION: Estonia

The 20th SS Grenadier Division was formed behind the lines of Army Group Center on the Russian Front in December 1943. Many of its soldiers were former members of the Estonian SS Brigade, which had been in combat since October 1943. The 20th SS received enough volunteers to reach full or almost full divisional strength. Transferred to Army Group North in early 1944, it took part in the retreat from Leningrad, the Battle of Narva, and the early Courland Pocket battles. It was evacuated to Germany and returned to the central sector of the Eastern Front in December. The unit was routed by the Soviets in their invasion of Silesia in late 1944 and early 1945. The 20th SS retreated into Bohemia and was surrounded with Army Group Center in the pocket east of Prague, where it was when the war ended. Like many former Soviet citizens who actively opposed the Communists during World War II, most of the division's survivors were put to death after they surrendered. SS Major General Franz Augsberger was the commander of the division in 1945.

SOURCES: Keegan: 104-05; OB 45: 346.

21st SS MOUNTAIN DIVISION "SKANDERBEG," OR (Albanische #1)

COMPOSITION: 50th (?) SS Mountain Infantry Regiment, 51st (?) SS Mountain Infantry Regiment, 21st SS Mountain Artillery Regiment, 21st SS Mountain Reconnaissance Battalion, 21st SS Mountain Anti-Tank Battalion, 21st SS Mountain Engineer Battalion, 21st SS Mountain Signal Battalion, 21st SS Anti-Aircraft Battalion

HOME STATION: Albania

This division was formed in the summer of 1944 from unreliable Albanian Muslims. It was never fully developed, however, because it would not operate outside of its own area, but preferred raping, pillaging, and massacring innocent Christian villagers to fighting the enemies of the Third Reich. This is why Himmler disbanded it later that year, before it was ever fully formed. The more reliable members of "Skanderbeg" were transferred to the 14th SS Mountain Regiment of the 7th SS Mountain Division. SS Major General August Schmidhuber (1944) was apparently the only commander the 21st SS ever had.

SOURCES: Keegan: 105, 157; OB 45: 346.

22nd SS VOLUNTEER CAVALRY DIVISION
"MARIE THERESIA" (Ungarische)

COMPOSITION: 52nd (?) SS Cavalry Regiment, 53rd (?) SS Cavalry Regiment, 54th (?) SS Cavalry Regiment, 55th (?) SS Cavalry Regiment, 22nd SS Artillery Regiment, 22nd SS Panzer Reconnaissance Battalion, 22nd SS Anti-Tank Battalion, 22nd SS Engineer Battalion, 22nd SS Signal Battalion, 22nd SS Anti-Aircraft Battalion

HOME STATION: Hungary

The 22nd SS Cavalry was formed in Hungary in mid-1944, when the 8th SS Cavalry Division "Florian Geyer" was divided. It took over two of the 8th SS Cavalry's four cavalry regiments, but which two is not clear, as its table of organization (above) indicates. The new division consisted mainly of Hungarian volunteers, and it soon reached full divisional strength. That October it was sent to northern Transylvania (in Rumania), where it fought the Soviets. Eventually surrounded in Budapest with the IX SS Mountain Corps, the 22nd SS fought bravely but was destroyed when the city fell in early February 1945. It was commanded by SS Major General August Zehender (1944-45).

NOTES AND SOURCES: Zehender, who was made an SS Brigadeführer during the last days of the Siege of Budapest, had formerly commanded a regiment in the 8th SS Cavalry Division (1943). Keegan: 157; Seaton: 500; Stein: 233; OB 45: 347.

23rd SS MOUNTAIN DIVISION "KAMA" (Kroatische #2)

COMPOSITION: 56th (?) SS Mountain Infantry Regiment, 57th (?) SS Mountain Infantry Regiment, 58th (?) SS Mountain Infantry Regiment, 23rd SS Mountain Artillery Regiment, 23rd SS Mountain Reconnaissance Battalion, 23rd SS Anti-Tank Battalion, 23rd SS Mountain Engineer Battalion, 23rd SS Mountain Signal Battalion, 23rd SS Anti-Aircraft Battalion

HOME STATION: Croatia

As with the other two Muslim SS divisions (the 13th and 21st), this unit was an unsuccessful experiment because its soldiers were too difficult to discipline. It was partially formed in the late summer of 1944 in Bosnia, from Moslem and Croat volunteers with cadres of German officers. Later that year Reichsführer Heinrich Himmler ordered it disbanded.

SOURCES: Keegan: 105, 158; OB 45: 347.

23rd VOLUNTEER SS PANZER GRENADIER DIVISION (Nederland)

COMPOSITION: See below

HOME STATION: The Netherlands

The second 23rd SS division was formed from a previously existing brigade of Dutch SS men in the last weeks of the war. Assigned to the 3rd SS Panzer Army on the Eastern Front, it fought in the Battle of Berlin and surrendered shortly afterward. The 23rd SS never exceeded regimental strength.

SOURCES: Keegan: 139; *Kriegstagebuch des OKW*, Volume IV: 1898; Lucas: 42.

24th SS MOUNTAIN DIVISION "KARSTJÄGER"

COMPOSITION: 59th (?) SS Mountain Infantry Regiment, 60th (?) SS Mountain Infantry Regiment, 24th SS Mountain Artillery Regiment, 24th SS Mountain Reconnaissance Battalion, 24th SS Anti-Tank Battalion, 24th SS Mountain Engineer Battalion, 24th SS Mountain Signal Battalion, 24th SS Anti-Aircraft Battalion

HOME STATION: Italy

This division was formed in the Istrian area of northern Italy by the expansion of the Karstjäger Battalion of the Waffen-SS. Its men were Italian Fascists in the service of Mussolini's rump republic, although many of its officers were Austrians who had formerly served with the 7th SS Mountain Division. The 24th SS confined itself to antipartisan activities and apparently never exceeded regimental strength. It was dissolved in 1945.

SOURCES: Keegan: 99, 158; OB 45: 347.

25th SS GRENADIER DIVISION "HUNYADI" (Ungarische #1)

COMPOSITION: 61st (?) SS Grenadier Regiment, 62nd (?) SS Grenadier Regiment, 63rd (?) SS Grenadier Regiment, 25th SS Artillery Regiment, 24th SS Füsilier Battalion, 24th SS Anti-Tank Battalion, 24th SS Engineer Battalion, 24th SS Signal Battalion, 24th SS Anti-Aircraft Battalion

HOME STATION: Hungary

Formed in late 1944 as the Russians invaded Hungary, this division was never fully organized and never reached anything like full strength. It disappeared as the Soviets overran Hungary.

SOURCES: Keegan: 158; OB 45: 348.

26th SS PANZER GRENADIER DIVISION (Ungarische #2)

COMPOSITION: 26th (?) SS Panzer Battalion, 64th (?) SS Panzer Grenadier Regiment, 65th (?) SS Panzer Grenadier Regiment, 66th (?) SS Panzer Grenadier Regiment, 26th SS Panzer Artillery Regiment, 26th SS Panzer Reconnaissance Battalion, 26th SS Anti-Tank Battalion, 26th SS Engineer Battalion, 26th SS Signal Battalion, 26th SS Anti-Aircraft Battalion

HOME STATION: Hungary

Himmler attempted to form this division in northwestern Germany in September 1944, by expanding the 49th SS Panzer Grenadier Brigade. Troops were also taken from the SS Panzer Brigade "Gross," which was disbanded in November 1944, and from young men (mostly Hungarians) who fled from Transylvania when the Russians overran that province. The unit disappeared with the fall of Hungary in early 1945; apparently the 26th SS was destroyed in that campaign.

SOURCES: Keegan: 158; OB 45: 348.

27th SS VOLUNTEER PANZER GRENADIER DIVISION "LANGEMARCK"

COMPOSITION: 27th SS Panzer Battalion, 67th SS Panzer Grenadier Regiment, 68th (?) SS Panzer Grenadier Regiment, 27th SS Panzer Reconnaissance Battalion, 27th SS Anti-Tank Battalion, 27th SS Engineer Battalion, 27th SS Signal Battalion, 27th SS Anti-Aircraft Battalion

HOME STATION: Belgium

The first attempt to form this division was made in September 1944 when Himmler ordered the 51st SS Panzer Grenadier Brigade expanded. There simply were not enough soldiers in this unit, however, so the divisional number 27th SS was given to the 6th SS Storm Brigade "Langemarck" later that year. This brigade was a Belgian SS Legion that had been activated in the fall of 1943 and had distinguished itself on the Eastern Front in the spring of 1944. The new 27th SS never exceeded regimental strength but served on the Russian Front in the retreats from Poland and Pomeria and in the Battle of Berlin.

SOURCES: Keegan: 96, 158; OB 45: 348.

28th SS VOLUNTEER PANZER GRENADIER DIVISION "WALLONIEN"

COMPOSITION: 69th SS Panzer Grenadier Regiment, 70th SS Panzer Grenadier Regiment, 28th SS Panzer Artillery Regiment, 28th SS Panzer Reconnaissance Battalion, 28th SS Anti-Tank Battalion, 28th SS Engineer Battalion, 28th SS Signal Battalion, 28th SS Anti-Aircraft Battalion

HOME STATION: Belgium

This division was formed for political and propaganda reasons from French-speaking Belgians, many of whom had been captured by the Germans in the Western campaigns of 1940 and volunteered to serve in the division in order to get out of Nazi prisoner-of-war camps. The unit was originally formed in 1941 as the 5th SS Sturm Brigade, which served on the Russian Front for three years and suffered heavy losses at Cherkassy. The new division, which never exceeded regimental strength, was officially activated in the summer of 1944 and trained in Hanover. It was defending the Bonn area in December 1944 but was sent east soon after and fought its last battle before Berlin in April 1945. Its commander was SS Major General Leon Degrelle (1944-45).

NOTES AND SOURCES: Degrelle had commanded the 5th SS Sturm Brigade "Wallonien" (1943-44) and held the Knight's Cross with Oak Leaves. Keegan: 96, 158; OB 45: 348.

(1) 29th SS GRENADIER DIVISION (Russische #1)

COMPOSITION: Believed to include the 71st SS Grenadier Regiment, 72nd SS Grenadier Regiment, and 73rd SS Grenadier Regiment

HOME STATION: See below

The first of two SS divisions to bear the number "29," this unit was formed in 1944 from Soviet prisoners-of-war. Later that year it was transferred to General Vlasov's army and served briefly on the Eastern Front. Many of its troops surrendered to the Americans but were subsequently handed over to the Soviets, who slaughtered them.

SOURCES: Keegan: 158; OB 45: 349.

(2) 29th SS GRENADIER DIVISION (Italienische #1)

COMPOSITION: Various sources in Italy

HOME STATION: northern Italy

The second 29th SS Grenadier Division was formed from Fascist Italians in Mussolini's rump republic in 1945. It probably never exceeded regimental strength, and it is even doubtful that it reached that level. The division disappeared in April 1945, when Army Group C collapsed.

SOURCE: Keegan: 99, 158

30th SS GRENADIER DIVISION (Russische #2)

COMPOSITION: 75th SS Grenadier Regiment, 76th SS Grenadier Regiment, 77th SS Grenadier Regiment, 30th SS Artillery Regiment, 30th SS Füsilier Battalion, 30th SS Anti-Tank Battalion, 30th SS Engineer Battalion, 30th SS Signal Battalion, 30th SS Anti-Aircraft Battalion

HOME STATION: See below

This division was formed from Russian personnel, many of whom had police experience, and with a small number of former German police. Activated in the summer of 1944, it was sent to eastern France in September but was withdrawn from the Western Front in October and returned to Germany. Most of its personnel were considered unreliable; nevertheless, the 30th SS was back in combat in Alsace in November and took part in the withdrawal across the Rhine. In 1945 it was transferred to General Vlasov's Free Russian Army and was sent east. It fell into Soviet captivity in 1945, which meant death for most of the soldiers of the division. SS Lieutenant Colonel Hans Siegling was apparently the last German commander of the division.

NOTES AND SOURCES: Obersturmbannführer Siegling was only 33 years old in 1945. Keegan: 158; OB 45: 349.

31st SS VOLUNTEER GRENADIER DIVISION
"BÖHMEN-MÄHREN"

COMPOSITION: 78th SS Grenadier Regiment, 79th SS Grenadier Regiment, 80th SS Grenadier Regiment, 31st SS Artillery Regiment, 31st SS Füsilier Battalion, 31st SS Anti-Tank Company, 31st SS Engineer Battalion, 31st SS Signal Battalion, 31st SS Anti-Aircraft Battalion

HOME STATION: Protectorate

The 31st SS Division, which consisted of Germans and Volksdeutsche, was formed in the Balkans in September 1944. Many of its troops came from the Bohemia and Moravia areas of the Protectorate (Czechoslovakia). It was in action on the Hungarian sector of the Eastern Front by December 1944 and ended the war in Czechoslovakia, where it surrendered to the Soviets in May 1945.

SOURCES: Keegan: 158; *Kriegstagebuch des OKW*, Volume I: 1146; OB 45: 349

32nd SS PANZER GRENADIER DIVISION "JANUARY 30"

COMPOSITION: Various units

NOTES AND SOURCES: Berlin (?)

Formed in 1945, the 32nd SS was made up of hastily inducted Germans and bore little resemblance to the former elite formations that bore the title "Waffen-SS." Like many of the later SS divisions, it never exceeded regimental strength. In February 1945 it was still half-formed and incompletely trained; nevertheless it was sent from Berlin to the training area of the 9th Army. Subsequently attached to the V Mountain Corps of Army Group Vistula, it was destroyed in the Battle of Berlin.

SOURCES: Keegan: 158; Ziemke 1959b: 34.

(1) 33rd SS CAVALRY DIVISION (Ungarische #3)

COMPOSITION: Various units

HOME STATION: Hungary

Organized in late 1944, this division was at regimental strength when the siege of Budapest began. Quickly committed to the fighting, the 33rd SS Cavalry was wiped out by February 13, 1945, along with most of the rest of the IX SS Mountain Corps.

SOURCES: Chant, Volume 17: 2371; Keegan: 159.

(2) 33rd SS GRENADIER DIVISION "CHARLEMAGNE"
(Französische #1)

COMPOSITION: Various units

HOME STATION: France

The forerunner of this division, the "Légion Volontaire Française," was formed in July 1941, by French-speaking Fascists as an anti-Bolshevik unit. Later it received half-hearted financial support from the Vichy government. It fought on the Russian Front until the spring of 1944, when it was sent to Prague and expanded into the SS Grenadier Brigade "Frankreich." The 33rd was further upgraded to divisional status in December 1944, probably at the Wildflecken Maneuver Area. Returned to the Eastern Front, the 33rd SS was annihilated in the Battle of Berlin. The Charlemagne Division never exceeded brigade strength and was given divisional status for political reasons only. Its last commander was reportedly SS Major General Puaun (1945).

NOTES AND SOURCES: Puaun was the former commander of the 638th Grenadier Regiment of the German Army. Keegan: 96, 159; OB 45: 350.

34th SS PANZER GRENADIER DIVISION
"LANDSTURM NEDERLAND"

COMPOSITION: 48th SS Panzer Grenadier Regiment "General Seyffardt," 49th SS Panzer Grenadier Regiment "De Ruyter," 54th SS Artillery Regiment, 54th SS Reconnaissance Battalion, 54th SS Anti-Tank Company (?), 54th SS Engineer Battalion, 54th SS Signal Company (Battalion?), plus anti-aircraft units

HOME STATION: The Netherlands

The 34th SS was formed in autumn 1943, in Germany, mainly from Dutch personnel. It apparently absorbed the 2nd SS Motorized Brigade, which had been fighting on the Eastern Front during the first half of the year. It also absorbed the 4th SS Brigade "Nederland." By November the division was in Yugoslavia but was sent to Army Group North in December. From that time on it was more or less continuously engaged, fighting against the Russian winter offensive of 1943-44, in the retreat through the Baltic States, and in the battles of the Courland Pocket. It was still in Courland when the war ended. SS Major General Jürgen Wagner was commanding the division in January 1945 and was apparently the last commander of the 34th SS. It had previously been commanded by SS Major General Joachim Ziegler (1944).

NOTES AND SOURCES: Ziegler later led the 11st SS Panzer Grenadier Division in the Battle of Berlin. Wagner had previously directed the 9th SS Panzer Grenadier Regiment of the 5th SS Panzer Division "Viking" on the Russian Front (1943). Keegan: 99, 159; OB 45: 350.

35th SS POLICE GRENADIER DIVISION

COMPOSITION: Various units

HOME STATION: Breslau (?)

This unit was organized from German policemen in early 1945. It reached regimental strength before being sent to the XL Panzer Corps, 4th Panzer Army, Army Group Center (formerly South). It served on the Eastern Front in the last weeks of the war and surrendered to the Russians east of Prague in May 1945.

SOURCES: Keegan: 159; *Kriegstagebuch des OKW*, Volume IV: 1896.

36th SS GRENADIER DIVISION "DIRLEWANGER"

COMPOSITION: Various sources

HOME STATION: Unknown

Formed as a division in 1945, this unit is better known as the Dirlewanger Brigade, which was its name before it was upgraded in the last weeks of the war. Most of its members were men taken from concentration camps; a few of its "soldiers" were Communists or political prisoners, but most were common criminals. Its commander, SS Colonel Doctor Oscar Dirlewanger, was a brutal drunkard who had once been expelled from the SS on a morals offense. The brigade was responsible for a number of atrocities, especially against the Poles and Jews during the Warsaw Ghetto uprising during the autumn of 1944. It also fought on the Hungarian sector of the Russian Front in late 1944. Both the division and its commander were considered notoriously unreliable by the German Army. It ended the war on the Eastern Front in 1945, although Dirlewanger himself fled and escaped capture by the Allies.

NOTES AND SOURCES: General Friessner, Commander-in-Chief of Army Group South Ukraine, once gave Dirlewanger orders on how to defend a sector against Russian attack. Returning later to check on how those orders were being carried out, he found that the brigade had departed the area without informing his headquarters or anybody else's and that the Soviets had occupied the positions he had assigned Dirlewanger to defend. Friessner himself narrowly avoided capture by the Russians by taking to his heels. Keegan: 159; Seaton: 456, 498-99; Ziemke 1966: 344. Also see Johannes Friessner, *Verratene Schlachten*, Holstein, Hamburg, 1956.

37th SS CAVALRY DIVISION "LÜTZOW"

COMPOSITION: Various units

HOME STATION: Unknown

Little is known of this unit. It was formed from ethnic Germans in the last days of the war, but never exceeded regimental strength. En route to Army Group South in Austria on March 1, 1945, the 37th SS fought on the southern sector of the Eastern Front and probably took part in the defense of Vienna. It capitulated soon after.

SOURCES: Keegan: 159; *Kriegstagebuch des OKW*, Volume IV: 1895.

38th SS PANZER GRENADIER DIVISION "NIBELUNGEN"

COMPOSITION: Various units

HOME STATION: Bad Tolz

Formed from SS officer cadets at the Bad Tolz SS Officers' School in the last days of the war, the 38th SS never exceeded regimental strength. It was thrown into battle on the southern sector of the Russian Front and was there when the war ended.

SOURCES: Keegan: 159; *Kriegstagebuch des OKW*, Volume I: 1147.

11

Miscellaneous Divisions

Brandenburg Division
see Panzer Grenadier Division "Brandenburg"

1st COSSACK CAVALRY DIVISION

COMPOSITION (1944): 1st Cossack Cavalry Regiment, 2nd Cossack Cavalry Regiment, 3rd Cossack Cavalry Regiment, 4th Cossack Cavalry Regiment, 5th Cossack Cavalry Regiment, 6th Cossack Cavalry Regiment

HOME STATION: Poland (?)

Formed in Poland in the late summer of 1943, this unit included Don, Kuban, Terek, and Siberian Cossacks, who had been operating in separate cavalry squadrons against Russian guerillas. At that time the division was composed of two brigades, each of three sabre squadrons and an artillery battalion. Subsequently sent to Yugoslavia in the fall of 1943, it was used in antipartisan operations along the middle stretch of the Zagreb-Belgrade Railroad. It was sent into action on the Eastern Front in early 1945 and by February was fighting on the Yugoslav-Hungarian border. It surrendered to the British 8th Army on the Italian-Yugoslav frontier in May 1945, but its men were subsequently turned over to the Soviets, who killed them. The division's commander, Lieutenant General Helmuth von Pannwitz (1943-45), was also turned over to a Soviet military tribunal, which had him executed on January 16, 1947, for leading White Russian troops.

NOTES AND SOURCES: General von Pannwitz took over the XV Cossack Cavalry Corps in February 1945. Von Mellenthin 1977: 49-52; OB 45: 285. Lucas, *War on the Eastern Front, 1941-1945*, New York, Stein and Day, 1980, 115.

2nd COSSACK CAVALRY DIVISION

COMPOSITION: Various units (see below)

HOME STATION: See below

Formed in France in September 1944, this division consisted of Soviet Cossacks released from P.O.W. camps or transferred from the 1st Cossack Cavalry Division. Some of the regimental headquarters of the 1st Cossack Cavalry were transferred to the 2nd also, but which ones are not clear (see Composition, 1st Cossack Cavalry Division). The 2nd Cossack Cavalry fought on the southern sector of the Eastern Front in Yugoslavia and Hungary but surrendered to the British 8th Army on the Italian border in May 1945. In accordance with the Yalta agreements, however, its personnel were turned over to the Russians, who executed them. The division's commander was Colonel Hans-Joachim von Schultz (1944?-45).

NOTES AND SOURCES: Schultz was the former Chief of Staff of the 1st Cossack Cavalry Division (1943-44) and probably also served briefly as Chief of Staff of the XV Cossack Cavalry Corps. Von Mellenthin 1977: 49-52.

18th ARTILLERY DIVISION

COMPOSITION: General Headquarters Artillery Units of Army Group South

HOME STATION: Army Group South (?)

This rare animal was the brainchild of Field Marshal Erich von Manstein and was created in the rear area of Army Group South in December 1943. Modeled on the Russian artillery divisions that were responsible for heavy German losses from late 1942, the 18th Artillery included eight tracked or motorized artillery battalions. It had a total strength of nine 210mm howitzers, thirty 150mm guns, forty-eight 105mm guns, and a dozen 100mm guns. The division first fought at Zhitomir as a part of XLVIII Panzer Corps and later played a major role in the destruction of the Russian 1st Tank Army south of Cherkassy in early 1944. In March 1944 it was defending near Tarnopol as part of the XLVIII Panzer Corps, 4th Panzer Army, when Hitler finally worked up the resolve to rid himself of the brilliant but independent-minded von Manstein. The division was dissolved a few weeks later, apparently on the orders of Field Marshal Model. Of the 18th Artillery, Peter Young wrote: "... much was expected of it. But it proved a disappointment and was disbanded after a few months." The experiment was not repeated, and no other German artillery divisions as such were created during the Second World War, although about a dozen Volks Artillery Corps of approximately regimental strength did appear on the Western Front in late 1944 and early 1945.

NOTES AND SOURCES: The 18th Artillery was led by Lieutenant General Thoholte. Manstein: 497, 509; Peter Young (ed.), *The Marshall Cavendish Illustrated Encyclopedia of World War Two*, Marshall Cavendish, New York, 1981: Volume 5: 1325.

VOLUNTEER DEPOT DIVISION

COMPOSITION: Eastern Battalions

HOME STATION: Lyons, France

This divisional headquarters was created at Lyons, France, to administer five depot regiments supplying "Eastern" (Ost) battalions in the occupied areas of western Europe, primarily in France. During the retreat from France in September 1944, it was temporarily redesignated 19th Army Security Division and controlled miscellaneous troops during the retreat from the French Mediterreanean coast to Alsace. That fall it was reestablished as the Volunteer Depot Division, headquartered at the Ohrdruf Maneuver Area in Wehrkreis XIII. It apparently remained in operation until the last days of the war.

SOURCE: OB 45: 285.

Appendices

APPENDIX I
CHARACTERISTICS OF GERMAN TANKS

Model	Weight (in tons)	Speed (m.p.h.)	Range (miles)	Armament	Crew
PzKw II	9.3	25	118	1 20mm 1 MG	3
PzKw III	24.5	25	160	1 50mm 2 MGs	5
PzKw IV	19.7	26	125	1 75mm 2 MGs	5
PzKw V "Panther"	49.3	25	125	1 75mm 2 MGs	5
PzKw VI "Tiger"	62.0	23	73	1 88 mm 2 MGs	5

APPENDIX II
TABLE OF EQUIVALENT RANKS

U.S. Army	German Army
General of the Army	Field Marshal *(Generalfeldmarschall)*
General	Colonel General *(Generaloberst)*
Lieutenant General	General *(General)*
Major General	Lieutenant General *(Generalleutnant)*
Brigadier General	Major General *(Generalmajor)*
Colonel	Colonel *(Oberst)*
Lieutenant Colonel	Lieutenant Colonel *(Oberstleutnant)*
Major	Major *(Major)*
Captain	Captain *(Hauptmann)*
First Lieutenant	Lieutenant *(Oberleutnant)*
Second Lieutenant	Lieutenant *(Leutnant)*

SS Rank	German Army Equivalent
Reichsführer SS (Himmler)	Commander in Chief of the Army*
None	Field Marshal
Oberstgruppenführer	Colonel General
Obergruppenführer	General
Gruppenführer	Lieutenant General
Brigadeführer	Major General
Oberführer	Major General
Standartenführer	Colonel
Obersturmbannführer	Lieutenant Colonel
Sturmbannführer	Major
Hauptsturmführer	Captain
Obersturmführer	First Lieutenant
Untersturmführer	Second Lieutenant

---

*Held by Field Marshal Werner von Blomberg (1933-38), Field Marshal Walter von Brauchitsch (1938-December 1941), and Hitler (December 1941-April 1945).

APPENDIX III
THE INDIVIDUAL WEHRKREISE

WEHRKREIS I

This Wehrkreis consisted primarily of East Prussia until 1939. Later it was expanded to include the microstate of Memel, and the Zichenau, Sudauen, and Bialystok districts of Poland. It gave up the Elbing district of West Prussia when Wehrkreis XX was created in late 1939. The Wehrkreis had an area of 78,731 square kilometers in 1944, with a population of 4,667,000. Wehrkreis Headquarters was located in Königsberg.

When the war broke out, the Wehrkreis created Replacement Division Staffs 141 and 151 to control its replacement-training units. From September 1940 to July 1941 these staffs conducted their training operations in Poland but then returned to East Prussia. When the Replacement Army was reorganized in the fall of 1942, Wehrkreis I lost much of its training mission. The 141st and 151st were upgraded to reserve division status, given training responsibilities separate from the Wehrkreis, and placed directly under the Home Army; in other words, Wehrkreis I lost them. The 141st was transferred to Lithuania and the 151st went to White Russia. Meanwhile, the Wehrkreis's replacement functions were taken over by Replacement Division Staffs 401 and 461, located at Königsberg and Bialystok, respectively. In 1944 the Wehrkreis regained its training mission, but all of its operations were disrupted when the Soviets invaded East Prussia in January 1945. The 401st Replacement Division, for example, went into combat in the Baltic States in late 1944. The Wehrkreis ceased to exist in March 1945 when Königsberg fell to the Soviets. Field divisions affiliated with this East Prussian Wehrkreis included the 1st Infantry, 1st Cavalry, 11th Infantry, 21st Infantry, 24th Panzer, 61st Infantry, 114th Jäger, 121st Infantry, 161st Infantry, 206th Infantry, 217th Infantry, 228th Infantry, 244th Infantry, 291st Infantry, 311th Infantry, 340th Infantry, 349th Infantry, 383rd Infantry, 395th Infantry, 399th Infantry, 542nd Infantry, and 714th Infantry.

WEHRKREIS II

This Pomeranian and Mecklenburger military district, which was headquartered at Stettin, had an area of 54,131 square kilometers and a population of about 3,251,000. When the war broke out it created Replacement Division Staffs 152 and 192 to control its replacement-training units. When the replacement and training functions were divided in the fall of 1942, the 152nd and 192nd went to Graudenz and Gnesen, Poland, respectively, and Wehrkreis II lost them and their subordinate training regiments. Meanwhile, the Wehrkreis created Replacement Division Staff 402 to control its replacement units. By late 1944 the military district had reassumed its training mission. This Wehrkreis was noted for its largely nondivisional artillery and antiaircraft schools and units. Its affiliated units included the 2nd Motorized, 12th Infantry, 12th Panzer, 32nd Infantry, 59th Infantry, 75th Infantry, 122nd Infantry, 162nd Infantry, 201st Security, 207th Infantry, 207th Security, 242nd Infantry, 258th Infantry, 272nd Infantry, 274th Infantry, 281st Security, 292nd Infantry, 302nd Infantry, 328th Infantry, 338th Infantry, 347th Infantry, 353rd Infantry, 549th Infantry, 551st Infantry, and 702nd Infantry divisions.

WEHRKREIS III

Consisting of the Berlin area and Brandenburg, Wehrkreis III had an area of 39,161 square kilometers and a population of about 7,250,000. It included a large number of school units, as well as special units and service organizations centering on the Third Reich's capital city. Immediately after the outbreak of the war, Wehrkreis Headquarters at Berlin set up Replacement Division Staffs 143, 153 and 233, to control the military district's replacement-training units. The 233rd directed motorized and panzer training and replacement units and was upgraded to a panzer reserve division in the fall of 1942. Some of the Wehrkreis's affiliated units were stationed in Poland, beginning in 1941. After the partial separation of the Replacement Army's training and replacement functions in the fall of 1942, the Wehrkreis's training units were sent to the northwestern Ukraine with the 143rd and to the Crimea with the 153rd; both of these units were upgraded to reserve divisions. The 233rd was transferred to Denmark and remained there until the end of the war. It was one of the few reserve divisions still conducting training in 1945. Meanwhile, Wehrkreis III formed Replacement Division Staff 463, in late 1942, to assume control of the remaining nonmotorized replacement units, and Replacement Division Staff 433 was later added to direct the motorized replacement units. These new divisions headquartered at Potsdam and Frankfurt-on-the-Oder, respectively. As the reserve divisions of the German Army were committed to combat in 1943-44, it became necessary for the Wehrkreis to reassume training responsibilities. Wehrkreis III met this problem initially by sending recruits to training units in Wehrkreis XX and then, in early 1944, by gradually added training companies to its organic replacement battalions. The replacement and training units of the elite Grossdeutschland Panzer Division, the Führer Begleit Brigade, and the Führer Grenadier Brigade were all controlled by the Grossdeutschland Motorized Replacement Brigade, which was subordinate to the III Military District from its (the brigade's) inception. Divisions affiliated with Wehrkreis III included the 3rd Light, 3rd Infantry, 3rd Motorized, 3rd Panzer, 5th Light, 8th Panzer, 21st Panzer, 23rd Infantry, 26th Panzer, 38th Infantry, 50th

Infantry, 68th Infantry, 76th Infantry, 90th Light, 90th Panzer Grenadier, 93rd Infantry, 123rd Infantry, 130th Panzer (Lehr), 153rd Field Training, 153rd Reserve, 163rd Infantry, 203rd Security, 208th Infantry, 218th Infantry, 257th Infantry, 273rd Infantry, 278th Infantry, 293rd Infantry, 333rd Infantry, 386th Motorized, 403rd Security, 563rd Infantry, 719th Infantry, and the Grossdeutschland Panzer.

WEHRKREIS IV

Wehrkreis IV included Saxony, most of the Prussian Province of Merseburg (the southern part of the former Prussian province of Saxony), a small district in eastern Thuringia and a small part of western Lower Silesia. In 1938 it was extended to include the former Czechoslovakian Sudetenland. It had an estimated population of 7,875,000 and an area of 30,357 square kilometers.

After the invasion of Poland in 1939, the Wehrkreis formed Replacement Division Staffs 154 and 174, to control its replacement and training units. In autumn 1941, some of these units were transferred to the Czechoslovakian Protectorate. The replacement elements of these units returned to Wehrkreis IV in the fall of 1942 when the Home Army divided the military districts' training and replacement functions. The 174th (now a reserve division) left for central Poland, and the 154th, which was also upgraded, followed shortly afterward. Wehrkreis Headquarters (which was located at Dresden) upgraded Special Administrative Division Staff 404 to a replacement division staff and created Replacement Division Staff 464 to replace them. In March 1944, elements of the 154th and 174th Reserve Divisions went into combat on the Eastern Front, but these divisions were not entirely committed to action until the end of the year. Wehrkreis IV meanwhile resumed its training missions under its new replacement division staffs and the IV Panzer Command, a brigade-sized headquarters that was also subordinate to the Wehrkreis. The military district was overrun by the Russians in the spring of 1945. Its affiliated divisions included the 4th Infantry, 14th Infantry, 14th Panzer, 18th Infantry, 18th Panzer, 24th Infantry, 56th Infantry, 87th Infantry, 94th Infantry, 104th Jäger, 134th Infantry, 164th Infantry, 164th Light Afrika, 209th Infantry, 223rd Infantry, 255th Infantry, 256th Infantry, 275th Infantry, 294th Infantry, 304th Infantry, 336th Infantry, 372nd Infantry, 384th Infantry, 568th Infantry, and 704th Infantry.

WEHRKREIS V

This military district included all of Hohenzollern and all but the northern sections of Württemberg and Baden. After the fall of France in 1940 it absorbed Alsace. In mid-1944 it had an area of 38,814 square kilometers and a population of about 5¾ million people. Stuttgart was the headquarters of the Wehrkreis.

After the outbreak of hostilities, V Military District established Replacement Division Staffs 155 and 165, to control its replacement-training units. The 155th consisted of motorized and panzer elements. From November 1939 until September 1940, these units were stationed in the Protectorate (formerly Czechoslovakia). In early 1942 the replacement units were transferred to Alsace, and Special Administrative Division Staff 405 was upgraded to replacement division status to control them. Meanwhile, Colonel General Fromm, the Commander-in-Chief of the Replacement Army, partially divided the replacement and training missions of the Wehrkreis in early 1942 in an experimental measure that was later adopted in all the Wehrkreise. Replacement Division Staff 165 became the original reserve division and moved to the Epinal area of eastern France with approximately half of Wehrkreis V's training units. Later it was transferred to Holland. Meanwhile, the Wehrkreis created Replacement Division Staff 465 to take over the nonmotorized replacement elements left by the 165th. In late 1943 the military district also lost its panzer and motorized training units when the 155th Reserve Panzer Division was created from the former replacement division, and was sent to northwestern France.

In May 1944, the 155th Reserve Panzer was absorbed by the 9th Panzer Division; two months later the 165th Reserve Division was disbanded, its personnel sent to several divisions on the Western Front, and its Headquarters used to form the 70th Infantry Division. The loss of these two divisions meant that Wehrkreis V had to resume its own training operations under the 465th and newly formed Replacement Division Staff 405. Parts of these divisions were in action in September 1944 when the Western Allies invaded Alsace. Elements of the 405th Replacement Division worked on fortifications in the Vosges Mountains and later held defensive positions on the eastern bank of the Rhine, before withdrawing into the interior. The entire V Military District was overrun by the Americans and the French in the spring of 1945. Field divisions affiliated with this Wehrkreis included the 5th Infantry, 5th Jäger, 10th Panzer, 23rd Panzer, 25th Infantry, 25th Panzer Grenadier, 35th Infantry, 77th Infantry, 78th Infantry, 101st Jäger, 125th Infantry, 198th Infantry, 205th Infantry, 215th Infantry, 245th Infantry, 260th Infantry, 266th Infantry, 271st Infantry, 282nd Infantry, 305th Infantry, 307th Infantry, 323rd Infantry, 330th Infantry, 335th Infantry, 344th Infantry, 355th Infantry, 364th Infantry, 365th Infantry, 372nd Infantry, 554th Infantry, and 715th Infantry.

WEHRKREIS VI

This large military district encompassed almost all of Westphalia, the northern half of Rhenish Prussia, and part of western Hanover. It had an area of just over 40,000 square miles and a population of 12,100,000.

Wehrkreis Headquarters was located in Münster. When the war broke out, the VI Military District set up Replacement Division Staffs 156, 166, and 176. Most of the subordinate replacement-training units of these divisions were posted in Wehrkreis XX from November 1939 until September 1940. When the Home Army split the Wehrkreis's training and replacement functions in the autumn of 1942, the training units in the southwestern part of the District moved into eastern Belgium under the 156th Reserve Division, which eventually became the 47th Infantry. The training units in the northeastern part of the Wehrkreis were transferred to Denmark under Replacement Division Staff 166 (later 166th Reserve Division) early the following year. The rest of the training elements of the Wehrkreis remained subordinate to the Münster headquarters and generally concentrated in western Westphalia, although some of them operated as far away as the Netherlands. Within the Wehrkreis, the 176th Replacement Division absorbed the remaining replacement units of the 166th, and the 526th Frontier Guard Division Headquarters was converted to a replacement division staff to replace the 156th Division. The VI Panzer Command, a brigade-sized headquarters that was probably formed prior to the start of the war, remained at Warendorf and never gave up its training units, although it did set up bases in eastern Holland.

After the British and Canadians entered Belgium in August and September 1944, the 176th and 526th Replacement Divisions were both committed to combat, although their unfit, convalescent, and untrained personnel remained behind under Wehrkreis control. The 526th also left a "reserve" or cadre staff behind at Wuppertal-Vohwinkel and possibly at Cologne as well. The 526th was eventually dissolved and its personnel distributed among several divisions. On the other hand, the 176th was upgraded to an infantry division in November 1944, while the VI Panzer Command also sent a battle group into action in the Low Countries. The Wehrkreis was still performing its mission on a reduced scale until just before the end of the war, when it was overrun by Montgomery's armies.

The field divisions affiliated with Wehrkreis VI included the 1st Light, 6th Infantry, 6th Panzer, 16th Infantry, 16th Panzer Grenadier, 16th Panzer, 25th Panzer, 26th Infantry, 39th Infantry, 47th Infantry, 64th Infantry, 69th Infantry, 84th Infantry, 86th Infantry, 95th Infantry, 106th Infantry, 116th Panzer, 126th Infantry, 176th Infantry, 196th Infantry, 199th Infantry, 211th Infantry, 227th Infantry, 253rd Infantry, 254th Infantry, 264th Infantry, 306th Infantry, 326th Infantry, 329th Infantry, 361st Infantry, 371st Infantry, 385th Infantry, 386th Infantry, 393rd Infantry, 569th Infantry and 716th Infantry.

WEHRKREIS VII

The VII Military District, which had an area of 32,000 square kilometers and a population of 3,200,000, included Upper Bavaria, the southern parts of Lower (northern) Bavaria, and the Upper Palatinate, most of Swabia, and minor parts of Upper and Central Franconia. Its headquarters was in Munich.

Replacement Division Staffs 147 and 157 were established after the outbreak of the war to control the rapidly growing number of replacement-training units in the District. The infantry and mountain training elements of the Wehrkreis went to eastern France under the 157th, when it was upgraded to a mountain reserve division in the fall of 1942. In early 1943 the 147th was also upgraded to reserve division status and was transferred to the Ukraine by the Home Army. Wehrkreis VII formed Replacement Division Staffs 407 and 467, at Augsburg and Munich, respectively, to replace them.

The 147th Reserve Division became the 147th Field Training Division in 1943 and was destroyed in 1944. The 157th became a mountain division in 1944 and was engaged in southern France by August. It thus became necessary for the Wehrkreis to begin training its own recruits, and its replacement units became replacement-training formations once more. The VII District continued to conduct operations until it was overrun—mainly by the Americans—at the end of the war. Its affiliated divisions included the 1st Mountain, 4th Mountain, 7th Infantry, 17th Panzer, 27th Infantry, 57th Infantry, 88th Infantry, 97th Jäger, 147th Field Training, 157th Mountain, 167th Mountain, 212th Infantry, 268th Infantry, 277th Infantry, 337th Infantry, 362nd Infantry, 367th Infantry, 376th Infantry, 387th Infantry, and 707th Infantry.

WEHRKREIS VIII

The VIII Military District consisted of almost all of Silesia. In 1938 it absorbed part of the Sudetenland, and the next year it was extended to include Polish Eastern Upper Silesia and the Teschen district of Poland. In 1944 this Wehrkreis had a population of 8,441,000 and an area of 56,000 square kilometers. The headquarters was located at Breslau.

Replacement Division Staffs 148, 158, and 178 were formed in 1939 to control the replacement-training units of this Wehrkreis. The 178th was a motorized/panzer unit. In February 1941, the 148th moved to Lorraine and the 158th was posted in Alsace, but both remained subordinate to the VIII. In the latter part of 1942 these divisions returned their replacement elements to Wehrkreis VIII, were upgraded to reserve divisions, and separated from the District. Special Administrative Division Staffs 408 and 432 were converted to replacement division headquarters to control the replacement units released by the new reserve divisions. The 178th Panzer Replacement Division retained both its training and replacement missions to the end and never left the Wehrkreis.

After D-Day, the 158th and 189th were both committed to battle on the Western Front, and the Wehrkreis reassumed training responsibilities for its nonmotorized recruits. Wehrkreis VIII ceased operations in early 1945 and committed its units to action against the Russians when Breslau came under siege. The city held out until May, even after Berlin had fallen. The field divisions affiliated with Wehrkreis VIII included the 5th Panzer, 8th Infantry, 8th Jäger, 11th Panzer, 16th Infantry, 18th Infantry, 18th Panzer Grenadier, 28th Infantry, 28th Jäger, 62nd Infantry, 81st Infantry, 102nd Infantry, 148th Infantry, 168th Infantry, 213th Infantry, 213th Security, 221st Infantry, 221st Security, 226th Infantry, 230th Coastal Defense, 239th Infantry, 252nd Infantry, 298th Infantry, 320th Infantry, 332nd Infantry, 358th Infantry, 370th Infantry, 442nd Security, and 708th Infantry.

WEHRKREIS IX

This military district consisted of almost all of Thuringia, the Prussian province of Hesse, northern and eastern Hesse, eastern Nassau, a part of western Merseburg, and small sections of southern Westphalia, southern Hanover, and western Lower Franconia. Its area was 37,654 square kilometers and its population was estimated at 5,427,000 in early 1945. District Headquarters was located at Kassel.

Wehrkreis IX set up Replacement Division Staffs 159, 179, and 189 when the war broke out in 1939. After the separation of the District's replacement and training elements in 1942, the 159th and 189th became reserve divisions and left for France with the nonmotorized training units that had formerly belonged to the Wehrkreis. The 179th was upgraded to a reserve panzer division and left for France with its subordinate training units in autumn 1943. Wehrkreis IX did not have primary training responsibility again until 1944, when the 159th and 189th became engaged in combat on the Western Front, and the 179th was merged with the depleted 16th Panzer Division to form the 116th Panzer. Replacement Division Staff 409 and IX Panzer Command assumed the missions formerly conducted by the three reserve divisions. In 1945 the Soviets occupied the eastern sectors of this district, and the Western Allies overran the rest. The 1st Panzer, 2nd Light, 7th Panzer, 9th Infantry, 15th Infantry, 20th Panzer, 27th Panzer, 29th Motorized, 52nd Infantry, 52nd Security, 82nd Infantry, 129th Infantry, 159th Infantry, 169th Infantry, 189th Infantry, 214th Infantry, 232nd Infantry, 251st Infantry, 299th Infantry, 319th Infantry, 339th Infantry, 345th Motorized, 346th Infantry, 356th Infantry, 363rd Infantry, 377th Infantry, 559th Infantry, and 709th Infantry Divisions were affiliated with Wehrkreis IX.

WEHRKREIS X

Located just south of Denmark, this Wehrkreis included Schleswig-Holstein, Oldenburg, Hamburg, Bremen, and northern Hanover. It had an area of 39,143 square kilometers and a population of about 5.5 million. Hamburg was the district headquarters.

After the invasion of Poland began, the X formed Replacement Division Staffs 160, 180, and 190, to control its replacement-training units. From 1940 to 1942 most of the Wehrkreis's subordinate units were billeted in Denmark, except for those elements native to Oldenburg, which were mainly stationed in the Netherlands. After the Home Army reorganized in 1942, the 160th became a reserve division, while the 180th and 190th returned to Wehrkreis control, directing the district's replacement units. By 1944 they included substantial numbers of combined replacement-training units.

In mid-September 1944, the 180th and 190th were hastily committed to combat as infantry units against Allied ground forces that were driving on the Arnhem area, where the British 1st Airborne Division was trying to hold off the II SS Panzer Corps. By delaying the Allied advance, the 180th and 190th probably contributed more to the success of a major operation than did any other units that were affiliated with a Wehrkreis. These divisions never returned to Hanover, for they were both upgraded to infantry divisions in November 1944. The X probably established a new replacement division headquarters to control its remaining replacement-training battalions, but this is not certain. The X Military District was not completely overrun until May 1945 and seems to have operated (with declining intensity) until the very end. Field divisions affiliated with Wehrkreis X included the 20th Panzer Grenadier, 22nd Infantry, 30th Infantry, 58th Infantry, 83rd Infantry, 89th Infantry, 110th Infantry, 170th Infantry, 180th Infantry, 190th Infantry, 225th Infantry, 269th Infantry, 270th Coastal Defense, 290th Infantry, 416th Infantry, 560th Infantry, and 710th Infantry Divisions.

WEHRKREIS XI

Consisting of Brunswick, Anhalt, the southern part of Hanover, the Province of Magdeburg and the small region of Schaumburg-Lippe, this Wehrkreis covered 33,040 square kilometers and had a population of 4,149,000. The city of Hanover was the district capital.

In 1939, the XI formed Replacement Division Staffs 171 and 191, which stayed within the Wehrkreis until the fall of 1942, when they were upgraded to reserve division status and sent to the coast of the English Channel. Replacement Division Staff 471 was formed in late 1942 to control the replacement units left behind by the reserve divisions.

By early 1944 the 171st and 191st Reserve Divisions had ceased training operations and were redesignated the 48th and 49th Infantry Divisions, respectively. The Wehrkreis, therefore, had to resume training within its borders. To do this, it converted most of its replacement units to replacement-training units. These forces continued in operation until the end of the war.

Wehrkreis XI was the home of several important schools, as well as a number of parachute replacement and training units. Its affiliated field divisions included the 13th Motorized, 13th Panzer, 19th Infantry, 19th Panzer, 31st Infantry, 48th Infantry, 49th Infantry, 71st Infantry, 96th Infantry, 111th Infantry, 131st Infantry, 181st Infantry, 216th Infantry, 265th Infantry, 267th Infantry, 272nd Infantry, 276th Infantry, 295th Infantry, 321st Infantry, 352nd Infantry, 390th Field Training, 541st Infantry, 553rd Infantry, and 711th Infantry.

WEHRKREIS XII

The XII Military District, which headquartered at Wiesbaden, included the southern part of Rhenish Prussia, the western parts of the State of Hesse and Prussian Nassau, the Bavarian Palatinate, the vital Saar Industrial district, and a small part of northern Baden. It was expanded after the fall of France to include Lorraine and Luxembourg. The Wehrkreis's area was 36,471 square kilometers, with a population of 6,240,000.

The District created Replacement Division Staffs 172 and 182 to direct its replacement-training units when the war broke out. These divisions went to Poland in November 1939 but returned to the Wehrkreis in September 1940. In 1941 and 1942 elements of these units were stationed in the Nancy area of eastern France. In the fall of that year, these elements returned their replacement components to Germany and were joined by other training battalions under the headquarters of the 182nd, which had been redesignated a reserve division. Later these forces were transferred to the Channel coast. Meanwhile, Wehrkreis XII created Replacement Division Staff 462 to control the returning replacement battalions.

In August 1944, the 182nd Reserve was disbanded and its personnel scattered among a number of combat divisions. Wehrkreis XII thus regained its training responsibilities, which it met by expanding its existing regiments.

The 462nd Replacement Division was upgraded to a field (Volksgrenadier) division in September 1944, went into action in eastern France, and was subsequently destroyed at Metz. Shortly thereafter, the entire Wehrkreis became a battleground and the District's operations were seriously disrupted. Until this time the motorized and panzer units were trained and administered by Replacement Division Staff 172 and the XII Panzer Command, which had ceased to exist by early 1945. The 999th Replacement Brigade, which consisted mainly of political prisoners and ordinary criminals, was also administered by this Wehrkreis until the Western Allies overran it in 1945. Its affiliated field divisions included the 15th Panzer, 15th Panzer Grenadier, 22nd Panzer, 33rd Infantry, 34th Infantry, 36th

Infantry, 36th Panzer Grenadier, 65th Infantry, 72nd Infantry, 79th Infantry, 85th Infantry, 91st Infantry, 112th Infantry, 132nd Infantry, 197th Infantry, 246th Infantry, 263rd Infantry, 342nd Infantry, 348th Infantry, 389th Infantry, 391st Field Training, 444th Security, 462nd Infantry, 556th Infantry, 712th Infantry, and 999th Infantry.

WEHRKREIS XIII

This district consisted of most of Franconia, Lower Bavaria, the Upper Palatinate, and small sections of southern Thuringia, northern Baden, Württemberg, and Swabia. In 1938 it annexed part of Czechoslovakia. The Wehrkreis, which had its headquarters in Nuremberg, had an area of 49,900 square kilometers and a population of 4,771,000.

When the war started, the XIII established Replacement Division Staffs 173 and 193 to control its replacement-training units. In the fall of 1943 the 173rd was redesignated a reserve division, transferred to eastern Croatia with most of the Wehrkreis' training units, and placed directly under the control of the Home Army. The 193rd Replacement Division, which was now in Bohemia, remained under Wehrkreis control with some of the training units. Replacement Division Staff 413 was created at Nuremberg in 1943 to assume command of the replacement units left behind by the 173rd. The District's motorized and panzer training units were assigned to the 273rd Reserve Panzer Division in late 1943 and lost to the Wehrkreis.

By spring 1944, both the 173rd Reserve and 273rd Reserve Panzer Divisions had been dissolved, and the Wehrkreis regained all the training responsibilities it had lost the year before. To meet these responsibilities, the Wehrkreis enlarged its existing replacement regiments, which continued operating until the end of the war.

In 1945, the eastern parts of this Wehrkreis were overrun by the Soviets, and the western sections were captured by the Americans and the French.

The following field divisions were affiliated with Wehrkreis XIII: 1st Ski Jäger, 4th Panzer, 7th Mountain, 10th Infantry, 10th Panzer Grenadier, 17th Infantry, 46th Infantry, 73rd Infantry, 98th Infantry, 99th Jäger, 113th Infantry, 183rd Infantry, 231st Infantry, 237th Infantry, 271st Infantry, 296th Infantry, 334th Infantry, 343rd Infantry, 565th Infantry, and 713th Infantry.

WEHRKREIS XVII

With an area of 38,934 square kilometers and an estimated population of 4,604,000 in 1944, this Wehrkreis consisted of the northeastern part of what had once been Austria. It was headquartered in Vienna.

The District, which was formed in 1938, set up Replacement Division Staffs 177 and 187 shortly after the invasion of Poland, to control its replacement-training units. Many of these were transferred to Moravia in 1941 under the HQ of the 177th or the XVII Panzer Command, both of which remained under Wehrkreis control. The western part of Slovakia was also used by the Wehrkreis as a training area.

In the fall of 1942 the XVII District lost much of its training mission, as well as the 187th Division, which was redesignated a reserve unit and sent to Croatia with the training units. Replacement Division Staff 487, however, was formed at Linz to control the replacement units left behind by the 187th. When the 187th ceased training and was redesignated a jäger division in autumn 1943, Wehrkreis XVII, which had never completely ceased training (unlike some other districts), simply enlarged its existing replacement-training facilities and expanded its capabilities with a minimum of difficulty. The Wehrkreis was overrun by the Russians in April 1945.

Wehrkreis XVII also directed the Croatian Training Brigade for most of the war. This brigade provided trained replacements for the 369th, 373rd, and 392nd Croatian Infantry Divisions of the German Army, as well as for their German cadres. Divisions affiliated with Wehrkreis XVII included the 2nd Panzer, 4th Light, 9th Panzer, 42nd Jäger, 45th Infantry, 92nd Infantry, 100th Jäger, 117th Jäger, 137th Infantry, 243rd Infantry, 262nd Infantry, 277th Infantry, 297th Infantry, 327th Infantry, 331st Infantry, 351st Infantry, 369th Infantry, 373rd Infantry, 392nd Infantry, 564th Infantry, and 717th Infantry.

WEHRKREIS XVIII

Created with the annexation of Austria in 1938, this mountainous district included most of the territory of what was formerly Austria, but less than half of its population. It consisted of southern and western Austria, the Tyrol region, and (as of 1941) the Upper Carniola and Lower Styria districts of Yugoslavia. It had a population of 3,000,000 and an area of almost 59,000 square kilometers in 1944.

With the outbreak of hostilities, the XVIII set up Replacement Division Staff 188 to control its replacement-training units, which were almost all mountain forces. In autumn 1943 this division was transferred to northern Italy as a reserve division, and its training units were lost to the Wehrkreis. To control the remaining replacement units, the XVIII set up Replacement Division Staff 418 at Salzburg, which was also the headquarters of the Wehrkreis. When the 188th was upgraded to a regular mountain division in late 1944, Wehrkreis XVIII reassumed its normal training duties, in so far as that was possible in the fifth year of the war. The District was occupied, largely by the Western Allies, in the spring of 1945.

The 2nd Mountain, 3rd Mountain, 5th Mountain, 6th Mountain, 8th Mountain, 118th Jäger, 188th Mountain, and 718th Infantry Divisions were all affiliated with Wehrkreis XVIII.

WEHRKREIS XX

This Wehrkreis, which consisted of Danzig, the Elbing area of West Prussia, and sections of northern Poland, was created in the winter of 1939-40. Its Danzig headquarters administered an area of 26,000 square kilometers, which were inhabited by 2,259,000 people, most of whom were Poles. It never set up any replacement or reserve divisions of its own, although Replacement Division Staff 152 of Wehrkreis II was attached to it in the fall of 1942. The XX Military District also controlled the "Feld-herrnhalle" Motorized Replacement Brigade, which provided replacements for the 60th Panzer Grenadier and 13th Panzer Divisions. Most of these men were former S.A. (Brownshirt) members.

General of Artillery Bodewin Keitel, the younger brother of Field Marshal Wilhelm Keitel, was the commander of this Wehrkreis for most of its existence. The District was overrun by the Russians in January 1945.

WEHRKREIS XXI

The XXI Military District was created in northern Poland in 1939-40. Headquartered at Posen, it controlled an area of 44,000 square kilometers and had a population of 4,635,000, most of which were Poles. Because of its foreign composition, the XXI never set up its own units but did provide facilities for other Wehrkreise training elements, principally the 192nd Replacement Division of Wehrkreis II. The XXI District was overrun by the Russians in late 1944 and early 1945.

WEHRKREIS GENERAL GOUVERNEMENT

Officially formed in central and southern Poland on November 1, 1943, this District had, in fact, been functioning since 1939. With 142,207 square kilometers and 18 million people, it was easily the largest and probably the least German of the Wehrkreise. Warsaw was the District Headquarters. The Wehrkreis's main function in World War II was to provide training facilities for the reserve divisions. It had a limited internal organization and no affiliated divisions.

WEHRKREIS BOHEMIA AND MORAVIA

With an area of 48,902 square kilometers and a population of 7,500,000, this Czechoslovakian district was headquartered at Prague. It was created in 1939 but never produced a field division; however, it provided facilities, administrative support, and training areas to no less than five Wehrkreise, as well as Luftwaffe and Waffen-SS units, which tended to concentrate here. It did not cease operations until Czechoslovakia became a battleground in 1945.

APPENDIX IV
THE HIGHER HEADQUARTERS

The German divisions in the field were, generally speaking, controlled by three types of higher headquarters: the army group, the army, and the corps or corps command. The corps command differed from the corps in that it was usually formed as special headquarters for defensive missions, mainly in occupied territories. Most of the corps commands were upgraded to corps as the war progressed, and, indeed, there was little difference in them and corps headquarters. As early as 1942, for example, U.S. Intelligence reported of them: "While not composed of a high percentage of offensive combat arms, they can give a good account of themselves in battle. In some cases, they have been used for offensive missions" (OB 42: 52).

An army group headquarters usually controlled two or more armies, but never more than seven. Armies directed the operations of two or more corps, and corps controlled two or more divisions. Each headquarters had various combat and support units organic to it, as well as attached combat divisions. An army group, for example, included a Commander of the Army Group Rear Area (Befehlshaber des rückwärtigen Heeresgebiets), and each army had a Commandant of Army Rear Area (Kommandant des rückwärtigen Armeegebiets), whose task was to supervise the administration of the communications zone so that the army group or army commander could concentrate on field operations. Both commandants were in charge of security units (divisions or regiments), as well as administrative and supply units, and GHQ formations.

General Headquarters units organic or attached to armies and army groups included special duty infantry battalions, security and motorized security regiments or brigades, special Jagdkommandos (raiding detachments), motorized machine gun battalions, antiaircraft units, reconnaissance battalions, and special disciplinary battalions (Sonderbataillons)—units to which insubordinate soldiers were sent. Usually they were employed in areas of the Russian Front where heavy fighting was expected.

Each army also had an infantry equipment park, as well as other parks for medical and veterinary services, heavy transport equipment parks (one per army), and other maintenance detachments. Independent tank, heavy anti-tank, and tank flame-thrower battalions were also organic to some army and army group headquarters and were often attached to corps or divisions, in accordance with the tactical judgment of the army or army group commander.

Other GHQ units included (but were not limited to) artillery regimental staffs (all fully motorized, except for coastal defense artillery), super heavy artillery units, all varieties of artillery, artillery observation battalions (i.e., forward observers), armored assault gun battalions, survey and mapping units, observation balloon units, meteorological platoons, artillery parks, chemical units (including projector, or rocket units), decontamination battalions, gas defense units, combat, fortress, and railway engineer units, engineer landing companies (amphibious), assault boat companies, bridging units, technical battalions (used for the production and treatment of oil, coal mining, etc.), signal units, motor transport regiments and battalions, tank repair battalions, motor maintenance workshops, field workshops, motor transport park companies, supply battalions and special supply staffs, GHQ or army medical battalions, hospital detachments, veterinary parks and units, construction staffs, military police battalions (one per army), and local defense units—which were usually assigned to guard prisoners of war.

Corps-type units varied with the type of corps, of which there were several, including infantry (or "armeekorps"), panzer, mountain, reserve, parachute, SS, and corps commands. They contained fewer GHQ units than army or army group headquarters, but included supply, signal, military police, artillery, security, field postal, and other units.

One other type of major headquarters must be mentioned, and that is the Oberbefehlshaber, or OB. It frequently controlled army groups, although sometimes it just controlled armies. OB West was the most famous Oberbefehlshaber, and it was responsible to OKW (see chapter 2) and to Hitler for directing the war on the Western Front in 1944-45.

OB EAST*
October 1939: formed in Poland to guard Germany's eastern territories against a possible Russian surprise attack while Hitler overran France and the Benelux countries. It controlled a dozen third- and fourth-wave divisions plus a cavalry brigade.
July 1940: dissolved.

OB NORTHWEST
April 6, 1945: created to control the remnants of the 1st Parachute and 25th armies, plus naval and Luftwaffe units, in Holland and northwestern Germany.
May 1945: surrendered

OB SOUTH (also known as OB SOUTHWEST)
late 1941: formed to direct German military activities in Italy and North Africa
August 1943: included Rommel's Army Group B in northern Italy, Hube's forces fighting the Allies in Sicily, and a few German units in central Italy, Sardinia, and Corsica

---

*The purpose of this book is to describe the German ground divisions. The histories of the higher headquarters will be discussed in thumbnail sketch form only.

May 1944: directed the 10th and 14th armies on the Italian Front, plus Army Detachment von Zangen in northern Italy

April 1945: in charge of army groups G, C, and E

OB SOUTHEAST (and simultaneously ARMY GROUP F)

August 1943: created at the time of the Italian surrender. Included Army Group F (in Yugoslavia and Albania) and Army Group E (in Greece and the Mediterranean islands)

late 1944 or early 1945: dissolved

OB WEST

1942: formed in Paris (also known as Army Group D, a headquarters it eventually absorbed)

1944-45: controlled army groups B, G, and H on the Western Front

ARMY GROUP A

early 1942: activated on the southern sector of the Russian Front, when Army Group South was divided

1942-43: directed the drive on and retreat from the Caucasus; fought on the southern flank of the Russian Front

April 1944: redesignated Army Group South Ukraine; eventually renamed Army Group South and, in April 1945, Army Group Ostmark

May 1945: surrendered

ARMY GROUP B

spring 1942: formed to control armies advancing on Stalingrad early 1943: dissolved

August 1943: reformed in southern Germany under Rommel

late 1943: controlled German units in northern Italy

January 1944: sent to France; controlled 7th and 15th armies and Armed Forces Netherlands HQ

June 1944: Normandy

August 1944: crushed at Falaise

December 1944: commanded Ardennes counteroffensive

April 1945: destroyed in the Ruhr Pocket

ARMY GROUP C

November 1943: formed in southern Italy

1943-45: directed German combat operations in Italy, controlling 10th and later 10th and 14th armies

May 4, 1945: surrendered

ARMY GROUP CENTER

1939: formed as Army Group North; invaded Poland

1940: overran Low Countries as Army Group B
1941: redesignated Army Group Center; invaded Russia; defeated at Moscow
1943: Kursk
1944: crushed in Vitebsk-Minsk area: retreated through Poland
January 26, 1945: redesignated Army Group North; fighting in East Prussia
April 2, 1945: disbanded

ARMY GROUP COURLAND

1939: formed as Army Group C on Siegfried Line
1940: opposed French forces in Maginot Line
1941: redesignated Army Group North for Russian invasion: conquered Baltic States
1941-January, 1944: maintained Siege of Leningrad and fought in the Lake Ilmen area
1944: withdrew to Narva River-Lake Peipus line
September 1944: retreated into Courland Pocket
late 1944: redesignated Army Group Courland
May 1945: surrendered to the Soviets

ARMY GROUP D

1941: formed to control German armies stationed in France, Belgium, and Holland
early 1944: absorbed by OB West

ARMY GROUP DON

November 1942: formed from HQ, 11th Army; directed Stalingrad relief operation
February 1943: redesignated Army Group South; later renamed Army Group North Ukraine, Army Group A, and Army Group Center
April 1945: surrounded in Czechoslovakia; surrendered to the Russians early the following month

ARMY GROUP E

1942-43: formed in the Balkans by the expansion of the 12th Army
1944: withdrew from southern Balkans
1945: surrendered in Croatia

ARMY GROUP F

Summer 1943: formed to control German occupation forces in the Balkans
Autumn 1944: retreated from southern Balkans
Winter 1944: gave up control of most of the units of Army Group E
early 1945: dissolved

ARMY GROUP G
May 1944: formed in southern France
1944-45: retreated across southern France and southern Germany
May 6, 1945: surrendered

ARMY GROUP H
autumn 1944: formed on northern sector, Western Front
1945: retreated across northwestern Germany
April 6, 1945: deactivated; became OB Northwest

ARMY GROUP NORTH
see Army Group Courland

ARMY GROUP SOUTH
1939: formed to control German forces invading Poland
1940: as Army Group A, played the major role in the conquest of France
1941: once again designated Army Group South; overran the Ukraine, the
    Donets, and most of the Crimea; turned back at Rostov
spring 1942: divided into army groups A and B; ceased to exist

ARMY GROUP VISTULA
January 25, 1945: created for the defense of western Prussia, Pomerania,
    and Berlin
April 1945: crushed in Battle of Berlin
May 2, 1945: surrendered

1st ARMY
1940: French campaign
1940-44: occupation duties, southwestern France
1944: withdrew across southern France; fought along the Loire and upper
    Seine
early 1945: fought in the Saar; retreated across southwestern Germany
May 1945: surrendered south of Munich

1st PARACHUTE ARMY
early 1944: formed in eastern France as a training headquarters from HQ,
    XI Air Corps
autumn 1944: became operational; fought in Belgium and Holland
early 1945: in eastern Holland
May 1945: surrendered in Oldenburg area, northwestern Germany

1st PANZER ARMY
summer 1939: formed as XXII Corps
September 1939: Poland
1940: fought in Western campaign as Group von Kleist

1941: fought in Balkans as 1st Panzer Group
late 1941: redesignated 1st Panzer Army
1941-45: fought on Eastern Front

2nd ARMY
1939: Poland
1940: Western campaign
1941: Balkans
1941-44: Russian Front
autumn 1944: Poland
1945: fought in East Prussia and Vistula delta
May 9, 1945: last elements surrendered to the Russians on the Hela peninsula

2nd PANZER ARMY
May 1939: formed as XIX Motorized Corps
September 1939: Poland
1940: Western campaign; redesignated Group Guderian
1941: redesignated 2nd Panzer Group; upgraded to panzer army status in December
1941-43: Eastern Front
late 1943: transferred to Balkans
late 1944: engaged in Croatia and subsequently fought the Russians in Hungary
1945: ended the war on the southern sector of the Eastern Front

3rd ARMY
1939: formed from elements of HQ, I Corps and Wehrkreis I: Poland
late 1939: disbanded; probably used to form HQ, 18th Army

3rd PANZER ARMY
1937: formed in Jena as XV Corps, to control the original three German light divisions
1939: Poland
1940: Western campaign (as XV Motorized Corps and later as Group Hoth)
1941: Eastern Front as 3rd Panzer Group
late 1941: redesignated 3rd Panzer Army
1941-45: fought on central sector, Russian Front, and in Poland, East Prussia, and northeastern Germany

4th ARMY
1939: Poland
1940: Western campaign
1941-44: central sector, Russian Front
1944: crushed by Soviet summer offensive

1945: East Prussia; mostly destroyed at and in vincinity of Königsberg

4th PANZER ARMY

1937: formed in Berlin as XVI Corps to control the original panzer divisions
1939: Poland
1940: West
1941: Russia (as 4th Panzer Group)
late 1941: upgraded to panzer army status
1941-45: central and southern sectors, Eastern Front. Retreated across the northern Ukraine, Poland, and Silesia
1945: ended the war in eastern Germany

5th ARMY

1939: controlled units along the western German frontier during the Polish campaign
October 1939: transferred to occupied Poland
late 1939: disbanded

5th PANZER ARMY

December 1942: formed in Tunisia
May 1943: destroyed
August 6, 1944: reformed in Normandy from HQ, Panzer Group West, fought in Normandy, Falaise, the retreat through France and in the Ardennes
April 1945: destroyed in the Ruhr Pocket

6th ARMY

1939: formed as 10th Army: Poland
early 1940: redesignated 6th Army
May 1940: destroyed Belgian Army
1941-43: southern sector, Russian Front
January 1943: surrendered at Stalingrad
early 1943: reformed in southern Russia
1943-45: on Eastern Front; suffered heavy losses on lower Dnieper and in Hungary; ended war on southern sector

6th SS PANZER ARMY

autumn 1944: formed as 6th Panzer Army in the vicinity of Paderborn, northwestern Germany; in charge of refitting panzer divisions smashed in French campaign
late 1944: Ardennes offensive
early 1945: Hungary
April 1945: defeated by the Russians in the Battle of Vienna

7th ARMY
1940: Western campaign
1940-44: occupation duties, western France
1944: fought in Normandy, at Falaise, and in the Ardennes offensive
May 1945: surrendered to the Americans in Czechoslovakia

8th ARMY
1939: formed from HQ, Army Group 3: Poland
1940: disbanded
July 1943: reformed on southern sector, Russian Front
February 1944: smashed west of the lower Dnieper
1944: retreated through eastern Carpathians, lower Dnestr, Transylvania, and Hungary
1945: ended the war on the southern sector, Eastern Front

9th ARMY
early 1940: formed from OB East
1940: Western campaign
1941-44: central sector, Russian Front
summer 1944: smashed by Soviets
1944-early 1945: retreated across southern and central Poland
1945: destroyed in Battle of Berlin

10th ARMY
1939: formed: Poland
early 1940: redesignated 6th Army (see 6th Army)
August 1943: reformed in southern Italy
1943-45: Italian campaign

11th ARMY
late 1940: formed
1941-42: southern sector, Russian Front; conducted Siege of Sevastopol
August 1942: shifted to northern sector, Eastern Front
December 1942: redesignated Army Group Don
April 1945: reactivated after Ruhr encirclement; quickly overrun by Western Allies

11th SS ARMY
February 1945: formed; defeated in futile counterattack at Stargard: HQ pulled out of the line to collect stragglers; continued to operate in northern Germany until the end of the war

12th ARMY
spring 1940: formed

1940: Western campaign
1941: Sent to Balkans; remained there
winter of 1942-43: expanded to Army Group E
April 1945: reactivated in Harz Mountains to relieve Berlin
May 1945: surrendered

14th ARMY
1939: Poland
late 1939: disbanded
autumn 1943: formed in northern Italy to control forces formerly under
  Army Group B
February 1944: committed to battle at Anzio
1944-45: Italian Front

15th ARMY
late 1940: formed to control units in northern France and Belgium
September 1944: in action on Western Front; retreated into Holland
late 1944: shifted to Aachen sector
April 1945: destroyed in Ruhr Pocket

16th ARMY
spring 1940: formed
1940: Western campaign
1941-45: northern sector, Eastern Front
May 1945: surrendered in Courland Pocket

17th ARMY
late 1940: formed
1941-43: southern sector, Eastern Front; in Caucasus campaign
late 1943: withdrew into Crimea
April 1944: largely destroyed at Sevastopol; HQ evacuated
September 1944: reappeared in the Krakow sector, Poland; fought on the
  southern sector of the Eastern Front for the rest of the war

18th ARMY
spring 1940: formed, probably from Headquarters, 3rd Army
1940: Western campaign; took Paris
1941-45: northern sector, Eastern Front; besieged Leningrad
May 1945: surrendered in Courland Pocket

19th ARMY
February 1943: formed at Avignon, southern France, absorbing Headquarters, LXXXIII Corps, as well as Army Detachment Felber, which had
  occupied Vichy France in November, 1942

1942-44: controlled German troops in Mediterranean France

August 1944: withdrew north

1945: retreated across southwestern Germany; largely destroyed by the French and Americans in the Black Forest

May 5, 1945: surrendered at Innsbruck

20th MOUNTAIN ARMY

1941-42 (winter of): formed in northern Finland as the Army of Lapland

summer 1942: redesignated 20th Mountain Army

1941-44: fought in Murmansk sector in extreme northern Russia

autumn 1944: withdrew from northern Russia and northern Finland into northern Norway

late 1944: absorbed 21st Army; controlled all German Army troops in Norway

May 8, 1945: surrendered

21st ARMY

1939: formed as XXI Corps: Poland

1940: conquered Norway as Group XXI

summer 1941: expanded to Army of Norway, absorbing Headquarters, LXIII Corps Command

1941-42: responsible for German operations in Finland and the Murmansk region of northern Russia until the formation of the 20th Mountain Army

late 1944: absorbed by 20th Mountain Army

April 1945: a second 21st Army formed north of Berlin

May 2, 1945: surrendered to Americans at Ludwigslust

24th ARMY

late April 1945: created in the Tyrol region to block Allied drive from northern Italy into southern Germany; experienced little success

May 1945: surrendered to the Allies near Arlberg Pass in extreme southern Germany

25th ARMY

late 1944: formed in Holland from Headquarters, Armed Forces Netherlands (a cross between a corps and an Army HQ), after the 15th Army's Headquarters was transferred to the Aachen sector

1944-45: fought in Holland and northwestern Germany

ARMY OF LIGURIA

August 3, 1944: formed in northern Italy to control German and Italian Fascist troops; the army was commanded by Italians

April 1945: largely destroyed in Po River campaign

ARMY OF NORWAY
December 19, 1940: created
1940-44: administered occupied Norway
December 18, 1944: absorbed by 20th Mountain Army

PANZER ARMY AFRIKA
June 1941: formed as Panzer Group Afrika
1941-43: directed Axis operations in Libya and Egypt; retreated to Tunisia
May 1943: destroyed

I CORPS*
1921: formed as an integral part of Headquarters, Wehrkreis I
1939: Poland
1940: France
1941-45: northern sector, Eastern Front
1945: surrendered in Courland Pocket

I LUFTWAFFE FIELD CORPS
late 1942 or early 1943: formed
1943 (?): disbanded; this corps never saw active field operations

I PARACHUTE CORPS
early 1944: formed in central Italy
1944-45: fought on Italian Front

I SS PANZER CORPS
1942: formed in Germany
1943: southern sector, Russian Front
1944: Western Front (Normandy, Falaise, Ardennes)
January 1945: sent to Eastern Front; fought in Hungary and Austria

II CORPS
1921: formed as a part of Headquarters, Wehrkreis II
1939: Poland
1940: West
1941-45: northern sector, Eastern Front
1945: surrendered in Courland Pocket

II LUFTWAFFE FIELD CORPS
early 1943: formed
1943-early 1944: Eastern Front, mainly on central sector
early 1944: disbanded; part of staff used to form I Parachute Corps

---

*Unless otherwise designated, all German corps were understood to be infantry corps.

II PARACHUTE CORPS

late 1943: formed in France, where it was responsible for forming new Luftwaffe Field and parachute divisions

June 1944: committed to combat in Normandy; almost continuously in action on the Western Front thereafter

1945: fought in Holland and northwestern Germany

II SS PANZER CORPS

May 1942: formed in Germany; sent to northern France in July

January 1943: sent to southern sector, Eastern Front

August, 1943: transferred to Italy

December 1943: returned to France

March 1944: returned to Eastern Front; fought at Tarnopol on southern sector

June 1944: rushed to Normandy sector of France

August 1944: surrounded at Falaise and Mons; broke out with heavy casualties; sent to Arnhem, The Netherlands, to reform

September 1944: smashed British 1st Airborne Division at Arnhem

December 1944: in Ardennes counteroffensive

1945: Eastern Front; fought in Hungary and Austria

III LUFTWAFFE FIELD CORPS

1942-43 (winter of): formed

1943: Eastern Front, mainly on northern sector

October 1943: dissolved. Staff used to form II Flak Corps

III PANZER CORPS

1921: formed as an integral part of Headquarters, Wehrkreis III

1939: fought in Poland as an infantry corps

1940: France

1941: redesignated III Panzer Corps

1941-45: Eastern Front, mainly on southern sector

III SS Corps

April 1943: formed to control the training and subsequent operations of new Scandinavian and Dutch SS divisions

Sept.-Dec. 1943: in Croatia

December 1943-1945: northern sector, Eastern Front

IV LUFTWAFFE FIELD CORPS

see XC Corps

IV PANZER CORPS

1921: formed as part of Headquarters, Wehrkreis IV

1939: Poland, as an infantry corps
1940: Western campaign
1942-43: Eastern Front; destroyed at Stalingrad
summer 1943: reformed
1943-45; southern sector, Eastern Front
early 1945: reformed as a panzer corps

IV SS PANZER CORPS

summer 1943: formed in France to control SS divisions forming at that
    time
August 1944-45: southern sector, Russian Front

V CORPS

1921: formed as part of Headquarters, Wehrkreis V
1940: Western campaign
1941-44: southern sector, Eastern Front
April 1944: evacuated from Crimea
1945: reportedly in action on Eastern Front

V SS MOUNTAIN CORPS

summer 1943: organized in Yugoslavia
1943-44: engaged in antipartisan operations
late 1944: transferred to Germany
1945: destroyed in the Battle of Berlin

VI CORPS

1921: formed as part of Headquarters, Wehrkreis VI
1939: Poland
1940: Western campaign
1941-44: Eastern Front (southern sector until early 1944)
July 1944: destroyed by Russian summer offensive
late 1944: reformed
1945: northern sector, Eastern Front

VI SS CORPS

late 1943: organized in Latvia to control Latvian SS divisions
1944-45: northern sector, Eastern Front

VII CORPS

1921: formed as part of Headquarters, Wehrkreis VII
1939: Poland
1940: Western campaign
1941-45: Russian Front, mainly on central sector
1945: Silesia; managed to surrender to the Americans

VIII CORPS
1935: formed as a corps HQ and a Wehrkreis from HQ, 2nd Cavalry Division
1939: Poland
1940: West
1941-43: Eastern Front; destroyed at Stalingrad
summer 1943: reformed
1943-45: Eastern Front, southern, northern, and central sectors

IX CORPS
1935: formed as a corps headquarters and a Wehrkreis from HQ, 3rd Cavalry Division
1940: Western campaign
1941-45: Eastern Front
1945: East Prussia

IX SS MOUNTAIN CORPS
early 1944: formed in Croatia
late 1944: transferred to Hungary; in action, Eastern Front
February 1945: destroyed in Siege of Budapest

X CORPS
1935: formed as a corps headquarters and a Wehrkreis
1939: Poland
1940: West
1941-45: northern sector, Eastern Front

XI CORPS
1936: formed as a corps headquarters and a Wehrkreis
1939: Poland
1940: West
1941-43: Eastern Front; destroyed at Stalingrad
summer 1943: reformed; back to southern sector
February 1944: smashed at Cherkassy
1944: reformed in Poland; still in southern Poland in August
1945: Upper Silesia; surrendered to the Russians in Czechoslovakia

XI AIR CORPS
summer 1940: formed to control expanding parachute units
1941: Crete
1942: in southern France
April 1943: Italy (in Rome area)
March 1944: upgraded to 1st Parachute Army at Nancy, France

XI SS PANZER CORPS
1944: created
late 1944: southern Poland
1945: Pomerania; destroyed in the Battle of Berlin

XII CORPS
1936: formed as a corps headquarters and a Wehrkreis
1939: West Wall
1940: France
1941-44: central sector, Russian Front
July 8, 1944: remnants surrendered to Soviets at Minsk
March 1945: recreated from Headquarters, Wehrkreis XII in southwestern Germany
May 1945: surrendered to the Americans near Pilsen, Czechoslovakia

XII SS CORPS
1944: created
1944-45: northern sector, Western Front
April 1945: destroyed in the Ruhr Pocket

XIII CORPS
1936-37: formed as a corps headquarters and a Wehrkreis
1939: Poland
1940: West
1941-44: Eastern Front
July 1944: destroyed in Soviet summer offensive
late 1944: Corps Felber on Western Front given designation XIII Corps
December 1944: fought in the Ardennes counteroffensive
April 25, 1945: destroyed by U.S. forces southwest of Stuttgart

XIII SS CORPS
August 1944: formed at Breslau
autumn 1944-45: Western Front
May 1945: surrendered in Munich

XIV PANZER CORPS
1936-37: formed as motorized corps to control units in the process of motorization
1939: Poland
1940: West
late 1940: redesignated XIV Panzer Corps
1941: Balkans
1941-43: Eastern Front; destroyed at Stalingrad

summer 1943: reformed in Sicily
1943-45: Italy

XV COSSACK CAVALRY CORPS
February 1, 1945: formed
1945: fought on Yugoslav-Albania border
May 1945: surrendered to the British; handed over to the Soviets

XV CORPS
see 3rd Panzer Army

XV MOUNTAIN CORPS
summer 1943: formed
early 1944: sent to Croatia
late 1944: on Dalmatian coast (northwestern Yugoslavia); responsible for
  coastal defense and line of communication duties

XV SS CORPS
1944: formed
1944-45: fought Tito's partisans in Yugoslavia
April 1945: surrendered to Western Allies in Austria but turned over to the
  Russians; disappeared

XVI MOTORIZED CORPS
see 4th Panzer Army

XVI SS CORPS
late 1944: formed
1945: on Eastern Front (in eastern Germany)

XVII CORPS
1938: formed in Vienna as a corps headquarters and a Wehrkreis after the
  annexation of Austria
1939: Poland
1940: West
1941-45: southern sector, Eastern Front

XVIII MOUNTAIN CORPS
1938: formed at Salzburg as a corps headquarters and a Wehrkreis
1939: Poland
1940: West
1941: Balkans
1941-44: in northern Finland; fought on Murmansk sector of the Eastern
  Front

autumn 1944: retreated to Norway; remained there the rest of the war

XVIII SS CORPS
1944: created
1945: southern sector, Western Front
May 1945: surrendered to 1st French Army near Swiss border

XIX MOTORIZED CORPS
see 2nd Panzer Army

XIX MOUNTAIN CORPS
summer 1940: formed as Mountain Corps Norway
latter part of 1942: redesignated XIX Mountain Corps
1941-44: fought on Murmansk sector of Eastern Front
autumn 1944: retreated across northern Finland to Norway; ended the war
   there

XX CORPS
1939: formed in Danzig: Poland
1941-45: Eastern Front, mainly on central sector
May 5-7, 1945: surrendered to the Americans

XXI CORPS
see 21st Army

XXI MOUNTAIN CORPS
late summer 1943: formed in Balkans
1944: in Albania and Montenegro
late 1944: heavily engaged against partisans; withdrew to Sarajevo
1945: southern sector, Eastern Front

XXII CORPS
see 1st Panzer Army

XXII MOUNTAIN CORPS
late summer 1943: formed in Greece
September 1944: withdrew through Yugoslavia
December 1944: Hungary
1945: southern sector, Eastern Front

XXIII CORPS
1938: part of peacetime army as Frontier Command Eifel, headquartered at
   Bonn
1939: redesignated XXIII Corps

1940: West
1941-45: central sector, Eastern Front

XXIV PANZER CORPS
1938: part of the peacetime army as Frontier Command Saarpfalz, headquartered at Kaiserslautern
1939: redesignated XXIV Corps: Poland
1940: West
1941: redesignated XXIV Panzer Corps
1941-45: Eastern Front
1945: surrendered in Czechoslovakia

XXV CORPS
1938: part of peacetime army as Frontier Command Oberrhein at Baden-
Baden
1939: redesignated XXV Corps
1940: West
1940-44: occupation duties in France
August 1944: isolated in Brittany
May 1945: surrendered

XXVI CORPS
1939: formed: Poland
1940: West
1941-44: northern sector, Eastern Front
early 1944-45: central sector, Eastern Front

XXVII CORPS
1939: formed
1940: West
1941-45: Eastern Front
July 1944: heavy losses at Minsk

XXVIII CORPS
early summer 1940: formed
1941-45: Eastern Front
May 1945: surrendered in Courland Pocket

XXIX CORPS
early summer 1940: formed
1941-45: southern sector, Eastern Front

XXX CORPS
1939: formed: Poland
1940: France

1941-44: Eastern Front
February 1944: suffered heavy losses during evacuation of Nikopol bridge-
    head on the lower Dnieper
August 1944: heavily engaged west of the Dnestr
January 1945: transferred to Holland
1945: on Western Front

XXXI CORPS COMMAND
see LXXX Corps

XXXII CORPS COMMAND
see LXXXI Corps

XXXIII CORPS COMMAND
late 1939: formed
summer 1940: sent to Trondheim area, central Norway; remained there
    throughout the war

XXXIV CORPS
late 1939: formed in Poland as XXXIV Corps Command
1941: upgraded
1941-43: central sector, Eastern Front
1944: in Balkans withdrawal
January 1945: reformed in northern Yugoslavia; fought between the Drava
    and Sava

XXXV CORPS
late 1939: formed in Poland as XXXV Corps Command
May 1942: upgraded
1942-44: central sector, Eastern Front
July 1944: destroyed

XXXVI MOUNTAIN CORPS
October 5, 1939: formed as XXXVI Corps Command in Poland
summer 1940: in Norway
June 1941: transferred to northern Finland; fought in the Murmansk sector
October 1941: upgraded to XXXVI Mountain Corps
autumn 1944: withdrew through northern Finland to Norway

XXXVII CORPS COMMAND
see LXXXII Corps

XXXVIII CORPS
1939: formed: Poland
1940: West

1941-45: northern sector, Eastern Front

XXXIX PANZER CORPS
late 1939: formed
1940: France
1941-44: Eastern Front
July 8, 1944: surrendered to Soviets near Minsk
autumn 1944: reconstituted
December 1944: on Western Front in Ardennes counteroffensive
early 1945: transferred to northern Alsace

XL PANZER CORPS
late 1939: formed
1940: West
1941: Balkans
1941-45: Eastern Front, mainly on southern sector

XLI PANZER CORPS
late 1939: formed
1940: West
1941: Balkans
1941-44: central sector, Eastern Front
July 1944: destroyed
late 1944 (?): reconstituted
April 1945: surrendered to the Western Allies near Magdeburg

XLII CORPS
1939: formed: Poland
1940: West
1941-44: Eastern Front
April 1944: reorganized in Poland after suffering heavy losses during the
   Dnieper withdrawal
September 1944: southern Poland

XLIII CORPS
early summer 1940: formed
1940: West
1941-44: Eastern Front
July 1944: smashed on central sector

XLIV CORPS
early summer 1940: formed
1940: West

1941-45: Eastern Front

XLV CORPS COMMAND
see LXXXIII Corps

XLVI PANZER CORPS
early summer 1940: formed
1941: Balkans
1941-45: Eastern Front
August 1944: cited for distinguished defensive action on Vistula and north-
    east of Warsaw
early 1945: heavily engaged in Silesia

XLVII PANZER CORPS
1940: formed in Danzig as an infantry corps: dissolved
summer 1940: formed as a panzer corps
1941-44: Eastern Front
June 1944: transferred to France
1944-45: fought in Normandy, at Falaise, and in the Ardennes
April 1945: destroyed in Ruhr Pocket

XLVII PANZER CORPS
1940: formed as XLVIII Corps in Posen, Wkr. XXI
summer 1940: reformed as a panzer corps
1941-45: Eastern Front
1945: surrendered to Western Allies

XLIX MOUNTAIN CORPS
early summer 1940: formed in the Protectorate
1941: Balkans
1941-45: southern sector, Eastern Front; suffered heavy losses in the
    Crimea 1944
May 1945: surrendered to Soviets in Czechoslovakia

L CORPS
late 1940: formed
1941: Balkans
1941-45: Eastern Front
October 1944: isolated in the Courland Pocket; remained there

LI MOUNTAIN CORPS
1940: formed as an infantry corps
1941-43: Eastern Front; destroyed at Stalingrad

summer 1943: reformed in southern Germany
1943-45: Italian Front; destroyed in Po River campaign

LII CORPS
late 1940: formed
1941-44: southern sector, Eastern Front
August 1944: heavy losses in Dnieper and Dnestr withdrawals; subsequently disbanded

LIII CORPS
late 1940: formed
1941-44: central sector, Eastern Front
July 1944: destroyed at Vitebsk
1944: reformed; subsequently fought on Western Front
April 1945: destroyed in Ruhr Pocket

LIV CORPS
1940: formed as a corps command
spring 1941: upgraded to corps headquarters
1941-45: Eastern Front (southern, then northern sector)

LV CORPS
spring 1941: formed
1941-45: central sector, Eastern Front

LVI PANZER CORPS
late 1940: formed
1941-45: Eastern Front
early 1945: withdrew into Silesia
May 1945: surrendered in Berlin

LVIII PANZER CORPS
1943: formed as LVIII Reserve Panzer Corps in France
early 1944: upgraded
August 1944: southern France
December 1944: fought in the Ardennes

LIX CORPS
spring 1941 (?): formed
1941-45: Eastern Front
March 1944: cited for distinguished action on the southern sector
May 1945: surrendered to the Russians in Czechoslovakia

LX CORPS COMMAND
see LXXXIV Corps

LXI RESERVE CORPS
September 1942: formed in Poland
early 1944: dissolved

LXII RESERVE CORPS
September 1942: formed in Poland
early 1944: transferred to southern France
August 1944: destroyed in southern France

XIII CORPS
late 1940 or early 1941: formed in Norway as LXIII Corps Command
1941: absorbed by Headquarters, 21st Army
1944: reformed
November 1944: in action on Western Front
January 1945: resisting in the Vosges
April 1945: surrendered in Ruhr Pocket

LXIV CORPS
early 1941 (?): formed as the LXIV Corps Command
autumn 1942: converted to LXIV Reserve Corps
early 1944: in southeastern France
autumn 1944: upgraded
early 1945: in southern Alsace
March 1945: largely destroyed in Colmar Pocket
April 1945: finished off by French in the Black Forest

LXV CORPS z.b.V.
early 1941: formed
May 1941: at Belgrade, Serbia
1941 (?): dissolved
1943: reformed
1943-45: controlled artillery staffs connected with use of the "V" weapons

LXVI CORPS
autumn 1942: formed as LXVI Reserve Corps
1943: on Eastern Front
early 1944: sent to southeastern France
August 1944: took part in the withdrawal from the Mediterranean coast
autumn 1944: upgraded
late 1944: fought in the Ardennes
April 1945: destroyed in Ruhr Pocket

LXVII CORPS
1940 (?): formed as the LXVII Corps Command
autumn 1942: converted to LXVII Reserve Corps in France

summer 1944: transferred to Somme area; took part in the withdrawal from
    France
autumn 1944: upgraded
late 1944: in Aachen sector
early 1945: smashed at Eifel and Remagen

LXVIII CORPS
summer 1943 (?): formed in Balkans
early 1944: in Greece
September 1944: evacuated Athens and withdrew through Yugoslavia
late 1944: sent into action on Eastern Front; fought at Lake Balaton and on
    the Drava

LXIX CORPS
late 1942: formed in the Balkans
1942-44: served mainly in Croatia
September 1944: still in Croatia

LXX CORPS COMMAND
autumn 1941: formed in southern Norway
October 1944: still in Oslo area; almost certainly remained there until the
    end of the war

LXXI CORPS COMMAND
spring 1942: formed in northern Norway
1944: took part in withdrawal from Finland
late 1944: transferred south to Harstad
1945: ended the war in Norway

LXXIII CORPS
summer 1944: formed in Italy as Venetian Coast Command
latter part of 1944: Italian Front
December 1944: upgraded to LXXIII Corps

LXXIV CORPS
early 1944: in Brittany
1944-45: on Western Front
April 1945: destroyed in Ruhr Pocket

LXXV CORPS
early 1944: formed in northern Italy; subsequently assigned to the Army of
    Liguria
1944-45: responsible for the defenses on the Franco-Italian frontier

LXXVI PANZER CORPS
summer 1943: formed in Italy
1943-45: remained on Italian Front
April 24-25, 1945: destroyed in Po River campaign

LXXX CORPS
September 1939: formed as "Grenzkommando I" in Poland
November 1939: converted to XXXI Corps Command
April 1940: Denmark
summer 1940: fought in Western Campaign; remained in France
1941-42 (winter of): converted to LXXX Corps
1944-45: Western Front

LXXXI CORPS
October 1939: formed as XXXII Corps Command in Poland
April 1940: sent to Copenhagen, Denmark
summer 1942: sent to northwestern France; upgraded to LXXXI Corps
1944-45: Western Front
April 1945: destroyed in Ruhr Pocket

LXXXII CORPS
1939: formed as XXXVII Corps Command
1940: France; remained there
summer 1942: upgraded to LXXXII Corps
1944-45: Western Front; fought in Saar
May 1945: surrendered northeast of Munich

LXXXIII CORPS
early 1940: formed as XLV Corps Command
summer 1942: upgraded LXXXIII Corps
November 1942: took part in the occupation of Vichy France
spring 1943: expanded to form Headquarters, 19th Army

LXXXIV CORPS
late 1940: formed as LX Corps Command
summer 1942: upgraded to LXXXIV Corps in northwestern France
June 1944: met Normandy invasion
August 1944: destroyed at Falaise

LXXXV CORPS
1940: formed
1940-44: on occupation duties, mainly in southern France
1944-45: southern sector, Western Front

May 1945: surrendered to Western Allies near Pilsen, Czechoslovakia

LXXXVI CORPS
late 1942: formed in southwestern France
1944: retreated across southern France
January 1945: on northern sector, Western Front; served there until the end
of the war

LXXXVII CORPS
late 1942: formed in France
latter part of 1943: moved to northern Italy
autumn 1944: dissolved; staff probably absorbed the Headquarters, Army
of Liguria

LXXXVIII CORPS
early summer 1942: formed in Holland
1944-45: northern sector, Western Front

LXXXIX CORPS
summer 1942: formed as the "Scheldt" Corps in **Belgium**
December 1942 (or January 1943): upgraded to **LXXXIX** Corps
1944-45: Western Front
early April 1945: destroyed

XC CORPS
1942-43 (winter of): formed as IV Luftwaffe Field Corps
1943-early 1944: southern sector, Eastern Front
early 1944: transferred to French Mediterranean coast
August 1944: took part in the retreat to Alsace
late 1944: redesignated XC Corps
1945: southern sector, Western Front
March 1945: destroyed west of the Rhine (a previous XC Corps z.b.V. had
fought in Tunisia in November and December 1942)

XCI CORPS
autumn 1944: formed to control units withdrawing from Greece
late 1944: conducting rearguard actions south of Sarajevo
early 1945: Hungary
1945: reportedly destroyed in the Battle of Berlin

XCVII CORPS
late 1944 or early 1945: created in Italy
1945: on coastal defense duties along the Gulf of Venice

March 1945: transferred to Army Group E on southern sector, Eastern
  Front

AFRIKA KORPS
spring 1941: formed in western Libya
1941-43: fought in Libya and Egypt
May 1943: destroyed in Tunisia

PANZER CORPS "FELDHERRNHALLE"
early 1945: formed
1945: southern sector, Eastern Front

PARACHUTE PANZER CORPS "HERMANN GÖRING"
late 1944: formed
1944-45: fought in East Prussia; destroyed there

PANZER CORPS "GROSSDEUTSCHLAND"
early 1945: formed
1945: East Prussia

MOUNTAIN CORPS NORWAY
see XIX Mountain Corps

APPENDIX V
THE FLAK DIVISIONS

General. The Flak divisions belonged to the Luftwaffe and were used in one of two roles: either they were assigned a territorial sector in Germany or in occupied Europe, or they were assigned a sector of the front, where they operated more or less independently of Army control. Because of their wide distribution, it is impossible to discuss their unit histories in the same manner as was possible with the infantry and other divisions; therefore, only a brief discussion of them will be given.

Unit	Area of Responsibility (1944)
1st Flak Division	Berlin
2nd Flak Division (Motorized)	Paris; then transferred to northern sector of the Russian Front in early 1942
3rd Flak Division	Hamburg
4th Flak Division	Düsseldorf
5th Flak Division	Frankfurt-am-Main; transferred to Darmstadt, western Germany, in 1942 and to southeastern Europe in late 1943.
6th Flak Division (Motorized)	Western Europe; transferred to northern Russia in 1942
7th Flak Division	Cologne
8th Flak Division	Bremen
9th Flak Division	Paris; then transferred to central sector of the Russian Front in 1942 and to the Crimea in 1943
10th Flak Division (Motorized)	Rumania and Bulgaria (1941); southern sector of the Russian Front (1942-on)
11th Flak Division (Motorized)	Rennes-Paris area of northern France; then transferred to southern France in late 1942
12th Flak Division (Motorized)	central sector, Russian Front
13th Flak Division	Caen, France
14th Flak Division	Leipzig
15th Flak Division (Motorized)	Rumania (1941); transferred to southern Russia in 1942
16th Flak Division	Lille
17th Flak Division (Motorized)	southern sector, Russian Front
18th Flak Division (Motorized)	central sector, Russian Front
19th Flak Division (Motorized)	North Africa; virtually destroyed, 1943; reformed in Greece, 1943
20th Flak Division (Motorized)	North Africa; virtually destroyed, 1943; reformed in the Balkans
21st Flak Division	Southwestern Germany
22nd Flak Division	Western Germany

Bibliography*

Baumann, H. *Die 35 Infanterie Division im Zweiten Weltkrieg*. Karlsruhe: G. Braum, 1964.

Benoist-Mechin, Jacques. *Sixty Days That Shook the West: The Fall of France*. New York: G. P. Putnam's Sons, 1963.

Bernadotte, Count Folke. *The Curtain Falls: The Last Days of the Third Reich*. New York: Alfred A. Knopf, 1945.

Blumenson, Martin. *Breakout and Pursuit*. United States Army in World War II, European Theater of Operations, Office of the Chief of Military History, U.S. Department of the Army. Washington, D.C.: United ed States Government Printing Office, 1960.

––––––. *Salerno to Cassino*. United States Army in World War II, European Theater of Operations, Office of the Chief of Military History, U.S. Department of the Army. Washington, D.C.: United States Government Printing Office, 1969.

Brett-Smith, Richard. *Hitler's Generals*. San Rafael: Presidio Press, 1976.

British Military Intelligence Interrogation Reports. Historical Research Center, Air University, Maxwell Air Force Base, Alabama.

Carell, Paul. *The Foxes of the Desert*. New York: E.P. Dutton, 1960.

––––––. *Hitler Moves East, 1941-43*. Boston: Little, Brown and Company: 1965 (republished by Bantam Books, New York: 1966).

––––––. *Scorched Earth*. Boston: Little, Brown and Company, 1966 (republished by Ballantine Books, New York: 1971).

––––––. *Invasion: They're Coming*. New York: E.P. Dutton, 1963 (republished by Bantam Books, New York: 1973).

Chant, Christopher, ed. *The Marshall Cavendish Illustrated Encyclopedia of World War II*. 25 Volumes. New York: Marshall Cavendish Corporation, 1972.

––––––. et al. *Hitler's Generals*. New York: Chartwell Books, Inc., 1979.

*Author's earliest works appear first.

521

Chapman, Guy. *Why France Fell: The Defeat of the French Army in 1940.* New York: Rinehart and Winston, 1968.

Clark, Alan. *Barbarossa: The Russian-German Conflict, 1941-45.* New York: William Morrow and Company, 1965.

Cole, Hugh M. *The Lorraine Campaign.* United States Army in World War II, European Theater of Operations, Office of the Chief of Military History, United States Department of the Army. Washington, D.C.: United States Government Printing Office, 1950.

————. *The Ardennes: The Battle of the Bulge.* United States Army in World War II, European Theater of Operations, Office of the Chief of military History, United States Department of the Army. Washington, D.C.: United States Government Printing Office, 1965.

Cooper, Matthew. *The German Army: 1933-1945.* Briarcliff Manor, N.Y.: Stein and Day/Publishers, 1978.

Deighton, Len. *Blitzkrieg: From the Rise of Hitler to the Fall of Dunkirk.* New York: Alfred A. Knopf, 1979.

Edwards, Roger. *German Airborne Troops, 1939-45.* New York: Doubleday and Company, 1974.

Eisenhower, John S.D. *The Bitter Woods.* New York: G.P. Putnam's Sons, 1969.

Ellis, L.E. *Victory in the West.* Volume II, *The Defeat of Germany.* London: Her Majesty's Stationery Office, 1968.

Fisher, Ernest F., Jr. *Cassino to the Alps.* United States Army in World War II, Mediterranean Theater of Operations, Office of the Chief of Military History, United States Department of the Army. Washington, D.C.: United States Government Printing Office, 1977.

FitzGibbon, Constantine. *20 July.* New York: W.W. Norton and Company, 1956.

Forman, James. *Code Name Valkyrie: Count von Stauffenberg and the Plot to Kill Hitler.* New York: Laurel-Leaf Library, 1975.

Friessner, Hans. *Verratene Schlachten.* Hamburg: Holstein, 1956.

Galante, Pierre. *Operation Valkyrie: The German Generals' Plot Against Hitler.* New York: Harper and Row, 1981.

Garland, Albert N. and Howard McG. Smyth. *Sicily and the Surrender of Italy.* United States Army in World War II, Mediterranean Theater of Operations, Office of the Chief of Military History, United States Department of the Army. Washington, D.C.: United States Government Printing Office, 1965.

German Order of Battle, 1944. London: Arms and Armour Press, 1975.

Goebbels, Paul Joseph. *The Goebbels Diaries.* Garden City, New York: Doubleday and Co., Inc., 1948. Edited and translated by Louis P. Lochner (republished by Universal-Award House, Inc., New York: 1971).

Goralski, Robert. *World War II Almanac, 1931-1945*. New York: G.P. Putnam's Sons, 1981.

Görlitz, Walter. *Paulus and Stalingrad*. Westport, Conn.: Greenwood Press, Publishers, 1963.

Goutard, A. *The Battle of France, 1940*. New York: Ives Washburn, 1959.

Guderian, Heinz. *Panzer Leader*. New York: Ballantine Books, 1957.

Harrison, Gordon A. *Cross-Channel Attack*. United States Army in World War II, The European Theater of Operations, Office of the Chief of Military History, United States Department of the Army. Washington. D.C.: United States Government Printing Office, 1951.

Hart, B.H. Liddell. *History of the Second World War*. 2 vols. New York: G.P. Putnam's Sons, 1972.

Hartmann, Theodor. *Wehrmacht Divisional Signs, 1938-45*. London: Almark Publishing Company, 1970.

Hassell, Ulrich von. *The von Hassell Diaries, 1938-1944*. Westport, Conn.: Greenwood Press, Publishers, 1979.

Hastings, Max. *Das Reich*. New York: Holt, Rinehart and Winston, 1981.

Hoffman, Peter. *The History of the German Resistance, 1933-1945*. Cambridge, Mass.: M.I.T. Press, 1977.

Höhne, Heinz. *Canaris*. Garden City, New York: Doubleday and Company, 1979.

Horne, Alister. *To Lose a Battle: France, 1940*. Boston: Little, Brown and Company, 1969.

Irving, David. *The Trail of the Fox: The Search for the True Field Marshal Rommel*. New York: E.P. Dutton, 1977.

Jackson, W.G.F. *The Battle for North Africa*. New York: Mason/Charter, 1975.

Jacobsen, Hans-Adolf, ed. *July 20, 1944*. Bonn: Federal German Government Press and Information Office, 1969.

Jenner, M. Die *216/272 Niedersächsische Infanterie-Division*. Bad Nauheim: Podzun, 1964.

Keegan, John. *Waffen-SS: The Asphalt Soldiers*. New York: Ballantine Books, 1970.

Kemp, Anthony. *The Unknown Battle: Metz, 1944*. Briarcliff Manor, N.Y.: Stein and Day Publishers, 1981.

Kennedy, Robert M. *The German Campaign in Poland (1939)*. United States Department of the Army *Pamphlet 20-255*. Washington, D.C.: United States Department of the Army, 1956.

Kesselring, Alfred. *A Soldier's Record*. Westport, CT: Greenwood Press, 1970. .

Kriegstagebuch des Oberkommando der Wehrmacht (Wehrmachtführungsstab). 4 vols. Frankfurt-am-Main: Bernard und Graefe Verlag für Wehrwesen, 1961.

Lange, Wolfgang. *Korpsabteilung C*. Neckargemünd: Vowinckel, 1961.

Lewin, Ronald. *Rommel as a Military Commander*. New York: Ballantine Books, 1970.

Lucas, James. *Alpine Elite: German Mountain Troops in World War II*. New York: Jane's Publishing Company, 1980.

_____. *War on the Eastern Front, 1941-1945: The German Soldier in Russia*. New York: Stein and Day Publishers, 1980.

MacDonald, Charles B. *The Siegfried Line Campaign*. United States Army in World War II, European Theater of Operations, Office of the Chief of Military History, United States Department of the Army. Washington, D.C.: United States Government Printing Office, 1963.

_____. *The Last Offensive*. United States Army in World War II, European Theater of Operations, Office of the Chief of Military History, United States Department of the Army. Washington, D.C.: United States Government Printing Office, 1973.

Manstein, Erich von. *Lost Victories*. Chicago: Henry Regnery, 1958.

Manvell, Robert, and Heinrich Fraenkel. *The Men Who Tried to Kill Hitler*. New York: Coward-McCann, 1964.

Mellenthin, F.W. von. *Panzer Battles*. Norman: University of Oklahoma Press, 1956 (republished by Ballantine Books, New York: 1971).

_____. *German Generals of World War II*. Norman: University of Oklahoma Press, 1977.

Mitcham, Samuel W., Jr. *Rommel's Desert War: The Life and Death of the Afrika Korps*. Briarcliff Manor, N.Y. : Stein and Day Publishers, 1982.

_____. *Rommel's Last Battle: The Desert Fox and the Normandy Campaign*. Briarcliff Manor, N.Y.: Stein and Day Publishers, 1983.

_____. *Triumphant Fox: Erwin Rommel and the Rise of the Afrika Korps*. Briarcliff Manor, N.Y.: Stein and Day Publishers, 1984.

Müller-Hillebrand, B. *Das Heer, 1939-1945*. Frankfurt-am-Main: E. S. Mittler und Sohn, 1954.

Munzel, O. *Die Deutschen Panzer Truppen bis 1945*. Herford und Bonn: Maximilian, 1965.

Neumann, Peter. *The Black March*. New York: Bantam Books, 1960.

Oberkommando des Heeres (High Command of the [German] Army), Chief of the Replacement Army. "Frontnachweiser." Several editions, the last of which was dated 15 December 1944, with pen and ink entries made later. On microfilm at U.S. National Archives.

Payne, Robert. *The Life and Death of Adolf Hitler*. New York: Praeger Publishers, 1973.

Pertinax. *The Gravediggers of France*. Garden City, New York: Doubleday and Company, 1944.

Playfair, I.S. O. *The Mediterranean and the Middle East*. Vol. 3. London: His Majesty's Stationery Office, 1960.

Plocher, Hermann. *The German Air Force Versus Russia, 1941*. United States Air Force Historical Studies: Number 153, Aerospace Studies Institute, Air University, 1965. Published in hardback form by Arno Press, New York: 1968.

————. *The German Air Force Versus Russia, 1942*. United States Air Force Historical Studies: Number 154, Aerospace Studies Institute, Air University, 1966. Published in hardback form by Arno Press, New York: 1968.

————. *The German Air Force Versus Russia, 1943*. United States Air Force Historical Studies: Number 155, Aerospace Studies Institute, Air University, 1967. Published in hardback form by Arno Press, New York: 1968.

Rommel, Erwin. *The Rommel Papers*. New York: Harcourt Brace Jovanovich, 1953 (edited by B.H. Liddell Hart).

Rowe, Vivian. *The Great Wall of France: The Triumph of the Maginot Line*. New York: G.P. Putnam's Sons, 1967.

Ruge, Friedrich. *Rommel in Normandy*. San Rafael, California: Presidio Press, 1979.

Ryan, Cornelius. *The Last Battle*. New York: Popular Library, 1966.

Salisbury, Harrison E. *The 900 Days: The Siege of Leningrad*. New York: Harper and Row, Publishers, 1969.

Seaton, Albert. *The Russo-German War, 1941*. New York: Praeger Publishers, 1970.

Shaw, John, et al. *Red Army Resurgent*. Time-Life Books, World War II Series, Vol. 20. Chicago: Time-Life Books, 1979.

Shirer, William L. *The Rise and Fall of the Third Reich*. New York: Simon and Schuster, 1960.

Snydor, Charles W., Jr. *Soldiers of Destruction: The SS Death's Head Division, 1933-1945*. Princeton, New Jersey: Princeton University Press, 1977.

Speidel, Hans. *Invasion, 1944*. New York: Paperback Library Edition, 1968.

Stein, George. *The Waffen SS*. New York: Cornell University Press, 1966.

Taylor, Telford. *Sword and Swastika: Generals and Nazis in the Third Reich*. Chicago: Quadrangle Paperbacks, 1969. Originally published by Simon and Schuster, New York: 1952.

Teske, Hermann. *Bewegungskrieg: Führungsprobleme einer Infanterie-Division im Westfeldzug, 1940*. Heidelberg: Scharnhorst Buchkameradschaff, 1955.

The German Campaign in the Balkans (Spring, 1941). Washington, D.C.: U.S. Department of the Army, 1953.

Thorwald, Jürgen. *Defeat in the East*. New York: Bantam Books, Inc., 1980.

Toland, John. *Adolf Hitler*. New York: Ballantine Books, 1977 (originally published by Random House, New York: 1976).

Tornau, G., and F. Korowski. *Sturmartillerie Fels in der Brandung*. Hereford and Bonn: Maximilian, 1965.

United States Department of the Army. *The German Campaign in the Balkans (Spring, 1941)*. United States Department of the Army *Pamphlet 20-260*. Washington, D.C.: United States Department of the Army, 1953.

United States Military Intelligence Division. "The German Replacement Army (Ersatzheer)." Washington, D.C.: United States Army War Department, 1945.

United States Military Intelligence Service. "Order of Battle of the German Army." Washington, D.C.: United States War Department General Staff, 1942.

————. "Order of Battle of the German Army, 1943." Washington, D.C.: United States War Department General Staff, 1943.

————. "Order of Battle of the German Army, 1944." Washington, D.C.: United States War Department General Staff, 1944.

————. "Order of Battle of the German Army, 1945." Washington, D.C.: United States War Department General Staff, 1945.

Vormann, Nikolaus. *Tscherkassy*. Heidelberg: Vowinckel, 1954.

Warlimont, Walter. *Inside Hitler's Headquarters, 1939-45*. New York: Frederick A. Praeger, Publishers, 1964.

Wheeler-Bennett, Sir John W. *The Nemesis of Power: The German Army in Politics, 1918-1945*. New York: The Viking Press, 1967.

Whiting, Charles. *Bloody Aachen*. Briarcliff Manor, New York: Stein and Day Publishers, 1976.

————. *Hunters from the Sky: The German Parachute Corps 1940-1945*. Briarcliff Manor, New York: Stein and Day Publishers, 1974.

Wistrich, Robert. *Who's Who in Nazi Germany*. New York: Macmillan Publishing Company, 1982.

Young, Desmond. *Rommel: The Desert Fox*. New York: Harper and Row, Publishers, 1965.

Young, Peter (ed.). *The Marshal Cavendish Illustrated Encyclopedia of World War II*. New York: Marshall Cavendish, 1981.

Ziemke, Earl F. "The German Northern Theater of Operations, 1940-45." United States Department of the Army *Pamphlet 20-271*. Washington, D.C.: United States Department of the Army, 1959.

————. *Stalingrad to Berlin: The German Defeat in the East*. Office of the Chief of Military History, United States Department of the Army. Washington, D.C.: United States Government Printing Office, 1966.

————. *Battle for Berlin*. New York: Ballantine Books, 1968.

Zimmermann, Erich, and Hans-Adolf Jacobsen. *Germans Against Hitler*. Bonn: Federal German Government Press and Information Office, 1960.

Index

527